The Blackwell Companion
to Protestantism

Blackwell Companions to Religion

The Blackwell Companions to Religion series presents a collection of the most recent scholarship and knowledge about world religions. Each volume draws together newly commissioned essays by distinguished authors in the field, and is presented in a style which is accessible to undergraduate students, as well as scholars and the interested general reader. These volumes approach the subject in a creative and forward-thinking style, providing a forum in which leading scholars in the field can make their views and research available to a wider audience.

Published

The Blackwell Companion to Judaism
Edited by Jacob Neusner and Alan J. Avery-Peck

The Blackwell Companion to Sociology of Religion
Edited by Richard K. Fenn

The Blackwell Companion to the Hebrew Bible
Edited by Leo G. Perdue

The Blackwell Companion to Postmodern Theology
Edited by Graham Ward

The Blackwell Companion to Hinduism
Edited by Gavin Flood

The Blackwell Companion to Political Theology
Edited by Peter Scott and William T. Cavanaugh

The Blackwell Companion to Protestantism
Edited by Alister E. McGrath and Darren C. Marks

The Blackwell Companion to Modern Theology
Edited by Gareth Jones

The Blackwell Companion to Religious Ethics
Edited by William Schweiker

The Blackwell Companion to Christian Ethics
Edited by Stanley Hauerwas and Sam Wells

Forthcoming

The Blackwell Companion to the Study of Religion
Edited by Robert A. Segal

The Blackwell Companion to Eastern Christianity
Edited by Ken Parry

The Blackwell Companion to Christian Spirituality
Edited by Arthur Holder

The Blackwell Companion to the New Testament
Edited by David Aune

The Blackwell Companion to Protestantism

Edited by

Alister E. McGrath and Darren C. Marks

Blackwell
Publishing

350 Main Street, Malden, MA 02148-5020, USA
108 Cowley Road, Oxford OX4 1JF, UK
550 Swanston Street, Carlton, Victoria 3053, Australia

First published 2004 by Blackwell Publishing Ltd

Library of Congress Cataloging-in-Publication Data

The Blackwell companion to Protestantism / edited by Alister E. McGrath and
Darren C. Marks.
     p. cm. – (Blackwell companions to religion)
   Includes bibliographical references.
   ISBN 0-631-23278-8 (alk. paper)
    1. Protestantism. I. McGrath, Alister E., 1953– II. Marks, Darren C. III. Series.
  BX4811.3.B57 2003
280′.4 – dc21

                         2003008185

A catalogue record for this title is available from the British Library.

Set in 10.5 on 12.5 pt Photina
by SNP Best-set Typesetter Ltd., Hong Kong
Printed and bound in the United Kingdom
by T.J. International, Padstow, Cornwall

For further information on
Blackwell Publishing, visit our website:
http://www.blackwellpublishing.com

The editors and publishers gratefully acknowledge the permission granted to reproduce the
following copyright material on page 268 of this book: Thomas, R.S. (1995). The Minister.
In *Collected Poems 1945–1990*. London: J.M. Dent.

Contents

Contributors   ix

Foreword   xiv
Alister E. McGrath and Darren C. Marks

Introduction: Protestantism – the Problem of Identity   1
Alister E. McGrath and Darren C. Marks

**Part I   The Formation of Protestant Identity:
History and Ideology**   21

European Protestantism

1 Protestantism in German-speaking Lands to the Present Day   23
    Randall C. Zachman

2 Shapers of Protestantism: Martin Luther   40
    Graham Tomlin

3 Shapers of Protestantism: John Calvin   53
    Alister E. McGrath

4 Shapers of Protestantism: F. D. E. Schleiermacher   66
    Nicholas Adams

5 Shapers of Protestantism: Karl Barth   83
    John Webster

6 English Protestantism to the Present Day   96
    Gerald Bray

7 Scottish Protestantism to the Present Day   109
    Kenneth B. E. Roxburgh

8   Welsh Protestantism to the Present Day   120
    D. Densil Morgan

9   Irish Protestantism to the Present Day   123
    Alan Ford

10 Nordic Protestantism to the Present Day   130
    Aasulv Lande

11 Protestantism in the Netherlands to the Present Day   147
    Peter van Rooden

12 Protestantism in Eastern Europe to the Present Day   155
    Parush Parushev and Toivo Pilli

13 French Protestantism to the Present Day   161
    Alister E. McGrath

14 Italian Protestantism to the Present Day   163
    Alister E. McGrath

North American Protestantism

15 Protestantism in the United States of America to the Present Day   165
    John Corrigan

16 Shapers of Protestantism: Jonathan Edwards   181
    Stephen R. Holmes

17 Canadian Protestantism to the Present Day   189
    Darren C. Marks

Asia and Australasia

18 Indian Protestantism to the Present Day   201
    Ivan Morris Satyavrata

19 South-East Asian Protestantism to the Present Day   206
    Yung Hwa

20 Japanese Protestantism to the Present Day   210
    Nozomo Miyahira

21 Korean Protestantism to the Present Day   216
    Young-Gi Hong

22 Chinese Protestantism to the Present Day   222
    Carver T. Yu

23 Protestantism in Australia, New Zealand and Oceania to the
    Present Day   232
    Ian Breward

Africa

24 African Protestantism to the Present Day   239
    John S. Pobee

**Part II Protestantism and Present Identity:
Relations and Influence**   249

Protestantism and its Relations

25 Protestantism and the Bible   251
    R. Kendall Soulen

26 Protestantism and the Arts   268
    Trevor Hart

27 Protestantism and Politics, Economics, and Sociology   287
    J. Philip Wogaman

28 Protestantism, Law and Legal Thought   298
    John Witte Jr.

29 Protestantism and the Sciences   306
    Ted Peters

Protestantism and its Influence

30 Protestantism and Liberalism   322
    Mark D. Chapman

31 Protestantism and Feminism   332
    Cynthia L. Rigby

32 Protestantism and Fundamentalism   344
    William V. Trollinger Jr.

33 Protestantism and Racism   357
    Paul R. Griffin

34 Protestantism and Judaism   372
    Clark M. Williamson

35 Protestantism and Spirituality   382
    Bradley P. Holt

36 Protestantism and Missions   392
    Werner Ustorf

Part III The Future of Protestantism   403

37 The Future of Protestantism: Ecumenism and the Mainline
    Denominations   405
    Alan D. Falconer

38 The Future of Protestantism: Evangelicalism 421
Mark A. Noll

39 The Future of Protestantism: The Rise of Pentecostalism 439
Allan Anderson

40 The Future of Protestantism: Postmodernity 453
Graham Ward

41 The Future of Protestantism: The Non-Western Protestant World 468
Allan Anderson

Index 483

Contributors

Alister E. McGrath is Professor of Historical Theology at Oxford University, and Principal of Wycliffe Hall, Oxford. He studied at the Universities of Oxford and Cambridge, and served in a parish in Nottingham before joining the staff at Wycliffe, where he now teaches in the area of systematic theology, science and religion, spirituality, and apologetics. His most recent publications are the three-volume work, *A Scientific Theology* (2001–3), and *The Intellectual Origins of the European Reformation* (2nd edn., 2003). He is also the author of numerous best-selling books, including *A Brief History of Heaven* (2003), *Christian Theology: An Introduction* (3rd edn., 2001), *The Christian Theology Reader* (2nd edn., 2001), *Christian Spirituality* (1999), *Reformation Thought* (3rd edn., 1999), *Science and Religion* (1998), *Historical Theology* (1998), and *An Introduction to Christianity* (1997), all available from Blackwell Publishing.

Darren C. Marks lectures in systematic theology and religious studies at Huron University College at the University of Western Ontario in Canada. He holds degrees in science and theology from the University of Toronto (Victoria and Wycliffe College) and advanced degrees in theology from the University of Oxford (St Hugh's College) under the supervision of Professor J. Webster. He has also studied at the Friedrich Wilhelms Universität (Bonn) under Professor Dr G. Sauter. He is the author of numerous articles in systematic theology, Canadian ecclesiastical history, and the editor of *Shaping a Theological Mind* (2003). His primary research area is contemporary systematic theology although his doctoral work dealt with nineteenth-century German Protestant theology (Julius Müller and the Mediating Theology). Dr Marks is currently working on several publishing projects, including a text on seventeenth- and eighteenth-century theologians, a work on the doctrine of sin, and articles including *George Grant and the Theologia Crucis*, as well comparing the possibilities of a Christomorphic metanoia in James H. Cone and Dietrich Bonhoeffer.

Nicholas Adams is a lecturer in systematic theology and theological ethics at the University of Edinburgh. He writes on German philosophical issues in theology, and is currently writing a book on Jürgen Habermas and theology.

Allan Anderson is Senior Lecturer in Pentecostal Studies at the Graduate Institute for Theology and Religion, University of Birmingham, UK. He is the author of five books on African Pentecostalism, including *Zion and Pentecost* (2000) and *African Reformation* (2001).

Gerald Bray is Anglican Professor of Divinity at Beeson Divinity School, Samford University, Birmingham, Alabama, USA. He was formerly tutor in Christian doctrine at Oak Hill College, London. He is the author of several books, including *The Doctrine of God* (1993) and *Biblical Interpretation, Past and Present* (1996).

Ian Breward is Emeritus Professor of Theology at the United Faculty of Divinity, University of Melbourne.

Dr Mark D. Chapman is Vice-Principal, Ripon College, Cuddesdon, UK.

John Corrigan is Edwin Scott Gaustad Professor of Religion and Professor of History, and Director of the Institute for the Study of Emotion, Florida State University.

Alan D. Falconer, a Church of Scotland minister, has been Director of the Faith and Order Commission, World Council of Churches since 1995. He was formerly Director of the Irish School of Ecumenics (1990–95) and served on a number of international dialogues as a representative of the World Alliance of Reformed Churches.

Alan Ford is Professor of Theology and Head of the School of Humanities at the University of Nottingham, UK.

Dr Paul R. Griffin is Professor of Religion and Director of African and African-American Studies at Wright State University, Dayton, Ohio, USA and founder and Director of the Wright State University *National Conference on the Future Shape of Black Religion* which ran from 1990 to 2001. His most recent book is *Seeds of Racism in the Soul of America* (1999).

Trevor Hart is Professor of Divinity, Principal of St Mary's College and Director of the Institute for Theology, Imagination and the Arts in the University of St Andrews, UK. His publications include *Faith Thinking: the Dynamics of Christian Theology* (1995), *Regarding Karl Barth* (1999) and (with Richard Bauckham) *Hope Against Hope: Christian Eschatology at the Turn of the Millennium* (1999). He is also General Editor of *The Dictionary of Historical Theology* (2000). He is a priest in the Scottish Episcopal Church and Convener of its Doctrine Committee.

Revd Dr Stephen R. Holmes is a Baptist minister, Lecturer in Christian Doctrine at King's College London, and an Associate Lecturer at Spurgeon's College. His publications include *God of Grace and God of Glory: An Account of the Theology of Jonathan Edwards* (2000), and *Listening to the Past: The Place of Tradition in Theology* (2002).

Bradley P. Holt is Professor of Religion at Augsburg College, Minneapolis, Minnesota, USA.

Dr Young-Gi Hong earned his Ph.D. at the Oxford Centre for Mission Studies with Wales University. He is the president of the Institute for Church Growth in Korea, and teaches missiology at Hansei University.

Aasulv Lande is Professor in Missiology with Ecumenical Theology at the Centre for Theology and Religious Studies, University of Lund, Sweden.

Nozomo Miyahira is currently Associate Professor of Christian Theology at Seinan Gakuin University, Fukuoka, Japan. He is author of *Towards a Theology of the Concord of God: A Japanese Perspective on the Trinity* (2000) and *God Who Takes Responsibility and Gives Meaning: A Japanese Christianity in the 21st Century* (2000, in Japanese).

D. Densil Morgan is Reader in the Department of Theology and Religious Studies, University of Wales, Bangor, UK.

Mark A. Noll is McManis Professor of Christian Thought at Wheaton College, Illinois, USA. He is the author of *America's God, from Jonathan Edwards to Abraham Lincoln* (2002), *The Old Religion in a New World: The History of North American Christianity* (2002), and *American Evangelical Christianity* (Blackwell, 2001).

Parush Parushev is the Academic Dean and the Director of Applied Theology of the International Baptist Theological Seminary of the European Baptist Federation in Prague, Czech Republic. He is a faculty member of the Bulgarian Evangelical Theological Institute in Sofia and of the California Christian College, USA.

Ted Peters is Professor of Systematic Theology at Pacific Lutheran Theological Seminary and the Graduate Theological Union in Berkeley, California, USA. He is editor in chief of *Dialog, A Journal of Theology*, and he co-edits *Theology and Science* for the Center for Theology and the Natural Sciences.

Toivo Pilli is Director of Baptist and Anabaptist Studies at the International Baptist Theological Seminary, Prague, Czech Republic.

Rev. Canon Professor Emeritus John S. Pobee, University of Ghana was formerly Co-ordinator of Programmes on Theological Education and Ministerial Formation, World Council of Churches, Geneva. His publications include *Towards an African Theology* (1979) and *Persecution and Martyrdom in the Theology of Paul* (1985).

Cynthia L. Rigby is W. C. Brown Associate Professor of Theology at Austin Presbyterian Theological Seminary, Texas, USA.

Dr Kenneth B. E. Roxburgh is Chair of the Department of Religion at Samford University, Birmingham, Alabama, USA.

Ivan Morris Satyavrata is President and Professor, Department of Theology, Southern Asia Bible College, Bangalore, India.

R. Kendall Soulen is Professor of Systematic Theology, Wesley Theological Seminary, Washington, DC. He is the author of *The God of Israel and Christian Theology* (1996) and co-author with Richard N. Soulen of *Handbook of Biblical Criticism* (3rd edn., 2001). He is an ordained elder in the United Methodist Church.

The Revd Dr Graham Tomlin is Vice Principal and Tutor in Historical Theology and Evangelism at Wycliffe Hall, Oxford. He is the author of *The Power of the Cross: Theology and the Death of Christ in Paul, Luther and Pascal* (1999), *Walking in His Steps: A Guide to Exploring the Land of the Bible* (2001), *The Provocative Church* (2002) and *Luther and his World* (2002).

William V. Trollinger Jr. is Associate Professor of History at the University of Dayton, Ohio, USA.

Werner Ustorf is Professor of Mission at the University of Birmingham, United Kingdom, and Director of the Centre for Missiology and World Christianity. His publications include *Sailing on the Next Tide. Missions, Missiology, and the Third Reich* (2000), and *Bremen Missionaries in Togo and Ghana, 1847–1900* (2002).

Peter van Rooden is a Reader at the Research Center Religion and Society of the Universiteit van Amsterdam.

Graham Ward is Professor of Contextual Theology and Ethics at the University of Manchester. His books include *Barth, Derrida and the Language of Theology* (1995) *Cities of God* (2000) and *True Religion* (2002). He has edited *The Postmodern God* (1998), *The Certeau Reader* (1999) and the *Blackwell Companion to Postmodern Theology* (2001). He is senior executive editor of the journal *Literature and Theology*.

John Webster is Professor of Systematic Theology at the University of Aberdeen, UK.

Clark M. Williamson is Indiana Professor of Christian Thought, Emeritus, at Christian Theological Seminary in Indianapolis. His publications include *Has God Rejected His People? Anti-Judaism in the Christian Church* (1982), *A Guest in the House of Israel: Post-Holocaust Church Theology* (1993), and *Way of Blessing, Way of Life: A Christian Theology* (1999).

John Witte, Jr. (J. D. Harvard, 1985), is Director of the Law and Religion Program, and Director of the Center for the Interdisciplinary Study of Religion, Emory University, Atlanta, Georgia, USA.

J. Philip Wogaman is Professor Emeritus in Christian Ethics, Wesley Theological Seminary, Washington, DC.

Dr Carver T. Yu is Professor in Dogmatic Theology and Vice President, China Graduate School of Theology, Hong Kong. He is also a member of the Center of Theological Inquiry, Princeton, USA and is an ordained minister in the Cumberland Presbyterian Church.

Dr Yung Hwa is Director of the Centre for the Study of Christianity in Asia, Trinity Theological College, Singapore.

Randall C. Zachman is Associate Professor of Reformation Studies at the University of Notre Dame, Indiana, USA. His areas of interest are in the history of Christian thought from the Reformation period to the present, with particular attention to the theological trajectory traced by the theology of John Calvin, Friedrich Schleiermacher, and Karl Barth. He is author of *The Assurance of Faith: Conscience in the Theology of Martin Luther and John Calvin* (1993).

Foreword

Any work that attempts to define a multifaceted movement such as Protestantism faces several Herculean tasks. Aside from the sheer immensity of its history across the entire globe and its unique manifestations and impact therein, one also has to face the post-modern charge that Protestantism is nothing more than religious modernity. Implicit in this charge is the denuding of what most Protestants would claim central to their faith, the presence of God's redeeming activity in and through the church, in favour of a presentation of Protestantism as an ideological movement – complex to be sure, but nothing more than a series of ideas and repercussions in a steady ebb and flow that eventually threaten in the west to run out of steam, and which elsewhere seems alien or imposed. Protestantism, then, is both a church movement (or better yet an expression of a faith-based church) but also a cultural phenomenon that has been shaped and has shaped that which surrounds it. It is with this multiplicity in mind that this *Companion* has been designed. The *Companion* tries to treat Protestantism as both a church-based movement and a cultural phenomenon. It gives prominence to the theology and churches of Protestants but also looks to how each has intermingled, positively and negatively, within a wider cultural milieu that still resonates today.

Adding another layer of difficulty to the project is that Protestantism, almost from its inception and certainly from the seventeenth century onwards, is pan-global and in each locale, micro and macro, has encountered and assimilated indigenous movements and fostered new expressions. Many of these continental, national and local histories, especially in what the African theologian John Pobee calls the 'North Atlantic Captivity' of Europe and North America, are well studied, while many histories are overlooked or largely ignored. We have tried to address this imbalance and the very needful recognition that Protestantism is pan-global in influence (and that most Protestants now are not European or North American) by having native scholars author their own histories and by looking to the future of Protestantism as a non-western European movement and phenomenon.

The shape of the text reflects this triad of concerns: Protestantism as pan-global, theological and ideologically loaded. The Introduction is an attempt to provide a historical theological background, from Protestantism's own confessions, of what Protestants believe and how they organize themselves as a consequence in their church polity. Complementing this introduction is the final part, on 'The Future of Protestantism'. In this part, the essays attempt to define and analyse the offspring of Protestantism – post-modernism, Pentecostalism, Evangelicalism; the emergence of Asian, African and South American Protestant forms; and the situation of historic western Protestant denominations. The Introduction and final part begin and end (at least for the present) the conversation about what Protestantism is in terms of its origins and its future.

Sandwiched between the Introduction and 'The Future of Protestantism' are two further major parts. The first, 'The Formation of Protestant Identity: History and Ideology', is a magisterial survey of Protestantism in various regional and national identities, as well as an opportunity for several major Protestant thinkers to be explored. The brief given to each author was not only to give a landmarked history but also to attempt a synthesis of the implications of that history within the life of the region or nation. This is purposed on two fronts. First is to avoid the catalogued rehearsal of facts covered in other works. Secondly, and more importantly to the ethos of the text, is the attempt to grapple with two of our triad of concern – that we present each history as the result of a church or faith movement that in turn impacts and is impacted by its surrounding culture. The importance of indigenous authors was paramount in this regard. Of course, while every attempt has been made to present as much of the rich diversity of Protestant identities, not all nations and histories are accounted for. To this the editors can only plead 'guilty' and offer space considerations (as well as target audiences) in defence, but meanwhile hoping that bibliographies offset some of the selection. Likewise, the list of who could have been highlighted, apart from the 'big five' of Luther, Calvin, Edwards, Schleiermacher and Barth, is disputable. It was felt, and is mitigated by the historical essays themselves in which other notable figures (and ideas) are introduced, that these five thinkers are foundational to any discussion of Protestantism in any form or context. A similar defence of space is proffered.

The next major part, 'Protestantism and Present Identity', is broken down into two components. Once again, these reflect the triadic concern that drives the text. 'Protestantism and Its Relations' frames the conversation that Protestantism has had (and continues to have) with major segments of human enterprise and culture (usually in the western context). The relationship of Protestantism to science, art, politics and law as well as itself via its Bible-centred commitments is explored, highlighting the interplay between the 'religious' or 'theological' and other presumably secular human enterprise and creations. 'Protestantism and its Influence' furthers this conversation by addressing Protestantism to various movements that dominate much of the present situation and constitute the grounds of future conversations elsewhere. The section explores Protestant responsibility for (and resources to combat) anti-Semitism, racial and sexual inequality, and presents two of the major Protestant variations (or reactions) in liberalism and fundamentalism. In looking forward to the 'new Protestantism' of the twenty-first century in new climes it seems imperative that Protestantism learns of its own critique well, if only to avoid repeating the same mistakes in new situations. This section also examines 'how' Protestantism has exported itself in missions and its spirituality. Again, these essays indicate how the interplay between idea theology and wider culture is transferred into real concrete situations in both pleasantly surprising and woefully shattering ways.

Having nearly 40 different contributors, many writing in a second or even third language, makes for some stylistic variance, and we have retained the contributors' spelling and punctuation style, whether UK or US. References and up-to-date further reading lists have been provided as springboards for further study. The reader is also encouraged to use the index as a means of maximizing the interpenetration of movements and individuals across the rich history of Protestantism.

It is the hope of the editors that the chapters be understood not merely as dictionary accounts, but as arguments, although well-researched and documented ones, which will induce fuller and more profound conversations as to the past, present and future of Protestantism in all its forms.

Finally, it is impossible to acknowledge the contribution of all the scholars who have had a hand in the shaping of this volume. A rigorous process of consultation and recommendation allowed the editors to cull the best authors in a range of topics and expertises (far outside our own). Many have assisted in this process but two are notable: Prof Ellen Charry (Princeton Theological Seminary) and Dr Chris Sugden (Oxford Centre for Mission Studies) both nominated many excellent choices who found their way into the volume. To them, and the many unnamed others who nominated scholars during the project, our thanks are given.

The Editors

Introduction: Protestantism – the Problem of Identity

Alister E. McGrath and Darren C. Marks

Protestantism is traditionally understood to designate the churches and denominations that have received their inspiration from the Reformation, including the whole unfolding of that history from the sixteenth century down to the present day. This understanding of the notion informs this *Companion*, which aims to explore the many facets of this development, especially within Western culture. Yet it must be conceded that 'Protestantism' remains obstinately resistant to more precise definition. As by far the most diverse form of contemporary Christianity, it is more susceptible to description rather than definition. Its intrinsic resistance to any concept of centralized authority corresponding to the Roman Catholic *magisterium* has led to a remarkable degree of diversification at both the theological and sociological levels. Even though certain important patterns of commonality may be discerned, contemporary Protestantism is perhaps at least as notable for its divergences as for its shared historical roots and theological agendas.

The rapid growth of Protestant denominations in the twentieth century, given further impetus through the remarkable development of charismatic and Pentecostal groupings, has made it increasingly difficult to speak convincingly of the 'essence of Protestantism'. While there are important debates within the movement over what its core identity and values might be, empirical observation of the movement suggests that the self-understandings of the movement have become increasingly fluid since the Second World War. The rapid expansion of the movement in its Pentecostal and charismatic forms, particularly when set against the backdrop of the decline of traditional Protestant denominations in the West, suggests that the profile of Protestantism is likely to undergo highly significant changes in the twenty-first century.

In recent times, 'Protestant' has increasingly become a shorthand term for a number of seemingly disparate Christian denominations and general cultural attitudes, which need to be parsed carefully. Even its more notorious and disparaged nonreligious caricatures contain at least some truths about the nature of the movement. Thus Friedrich Nietzsche, Max Weber and H. Richard Niebuhr argued that 'Protestantism' designates an ethos that has certain specific political and economic overtones, namely those associated with Western European capitalism and politics and present-day American-style democracy. All argue with differing stresses that there are specific ideas, disguised and given authority as specific doctrines, inherent in the mainline or 'magisterial' Reformation that were and are catalytic to forms of the modern Western world and which have also contributed much of the woes of that culture. The commonality is the stress on the ideological penetration, usually thought of as negative, embedded in its theology, of Protestantism in the nontheological (or seemingly so) areas of politics, culture and economics.

In its strictest sense, the term 'Protestant' refers to the group of German princes and cities who 'protested' in April 1529 against the re-entrenchment by the Diet of Speyer of the Diet of Worms's active policy of persecution of Lutheranism and Zwinglism (1521). Prior to the Diet of Speyer, those church groups which are now understood to be Protestant – namely, the Lutheran and Reformed (later to be known as Calvinist) communities – were commonly referred to as 'evangelical' (*evangelisch* or *évangélique*), thus stressing its centre of biblical exegesis (*sola scriptura*) and its doctrinal core in a faith-based redemptive Christology. At this early stage, issues of church identity were seen as subordinate to the greater question of the recovery of an authentic and biblical understanding of the gospel itself. Yet a debate over the nature of these ecclesial groupings could not be postponed. Throughout the 1530s, the issue of evangelical self-definition became of increasing importance, both to the evangelical movement itself and its increasingly concerned critics.

The question of Protestant self-definition was made more complex through the rise of what is now generally referred to as the 'Radical Reformation'. The historical roots of this movement are complex, and interlock to no small extent with the emerging Lutheran and Reformed churches. These radicals argued that the mainline reformers – such as Luther and Zwingli – had been inconsistent or negligent in their application of their reforming principles and agendas. For example, it was argued that Luther had retained a number of traditional beliefs and practices (such as infant baptism) which were not adequately grounded in the Bible, and which ought therefore to be rejected. Furthermore, radical reformers objected to the close and positive links that Luther, Zwingli and Calvin encouraged between the church and the magistracy (hence the term 'magisterial Reformation'), and argued that authentic Christian existence could only be attained through a return to the pre-Constantinian situation, in which the church was radically separated from the state and its values. Although small in numbers, such radical communities are of considerable interest to both historians and theologians, not least on account of the challenge they pose to the assumption that Protestantism is by definition world-affirming and prone to social assimilation.

Important though the Radical Reformation is historically, particularly in relation to the emergence of the significant and influential Baptist and Mennonite communities in North America, its emphasis upon the separation of church and state limited its impact upon the development of Western culture. For much of its history, Anabaptism's instinctive attitude was that of social disengagement, in order to focus on spiritual and social issues within their own communities, which were often conceived as profoundly countercultural creations. As this *Companion* is concerned with every aspect of Protestant life and thought, it is perhaps inevitable that it should focus primarily upon the numerically larger and more socially engaging magisterial Reformation.

We have tried to avoid any hint of the hagiographical historiography of Protestantism, usually associated with the nineteenth century and its sociopolitical and even missionary agendas, which portrayed Protestantism as the zenith of human culture. The magisterial Reformers, according to this view, are not only founders of a theological movement but are agents of God's providential hand in resisting a spiral of decay that continually threatens human culture. This approach to Protestantism often leads to the simple equivocation of all things good with Western European culture – an assumption that many regard as fundamental to the colonialism of the period – as well as encouraging the implicit demonization of both the non-Christian world and Catholic Europe. In terms of its view of history, this approach saw the Reformation as representing divine intervention in history, without precedent and independent of all other factors except God's will. Its heroes became noncontextualized figures, devoid of any background in Catholic thought or history, and its opponents were often treated as deliberate opponents of the divine will. An increasing awareness of the complexity of the intellectual and social origins of the Reformation has largely dispelled such misleading stereotypes, except in popular polemical literature.

Protestantism is best regarded as a heterogeneous movement with shared theological roots that largely began in central and northern Europe, and quickly developed political, economic and social dimensions on account of its interaction with the specific societal structures and norms within which it first took root. The roots of the movement are to be sought in medieval Europe, and its theology in secular philosophical and philological movements such as Renaissance humanism, as well as in wider shifts in contemporary European culture from largely rural feudalism to urban-based economies and political structures. Each of these can be rightly considered as both connected and important to an understanding of the emergence and identity of 'Protestantism'. For example, Protestantism was widely regarded as liberating by the increasingly important middle classes of the imperial cities of Europe, who saw the new understanding of the Christian faith as marking a break with the traditional structures of the past and offering them theological legitimization for their social and political agendas.

It will be clear that the term 'Protestantism' now designates a wide range of significantly different theological emphases and church structures. These are often described under four general headings, as follows:

1   Classical Protestant denominations, which trace their historical origins and theological pedigrees back to the Reformation of the sixteenth century. Lutheran, Reformed and Anglican forms of Protestantism might all reasonably be located in this category. Such denominations are often characterized by a concern with classical creedal formulations, as well as the distinctive traditional characteristic emphases of the denomination, often embodied in certain specific 'confessions of faith', such as the Formula of Concord, the Westminster Confession of Faith or the Thirty-nine Articles. Within such denominations, there is often tension between liberals and traditionalists, with the former seeking to explore and develop approaches to theology and church life which are more responsive to societal and cultural changes, often seeing traditional formulations of faith and understandings of church structure as impeding such an engagement. Traditionalists, on the other hand, argue that the identity and distinctive ethos of the denomination is defined and safeguarded by traditional formulations of faith. To meddle with such 'givens' is potentially to forfeit the denomination's reason for existence, leading to a loss of theological vision and social identity.

2   Denominations and movements which trace their history and derive their theological moorings, at least in part, from the Radical Reformation of the sixteenth century. The Mennonite communities in North America are a particularly luminous example of such a denomination. However, it is also reasonable to suggest that the highly influential consortium of Baptist churches trace their origins to this sixteenth-century movement, even if that historical connection is complex, based partly on English independent churches of the early seventeenth century. Once more, tensions exist between liberals and traditionalists within these churches.

3   Denominations and movements which have arisen from tensions within mainline Protestantism, and see themselves as recapturing at least something of its original theological vision, above all a firm rooting in the Bible. Perhaps the most obvious example of such a development is the phenomenon of evangelicalism, which emerged in both the United Kingdom and the United States during the eighteenth century, and has gone on to become one of the most significant forces in contemporary English-language Protestantism. While many evangelicals see their natural ecclesiological habitat as being within mainline denominations, within which they can function as an *ecclesiola in ecclesia*, others have sought to create avowedly evangelical denominations in their own right.

4   Charismatic and Pentecostal groupings, whose origins lie in the twentieth century. While some charismatic Protestants are content to operate within mainline Protestant denominations, the majority operate within specifically charismatic denominations or organizations, such as the Assemblies of God.

Although relatively recent arrivals on the scene, there are persuasive indications that this style of Protestantism is coming to be of major importance in the emerging world.

Individual articles in this volume will consider these movements and their distinctive identities, regional variations and developments in agendas, and specific issues with which Protestantism has been forced to engage throughout its history. It is, however, also important to attempt to identify at least some of the leading themes that have characterized Protestantism since its emergence in the sixteenth century, not least because these are often intimately linked with the distinctive identity and agenda of the movement.

The Contours of Classical Protestant Thought

The contours of classical Protestant theology were shaped during the sixteenth century, and may be regarded as the outcome of the confluence of the ideas and methods of leading reformers and the manner in which these were received and expounded by Protestant communities. The two most significant theological epicentres of the first phase of the Reformation were at Wittenberg and Zurich. Martin Luther's vision of the Christian gospel, which was given more systematic expression by his colleague Philip Melanchthon, focused on the evangelical proclamation of justification *sola fide* (by faith alone), with an emphasis upon the supreme authority of the Bible in matters of Christian doctrine – a notion which subsequently came to be expressed in the slogan *sola scriptura* (by Scripture alone). Although Luther was not the most systematic of writers, his ideas were widely disseminated through his two *Catechisms* (1529), and especially through Philip Melanchthon's *Loci Communes*, which first appeared in 1521.

The Swiss city of Zurich was the centre for a quite distinct understanding of the Christian life, which initially made no reference to the notion of justification *sola fide*. For Zurich's reformer Ulrich Zwingli, the life and morality of the church was to be reformed through a return to the vision of the Christian life. While Luther and Zwingli shared a common commitment to the authority of the Bible (and a corresponding rejection of the notion of absolute papal authority), they initially diverged significantly over how Scripture was to be interpreted, and whether the reforming agenda should focus on the doctrine or ethics of the church. A degree of convergence was achieved through the mediating influence of the second generation reformer John Calvin, and the rise of the city of Geneva as a centre for reformed theological education and evangelism, especially in Calvin's native France. Under Calvin, a coherent vision of the Reformation as a biblically grounded reformation of both the life and thought of the church emerged, given systematic articulation in Calvin's highly influential *Institutes of the Christian Religion*, first published in 1536, which appeared in its definitive form in 1559.

Important though Luther and Calvin are for any evaluation of the distinctive ideas of Protestantism, two important qualifications of their authority must be noted. First, both Lutheran and Reformed communities chose to define themselves, not specifically with reference to the writings of either Luther or Calvin, but with reference to certain 'confessions of faith'. These confessions were regarded as subordinate to both the Bible and the historic creeds of the Christian church, and were understood to clarify the distinctive vision of the Christian faith associated with the Lutheran and Reformed communities. Within Lutheranism, the *Augsburg Confession* (1530) initially played a highly influential role, although this was gradually supplanted following the publication of the *Formula of Concord* (1578). Reformed communities throughout Europe drew up confessions of faith which expressed their leading theological commitments, above all to the supreme authority of the Bible in matters of faith and doctrine. The Westminster Confession of Faith (1647) may be taken as representative of this general trend:

> The whole counsel of God, concerning all things necessary for his own glory, man's salvation, faith and life, is either expressly set down in Scripture, or by good and necessary consequence may be deduced from Scripture; to which nothing at any time is to be added, whether by new revelations of the Spirit, or traditions of men.

Among these Reformed confessions, the following are of particular interest: the Ten Theses of Berne (1528), the Tetrapolitan Confession of 1530, the Lausanne Articles and the Geneva Confession of 1536, the Second Helvetic Confession (1566).

In what follows, we shall explore some of the basic ideas that emerge as characteristic of magisterial Protestantism in this formative period.

An exegetical Christological foundation

The two slogans that are usually thought to lie at the heart of the theological vision of the magisterial Reformation are *sola fide* and *sola scriptura* – the doctrine of justification by faith and the claim that the life and thought of the church must find their basis in the Bible alone. Both of these slogans can be argued to be subsidiary to a more fundamental doctrine that is derived from an *exegetical Christology* that many modern theologians regard as the true (but not exclusive) purview of the Reformation in general, and of both Luther and Calvin in particular.

Luther and Calvin were primarily exegetes of the Bible and saw in its message the announcement of the gospel as revealed fully in Christ. This message was nothing more than the promise of God to forgive sinners. The authority and the guiding hermeneutical principle thus reside in the Bible, understood as the witness to God's objective declaration of salvation in Christ Jesus. Both theologians saw in the Bible the truth that the Christian shares a radical new relationship with God because of Christ, and that this saving work – our justifica-tion – therefore lies wholly beyond any human possibility and capacity. Salva-tion is an act of grace given in the economy of the Triune God, of which Jesus Christ is the mediator between God and humanity.

Both Luther and Calvin can be argued to share a radical vision of Christo-centrism – often summarized in the slogan *soli Christo* – derived from their reading of the Bible. Both emphasize that God's gift to humanity in Christ is nothing less than Christ himself, wherein human beings are engrafted into that which properly only belongs to the God-man in all his life, death, resurrection, ascension and heavenly ministry. Both stress that humans can do nothing to merit divine forgiveness or to assuage divine wrath. As a consequence, the bond between Christ and his church is established solely on the merit of Christ alone and subsequently in the work of the Triune God as justifier, sanctifier and regen-erator. The remainders of their respective theologies can be regarded as footnotes to this radical Christocentrism derived from their biblical exegesis, and its sub-sequent application to the life and witness of the church.

On the nature of justification

A comparison of Luther's doctrine of justification with Calvin's treatment of the matter suggests that Luther held a more prescriptive view of the doctrine than Calvin, who tends to adopt a largely descriptive approach. Both, nonetheless, stress the basic insight that Christ meets us in and through his Word, and that this transformative action is grounded in God's freedom, which is totally inde-pendent of human merit or capacity. It is possible to misunderstand Luther by placing an emphasis upon faith, rather than Christ; to stress the role which human faith itself plays (*pisteology*) is to reduce Luther's emphasis that salva-tion is wholly the work of God, which is received by faith. As Luther and Melanchthon both stressed, justification takes place *propter Christum per fidem* (on account of Christ, through faith), where a false reading of Luther holds it to take place *propter fidem*. According to this misunderstanding, the Christian repents and has faith in God's promises, which then brings about new life. This preoccupation with subjectivity – as one's sense of status before God – has been often argued as a central motif of modernity and as the theological parent of the Enlightenment's conception of the autonomous self.

Calvin roots justification more centrally into the notion of covenant and the Lordship of Christ, making the question of justification rest not on one's faith but rather on the faithfulness of faith's object. With the context of the Christian's incorporation into Christ, Calvin argues that the Christian is made 'holy' objectively in God, so that justification and sanctification are to be seen as the double unfolding (*la double grâce*) of that objective promise. Faith is a response or the working out of our radical new justified existence in the obedience of that alteration by God, as the Holy Spirit works on the human will. For Calvin, the consequence of faith is thus worship and repentance. In contrast to Luther,

Calvin argues that faith is given in our union with Christ, not as a part or pre-condition of that union. To think otherwise would represent a challenge to Christ's Lordship, the simple Trinitarian understanding that in Christ God is fully present, and to the covenant of God that in the work of the Son God redeems and thereby shares with humanity the *beneficia Christi*. Calvin, as we shall see, thus goes on to root his doctrine of justification in a robust notion of predestination or election. The prominence of election is thus ultimately derived from his more foundational doctrine of justification. Sanctification and justification are simultaneous in the gifting of grace, in that the presence of Christ is always dependent on God's prevenience.

On the nature of predestination or election

Classically the two major differences between Calvin and Luther are held to be located in their Eucharistic theology and in the doctrine of predestination. According to this viewpoint, Christological differences are the source of contention in the Eucharist while the doctrine of election is due to Calvin's working from a doctrine of God that emphasizes the free objectivity of God over Luther's starting point of subjectivity and faith. There is much to be commended in this view but the differences seem to be more rooted in Christology than in competing views of the doctrine of God or justification's keynotes. Luther, for example, in his *de Servo Arbitrio* argues for a doctrine of predestination, derived from Augustine, that corresponds closely to Calvin's later doctrine. Luther, here opposing Erasmus and a perceived threat of Pelagianism, argues that not only does God elect those who are to be saved but also that God actively hardens those who reject the gospel. This is a form of double predestination, that God elects both the saved and the condemned independent of human action. Regardless of their respective starting points, both use the doctrine as a foundation of the believer's confidence that God has prepared a way of grace independent of human merit.

The source of difference, however, lies primarily in the application of their exegetically derived Christology. Luther is much more attuned to the biblical position that the will of God revealed in Christ is primarily a will to save. In short, Christology is a reflection on the grace of God as revealed in Christ. For Luther, to seek the grounds for this decision by God, the so-called 'secret will' of God, is to miss or misunderstand the basic comfort of the gospel that God has come for sinners in Christ. Luther's Christology is preoccupied with the reality that Christ is God and demonstrates God's will for humanity, which is the promise of forgiveness and union with Christ as known to the believer. Predestination is a secondary aspect of the guiding principle of Luther's Christology as the justifying Saviour known by faith. Calvin, on the other hand, is more rigorous in the application of his Christology. The biblical identification of Christ with God – not merely as God's revelation but as the Lord – is understood by Calvin as not only to relate to the application of salvation (here following Luther), but to represent a fundamental statement concerning divine Trinitarian ontology. For Calvin, Luther threatens the unity of divine ontology, God as Triune, by raising the possibility of two wills in God, one hidden in the pre-Creation will of God, and the other revealed in Christ. For Calvin, to think that somehow Christ represents a different expression of God's will is to challenge not only the coherence of a doctrine of God but also his Christology and its simple identification of Christ as the Lord. Predestination can thus be seen as an integral aspect of Calvin's application of his Christology: in Christ the whole being and will of God including God's transcendental freedom above creation is made known, fully and reliably.

Developments within later Lutheranism might seem to lend some weight to Calvin's concerns. Lutheran scholasticism, apparently borrowing from the Jesuit doctrine of *scientia media*, came to distinguish a unity of purpose from a nonabsolute and therefore contingent divine will in relation to the application of salvation. According to this view, while God desires all to be saved, God knows beforehand that some will reject salvation and therefore excludes them in reality from the application of Christ's work. This 'middle-knowledge', with its distinction between passive foreknowledge (*praescientia*) and active foreordination (*praedestinatio*) effectively bifurcates the divine will, forcing a distinction between a general and absolute will to save (*voluntas universalis sive antecedens*), and a more restricted will by which God foresees (*praevisio*) the concrete and contingent application of salvation won by Christ (*voluntas specialis sive consequens*). This is more a doctrine of the human election of God than a doctrine of how in Christ God comes to humanity. Particularly in nineteenth-century Lutheranism the manifestation of the two Christological stresses becomes a foundation for an anthropologically based liberalism, and the increasing evaluation of theology as nothing more than anthropology. Religion, including Christianity, is thus to be construed as an expression of the human need or experience of God. In reaction to this development, it is to Karl Barth's credit that his theology represents a return to both Luther and Calvin's insistence that whatever election is, it must be a reflection of Christology and not another theological starting point.

On the nature of the gospel and law dialectic

A fundamental difference in Christological emphasis can also be argued to underlie the different understandings of Luther and Calvin on the relationship to law and gospel. Both Luther and Calvin root law in their respective Christologies, holding that in Christ the compulsion and curse of the law is removed and, despite their moral imperfections, foolish and hopeful sinners can find comfort and sustenance for their ethical lives. Luther's law–gospel dialectic is a reflection of his preoccupation with the application of his Christological rule that Christ saves. Before the comfort of the gospel, humanity stands in a negative relationship to God and knows only the law, and the law condemns.

Humanity stands under the wrath of God. Law, understood as not only con-science but primarily as the revelation of the Old Testament, functions to demon-strate sin and is an expression of original sin. However, paralleling his incipient double-will theology, Luther thinks that law is an 'alien work' (*opus alienum*), when compared with the 'true work' (*opus proprium*) of Christ – that is, the comfort of the gospel. Law, therefore, has an apparently different function before and after conversion. Before conversion law has a pedagogical and a political use; it prepares for grace and restrains sin, particularly in its manifestation as soci-etal precepts as found in the Mosaic commandments and the Noachic orders of creation such as the role of the family. After conversion, the law possesses a *usus normativus* by which it directs and informs the Christian life, enabling believers, with the assistance of the Holy Spirit, to fulfil God's will for their lives. Once again, it is Luther's application of his Christology understood as connected to the notion of justification that drives his understanding. Law is understood in light of the Christological maxim 'Christ justifies'.

Calvin, likewise, works from his Christological maxim that Christ is God, and rejects Luther's abstraction of law from Christology for the reasons given in his doctrine of election. To posit that law – originating in God as God's will for humanity – is different from gospel, is to abstract God from Christ. There is no abstract law as a means to or reflection of God but only God in Christ. Law, for Calvin, must rest firmly in the covenant faithfulness of God found in Christ. Law is explained in Christology. Calvin thus only accepts Luther's 'third' use of the law (*usus normativus*) where Luther argues that once joined to Christ our works, as obedience, are able to fulfil God's mandate and then only because of Christ's promise of Spirit.

On the Eucharist

There is little doubt that one of the most significant divergences between Luther and Calvin related to the Eucharist. Numerous attempts to find an evangelical compromise, urged upon them by the conciliatory Philip Melanchthon and Martin Bucer, were rejected by Luther himself, and later by the Formula of Concord. It is here that their respective Christological differences find clearest expression. Despite their differences on this matter, however, both Luther and Calvin rejected Zwingli's earlier 'memorialism' as an inadequate account of the Eucharistic event, arguing that his portrayal of the Eucharist as an act of remembrance of Christ's sacrifice reduces the Eucharist to a human act, and therefore by implication our *unio mystica* is not a statement of God's grace but is tied to human effort. For both Luther and Calvin, whatever the Eucharist sym-bolizes, it is at the most profound level a reflection of their Christology and the common magisterial Reformation principle that God alone, in Christ, justifies independent of human merit. Both Eucharistic theologies stress the objectivity of the sacrament – that its effectiveness and meaning stands outside human merit or understanding and is based in God's promises in Christ.

Luther's Eucharistic theology is often referred to in terms of 'consubstantiation', thus emphasizing its contradistinction to the Roman Catholic doctrine of transubstantiation. According to this doctrine of transubstantiation, the consecrated bread and wine substantially become in property or substance the body and blood of Christ. This had two unacceptable implications for Luther. First is that the elements themselves became improper objects of worship; second, that the mass is seen as another aspect of what Christ singularly did in his vicarious action on the cross. Luther rejected the doctrine of transubstantiation, and in its place offered a doctrine of consubstantiation which takes as its starting point the declaration that while the elements are not transmuted materially, they are nevertheless more than just bread and wine. Luther develops this important notion in two ways. First, Luther argued that the elements derive their meaning solely due to the Word itself. It is because Christ commanded the elements to be celebrated that they have any meaning at all. Second, and more centrally, because of the Word they come to be more than bread and wine (but not transformed into the body and blood) in that in and through them we really receive the promise (and therefore substance) of Christ, meaning forgiveness.

In his controversy with Zwingli, Luther was clear to argue (and possibly overstate) that the elements were not merely instruments through which faith was strengthened on the basis of Christ's work; in some way, they also conveyed Christ. The Eucharist becomes a 'means of grace' as the elements become the body and blood of Christ 'in, with and under' the bread and wine. Luther's Eucharistic theology is driven by his simple equivocation of the mode and form of Christ with that of the elements, so that he needs to use another doctrine to explain how Christ can be 'in, with and under' the elements and yet remain both God and human. The material – the elements – can be understood as competing with the primary stress of promise as found in the Word. The key area that comes under scrutiny is not whether Christ is God, and therefore can be ubiquitous in presence, but what happens to his humanity in the supper. The question is whether this 'repletive' mode of presence extends only to Christ's divine nature or whether his human nature is likewise able to be everywhere at once. For Luther's critics, the employment of the *communicatio idiomatum* (a statement that in the incarnation both natures of Christ are mutually penetrating so that humanity shares divinity and vice versa) in his Eucharistic theology threatens the human nature of Christ and therefore his role as saviour and mediator and his ongoing ministry to the church. Christ's human nature, the basis of our *unio mystica*, if having the property of ubiquity (being in all places at all times), cannot be said to be like any other human nature. This raises the question of what is human nature, both fallen and redeemed, and threatens the entire unity of God to creation and Christ's role as mediator and as saviour. Later Lutheran theologians would pick up this theme in Luther with the two state theologies of humiliation and exaltation and the doctrine of *kenosis*. The incarnation, Christ's humiliation, is either an emptying or a concealment of divinity and threatens the equation of Christ to God and reduces his sufferings and work to that of an illusion. What is lost is the solidarity of Christ to human-ity. As ever, the theological issue is one of Christology.

What Luther is at pains to avoid in his Eucharistic theology is the transfor-mation of the Eucharist into either a human symbol (as in Zwingli's account) or into another Christ (as in the doctrine of transubstantiation). Luther is keen to preserve the fact, derived from his exegetical Christology and founded on his notion of *unio mystica*, that the gift in the elements is Christ himself. This spiri-tual presence, 'in, with and under' the elements, is due to God's promise and action in Christ. The Eucharist is boldly claimed by the Christian as nothing less than Christ, and therefore the promise of forgiveness which in turn shapes the Christian's life in reality.

Calvin, likewise, roots his Eucharistic theology in the primacy of God's action and promise in Christ. The elements are signs, God's sensual accommodation to us, of the true spiritual reality which is becoming true in faith. The content of that reality is Christ and the symbols are portents of that reality. The elements are not the substance of Christ, but instruments pointing to that reality. They are nonetheless spiritual food in that they are the gift of the union with the Mediator, but this action is founded on the Trinitarian life of God, as it is the Spirit of Christ that bonds us and not our faith. In the elements, God condescends in the Spirit to fulfil the promise of Christ's presence to his church. In contradistinction to Luther, it is not 'by mouth', meaning the physical elements, that we partake of Christ but the Spirit's filling the vessel of faith.

Calvin's distinctive teaching is that Christ's human nature subsequent to the ascension remains human. Central to Calvin's Eucharistic theology is the recog-nition that it is not necessary to explain the mechanism of the mystery of Christ's *corporalis praesentia*. This distinguishes him from Luther. What distin-guishes him from Anabaptism and Zwinglianism is his insistence with Luther that the ground of the Eucharist (and baptism) is the objectivity of God so that in the sacraments the content or substance, spiritually or instrumentally, is nothing less than Christ. This removes the requirement of piety or its attestation as a factor in salvation or faith. For both magisterial reformers, working from their exegesis of the Bible, the focus of the sacraments is the reality of that person whom they signify, and the gift of Christ therein to the church.

On the doctrine of the church and the priesthood of all believers

From what has been said thus far, the importance of the church to both Luther and Calvin will be obvious. Both theologians understand the church as the unique place in which God manifests the promise of Christ to the world. The church is not merely a society of like-minded people but absolutely central in its function as witness through sacrament and ministry of the Word (primarily preaching as exegesis of the Bible) to the objectivity of God and redemption. The defining marks of the church are thus identified as the preaching of the gospel, and the proper administration of the sacraments. Both see the church as visible and invisible, in that the invisible are those chosen in God (election) and that within the 'visible' or earthly church there is both elected and nonelected. The church's task is the preaching of the gospel, meaning Christ, which in turn calls Christians to the sacraments wherein faith is strengthened. Preaching is the exegesis of the Bible and its Christologically controlled claims on all aspects of human existence within the church. The church is the radiating centre of God's action within the whole world. For both theologians the church is not necessary in the sense that God is confined to the church, but it is necessary in the sense that God binds us to it in its function as the place in which Christ is witnessed to as the Lord. Both therefore hold that there is no salvation outside the church.

This vision of the church is a statement against the often misunderstood doctrine of separation of church and state. In fact, the term *magisterial* refers explicitly to the interpenetration of the church into the state by the reformers. The question is: what is the nature of this interpenetration? Both reformers saw the church and state as different means to a similar end, which was to bring the entire creation into proper service and worship of God. The role of the state was to restrain evil and to provide a nursery from which the message of the gospel could thrive. The role of the church is its primary function of witness, but also as it performs that role the church must anchor itself in the secular and thereby transform it. For both, and developed in later manifestations of their traditions, the separation of church and state was illusory as the church needed to be faithful in the real world and the state needed to be shown the true content of justice as love. It must be underscored, however, that neither Luther nor Calvin thought that the church was Christ, that Christianity was the same as Christ and that the church should enjoy privilege on the basis of being the church. In fact, this was a primary complaint against their Catholic opponents. Instead, both understood the role of the church as that place wherein Christ, through the ministry of the Word and sacraments, was witnessed to as the Lord. The leitmotifs of the church are service and worship, not prestige and privilege. Nonetheless, it is also true that this fine line was crossed by both men in some of their dealings, famously by Luther on the Jewish presence and by Calvin in his treatment of Servetus and other Anabaptists, and by later generations of Christians in their respective traditions.

The inevitable outcome of both Luther and Calvin's exegetical and Christological theology is the doctrine of the priesthood of all believers. Every believer, by virtue of his or her baptism, has the status of a priest in the church of God. This doctrine held that each Christian, in praxis and faith, is brought through the vicarious action of Christ into a new life and responsibility before God and that access to this new life is unmediated in the sense that it falls solely on Christ alone. While the church is absolutely central for this life, it is not absolutely critical as the bearer of salvation. The individual's own status before God and direct access to God through Christ means that all Christians are equally 'priests', that is, called to minister and witness to the Word and live in sacramental grace without ontological or theological distinction. The magisterial Reformers, however, as we shall see, despite the universality of access through Christ did recast polity (order) in parallels to Catholic structures of priest and laity, especially in terms of administering 'gifts' (charisms) of offices and the sacraments. The interpretation of the 'priesthood of all believers', originally a mark of Christ's uniqueness and claim on the Christian as Lord, is quickly shifted in its gravity to a reflection on polity.

The 'Protestant Problematic'

The problem in trying to 'identify' Protestantism is, in part, due to its origins as a breakaway movement from a larger ecclesial grouping, which tended to define and conceptualize itself theologically, rather than institutionally. Once this decisive transition had been made, the essence of Protestant identity shifted from a specific institutional affiliation to adherence to a set of ideas, which in turn legitimated further fissure and division within Protestantism. The 'Protestant problematic' (Karl Rahner) is that it places priority on individual conscience in response to revelation – in the Bible and the experience of salvation – as its defining characteristics. As such it must create the possibility, but not the necessity, of interpretative difference in doctrine, practice and polity. Running alongside this 'Protestant problematic' is that it is a historical human movement riddled, despite claims to the contrary, with human conditionality and fraility. A brief survey of issues, currently in discussion but not unique in Lutheranism in regard to its definitive *Augsburg Confession*, serves to illustrate the problems.

Although clear attempts to define the distinguishing beliefs of the Wittenberg evangelical faction were under way by the late 1520s, it was not until 1530 that a comprehensive statement of Lutheran theology was drafted in the *Augsburg Confession*. This *Confession* can be understood in one of two, often competing, ways. First, it can be seen as an essentially *sociological* document born out of the political expediencies of its period, rather hastily and haphazardly patched together from previous, usually theologically charged works by Luther and Melanchthon, with the primary objective of securing peace. According to this version of things, the summoning of Luther, Melanchthon, Justus Jonas and John Bugenhagen to Augsburg by Emperor Charles V (21 January 1530) is to be seen as the result of external forces. The failure of the Protestant princes to guard against either Turkish or Catholic armies meant that the 'priests' squabbles' between Lutheran and Zwinglian or Lutheran and Catholic camps had to be resolved in order that the business of self-preservation might proceed. This interpretation, however, minimizes earlier attempts of self-identification and even nascent intra-Protestant ecumenism, such as the *Schwabach Articles*, the *Marburg Colloquy* (October 1529) and the presence of an already formed Lutheran theology such as that of Melanchthon's *Loci Communes* (1521), let alone Luther's own work.

The second way of understanding the *Augsburg Confession* is to view it as the culmination of earlier attempts by Luther and Melanchthon at self-identification, which may well have been *occasioned* by greater political needs but was not *defined* by them. In regard to early Lutheranism, self-definition was less about matters of institutional form or church polity, although these were important; rather, it was mainly concerned with a statement about the fundamental matters of faith. It is this latter understanding of the evolution of the *Augsburg Confession* that seems the more viable. The *Augsburg Confession* is best understood as the fruit of a maturing tree, with its origins in Luther and Melanchthon's earlier occasional and systematic writings and the attempts at self-identification they proposed. It is not *merely* an occasioned or historical document, whether through political or military threat or even in theological dispute, but rather is a positive exposition of Lutheran theological construction and identity.

Alongside Luther's *Small Catechism*, the *Augsburg Confession* is the most widely recognized Lutheran confession. The *Confession*'s stature is not merely due to its historical cogency; it is also affirmed because of its relationship to Scripture and to the central tenet of Luther's theology in justification by faith. Its normative status is derived from its function as a witness to what Lutherans believe is the crux of the Christian message of Scripture and of living Spirit – the forgiveness of sins won by Jesus Christ. The *Confession*'s status is such that it is 'not subject to the regulations of the church'; it is thus to be understood as constitutive – not solely foundational – in relation to Lutheran ecclesiology. This claim to normative status has been contested throughout history. The precise status of the *Confession* was so earnestly disputed by second-generation Lutherans that a second central confessional self-understanding proved necessary; this was drafted in 1578–80 and published as the *Formula of Concord* (1578) and the *Book of Concord* (1580). The *Book of Concord* is the attempt of subsequent Lutheran scholars such as James Andreae and Martin Chemnitz to unify Lutheranism, and place it within a new stable context, theologically and politically removed from the turbulence of the early years of the Reformation. Second-generation Lutheranism also distances itself somewhat from the *Augsburg Confession* through its conscious attempt to distinguish Lutheranism from the increasingly significant Reformed tradition, particularly those forms of eucharistic 'crypto-Calvinism' thought to be associated with Melanchthon.

Most famously, Friedrich Schleiermacher (*The Christian Faith* § 26) argued that historical confessions were to be classified as 'occasional (and therefore contingent) writings'. Although a Reformed theologian, Schleiermacher, in contrast to earlier Protestant scholastic theologians, shifts the authority of the *Confession* from that of the document's *theological or doctrinal meaning* to the *act of confessing* by its authors. Its normative status is found in its witnessing function, not its content. This has become the favoured understanding of the *Confession*. By recovering the notion of witness along with justification by faith as a leitmotif in the *Confession*, contemporary Lutheranism believed that it could avoid the polarizing dogmatism (*corpus doctrinae*) of the eighteenth and early nineteenth centuries in favour of a more ecumenically suitable tool by affirming that the *Confession* is only meaningful as it is used to call the church into being, or dependent on the gathered community which in turn carries out the mission of the *Confession* of faith, hope and love.

Yet the stability of any attempt to define 'Protestantism' on the basis of such a confessional document is now increasingly problematic. A number of factors create severe difficulties for such attempts at Protestant self-definition. Two are of particular importance. Although notionally specific to the *Augsburg Confession*, these concerns possess a wider validity, allowing them to be transferred to other confessional approaches.

In the first place, the *Augsburg Confession's* claim to be universally valid is undermined by its historical particularity in formation and intent. The *Book of Concord*, which is intended to further exclude the Reformed tradition, is likewise a text born out of historical circumstances. How then can they provide the foundation for a *contemporary* concord with both Catholic and Reformed faiths? The increasing recognition of the *Standordsgebundenheit* (historically situated nature) of Protestant Confessions of Faith raises serious difficulties for their contemporary application and usage, in that they are widely accepted to be the response to a specific, but now past, historical context.

In the second place, the reconceptualization of the *Confession* primarily as a 'witness', rather than as a 'doctrinal norm,' leads to an emphasis being placed upon the confessional activity of the community of faith, rather than upon what that community actually confesses. This emphasis upon the community as a *confessing* entity has opened the door for the elevation of a doctrine of the church (ecclesiology) over and against what seems to be the intent of the *Confession's* Christocentric core. What, in short, is the relationship to 'historic Lutheranism' (in terms of new issues such as homosexuality and the ordination of women, let alone non-Western forms of Protestantism) when one assumes that it is the church's *confession* which is the leitmotif of its identity, rather than the doctrines which it confesses? How is orthodoxy to be determined, when the emphasis is placed firmly on the communal action of confessing, rather than what is actually confessed by the community?

Other concerns may also be noted. For example, each Protestant theological community has inherited a series of debates and issues which were seminal at various points in its history, but which are now increasingly regarded as of largely historical interest. In the case of Lutheranism, an example may be found in the 'strict' form of the Lutheran two-kingdom theology, which has become increasingly problematic in recent Lutheran history, not least on account of the German Church Crisis of the 1930s. Recent Lutheran scholars, such as Helmut Thielicke and Jürgen Moltmann, have tried to revive or retrieve the two-kingdom theology in terms of an eschatological framework, within which Jesus's ministry is seen as the breaking in of a kingdom of justice to which Christians are bound in both act and critique. This, it is argued, avoids the insipient dualism inherent in Luther's assumptions of the kingdom of God and kingdom of Satan and allows Lutherans to dialogue with Catholics and others on the basis of a doctrine of creation or natural law. Other traditions have equally problematic 'historical' doctrinal fossils that seem to be connected to 'historical' embarrassments, or causes of woe, that the current forms are eager to rehabilitate or renounce. How does each tradition face its own *practical* critical history?

This short survey of issues in regard to Lutheranism and its creedal identity point to the problem and future challenge of Protestantism. The traditional insistence that Protestantism rests upon the double foundation of the doctrine of justification by faith alone and a complete reliance on the Bible is now seen as neither constituting a sufficient definition for the movement, nor offering a foolproof prescription for its future health. A critical reading of church history readily demonstrates that other marks crept in and competed for the centre of familial definition – such as church–state relationships, freedom of conscience, freedom in polity, sanctification and so on. As the reader will note in the following chapters, Protestantism, regardless of its historical or geographical location, is best seen as a continuous attempt to reform the church in response to its situation and the call of the gospel as found in the Bible, tradition and one's experience of grace. The *ecclesia reformata*, as the slogan has it, must be *ecclesia semper reformanda*. That is to say, to be a reformed church is to be committed to a continuous process of reformation, rather than to one specific moment in that history, or to a conception of reformation which sees it as a once-for-all event, rather than an ongoing process. Perhaps this is the best definition – and therefore not exclusive to Protestantism – that Protestantism is an attempt of faithful, but erring, Christians who strive to live as witnesses to Christ and who, like Jacob, grapple with and against God in the hope of securing God's blessing, not only for themselves but for the entire world.

References

Rahner, Karl (1973). Authority in the Church. An Exchange Between Hans Küng and Karl Rahner. *The Tablet* 227: S. 597–8.
Schleiermacher, Friedrich (1989). *The Christian Faith*, H. R. Mackintosh and J. S. Stewart (eds.). Edinburgh: T & T Clark.

Further Reading

General
Barth, Karl (1957). *Die Protestantische Theologie im 19. Jahrhundert*. Zurich: Evangelischer Verlag.
Bebbington, David (1989). *Evangelicalism in Modern Britain: A History from the 1730s to the 1980s*. London: Hyman.
Dillenberger, John and Welch, Claude (1988). *Protestant Christianity: Interpreted Through its Development*. New York: Macmillan.

Forni, Guglielmo (1995). *The Essence of Christianity: The Hermeneutical Question in the Protestant and Modernist Debate (1897–1904)*. Atlanta, GA: Scholars Press.

Kegley, Charles W. (1965). *Protestantism in Transition*. New York: Harper.

McClendon, Muriel C., Ward, Joseph, and MacDonald, Michael (1999). *Protestant Identities: Religion, Society, and Self-fashioning in Post-Reformation England*. Stanford, CA: Stanford University Press.

Martin, David (1990). *Tongues of Fire: The Explosion of Protestantism in Latin America*. Oxford: Blackwell.

Rupp, George (1977). *Culture-Protestantism: German Liberal Theology at the Turn of the Twentieth Century*. Missoula, MT: American Academy of Religion.

Stoll, David (1990). *Is Latin America Turning Protestant? The Politics of Evangelical Growth*. Berkeley: University of California Press.

Tavard, George H. (1959). *Holy Writ or Holy Church: The Crisis of the Protestant Reformation*. London: Burns & Oates.

Tillich, Paul (1957). *The Protestant Era*. Chicago: University of Chicago Press.

Ward, W. R. (1992). *The Protestant Evangelical Awakening*. Cambridge, UK: Cambridge University Press.

Welch, Claude (1985). *Protestant Thought in the Nineteenth Century*. New Haven, CT: Yale University Press.

Specific Protestant traditions

LUTHERAN

Braaten, Carl F. (1983). *Principles of Lutheran Theology*. Philadelphia: Fortress.

Burgess, Joseph A. (ed.) (1980). *The Role of the Augsburg Confession: Catholic and Lutheran Views*. Philadelphia: Fortress.

Gassman, G. and Hendrix, S. (1999). *Fortress Introduction to the Lutheran Confessions*. Philadelphia: Fortress.

Grane, Leif (1987). *The Augsburg Confession: A Commentary*, trans. J. Rasmussen. Minneapolis: Augsburg.

Gritsch, Eric and Jenson, Robert (1972). *Lutheranism*. Philadelphia: Fortress.

Maurer, Wilhelm (1986). *Historical Commentary on the Augsburg Confession*, trans. H. George Anderson. Philadelphia: Fortress.

Mildenberger, Friedrich (1983). *Theologie der Lutherischen Bekenntnisschriften*. Stuttgart: Kohlhammer.

Tappert, Theodore G. (ed.) (1959). *The Book of Concord: Confessions of the Evangelical Lutheran Church*. Philadelphia: Muhlenberg.

REFORMED THEOLOGY

Cochrane, Arthur C. (ed.) (1966). *Reformed Confessions of the 16th Century*. London: SCM.

Kendall, R. T. (1979). *Calvin and Calvinism to 1649*. Oxford: Oxford University Press.

Niesel, William (1960). *Das Evangelium und die Kirchen: Ein Lehrbuch der Symbolik*. Neukirchen: Kries Moers.

Rohls, Jan (1998). *Reformed Confessions: From Zurich to Barmen*, trans. J. Hoffmeyer. Louisville, KY: John Knox Press.

Torrance, T. F. (1959). *The School of Faith: Catechisms of the Reformed Church*. Edinburgh: T & T Clark.

PRESBYTERIAN

Henderson, G. D. (ed.) (1960). *The Scots Confession 1560*. Edinburgh: St Andrew's Press.

Hendry, George (1960). *The Westminster Confession for Today*. London: SCM.

Rogers, J. B. (1992). *Presbyterian Creeds: A Guide to the Book of Confession*. Louisville, KY: John Knox Press.

CONGREGATIONALIST

Matthews, A. G. (ed.) (1959). *The Savoy Declaration of Faith and Order 1658*. London: Independent Press.

Walker, Williston (1960). *The Creeds and Platforms of Congregationalism*. London: Harper Collins.

BAPTIST

George, Timothy (2001). *Theologians of the Baptist Tradition*. Nashville, TN: Broadman.

Lumpkin, William L. (1959). *Baptist Confessions of Faith*. Chicago: Judson Press.

ANGLICAN

Bicknell, E. J. (1955). *A Theological Introduction to the Thirty-Nine Articles of the Church of England*. London: Longmans.

Evans, G. R. and Wright, J. R. (eds.) (1991). *The Anglican Tradition: A Handbook of Sources*. London: SPCK.

O'Donovan, Oliver (1986). *On the Thirty-Nine Articles: A Conversation with Tudor Christianity*. Oxford: Paternoster.

Tyacke, Nicholas (2001). *Aspects of English Protestantism c 1530–1700*. Manchester, UK: Manchester University Press.

METHODIST

Davies, R. and Rupp, G. (eds.) (1965). *A History of the Methodist Church in Great Britain*, 4 vols. London: Epsworth Press.

Halévy, Elie (1970). *The Birth of Methodism in England*, trans. B Semmel. Chicago: Univesity of Chicago Press.

Hempton, David (1996). *The Religion of the People: Methodism and Popular Religion c 1750–1900*. New York: Routledge.

ANABAPTIST

Dyck, Cornelius J. (ed.) (1993). *An Introduction to Mennonite History*. Scottsdale, AZ: Herald Press.

Harder, Leland (1985). *The Sources of Swiss Anabaptism*. Scottsdale, AZ: Herald Press.

Snyder, Arnold C (1995). *Anabaptist History and Theology*. Kitchener, Ontario: Pandora Press.

PART I

The Formation of Protestant Identity: History and Ideology

European Protestantism

1	Protestantism in German Speaking Lands to the Present Day	23
2	Shapers of Protestantism: Martin Luther	40
3	Shapers of Protestantism: John Calvin	53
4	Shapers of Protestantism: F. D. E. Schleiermacher	66
5	Shapers of Protestantism: Karl Barth	83
6	English Protestantism to the Present Day	96
7	Scottish Protestantism to the Present Day	109
8	Welsh Protestantism to the Present Day	120
9	Irish Protestantism to the Present Day	123
10	Nordic Protestantism to the Present Day	130
11	Protestantism in the Netherlands to the Present Day	147
12	Protestantism in Eastern Europe to the Present Day	155
13	French Protestantism to the Present Day	161
14	Italian Protestantism to the Present Day	163

North American Protestantism

15	Protestantism in the United States of America to the Present Day	165
16	Shapers of Protestantism: Jonathan Edwards	181
17	Canadian Protestantism to the Present Day	189

Asia and Australasia

18	Indian Protestantism to the Present Day	201
19	South-East Asian Protestantism to the Present Day	206
20	Japanese Protestantism to the Present Day	210
21	Korean Protestantism to the Present Day	216

22 Chinese Protestantism to the Present Day   222
23 Protestantism in Australia, New Zealand and Oceania to the
    Present Day   232

Africa
24 African Protestantism to the Present Day   239

CHAPTER 1

Protestantism in German-speaking Lands to the Present Day

Randall C. Zachman

The rise of Protestant theology in German-speaking lands took place by means of an unprecedented turn of events within the Latin theological tradition. From the earliest days of the Christian community, the assumption had been that what one received from the authoritative bearers of the Christian faith, namely the bishops, was both catholic and apostolic in nature, and was therefore unquestionably true and in harmony with the teaching of the prophets and apostles in Scripture. Beginning with Martin Luther, however, that assumption was deeply shaken by the claim that the teaching authorities of the Church, including university professors of theology as well as bishops and the Pope, were no longer teaching the truth of God, but rather were teaching the lies of Satan. More specifically, Luther claimed that there was a clear contradiction between the teaching of Scripture and the teaching of the Roman Church. In such a situation, one could no longer take the teaching of the Church as the given foundation on the basis of which theological reflection would proceed, but one would first have to test all of received tradition by the clear teaching of Scripture, in order to hold fast what withstands the test, and to reject all the rest as lies and deception. The result of such testing and critique would be to *restore* catholic and apostolic teaching to the Church, after the bishops and teachers of Rome had lost it. None of the Reformers wanted to be "Protestant" instead of "Catholic," as we tend to think today; rather, they wanted to be "Catholic" instead of "Roman." They radically criticized the teaching of the Roman Church in order to discover anew the teaching of the Catholic Church, and to hand that teaching on to posterity.

However, once one accepts the claim that the tradition one receives is distorted by lies and deceptions, it is almost inevitable that the teaching that one reforming theologian hands on as catholic and apostolic will be evaluated by another reforming theologian as still being infected with the error and falsehood of the previous Roman tradition. The reason for this would lie in the differing criteria or authorities advanced by different German theologians by which to distinguish truth from falsehood, giving rise to different visions of true Christian faith and life. The history of German Protestant theology is the story of the endless and relentless criticism of received tradition, on the basis of differing and often mutually exclusive sources of authority, in order to restore the true apostolic teaching and faith in a church that had fallen into error.

As we will see below, the story of Protestant theology goes through several distinct phases of development. The first phase is the attempt to recover the genuinely catholic teaching of the church by means of the radical criticism of all received tradition by means of the Word of God in Scripture. This period culminates in the confessional divisions between the Lutheran, Reformed, and Anabaptist traditions, and the development of confessional orthodoxy in the sixteenth and seventeenth centuries. The second period, located in the seventeenth and eighteenth centuries, is marked by the criticism of confessional orthodoxy, either by means of genuine and living faith in the heart, versus false faith created by assenting to true ideas; or by means of the criticism of all alleged revelation by means of the universal and necessary truths of reason. The third period, beginning at the end of the eighteenth century, responded to the rational and historical criticism of Christian revelation by seeking to interpret Christian symbols by means of their proper referent in the human person, be that practical reason, speculative reason, or immediate feeling. The fourth phase, at the dawn of the twentieth century, finds these interpretations of Christian symbols to be deficient, and seeks to reconnect contemporary theology with the theology of the Reformers by means of a critically revised understanding of the Word and work of God in Christ.

The Criticism of Tradition by the Word of God

According to Martin Luther (1483–1546), the Roman Church had taken the Catholic Church captive by replacing the gospel of Christ with the law invented by human reason. Luther claimed that reason could only see God as a righteous Judge who gives the Law, so that we might be able to remove the sense of sin from the conscience by doing works of the Law. By following reason, the Roman Church urged those plagued by the sense of sin in their conscience to do works commanded by the Church until the sense of sin disappeared. However, according to Luther's interpretation of the apostolic teaching of Paul, the Law is powerless to remove sin, as God gave it with the sole purpose of revealing sin, in order to humble us and remove all self-righteousness. Only Christ, true God and true human, has the power to remove sin, by taking our sin into his body and giving us his righteousness in its place. Christ is offered to us in the gospel to be received by faith, not by our works. The true apostolic church should teach the gospel of Christ alone, both in preaching and in the sacraments of baptism and the Lord's

Supper (as well as in private confession), so that terrified consciences might be freed from the curse of the Law and set at peace.

Luther's colleague at the University of Wittenberg, Andreas Bodenstein von Karlstadt (1480–1541), agreed with Luther that the Roman Church had taken the Christian church captive, but he thought that Luther had not gone far enough in his restoration of the apostolic faith, and intensified his criticism of the direction of Luther's reforms from 1522 onward. Karlstadt was deeply troubled by the worship of images in the Roman Church, and thought that they should be removed from all places of worship. The veneration of the sacrament as the body and blood of the eternal Son of God also dismayed Karlstadt. Karlstadt claimed that Christ was pointing the faithful not to the bread and wine, but to his death on the cross for their redemption, which they were to remember with fervent devotion and love. Karlstadt also thought that the presence of theologians in the university made them proud of their learning and elitist when compared to ordinary Christians; hence he left the university and sought to learn from the members of his congregation in Orlamünde, in the trust that all Christians are taught by God through the Holy Spirit.

Philip Melanchthon (1497–1560), Luther's colleague at the University of Wittenberg, defended university-based theology against Karlstadt's criticisms by insisting that the recovery of the gospel by Luther was essentially and necessarily linked to the recovery of letters by learned people in his day. According to Melanchthon, the gospel could only flourish where the teaching of literature and languages also flourished. Melanchthon thought that Christian teachers had a great deal to learn from classical pagan teachers like Plato and especially Aristotle about the right method and order of teaching, even if the content of their teaching could come only from the Word of God. Melanchthon developed his own method of teaching in his *Loci Communes* (Melancthon, 1988), which he edited several times during his life. Melanchthon was also very interested in defending the catholicity of the teaching of Martin Luther, and so in later editions of the *Loci* he took the topics to be covered in his book from the consensus of the prophets, apostles, and Greek and Latin fathers of the patristic period, so that he might be able to defend the doctrine of the Trinity against those like Servetus who denied it could be found in Scripture. His attention to the Greek fathers in particular led him to teach after 1531 that there are three causes of true faith in the believer: the Word, the Holy Spirit, and the assent of free will.

Ulrich Zwingli (1484–1531) thought that Luther was right to place the Word of God above all the teaching of the Roman Church, as the one true sign of apostolic teaching. However, for Zwingli, the Word of God was closely identified with the freely given illumination of the Holy Spirit, as Christ had promised that all believers would be taught by God, and not by human teachers. For Zwingli, the problem with human teaching is not that it leads us to rely on works to free us from sin, as Luther taught, but rather that it leads us to rely on creatures rather than the Creator. According to Zwingli, only the Creator can freely reveal himself to the pious by the Holy Spirit. The Creator is revealed to be the free, self-giving source of all good things, who created us with the sole design of imparting Godself to us. The spiritual nature of God makes impossible the representation of God or Christ in images; hence Zwingli agreed with Karlstadt that images should be removed. Once the Spirit reveals the self-giving goodness of the Creator to us, the Spirit then dives deeply into our hearts and souls and reveals us to be sinners in bondage to self-love, who contradict God by doing everything in reference to ourselves. Once we see the depth of our sin by the Spirit, we are terrified in our consciences, and flee for refuge to the goodness of the Creator we have come to know. However, the justice of God now blocks our access to the Creator, and will not allow sinners to have access to the mercy and goodness of God. At this point, when the sinner is on the verge of despairing of all help, God sends his Son to die for us, so that the justice of God might be satisfied (echoing Anselm), and we might have access to God. The sending of the Son is the sole pledge that God loves us, and the sole means by which God frees us from sin. The sacraments of baptism and the Lord's Supper signify the sending of the Son, whom we have already come to know by the revelation of the Spirit, but they do not pledge the love of God to us, nor do they bring the Holy Spirit.

Zwingli was first supported and then attacked by some of his closest followers, especially Balthasar Hubmaier (1485–1528). Hubmaier agreed with Zwingli that the sacraments do not convey grace or pledge God's love to us; but from this he drew the conclusion that the sacraments should not be administered to any who had not first come to living faith by the Holy Spirit. Hence Hubmaier denied that infant baptism was baptism at all, for according to the Word of God in Scripture Jesus commanded that we should be taught and come to faith before we are to be baptized. Moreover, the baptized devote themselves to following Christ, and hence do not practice violence against each other any more, in contrast to the way Zwingli relied on the Zürich civil authorities to punish his opponents (including Hubmaier). Zwingli responded to Hubmaier by denying that there was any necessary relationship between water baptism and the sending of the Spirit. The Spirit may be given before, during, or after water baptism – the two are utterly distinct events. Water baptism is given to infants because baptism, like circumcision, is a sign of the covenant, and the children of believers are born into the new covenant just as Jews were born into the covenant made with Abraham. This does not mean that water baptism removes original sin, for Zwingli taught that only Christ removes the sin of Adam, as taught by Paul in Romans 5 : 12 ff.

Though Zwingli appreciated Luther's emphasis on the Word of God and faith in Christ, he thought that Luther's teaching on the Lord's Supper was no better than that of the papacy. Since Zwingli taught that sacraments are signs of the sending of the Son to open access to God for sinners, he denied that the body and blood of Christ are present under the appearance (Rome) or reality (Luther) of the bread and wine of the Lord's Supper. The body and blood of Christ cannot be present in the Lord's Supper, because Christ's body is at the right hand of God in heaven, and human bodies can only be in one place at one time. Moreover,

Christ himself taught that the flesh profits nothing, including the flesh of Christ were it to be eaten with the mouth. What profits our souls is our faith in the sending of the Son to die for us, and not our eating of the body and blood of Christ with our mouths. By insisting that the body and blood of Christ are truly offered and eaten in the bread and wine of the Lord's Supper, Luther according to Zwingli was no better than Rome.

John Calvin (1509–64) was not himself a German-speaking theologian, but his theology, available to German theologians through the Latin in which they all wrote, had a decisive impact on the future direction of German Protestant theology. Calvin sought to reunite the followers of Luther and Zwingli by means of his teaching on the sacraments. Like Luther, Calvin taught that the sacraments are pledges of God's grace to establish consciences in the promise of God, and are used by God as instruments to convey God's grace to us. The sacraments are not naked signs, as Calvin thought Zwingli had taught, but truly offer what they represent. However, like Zwingli, Calvin taught that the body of Christ is in heaven, not in the sacrament, so that we are to feed on the body of Christ by faith, not by eating with the mouth. Calvin sought to reunite Zürich and Wittenberg by means of this teaching, especially by means of his friendship with Bullinger and Melanchthon. Calvin succeeded in coming to an agreement with Zürich, in the Zürich Consensus of 1551, but this agreement itself was attacked by students of Melanchthon in Germany, and was never publicly defended by Melanchthon himself, although Melanchthon and others were suspected by some of being "crypto-Calvinists." The attack by German theologians on the Zürich Consensus further widened the rift already created by Luther and Zwingli, and set the stage for later developments within each theological trajectory.

Calvin is perhaps best known for his defense of the doctrine of election, especially once that doctrine had been attacked by the Genevan physician, Bolsec. Calvin taught that every good thing offered to us by God in Christ through preaching and the sacraments can only truly be received by the gift of the Holy Spirit, which is freely given to the elect, and freely withheld from the reprobate, by the good pleasure of God. Bolsec attacked this teaching as making God into a tyrant. Calvin once again sought support from his friends Bullinger and Melanchthon, but in vain. Bullinger thought Calvin should only teach election, and drop his insistence on reprobation. Melanchthon thought that Calvin's doctrine of election reintroduced Stoic necessity into Christian doctrine, and undermined the confidence the faithful should have in the mercy of God promised in the gospel. The Bolsec controversy convinced Calvin that the doctrine of election should have confessional status, leading him to urge its inclusion in the French Confession of 1559, which was later imitated by the Belgic Confession.

The controversies over the person of Christ, the Lord's Supper, and the doctrine of election set the Lutheran and Reformed traditions in a polemical relationship to one another, even as they were both polemically related to Rome and the Anabaptists. The period following Luther, Melanchthon, and Calvin was defined both by the theological method of Melanchthon and Calvin, as well as by the confessions that were developed by each community in the latter half of the sixteenth century. As noted above, Melanchthon had attempted to restore catholic and apostolic teaching to the church by gathering together in an orderly way the chief topics or *loci* of Christian doctrine, including by 1543 topics that came from the Greek and Latin churches of the first five centuries, supported by testimonies from the prophets, apostles, and Greek and Latin fathers. Calvin adopted this method as his own in the *Institutes* from 1539 to the final edition of 1559 (see Calvin, 1960), although he took his topics exclusively from the prophets and apostles, and saw the conciliar decisions as interpretations of Scripture, and not as topics in their own right. Calvin also engaged much more directly in polemical disputation with his theological opponents, whereas Melanchthon thought that the theologian should avoid such polemics and teach the topics of theology in a clear and edifying way. Subsequent Lutheran and Reformed theology developed along the lines laid down by both Melanchthon and Calvin, with both sides combining both the orderly presentation of the chief topics of Christian doctrine along with a polemical refutation of the teaching of their opponents, supported by the testimony of Scripture and the fathers. Melanchthon and Calvin had balanced this aspect of teaching with commentaries on complete books of Scripture; but the subsequent theological tradition emphasized the doctrinal topics virtually to the exclusion of biblical commentaries.

The summaries of topics were also guided by the confessional and catechetical literature that emerged by the end of the sixteenth century. The controversy over the person of Christ and the Lord's Supper made it necessary for the Lutheran community to place the Augsburg Confession and its Apology in the context of Luther's theological refutation of the teaching of Zwingli, and not in the context of Melanchthon's own work, which his opponents thought verged too closely on Calvin's position. The Formula of Concord of 1577 was offered by Lutheran theologians as being the definitive interpretation of the Augsburg Confession, along with the Large and Small Catechisms of Martin Luther. Luther's arguments against Zwingli – especially his insistence that the humanity of Christ is everywhere that his divinity is by the unity of the person of Christ, and his insistence that even unbelievers eat the body and blood of Christ with their mouths in the Lord's Supper – attained a confessional authority and status they did not have in his lifetime. Calvin's failure to unite Zürich and Wittenberg led to the formation of an independent confessional tradition, aided in large part by the decision of Frederick II to side with Calvin and Melanchthon in the ongoing polemics over the Lord's Supper at the University of Heidelberg. Both the Second Helvetic Confession (1566) and the Heidelberg Catechism (1562) were adopted by Frederick, and by subsequent Reformed theologians, as the major confessional texts guiding their summaries of theological topics, with both reflecting the position of the Zürich Consensus regarding the presence of the humanity of Christ in heaven and the spiritual, but not oral, eating of the body and blood of Christ in the Lord's Supper.

The Criticism of Revealed Truths: Pietism and Rationalism

The increasing emphasis on the teaching and polemical defense of right doctrine by the Lutheran and Reformed theological traditions led to two different kinds of criticism in the seventeenth and eighteenth centuries, which attempted both to free theology from unnecessary conflict and to free ordinary believers from being dominated by prejudice and passion. The first of these movements, commonly called "Pietism," took its impetus from the distinction made by Luther in his Preface to Paul's Epistle to the Romans between faith as an idea created by the mind, and faith created in the heart by the work of God. Faith as a divine work creates an entirely new person who lives a new life of love and service to the neighbor, and who daily dies to the sins and passions that dominated their former life. Faith as an idea created by the mind leads ordinary Christians to believe that faith is essentially related to right doctrine, and to the polemical refutation of those who differ doctrinally. Faith as a divine work in the heart leads us to love even those whom we know to differ from us doctrinally, in the hope that we may be one in Christ and the Spirit even if we are not fully one in doctrine and confession.

Various strategies were created by which such living divine faith might be both created and nurtured. Philipp Jakob Spener (1635–1705) echoed Luther by turning to the Word of God as the source of all reform and renewal in the church but, unlike Luther, Spener turned to the exhortative passages of Paul in which Paul urges us to walk and live according to the Spirit and not the flesh, and to be renewed in the inner person. Spener attempted to revive Luther's teaching of the priesthood of all believers, in the hope that if the whole community would both study and teach the Word of God, it would enkindle genuine piety in their hearts. August Francke's (1663–1727) experience taught him that even the Word of God in Scripture was not enough to conquer the pride of human reason in its own idea of faith. What is needed is genuine repentance before God, including praying and weeping on our knees, so that God might conquer our proud reason and enkindle faith in our hearts. Francke, like Spener, was convinced that the preaching and testimony of one in whom God created faith would act as a flame enkindling such faith in others, as one candle brings light and heat to another.

Nicholas Ludwig, Count von Zinzendorf (1700–60), found all such methods of creating or enkindling faith to border on the ridiculous, for they bind the freedom of Christ to act when and where Christ wills. True faith is not created by teaching or preaching the Word of God, nor by praying and weeping, nor by the testimony or doctrine of others. True faith is only created when the Creator and Savior of the world appears before the heart in his blood and wounds, leading the heart to realize that it is in distress and has no Savior, while simultaneously giving the heart the certainty that the one who appears wounded and bloody before it desires to save it, and will save it. Such a heart falls in love with the one who appears before it, even without knowing his name; and this faith in love is sufficient to save it, even if it never comes to know who the Savior is. According to Zinzendorf, the whole language of the Christian community, from the Lord's Prayer to the doctrine of the Trinity, is nothing but the unfolding and explication of this faith in the heart, and so it means nothing to the one who has not first fallen in love with the suffering Creator and Savior.

The fracturing of evangelical Christianity into competing confessional camps, all of whom appealed to the true meaning of Scripture and to true Christian faith and piety, led others to abandon confidence in Scripture and emotionally charged faith altogether, and to follow the lead of Descartes in seeking to discover all truth by the clear light of reason. Over against Luther and Francke, who wanted Christians to humble their reason with the awareness of their sin to make room for faith, John Locke (1632–1704) asked all Christians to use their God-given reason to be able to distinguish between true and false claims of divine revelation. Locke combined this rational test of revelation with a simplification of the articles of faith. According to Locke, nothing could be made an article of faith that was not found in the preaching of Jesus and the apostles in the Gospels and Acts. Locke thereby introduced the distinction between the preaching of Jesus and the preaching of Paul, which would remain with Protestant theology to this day. According to Locke, there is only one article of saving faith, namely faith in Jesus as the Messiah. Locke understood the Messiah to be a kind of philosopher-king who teaches the law by authority, and who seeks to bring all to obedience to God, even though their own incomplete obedience can only be completed by faith in his perfect obedience. Such faith is rational, both because the teaching of Jesus is the same as the natural law found in universal human reason, and because the authority of Jesus is warranted by miracles that are above, but not contrary to, reason, especially the miracle of his resurrection. Locke sought in this way to free Christian teaching from the complexity of dogma it had developed in the confessional and orthodox period, and to free it from the emotional enthusiasm and subjectivism it was attaining under the influence of the Pietists.

Hermann Samuel Reimarus (1694–1768) agreed with Locke that Scripture should be read with the clear and critical eye of reason, but unlike Locke, Reimarus did not think that such a reading of Scripture would lead one to conclude that faith in Jesus as the Messiah is rational. Reimarus understood the Messiah not as the philosopher-king of Locke, but as the Davidic ruler of the Hebrew Bible, who was to free the people of Israel from their earthly enemies so that they could live at peace in the land promised to them by God. According to Reimarus, both Jesus and his followers thought that he was such a Messiah, and called on the Jews in Galilee and then in Judea and Jerusalem to have faith in him as the Son of David who had come to rule his people, culminating in his dramatic entrance into Jerusalem during Passover. However, Jesus did not succeed in overthrowing the Jewish authorities in Jerusalem, and they quickly had him put to death. Jesus lost all hope that he was the Messiah, crying out that God had forsaken him. The disciples also initially lost their hope, but they soon came up with a grand hoax to tell the people so as to save face and retain their support and authority. They invented the story that God had raised Jesus from the dead, and that God had made him not the political ruler of the Jews, but the spiritual Savior of both Jews and Gentiles. Reimarus was convinced that reason could easily unmask the hoax of the resurrection, due to the presence of innumerable contradictions between the alleged witnesses to the resurrection. Faith in Jesus as the Messianic King of the Jews is therefore falsified by his death, and faith in Jesus as the Messianic Savior of Jews and Gentiles is falsified by the self-contradictory nature of the historical accounts of the resurrection.

Gotthold Lessing (1729–81) published the writings of Reimarus in order to direct attention away from the historical verification of Christian revelation, so that the proper task might be taken up, that of converting revealed truths into rationally demonstrated truths. According to Lessing, there is a categorical difference between the necessary truths of reason, among which is the idea of God, and the contingent truths of history. Because they are contingent, historical events can never become the basis for changing the necessary truths of reason, as in the familiar Christian claim that because God raised Christ from the dead by the Spirit, we must now believe that God is three persons in one essence. According to Lessing, God did not reveal truths so that we might seek to confirm them historically – something that is impossible, as he thought Reimarus had shown once and for all – but rather so that we might reflect on them in the attempt to convert revealed truths into truths that can be demonstrated rationally. Such reflection has as its goal the moral transformation of the human race, gradually ridding humanity of its selfishness so that it begins to practice virtue first for the sake of temporal rewards (Moses), then for the sake of eternal rewards (Jesus), until it finally reaches the eternal Gospel of practicing virtue for the sake of virtue alone (Paul).

The Proper Interpretation of Christian Symbols

If Martin Luther created an unprecedented crisis in the Christian tradition by pitting the Word of God in Scripture against the received tradition of the church, Reimarus and Lessing created another unprecedented crisis by using a rational reading of Scripture to undermine any attempt to verify Christian revelation historically. If Christian faith was to be verified, it could no longer be done by appealing to the truth of inspired Scripture, for Reimarus had shown that Scripture itself was historically unreliable and self-contradictory; nor could it be done by means of historical events like miracles, for Lessing had shown that the contingent truths of history can never become the proof of the necessary truths of reason. The generation after Reimarus and Lessing basically offered three distinct ways by which the symbolic language of revelation could be both interpreted and verified; by appealing to practical reason and morality (Kant), by appealing to speculative reason and knowledge (Hegel), or by appealing to the immediate self-consciousness of God and the inwardly certain fact of redemption by Jesus (Schleiermacher).

Immanuel Kant (1724–1804) attempted to free both philosophy and theology from the error of thinking that God could be known, and that the idea of God was the source of all true ideas, including the natural law. According to Kant, all knowledge is oriented to what we can intuit with our senses, and is rooted in the way our understanding orders our sense experience. Whatever cannot be sensibly intuited cannot be known, and this includes God. However, the elimination of God from the realm of pure reason was meant to point us to the right locus for speaking about God, namely in practical reason. According to Kant (1960), reason both gives itself the law, and represents to itself the archetype of the person who completely follows the law, no matter how much opposition that person faces. The law should be obeyed out of reverence for it, which arises within practical reason when reason gives the law and the archetype to itself. However, reason cannot but wonder what the consequences of such obedience will be, even if it cannot adopt such consequences as an incentive for obedience (for that would be self-serving). The term "God," properly understood, has to do with the one who alone can bring our obedience into correspondence with the causal order of nature, which would result in happiness. All language about God, both in Scripture and in tradition, has its true meaning in practical reason, and is rightly understood only when it is referred to practical reason. Thus the Pauline and Augustinian doctrine that "all have fallen in Adam" is properly understood to describe the way each and every one of us experiences the perversion of freedom by freedom itself, giving rise to radical evil within the ground of freedom that cannot be expunged by our own efforts. The "sending of the Son to redeem us" properly refers to the mysterious way that reason, even in the midst of radical evil, nonetheless represents to itself the archetype of the person well pleasing to God, who obeys the law for the sake of the law over against all other incentives, leading us to "practical faith" in the Son of God, by means of which we attain the confidence that we can free ourselves from radical evil because we ought to do so.

G. W. F. Hegel (1770–1831) agreed with Kant that the symbols of Scripture and tradition needed to be interpreted and verified in light of reason, but he disagreed with Kant's claim that God could not be known. Hegel thought that such a claim revealed the deficiency of an old way of construing the truth by means of identity predication, that is, A is A and not non-A. Thus, for Kant, God is infinite, supersensible, and numinous, and hence cannot be known. For Hegel, this is not the living God, but rather a dead god. According to Hegel, the truth is not the static isolation of self-identity, so that one is what one is and cannot be anything else. Rather, truth is the dynamic movement wherein A posits itself as not-A in order to overcome the antithesis and return to itself as A. This truth is first revealed in history in the symbolic language of Scripture and the church, especially in the doctrine of the Trinity. The doctrine of the Trinity claims that God created all things through the Word in the unity of the Spirit, and that God reconciled the world to Godself by sending the Son to die on the Cross, and by raising the Son from death by the Spirit, in order to unite the world to God by the bestowal of the Spirit. Faith recognizes the truth of these claims without being able to conceptualize this truth; but after Reimarus only philosophy can verify the truth of these symbols, by means of the concept of "spirit." Spirit is that which posits itself as its opposite in order to return to itself as itself. Infinite spirit posits itself as finite spirit, living spirit posits itself in death, in order to return to itself through finitude and death as infinite spirit. Spirit does not avoid death, but rather posits itself in death, in order to pass through death to return to itself as spirit. Spirit does not avoid all opposition and estrangement in static self-identity, but rather posits itself as its opposite in estrangement from itself (symbolized in the Church's teaching of the fall of Adam into sin and death), in order to reconcile itself with itself by overcoming the opposition in itself (symbolized in the Church's teaching of reconciliation by means of the death and resurrection of Christ).

Friedrich Schleiermacher (1768–1834) agreed with Kant and Hegel that the symbolic language of Scripture and the church needed to be interpreted in light of its proper referent, but he rejected the way both of them made such interpretation the task of philosophy, and not of ecclesial theology. According to Schleiermacher (1989), the presence of religious communities does not express an irrational deception from which reason can now free us, nor does it represent a more primitive level of the truth now attained by philosophy. Rather, religious communities are essential to the development of the human race, precisely as religious communities. Hence there must be something essential to all human persons that can only come to expression and fruition by means of such religious communities. According to Schleiermacher, the form of consciousness that leads us to join religious communities cannot be a form of knowing, for that would lead to Hegel; nor can it be a form of doing, for that would lead to Kant. Hence, it must be a form of feeling, understood in terms of an immediate self-consciousness of being absolutely dependent. Moreover, people are drawn to the Christian community by their experience within that community of themselves as sinners in need of redemption, and of Christ as the one who will bring this need to an end. Such faith could never tolerate the idea that the historical person of Jesus the Redeemer could be replaced by practical faith in the archetype of reason or by the concept of spirit. Hence one must ask what must be true about Christ in order for him to be the one irreducible cause of this experience in all who join the Christian community, from the earliest disciples to today. Schleiermacher concluded that Jesus must have been the one person in history who did not need redemption, and who therefore had an absolutely potent God-consciousness that combined sinlessly with all moments of his conscious life. Christ is the sinless archetype, but within history, not within reason, according to Schleiermacher, and his influence within history, by the mediation of the Christian community, brings about our experience of needing redemption and of Christ as the one who will bring such a need to an end.

The solutions proposed by Hegel and Schleiermacher were themselves radically critiqued by their students. David Friedrich Strauss (1808–74) was a student of both Hegel and Schleiermacher. Strauss appreciated Schleiermacher's desire to describe Christian faith both scientifically and ecclesially, but he thought that his attempt to combine both radical criticism and genuine piety did not go far enough to meet the challenges posed to Christian faith by historical criticism. According to Strauss, the claim that Jesus alone is the sinless arche-type of the God-consciousness is no less supernatural or miraculous than is the traditional claim that Christ is divine and human in one person. The ascription of divinity or unsurpassable perfection to Jesus comes from the mythologizing tendencies of oral traditions, according to Strauss. If a higher level of con-sciousness does emerge in history, it must emerge socially, and not in one unsur-passable individual.

Ludwig Feuerbach (1804–72) was a student of Hegel's, but he was equally critical of Hegel and Schleiermacher. According to Feuerbach (1989), Hegel was correct in seeing the doctrine of the Trinity as the central religious symbol embodying the truth of all religiousness. However, for Feuerbach, all religious symbols are really projections of particular human needs into the sphere of the "divine," to which we then turn to bestow these needs upon us. The basic human need for all people is the need to love and be loved by other people in a genuine I–Thou relationship. The Christian tradition succeeds in projecting the essential human need into "God" in the symbol of the Trinity, which itself is seen as the I–Thou relation between the Father and the Son in the Spirit. Feuerbach thought that the social world of his day was now ready to begin exercising that love in the human community, thereby eliminating the need to keep projecting it into divinity. When we are speaking about "God," we are really speaking about our need to love and be loved by others in society.

Karl Marx (1818–83) agreed with Feuerbach that language about God is really language about human social relations, but he thought that Feuerbach's emphasis on the I–Thou relation focused thinking too much on bourgeois ideas of romantic love, for which the workers of the world had no time. Marx thought that the essential estrangement of his time lay not in the lack of I–Thou rela-tions, but in the way the workers did not own the means of production in which they labored. To be human is not to love, as Feuerbach thought, but to produce, and the goal of history will not be attained until workers themselves own and control the means of production, which are currently owned and controlled by the capitalists.

Strauss, Feuerbach, and Marx seriously challenged the interpretations of Christian faith proposed by Hegel and Schleiermacher. One now had to show that symbols of God really did refer to something other than a projection of human need, and that symbols of the unsurpassability of Christ were not pro-jections of the attainments of social groups to a higher level of consciousness in history, or the ideology of the bourgeoisie. Albrecht Ritschl (1822–89) returned to the religious philosophy of Immanuel Kant, and to the biblical picture of Christ, in order to answer the criticisms of Strauss and Feuerbach, and to set Christian faith on its proper biblical and confessional foundation. Ritschl agreed with Kant that God is the Moral Creator and Ruler of the world, who alone can unite the moral and natural goals of the world in Blessedness. Ritschl went beyond Kant by seeing this view of God as being both theoretical as well as practical, giving rise to spiritual as well as moral values, to which all religious language refers. The revelation of God in Christ is of a Loving Will whose personal end is also the end of the human race, that is, Blessedness in the Kingdom of God. Christ is the unique revelation of God, as his personal end completely coincides with God's personal end. Faith in Christ satisfies the need of humanity to see the individual as of more worth than the whole of nature, while also summoning the faithful to the task of creating the Kingdom of God in a community of universal love. Faith in God avoids Feuerbach's criticism because it is always linked with the moral duty to love others, therefore avoiding the selfishness of meeting our own needs. Faith in Christ avoids the criticisms of Strauss because such faith is not verified historically, but rather ethically and religiously, by Christ's dedication to the Kingdom and his freedom from the world even in the midst of suffering.

The portrayal of the Kingdom of God proposed by Ritschl, which was pivotal to his understanding of God and Christ, faced its most serious challenge from a member of his own school. Johannes Weiss (1863–1914) returned to the problem first posed so effectively by Reimarus: namely, what would Jews of the Second Temple period have understood Jesus to mean when he proclaimed the coming of the Kingdom of God? According to Weiss, Jesus did not speak of the Kingdom as a political reality, as Reimarus had argued, but rather drew on contemporary Jewish eschatological and apocalyptic thinking in his preaching. Weiss argued that the Kingdom of God was not the moral task of a universal community of love described by Ritschl, but was rather the supernatural work of God alone, bringing to end the old world and creating a new heaven and a new earth. Such a Kingdom could not be harmonized with any human project, either political or moral; it could only be the work of God, beyond any human control, coming from the future into the present.

At the same time that Weiss was having an impact on the school of Schleiermacher and Ritschl, German theology was at last coming to grips with the criticism of Hegel and Schleiermacher found in the relentlessly dialectical theology of Søren Kierkegaard (1813–55). Kierkegaard agreed with Schleiermacher over against Hegel that Christ was a singular individual who could not be sublated into a concept of reason. However, he disagreed with Schleiermacher's description of the person of Christ. Christ was not the archetype of perfect human piety whose influence magnetically draws human beings into the Christian community. Rather, Christ is an individual human being who claims to be God. Over against Hegel, Kierkegaard insisted that mature human reason recognize that there is an infinite qualitative distinction between God and the world, a distinction that can never be sublated by the dialectics of reason. For an individual to claim to be God brings human reason to the possibility that it may be offended by the unresolvable paradox of the claim. The possibility of offense is intensified by the kind of individual Jesus is portrayed to be in the sacred history of the Gospels (especially Matthew and

John), which Kierkegaard, like Locke and Reimarus, distinguished from the teaching of Paul. Jesus comes with the offer to give us rest in his own person, yet those who accept his offer of help are made to suffer simply because they let themselves be helped by him. He claims to be divine compassion itself, yet both he and those who follow him are made to be a sacrifice in this life, with no discernable benefit in return. Jesus' claim to be the saving God, combined with his call to suffer voluntarily for the sake of his Name and to be made a sacrifice by the love of God, brings human reason and understanding to a standstill, making it necessary for us to decide: will we be offended, or will we believe? Kierkegaard thought that the Lutheran Church of his day had removed the possibility of faith by removing the possibility of offense, by replacing the paradox of Jesus with a human portrayal of sympathy, compassion, and success.

The influence of Kierkegaard was intensified by the revival of interest in the theology of Martin Luther at the dawn of the twentieth century, provoked in particular by the discovery and publication of Luther's *Lectures on Romans* (1515–16), which had never been published before. In this period of his career, Luther argued that human beings are so perverted by self-love, so turned in on themselves, that they pervert every good thing that God gives them by their selfishness. The gravity of self-love is so great that it would even pervert the grace of God, if reason could detect the presence of such grace in the person. In order to free us from the bondage of self-love, God hides the infusion of saving grace under an appearance that completely contradicts it, namely the awareness of sin, death, and wrath. When we are the objects of God's love, we feel that we are objects of God's wrath; when we are justified by the gift of God's grace, we feel that we are being condemned as sinners. True love for God in this life manifests itself in the candid confession that we are sinners deserving nothing but wrath and hell, so that we consign and resign ourselves to hell, with Christ crucified, out of love for God.

The Word and Work of God in the Modern World

Rudolph Bultmann (1884–1976) used the insights of Weiss, Kierkegaard, and early Luther to return to a project first attempted by Schleiermacher, namely to describe true Christian faith in a way that avoids unnecessary conflict with science. Bultmann agreed with Weiss that Jesus expected the coming of a supernatural work of God that would radically end the old world in a cataclysmic judgment, and would create a new world in harmony with God. From Kierkegaard, Bultmann adopted the insight that Jesus summons every individual of every time and place to decision: will we be offended, or will we believe? In order for such a decision to be made possible, the message of Jesus and his apostles must be interpreted in such a way that it can address every individual here and now with the summons to decision. From early Luther, as well as from his teacher Wilhelm Herrmann (1846–1922), Bultmann arrived at a description of faith that opposed faith to all worldly security. Faith believes in the love of God despite what we see and feel, and this "in spite of" is never resolved in this life. Bultmann clarified his thinking of the "in spite of" by means of his reading of early Heidegger, for whom authentic existence is to be open to the future in every free decision between the past and the future, in spite of the inevitable approach of death and nothingness. For Bultmann, the message of the gospel does not inform us in a mythological way of what God has done in the past to secure our existence in this world and the next; rather, the gospel summons us to the decision to be crucified with Christ, to let go of all worldly security, to find our hope only in the future coming of God in love, in spite of the appearance of death and nothingness.

Karl Barth (1886–1968) was a fellow student of Wilhelm Herrmann, but unlike Bultmann he saw both Schleiermacher and Bultmann as leading Protestant theology into a dead end. Barth became convinced that all attempts to describe Christian faith as the fulfillment of universal human nature fall subject to Feuerbach's criticism of all human religiousness. The truth of Christian faith could not be found in the nature of humanity, but rather in the nature of God, echoing Anselm's method of doing theology. However, unlike Anselm, Barth (1957–75) denied that human reason has any idea of the true nature of God. All rational ideas of God – especially of God's power and freedom – which are seen to be absolute and arbitrary are really projections of human pride, which seeks such power and freedom for itself. With Kierkegaard, Barth insisted that the self-revelation of God in Christ contradicts all human ideas of God; but with Hegel, Barth thought that it was possible, indeed necessary, to come to know the true nature of God by beginning with the death of Jesus Christ. Barth thought that he could escape imposing rational necessity on the work of God, as Hegel had done, by placing the death of Christ in the context of God's free election, and of God's gracious covenant with Israel. According to Barth, the only way that the identification of Jesus both with God and with sinful Israel can avoid being a contradiction in the being of God is if we understand God to be the One who loves in freedom. God elects to take upon himself, in the person of the Son, the future that humanity had elected for itself in Israel – a future of suffering, death, and annihilation by the wrathful love of God – in order to give to humanity the future God elects to give to us, eternal life with God. Our reconciliation with God is not due to our own free decision to believe or be offended, as with Kierkegaard and Bultmann, but with God's free decision to make our own lost plight God's own. A God who is the Whence of the feeling of absolute dependence could not act in this way, according to Barth, but only the God who loves in freedom and is free in his love.

The history of Protestant theology is the story of the relentless criticism of tradition in the hope of restoring genuinely catholic and apostolic teaching, in order to restore and renew the church. Its greatest promise, as we have repeatedly seen, is also its greatest peril, as each theologian's proposal for the restoration of true apostolic and catholic teaching is itself radically criticized by those who follow him.

References

Barth, Karl (1957–75). *Church Dogmatics*, volume IV, part 1, trans. and ed. G. W. Bromiley and T. F. Torrance. Edinburgh: T & T Clark.
Calvin, John (1960). *Calvin: Institutes of the Christian Religion*, ed. John McNeill, trans. Ford Lewis Battles. Philadelphia: Westminster Press.
Feuerbach, Ludwig (1989). *The Essence of Christianity*, trans. George Eliot. Buffalo, NY: Prometheus.
Kant, Immanuel (1960). *Religion within the Limits of Reason Alone*, trans. T. M. Greene & H. H. Hudson. New York: Harper & Row.
Philip Melanchthon (1988). *Loci Communes 1543*, trans. J. A. O. Preus, Saint Louis: Concordia Publishing House.
Schleiermacher, Friedrich (1989). *The Christian Faith*, ed. H. R. Mackintosh and J. S. Stewart. Edinburgh: T & T Clark.

Further Reading

Book of Confessions (1999). Louisville, KY: Westminster John Knox Press.
Bultmann, Rudolph (1958). *Jesus Christ and Mythology*. New York: Charles Scribner's Sons.
Erb, Peter C. (ed.) (1983). *Pietists: Selected Writings* (1983). New York: Paulist Press.
Hegel, G. W. F. (1988). *Lectures on the Philosophy of Religion, 1827*, ed. Peter C. Hodgson. Berkeley, CA: University of California Press.
Hubmaier, Balthasar (1989). *Balthasar Hubmaier, Theologian of Anabaptism*, trans. and ed. H. Wayne Pipkin and John H. Yoder. Scottsdale, PA: Herald Press.
Karlstadt, Andreas Bodenstein von (1978). *Karlstadt's Battle with Luther*, ed. Ronald J. Sider. Philadelphia: Fortress Press.
Karlstadt, Andreas Bodenstein von (1995). *The Essential Karlstadt: Fifteen Tracts*, trans. and ed. E. J. Furcha. Scottsdale, PA: Herald Press.
Kierkegaard, Søren (1991). *Practice in Christianity*, ed. Howard and Edna Hong. Princeton, NJ: Princeton University Press.
Robert Kolb and Timothy Wengert (eds.) (2000). *The Book of Concord: The Confessions of the Evangelical Lutheran Church*, trans. James Schaffer. Minneapolis, MN: Fortress Press.
Lessing, Gotthold (1956). *Lessing's Theological Writings*, ed. and trans. Henry Chadwick. Stanford, CA: Stanford University Press.
Locke, John (1958). *The Reasonableness of Christianity*, ed. I. T. Ramsey. Stanford, CA: Stanford University Press.
Luther, Martin (1955–86). *Luther's Works* [*LW*], American edn., Jaroslov Pelikan and Helmut T. Lehmann (eds.), 55 volumes. St. Louis and Minneapolis: Concordia and Fortress.
Luther, Martin (1957). *The Freedom of the Christian, LW* 31.
Luther, Martin (1959). *The Babylonian Captivity of the Christian Church, LW* 36.
Luther, Martin (1963). *Lectures on Galatians, 1535, LW* 26–27.
Luther, Martin (1972). *Lectures on Romans, 1515–1516, LW* 25.
Marx, Karl (1998). *The German Ideology, Including Thesis on Feuerbach*. Amherst, NY: Prometheus Books.
Reimarus, Hermann Samuel (1985). *Fragments*, ed. Charles H. Talbert, trans. Ralph S. Fraser. Chico, CA: Scholars Press.

Ritschl, Albrecht (1902). *The Christian Doctrine of Justification and Reconciliation*, ed. and trans. H. R. MacIntosh and A. B. MacAulay. Edinburgh: T & T Clark.

Strauss, David Friedrich (1977). *The Christ of Faith and the Jesus of History: A Critique of Schleiermacher's* The Life of Jesus, trans Leander Keck. Philadelphia: Fortress Press.

Zwingli, Ulrich (1981). *Commentary on True and False Religion*. Durham, NC: Labyrinth Press.

CHAPTER 2

Shapers of Protestantism: Martin Luther

Graham Tomlin

As the instigator of the Protestant Reformation through the events following his famous protest about the abuse of indulgences in 1517, Martin Luther occupies a pivotal role within Protestantism and has exercised a continuing, though not unquestioned, authority within it. Born in 1483, in Eisleben, Germany, he matriculated at the university of Erfurt in 1501. A dramatic experience in a thunderstorm in 1505 led to entry into the monastery of the Augustinian Order in Erfurt to begin life as a friar, an event which did not indicate a termination of his study, merely a redirection into the pursuit of theology. Erfurt was increasingly becoming known as a stronghold of northern European humanism; however, within the faculty of theology, the predominant type of theology and philosophy which Luther learnt was the Ockhamist style associated with the *via moderna*. He was ordained priest in 1507, and transferred formally to the new university of Wittenberg in 1511 to become Professor in Biblical Studies, a post he held until he died.

Luther's Break from Late Medieval Theology

The nature and timing of Luther's rejection of late medieval patterns of thought, and his adoption of a new Reformation theology, are both contested and complex. On one level, his shift can be seen as a new approach to a central medieval theological question, concerning the correct preparation for receiving God's grace. His early theological writings reflect fairly faithfully the concerns and perspectives of the *via moderna*, associated with William of Ockham and Gabriel Biel, with its soteriological emphases on the *pactum* or covenant, whereby God promises to reward those who do what is in them (*quod in se est*) with the gift of infused grace. This grace will then enable works to be performed which are worthy of full (condign) merit and the gift of salvation. Over the years of Luther's early work on the Bible, as he worked through lectures in Wittenberg on the Psalms and the book of Romans from 1513–16, he can be seen gradually to take leave of this position. In these writings an increasing focus is discernible, drawn both from popular piety and from monastic theologians such as Bernard of Clairvaux, on the cross of Christ as the pattern of God's work in saving sinners. This led Luther to a perception that preparation for grace consists not in producing works which are rewarded by infused grace, but that God himself works preparation for grace by leading the sinner to an awareness of his or her own emptiness before God. Sinners can only prepare for grace by becoming passive, not active, in salvation, giving up the attempt to perform works which merit salvation. As he pointed out in the famous '95 Theses on Indulgences', it is suffering, and not works, that constitutes the proper preparation for grace.

Another related aspect of the 'Reformation breakthrough' was a new understanding of the 'righteousness of God' (*iustitia dei*). Luther referred to this in a later recollection, the famous 'autobiographical fragment' of 1545. As he pondered the scriptural use and meaning of the phrase, particularly its occurrence in Romans 1.17, Luther turned from a view, common within systematic works of theology at the time, of this as 'active righteousness', or God's own righteousness by which he actively condemns sinners. Instead he began to understand it as 'passive righteousness', a righteousness which God works in sinners, and which is received by faith. Hence God's *iustitia* became for Luther not demand but gift. Acceptance of sinners by God as truly righteous came at the start of, and as the essential precondition for, the grateful living of Christian life, rather than a goal to be achieved at the end of it. Christians were not partly righteous and partly sinful, with the Christian life as the slow process, to be completed in purgatory, whereby such sin as remained could be removed, until final acceptance by God was achieved. Instead, Christians were, in Luther's well-known phrase, 'at the same time righteous and sinful': fully righteous by virtue of the righteousness of Christ received by faith, despite and yet simultaneous with the real presence of sin.

A third aspect of the formation of Luther's distinctive theology was an increased focus upon the Word of God, both as the object of faith, and the means by which it is evoked. This comes into focus in Luther's thought over the years 1517–20, beginning especially in his lectures on the book of Hebrews in 1517. Here, the emphasis falls upon faith as 'hearing the Word of God'. Faith is the capacity to hear the promise of God and simply believe it. Faith therefore includes both a positive and negative aspect. Positively, it lays hold of and clings tightly to the Word of promise which offers forgiveness and grace; negatively, it refuses to try to earn any kind of personal merit before God on the basis of which a claim might be made for his favour. Faith resolves to take God at his word that he justifies not the godly, but the ungodly (Romans 5.6). Faith therefore eschews the attempt to impress God with works: it is by definition the opposite of 'works' – passive receptiveness of grace, not active co-operation with it. Alongside

Luther's developing understanding of the sacraments during this period, the Word of God, which takes form in both preaching and sacraments, became for him the actual presentation of grace, the means through which it was conveyed to the sinner, a factor which became increasingly important and distinctive in Luther's theology.

A fourth aspect concerned the 'external' nature of the righteousness by which Christians are justified. All previous versions of scholastic soteriology suggested to varying degrees that the granting of salvation required the actual and gradual transformation of penitents from within, with the help of God's grace, so that they became meritoriously righteous within themselves, and it was on the basis of this internal righteousness, once it was complete, that the gift of justification was bestowed. Luther, however, insisted that the righteousness which justifies a Christian is not his or her own internal righteousness, but is instead an external or strange righteousness (*iustitia externa* or *aliena*), the righteousness of another, namely Christ. To be sure, the believer is subsequently transformed by the power of grace and in the practice of good works, but this has nothing to do with justification, which is achieved solely by the alien righteousness of Christ. While all scholastics from Aquinas to Scotus to Biel held that salvation was granted as a result of the performance of various kinds of meritorious works (though all agreed that such works could only be performed with the help of God's grace), Luther broke from this system of merit altogether. Salvation did not depend on the performance of meritorious works, even those performed with the assistance of grace. In this he was followed by all subsequent Protestant Reformers, including Melanchthon and Calvin, in holding that justification was granted solely on the basis of the merits of Christ, imputed to the believer through faith alone.

The 'Reformation Breakthrough' and the Split from Rome

Precisely when the Reformation 'breakthrough' took place (if indeed it can be seen as a single event at all) is still hotly disputed, and it is hard to see any clear agreement forthcoming on the question. The best that can be said is that over the period between 1514 and 1520, Luther's theology was transformed in a way which includes a number of different but interlocking factors, and which led to a decisive break from the theology and piety of his contemporaries, and eventually from the papal church itself.

However, more recent scholarship has tended to emphasize the continuities between Luther's theology and late-medieval belief and practice. Quite clearly he was not conscious of rediscovering a gospel lost since New Testament times, but instead reclaiming insights from patristic writers such as Augustine and medievals such as Bernard of Clairvaux, which had been obscured by more recent developments in scholastic theology. At the same time as marking a clean break from some aspects of late medieval theology, Luther must also be seen as restoring some truly 'catholic' insights from the past, such as the priority of grace, the rejection of semi-Pelagian notions of salvation, the sacramental nature of God's offering of himself to believers and the centrality of the cross to Christian piety and theology.

This developing theology became controversial in rather accidental fashion in 1517. In the summer of that year, Luther wrote 97 theses as a strong attack on Gabriel Biel's soteriology in particular, and scholastic theology in general. Whether *via antiqua*, or *via moderna*, he felt it had become infected by the same semi-Pelagian disease. These were followed by his more famous (but actually less radical) '95 Theses on Indulgences'. Indulgences were certificates issued by the church which remitted punishments imposed as part of the penitential system. More recently, indulgences had begun to be applied not only to the church's 'temporal' punishments, but to the punishments to be endured in purgatory as well. They could even be applied to deceased relations who were already believed to be suffering the torments of purgatory. An indulgence backed by Archbishop Albrecht of Mainz, and being preached near Wittenberg by the renowned indulgence-seller Johann Tetzel drew Luther's fire – his basic complaint was that these certificates offered a form of cheap grace, 'false assurance', and encouraged people to trust in letters of indulgence rather than God's mercy, worked in the life of a penitent through suffering. They encouraged Christians to avoid the true and painful contrition which alone rendered the sinner receptive to God's grace.

Luther's protest was eventually taken up by a series of papal representatives, and interpreted as an attack both on clear conciliar teaching and papal authority, attacks which Luther seems not to have intended when the indulgence controversy began. Over this period from late 1517 to 1520, in dispute with able papal theologians such as Cajetan, Prierias and Eck, the implications of Luther's theology of faith and the Word were slowly drawn out. The similarities between his ideas and those of the executed Bohemian heretic Jan Hus were brought to his attention, as was the clear water between his own teaching and that of recent councils (especially the Council of Constance in 1415) and papal decretals. The result was excommunication in January 1521, followed by an appearance before the emperor Charles V at the Diet at Worms later the same year, after which Luther was placed under the imperial ban, an edict which however was never fully implemented in Luther's lifetime.

The Reforming Programme

In a series of writings in 1520, Luther echoed humanist concerns by appealing over the heads of the clergy to the German nobility to reform the church in their territories, on the basis of the idea of universal priesthood. It was not ordination, but baptism, which made priests in the church of God, a doctrine which in Luther's hands spoke not so much of the individual's right to stand alone before God without other human mediators, but rather of the communal nature of the church, and the responsibility each baptized person had to act for the benefit of other Christian brothers and sisters. On this basis, the nobility had the full right and responsibility to introduce reform when the clergy were unwilling to do so. Alongside this, he proposed radical changes to the sacramental system of the church, including the administration of the mass in both kinds (*both* bread *and* wine given to the laity, not just bread as was the custom), clerical marriage, the abolition of masses for the dead, and a virtual removal of the role of the papacy in the administration of the church in Germany. Universities were also to be reformed, eliminating both the study of Aristotle, the foundational framework of all scholastic theology, as well as the use of the 'Sentences' of Peter Lombard (a heavily annotated edited selection of earlier Christian writing), and their replacement with the study of the Bible, biblical languages and Augustine. All these reforms were advanced on the principle that everything in the church should be conducive to the hearing of the Word and the proper response of faith. The Word, in both spoken and sacramental forms, needed to be placed at centre stage, and everything which obscured or confused it had to be eradicated. At the same time, anything that encouraged a trust in any form of works (such as pilgrimages, relics or indulgences) rather than the simple response of faith in that word of promise should be discouraged.

For the next few years, Luther's own position within the Reformation movement was unrivalled, even during his post-Worms 11-month 'exile' in the Wartburg castle near Eisenach. The Reformation made significant advances in towns all over Germany and the reforms Luther proposed seemed destined to spread rapidly across Germany. However, Luther's own personal reputation took a number of severe blows from the middle of the decade onwards, through three separate, but related controversies.

Reformation Divisions

While Luther had been in the Wartburg in 1521–2, his erstwhile colleague Andreas Karlstadt began to introduce reforms to the church in Wittenberg similar to those Luther had envisaged, but involving a measure of anti-clericalism and iconoclasm. On his return in March 1522, Luther insisted successfully that these reforms be turned back, until the reasons for the changes had been fully understood by the people. Reluctant to replace catholic legalism with a new evangelical form of the same thing, he insisted that such changes must be freely chosen and not forced upon an unwilling and confused people. Rightly or wrongly, this action won for Luther the reputation in some reforming circles that he was unwilling to pay the inevitable price of reform, and was after all an unreconstructed conservative. In 1524–5, a grassroots movement of the disenfranchised and disconnected 'common man' began to demand changes both to the structure of society and the church, all in the name of Luther's newly rediscovered gospel. Fuelled by the radical teaching of figures such as Karlstadt and the fiery Thomas Müntzer, the 'peasants' as they were known, not only demanded such change, they began to organize, march and prepare for battle to achieve it. While Luther was clearly sympathetic to their demands, he disagreed intensely with their methods and came out strongly against this 'insurrection', on the basis that the private Christian's true weapons were prayer, confession and suffering, not swords and clubs. Luther's infamous advice to the nobles to put down the rebellion with as much force as necessary, making no distinction between those innocent or guilty of actual violence, distanced him from many associated with this mass movement and strengthened the suspicion of many that he did not have the courage of his own convictions. Just as the peasants were being struck down in their thousands at the battle of Frankenhausen in 1525, Luther appeared to be siding with the aggressive and unjust nobility – his decision to get married to an ex-nun during these same months did little to enhance his standing either.

Around the same time, another major controversy erupted, which concerned the question of the freedom of the will, and involved a falling-out with the Dutch humanist, Erasmus. Early relations between the two had been respectful, even supportive at times, but distant. Urged on by others, Erasmus wrote a thinly veiled attack in 1524 on Luther's doctrine of the will, entitled *A Discourse Concerning Free Choice*. Erasmus advocated a certain simple freedom for the human will to choose to turn towards God or not, and stated his belief that further precision on such questions was impossible due to the lack of clarity of Scripture on these points. For Luther, this position was untenable on two main counts. First it reopened the door to uncertainty in the doctrine of salvation. If any part of the transaction of salvation was dependent on human action or choice, it introduced a subjectivity and hence an uncertainty, which robbed the sinner of the joyful certainty of God's grace and promise. Second, it undermined the clarity of Scripture. Only if the promise of Scripture was clear and unequivocal could it be trusted and hence bring security and peace. For Luther, Erasmus's casual assertion of Scripture's opaqueness on such questions removed the Christian's hope and freedom.

The Reformation in Switzerland under Zwingli and Calvin always retained a humanist character, partly due to the humanist training of these reformers. Luther's dispute with Erasmus, however, revealed deep ideological differences between them which meant that, despite Melanchthon's influence, the Lutheran reformation was alienated from the main channels of humanist thought. Luther seemed to have made an enemy of someone who might have been a natural ally, isolating him even more from other reforming programmes within the church.

From 1526 onwards, he found himself embroiled in further disputes, this time with other reformers within the evangelical movement itself. These debates were to divide the Reformation movement even more profoundly, and centred on the sacraments. Earlier, Luther had clashed with Karlstadt over the interpretation of the mass or Lord's Supper, but now he faced stronger opposition from Swiss theologians, particularly Ulrich Zwingli from Zürich, over the same issue. While Luther had long abandoned the medieval doctrine of transubstantiation as an unnecessary piece of speculative Aristotelian theory, he consistently held to the idea of Real Presence, the notion that 'in the Supper we eat and take to ourselves Christ's body truly and physically'. Zwingli however denied the real bodily presence of Christ in the elements of bread and wine, insisting that the Lord's Supper was primarily a communal meal whereby Christians pledge their allegiance both to Christ and one another.

A series of lengthy treatises and counter-treatises culminated in the 'Marburg Colloquy' called by one of the most influential Protestant laymen, Philip of Hesse, anxious to establish a common front against the growing menace of imperial force which was threatening to implement more fully the Edict of Worms. The colloquy brought together the main figures in the evangelical movement at the time including Luther, his close Wittenberg colleague Philip Melanchthon, Zwingli, Bucer, Oecolampadius and Osiander. The debate was inconclusive. While agreement was acknowledged on a remarkably wide range of theological issues, over the contentious issue of sacramental presence, the parties agreed, reasonably amicably, to differ. Even so, it became clear in time that both still felt the gospel was at stake. Luther thought Zwingli's refusal to recognize the embodied way in which God presents himself to us in sacraments was an implicit denial of the incarnation, and so jeopardized the reality of the gift of Christ to us. Zwingli thought Luther's insistence on the real bodily presence of Christ in the sacrament encouraged a false trust in the elements themselves rather than in Christ, and compromised God's spiritual freedom to act as he chooses, independent of physical forms.

The result was a split between two forms of Protestant theology and church life which remains to this day. Lutheran and Reformed churches differ over a number of issues, yet this understanding of the sacraments is the place where their divisions come to the surface most acutely and visibly.

For the remainder of Luther's career, he was based in Wittenberg. From a distance in Coburg, he influenced the Diet of Augsburg in 1530 (he was still under the imperial ban, hence not allowed to be present). Here, the Augsburg Confession, largely drafted by Melanchthon, was presented as a declaration of Lutheran theology before the imperial estates, yet without any success in finding reconciliation with Catholic theology or polity. Luther spent many hours and words working on the reformation of the church in Saxony, his home region, and in a project which was always among the closest to his own concerns, the translation of the Bible from the original languages into a colloquial and accessible German. This translation was to be a vital step in the creation of modern High German, and remains Luther's most enduring legacy to the German church in the coming centuries.

Themes in Luther's Theology

Revelation

While Luther always said that it was the doctrine of justification, as discussed above, by which the church stood or fell, a number of other structural themes in his theology determine the distinctive nature of his thought. One key area is his understanding of revelation. For Luther both salvation and revelation are in 'Christ alone' (the essence of this insight is expressed most fully in the *Heidelberg Disputation* of 1518). As we have seen above, it is through the merits of Christ alone, and not any merit of our own that justification comes. Christ is at the same time the central point of God's revelation to the world, and it is a grave mistake to begin seeking for God anywhere else, whether in mystical experience, speculation, good works or human reason. The way in which God dealt with Christ (first crucifying and then raising him) is the same way he deals with Christians (first humbling them through the law, then justifying them through the gospel). Salvation and revelation are therefore joined at the point of the crucified Christ – it is in Christ that God's salvation occurs and the pattern of his dealings with humanity is revealed. However, Luther points out that this runs counter to everything that human reason expects. Whereas reason expects the justification of the godly through works, the gospel speaks of the justification of sinners through faith alone. Reason expects God to be revealed in glory, strength and power. The gospel says that he is revealed in the weakness of the cross. As a result, while acknowledging the role of reason in the ordinary matters of life, when it comes to our knowledge of God, Luther is deeply suspicious of the competence of human reason. This insistence that Christian theology must begin with God's revelation in Christ, and in particular in the crucified Christ, lies at the foundation of many Protestant doctrines of revelation. Characteristically, Protestant theology has favoured revealed as opposed to natural theology, retaining a strong sense of the radical effects of the fall upon natural human reason, and much of this suspicion can be traced back to Luther's own understanding of revelation.

Scripture

Related to this, and another key area where Luther's theological emphases have left a lasting mark on Protestantism, is his doctrine of Scripture. Luther's focus on 'Scripture alone' as the final authority for Christian life and thought emerged from two distinct but related aspects of his early development. We have already noted his role as Professor of Holy Scripture at Wittenberg, and the vital role played by his early lectures on the Psalms, Romans, Galatians and Hebrews in the emerging shape of his theology. During the course of his controversy with papal representatives such as Cajetan, Prierias and Eck, Luther appears to have been surprised by their failure to tackle him on the grounds he wanted to argue – the teaching of the Bible. Instead, all he encountered was the repeated charge that his ideas were opposed to both papal and conciliar teaching, and therefore to be condemned. While he began the indulgence controversy with a somewhat naïve expectation that Scripture, pope, councils and canon law would be seen to be in agreement, these controversies soon drove a firm wedge between Luther's reading of Scripture and these other authorities. The failure of his opponents to answer him with Scripture compelled him towards asserting the authority of Scripture over against these other authorities, rather than complementary with them.

The other force which shaped his emerging doctrine of Scripture was experiential. Luther's experience of Christian life from early times, and subsequently in the monastery, was marked by what he later called *Anfechtung*, the experience of doubt and despair, especially focused on the question of whether God looked on him with favour or condemnation. His theological development did not banish these experiences, they simply gave him means of dealing with them. Such experiences were particularly acute during the controversy with the papacy, and the consequent need for reassurance which could be trusted. *In extremis*, Luther found that a human word such as papal teaching, the pronouncement of a council or the word of eminent theological authorities could not give him the solid ground he needed. Only a word from God in Scripture presented itself as an unyielding foundation on which he could stand firm while the storms of conflict or conscience raged around him.

Eventually, Luther took his famous declaration at Worms before the emperor Charles V, that he was '. . . bound by the Scriptures I have quoted and my conscience is captive to the Word of God'. Luther's stand on the authority of Scripture as supreme and final when it comes into contradiction with other church authority has bequeathed a seminal and determining legacy to later Protestantism. One of the central and uncontested principles of Protestant theology has been an adherence to the final authority of Scripture, and Luther's own history played a formative role in the establishment of that as one of the abiding marks of later Protestantism. The question of the interpretation of Scripture is, of course, another matter. The debate with Zwingli over the Eucharist showed the inability of Evangelicals who held in common the final authority of Scripture always to agree on what it meant, or the central principles by which it should be interpreted. However, this does not gainsay the vital role played by Luther in establishing the central role of Scripture within Protestantism, and the principle of the role of theology as exegesis – that theology is essentially a response to the prior Word of God revealed in Christ and in the Scriptures, a human word in response to God's word.

Christology

Although Luther clearly played a pivotal role in the beginnings of the Reformation, and continued all his life to enjoy the reputation of the one who had instigated the break from Rome, from the mid-1520s onwards, there is a distinct sense that the Reformation went its own way, and chose paths different from Luther. This was true not only of such reformers as Zwingli, but also the more radical groupings which sprang up on the fringes of the Reformation across northern Europe. If Luther's doctrines of Revelation and Scripture had a profound effect on subsequent Protestant theology, other areas of his thought remain distinct from others in the evangelical movement, and served to identify an emerging 'Lutheran' style of theology and church life (although of course Luther himself always hated the use of such a term). One such area was Christology. Luther always held to a strongly 'Alexandrian' Christology; in other words, holding that Christ's divine and human natures were not separate entities co-existing within the same body, but a unified substance – a divine–human nature. This preserved for Luther the notion that Jesus's human life and nature expressed perfectly the nature and heart of God. The incarnation, as God's gift of Christ to us, to be received by faith, is a true expression of the heart of God as turned towards humanity in love and favour. It reveals once and for all the innermost heart and will of God, not as the demanding judge, but as the generous giver. It is how we know what God is like. In addition this Christology profoundly affected his understanding of the way God communicates himself to humankind. As we have seen, justification consists in the promise and gift of the righteousness of Christ to sinners, received only by faith. Because Luther could not conceive of any separation between Christ's divine and human nature, this gift could not be thought of as just a spiritual thing, but it had to take embodied form, just as in the incarnation. Hence, Luther thought of God's approach and availability in very physical forms.

It is this Christological perspective that lies at the root of Luther's insistence on the real presence of Christ in the elements of bread and wine in the mass. God's word of promise, which comes in the form of both preaching and sacrament, does not just refer to the gift of Christ, it actually conveys what it promises. It is no mere legal fiction, but effects a real union between the believer and Christ at the most intimate level, in which the believer's sin is exchanged with Christ's righteousness. If, as Luther insists, Christ is one human/divine nature, then it cannot be that Christ is offered to us spiritually, while his physical presence or flesh is elsewhere. Both belong together, and Christ and his benefits are offered to us bodily in the sacrament, to be received in faith. In fact, Luther goes as far as to say that 'the Spirit cannot be with us except in material and physical things, such as the Word, water and Christ's body and in his saints on earth'.

This insistence on the embodied nature of the Spirit's presence with us is a mark of Luther's and subsequent Lutheran theology that distinguishes it from Reformed theology. The Christology of Zwingli, and to a lesser extent Calvin, tended to take on a more 'Antiochene' form, making more of the distinction between Christ's divine and human natures, along with a more Platonic ontology, seeing the spiritual and physical as opposing qualities. Hence they tend to view Christ's presence in the Eucharist as either in some sense 'spiritual' (Calvin), or merely in the hearts of the believers (Zwingli). For Luther, this was to compromise the heart of the gospel – it effectively denied that God actually gives us Christ as a gift. As Luther saw it, this position presented the Eucharist as pointing to the grace and righteousness of Christ, but not actually giving it to us. It indicated grace as something to be striven towards through an act of remembrance (works again!) rather than something graciously presented and received as gift.

Political theology

Another aspect of Luther's theology that distinguished him from other contemporary and subsequent reformers, was in the area of political theology. The Reformation, emerging as it did in a society in which church and secular authorities were inextricably entwined, had to engage with political reality and position itself over against various forms of secular authority. In particular, the staunchly Catholic Duke George, sovereign of neighbouring Albertine Saxony, banned the use of Luther's German Bible in his territories. In his advice to his own followers in those areas, Luther devised the theory of what became known as the 'Two Kingdoms', to set limits to the authority of secular princes such as Duke George. In an adaptation of Augustine's theory of the two cities, Luther depicted the world as divided into two kingdoms: the kingdom of God and the kingdom of the world. In the former stand the 'true believers who are in Christ and under Christ'. These need no external law or compulsion to obey the will of God, because they do so willingly from the heart, as a natural outworking of grace. In the kingdom of the world, however, stand all the 'unrighteous' and 'lawless'. These do need the coercive force of control, restraint and punishment to make them obey the law. To rule over these two different kingdoms, God has instituted two different forms of government. Those in the kingdom of God are ruled solely by the Word of God, which both teaches and evokes obedience. Those in the kingdom of the world cannot be ruled solely by the Word, but require the force of the sword of secular government to enforce obedience and order, otherwise social chaos would ensue. It is secular government's role to enforce the law and punish the disobedient, not to meddle in the kingdom of God. Rulers such as Duke George overstepped the legitimate range of their authority, trying to interfere in matters pertaining to the 'kingdom of God' such as the Bible in the vernacular.

Similarly, the argument was used to delineate the proper role of the clergy – their role focused around the Word of God, in preaching and celebrating the sacraments. Interference in secular political affairs, such as was common among the prince-bishops, ecclesiastical estates and a politicized papacy, was simply not their job – they too had overstepped the proper areas of their activity. This was an argument primarily about religious toleration, insisting that there were limits to both secular and ecclesiastical authority (hence the title of Luther's work of 1523 – *On Secular Authority – To What Extent Should It Be Obeyed?*). As such it was reasonably successful. However, as a total political theology it was less so. The theory led to some confusion, partly due to Luther's own ambiguous use of terminology, and partly due to the impression it gave that life was divided into two spheres, one secular and political, the other spiritual and ecclesiastical, and that neither could really address the other. In fact, Luther saw both governments equally as God's means of ruling the world. He also saw a valid and proper role for Christians in both, making a decisive break from the implicit assumption of the superiority of the spiritual over the temporal in much medieval Christianity. However, Luther's tendency to confuse 'secular' with 'worldly' (the German word *weltlich* can mean both), and his interchangeable use of 'authority' (*Oberkeit*) and 'power' (*Gewalt*) tended to imply that secular government was inevitably oppressive and had little to do with God. The rest of the Reformation, especially as it developed outside Germany, left Luther's two kingdoms theory on one side, with very different configurations of the relationship between state and church emerging in Geneva, Zürich, Strasbourg and England.

Luther's Legacy

Since his death in 1546, Luther has continued to exert a powerful influence on Protestant thought. While his sacramental and political ideas had less impact on the wider Reformation, his articulation of the doctrine of justification by faith as central to the gospel, the denial of human merit in justification, the move to a vernacular liturgy and Scripture, and the placing of Scripture as the supreme authority for the church were all stamped indelibly upon Protestant consciousness from his time onwards. Some aspects of his thought were not picked up in the immediate history of the Reformation, but waited like seeds planted deep underground, to emerge into the light much later. For example, Luther's 'theology of the cross', the idea that the cross is the very heart of the revelation of God, hidden in the suffering Christ, was virtually ignored by Luther's own contemporaries, but was picked up in the twentieth century by theologians such as Jürgen Moltmann, Eberhard Jüngel and Kazoh Kitamori, as a vital resource in constructing a theology of God in a world of suffering after the Second World War, or when facing the apparent absence of God in the post-Enlightenment world.

Luther stands as a reminder of the distinctive and polemical nature of theology. His revolt against what he saw as the semi-Pelagianism of scholastic doctrines of salvation, his protest at the lack of accountability of the papal church as well as its distance from the suffering Christ, all show the power of theology to act not as a legitimization of ecclesiastical power, but a critique of it. Luther's theology was an attempt to recall the church to its true identity and its title deeds. Hence it draws attention to the subversive and polemical nature of theology in enabling the church to be *ecclesia semper reformanda*, always in the process of Reformation.

Further Reading

Brecht, M. (1985). *Martin Luther: His Road to Reformation 1483–1521*. Philadelphia: Fortress Press.

Brecht, M. (1990). *Martin Luther: Shaping and Defining the Reformation 1521–1532*. Minneapolis: Fortress Press.

Brecht, M. (1999). *Martin Luther: The Preservation of the Church 1532–1546*. Minneapolis: Fortress Press.

Ebeling, G. (1972). *Luther: An Introduction to his Thought*. London: Collins.

Lohse, B. (1999). *Martin Luther's Theology: Its Historical and Systematic Development*. Minneapolis: Fortress Press.

Oberman, H. A. (1989). *Luther: Man Between God and the Devil*. New Haven, CT: Yale University Press.

CHAPTER 3

Shapers of Protestantism: John Calvin

Alister E. McGrath

Although John Calvin (1509–64) was a French theologian working in the independent city of Geneva for much of his career, his impact on German-speaking Protestantism – and far beyond – has been immense. Calvin was born on 10 July 1509 in the cathedral city of Noyon, north-east of Paris. He was the son of Gérard Cauvin, who was in charge of the legal and financial business of the chapter of the local cathedral. ('Calvin' is the Latinized form of the French name 'Cauvin'.) At some point, possibly as early as 1521, Calvin left home to study arts at the Collège de Montaigu, University of Paris. It appears that his father intended him for an ecclesiastical career. This was rendered problematic when Cauvin became caught up in a series of financial controversies with the cathedral chapter. Charges of misappropriation of funds, arising from missing accounts, led to Cauvin's excommunication in 1528, and the end of any hopes his son might have had for an accelerated rise through the ecclesiastical ranks due to powerful local patronage.

Calvin now found himself having to consider alternative careers, and was directed by his father to study civil law, presumably with the aim of establishing himself in a potentially lucrative practice. The University of Paris only offered courses in canon law; Calvin accordingly moved to Orléans and Bourges, where he studied civil law, encountering the ideas of French legal humanism, particularly those of Guillaume Budé, in doing so. Calvin would have come to know at least something of Lutheran ideas during his time at Paris, when the university was actively engaged in their suppression. However, during his time at Orléans he encountered these ideas in a more sympathetic environment. It is thought that his cousin, Robert Olivétan, and his Greek tutor, Melchior Wolmar, may have helped him gain a deepened appreciation of Luther's leading ideas.

The death of Calvin's father in 1531 led to his return to Paris, and a growing interest in classical studies. In 1532, Calvin published a commentary on Seneca's *De clementia*, which some scholars suggest contains at least the germs of his reforming ideas, while nevertheless showing no obvious explicit commitment to an evangelical agenda. By the autumn of 1533, however, Calvin was publicly declared to be an evangelical by the city authorities, who took exception to a sermon preached by the new rector of the University of Paris, Nicholas Cop. A copy of this sermon exists in Calvin's handwriting, and it is thought that he may have authored the work himself. Calvin was obliged to flee Paris in some haste, leaving his personal papers behind him. After a period of unsettled life, involving sojourns in cities in France and Italy, he settled in the Swiss city of Basle in 1535. By then, Basle had gained a reputation as a refuge for evangelicals, and Calvin clearly regarded it as a secure base from which he might consider his options for the future.

During his time in Basle, Calvin composed the *Institutes of the Christian Religion*. This work was occasioned by increasing hostility on the part of the French government to evangelicals within France, on account of the *affaire des placards* (October, 1534). The placing of evangelical posters in public places, including royal palaces, led to the evangelical community being regarded with increasing suspicion, and eventually discrimination. Calvin's work (which included a dedicatory epistle to the French king) was intended partly to demonstrate that French evangelicals were orthodox Christians, and owed nothing to the more radical ideas associated with the Anabaptists who had taken over the city of Münster in 1534, causing consternation throughout the region. This work, which was first published in Latin in March 1536, would go through many editions, culminating in the definitive edition of 1559.

In the summer of 1536, Calvin set off for Strasbourg, where he intended to settle down to a life of scholarship. However, the somewhat circuitous route he was obliged to take as a result of the Habsburg-Valois wars led him to spend a night in the independent city of Geneva. Here he was recognized, and pressed into the service of the Reformation in the city. Geneva had gained its independence from the neighbouring Duchy of Savoy in 1535, and had adopted the general principles of the Protestant Reformation. However, it needed someone to assist Pierre Viret and Guillaume Farel in consolidating its hold on the city, not least in matters of theology and Christian education. Calvin was persuaded to remain in the city, until the unpopularity of some of his reforms – such as the imposition of a confession of faith on each individual resident of the city – led to his being expelled from Geneva in April 1538.

Calvin now moved to Strasbourg, the original goal of his travelling in 1536. Under the benevolent mentoring of Martin Bucer, Calvin was appointed pastor to the French-speaking Protestant congregation of the city, allowing him to enhance his previously somewhat limited experience of church leadership. He also found time to work on the *Institutes*, producing both a French translation of the Latin original, as well as an expanded second edition of the work. He also composed a work of theological diplomacy – a *Little Treatise of the Lord's Supper*, designed to mediate between the somewhat entrenched positions associated with Luther and Zwingli, which had become the subject of considerable debate and acrimony.

In 1541, a changed political situation in Geneva brought about Calvin's recall to the city. Although his original intention was to remain in the city for a mere six months, he never left the city again until his death in 1564. During this period, Calvin sought to consolidate the Reformation in Geneva, and to extend and develop its theological foundations and political influence. Under his leadership, Calvinism quickly became an international movement. Missionaries were sent out from Geneva into Calvin's native France, achieving a significant impact on French religion and culture. The coming of the Wars of Religion in France can be seen as the direct outcome of the burgeoning influence of Calvinism in his homeland. Yet this pattern of growing influence is by no means limited to France; the rapid expansion of Calvinism in Germany, the Low Countries and England demonstrates the growing influence of this international movement on the shaping of Protestantism.

The phenomenon of the refugee and the place of refuge played no small part in the propagation of Calvinism. Geneva was one of a number of European centres (such as Frankfurt, Emden, and Strasbourg) which played host to Protestants who had been exiled from their homelands on account of their beliefs. During their period of exile, such refugees often absorbed Calvin's outlook, and, upon their return to their native lands, proceeded to propagate Calvinism. While French exiles were by far the most numerous, they were supplemented by others, particularly the 'Marian Exiles' – the English Protestants seeking safety from the persecutions launched by Mary Tudor. On returning to England after Mary's death, these individuals often went on to secure high office in both state and church. Thus 12 of the 18 bishops appointed by Elizabeth I in the aftermath of the mass resignations of 1559 had sought refuge in Europe during Mary's reign; most returned to England convinced Calvinists. Other countries, by receiving Calvinist refugees, nourished centres of Calvinist activities which had the potential to extend their influence beyond their congregations.

So what are the main ways in which Calvin's legacy has shaped Protestantism? A number of factors may be discerned.

Calvin's Influence on the Shaping of Protestantism

The growing reputation of Geneva as a centre of Calvinism led to a substantial number of future Protestant church leaders and theologians moving to the city to secure the educational benefits it so liberally provided, or attempting to replicate them in their homelands. The beliefs and practices of Geneva thus came to play an almost normative role in the development of Reformed thinking. As most of the innovations introduced in Geneva are directly due to Calvin's innovations, his personal influence on the development of international Protestantism must be regarded as immense. The main lines of that influence may be summarized as follows.

Educational

In part, Geneva's international reputation rested upon its academy, founded by Calvin in 1559, with the eminent theologian Théodore de Bèze as its first rector. Inaugurated on 5 June 1559, the academy embodied the model of theological education favoured by Calvin, including immersion in biblical studies and languages, a sustained engagement with systematic theology, the mastering of rhetoric as an essential prerequisite to effective preaching, and the fostering of a critical yet appreciative attitude towards secular philosophy. Calvin placed theological education on a new and rigorous footing, which influenced Protestant attitudes for at least 250 years, in both the old world and the new.

As Calvinism became an international movement, an increasing number of European universities became favourably disposed towards the new religion, and gradually came to overshadow the Genevan Academy. Thus the universities of Leiden and Heidelberg rapidly gained an international reputation, and were supplemented by the new Calvinist academies located strategically at cities such as Herborn in Hanau (the location of the celebrated Wechel presses). The Edict of Nantes, which offered safety to Calvinists in certain specified regions, led to the emergence of new and influential academies in Saumur and Sedan. The foundation of Harvard College (1636) established the intellectual hegemony of Calvinism in New England, ensuring the survival of the by then not so new faith in the new world.

With the passing of its monopoly on clerical education, Geneva's star slipped from the ascendancy. Calvinist pastors found cosmopolitan institutions at places such as Heidelberg, Saumur and Sedan more attractive than that of Geneva, despite the powerful and evocative links with Calvin which still lingered at that city. Yet these newer academies and universities nevertheless embodied and modelled a practice of theological education which was clearly due to Calvin. Although the influence of Genevan theological education diminished over time, the broader impact of Calvin's vision remained significant for many generations.

The structures of the church

Calvin's experience as a pastor in Strasbourg brought a new intellectual rigour and practical wisdom to the issue of the organization of the church. The importance of church structures to the international development of Calvinism can perhaps be appreciated best by comparing the very different situations within which Lutheranism and Calvinism came to be established in Western Europe and North America. Lutheranism generally advanced through the sympathy of monarchs and princes, perhaps not totally unaware of the important ecclesiastical role alloted to them by Luther's doctrine of the 'Two Kingdoms'. Although Calvin was aware of the potential of winning over monarchs to his ideas (his particular ambition being to gain a sympathetic hearing within the French court), Calvinism generally had to survive and advance in distinctly hostile situations (such as France in the 1550s), in which both monarch and the existing church establishment were opposed to its development. Under such conditions, the very survival of Calvinist groups was dependent upon a strong and well-disciplined church, capable of surviving the hostility of its environment. The more sophisticated Calvinist church structures proved capable of withstanding considerably more difficult situations that their Lutheran equivalents, providing Calvinism with a vital resource for gaining ground in what might at first sight seem thoroughly unpromising political situations.

Calvin's *Ecclesiastical Ordinances* of 1541 established as normative the distinctive fourfold ministry of pastors, teachers (or 'doctors'), elders and deacons, as well as two committees – the Company of Pastors and the Consistory. Whereas Luther regarded the organization of the church as a matter of historical contingency, not requiring theological prescription, Calvin held that a definite pattern of church government was prescribed by Scripture, and insisted that the Reformed church should embody this fourfold ministry. The continuing influence of this understanding of the organization of the church remains powerful in contemporary Presbyterianism, and continues to be reflected in other sections of modern Protestantism, especially in Baptist communities.

The 'Company of Pastors' played a particularly important role in Calvin's conception of the church. It provided the eight pastors within the city of Geneva, and their colleagues in the rural area immediately around the city, with what was, in effect, a corporate episcopacy, ensuring unity of doctrine and policy. The Consistory, which included elders as well as pastors, acted as a court of ecclesiastical discipline. Although it rapidly fell into disrepute on account of the severity of some of its judgements, its very existence nevertheless affirmed the legitimate place of the church in shaping the moral life of the civil community – a theme which is repeatedly found in later Protestant accounts of the role of the church.

The emphasis upon the Bible

As William Chillingworth once memorably argued, 'The Bible is the religion of Protestants'. This influential perception was given credence largely through the influence of Calvin upon the intellectual habits of an emerging generation of Protestants. Calvin made three decisive contributions towards the consolidation of the place of the Bible within Protestant theology and spirituality.

1   The *biblical commentary* aimed to allow its readers to peruse and understand the Bible, explaining difficult phrases, commenting on issues of translation, identifying points of importance, and generally allowing its readers to become familiar with the thrust and concerns of the biblical passage. Calvin produced a series of biblical commentaries, dealing with virtually every book of the Bible, aimed at a variety of readerships, both academic and lay.

2   The *expository sermon* aimed to fuse the horizons of the scriptural texts and its hearers, applying the principles underlying the scriptural passage to the situation of the audience. Calvin's sermons at Geneva are a model of their kind. In particular, Calvin developed the practice of *lectio continua* – the continuous preaching through a scriptural book, rather than on passages drawn from a lectionary or chosen by the preacher. For example, during the period between 20 March 1555 to 15 July 1556, Calvin is known to have preached some two hundred sermons on Deuteronomy. The importance of preaching to Calvin's understanding of the Christian life can be appreciated by considering the architecture of St Peter's Cathedral, Geneva, in which the pulpit towers above the congregation, dominating the interior of the cathedral in the way that the Bible should dominate the lives of believers.

3   Works of *biblical theology*, of which the supreme example is Calvin's *Institutes*, aimed to allow their readers to gain an appreciation of the theological coherence of scripture, by bringing together and synthesizing its statements on matters of theological importance. By doing this, it enabled its readers to establish a coherent and consistent worldview, which would undergird their everyday lives. 'My object in this work,' wrote Calvin, 'is to so prepare and train students of sacred theology for the study of the word of God that they might have an easy access into it, and be able to proceed in it without hindrance' (*Opera Calvini*, 1. 255). In other words, the book is intended to be a guide to Scripture, functioning as an extended commentary to its often intricate and complex depths of meaning. Its impact on the consolidation of the Reformation was substantial. As the French historian Pierre Imbart de La Tour once commented: 'The first work of Calvin was a book – the *Institutes*. The second was a city – Geneva. Book and city complement one another. One is doctrine formulated; the other is doctrine applied.' For Calvin, scripture moulded doctrine, which in turned shaped the realities of Christian life.

Calvin's emphasis upon the importance of the Bible was taken up and developed by others. A small group of English exiles in Geneva in the late 1550s produced the Geneva Bible (1560), which combined a new English translation of the biblical text with extensive marginal notes, in effect providing a continuous theological commentary on the text of the Bible. This work rapidly became the Bible of preference for English-speaking Protestants, and retained this status until well into the seventeenth century, when the King James translation of 1611 gradually began to displace it, partly for political reasons.

Calvin's theological influence on Protestantism

It is widely considered that Calvin's greatest impact upon Protestantism lies in his theology. This influence can be located at two distinct levels: the ideas which Calvin develops, and the medium which he deployed in propagating them – namely, the *Institutes of the Christian Religion*.

In March 1536, the Basle printers Thomas Platter and Balthasar Lasius published the *Institutio Christianae Religionis*, usually known in English as the *Institutes of the Christian Religion*. The translation of the Latin title poses some problems. The word *Institutio* immediately suggests a parallel with the *Institutes* of Justinian, a foundational legal code of the classical period, familiar to Calvin from his Orléans period. In terms of its structure or content, however, the work bears little resemblance to a legal code. Erasmus employed the same Latin word to mean 'instruction', or perhaps even 'primer' (for example, his *Institutio principis Christiani* of 1516, which may have served as an inspiration for Calvin's title). The English word *Institution* conveys another of Calvin's concerns – to return to a more authentic form of Christianity than that encountered in the late medieval period. It is Christianity as originally instituted which concerns Calvin, not as it was developed (or deformed, in Calvin's view) in the Middle Ages. In practice, most English translations choose to render the Latin title as *Institutes of the Christian Religion*, despite the alternatives suggested by the Latin original.

It is clear that the first edition of the work was modelled on Luther's *Lesser Catechism* of 1529. Both its structure and substance indicate the extent to which Calvin has drawn upon this important educational work of the German Reformation. Its 516 small-format pages consist of six chapters, the first of which is essentially an exposition of the Ten Commandments (or Decalogue), and the second an exposition of the Apostle's Creed. After expositions of 'The Law', 'Faith', 'Prayer' and 'The sacraments', Calvin includes two chapters of a more polemical nature on 'False sacraments' and 'The liberty of a Christian'.

The second expanded edition of the *Institutes* dates from Calvin's Strasbourg period. Published in Latin in 1539, the volume was now three times as long as the first edition of 1536, with 17 chapters instead of six. Two opening chapters now deal with the knowledge of God and the knowledge of human nature. Additional material was added on the doctrine of the Trinity, the relation of the Old and New Testaments, penitence, justification by faith, the nature and relation of providence and predestination, and the nature of the Christian life. Although the work retained much material drawn from the earlier edition, it is evident that its character and status had changed. It was no longer a catechism; it was well on the way to being a definitive statement of the nature of the Christian faith, inviting comparison with the *Summa Theologiae* of Thomas Aquinas.

As already noted, a French edition of the *Institutes* was published in 1541. This is not actually a direct translation of the 1539 edition; there are several points at which material from the 1536 edition, although altered in 1539, has been included, in translation, in that of 1541. This has led to speculation that Calvin may originally have intended to produce a French translation of the 1536 edition, and, abandoning this project, included material already translated into the 1541 edition without the modifications introduced in 1539. The work shows numerous minor alterations, all of which may be explained with reference to the envisaged readership. Scholarly points likely to cause difficulty (for example, all

Greek words and references to Aristotle) are omitted, and additional material likely to be familiar to the intended readership (for example, French proverbs and idioms) are added.

A further Latin edition appeared in 1543, with a French translation in 1545. Now expanded to 21 chapters, it included as its most significant addition a major section on the doctrine of the church. Minor alterations include the addition of two chapters on vows and human traditions, and the creation of a separate chapter for the material relating to angels. The impact of experience upon Calvin's religious reflections is evident in this edition, particularly in the discussion of the importance of ecclesiastical organization. Despite the obvious merits of this edition, an inherent defect, already discernible in 1539, now becomes transparently obvious: the work is poorly organized. New chapters are added, without thought being given to the overall impact such addition has upon the structure and organization of the work. Many chapters are impossibly long, without any attempt to subdivide them into sections. The Latin edition of 1550, and the subsequent French translation of 1551, attempted to remedy this deficiency by subdividing their 21 chapters into paragraphs. A few additions may be noted, such as new sections dealing with biblical authority and human conscience. The fundamental flaw remains, however: the edition of 1550, like that of 1543, must be regarded as a remarkably poorly organized work.

Recognizing both the need for total revision and the limited time available in which to achieve this (illness was a recurring feature of Calvin's final years), the reformer decided to recast the entire work. While a few additions are made, the most significant change is the total reordering of the material, which virtually restores unity to what had almost degenerated into a series of unrelated fragments. The material was now distributed among four 'books', arranged as follows: the knowledge of God the creator; the knowledge of God the redeemer; the manner of participation in the grace of Jesus Christ; the external means or aids which God uses to bring us to Jesus Christ. The 21 chapters of 1551 are now expanded to 80 chapters, each carefully subdivided for ease of reading, distributed over these four books.

It is possible that Calvin had adapted the quadripartite structure of the edition of 1543 to create the new division of material; an alternative explanation, however, is that he had noticed and adapted the fourfold division of material in the *Four Books of the Sentences* of Peter Lombard, a seminal medieval theologian to whom Calvin often refers. Is Calvin setting himself up as the Protestant successor to Peter Lombard, and his *Institutes* as the Protestant alternative to his great theological textbook? We shall never know. What we do know is that the *Institutes* rapidly became firmly established as the most influential theological work of the Protestant Reformation, eclipsing in importance the rival works of Luther, Melanchthon and Zwingli.

The remarkable success of the 1559 *Institutes* partly reflects its superb organization. Philip Melanchthon established the definitive pattern for Lutheran works of systematic theology in 1521, through the publication of his 'Commonplaces' (*Loci Communes*). In its first edition, this work simply treated a number of subjects of obvious relevance to the Lutheran Reformation. Gradually, however, polemical and pedagogical considerations obliged Melanchthon to expand the work considerably. Melanchthon met this challenge in a surprisingly inadequate manner: he merely added additional material, regardless of the impression of lack of a unified structure this created. It soon became evident that this way of handling material was clumsy and disorganized, incapable of achieving the systematic analysis needed for the theological debates of the late sixteenth and seventeenth centuries. Calvin, however, bequeathed to his heirs an intensely systematic and organized structure, which proved ideally suited not merely to the needs of his own generation, but also for those of at least a century to come. Lutheranism never really recovered from the false start given to it by Melanchthon; the intellectual domination of Protestantism by theologians of the Reformed tradition is partly due to both the substance and structure of Calvin's final edition of the *Institutes*.

Yet the importance of the theological ideas mediated by the *Institutes* must not be overlooked. Calvin's theology stamped itself decisively upon the emerging mind of the Reformed church, totally displacing that of Zwingli, which – with the exception of his sacramental ideas – rapidly became relegated to the sidelines of theological debate. Limits on space prevent more than two of the most distinctive ideas bequeathed by Calvin to his successors within Protestantism being considered in what follows. The two topics chosen are to be regarded as illustrative of Calvin's approach, and indicative of the way in which he has been of such influence on the shaping of the Protestant theological mind.

Natural theology   Calvin affirms that a general knowledge of God may be discerned throughout the creation – in humanity, in the natural order, and in the historical process itself. Two main grounds of such knowledge are identified, one subjective, the other objective. The first ground is a general 'sense of divinity' or a 'seed of religion', implanted within every human being by God. God has endowed human beings with some inbuilt sense or presentiment of the divine existence. Something about or of God appears to have been engraved in the hearts of every human being. Calvin identifies three consequences of this inbuilt awareness of divinity: the universality of religion (which, if uninformed by the Christian revelation, degenerates into idolatry); a troubled conscience; and a servile fear of God. All of these, Calvin suggests, may serve as points of contact for the Christian proclamation.

The second such ground lies in experience of and reflection upon the ordering of the world. The fact that God is creator, together with an appreciation of his wisdom and justice, may be gained from an inspection of the created order, culminating in humanity itself. 'God has revealed himself in such a beautiful and elegant construction of heaven and earth, showing and presenting himself there every day, that human beings cannot open their eyes without having to notice him' (*Institutes*, I.v.1). Calvin makes no suggestion whatsoever that this knowledge of God from the created order is peculiar to, or restricted to, Christian believers. Calvin insists that anyone, by intelligent and rational reflection upon the created order, should be able to arrive at the idea of God. The created order is a 'theatre' or 'mirror' for displaying the divine presence, nature and attributes. Although God is invisible and incomprehensible, God chooses to become known under the form of created and visible things by donning the garment of creation.

Calvin thus commends the natural sciences (such as astronomy), on account of their ability to illustrate further the wonderful ordering of creation, and the divine wisdom which this indicates. This is widely seen as representing a historically significant incentive to the development of the natural sciences. Calvin's theological motivation for the study of nature is simple: this leads to an enhanced appreciation of the glory and wisdom of God. This theme is developed by Protestant confessional documents which have clearly been influenced by Calvin at this point. Thus the *Belgic Confession* (1561), a Calvinist statement of faith which exercised particular influence in the Lowlands (which would become particularly noted for its botanists and physicists), declared that nature is 'before our eyes as a most beautiful book in which all created things, whether great or small, are as letters showing the invisible things of God to us' (Müller, 1903: 233).

Predestination   One of the most distinctive themes of the Reformed tradition is the emphasis placed upon predestination – the subject of a particularly vicious dispute between Calvin and Jerome Bolsec in the 1550s. Although this doctrine became of increasing importance in the writings of Calvin's followers, such as Théodore de Bèze, it is far from clear that it possesses this significance in Calvin's writings. Calvin defines predestination as 'the eternal decree of God, by which he determined what he wished to make of every person. For God does not create everyone in the same condition, but ordains eternal life for some and eternal damnation for others' (*Institutes*, III, xxi, 5). Predestination is thus a doctrine which should induce a sense of awe within us. The *decretum horribile* is not a 'horrible decree', as a crude translation of the Latin might suggest; rather it is an 'awe-inspiring' or 'terrifying' decree.

Far from being arid and abstract theological speculation, Calvin's analysis of predestination begins from observable facts. Some do, and some do not, believe the gospel. The primary function of the doctrine of predestination is to explain why some individuals respond to the gospel, and others do not. It is an *ex post facto* explanation of the particularity of human responses to grace. Calvin's predestinarianism is to be regarded as *a posteriori* reflection upon the data of human experience, interpreted in the light of Scripture, rather than something which is deduced *a priori* on the basis of preconceived ideas concerning divine omnipotence. Belief in predestination is not an article of faith in its own right, but is the final outcome of scripturally informed reflection on the effects of grace upon individuals in the light of the enigmas of experience.

Experience indicates that God does not touch every human heart. Why not? Is this due to some failure or omission on God's part? In the light of Scripture,

Calvin feels able to deny the possibility of any weakness or inadequacy on the part of God or the gospel: the observable pattern of responses to the gospel reflects a mystery by which some are predestined to respond to, and others to reject, the promises of God. 'Some have been allocated to eternal life, others to eternal damnation' (*Institutes*, III.xii.5).

This is no theological innovation. Calvin is not introducing a hitherto unknown notion into the sphere of Christian theology. The late medieval Augustinian school exemplified by such leading medieval theologians as Gregory of Rimini and Hugolino of Orvieto had also taught a doctrine of absolute double predestination, insisting that God allocates some to eternal life, others to eternal condemnation, without any reference to their merits or demerits. Their fate rested totally upon the will of God, rather than their individualities. It is possible that Calvin has actively appropriated this aspect of late medieval Augustinianism, according to which salvation lies outside the control of the individual, who is powerless to alter the situation.

Calvin stresses that this selectivity is not in any way peculiar to the matter of salvation. In every area of life, he argues, we are forced to reckon with the mystery of the inexplicable. Why is it that some are more fortunate than others in life? Why does one person possess intellectual gifts denied to another? Even from the moment of birth, two infants may find themselves in totally different circumstances through no fault of their own: one may find a full breast of milk to suck and thus gain nourishment, while another might suffer malnutrition through having to suck a breast that is nearly dry. For Calvin, predestination is merely a further instance of a general mystery of human existence, in which some are inexplicably favoured with material or intellectual gifts which are denied to others. It raises no difficulties which are not already presented by other areas of human existence.

Does not this idea of predestination suggest that God is dispensed from common notions of goodness, justice or rationality? Although Calvin specifically repudiates the conception of God as an absolute and arbitrary power, his discussion of predestination has raised the spectre of a God whose relationship to the creation is whimsical and capricious, and whose conception and exercise of power is not bound to any law or order. In the end, Calvin argues that predestination must be recognized to rest in the inscrutable judgements of God. We cannot know, or hope to know, why God elects some and condemns others. God must be free to choose whom God wills, otherwise the divine freedom is compromised by external considerations. The creator would thus become subject to the creation. Calvin insists, however, that God's decisions reflect the divine wisdom and justice, which are upheld, rather than contradicted, by the fact of predestination.

This doctrine has played a significant role in the development of Protestantism. In the first place, it served to distinguish the Reformed church from its Lutheran counterpart. As intra-Protestant polemics became increasingly heated during the late sixteenth century, pressure developed to find clear lines of demarcation between the Lutheran and Reformed communities. The doctrine of predestination proved ideal for this purpose of differentiation, offering an unambiguous means of distinguishing them. Yet the doctrine was also of decisive importance in fostering the notion of the divine calling of the Reformed church. English Puritans settling in America, for example, saw themselves as God's chosen people, entering into a new promised land. As the recent history of Southern Africa has shown, there is a worryingly easy transition from the theological idea of election to the political idea of 'special privilege' and the racist idea of 'apartheid'. Yet this must be regarded as an aberration of this idea, rather than its authentic application. A further point of application lay in Calvin's work ethic, which celebrated the idea of activity within the created order as a means of demonstrating and celebrating the individual's divine calling. Max Weber argued that the key to understanding the historical link between Calvinism and capitalism lay in the new attitude to personal and economic activism encouraged by this doctrine. Controversial and problematic though Weber's theory may be, it highlights the relevance of this doctrine to the shaping of Protestant attitudes to the world throughout its history.

Although Calvin separated his discussions of predestination and providence in later editions of the *Institutes*, it is clear from earlier editions that he sees a close theological relationship between the two themes. Taken together, the two ideas express the sovereignty of God over all aspects of the created order, including both secular history and salvation history (if this somewhat nuanced distinction be permitted). The theme of God's providential government of both the world and the church plays a particularly significant role in later Protestant thought (for example, in relation to B. B. Warfield's positive take on Darwin's theory of evolution, which he regards as a special case of the exercise of providence within creation.)

In conclusion, it may be noted that Calvin's theological heritage has proved fertile perhaps to a greater extent than any other Protestant writer. Richard Baxter, Jonathan Edwards and Karl Barth, in their very different ways, bear witness to the pivotal role that Calvin's ideas have played in shaping Protestant self-perceptions down the centuries. While the scholarly debate over the nature and extent of Calvin's influence over the development of modern capitalism, the emergence of the natural sciences and the shaping of modern views of human rights will continue, there is no doubting Calvin's role in contributing to the shaping of modern Protestant attitudes in these areas. It is impossible to understand modern Protestantism without coming to terms with Calvin's legacy to the movement which he did so much to nourish and sustain.

Further Reading

Cottret, B (2000). *Calvin: A Biography*. Grand Rapids, MI: William B. Erdmans.
Bouwsma, W. J. (1988). *John Calvin: A Sixteenth-Century Portrait*. New York: Oxford University Press.

Higman, F. M. (1967). *The Style of John Calvin in his French Polemical Treatises*. London: Oxford University Press.

Höpfl, H. (1982). *The Christian Polity of John Calvin*. Cambridge, UK: Cambridge University Press.

Kingdon, R. M. (1956). *Geneva and the Coming of the Wars of Religion in France, 1555–1563*. Geneva: Librairie E. Droz.

McGrath, A. E. (1990). *A Life of John Calvin: A Study in the Shaping of Western Culture*. Oxford: Blackwell.

Müller, E. F. K. (ed.) (1903). Belgic Confession, article 2. In *Die Bekenntnisschriften der reformierten Kirche*. Leipzig: Böhme.

Parker, T. H. L. (1995). *Calvin: An Introduction to his Thought*. London: Chapman.

Prestwich, M. (ed.) (1985). *International Calvinism, 1541–1715*. Oxford: Clarendon Press.

Wendel, F. (1978). *Calvin: The Origins and Development of his Religious Thought*. London: The Fontana Library/Collins.

CHAPTER 4

Shapers of Protestantism: F. D. E. Schleiermacher

Nicholas Adams

Friedrich Daniel Ernst Schleiermacher (1768–1834), the 'father of modern theology', was a Moravian Pietist pastor and professor of theology whose work in Berlin in the early 1800s transformed Protestant theology in Europe. His legacy for theology in general, and Protestantism more particularly, is twofold. He left not only a large body of theological and philosophical writings, some of whose arguments will be summarized here, but also a conception of how theology is to be studied in the university.

Schleiermacher fundamentally shaped the way theology is studied in Western Europe and North America. Any seminary or faculty of theology or divinity which divides its subject matter into philosophical theology, doctrine, church history, biblical studies and ethics is following a pattern laid down by Schleiermacher in the early 1800s. The relationship between these different subject areas varies widely from institution to institution, of course, but the fundamental pattern of theological study represented by this division into separate areas of expertise is one of Schleiermacher's gifts to the university. The first section of this chapter will rehearse the main features of Schleiermacher's conception of theology.

The influence of Schleiermacher's particular theological and philosophical work can be divided up in a number of ways. In the second and third section we shall look briefly at two areas where his work continues to shape current thinking: his discussions of feeling and consciousness in relation to religion, and his understanding of hermeneutics and language. This means that relatively little weight will be given here to the detail of his dogmatic theology as found in *Der Christliche Glaube* (in English *The Christian Faith*). This is a shortcoming, but one that is compensated for significantly by Schleiermacher's own ordered thinking. His main dogmatic arguments are summarized in his 'Introduction' to *The Christian Faith* and are not so obscure as to require radical reinterpretation by subsequent readers. The discussion here will also pay little attention to his

Dialectics, Ethics, Aesthetics, Sermons or to his shorter works, which (especially his wonderful *Christmas Eve* dialogue) richly reward patient attention.

Schleiermacher had a massive influence on subsequent theologians, whether they agree with him or not. Perhaps the most noteworthy engagement with Schleiermacher is that by Karl Barth. Barth admired Schleiermacher's theology, wrestled with problems thrown up by Schleiermacher's way of conceiving theology, and attempted to repair Protestant theology through a renewed emphasis on God's initiative and sovereignty. The fourth section summarizes some of Barth's criticisms.

Theology as a Subject of Study

Schleiermacher's purpose in the *Brief Outline of Theology as a Field of Study* (Schleiermacher, 1990) is to attempt a set of broad generalizations without omitting or underplaying the particularities of the material he surveys. When Schleiermacher was writing (first edition 1811, revised 1830), great changes were underway in German universities, both in the way they structured the teaching of subjects, and in the content of those subjects themselves. The study of 'History', in the sense now familiar, was in its innovative and fascinating infancy; biblical interpretation was being transformed through the development of new critical methods; philosophy was dominated by the new experimental idealism of Fichte, Schelling and Hegel and the romanticism of Friedrich Schlegel and his colleagues. All of this was taking place against the backdrop of political conflict in Europe in the wake of the French Revolution and the rise to prominence of Napoleon Bonaparte. The relationships between state, church and university were thus topics urgently in need of ordered consideration.

The most arresting features of the *Brief Outline* are the description it gives of the purpose of theological study and the way it divides its subject matter. The purpose of theological study is startlingly simple: it is to serve 'church leadership'. The division is tripartite: (1) philosophical theology, (2) historical theology, (3) practical theology. These are terms with currency in theology today, and although they are to a significant extent influenced by Schleiermacher, some divergences and developments are quickly apparent. The purpose of 'philosophical theology' is to gain an overview or, as he says, a 'general concept', of religious communities or fellowships of faith (Schleiermacher, 1990: §33). Once one has an overview of what religious communities are (or might be), then one can compare actual existing examples with this 'idea'. This comparison is what philosophical theology attempts. The undertaking also has a therapeutic dimension: once one knows what Christianity 'is', one can diagnose deviations from this general concept. Schleiermacher recognizes that this is a risky enterprise, and draws attention to the temptation to identify the particularities of one's own particular tradition with Christianity *per se*. This, he says, is a mistake. Doing philosophical theology means recognizing that within the scope of Christianity as a general concept, there is room for diversity and disagreement. Without a generous conception of this diversity, it is impossible to make sense of the tasks of 'apologetics' and 'polemics'. These refer respectively to public speech from the particular community to a wider audience and argument within a particular community. At the same time, diversity does not mean lazy tolerance. On the contrary, it requires sustained argument in order to cure 'diseased conditions' in Christianity: that is why apologetics and polemics are required. One of the skills Schleiermacher requires of the theologian is an ability to tell the difference between genuine diversity within Christianity and sick deviation from it. This is not something that can be determined in advance of patient enquiry: Schleiermacher seeks to discern rules for how this might be conducted.

The kinds of task undertaken in philosophical theology are elucidation of the ways in which it is distinctive (which involves exploring the meaning of 'revelation' and 'inspiration'), the continuities and discontinuities thrown up by its history (involving 'canon' and 'sacrament') and the relationship of the church to other institutions (involving 'hierarchy' and 'church authority') (§§43–8). Schleiermacher seems to be making a distinction between asking what kind of thing 'revelation' or 'canon' is *in general* and asking what 'revelation' or 'canon' Christian theology claims for itself *in particular*. Philosophical theology has a certain grammatical job that is distinct from, but related to, historical theology. Philosophical theology tries to settle the categories for discussion; historical theology argues about what is placed in these categories. One can already see here the need for further clarifications (which Schleiermacher does not supply at this stage): for example, to what extent are *general* concepts peculiar to a *particular* tradition? It is clear from the acuteness of Schleiermacher's philosophical thinking in other contexts that he well understands the importance of this kind of question. He himself recognizes in other work that there is no 'universal language', but that nonetheless translation between them is possible. In the current context, Schleiermacher implies that it is indeed difficult to say how we get from particulars to generalities, and that general concepts are unstable and open to dispute, but that nonetheless *we do use general concepts*, and sometimes quite successfully. The fact that general concepts are disputable does not mean we should not use them. It does mean that some care is required in their exercise. And philosophical theology is a discipline that exercises precisely this care. There is admittedly a certain circularity here, but it is difficult to see how it could be avoided without giving up *all* attempts at generalization and therefore at any ordering of knowledge whatsoever.

'Historical theology' is the term Schleiermacher uses for those aspects of theological study which describe the particular contents of Christian belief and practice. Under its heading come 'exegetical theology', 'church history' and 'historical knowledge of the present'.

Exegetical theology encompasses questions about the canon of scripture and how it is to be interpreted. It roughly corresponds to what is currently called 'biblical studies', although for Schleiermacher its purpose is exclusively to serve the church. He subdivides it into various categories: 'higher criticism' (determining what the canon is), 'lower criticism' (reconstructing the original meaning of the text) and 'hermeneutics' (specifying the rules for interpreting the text).

Church history is, for Schleiermacher, a comprehensive category. He calls it 'historical theology in the narrower sense' and its purpose is 'knowledge concerning the total development of Christianity since its establishment as a historical phenomenon' (§149). Part of this means skilfully relating the minute details recorded in documents to what he calls 'a single picture of their inner reality'. Unless this 'picture' is borne in view, one has not history but merely 'chronicle' (§153). One can see that getting a grasp of this 'inner reality' is difficult, but Schleiermacher is clear that this is the task of church history. It has different aspects. One is a description of what he calls 'the church's life', which entails understanding the cultural resources for worship available to Christians at any particular time, and the ways in which being a Christian affects how people live their lives outside worship. Schleiermacher's discussion here (as in so many places) is concerned to avoid one-sidedness: there is a problem either if Christian life is identified with morality in everyday life while worship has become empty ceremony; or if Christian life is identified exclusively with what goes on in worship, while everyday morality is determined by alien non-Christian practices and beliefs. For Schleiermacher, worship and ethics are two aspects of one church life, and while they can be distinguished from each other for analytical purposes, they belong together.

The third subcategory, after 'exegetical theology' and 'church history', is 'historical knowledge of the present'. First in this category is doctrine. Again, 'dogmatic theology serves the leadership of the church' (§198) by showing how current doctrinal formulations arise from historical developments, and at the same time indicating how they inform practice in the present. Dogmatic theology rehearses historical debates so that old confusions are not repeated in the present. Beyond this, Schleiermacher advances some observations about the role and scope of disagreement in matters of doctrine. Schleiermacher is particularly interested in the relation between things that are fixed (and can be reduced to rules) and things that cannot be fixed (and which display spontaneity). In his discussion of doctrine, Schleiermacher explores the relationship between tradition and innovation, orthodoxy and heterodoxy. These are not mutually exclusive. They are two ends of a single continuum and are, moreover, equally important (§204). Tradition is the relatively stable, rule-bound element of doctrine: it can be preserved and handed down in a relatively fixed form. Innovation is the spontaneous, surprising element of doctrine: it is mobile and introduces new modes of expression. The enemy of good doctrine is one-sidedness: orthodoxy is needed for unity; heterodoxy is needed for development (§§203–6). This is obviously a formal point, which makes no attempt to make judgements about particular dogmatic formulations. What, then, are the criteria for testing them? Schleiermacher offers two: their consonance with Scripture and their consonance with other formulations. What form do dogmatic formulations take? Schleiermacher suggests this will depend on 'the existing condition of the philosophical disciplines' (§213). In general, 'dogmatic theology is endless' (§218).

Why? Each theologian has to digest all topics in theology, because they are all related to each other. Skill in dogmatic theology means grasping at some level what it is that binds them together, even if it is impossible to specify concretely what that something is.

This leads to Christian ethics. About this, Schleiermacher is very prescriptive: dogmatic theology has both speculative and practical sides, but this distinction is not an 'essential separation'; it is merely a division of labour between different theological emphases (§223). Schleiermacher notes with disapproval that some theologians fail to acknowledge this, and develop ethics and doctrine in isolation from one other. He diagnoses the problem's origin in the appeal to different kinds of philosophy: 'rational theology' for doctrine, 'philosophical ethics' for Christian ethics. This, he says, is a serious error which needs correcting. It can only be corrected, he suggests, by doing dogmatics properly, and that means that one's style of reasoning needs to be the same for both doctrine and ethics (§§225–7). The church needs one dogmatic theology divided into two aspects (doctrine and ethics), rather than two undivided but separate disciplines.

One cannot do theology without knowing what people in churches actually think. This means that the study of theology will include gathering information about what communities do, in fact, think. And not just one's local church, but all the major denominations at a particular time. This kind of knowledge helps communities correct any one-sidedness from which they may suffer. Schleiermacher calls this area of study 'church statistics' (§232ff.), the last of the subdivisions of 'historical theology'.

The third and final part of the *Brief Outline* after philosophical theology and historical theology concerns 'practical theology'. Practical theology is not to be separated from philosophical or historical theology, but is distinct from them by virtue of its particular emphasis. The practical theologian's job is to teach others about how the church can embody what is said in the more speculative or scholarly aspects of theology (§258). Practical theology is concerned with the relationship between clergy and laity, ecclesiastical hierarchy, the effectiveness of communication of theology and pastoral work.

Schleiermacher acknowledges the danger in saying that there is one discipline of theology, divided up into different aspects. The main danger he identifies is what we would call the problem of deciding the 'core' of theological education. Schleiermacher insists that there can be no definite specification of what counts as core and what counts as specialization (§335). This has to be judged on a case-by-case basis for each student.

Part of the aim of Schleiermacher's work, broadly conceived, is formal: to assist existing debates and provide resources for their development. Doing this requires an account of the rules of debate, the limits of discussion, and the adjudication of boundaries so that one can determine whether a discussion is really part of an existing debate or is better described as starting a new and different one. There is constant pressure in his writing to discern contrary tendencies and to find structures of thinking in which they correct each other rather than become one-sided. This is particularly obvious in his discussion of ethics. As we have seen, Schleiermacher argues strenuously against the tendency to split dogmatics into theoretical and practical sides. Even so, Schleiermacher's diagnosis here is largely negative: the idea of an integrated dogmatic study, with both speculative and practical dimensions, is something he can only imagine, and he leaves this as a task for future generations.

Schleiermacher's influence on the structure of contemporary university study of theology does not stop with his conceptions in the *Brief Outline*. His way of looking at human experience in *On Religion* is a major resource for some conceptions of what 'religious studies' is. The order of Schleiermacher's argument is from general observations to particular instances rather than the other way round. As we shall see, he starts with a general and universal experience ('feeling'), then moves towards how it is expressed in language, then moves towards how it finds particular expression in communities and finally says how it is expressed most perfectly in Christianity. Any study which begins with 'religion' as a general category, with 'religious language and practice' as a subheading, and then 'particular religious languages and practices' as a further specification follows Schleiermacher's lead here.

Feeling, Consciousness and Religion

The most important discussion by Schleiermacher of consciousness in relation to Christianity are his *On Religion: Speeches to its Cultured Despisers* of 1799 (revised 1830) and *The Christian Faith* of 1821 (also revised 1830). This section will take the main argument about feeling from these two works together (Schleiermacher, 1988, 1989).[1]

The main purpose of Schleiermacher's *On Religion* is to separate religion from metaphysics and morality (Schleiermacher, 1988: 22–3; Crouter, 1988: xiv; Bowie, 1998: xiv–xv). Why would he want to do this? The short answer is: because of issues raised by two massive influences on German thought, Spinoza and Kant. To understand Schleiermacher we need to understand what Spinoza and Kant had bequeathed to Schleiermacher's time.

Spinoza, in his *Ethics* (1677) argued that the only thing humans can know is the one substance, which is 'God or nature'. There is no separate God, known relationally as in the theological traditions of Judaism and Christianity. There is only the one unified substance, of which humans (and their thinking) are an integral part. Philosophy's task is to explicate the one substance, and explain how its unity is related to its different parts and to give an account of how it is thinkable in philosophy. Metaphysics which posits a separate God (whether known relationally or not) is based on misconceptions about what a 'substance' is or on other faulty premises whose mistakenness can be demonstrated.

Kant, in his *Critique of Pure Reason* (1781) and *Religion Within the Limits of Reason Alone* (1793), argued that the only things humans can know are the presentations of our minds. The only things of which we have such presentations are objects in the world. We have understanding when sense experience (provided by objects) and concepts (provided by the mind) are combined. God, however, is not the kind of object which provides us with sense experience. For that reason we cannot have knowledge of God. Rather, God is a product of reason, and is an idea by which we measure our actions in the world. Ideas are not known: they are posited by our minds. Nonetheless, God is an indispensable idea, and is an idea that guides our moral lives. Religion, as considered within philosophy, is the practice of having our lives guided morally by the idea of God.

Schleiermacher, in common with his contemporaries, learned from these philosophical arguments, and attempted to repair their shortcomings. Spinoza's arguments were powerful in demolishing the idea that philosophy can arrive at the idea of God, understood as a being separate from the world. Kant's arguments were powerful in the 'Copernican revolution' they created, in focusing not on the objectivity of objects, but on the activity of human thinking in 'constituting' objects of consciousness. After Kant, philosophers like Schleiermacher were concerned to show how consciousness (now, along with language, one of the foci of philosophy) could be explored and explained. Spinoza's account of the world lacked an adequate account of human freedom. It was good at describing the determined nature of reality, but was bad at doing justice to spontaneity, human creativity or moral freedom. Kant tried to address this by suggesting there were two realms: the determined realm of nature, and the free realm of human moral action. Kant, however, was left with the difficult task of showing how these realms related to each other. Both Spinoza and Kant were weak at showing how human feelings, relations and spontaneity are integral to experience. Early nineteenth-century German philosophy, especially romantic philosophy, to which Schleiermacher is a contributor, attempted to correct these defects by redescribing nature as itself spontaneous (and not merely 'active') as well as determined, and human action as freely creative as well as bound by rules. It is in discussions of consciousness and language that philosophers experimented with such corrections.

What romantic philosophers did less carefully was consider religion in the light of these changes. Once 'metaphysics' (i.e., the attempt in philosophy to know God) was abandoned, what might 'religion' entail? Was it to be reduced to morality (as in Kant, as it appeared to the romantics)? Some German philosophers at the beginning of the 1800s argued for a 'new religion' which would unite conceptual rigour and sensual experience; others turned to a worship of nature. Schleiermacher believed he could do justice to the history of Christianity by *redescribing it* in the wake of Spinoza and Kant, rather than having to abandon it in favour of something new (e.g. the erasure of religion by art). The task of *On Religion* and *The Christian Faith* is to show how it can be done.

Schleiermacher, then, set himself the task of a non-metaphysical and non-moral account of religion. He appealed to something his romantic contemporaries, the 'cultured despisers of religion', would have to agree upon: the power of human intuition and feeling. 'Intuition' (*Anschauung*) is a technical term in

German philosophy, and arguments about how it is conceived are a central concern of German philosophy in this period. Broadly, it describes the relationship between mind and world without splitting one from the other. It asks the question: how is the mind 'in' the world? For Schleiermacher, we have intuition because we are linked to the world in a way that transcends our cognitive and practical activity (Bowie, 1998: xvi). We are not merely Spinoza's mechanical effects of a self-relating universe, nor free agents who posit the world through our subjectivity (such as in Fichte). We are both active and receptive agents. We have an immediate feeling (intuition) of being both wholly individual and yet part of a whole that transcends us. This intuition is prereflexive, that is, it is what we have to think about, rather than itself being a product of our thinking (Crouter, 1988: xxxii). Religion is the practice of doing justice to this intuition. Schleiermacher's argument in *On Religion* is that the key category is experience. We experience our bond with the whole (the infinite) but we experience it individually (finitely). Religion is the interplay between the tug towards conceptual thinking (the finite) and the tug towards preconceptual intuition (the infinite). That means that thinking itself is inherently one-sided, and that truly religious understanding means, in a crucial sense, not 'thinking' at all but feeling. This is not irrational wooliness, but an attempt to describe the relation between finite and infinite, at the same time as redescribing Christian religious life. The remainder of *On Religion* tries to show how this general insight can be applied in more and more particular ways: to communication and language, to social life and communities, and finally to Christianity.

The Christian Faith continues this pattern. The 'Introduction' is a variation on the theme of *On Religion* followed by greater particularity. It attempts to redescribe the details of dogmatic theology in line with the fundamental insight that religion is feeling rather than thinking (in the above sense) and that theological reasoning is thinking in the light of this feeling. *The Christian Faith* insists, as its substantial claim about intuition, that faith has at its root a feeling of radical dependence (*Gefühl der schlechthinnigen Abhängigkeit*), which finds its highest expression as God-consciousness. This claim decisively separates Schleiermacher from the pneumatology of Hegel, for whom all experience is necessarily conceptually mediated. For Hegel the idea that there could be a non-mediated consciousness is a mistake. It is worth delving a little deeper here, as Schleiermacher is not at all persuaded by Hegel.

Hegel insists that any experience of the infinite or absolute is mediated by the finite or determinate. In trinitarian terms, following scriptural warrant, the Father is only known through the Son. Developing this insight experimentally, this relationship is universalized in the Spirit and encompasses all knowledge. Knowledge of God is thus knowledge of the Son. Schleiermacher does not agree. The two poles between which he wishes to steer are solipsism (i.e., we do all the world-constituting work in our pure individuality, as for Fichte) and naturalism (i.e., the world is self-constituted and we are just its effects, as for Spinoza). Schleiermacher addresses this by suggesting that we are dependent and receptive upon a prior world we did not create, but that the manner of our response is spontaneous and unique to each of us (Bowie, 1998: xvii). We have a (spontaneous, individual) feeling of radical (receptive, universal) dependence. The formula 'feeling of radical dependence' is designed to perform this double task. Schleiermacher associates the feeling of radical dependence with the concept of God, through an account of 'God-consciousness'. This means that 'God' refers both to what can be known (in so far as it is mediated) and what cannot be known (in so far as it is what gives rise to 'knowing', and therefore itself unknowable). For Hegel, this would require acknowledging that God is, at least, partly unintelligible, which he (with Spinoza) rejects. For Schleiermacher, it requires admitting that intelligibility rests upon the unintelligible, which he (with the early Schelling) accepts. Schleiermacher is therefore more Augustinian and less Spinozist here, in so far as he thinks theology involves speaking what cannot be spoken. What evokes our thinking cannot be thought, and we should not confuse the response that is evoked from us with the idea that we ourselves are the prevenient agent of the world's reality. The triumph of the concept in Hegel is a trinitarian theology dominated by the Word; the feeling of absolute dependence in Schleiermacher is a trinitarian theology oscillating brilliantly between Creator and Spirit, but (problematically for orthodox theology) with no intrinsic need for the Word. A properly trinitarian theology need not be forced into either position here: whether it finds itself concerned with intelligibility or unintelligibility, or with both in human action, depends upon which person of the Trinity is currently the focus of discussion.

The Christian Faith elaborates an interplay of opposites (God and world, sin and grace) and shows how they are handled *together* in human consciousness. Every major doctrine is to be redescribed, according to this pattern, as the elucidation of the consciousness we have of these opposites and how we respond in self-consciousness and action. This 'interplay of opposites' structure is Schleiermacher's substitute for trinitarian theology, and it has some startling consequences. Most strikingly, the order of topics does not follow the creed (Father, Son, Spirit, church, eschaton) but something quite different: creation, God, sin, grace. The order of the second section is particularly experimental: the state of humanity, the person and work of Christ, justification and sanctification, the church, Scripture, sacraments, the eschaton, redemption, Trinity. It is worth noticing that although Schleiermacher's theology is dominated by human action (consciousness and response), and although this topic normally comes under the topic of pneumatology, the Spirit is not itself a topic for Schleiermacher. This omission is interesting: is it because Schleiermacher is untrinitarian, and oblivious to the necessity of doing justice to the Spirit? Or is it because Schleiermacher is so attuned to the Spirit-filled nature of human action that the whole discussion is pneumatological, and thus the Spirit cannot be merely a topic in it?

Schleiermacher's focus on feeling is a way to avoid being trapped in a theology reduced to metaphysics or morality, and his handling of consciousness reflects romantic debates about how descriptions of knowledge and action are rooted in questions about how the infinite is related to the finite.

Hermeneutics and Language

Schleiermacher's contribution to hermeneutics continues to teach philosophers about key issues in language and meaning. Although Schleiermacher's work in this area was famously rehearsed and recovered in Hans-Georg Gadamer's *Truth and Method* of 1960, recent work by Manfred Frank and (in English) Andrew Bowie makes the relevant texts available in ways that throw the principal issues into sharp and informative relief (Schleiermacher, 1977; Bowie, 1998).

Schleiermacher loved rules. 'Pleasure in truth is pleasure in rules, joy in agreement of individual things with the rule' (Crouter, 1988: xxii). And more than rules, he loved exploring why having a good set of rules is insufficient for performing the task that the rules are for. Rules need to be applied, and applying rules is a skill or art (*Kunst*). A skill is something one learns by practice, not by learning more rules; if this were not so, there would be an endless regression with rules governing rules. The interpretation of texts, not least Scripture, is something governed by rules. It is the task of the philosopher to elaborate these rules in as succinct a way as possible. Schleiermacher's hermeneutics is partly such an elaboration. At the same time, rules are applied by specific persons at specific times in individual ways. They exercise skill and make judgements in ways that are not reducible to rules, but indicate the freedom and spontaneity of the interpreter. Schleiermacher's hermeneutics is partly an exploration of the implications of acknowledging such freedom and spontaneity.

Schleiermacher uses many pairs of words to develop his hermeneutics. Explaining their tasks highlights the central issues. The main pairs are: grammatical and technical interpretation, formal and organic function, intuition and feeling, receptivity and spontaneity, dialectic and hermeneutics, transcendental and transcendent, divinatory and comparative method (Bowie, 1998: vii–xxxi).

Grammatical and technical interpretation refer to the two poles of interpretation: the general and the individual. Grammatical interpretation concentrates on an individual *example* of a general usage. Technical interpretation concentrates on an *individual* example of a general usage. In grammatical interpretation, people are just users of language. In technical interpretation language is just the tool with which people express themselves individually.

The relationship between 'formal' and 'organic' function, a distinction from the *Dialectics* of 1811, addresses the question: how much of 'meaning' is provided by the world, and how much by each person? By 'organic' function, Schleiermacher draws attention to the way the world encounters each person differently: it cannot be specified in advance. By 'formal' function, he means the aspects that are clearly the same for each person. Judgement is what happens when the formal meets the organic. This means that the problematic distinction between 'analytic' and 'synthetic' judgements (Kant) can be repaired by *a single notion of judgement*, which includes a distinction between formal and organic functions (Bowie, 1998: xxi). One can speculate about the implications this has for scriptural interpretation. Instead of distinguishing 'literal' from 'imaginative' (allegorical, spiritual, figurative) interpretations, it makes more sense to have a single notion of interpretation, with both literal and imaginative functions always present. This means even the most literal approach has an imaginative aspect, and even the wildest fancy of the imagination is about *this* text rather than another.

Intuition and feeling, covered in the previous main section, are terms whose job is to describe the relationship between world and mind. The term 'feeling' (along with 'divination') is understood by some readers to indicate that Schleiermacher thinks interpretation is about empathetic identification between reader and author. This is a distortion. 'Feeling' describes a person's *being part of* the world in a way that defies thinking because it is what makes thinking possible. The relationship is 'intuited' rather than thought.

Receptivity and spontaneity refer, as a pair, to the fact that when we make judgements, we use rules. The rules are received. Our use is spontaneous. We do not make up the rules: if we did, others could not make sense of us. Our use of them is not rule-bound: if it were, there would be an endless regression of rules for using rules. Interpretation is the skill of using the rules of interpretation.

Hermeneutics and dialectic refer respectively to the individual and universal aspects of understanding. Hermeneutics is the business of determining what a particular person is trying to say. Dialectic is the business of determining the principles behind the skill of making judgements, or the foundations of the art of entering into dialogue. Hermeneutics is concerned with meaning of statements; dialectics is concerned with whether they are true. Truth is not a metaphysical entity 'out there', but the product of a certain kind of reasoning about whether statements accord with what a particular community takes to be true. Schleiermacher thus puts 'community' and 'universal' on the same level, in matters of making judgements of truth. Judgements of truth are always made according to the criteria of a particular community (Bowie, 1998: xx–ii).

The difference between 'transcendent' and 'transcendental' in Kant (*Critique of Pure Reason*, A296/B352–3) is made problematic by Schleiermacher. For Kant, 'transcendent' refers to the transgression of limits, and thus does not refer to objects of experience at all, whereas 'transcendental' refers to space, time and concepts – that which limits sense data in the conditioning of something thought. Schleiermacher does not make a separation between the 'transcendent basis' of our being and the 'transcendent basis' of our thinking. This is because thinking is part of being: it takes place *after* intuition, which is already the indication that mind is in the world. The conditions for judgement are the same as the conditions for there being a world. Because of the role played by 'feeling' in Schleiermacher's thought, 'transcendent' and 'transcendental' are, in some sense, the same thing (Bowie, 1998: xxiv–v).

The difference between divinatory and comparative methods concerns the relationship between rules and their application. Divination is the ability to understand what someone means without exhaustive rules. We have already seen how there cannot be exhaustive rules: skill is always needed to apply them. What is the character of this skill? 'The *divinatory* method is the one in which one, so to speak, transforms oneself into the other person and tries to under-stand the individual element directly' (Schleiermacher, 1998: 92). Notice the 'so to speak' in this phrase. It is an indication of the struggle Schleiermacher has to *explain* the aspect of interpretation that cannot be reduced to rules. It is con-trasted with 'comparative' method, which treats someone else as 'something universal' and measures whether and how far they depart from other things that are similarly universal. Comparing different performances of the same musical score would be an example of this. Divination draws attention to the fact that individuals can relate to others *as individuals* (rather than treating them as instances of something general). Comparison draws attention to the fact that individuals all share something *in common*. The crucial thing is that divina-tion and comparison belong together: they may not be separated from each other. Without comparison, divination has no way of knowing whether it has made a mistake: it is not subject to any higher criteria of correction. Without divination, comparison cannot know that an individual is, in fact, an example of something universal: it would just have an infinite regression of rules that determine whether something is an example, without ever applying this rule (Schleiermacher, 1998: 93). Taking divination and comparison together means one can make interpretations and test them.

How do all these matters affect actual interpretation of Scripture? This is an important question, not least because there does not seem much relationship between the interpretation of Scripture and *The Christian Faith*. In general, for Schleiermacher, philosophical considerations indicate that interpretation is an infinite task. The role of historical criticism is particularly interesting here. His-torical criticism is not undertaken in order to resolve difficulties or solve prob-lems about what something means: this cannot be done, because 'no language is completely present to us, not even our own mother tongue'. We cannot com-pletely eliminate difficulties about meaning even in everyday sentences. Rather, historical criticism is useful because it provides 'ongoing instructions' for inter-pretation: it keeps the debate about meaning alive (Schleiermacher, 1998: 14–15). Interpretation of Scripture is an infinite task because we do not have a secure starting point: 'Beginning in the middle is unavoidable' and 'we must be satisfied with arbitrary beginnings in all areas of knowledge' (Bowie, 1998: xxxvi, xxvii). Particular conceptions of what a passage of Scripture means are handed down, and can be tested against other interpretations. There are rules for doing this, but no rules for applying these rules: only the skill of the inter-preter. There is thus no theory for deciding whether an interpretation is any good, only particular judgements by other skilful interpreters.

In hermeneutics, Schleiermacher is more interested in the conduct of argu-ment and disagreement in scriptural interpretation than he is in actual inter-pretation of Scripture. Put differently, he is concerned to articulate the ethics of scriptural interpretation. This could mean that Schleiermacher abdicates his responsibilities as an interpreter in favour of endless generalizations about how interpretation might take place, should anyone actually wish to do any. This is not the case. Schleiermacher's context is one in which there is no shortage of scriptural interpretation, and it has been made more complex by the rise of historical criticism. He himself was a pastor, and he delivered sermons each Sunday. Many of them are published, and it is obvious that Schleiermacher did a great deal of scriptural interpretation in contexts of worship. In these one sees Schleiermacher's struggle to correlate his reading of Scripture with the theological task which he sees so clearly (assisting church leadership), a difficulty exemplified by his almost complete ignoring of the Old Testament (Barth, 1982: 16; DeVries, 1996: 55). The task of the hermeneutics is different. His task is to assist the community of interpreters to disagree well and argue fruitfully. Here, as in so many other places, it is clear that Schleiermacher considers the discipline of hermeneutics to be in the service of the leaders of the church.

Barth on Schleiermacher

Karl Barth's critique of Schleiermacher in his *Protestant Theology in the Nineteenth Century* is important (Barth, 1972; cf. Barth, 1982). While it is true that Barth did not possess the same facility in philosophy as Schleiermacher, and although one needs to acknowledge that Barth had neither the detailed knowledge of romantic philosophy, nor access to the texts readers enjoy today, his criticisms are worth hearing. They provide a great deal of help in understanding why Schleiermacher continues to fascinate and trouble theologians today. We will focus on Barth's account of Schleiermacher's handling of Christology and the Trinity.

The main question Barth asks is this: how do *On Religion* and the introduction to *The Christian Faith* relate to the substantial dogmatic discussions in *The Christian Faith*? Put differently, what is the relationship between Schleiermacher's general observations and overviews and the nitty-gritty? Barth's judgement is that the relationship is a problem. To summarize in advance, Barth thinks that Schleiermacher's general observations tend to prejudge dogmatic questions in a decidedly untheological fashion, and when they do not, they produce contradictions. We will now look briefly at how he arrives at this view.

'The Christology is the great disturbing element in Schleiermacher's doctrine of faith', Barth suggests (Barth, 1972: 431). 'Jesus of Nazareth fits desperately badly into this theology ... He obviously gives Schleiermacher ... a great deal of trouble!' (p. 432). Barth suggests that because of the grand sweep of Schleiermacher's theology, and its conception of dogmatics as the elucidation and elaboration of human *consciousness* of God, Jesus has to fit the scheme. Jesus fits badly and Barth notes that this is an indication of the high quality of Schleiermacher's theological instincts, because he does not quite allow the big overview to crush the particularity of Jesus. Barth suggests that although Schleiermacher wanted to proclaim Christ in the Christological sections of *The Christian Faith*, the overarching theme of consciousness makes this difficult. The difference between God and humanity (two different actors) gets subsumed into a single consciousness (of one human actor) (Barth, 1972: 431–2, 457–62). Barth insistently poses the question of difference: both God's trinitarian difference (between Father, Son and Spirit) and the ontological difference (between creator and creature). He even constructs a little test: in a genuinely trinitarian theology, when one describes the divinity of one person (for example, the *Logos*) one finds one's account inextricably describing the divinity of another (say, the Spirit). 'Reformation theology, starting in reverse fashion, from the *Logos*, passes this test: as a theology of the Word it is at once a theology of the Holy Spirit . . .' (Barth, 1972: 460). Schleiermacher's theology does not start with Christ, but starts with human consciousness. In trinitarian terms, it privileges human response to God, which makes it a theology of the Spirit. But whereas starting from the *Logos* ensures the divinity of the Spirit in Luther's theology, for example, it is not clear to Barth that starting from the Spirit in the way Schleiermacher does ensures the divinity of the *Logos*. Barth is emphatic: Schleiermacher does indeed insist on the divinity of the *Logos*, but this divinity *does not follow from Schleiermacher's argument*. Rather, it is asserted, and in a way that sticks out like a sore thumb (Barth, 1972: 461).

Barth's point is this: Schleiermacher manages to work out a modern Christology which is integrated into a broader modern theology but he finds it exceptionally difficult. It is to this difficulty that Barth wishes to draw attention: why so difficult? Schleiermacher, for Barth, does much good work in describing Christ as mediating God and humanity, but the notion of mediation does not itself tell us that Christ is divine. The Reformers did this much better: 'The sole mediation which enters into consideration there is the recognition of the Father in the Son through the Spirit in the strict irreducible opposition of these "persons" in the Godhead'. In other words, mediation is not enough: it is *how this mediation is described* that matters: 'Schleiermacher immunized the concept of revelation' (Barth, 1972: 464). How does this happen? By considering Christology under the broader heading 'The State of the Christian as Conscious of the Divine Grace' (*The Christian Faith*: §§91–105). Barth worries that putting things like this suggests that Christ gets functionalized as a way to determine the state of the Christian, albeit a special and the most important way. It is true that Schleiermacher uses words like 'only' as in the summary at the head of §91: '*We have fellowship with God only in a living fellowship with the Redeemer . . .*' but for Barth the force of this 'only' comes merely from the insistent tone used by Schleiermacher and is not intrinsic to his description of Christ (Barth, 1972: 471).

Good theology, as Barth sees it, needs constantly to remind itself and its readers that it is trying to do justice to something that is *other than itself*. Theology must always be open to correction, repair and revision and, more importantly, must be open to contradiction by God. Schleiermacher's account of dogmatics as a description of Christian consciousness is one-sided: it successfully captures the *thinkability* of human response to God but does insufficient justice to God's *objective revelation*. This is a significant shortcoming, because Christian hope is rooted in a salvation made possible precisely because God is different, and not subject to the world as we are. The more confidently theology 'knows' things, the less it gives cause for hope beyond what we know from our tragic historical experience.

Barth is by no means the last word on the matter. For example, Barth tended to see philosophy and theology as distinct disciplines: Schleiermacher could have taught him the need to develop *Christian philosophical arguments* rather than allow philosophy *per se* to be considered in opposition to dogmatic theology. It is important to correct Barth's criticisms by paying more attention to the romantic philosophy that gave Schleiermacher not only his vocabulary but provided his theology with its basic argumentative tools. Schleiermacher well understood the unthinkability of the infinite: it was a central topic in romantic philosophy. Like his contemporaries, he was concerned to show how the thinkable finite relates to this unthinkable infinite. He was sure that the parts of philosophy that address this question are theologically significant. In this, Schleiermacher stands in a line of theologians that include Augustine, Anselm and Aquinas: the question, of course, is how well his (untrinitarian) account of the Trinity discharged these tasks.

Schleiermacher's approach to hermeneutics is especially relevant to understanding how he conceives of the task of dogmatic theology. His skill in hermeneutics is probably unmatched by any prior or later figure. He understood that because Scripture is written and interpreted, there cannot, *pace* Barth, be any absolute 'over and against' between revelation and history, only a recognition that the infinite is knowable – although by definition not absolutely – through the finite. Instead of saying Schleiermacher fails to acknowledge God's objective difference, it might be better to say that he does not adequately elaborate the theological significance of God's *unthinkable difference from the world*. This retains Barth's insight – that purely human hope is almost no hope – and helps do justice to Schleiermacher's romantic conceptual heritage. Schleiermacher understands Christian dogmatics as *finite thinking in relation to the infinite*, and not as the elaboration of objective revelation over and against the fragility of merely human knowledge. Schleiermacher teaches that dogmatics is merely human knowledge, and that the interpretation of Scripture is a human art.

Perhaps the problem with Schleiermacher for contemporary theology is that grammatical questions sometimes concern him at the expense of substance and that at other times his substantial theology is too experimental. Substantiating this, however, requires detailed engagement with his work.

Conclusion

Schleiermacher was arguably the best philosophical theologian since Aquinas. Comparing Schleiermacher with Aquinas has its pitfalls, but it helps throw some of the main issues into relief. Three things are worth mentioning in this connection.

1   Schleiermacher tried to address the major topics in theological education of his day. Like Aquinas he suggested an order for tackling questions, and did so with a view to improving the quality of theological education, particularly in the area of theological reasoning.

2   Schleiermacher relied very heavily on philosophical reasoning that is not straightforwardly Christian. As Aquinas used Aristotle to help interpret Scripture, so Schleiermacher used German idealist and romantic philosophy. This accounts for his reliance on categories like 'consciousness' and 'subjectivity' and the elaboration of practices of artistic creativity and their relation to rules.

3   Schleiermacher is subject to the same queries and criticisms as Aquinas. What is the relationship between biblical interpretation and philosophical reasoning? To what extent do the particular philosophical resources not just assist but prejudge dogmatic questions? What are the limits to speculation? How far do the powerful structures overdetermine the particular questions under consideration? Asking these questions helps show why some critiques of Schleiermacher are so passionate: at stake is not merely whether his theology is persuasive, but whether it is genuinely theological.

Just as Aquinas is for many the authoritative voice of medieval Christian theology, so Schleiermacher is the authoritative voice of modern Christian theology. Theology in the twenty-first century has learned from both, but is no longer either medieval or modern. Yet the questions it tackles are inherited questions: what is the relationship between Christ and the *Logos*? How is the Trinity an image of the relationship between infinite and finite? What have human and divine action to do with each other? What is the difference between Christian and non-Christian descriptions of the world? Schleiermacher's voice is audible in many, if not all, twentieth-century engagements with these questions, but the answers he gives are perhaps not as decisive as the way he organizes their presentation and discussion.

Schleiermacher shows the fruitfulness of good Christian philosophical arguments. At the same time, he shows the thrill and danger of experimentation in doctrine. Whether or not one wishes to do the kind of theology Schleiermacher did, his work helps us to understand how modern theology has taken the form it has, and why it receives the criticisms one finds in post-modern theology, whether broadly orthodox or radically experimental, or both.

Note

1   In this section I rely heavily on the arguments in Bowie (1998) and Crouter (1988).

References

Barth, Karl (1972). Schleiermacher. In *Protestant Theology in the Nineteenth Century*, trans. B. Cozens & J. Bowden. London: SCM, pp. 425–73.

Barth, Karl (1982). *The Theology of Schleiermacher*, ed. D. Ritschl, trans. G. Bromiley. Edinburgh: T & T Clark.

Bowie, Andrew (1998). Introduction. In F. Schleiermacher, *Hermeneutics and Criticism and Other Writings*. Cambridge, UK: Cambridge University Press, pp. vii–xl.

Crouter, Richard (1988). Introduction. In F. Schleiermacher, *On Religion: Speeches to its Cultured Despisers*. Cambridge, UK: Cambridge University Press, pp. xi–xlv.

DeVries, Dawn (1996). *Jesus Christ in the Preaching of Calvin and Schleiermacher*. Louisville, KY: Westminster John Knox Press.

Schleiermacher, Friedrich (1977). *Hermeneutik und Kritik*, ed. Manfred Frank. Frankfurt am Main: Suhrkamp.

Schleiermacher, Friedrich (1988). *On Religion: Speeches to its Cultured Despisers*, trans. R. Crouter. Cambridge, UK: Cambridge University Press.

Schleiermacher, Friedrich (1989). *The Christian Faith*, ed. H. R. Mackintosh & J. S. Stewart. Edinburgh: T & T Clark.

Schleiermacher, Friedrich (1990). *Brief Outline of Theology as a Field of Study*, trans. T. N. Tice. Lampeter, UK: Edwin Mellen.

Schleiermacher, Friedrich (1998). *Hermeneutics and Criticism and Other Writings*, trans. A. Bowie. Cambridge, UK: Cambridge University Press.

CHAPTER 5

Shapers of Protestantism: Karl Barth

John Webster

The Swiss Reformed theologian Karl Barth (1886–1968) is widely considered to be the most significant Protestant dogmatic thinker since Schleiermacher at the beginning of the nineteenth century. In the period from the early 1920s to the late 1960s, Barth was a central protagonist in many of the major developments in German-speaking Protestant theology and church life. His theological work, which spanned a number of fields but was most notable in the area of Christian doctrine, effected a thorough reordering of the discipline, not only by the challenge which it presented to the theological conventions then dominant, but also by its sheer fecundity and the vividness of its portrayal of the Christian faith and its objects. Barth was an exceptionally prolific author. His chief literary legacy is the unfinished *Church Dogmatics* (when Barth ceased work on the project, he was preparing the 13th volume). This immense work is complemented by a great number of other writings, particularly commentaries on biblical, credal and confessional texts; studies in historical and practical theology; and occasional and polemical writings.

As might be expected in the case of a thinker of such considerable stature, there has been widespread disagreement about the nature and extent of Barth's contribution to Christian theology. The sheer range of Barth's work, and the controversial character of its fundamental claims, have almost inevitably generated divergent and often conflicting interpretations of his thought. Moreover, Barth has often been read very selectively, with the result that a part has often been taken for the whole, and inadequate maps of the territory drawn, often for the purpose of hostile criticism. Thus, for example, Barth's exegetical or ethical writings have rarely featured in accounts of his theology, and as a result he has been subjected to criticism for developing an account of Christianity dominated by abstract dogmatic concerns, or one in which human action has scarcely any role to play. Some such interpretations have acquired near canonical status in studies of Barth, and their authority can only be dislodged by scrupulous study of his writings both in depth and in breadth.

These schematic interpretations have often been tied to a particular account of the development of Barth's work which has come to serve as an interpretative filter. On this account, Barth's work can be divided into two phases. A first phase, stretching from the middle of the First World War to the end of the 1920s, is characterized by an emphatically contrastive account of the relation between God and the world, and by an accentuation of divine sovereignty and transcendence of such power that the mundane realities of history, culture and morality are all but erased. This phase is usually labelled 'dialectical'. In a second phase, stretching from the early 1930s to the end of Barth's career, it is claimed that he is more deeply committed to affirming the fellowship between God and his creation, most of all in the mature trinitarian and Christological materials in the fourth volume of the *Church Dogmatics*.

With slight variations, this account has provided the framework for many widely divergent accounts of Barth and for numerous studies of particular themes in his theology. It suffers, however, from two fatal flaws. One is that it is too simplified to be illuminating as a close reading of Barth's texts. It tends to arrange both exposition and criticism of Barth by proposing a trajectory of his development, placing on it what are considered to be his major writings and then analysing them by isolating certain general themes. A second problem is that this account of Barth's development – never very well-grounded – is now unsupportable in view of the considerable bulk of posthumous material now available in the collected works currently in process of publication. Some of the most crucial parts of this posthumous material consist of lecture texts from the 1920s. Among other things, these manuscripts demonstrate that many of what were often taken to be Barth's concerns only later in his career – above all, his interest in the human world, which the dominant interpretation usually assigned only to his work in the 1950s – can be found already in the 1920s, at the very point where Barth was thought to be excluding such interests. Far from being, therefore, a thinker whose work went through a series of shifts, Barth can be shown to be strongly consistent, most of all in his commitment throughout his career to articulating a vision of Christianity shaped by the biblical gospel and by a reading of the Reformed tradition as both theocentric and humane.

Life

Born in Basel in 1886, Barth was the son of a moderate pastor and biblical theologian whose gentle and pious commitment to Christian orthodoxy was quietly influential upon his son's later development. In Barth's early years the family moved to Bern, and there he began theological studies in 1904. From here he went to Berlin, at that time one of the centres of liberal Protestant scholarship under the magisterial leadership of Adolf von Harnack, whom Barth admired greatly. It was, however, Wilhelm Herrmann in Marburg who was Barth's chief early theological mentor. Herrmann enabled Barth to articulate a thoroughly modern account of Christianity, that is, one which took Kant's metaphysical scepticism and Schleiermacher's theology of Christian consciousness with great seriousness. But Herrmann also acted as a barrier against the collapse of Christianity into cultural immanence, of which Ernst Troeltsch was, for Barth, the paradigmatic instance. After finishing his studies and a brief period on the staff of a liberal theological periodical, Barth took up pastoral work in the small Swiss town of Safenwil.

In his 10 years in parish ministry, Barth experienced a complete *volte-face*, abandoning his moderate liberalism and discovering an account of Christianity oriented to the wholly miraculous and 'other' reality of God, and the sheer gratuity of God's relation to the world of human affairs. The shift was in some measure prepared for by Barth's involvement in the antibourgeois Swiss social democratic movement, and by his distaste at the collusion of mainstream Protestant liberalism with German state militarism. But above all, he discovered that the tradition in which he had been reared offered only scant resources for Christian proclamation. In effect, Barth found his operative theology crumbling. For help, he turned to the Bible, especially to Paul, finding there 'the world of God'. The Bible, that is, witnessed to a transcendent reality of overwhelming potency which set itself before its readers on its own terms, not as a solution to human problems or an adornment to worldly projects, but as pure divine self-presentation. Out of this study came a flood of articles, lectures and addresses, but above all Barth's commentary *The Epistle to the Romans*, first published in 1919 and then completely rewritten three years later – an explosive piece of theological writing whose reverberations were felt throughout European Protestantism.

In 1921, Barth took up the academic work which was to engage him until retirement, first as Professor of Reformed Theology in Göttingen. His four years there were a period of intensely concentrated development. Lacking a doctorate and largely unprepared for university teaching, Barth had to acquaint himself with the classical Christian tradition, especially in its Reformed expressions. At first he taught mainly courses of theological exegesis (notably the Gospel of John and 1 Corinthians) and historical theology. In the latter connection he gave a remarkable series of lectures on Schleiermacher (even at this early stage, his vigorous critique is deeply respectful of the thinker whom he honoured above all moderns), as well as introducing himself and his students to key Reformed texts and thinkers. Toward the end of his period in Göttingen he lectured for the first time on dogmatics; this lecture material (published posthumously as *The Göttingen Dogmatics*) already contains in early form some important theological judgements which would characterize his mature work. Alongside his teaching, Barth was also leader of what was to be (unhelpfully) named 'Dialectical Theology', a critical movement which associated him with figures such as Bultmann and Brunner. The journal *Zwischen den Zeiten* became the chief organ of the movement, and Barth its prophet.

Barth moved to Münster in 1925, staying there for five years. Consolidating the theological positions sketched out in the first half of the decade, Barth continued his exegetical and historical teaching. A finely drawn depiction of the history of Protestant theology in the nineteenth century derives from lectures first given at Münster. But Barth became increasingly preoccupied with dogmatics and ethics, two areas of theology he considered to have a differentiated unity, corresponding to the integration of gospel (doctrine) and law (morals) which he took to be the particular genius of the Reformed confession. In 1927 he published the first volume of his *Christian Dogmatics*; though the project was quickly abandoned, it constituted a necessary stage in the preparation of the *Church Dogmatics*. He also lectured at length on ethics; although the full text was only published after Barth's death, some of the material was adapted for inclusion in the *Church Dogmatics*. Barth's fascination with dogmatics was a major factor in the dispersal of the circle around him: Bultmann and others thought that Barth had become a scholastic. Barth judged them to be trying to reinvigorate the anthropocentrism of Protestant liberalism.

Moving to Bonn in 1930, Barth rewrote his first published attempt at a dogmatic prolegomena, and so started the production of the *Church Dogmatics* which was to occupy him for the rest of his theological career. By the early 1930s, he was established as the commanding Protestant theologian in Germany. Free from anxiety about the viability of the theological task, and possessed of a thorough knowledge of great tracts of the exegetical and doctrinal traditions of Western Christianity, Barth worked at constructive doctrinal theology with increasing confidence and relish. He was a key figure in Protestant resistance to the Nazi regime, both in a flood of occasional writings and in his participation in the formation of the Confessing Church (Barth played a major role in drafting the *Barmen Declaration* in 1934). Dismissed from his post in 1935, he returned to his native Basel, where he remained for the rest of his life. Here the *Church Dogmatics* occupied the central place in Barth's intellectual work. As he wrote, its bulk increased exponentially. He found himself not only having to work out a fresh position on exegetical and historical questions, but also having to think out from the beginning some crucial tracts of Christian teaching (revelation, Trinity, predestination, creation, atonement, and much else). And, furthermore, he discovered that he could only do descriptive justice to his material by writing at considerable length. This proved to be a major factor in the noncompletion of the project, which is broken off in the middle of the fourth volume.

Despite his absorption with the *Church Dogmatics*, Barth did give himself to other tasks. He was an influential figure in postwar ecumenical endeavours; he was a devoted teacher to crowds of students from around the world; he was in great demand as lecturer, teacher and correspondent; he gave voice to his – frequently controversial – views on political and church life, to the dismay of the establishment. After retiring in 1962, Barth travelled to the USA, but shortly after his return suffered a long period of ill health which left him unable to work on major tasks for the rest of his life. Work on the *Church Dogmatics* (apart from a final fragment) had already effectively ceased when his long-time assistant Charlotte von Kirschbaum became permanently ill. He continued to teach a little, and to write minor pieces. Barth died on 10 December 1968.

Barth was a complex and powerful personality. He possessed a strong sense of public vocation, from which he derived a firm sense of his own identity. At various points in his life, his self-assurance and uncompromising adherence to hard-won conviction led to strained or broken relations with others, a situation to which Barth sometimes responded by presenting himself in the role of misunderstood outsider. Alongside this vigorously active and sometimes conflict-laden external life, Barth also maintained the remarkable interior concentration necessary for his intellectual work, and he was able to write (both in his theological work and in his correspondence) with pastoral sensitivity, gentleness and, at times, humane serenity.

Earlier Work

The conventional account of Barth has it that, after his break with Protestant liberalism around 1916, his theology was dominated by a radically polarized understanding of God's relation to humanity, one in which Barth assembled all manner of theological themes (eschatology, revelation, divine aseity, sin and grace) and some more abstract ideas (the absolute, origin, crisis, that which is 'other') into a colossal protest against the religion and theology of immanentism. Not only does this account fail to do justice to the full range of Barth's writing in the 1920s; it also mischaracterizes his fundamental intentions in the period. For all its polemic, Barth's earlier work is no mere volley of protest or negation; it is driven by a positive intent, namely to articulate the fundamental relatedness of God and his human creatures, in a way which does justice both to divine sovereignty and the human realities of history, culture and morality. The protest is not against the relation of God and humanity so much as against theologies which considered that relation to be grounded in, managed by or within the competence of the human subject.

As Barth struggled to give shape to these convictions in his last years as pastor and his first years as professor, he found himself working on three related fronts: biblical exegesis; a critical account of liberal Protestant religious culture, and especially of its theology; and the interpretation of the thinkers and texts of the Reformed tradition.

The Epistle to the Romans is undoubtedly the most significant exegetical work from this period, yet it remains largely misunderstood. It is frequently read either thematically, as a source book for Barth's own 'dialectical' views, or as a hermeneutical manifesto protesting against the hegemony of the historical-critical method. Neither reading takes account of the fact that the book is a *commentary* – not a treatise on Paul or on Barth's own theology, but an attempt to give a sequential exposition of what Paul said in Romans as the medium of what

God now says to the churches. Certainly, Barth does not stop short at describing the historical background and linguistic form of Paul's text, and in the prefaces to the various editions of the commentary he is sharply critical of the cramping effect of the concentration on such matters by his exegetical colleagues. But this does not mean that he is merely composing free variations on themes from Paul. He is attempting a conceptual paraphrase of Romans; the aim is to attend to and rearticulate Paul's thought, not to treat it as raw material for theological construction. Implicit within what Barth is attempting is a theological conviction that the biblical text is not a religious artefact enabling reconstruction of the circumstances of its production or of its author, but the instrument of a divine action of communication in which the reader is summoned and judged.

As Barth recovered a way of reading Scripture which was interested above all in the content of the biblical text and its function as medium of revelation, he found himself increasingly distanced from liberal Protestant theology. One of his major tasks when he turned to theological teaching was thus to develop an interpretation of the history of modern theology. He did this, however, not in order to dismiss or abandon its tasks, but in order to be instructed by it and to learn, by both agreement and interrogation, about the contemporary responsibilities of Christian theology.

Many of those associated with Barth adopted his critical tone and announced the end of the liberal era; Barth's own judgements were more complex, reserved and self-questioning. This can be seen from his lectures on *Protestant Theology in the Nineteenth Century* (Barth, 2001), first given in the late 1920s and then refined and eventually published shortly after the end of the Second World War. But even at the beginning of his teaching career, Barth showed himself to be a nuanced and respectful reader of the tradition, even when most puzzled or even repelled by it. His 1923/4 lectures on *The Theology of Schleiermacher* are a case in point. Barth had deep reservations about Schleiermacher's project; but Schleiermacher remained for him *the* living voice of Christian theology, one whose arguments often set the terms of debate, and one whose vision of a humane, churchly and Christocentric faith Barth shared, even when he sought to reground and reconstruct it. Barth feared that Schleiermacher ran together Christology and anthropology too easily, in such a way that the specificity of Jesus's existence is imperilled, and the Christ reduced to being a mere modification of a general realm of religious feeling. And he feared that for all his greatness Schleiermacher offered the initial impulse to a tradition which, in its late nineteenth-century phase, rendered the Christian gospel immanent within human moral and religious culture. Barth did not dispute Schleiermacher's conviction that the Christian faith is concerned with both God and humanity; his protest was against the distortions introduced by making the first term a function of the second, thereby allowing the human factor to acquire axiomatic status.

By way of response, Barth sought to develop a theology of God's relation to humanity in which the twin foci (God and creatures) were retained but redefined and related in an entirely different way. His primary resource for constructing such a theology was the Reformed tradition, which came to expression in the exegetical, doctrinal and confessional texts of Calvin and his successors. Barth had little deep knowledge of this tradition before he was required to teach it in Göttingen, but delved into it with great zeal, lecturing on Zwingli, Calvin, the *Heidelberg Catechism* and the Reformed Confessions in his first two years as professor. What he found in this tradition was a theology which held together both an emphasis on the free sovereignty of divine grace and the reality of human life as a historical project undertaken in active obedience to the saving will and presence of God. This ordering of grace and ethics, the vertical and the horizontal, the divine and the humane, quickly established itself as one of Barth's deepest intellectual and spiritual instincts, not only shaping his interpretation of the Calvinist tradition, but also providing one of the leading motifs of the later *Church Dogmatics*, namely, the theme of covenant fellowship.

When Barth first ventured to lecture on dogmatics in Göttingen, he sketched in rudimentary form some of the material which he would later develop in his mature dogmatic writings. Such themes as the tight linkage of the doctrine of the Trinity and revelation, the distinctly Reformed account of justification and sanctification – or the rejection of double predestination – already appear in the mid-1920s. Moreover, Barth has a clear conviction that theology takes place within the sphere of the church and its confession; it is not inquiry into the possibility of the Christian religion, but inquiry into the adequacy of the church's act of proclamation when measured against the church's ground and norm, which is the self-communication or Word of God. Far from being concerned with history, universal reason, morals or experience, theology is situated alongside the preacher, sharing the same responsibility before the prophetic and apostolic witness.

Barth's interpretation of the Reformed tradition enabled him to give theological grounding to his interest in the sphere of the ethical. In some early lectures and articles from the period when Barth was extricating himself from his liberal inheritance, he appeared to be a negative moralist, undercutting emphasis on human social action by vivid depiction of the wholly transcendent rule of the divine work. His aim, however, was not to dissolve the ethical but to relativize it, and precisely thereby to establish its basis in the presence and action of God. In the late 1920s, Barth gave a full-scale cycle of lectures on moral theology, published posthumously as *Ethics* (Barth, 1991). One of his major preoccupations there was to explain the correct ordering of grace and human moral activity, and thus to clarify the relation of dogmatics to ethics. He argued that Christian theology is at all points determined by the triune God's self-revelation. That revelation is, however, both indicative and imperative. Accordingly, ethics is inseparable from dogmatics, for a theology of human action emerges from the gospel's proclamation of the acts of God which dogmatics portrays. But, alongside this, dogmatics must be completed by ethics, because revelation is also command. Barth structures his ethics in a trinitarian way, treating in sequence the command of God as creator (Father), reconciler (Son) and redeemer (Spirit), and within this structure handles detailed topics such as marriage, sexuality, politics, education and much more. This trinitarian pattern was retained as the structure for the *Church Dogmatics.*

The *Church Dogmatics*

Reading the *Church Dogmatics* is no easy matter. Quite apart from the sheer scale and argumentative and conceptual complexity of the work, Barth's rhetoric is very demanding – in the literal sense that Barth writes in such a way as to place his readers in the presence of and under the claim of the gospel which he seeks to indicate. The style of the *Dogmatics* is in important respects closer to that of preaching than to that of conventional scholarly discourse, for Barth seeks not only to elicit an intellectual judgement from his readers, but to persuade, console, delight and exhort them. He writes neither as apologist, nor, despite the immense erudition of the work, as technical scholar, but as church theologian, making his case by extensive appeal to and exposition of Scripture and the derivative texts of the classical Christian tradition. He is only incidentally engaged in nontheological conversations; though he discusses philosophical texts at some length, he does not accord them foundational significance, preferring to give himself to the task of instructing the reader in the absorbing and utterly compelling reality of the works and ways of the triune God. The primacy of description helps explain the bulk of the *Dogmatics*, for Barth describes not by condensing his subject matter into concepts, but by cumulative depiction, establishing a conviction by manifold portrayal, recapitulation and rephrasing. The work has to be read at length in order to see how its various parts build into a coherent portrait of the Christian gospel, one which is, moreover, not static, but rather the attempt to indicate the living history of God with us. It also has to be read as a project which developed over the course of the 30 years in which Barth was at work on it, so that it has the unity not of a single statement but of a direction or of an integrated though complex and evolving vision.

The *Church Dogmatics* is divided into four volumes (the doctrines of the Word of God, God, creation and reconciliation; a fifth volume on the doctrine of redemption was never begun), each subdivided into part-volumes. The two parts of *Church Dogmatics* I (1932, 1938) begin and end with discussion of the nature and functions of dogmatics; the discussion is rooted, however, in an extensive account of revelation and the being and activity of the triune God. Barth makes the doctrine of the self-revealing Trinity do the job which for many other theologians is undertaken by theological prolegomena, namely that of establishing the grounds on which the theological task is possible. Instead of starting from, for example, a concept of religion or history, or an ontology or anthropology, Barth sets out from the given reality of revelation as it occurs in the sphere of the church. His first task, therefore, is an account of the 'Word', that is, the revelatory presence of God. God's Word is neither a deposit of truth nor a set of statements, but a divine act, namely, the event in which God has spoken, speaks now, and will speak, and which encounters us through the human instrument of Scripture and its proclamation in the church. Both preaching and Scripture are functions of God's majestic self-utterance in which, with utter dignity, aseity and spontaneity, God presents himself as lord of all reality. As self-revealing Lord, moreover, God establishes the human conditions for the reception of revelation, such that from start to finish – from its objective grounds to its subjective realization – revelation is the work of God. One of the crucial functions of trinitarian language about God is to state how in its entire scope, the work of self-revelation is a wholly sovereign divine undertaking.

Barth's interweaving of revelation and Trinity has often been judged to subsume the doctrine of the Trinity under that of revelation; the resulting idiom (of a single self-manifesting divine subject) is also thought to lead to an underplaying of the personal differentiations between Father, Son and Spirit and to challenge the fittingness of the term 'person' in a trinitarian context. In fact, the opposite is more nearly the case: Barth absorbs revelation back into Trinity, and does not have an independent doctrine of revelation so much as an account of the Father, Son and Spirit and of the differentiated unity in which they act and so communicate their presence. This theme is given two lengthy portrayals in *Church Dogmatics* I. I/1 describes the work of revelation proper to each mode of God's being. As Father, God reveals himself as creator and Lord; as Son, God reveals himself as reconciler, overcoming human enmity; as Spirit, God reveals himself as redeemer, making real our reconciliation to God. *Dogmatics* I/2 delves more deeply into the same matters in an extended treatment of incarnation and Spirit, which constitutes the first truly great piece of writing in the work. The overarching aim of the exposition is to propound that in the work of Christ and Spirit, God is both the objective and the subjective reality of revelation: both the divine gift and its reception proceed from God alone. The volume is then rounded out by a discussion of the nature of Scripture as prophetic and apostolic witness to revelation, and by a concluding presentation of the role of dogmatics in the church which seeks to hear and speak the gospel.

Four related themes are handled in the treatment of the doctrine of God in *Church Dogmatics* II: knowledge of God, the reality of God, divine election and the divine command. Barth's starting point in discussing knowledge of God is not the critical question of whether knowledge of God is possible, but rather the objectivity in which God knows himself. Human knowledge of God is gracious participation in divine self-knowledge through the mediation of the creaturely signs which serve God's self-manifestation. For such knowledge, humanity has no capacity other than that bestowed by God in Christ through the Spirit. From here, Barth moves to the central exposition of the divine reality, concentrating not on questions of the existence of God but on God's character, thereby keeping his attention fixed on the particular identity of the triune God enacted in the drama of creation and reconciliation. God's essence is to be determined out of his works, those acts in which God 'names' himself, declaring his identity as Father, Son and Spirit. In his works, God manifests that his being is directed to the establishment of fellowship with creatures, and so that he is one who loves in freedom: freedom is the depth of the divine love, and love is the actuality or shape of God's freedom.

The twin themes of freedom and love are further explored in a thorough reworking of some traditional conceptions of God's attributes (which Barth calls divine 'perfections'). The reworking continues in even more radical form in the doctrine of election. Barth seeks to detach the theology of election from the notion of an abstract, omnipotent divine will, and to reintegrate it into the particularity of God manifest in Christ. Talk of election is, in effect, an expansion of the name of Jesus, that is, of his sovereign work of reconciling love. Election is thereby linked, first, to God's self-election: as the God who elects, God determines that from all eternity he will be gracious. Second, election is the election of humanity, not simply for a certain fate (as in the older doctrine of divine decrees) but to a form of life and action. Accordingly, the doctrine of God closes with a lengthy treatment of ethics as rooted in the command of God. Election means covenant, and covenant entails a mutuality in which God is encountered by his creatures not as mere cause or force but as Lord by whom all things are made possible and to whom obedience is owed.

The third volume of the *Dogmatics*, on the doctrine of creation, is a point at which Barth diverges very markedly from the more conventional modern treatments of creation and anthropology. He is reluctant to allow this material to furnish a pretheological entrée to Christian language about God, and instead expounds them as doctrines which derive from prior teaching about God's identity. Thus, for example, he resists the metamorphosis of the Christian doctrine of creation into a generic account of origins, arguing that talk of God as creator is as much an assertion of faith as other pieces of Christian teaching. In particular, knowledge of the creator is Christologically derived. The point is summed up in Barth's proposal that creation is to be understood in terms of its purpose (what Barth calls its 'inner ground'), namely covenant, the fellowship between creator and creature. Similarly, in treating anthropology, Barth maintains the ontic and noetic priority of Christology: to be human and to know what it is to be human are grounded in the fact of the man Jesus. There are many ramifications here: a distinctive understanding of soul and body, an understanding of relation as humanly definitive, and a highly complex account of human temporality. A theology of providence is set out in *Church Dogmatics* III/3, where once again Barth is at pains to be Christianly specific. This means that the content of belief in providence is not a world picture or philosophy of history but the active conservation, accompaniment and governance of creaturely reality by God, spiritually perceived. A final part-volume turns to ethical themes, again in line with Barth's overall conception of the ethical character of dogmatics. Under the overarching theme of freedom, it considers life before God, life in fellowship, respect for and protection of life, and the limitations of humanity.

Because the fourth volume, on the doctrine of reconciliation, bulks so large in the whole work, and because it contains some of the most mature and expansive expression of Barth's convictions, it is tempting to read the *Dogmatics* backwards, and see the earlier volumes as mere stages on the way (especially for those who see Barth as steadily moving away from transcendentalism to a mellow humaneness). In fact, the doctrine of reconciliation presupposes the earlier materials, which it does not supplant but bring to full fruition. The intellectual structure of the material is extremely intricate, no section being fully understandable without reference to all the others. Its scope is vast, treating not only salvation, but also the person of Christ, the doctrine of sin, pneumatology, the theology of the church and of the Christian life, and ending with a fragmentary exposition of baptism and the Lord's Prayer as its ethical conclusion.

Barth does not follow the traditional sequence of Christology, soteriology, and Spirit in the church and the believer. Instead, all the topics are assembled in three long passages of argument in the first three part-volumes, each with a matching structure, and together forming a carefully constructed set of repetitions, echoes and variations. Each part-volume begins with a substantial treatment of the person and work of Christ (which Barth stubbornly refuses to separate). In IV/1, the theme is 'Jesus Christ, the Lord as Servant', in which the obedience of the Son of God is portrayed as his bearing of divine judgement, followed by his vindication at the resurrection. Here Barth pulls into one complex pattern the credal notion of Jesus as 'true God', and the classical Protestant notions of the Son's 'state of humiliation' and his priestly office. IV/2 treats the 'exaltation of the Son of Man'. Here the paradox of Jesus's lowly deity as the servant Lord is reversed, and his humanity is manifest in the triumphant 'homecoming of the Son of Man'; the tradition's confession of Jesus as 'true man' is thus linked to his 'state of exaltation' and to his kingly office. IV/3 rounds out the portrait by looking at the unity of the two natures of Christ and at Jesus as 'the true witness', the light of life in his office as prophet.

Having expounded this integrated account of the being and act of Jesus Christ as the divine-human agent of reconciliation, each part-volume then considers the effectiveness of the work of reconciliation in overcoming human sin. As the obedient Son of God, Jesus Christ exposes sin as pride, which is the antithesis to his humble self-offering; as the victorious Son of Man, Jesus Christ exposes sin as the sloth which refuses the calling of God; as the true witness, Jesus Christ exposes sin as falsehood. Thereafter, Barth expounds the ways in which the work of reconciliation effects the renewal of human life: as justification, sanctification and vocation; as the gathering, upbuilding and sending of the community in the Spirit's power; and as the individual believer's acts of faith, love and hope.

Conclusion

Barth's work continues to generate a considerable literature of commentary and criticism. Because he looms so large in twentieth-century theology, most major Protestant theological thinkers and movements have positioned themselves with regard to his work, and there is, in addition, a large body of Roman Catholic commentary, much of it appreciative. Current work on Barth demonstrates a number of concerns. Many have attempted to interpret Barth in terms of his context – whether by setting him in the wider history of modernity (of which he is considered by some to be the sternest of critics and by others a late example), or by envisaging him (especially in his earlier work) as a postmodern thinker *avant la lettre*, or, more successfully, by detailed historico-genetic study of the sources and evolution of Barth's thinking. Others continue to assess Barth's dogmatic achievements; in recent scholarship, his doctrine of the Trinity and his pneumatology have been heavily criticized as a late flowering of the putative Western monistic tradition, though these criticisms are difficult to sustain from the full range of his thinking. Similarly, his doctrine of the church has been debated, and by some judged to be too occasionalist, lacking in a sense of the church as a human project by which the presence and activity of God is brought to bear upon the world. It remains the case, however, that the best critical interpretations of Barth have been those which engage in scrupulous study of his texts and are alert to his character as a modern biblical and church dogmatician and moralist in the tradition of open Reformed Christianity.

Bibliographical Information

There is a full bibliography of primary and secondary materials in Wildi (1989–94). Barth's collected works (*Gesamtausgabe*) are currently under publication in Switzerland (Zurich: Theologischer Verlag Zurich). Besides the *Church Dogmatics* (1956–75), attention should also be paid to the other major lecture cycles (most published posthumously): see Barth (1982, 1990-, 1991, 1992, 2001). There are also many collections of essays: see Barth (1928, 1954, 1961, 1962, 1971). Among the biblical studies, see Barth (1933a, 1933b, 1986, 2002). Commentaries on credal and confessional texts include Barth (1938, 1956, 1960a, 1960b, 1964). There is also an important commentary on Anselm (Barth, 1960c).

The secondary literature on Barth is vast and multilingual. A good account of his life and work is offered in Busch (1976). Introductions include Hunsinger (1991) and Webster (2000a, 2000b), where more detailed bibliographies can be found.

References

Primary literature
Barth, K. (1928). *The Word of God and the Word of Man*. London: Hodder and Stoughton.
Barth, K. (1933a). *The Epistle to the Romans*. London: Oxford University Press.
Barth, K. (1933b). *The Resurrection of the Dead*. London: Hodder and Stoughton.
Barth, K. (1938). *The Knowledge of God and the Service of God*. London: Hodder and Stoughton.

Barth, K. (1954). *Against the Stream*. London: SCM.

Barth, K. (1956). *Credo*. London: Hodder and Stoughton.

Barth, K. (1956–75). *Church Dogmatics*. Edinburgh: T & T Clark.

Barth, K. (1960a). *The Faith of the Church*. London: Collins.

Barth, K. (1960b). *Dogmatics in Outline*. London: SCM.

Barth, K. (1960c). *Anselm. Fides Quaerens Intellectum*. London: SCM.

Barth, K. (1961). *The Humanity of God*. London: Collins.

Barth, K. (1962). *Theology and Church*. London: SCM.

Barth, K. (1964). *Learning Jesus Christ through the Heidelberg Catechism*. Richmond, VA: John Knox Press.

Barth, K. (1971). *Fragments Grave and Gay*. London: Collins.

Barth, K. (1982). *The Theology of Schleiermacher*. Edinburgh: T & T Clark.

Barth, K. (1986). *Witness to the Word*. Grand Rapids, MI: Eerdmans.

Barth, K. (1990–). *The Göttingen Dogmatics*. Edinburgh: T & T Clark.

Barth, K. (1991). *Ethics*. Edinburgh: T & T Clark.

Barth, K. (1992). *The Theology of Calvin*. Edinburgh: T & T Clark.

Barth, K. (2001). *Protestant Theology in the Nineteenth Century*. London: SCM.

Barth, K. (2002). *The Epistle to the Philippians*. Louisville, KY: Westminster John Knox Press.

Secondary literature

Busch, E. (1976). *Karl Barth*. London: SCM.

Hunsinger, G. (1991). *How to Read Karl Barth*. Oxford: Oxford University Press.

Webster, J. (2000a). *Karl Barth*. London: Continuum.

Webster, J. (ed.) (2000b). *The Cambridge Companion to Karl Barth*. Cambridge, UK: Cambridge University Press.

Wildi, M. (1989–94). *Bibliographie Karl Barth*, 3 vols. Zurich: Theologischer Verlag Zurich.

CHAPTER 6

English Protestantism to the Present Day

Gerald Bray

Origins

Although Protestantism as we know it originated in Germany and Switzerland, there is a sense in which its true origin lies in fourteenth-century England, where the Oxford don, John Wycliffe (1330–84) first taught many of the doctrines which would later characterize the German Reformation. Among other things, Wycliffe denied the real presence of Christ in the Eucharist, and said that the true church consisted only of the elect, and was therefore invisible. He also believed that it was necessary to translate the Bible into the spoken language and preach its message to the common people. Wycliffe's followers, known as 'Lollards', from an old word meaning 'to mumble', took up his precepts and made two separate translations of the Bible into English. They organized cells all over England, and in the early fifteenth century they attracted some prominent supporters. But persecution, which included the introduction of burning as punishment for heresy, drove the Lollards underground, and they were soon reduced to impotence. By the time the reformation reached England they were a scattered remnant, which quickly merged into the newly arrived Protestantism.

Wycliffe's ideas, however, circulated all over Europe, and were particularly influential on the Bohemian reformer, Jan Hus. Through him they reached Martin Luther and influenced his thought long after they had been forgotten in English university circles, where reforming ideas first reappeared through the influence of Renaissance humanism. Erasmus (1466–1536), its leading exponent, spent some time in Cambridge and attracted a small but important following there, as well as in London and Oxford. Men of the calibre of John Colet, dean of St Paul's cathedral, advocated serious reform along Erasmian lines, and when German Protestant literature began to appear in the 1520s, it was avidly read in English academic circles. William Tyndale (c.1494–1536) was moved to propose a translation of the Bible into English, but as that was illegal he was forced to flee the country. He went to Wittenberg, where he became one of Luther's most devoted disciples. In 1526 he published an English New Testament, complete with a series of prefaces to the different books, although these were little more than translations of the ones which Luther had produced for his German Bible.

Tyndale's work was banned in England, and probably would have had no influence there had it not been for King Henry VIII's looming marital difficulties. The king needed a credible male heir if his dynasty was to be secure, but his wife, Catherine of Aragon, had produced only a daughter and was rapidly growing too old to have further children. Henry decided to apply for an annulment of the marriage, on the rather specious grounds that Catherine had previously married his older brother Arthur (who had died shortly afterwards) and that his own marriage therefore fell foul of Leviticus 20:21, which says that if a man marries his sister-in-law the union will be childless. Weak though his case was, Henry was determined to pursue it and did all he could to secure the required papal annulment. Unfortunately for him, Catherine was the aunt of Charles V, King of Spain and Holy Roman Emperor, to whom she appealed for help. Charles was then in the process of conquering Rome and making the Pope his prisoner, so there was no possibility that Henry's request would be granted, in spite of indications that the Pope was willing to do so. Henry's patience ran out in 1529, when he decided to summon a parliament in which he stirred up anti-clericalism among the laity. He dismissed his chief adviser, Cardinal Thomas Wolsey, and advanced Thomas Cromwell, a layman who was sympathetic to the desire for ecclesiastical reform. Through Cromwell, he came in contact with Thomas Cranmer, a Cambridge don who had written a tract supporting the king's desire for an annulment, and when the archbishopric of Canterbury fell vacant in 1532, Cranmer was appointed to it.

After a long campaign, designed to wear down the clergy's resistance and persuade as many people as possible that the church was hopelessly corrupt, Henry finally engineered the break with Rome in 1534, when he had both the church and the parliament declare that he was 'supreme head in earth' of the Church of England. This declaration was immediately followed by the suppression of the canon law faculties in the universities and soon afterwards by the dissolution of the lesser monasteries. There were some who objected to the king's policies, especially in the north of England where rebellion broke out, but Henry was strong enough to crush the opposition and to carry the country with him. The dissolution of the greater monasteries went ahead in 1538–40, and Henry bought the support of the rising middle class by selling off large amounts of monastic land to them. This created a landed gentry with a vested interest in protecting the new order of things, a development which would prove to be invaluable later on, when a catholic reaction set in and threatened the progress of reformed ideas in the church.

Theologically speaking, Henry's break with Rome can scarcely be called a Protestant Reformation. There was no change at all to the liturgy and theology of the church. Mass continued to be said in Latin, and priests were not permitted to marry. An English translation of the Bible was authorized in 1538, but even that was not printed after 1541, by which time it had become illegal to deny such things as transubstantiation and priestly celibacy. From 1536 to about 1538 there was an attempt to forge an alliance between England and the Protestants of Germany, but this foundered on the mutual dislike of Henry and Luther as well as on the fact that the king did not accept the theological innovations which Protestantism entailed. When Henry died in 1547 very little had changed in the Church of England, and a number of Protestant sympathizers, including Thomas Cromwell, had lost their lives at the hands of an essentially Catholic king.

The English Reformation

The English reformation began in earnest only after Henry VIII died. His nine-year old son, Edward VI, who had been given Protestant tutors, succeeded him. The regency council included Thomas Cranmer, who was thus free to make some far-reaching reforms. He quickly produced an English-language liturgy which was designed to emphasize the Protestant doctrine of justification by faith alone. The Book of Common Prayer, as this liturgy was called, was introduced at Pentecost 1549, but it was sufficiently conservative that the anti-Protestant bishops were able to claim that it was acceptably Catholic in content. This was not what Cranmer and his close associates, who by then included a number of European divines whom he had invited to England, wanted to hear, and he was soon engaged on a revision of the prayer book. Before that appeared however, he got parliament to legislate for clerical marriage and produced new ordination services (the Ordinal), which emphasized the Protestant value of a learned ministry. He also published a series of sermons (the Homilies) which taught the basic doctrines of Protestantism, and which the clergy were ordered to read from their pulpits every Sunday. The revised prayer book came out in 1552 and was a clearly Protestant work. The traditionalist bishops could not accept it, but by then many of them had been deprived of their sees and sent into enforced retirement. A few months after the second prayer book came out, Cranmer produced 42 'articles' of faith, in which he outlined his own form of Protestant teaching. This owed much to Martin Luther, but even more to Martin Bucer and the emerging 'Reformed' theology which later came to be called 'Calvinism' after its leading exponent.

Cranmer also wanted to reform the church's administration and discipline, but he was prevented from doing so both by powerful opposition among the aristocracy, which may have feared an ecclesiastical dictatorship, and by the premature death of the King, which brought his half-sister Mary, daughter of the rejected Catherine of Aragon, to the throne in July 1553. Mary soon had Cranmer arrested on the ground that he had supported the claims of the

Protestant Lady Jane Grey to the crown, and many prominent reformers left the country. Parliament agreed to return to the Roman obedience, but only after it had extracted a promise from the queen that there would be no attempt made to recover the old monastic lands for the church. The dispossessed bishops were reinstated, and their Protestant substitutes were arrested along with Cranmer. There followed a show debate at Oxford, in which Cranmer was obliged to defend his Protestant views against the now dominant Catholic opposition, and that paved the way to his eventual trial for heresy. He was eventually burnt at the stake in 1556, by which time the flames had already claimed a number of other victims, including Nicholas Ridley and Hugh Latimer, both prominent reformers. Not content with punishing a few leaders, Mary did her best to extirpate Protestantism wherever she could find it, and over 200 ordinary people met their deaths for their beliefs. This struck public opinion as unwarranted savagery, and did much to discredit Catholicism in the eyes of the English people. Mary's marriage to Philip II of Spain did not help either, because it embroiled the country in an unwanted war with France, which caused England to lose Calais, its last remaining possession in that country. Mary also tried to restore the monasteries, and the fear grew that she would compel the gentry to surrender their recently acquired lands. Most seriously of all, her marriage to Philip was childless, and it soon became clear that the Catholic revival had no future. When Mary died in 1558, she was succeeded by her Protestant half-sister Elizabeth, and the reformation was re-established on what would turn out to be a permanent basis.

The Elizabethan Settlement and Puritanism

Elizabeth's strategy was to restore Protestantism as it had been at the death of Edward VI, but to do so in a way which reconciled as many traditionalists as possible to the new order. She issued a new prayer book, based on Cranmer's 1552 version but with somewhat more ritual than he had prescribed. Most of the bishops refused to support her, so she forced them out and appointed men who were prepared to do her bidding, but the population as a whole was ready to back her. By 1563 there was a second book of Homilies and a revised set of articles, their number reduced to 39. There was also a catechism for use in schools and a detailed set of instructions (known as 'injunctions') which determined how the new settlement was to be implemented at parish level. As Elizabeth was not immediately excommunicated by the Pope, many English traditionalists continued to worship in the church, which is exactly what the queen wanted. When her excommunication finally came (in 1570) it was accompanied by a papal order that all loyal Catholics should do their best to assassinate the 'heretical' queen. This outrageous demand turned many traditionalists against the papacy, and forced the government to persecute those who continued to waver in their allegiance. Though it was never wiped out completely, Catholicism came to be regarded as a foreign element in English life, and Protestantism began to make the steady progress which was to assure its place as the national faith of the English.

Yet as this happened, the character of English Protestantism became much more complex than it had been at the start of Elizabeth's reign. Under Mary, significant numbers of Englishmen had taken refuge abroad, and it was there that they came into real contact with European Protestantism for the first time. In Frankfurt, the English exile community split between those who were loyal to the 1552 prayer book and those who wanted more radical reforms, along continental lines. The conservatives won the argument, but the radicals went to Geneva where they were welcomed and encouraged to plan for a future reformation in England. They abandoned set forms of worship and began a fresh translation of the Bible, which was based on the latest critical texts. The Geneva Bible was known mainly for its marginal notes, which provided a radical Protestant interpretation of Scripture. For example, the name 'Antichrist' was applied without hesitation to the pope, and Catholics were identified with Old Testament idolaters. It was also famous for being printed in cheap pocket editions, which made it possible for ordinary people to own a copy of the Scriptures. It was this factor, more than any other, which made the Geneva Bible the translation of choice in late sixteenth-century England, and which opened the door to a more uncompromising form of Protestantism.

When Elizabeth came to the throne, these exiles hastened back to England, and for a while they were her most reliable supporters. She put several of them in high positions, and their outlook influenced the revision of the articles of religion mentioned above. But whereas Elizabeth saw her settlement as final, these radicalized Protestants regarded it as merely transitional. Soon they were agitating for further reforms which would 'purify' the church of its remaining Romish corruptions. These people called themselves the 'godly', but their enemies nicknamed them 'puritans', and the latter term has prevailed in common parlance. The Puritans had significant support in the House of Commons, a fact which led to increasing conflict between the lower house of parliament and the crown. They concentrated on trying to raise the educational level and preaching standard of the clergy, and this gained them considerable support. Even the queen may have agreed with them in principle, but her methods were those of gradualism, not of revolution. That this was essentially a difference of opinion among allies can be seen from the fact that when it became clear that England was threatened by a Catholic invasion, the Puritans abandoned their opposition to the government, and agreed to accept the existing establishment as by far the lesser of two evils. But after the Spanish Armada, on which Catholic hopes were pinned, was defeated (1588), the old Puritan demands re-emerged in an even more radical form.

In 1589–90 a series of tracts was published under the pseudonym of Martin Marprelate, which attacked the church hierarchy with unprecedented ferocity. A handful of radicals were rounded up and executed, but the identity of Martin Marprelate was never revealed. Moderate Puritans tried to persuade the hotheads to be patient and wait for the queen's death, when it was widely expected that the reforms they desired would be introduced by her successor, who was James VI, the Calvinist king of Scotland. The majority followed this advice, but some came to believe that the Church of England was unreformable and they left it altogether. These extremists came to be called 'separatists', and many of them went to Holland, where they were granted almost complete freedom of worship. It was in Holland that some of the separatists met groups of Mennonites, who persuaded them that infant baptism was unjustifiable on biblical grounds. Thus originated the English Baptists, some of whom felt obliged to return home to preach their new understanding of the gospel.

Civil War Over Religion

By then, the queen was long dead and James had ascended the English throne as James I (1603–25). The Puritan leaders immediately petitioned him to reform the Church of England along Scottish (Presbyterian) lines, but James would not agree to that. Instead, he sponsored a Puritan project to produce a new translation of the Bible, based on the latest critical texts. The one condition which he imposed was that the new translation should have no marginal notes accompanying it. A series of committees were set up to do the work, which was finally completed in 1611. It was immediately authorized for use in church, and within a generation it had completely displaced all earlier translations, to become the classic Bible of the English-speaking world. It was a translation acceptable to all shades of church opinion, a fact which was vitally important in a church which defined its faith as grounded on Scripture alone. So significant was this achievement that, although the King James Bible is no longer widely used in Protestant churches, the tradition of non-denominational Bible study and translation has continued in England to the present day. Whatever their other differences, English Protestants have always been one in their study of the Scriptures, and this has given them a unity and cohesion which has served to counteract the sometimes sharp denominational divisions in the church.

James I did his best to maintain the Elizabethan settlement in the face of Puritan pressure to change it, but because the moderate Puritans respected him for his Calvinist theology, they were usually willing to tolerate his compromising policies in other areas. This changed under his son and successor, Charles I (1625–49). Charles wanted to enforce the letter of the Elizabethan settlement of 1559, and he had little sympathy with Calvinism. In 1629 he shut down the Protestant-leaning parliament and four years later he was able to appoint the like-minded William Laud as Archbishop of Canterbury. Before long, even the more moderate Puritans were being openly persecuted, and many fled to New England. Those who remained behind could do little as long as the king was firmly in control, but in 1637 a revolt against Laudian policies in Scotland forced

Charles to raise an English army to crush it. The campaign went badly, and in 1640 the king was obliged to recall parliament.

The pent-up frustrations of a decade were suddenly unleashed, and the Puritans were soon demanding religious freedom. In 1641 Archbishop Laud was arrested, and a few months later, civil war broke out between the king on the one side and the Puritan House of Commons on the other. By 1643 it was clear that the Puritans were winning, but the king would not surrender. Even after he was captured, Charles played for time by making false promises to his captors. In the end, he was put on trial and executed, and the monarchy was abolished (1649).

By then, Archbishop Laud had been put to death (1645) and the Episcopal Church of England had been dismantled (1646). More significantly in the long term, an assembly of theologians at Westminster had drawn up a new confession of faith, two catechisms and a Presbyterian form of church order which parliament adopted in 1647. These documents were intended to be the basis for the union of the churches of England, Scotland and Ireland. Although they were rescinded when the monarchy was restored in 1660, they were afterwards adopted once more in Scotland (1690) and also became the fundamental confession of faith on which classical English Presbyterianism was built.

The Collapse of Puritanism and the Division of English Protestantism

In 1649 English Puritanism was firmly in control of parliament and the country, but it was rent by internal divisions. After 1640 religious censorship was no longer effective, with the result that a plethora of new sects emerged. Most of these proved to be ephemeral, but a few, like the Quakers, have survived to the present day. The main division was between the Presbyterians, supported by the Scots, and the so-called 'Independents', who wanted a congregational form of church government. To make things even more complex, some of these Independents rejected the practice of infant baptism, thereby becoming the nucleus of the future Baptist church. But even these early Baptists were divided into Calvinists, who agreed with the Presbyterians on most doctrinal matters, and the so-called 'Arminians', named after the Dutch theologian Arminius (1560–1609), who rejected the doctrines of unconditional election and predestination. Before long, the Puritan movement was divided along many criss-crossing lines, and all too often the Puritans fought each other rather than their common enemies.

Parliament was largely Presbyterian in complexion, but the army generally supported the Independents, and Oliver Cromwell, its commander-in-chief, tried to implement a broad-based toleration based on a Congregationalist principle. Unfortunately, it was an idea ahead of its time and almost nobody was satisfied with it. As time went on, Cromwell became increasingly dictatorial, thereby alienating many of his own followers. After his death, there was no one able to succeed him, and in 1660 King Charles II (1660–85) was restored with the backing of the Presbyterian faction in the army, which had gradually ousted the Independents.

Charles II promised toleration, but his more fanatical supporters were determined to avenge their defeat and humiliation during the civil war. They would not countenance anything less than a near-complete restoration of the old Episcopalian Church of England, with only token concessions to Puritanism. This was unacceptable to most of the Puritans, and when the new order was imposed in 1662, about 2,000 ministers left the church. Laws were quickly past to restrict their activities, and legal penalties against dissenters, as their supporters were called, were also introduced. Persecution soon followed, but it was of limited effectiveness. The king tried to find a compromise, but the fear that any move towards toleration would also benefit Roman Catholics ensured that all such attempts would fail. Charles was succeeded by his brother James II (1685–8) who had converted to Catholicism in 1672 and who was naturally inclined to favour his co-religionists whenever possible.

The ensuing crisis drew both conforming and dissenting Protestants together and James was forced to flee the country, leaving the crown to his Protestant daughter Mary II (1689–94) and her Dutch husband, William III (1689–1702). The constitutional settlement that emerged from these events guaranteed the position of the Church of England, and future sovereigns would be obliged to enter into communion with it. At the same time, the church's monopoly was compromised by an act of toleration, which granted certain limited rights to dissenters. Furthermore, in 1695 religious censorship was effectively abolished, which gave dissenters freedom to propagate their beliefs.

The Protestant State

From 1689 to 1832 England was an officially Protestant state to a degree that it had not been before and has not been since. Roman Catholicism declined into insignificance and the Church of England's Protestant character was loudly proclaimed on every possible occasion. It controlled both the law and education to such an extent that in 1753 it was given a monopoly over marriages (except those of Jews and Quakers, for whom there were special provisions). Dissent also declined, not least because it was possible to hold all the essential tenets of Calvinism and remain within the established church. But dissent also suffered from scepticism, which was spread under the guise of 'enlightenment'. By 1720 almost all the surviving Presbyterians and a large number of independents had become Unitarians, and those who resisted the trend were marginalized and ineffective.

This situation might have continued indefinitely had it not been for the 'evangelical revival', a movement of spiritual renewal that got underway about 1740.

Its most prominent figure was John Wesley (1703–91), who was converted in 1738 and soon became an indefatigable outdoor preacher. The revival had its own internal divisions, caused mainly by the fact that Wesley rejected the Calvinist doctrines of election and predestination, but its impact was unstoppable. By the end of the eighteenth century, Wesley's followers had become clearly defined as 'Methodists', so called because they practiced a methodical spiritual discipline, and they were virtually separate from the Church of England. The Calvinistic revivalists, on the other hand, remained within the established church, where they formed an 'evangelical' tradition which continues to the present day. The revival's most noticeable innovation was the introduction of popular hymn singing. So successful was this that today most English people regard the singing of hymns as the main ingredient of public worship, something that would have astonished the first reformers.

The revival also served to reanimate the older dissenting traditions, making them more like one another in the process. Preaching for conversion and congregational hymn singing became the order of the day, and by 1800 a palpable renewal of English Protestantism was discernible right across the denominational spectrum. One result of this was a new emphasis on social and political reform, including the abolition of slavery. Another was the explosion of a worldwide missionary movement, of which the interdenominational British and Foreign Bible Society (founded 1804) was the most prominent manifestation.

Ironically, the chief casualty of the revival was the country's Protestant constitution. The Church of England was widely criticized for its apparent lethargy, and its willingness to support the *status quo* in the state. Because of this, it was regarded as one of the chief obstacles to reform, and disestablishing it became one of the great revivalist causes of the nineteenth century. This process began with the emancipation of Protestant dissenters (1828) and Roman Catholics (1829) and continued with a series of revolutionary measures which greatly weakened the Church of England's hold on the country's life. Civil registration of births and marriages was introduced in 1837, tithes were generally abolished in 1836, the church courts which handled matrimonial and inheritance disputes were deprived of those jurisdictions (1858) and finally the ancient universities were opened to all without discrimination (1871).

Religious Pluralism and Secularization

By then the Church of England had to all intents and purposes become a voluntary society not unlike the nonconformist denominations, though it was not disestablished. It remained larger than all the other churches put together, and underwent its own renewal process that strengthened its ability to defend itself against secularist attacks. New dioceses were created, ancient sinecures and anomalies in its administration were ironed out, and a limited form of self-government was introduced. The evangelical wing of the church remained strong, but the main impetus for internal reform passed to a new group, the so-called 'Anglo-Catholics' who emerged after 1833. The Anglo-Catholics began by issuing a series of 90 tracts in which they advocated a church which would be spiritually independent of the state and which would recover its pre-Reformation heritage. The more extreme advocates of this school of thought began to blame the Reformation for being the root cause of the heresies and secularization which they saw all around them, and after 1845 there was a steady stream of conversions to the Church of Rome from among this group.

Anglo-Catholicism was stoutly resisted by the Protestant mainstream, but the real danger to English Protestantism came from elsewhere. It was not Roman conservatism but secular liberalism which made the greatest inroads on all the Protestant churches, and led to a steep decline in their intellectual vigour and influence. At first there was a fairly united front against such things as Charles Darwin's *On the Origin of Species* (1859), but by 1900 most prominent church leaders and departments of theology in the universities had accepted the new liberalism. Orthodox Protestants joined forces with like-minded people in North America to produce a series of tracts called *The Fundamentals* (1912), but the only result of this was the appearance of a new (and pejorative) term to describe traditional orthodoxy – 'fundamentalism'. Despite the high quality of much conservative scholarship, 'fundamentalism' was soon regarded as obscurantist and excluded from church government in almost all the denominations.

By 1914 the churches were losing ground, though this had not yet translated into a corresponding loss of social and political influence. Social reform and missionary endeavour remained characteristic of all the churches, and almost no one questioned the public role of Protestantism as England's official ideology. The First World War (1914–18) transformed this situation, but its long-term effects were not immediately felt. The churches were enthusiastic recruiters for the war effort, and dead soldiers were frequently compared with Christ himself, because they sacrificed their lives for their fellow citizens. But as the futility of war and the failure to establish a lasting peace became obvious, the church's earlier enthusiasm turned many people against it. Some church leaders joined the rising labour movement and advocated a form of Christian socialism, but most did not and Protestantism came to be associated with social conservatism to a degree that was altogether new in its history.

Church attendance continued to decline, but ironically the churches' influence on social policy seems to have increased in the mid-twentieth century. A clear example of this can be seen in the 1944 Education Act, which made religious instruction (by which was meant an undenominational basically Protestant Christianity) compulsory in all state schools. Religious broadcasting was also a prominent feature of this period, and it too, was mainly Protestant in character.

Secularization in the modern sense did not begin to affect English society until after 1960, by which time churchgoing had become the preserve of a small minority. The Christian morality which had traditionally shaped the law of the land was challenged and then abandoned, as divorce and abortion became easily obtainable. Religious education was transformed into ethics or the study of world religions, and some prominent church leaders denied the basic tenets of Christianity without being disciplined for it. By 2000 all the main Protestant churches had become so pluralistic in both doctrinal and ethical matters that it was difficult to see any relationship between them and the Protestant beliefs which had originally brought them into being.

Having said that, it is also true that all the Protestant churches were affected by a conservative evangelical revival, which after 1970 was increasingly tinged with a 'charismatic' spirituality, which emphasized the importance of exercising spiritual gifts like speaking in tongues, prophecy and faith healing. Traditional forms of worship were widely abandoned in favour of largely unstructured services with a high level of congregational participation. The Authorized Version of the Bible celebrated its 350th birthday in 1961 as the still-dominant translation throughout the English-speaking world, but by 2000 it had been replaced almost everywhere by a vast range of new translations, none of which had a clear edge over the others. The loss of a common Bible had severe effects on Protestants, who no longer had a familiar reference point which they shared, but it must be emphasized that this change was in no sense denominational, nor was it confined to England.

In fact, probably the most significant development in English Protestantism since 1945 has been its increasing exposure to worldwide Christianity. As the traditional missionary movement contracted dramatically, so the churches founded by missionaries in different parts of the world began to appear in Britain. Immigrants brought them from the West Indies and Africa, and mass communications ensured that when a church in Toronto 'sneezed' with a new form of charismatic blessing in the early 1990s, many English congregations immediately caught cold! Similarly, the ordination of women and the granting of full recognition to practising homosexuals in North America and Australasia has had a powerful knock-on effect in England, although there is still a native traditionalism which does what it can to resist such trends. English Protestants have embraced some aspects of Americanization wholeheartedly but they have also resisted others, most notably the American fascination with apocalyptic millenarianism, which remains a fringe interest in England. In a sense, it would not be too much to say that a distinctively 'English' Protestantism no longer exists. It has become part of a global phenomenon in which the English-speaking world as a whole may be dominant, but in which England itself plays only a supporting role, contributing significantly in some areas (especially church music), but in many others absorbing and reflecting what are in reality worldwide trends.

The Current Scene

In the light of the above, it can be said that Protestantism remains the dominant religious influence in England, but that it no longer enjoys the monopoly that it had before 1960. Roman Catholicism is numerically almost as strong as the Church of England, but it has undergone its own internal reforms which have produced a situation similar to that found in the main Protestant churches and is therefore no longer the threat to Protestantism that it once was. Non-Christian religions have become prominent through immigration, but it is still too early to tell how long that will last. As immigrant children integrate into English society, they may lose contact with their ancestral cultures and religions, which would nullify their apparent gains. On the other hand, they may succeed in domesticating Islam or Hinduism, so that an authentically English form of these religions will emerge. The vast majority of English people have no formal attachment to any religious body, but to the extent that they participate in religious activities at all, it is usually to some form of Protestantism that they turn. Committed Protestants deplore the lingering popular attachment to such politically incorrect hymns as William Blake's *Jerusalem* or *Onward Christian Soldiers*, but the fact that such an attachment still exists bears witness to the residual Protestantism of English popular culture. Similarly, religious broadcasting remains basically Protestant, and it is not unusual for Church of England clergy to appear in radio or television soap operas as part of the local landscape.

Theology continues to be taught at several state universities, and the emphasis on biblical studies points to its fundamentally Protestant character. There is a growing academic interest in the English Reformation that has both challenged and reaffirmed the Protestant character of the English nation and people. Perhaps more significantly, the state's growing inability to provide adequate social services and education has led to a revival of church-related activity in these spheres, not least in inner-city areas where the churches are often the only social agencies rooted in the locality. It is still uncommon for prominent public figures to profess any form of Christianity, and media hostility to the church remains strong, but reporters frequently express surprise at the strength of grassroots faith, which is after all what really counts, and the BBC's hymn-singing *Songs of Praise* retains its enormous popularity.

Protestant denominationalism is much weaker than it has ever been, and a practical pan-Protestant ecumenism is now all but universal in England, especially among lay people. Presbyterians and Congregationalists joined together to form the United Reformed Church in 1972, although a similar scheme to unite Anglicans and Methodists was a failure. Even so, forms of worship have converged to a significant extent, and parachurch organizations like Tear Fund (relief work) and Spring Harvest (events, conferences, etc) play a prominent role in shaping Protestant attitudes. The main internal divisions in all the churches are between liberals and conservatives on the one hand, and between charismatics and non-charismatics on the other. As these divisions cut right across denominational boundaries, interdenominational co-operation between the like-minded is strengthened and denominational labels become even less important. Today, homosexuality is far more likely to divide Protestants from one another than episcopacy or infant baptism are, and there is no indication that that trend will be reversed in the near future. Similarly, charismatic experiences cause more ripples than a new Bible translation does, however great an improvement it may be on its various rivals.

English Protestantism will survive, and in all probability it will continue to shape the country's religious culture for the foreseeable future. At the beginning of the third millennium, the real question is whether a new synthesis of doctrine, spirituality and social witness will emerge which can reunite what have become competing forces within Protestantism, and make a genuine impact on the nation as a whole.

Further Reading

Bebbington, D. W. (1989). *Evangelicalism in Modern Britain*. London: Unwin.

Bosher, R. S. (1951). *The Making of the Restoration Settlement. The Influence of the Laudians, 1649–1662*. London: Dacre Press.

Bray, G. L. (1994). *Documents of the English Reformation*. Cambridge, UK: James Clarke.

Brigden, S. (1989). *London and the Reformation*. Oxford: Oxford University Press.

Clark, J. C. D. (2000). *English Society 1660–1832*, 2nd edn. Cambridge, UK: Cambridge University Press.

Collinson, P. (1990). *The Elizabethan Puritan Movement*, 2nd edn. Oxford: Oxford University Press.

Davies, H. (1996). *Worship and Theology in England*, 3 vols, Grand Rapids, MI: Eerdmans.

Dickens, A. G. (1989). *The English Reformation*, 2nd edn. London: Batsford.

Fincham, K. (1990). *Prelate as Pastor. The Episcopate of James I*. Oxford: Oxford University Press.

Hughes, P. E. (1980). *Theology of the English Reformers*, 2nd edn. Grand Rapids, MI: Baker.

Hylson-Smith, K. (1988). *Evangelicals in the Church of England*. Edinburgh: T & T Clark.

Hylson-Smith, K (1993). *High Churchmanship in the Church of England*. Edinburgh: T & T Clark.

Paul. R. S. (1985). *The Assembly of the Lord*. Edinburgh: T & T Clark.

Rupp, E. G. (1986). *Religion in England 1688–1791*. Oxford: Oxford University Press.

Trueman, C. (1994). *Luther's Legacy. Salvation and the English Reformers 1525–1556*. Oxford: Oxford University Press.

Tyacke, N. (1987). *Anti-Calvinists. The Rise of English Arminianism, c. 1590–1640*. Oxford: Oxford University Press.

White, P. (1992). *Predestination, Policy and Polemic. Conflict and Consensus in the English Church from the Reformation to the Civil War*. Cambridge, UK: Cambridge University Press.

CHAPTER 7

Scottish Protestantism to the Present Day

Kenneth B. E. Roxburgh

The emergence of Scottish Protestantism can be traced to 1525, when the Scottish parliament tried to prevent Lutheran literature from entering the country. Beginning with instances of individual conversions to the Reformed faith, Protestantism eventually became closely associated with Scottish religious identity.

The Scottish Reformation

The Reformation in Scotland of 1559–60 came later than in most countries in Europe and marked a decisive rejection of Rome, the Latin mass, the papacy, priesthood and much else.

Accounts of the life of the church, prior to that time, differ according to the perspective of the writer. Traditional accounts feel that at the parish level the church was ill served: many priests were illiterate and greedy and the higher clergy were effectively appointed by the crown and drawn largely from the influential families. They practised simony and their moral conduct was not to be admired. It seems that easy generalizations are difficult to make as the spiritual health of different religious houses may have varied considerably.

Early Protestants

As early as 1494 a number of Ayrshire lairds and tenants were summoned before the Lords of the Council accused of unorthodox opinions, although they were confined to Kyle (Sanderson, 1997: 36ff.). A parliamentary act in 1525 attempted to curb any opinions contrary to the established Christian faith, and all discussion of Luther's teachings were prohibited, unless of course they were being condemned.

Patrick Hamilton arrived in Scotland in 1523 after studying in Paris and Louvain where academic disputes had taken place on Luther's views. In 1527 Hamilton was charged with 'disputing, holding and maintaining divers heresies of Martin Luther . . . repugnant to the faith' and on returning in 1528 from a time in Marburg he 'taught and disputed openly in the university' at St Andrews. Hamilton was the most striking example of an early Lutheran evangelical but he was by no means the only one. Others were persecuted and many subsequently fled to Cromwell's England. Lutheran books were imported, especially to St Andrews and Edinburgh, and in the 1530s there is a report of an unnamed 'woman of Leith' who, in childbirth, refused to invoke the Virgin's help, praying instead directly to Christ 'in whose help I trust'. She did finally recant her heresy. These early prosecutions, convictions and abjurations reveal a curious blend of early Lollard belief and Lutheran heresy.

John Knox

In 1547, John Knox preached at St Andrews against Roman Catholicism. Following a military defeat to the French, Knox was imprisoned in the French galleys for 19 months and then spent time in England from 1549 to 1554, again going into exile when Mary Tudor came to power and spending formative years in Geneva. He returned briefly to Scotland in the winter of 1555–6, eventually settling in May 1559 at the invitation of Protestant Lords of the Congregation.

During the 1550s, house cells of Edinburgh's Protestants were beginning to be organized on a more formal footing. These 'privy kirks' spread under the patronage of sympathetic lairds. The result was that small isolated groups became well-organized and militant. In 1556 John Knox, writing from Geneva, had encouraged these groups of believers to meet once a week as a 'congregation' for the 'reading, exhorting and in making common prayers' (Kirk, 1989: 1–16).

In April 1558 Mary, Queen of Scots, married the Dauphin Francis, leading to the prospect of a union of the Scottish and French crowns, and heightened the nobility's fears that the administration would become dominated by French interests. John Knox's preaching encouraged people to pull down images, altars and altar-pieces in the parish churches and to burn them. By 2 July a cross-section of society from nobles to lairds and burgesses had 'purged' a series of towns of Roman Catholicism and Knox was established as the first Protestant minister in Edinburgh. Parliament met and abolished the mass, proscribed the jurisdiction of the Pope, repealed anti-heresy laws, and adopted a Protestant Confession of Faith.

The Reformers stressed the importance of the parish, their ministers conducting a radically different type of service from before, based on lengthy sermons expounding biblical texts. The ritual of the mass disappeared and the number of sacraments was reduced to two. However, the actual provision of ministers was hindered by a lack of supply in many areas. Most parishes had to make do with a 'reader', not a minister, for at least a generation. The result of this meant that in many respects the progress of the Reformed Church after 1560 depended on a series of local Reformations, each moving at its own pace and with its own distinctive problems to surmount.

The Post-Reformation Period

The period following the Reformation was characterized by conflict between church and state with competing forms of church government, namely those of Presbyterianism and episcopacy. James VI was anxious not only to unite the crowns of Scotland and England, but also to unite the churches. Episcopacy, for many Scottish Protestants, was too reminiscent of 'Romish' religion and the policy of the Stuarts brought turmoil to Scottish politics and religion.

Covenanters: 1638–89

In 1638, opponents of the royal policy drafted the National Covenant, upholding 'true Reformed religion'. Nobles, ministers, burgesses and common people in various parts of the country signed the Covenant, backed by popular enthusiasm. At a November meeting of the General Assembly in Glasgow all opposition to Presbyterian and Puritan conviction was silenced and episcopacy was rejected. The Covenanters' victory against the King in the Bishops' Wars of 1639 and 1640 forced Charles I to accept Presbyterianism within Scotland.

When Charles II was restored to the throne in 1660 it soon became clear that the king would not support Presbyterianism, and an Erastian episcopacy was established by 1662. Over 270 ministers were deprived of their livings and conflict eventually erupted into military action between the crown and the Covenanting forces. The 'killing times' embittered many Presbyterians against any form of episcopacy.

The Glorious Revolution of 1688, which brought about the flight of James VII and the accession of William and Mary to the throne, was an event of religious as well as political significance. It was perceived probably by the majority of the Scottish population, at least in the Lowlands, as a rejection of James VII's attempts to reintroduce the practice of Roman Catholicism. The reinstatement of 'the antediluvians', 60 Presbyterian ministers who had been deposed since 1661, and their restoration to their parishes, whether held by someone else or

not, led to the beginnings of an expulsion of Episcopal ministers and the abolition of episcopacy. This was followed in 1690 by the re-establishment of full
Presbyterian government in the Church of Scotland.

The Eighteenth Century

The eighteenth century was a crucial period in the development of Scottish
national identity. Within this period, religion played an important part in
national, as well as individual, experience of what it meant to be Scottish at a
time when many political, economic and cultural changes were taking place.
Religion, in the form of Scottish Presbyterianism, continued to influence the lives
of most Scots as it pervaded the whole of Scottish society in the eighteenth
century.

Presbyterianism became the dominant force throughout the land. The vast
majority of clergy were now committed to a Presbyterian church government,
along with a subscription to the *Westminster Confession of Faith* for retaining
soundness and unity of doctrine. The Church of Scotland's claim to be the
national church of the Scottish people was largely unthreatened. However, this
would change. The middle decades of the eighteenth century would witness the
disruption of that unity as the result of the 1733 Secession and the formation
of the Relief Church in 1761. By the end of the century, there would be seven
different Presbyterian Churches within Scotland.

The Secession Church

Patronage was one of the issues which caused great debate and division within
the Church of Scotland during the eighteenth century. Despite the guarantee
made at the *Act of Union* of 1707, the British parliament in 1712 passed the 'Act
concerning patronage', which restored the rights of lay patrons to appoint ministers to charges within their gift. Many viewed the act with great alarm, and
problems arose when patrons not only insisted on their rights of presentation,
but also presented unwanted men. In 1729 the Assembly provided special committees to induct unpopular presentees who were being opposed. These became
known as 'Riding Committees', partly because they were seen as trampling over
the decisions of presbyteries and also because they moved about the country
conducting inductions, riding in and out of parishes. In the Assembly of 1731
an overture was presented which many people believed would restrict the call of
a minister to the heritors and elders of a congregation (Fraser, 1831: 358–60).
This overture became an act of church law in 1732, despite being opposed by
the majority of presbyteries who responded to the overture. It was also fiercely
resisted by a number of ministers, headed up by Ebenezer Erskine, Minister of
Stirling. Erskine was at this time the Moderator of the Synod of Perth and

Stirling. On 10 October 1732 he preached a blistering sermon attacking the new measure. Erskine was rebuked for this intemperate sermon by the Synod in 1732. When he appealed to the Assembly of 1733, the rebuke was upheld and Erskine, along with William Wilson of Perth, Alexander Moncrieff of Abernethy and James Fisher of Kinclaven were suspended from the ministry. They held to their charges and churches nevertheless, and continued to preach. In December 1733, they constituted themselves as the Associate Presbytery, thereby beginning the first secession from the Church of Scotland. By 1742 the Secession Church had 20 ministers and 36 congregations and by 1745 it had a synod of three presbyteries.

The Relief Church

From 1749 until 1752, many members of the evangelical party within the presbytery of Dunfermline supported the rights of the Inverkeithing congregation in their opposition to the settlement of Andrew Richardson as their minister. They consistently refused to obey the General Assembly of the Church of Scotland and perform an induction service. Several members of the emerging Moderate party within the Church of Scotland were determined to use the Inverkeithing case to uphold the case for ecclesiastical law and order, by disciplining those who refused to obey the orders of the Assembly. During the General Assembly of 1752, a motion was carried that one of the six ministers of the presbytery of Dunfermline who had refused to induct the new minister to Inverkeithing should be deposed, and Thomas Gillespie, a leading evangelical, was deposed from the ministry of the church. The decision of the General Assembly confirmed the power of the Moderates within the Church of Scotland (Roxburgh, 1999).

Following further disputed settlements, Thomas Boston, minister of Jedburgh, joined Thomas Gillespie at the induction of Thomas Colier to the newly formed congregation at Colinsburgh in Fife. On 22 October 1761, following the induction services, the three ministers and an elder from each of the three congregations met together and constituted themselves into the Presbytery of Relief. They stated that they were acting 'for the relief of oppressed Christian congregations' and that the presbytery would fulfil the same purpose as that of 'members of the Established Church of Scotland' (Struthers, 1843: 160). They believed that each individual, regardless of economic background or educational attainment, was of equal value in the eyes of God and should have a voice in the affairs of the Church.

From the three congregations which existed in 1761, the presbytery grew to 19 congregations by the time of Gillespie's death in January 1774. In 1800 the Relief Church had 60 congregations and 36,000 members, and by 1847 it had grown to 136 congregations. In May 1847, when it joined with the United Secession Church to form the United Presbyterian Church in Scotland, it became the largest single denomination in Glasgow and accounted for slightly less than one-fifth of churchgoers in Scotland (Roxburgh, 1999).

Revival

Whereas the leaders of the emerging Moderate party within the Church of Scotland devoted their time and energy to gaining positions of influence within the General Assembly of the Church of Scotland in order to effect change, members of the Popular party believed that only a spiritual awakening could reverse the spiritual malaise that prevailed within the country. In an age when various changes were taking place in society, many people were seeking a refuge in a Protestant identity associated with the familiar security of past generations, which harkened back to past experiences of religious fervour and spiritual vitality such as the Scottish Reformation and the Covenanting movement.

The revival tradition in Scotland was one that was intimately woven into the experience and expectation of evangelicals in the Church of Scotland. Accounts of the Scottish Reformation under John Knox, as well as later spiritual awakenings in the seventeenth century, were recalled in the early 1740s as news of a fresh awakening in New England through the ministry of George Whitefield and Jonathan Edwards was eagerly received on the Scottish side of the Atlantic. By 1741 expectations were nourished that Scotland could also experience a similar outpouring of the Holy Spirit, one which would recapture the glorious days when the Scottish experienced the blessing of God.

The message that Whitefield and others preached was well received by several people of 'great rank', particularly the Earl of Leven and the Marquis of Lothian. However, it was among the ordinary people of Edinburgh, Glasgow, Aberdeen, and Dundee that the Revival had its greatest impact. Although revival eventually reached a number of towns and villages throughout Scotland, the early hope that it was the herald of some millennial 'latter day glory' was never realized. However, almost 20 years after the revival began, the church at Cambuslang kept a day of fasting and thanksgiving 'in commemoration of the Reformation Work . . . in this place . . . about twenty years ago'. These memories encouraged them to believe that their identity as Scots could not be divorced from their spirituality as Presbyterians, Protestants and evangelicals.

The Nineteenth Century

The eighteenth and nineteenth centuries witnessed the growth of other non-Presbyterian Protestant denominations in Scotland: the Evangelical Union, the Baptists and the Christian Brethren.

The Evangelical Union

James Morison entered the Theological Hall of the United Secession Church in Glasgow in 1834 and was ordained and inducted to the Kilmarnock congregation in 1840. He began to preach 'the doctrine of a Universal Atonement, and consequently a free and unlimited offer of salvation to all and sundry'. Morison was questioned over the theological views propounded in the tract and 'accused of heresy' by some members of the Presbytery. In May 1843, following his deposition from the ministry of the Secession Church, Morison formed the Evangelical Union. The new denomination grew very quickly, with accessions from several ministerial students and ministers from the Congregational Union who had been deposed for their anti-Calvinist views, and by the end of 1843 there were 13 churches in the Union. By 1875, this number had increased to 82 and by 1896 to over 90 churches. The Evangelical Union was founded 'for mutual countenance, counsel and co-operation in supporting and spreading the glorious, simple, soul-saving and heart-sanctifying gospel of the grace of God'. The Union consisted of some churches that were Presbyterian in government and others that were Congregational in church polity. However, in 1896, the Evangelical Union united with the Congregational Union to form the Congregational Union of Scotland. By that time, Scottish theology had followed Morison's lead in abandoning the Calvinism of the Reformers and adopted a more inclusive evangelicalism.

Baptists

There had been a Baptist presence in Scotland since the 1650s during the Cromwellian era. This presence had disappeared by the end of the seventeenth century and re-emerged in Keiss in Caithness when Sir William Sinclair, influenced by Baptists in England, established a congregation in the area.

In the eighteenth century, Baptists made up a very small number of the churchgoing population of Scotland. By 1800 there were two Baptist groups operating in Scotland: the 'English' Baptists of 42 members and up to 100 hearers and the Scotch Baptists with around 400 members and approximately 1,000 hearers. Scotch Baptists affirmed the plurality of elders and deacons in contrast to the sole pastor and diaconal model of the 'English' Baptists. They also believed that pastors/elders should be present when the Lord's Supper was celebrated. They sought to maintain uniformity of practice within their congregations. The 'English' Baptists preferred a single pastor in charge of the congregation.

In the period 1800–27 there were three streams of Baptists in Scotland: Scotch, Haldanite and 'English' Baptists. The Haldane movement was strongly evangelistic, as were the English Baptists, and by the 1830s they were the strongest force of Baptists in Scotland. The division among Scotch Baptists in 1834 over the necessity of elders being present at the Lord's Table fatally weakened the connexion and, although once the dominant grouping of Baptists, they played a minor role in the subsequent history of Baptists in Scotland.

The Haldane brothers   James Haldane and his older brother Robert became itinerant evangelists in 1797, having an interest and involvement in evangelism in Britain and overseas. As members of the Established Church of Scotland they developed ecumenical contacts with other Christian leaders in the Church of England such as Charles Simeon, as well as Independents like David Bogue, believing that the success of evangelism depended on Christians co-operating together in propagating the gospel message. Robert began to use his wealth to establish the Society for the Propagation of the Gospel at Home.

In 1798 Robert Haldane sold a large part of his Airthrey estate near Stirling to finance the work of home evangelism and began to open preaching centres, where evangelicals of different denominations preached to the poor. The Haldane connection grew rapidly. By 1805 there were 25 congregations in existence and by 1808 the number had grown to 85. The Edinburgh congregation drew crowds of more than two thousand and in 1801 they moved to larger premises at the head of Leith Walk, the average attendance for a Sunday evening service being about 3,600. To provide pastors the Haldanes founded academies for the training of catechist-preachers in Glasgow, Edinburgh, Dundee and Elgin, whom they maintained at their own expense.

Both brothers became Baptists in 1808. Although a considerable number left the church at this time and formed an independent church, the Haldane brothers never made baptism an issue which barred people from communion or membership. In 1808 the Haldanes set up their own Baptist home missionary society that led, in 1827, to the establishment of the Baptist Home Missionary Society for Scotland. The influence of the Haldanes in Scotland in the first half of the nineteenth century was pervasive. In their vision for the spread of evangelical Christianity, assisted by ministerial friends from England, an extraordinary transformation of Scottish church life was achieved within a few short years.

The Christian Brethren

The Brethren movement originated in or about the year 1825. It grew out of Protestant evangelicalism and shared its defining characteristics of biblicism, conversionism, activism and crucicentrism. Beginning in Dublin and Plymouth, the movement spread north of the border. The 1859 revival provided a catalyst for significant growth; by 1878 there were 78 meetings and 115 meetings were established by 1885. A democratizing of society, as well as revival influences, was changing people's perception, and the involvement of the laity within the Brethren movement proved to be popular in drawing people from other denominations. Revivalism piety, a simple message and zeal in spreading it were the hallmarks of early growth among assemblies.

Brethren spirituality found its fullest expression in the weekly breaking of bread service. It was marked by simplicity, solemnity, a lack of ritual and an openness to the impulse of the spirit. By 1930 there were some 30,000 Brethren assemblies, comprising only 1.95 per cent of all Protestant church members and yet with a significant influence within Scottish Christianity.

Presbyterian divisions

18 May 1843 witnessed the destruction of the Church of Scotland. Many of the economic, social and cultural forces which were changing Scotland became evident at this time. The central issue that dominated the one leading up to the Disruption was that of the imposition of a minister upon a parish church. Some 454 ministers out of 1195 (37.9%), many elders and as much as half the lay members of congregations left the security of the established church for the sake of religious freedom and self-determination. Within a few years the Free Church had created an alternative national church, covering nearly the whole of Scotland. By 1847 the church had erected over 730 places of worship and supported 513 teachers with over 44,000 children in their schools. In 1847 it founded New College in Edinburgh and in the mid-1850s had two other colleges in Aberdeen and Glasgow. With one exception all their missionaries joined the new church.

Free Presbyterian Church of Scotland　As the Free Church moved into the second half of the nineteenth century some members appeared to be quite willing to relax their commitment to state connection as a principle of the church, while others maintained that it was a central issue of the Free Church. Forms of worship were changed by the introduction of hymns and instrumental music instead of the exclusive use of the Psalms. Additional tension was found in the debates between the supporters of higher critical methods with regard to the Bible, which were introduced into the Free Church colleges.

The Free Presbyterian Church was founded in 1893 as a result of the liberalization of Calvinist doctrine in the 1890s. It created a Second Disruption, during which many thousands of Gaelic-speaking Highlanders left the Free Church. The Free Presbyterians made exclusive use of psalmody and still allow no instrumental music in public worship. The Church retained the Westminster Confession of Faith as its credal statement. They maintained the belief that the whole Bible is inspired and infallible. The 1893 Free Presbyterian Church initially comprised two ministers and some 7,000 people. By July 1895 they had seven ministers, 18 students, 40 missionaries and 20,000 people connected to the new church. By 1900 the Free Presbyterian Church had 75 charges and mission stations, 70 of which were located in the Highlands.

Twentieth Century Developments

The twentieth century opened with the union of the Free Church and the United Presbyterian Church. In 1900 the four Highland synods of the Free Church had

239 ministers; 19 ministers remained in the Free Church and 220 went into the United Free Church. By 1905 30,000 people remained in the Free Church and over 600,000 were now connected to the United Free Church.

Protestants and Roman Catholics

Catholics, the majority of whom are descended from Irish immigrants, have routinely experienced prejudice from the very beginnings of their stay in Scotland. In 1900 there were 450,000 Catholics in Scotland, about 10 per cent of the population. They were concentrated in the west of Scotland, with nearly 70 per cent to be found in Motherwell, Glasgow and Paisley – predominantly an urban and industrial focus. As late as the late 1920s and 1930s the General Assembly of the Church of Scotland waged a relentless campaign against the supposedly malign effects of Irish Catholic immigration that was seen to be a 'menace' to 'Scottish Protestant identity' (Devine, 2000). A movement involving many national church leaders incited popular hostility towards Irish Catholics. The campaign was both sectarian and racist in tone, not with the desire of evangelism but of isolating and driving off the population. Outbreaks of violence eventually led the Church of Scotland to bring its campaign to an end and the anti-Catholic interests committee was dissolved in 1937. The outbreak of war in 1939 led all the parties to combine to defeat the Nazi threat and fascism. However, the remnants of sectarianism continues to effect parts of the west of Scotland to the present time.

Protestantism continues to be a marked feature of Scottish Christianity. However, the state of the church in Scotland, facing decline in the midst of a secular society, means that for the majority of Christians the issue of protest against Roman Catholicism is not the most vital aspect of their identity as believers. Survival, rather than accentuating the divisions within the church, at present, is the major issue facing Protestants in various denominations.

References

Devine, Thomas (2000). *Scotland's Shame: Bigotry and Sectarianism in Modern Scotland.* Edinburgh: Mainstream.
Fraser, Donald (1831). *The Life and Diary of the Rev Ebenezer Erskine.* Edinburgh: W Oliphant.
Kirk, James (1989). *Patterns of Reform.* Edinburgh: T & T Clark.
Roxburgh, Kenneth (1999). *Thomas Gillespie and the Origins of the Relief Church in Eighteenth Century Scotland.* Berne: Peter Lang.
Sanderson, M (1997). *Ayrshire and the Reformation: People and Change, 1490–1600.* East Linton, UK: Tuckwell Press.
Struthers, Gavin (1843). *History of the Relief Church.* Glasgow: A Fullerton and Co.

Further Reading

Cameron, J. K. (1994). The Church in Scotland from the Reformation to the Disruption. In G. Gilley and W. J. Shiels (eds.), *A History of Religion in Britain*. Oxford: Blackwell, pp. 129–51.

CHAPTER 8

Welsh Protestantism to the Present Day

D. Densil Morgan

Protestantism in Wales, as in England, dates from Henry VIII's breach with Rome. Its real impact, though, was in Elizabeth I's appointment of resident Welsh-speaking bishops, who combined a deep commitment to traditional cultural mores with a zeal for Word-centred reform. The Welsh Prayer Book and New Testament of 1567, translated by Bishop Richard Davies (c.1510–81) and the Renaissance scholar William Salesbury (c.1520–84), and the Welsh Bible of 1588, translated by Bishop William Morgan (c.1541–1604), were exceedingly significant for the later development of the nation's life. Although a powerful group of Roman Catholic exiles kept alive the hope of reconverting Wales to the old faith, by the third quarter of the sixteenth century Reformation values had generally triumphed.

It was not until the 1630s that Puritanism began to manifest itself as nonconformity to the rituals and discipline of the established church. The first Independent (Congregational) church was gathered in 1639, and the first Baptist congregation was convened in 1649 though there had been less formal gatherings of believers outside the bounds of the establishment for some years before. By the Commonwealth period (1642–60), Puritanism in its Independent, Baptist, Quaker and Presbyterian guises, rooted itself in different parts of Wales, though it never became widely influential. The Restoration of the monarchy in 1660 brought the Puritan ascendancy to an end, though Protestantism in its Anglican form was re-established and the 39 Articles and Book of Common Prayer became normative for the bulk of Welsh Christians once more.

What united the Anglican Church and the older dissent was a shared commitment to the Protestant faith. Irenically minded Independents such as Stephen Hughes (1622–88) and the Anglican Society for the Propagation of Christian Knowledge (SPCK) disseminated Welsh Bibles and established schools. Educational work and a more vibrant evangelistic mission was undertaken by Griffith Jones (1683–1761), rector of Llanddowror, though a more pronounced spiritual renewal came about in 1735 with the dawning of the Evangelical Revival led by Daniel Rowland (1713–90) and Howell Harris (1714–73). Biblically based and emphasizing the Reformation doctrine of justification by faith alone, the revival broke the bounds of Welsh Anglicanism and created what became in 1811 the Welsh Calvinistic Methodist Connexion.

By then Protestant Nonconformity had been transformed into a widely popular religious movement. Its success in winning the allegiance of the ordinary working people was spectacular. What had been a minority movement was now a vibrant, energetic confederation of Methodists (Calvinistic and Wesleyan), Independents and Baptists, who together comprised the principal manifestation of Protestantism in Wales. Popular Nonconformity produced a generation of preachers of unequalled power, of whom the Baptist Christmas Evans (1766–1838), the Calvinistic Methodist John Elias (1774–1841) and the Independent William Williams of Wern (1781–1840) were the most celebrated. By the middle of the nineteenth century academic excellence and theological acumen were represented by the Calvinistic Methodist Lewis Edwards (1809–87), principal of Bala College, while political radicalism was spearheaded by the Independents David Rees (1801–69) and Gwilym Hiraethog (1802–83). Effective gospel preaching, the sovereignty of the Word of God and its application to the political sphere had turned Wales into 'a nation of Non-conformists'.

The later nineteenth century saw the renewal of Welsh Anglicanism, though its rejuvenation was only partly due to Protestant emphases. Although the evangelicals were active, Tractarianism became a definite force. Nonconformity, for its part, was beginning to show signs of strain. If the tradition of popular preaching still existed, the chapels were finding it progressively difficult to contend with the twin challenges of modernity and Anglicization. The widespread religious revival of 1904–5 led by Evan Roberts (1878–1951) proved more significant for the development of international Pentecostalism than in the renewal of Welsh Nonconformity. The crisis was exacerbated by the political struggle to disestablish the four Welsh dioceses, which pitched Nonconformist against Anglican, and between 1889 (when the controversy effectively began) and 1914 (when parliament passed the Welsh Church Act cutting the link between the Anglican Church and the state), Christian integrity on both sides suffered grievously. Disenchanted by religious disputes, many people came to feel that the values of the future would be more secular in nature.

Following the First World War Nonconformity still remained the principal manifestation of Welsh Protestantism, with as many as one in five of the population being baptized and communicant members of their respective denominations. Although Anglicanism remained weaker numerically than Nonconformity on the whole, it still drew some 13 per cent of the Welsh people to its services. Following disestablishment, the newly formed 'Church in Wales' was now more substantial than any one other single denomination.

By this time doctrinal liberalism threatened to eclipse orthodoxy as the Nonconformist creed, with such accomplished theologians as Thomas Rees

(1869–1926), John Morgan Jones (1873–1946) and D. Miall Edwards (1873–1941) convincing many that in order to survive, Protestantism would have to adapt to the norms of philosophical idealism and the values of the Enlightenment. Not all were convinced, and by the 1940s a spirited Calvinistic renewal, deeply indebted to the work of Karl Barth, had occurred. Theologians such as J. E. Daniel (1902–62) and preachers like Lewis Valentine (1893–1986) combined a Barthian emphasis with a deep commitment to the doctrinal standards of classical Welsh Nonconformity. Evangelicalism of a more conservative stripe was championed in Wales by the influential London-based preacher Martyn Lloyd-Jones (1899–1981).

By the late 1960s secularization was taking its toll on all the mainline denominations. Chapel culture was in retreat, while the Christian presence was more and more dominated by Catholicism and a catholic Anglicanism. The final quarter of the twentieth century witnessed steep statistical decline across the board, and the undoubted vitality of the charismatic movement and the establishment of newer evangelical or 'house' churches did little to stem the secular tide. Protestant convictions, however, still persist, and the twin ideals of biblical authority and the spiritually liberating doctrine of justification by faith preserve both a link with the past and a hope for the future.

Further Reading

Bassett, T. M. (1977). *The Welsh Baptists*. Swansea: Ilston Press.

Evans, Eifion (1985). *Daniel Rowland and the Great Evangelical Awakening in Wales*. Edinburgh: Banner of Truth Trust.

Jenkins, Geraint H. (1978). *Literature, Religion and Society in Wales, 1660–1730*. Cardiff: University of Wales Press.

Jenkins, Geraint H. (1992). *Protestant Dissenters in Wales, 1639–89*. Cardiff: University of Wales Press.

Morgan, D. Densil (1999). *The Span of the Cross: Christian Religion and Society in Wales, 1914–2000*. Cardiff: University of Wales Press.

Pope, Robert (1998). *Building Jerusalem: Nonconformity, Labour and the Social Question in Wales, 1906–39*. Cardiff: University of Wales Press.

Pope, Robert (1999). *Seeking God's Kingdom: The Nonconformist Social Gospel in Wales, 1906–39*. Cardiff: University of Wales Press.

Tudur, Geraint (2000). *Howell Harris: From Conversion to Separation, 1735–50*. Cardiff: University of Wales Press.

Williams, Glanmor (1997). *Wales and the Reformation*. Cardiff: University of Wales Press.

CHAPTER 9

Irish Protestantism to the Present Day

Alan Ford

Protestantism in Ireland is much more than a religion. It is inextricably linked
to political, cultural, even racial identity, defining as it does one half of that stark
divide which so dominates modern Irish history: Protestant versus Catholic. This
is evident from the earliest history of the Protestant church. It was created by a
political act – Henry VIII's decision to break with Rome was extended to Ireland
by the 1537 Irish Act of Supremacy. It became associated with Anglicization and
Englishness as Henry's Dublin government sought to enforce the Reformation.
And it gained most of its support from English emigrants to Ireland and their
descendants. At the same time, however, beneath these generalizations there
lurk much more complex realities: over the centuries, Irish Protestantism grew
and changed, becoming more than just a colonial church: it developed its own
distinctive and varied theological, political and cultural identities, reacting to
and being shaped by its Irish environment. These complexities are reflected in
the denominational development of Irish Protestantism, which followed that
familiar post-Reformation fissiparous trajectory of initial unity broken by
repeated separation and division.

Defining Irish Protestantism: The First Century: 1537–1640

The Church of Ireland as established by Henry VIII was initially limited to those
areas of the country controlled by the royal government in Dublin, and was
more concerned with enforcing royal supremacy than spreading Protestantism.
It was not until the reign of James I (1603–25), when English power was
extended to the whole island and the plantation of Ulster led to an influx of
English and Scots settlers, that it was possible to speak of the Church of Ireland
as a national Protestant church, with royally appointed bishops in every diocese.

Initially this church united all Irish Protestants by subtly adapting its English heritage to allow for a broader ecclesiological polity, accommodating Episcopalians and Puritans. Its confession of faith, the Irish Articles of 1615, went beyond its English model, the Thirty-nine Articles, by adopting Calvinist double-predestination, taking a more relaxed approach to episcopacy, and formally identifying the Pope with Antichrist. As a result, Presbyterian ministers who arrived in Ulster with the Scottish settlers after 1610 found that they could happily serve within the Church of Ireland.

The fact that the vast majority of the native inhabitants of Ireland remained committed to Catholicism placed Irish Protestants in a difficult position: though they claimed to be an established national church, they had the allegiance of only a minority of the population. Some responded to this difficulty by accepting that Protestantism in Ireland was essentially colonial, and that the Church of Ireland was an offshoot of the Church of England. But others, including, most notably the leading Irish Protestant scholar, Archbishop James Ussher of Armagh (1581–1656), sought to develop an alternative identity, which later became widely accepted in the Church of Ireland. Ussher sought to legitimize the Church of Ireland by tracing its ancestry back to the early Irish Celtic church – the church of St Patrick and the islands of saints and scholars – which was, he claimed, to all intents and purposes Protestant.

The unity and independence of the Church of Ireland was ended in the mid-1630s by the success of the new and firmly anti-Calvinist Archbishop of Canterbury, William Laud, in bringing the Church of Ireland into line with the Church of England. The English Thirty-nine Articles replaced the 1615 Irish confession in 1634, and new disciplinary canons eliminated Presbyterians from the Church of Ireland and began the fragmentation of Irish Protantism.

From Disaster to Disaster: 1641–89

The fragmentation of Irish Protestantism was accelerated by the disasters of the 1640s. In 1641 Irish Catholics in Ulster rose against the English settlers, attacking them and driving them out of the province with considerable loss of life. The savagery of the rebellion, and the exaggerated accounts of the number slaughtered, turned 1641 into an iconic event in the Irish Protestant imagination, symbolizing barbaric Irish Catholic cruelty towards godly Protestants. It also began a long period of military struggle between Irish Catholics and English and Scottish Protestants, which culminated in Cromwell's victories in Ireland in 1649–50. Under the Commonwealth the Church of Ireland was disestablished in 1647, and in its place a rich variety of Protestant sects gained a hold in Ireland, including Baptists, Independents, Quakers and, most importantly, Presbyterians. Thus, though the Restoration of the monarchy in 1660 saw the Church of Ireland also restored as the national church, the narrow basis of the

Protestant settlement in Ireland, as in England, ensured that the Church was now faced with opposition on two wings, from Catholics and dissenters, in particular, Presbyterians.

The post-Restoration consolidation of Protestant control of land and political power was challenged dramatically by the accession of a Catholic monarch, James II, in 1685: this placed Irish Protestants, like their counterparts in England, in the awkward position of opposing a divinely appointed English king. Any reservations were, however, soon quashed by the arrival of William of Orange as a military saviour, and his triumph over James II at the Battle of the Boyne in July 1689 would later become one of the symbols of Irish Protestant solidarity.

The Long Eighteenth Century 1690–1800

The defeat of James was followed by a lengthy period during which the Irish Protestant establishment set about securing its ascendancy. From the 1690s on a series of penal laws imposed penalties on Irish Catholics (and, to a lesser extent, dissenters) that excluded them from land, influence or political power. The Church of Ireland became the church of government, its bishops occupying prominent political positions, appointed by English governments often more on the basis of their political loyalty than their pastoral qualifications. Attitudes towards Protestant dissent varied, with some Whig prelates, such as Archbishop King of Dublin, being positively disposed, while their high church counterparts were more hostile towards those who rejected establishment and episcopacy.

Treatment of dissenters was mixed. All Irish nonconformists suffered under the provisions of the sacramental test imposed in 1714 (not repealed till 1780), which required all office holders to take Anglican communion. Though this excluded them from political life, dissenters' freedom to practise their religion had been secured by the Toleration Act of 1719. The Presbyterians had, in addition, secured a grant from Charles II in 1672, the *regium donum*, which was used to pay its ministers, an arrangement that survived until 1870. The Presbyterians were bedevilled by internal divisions, most notably between the Old Lights, conservative Calvinists, and the more liberal New Lights, who came to prominence in the 1720s, rejecting the need to subscribe to the Westminster Confession. The dominance of the New Lights led to some of the Old Lights allying themselves to the conservative Scottish 'Seceders' who had broken with the Church of Scotland in 1733. In the 1740s a new element was added to Irish Protestantism, with the growth of Methodism offering an evangelical Arminian theology and a new missionary zeal. Steady growth after the first visit of John Wesley to Ireland in 1747, mainly in areas of previous Church of Ireland strength in Ulster, saw the Methodists grow to 44,000 members by 1844.

The second half of the seventeenth century saw resurgence in Protestant self-assurance, with the restoration of legislative independence to the Irish parliament in 1760, and the repeal of some of the penal laws. The 1798 rising, however, dented that confidence, and it was followed by the Act of Union in 1800, which, as well as joining the two states, also joined the Church of Ireland to the Church of England.

Political Challenges: 1801–1922

The long nineteenth century faced Irish Protestantism with a series of political challenges that forced the churches to reaffirm and restructure their outlooks and institutions. The privileged established position of the Church of Ireland came under continued attack from Catholics and dissenters: the result was a series of concessions, often imposed by the state, which reformed the hated tithe system, saw the final lifting of the penal laws with Catholic emancipation in 1829, the reduction in the number of Church of Ireland bishoprics and, finally, the disestablishment of the Church of Ireland in 1870. This latter was an immense shock to the Church's members, being seen by many as a political betrayal. In fact, freed from its link to the state and the Church of England, the newly independent church was given an opportunity to redefine its role in Ireland, look again at its Irishness, and come to terms with the rapid political changes associated with the growth of the largely Catholic home rule movement. Though there was within the Church of Ireland a very small high church minority, some of whom proved influential in the development of the Oxford Movement in the 1830s and 1840s, the freedom to define its own prayer book and beliefs which came with disestablishment confirmed its distinctly low church character.

Within the Presbyterian church the main challenge was as always the preservation of unity: here the departure of the non-subscribing New Light ministers in 1830 to form the Remonstrant Synod, left the remaining conservative ministers free in 1840 to join with the seceders to form the dominant force in modern Irish Presbyterianism, the General Assembly of the Presbyterian Church in Ireland, which by the end of the century had its own theological colleges and a significant record in overseas missionary work.

The tenor of all the Irish Protestants in the nineteenth century was decidedly evangelical, as the revival which had begun with the Methodists in the eighteenth century spread amongst established and dissenting churches alike. The evangelical commitment to Reformation principles, biblical fundamentalism, the importance of conversion and personal religious experience, together with a marked hostility to Catholicism, all marked two of the major Protestant enterprises in the nineteenth century, the Second Reformation and the Great Revival of 1859. The former began around 1800 and reached its peak in the 1820s, as evangelical Protestants of all denominations sent out missionaries to even the remotest areas of Ireland in a new attempt to win over the Catholic population. The offer of free primary education, and even free food during the famine, produced some short-term gains, but ultimately the movement was more notable for the way in which it provoked sectarian bitterness than for the number of converts it gained. The Ulster Revival of 1859 epitomized the new spirit of Irish Protestantism, with its mass rallies, and scenes of great religious enthusiasm and excitement, which transcended denominational boundaries.

Dealing with the New Ireland: 1922 to the Present

In 1922 Irish Protestantism was split in two: becoming a minority in the newly established southern Irish Free State, while remaining a majority in the six counties of Ulster which chose to remain within the United Kingdom. Though Protestant churches remained all-Ireland institutions, the contexts in which they operated, north and south, became increasingly distinct. Within the strongly Catholic ethos of the southern state, Protestant numbers declined dramatically, from 207,000 in 1926 (7% of population) to 157,000 in 1946 (5.3%), to 107,000 in 1991 (3%, nearly all Church of Ireland). The fall is largely accounted for by emigration, but in the eyes of Irish Protestants the most significant cause was the 1908 *Ne Temere* papal decree that required that the children of mixed marriages must be brought up Catholic. Initially southern Protestants were unsure of where their allegiance lay, but under the firm leadership of Archbishop John Gregg of Armagh they committed themselves to the Irish state and, despite some notable setbacks, such as the Fethard on Sea boycott of 1957 (when Catholics, urged on by their parish priest, boycotted Protestant shops and businesses), Protestants and Catholics in the Republic were, by the end of the twentieth century, remarkably well-integrated, culturally, politically and religiously.

The same cannot be said for Northern Ireland. During the early twentieth century, politics and religion had fused in Ulster, as Protestants joined together in solemn league and covenant to oppose home rule. The whole purpose of creating the Northern Irish state in 1920 was to ensure that the Protestant majority in Ulster did not become a minority in an all-Ireland state. Political power and Protestantism, as a result, went hand in hand in Ulster until well into the twentieth century. The Orange Order, originally founded in the 1790s, and dedicated to sustaining the 'glorious and immortal memory' of William's victory at the Boyne, served as a crucial link between Protestant churches and the state in Northern Ireland, upholding anti-Catholicism and fundamentalist principles. Catholic resentment against discrimination led to the creation of the civil rights movement in 1967: escalating tensions led to the outbreak of violence in 1969 and the beginning of the Northern Ireland 'troubles' as paramilitary organizations exploited and reinforced the entrenched and hostile political and religious positions of the Catholic and Protestant communities.

The response of the churches to the troubles has been firm, with regular condemnations of the use of violence and calls for reconciliation. But the realities of sectarian bitterness in the North have often made it difficult for religious leaders on either side to translate these words into real changes in attitude within their own communities. This largely explains the slow pace of ecumenism in Ireland. Efforts to promote reunion of the Protestant churches in the 1930s foundered on the Church of Ireland's reluctance to recognize Presbyterian orders and sacraments; it was not until 1973 that formal ecumenical meetings between the Catholic and Protestant churches got under way. Even then, long-entrenched fundamentalist suspicion of Roman Catholicism made it very difficult for Protestant churches (and especially Presbyterians) to engage in ecumenical discussions or be seen to make concessions. The foundation of a small breakaway Free Presbyterian church in 1951 by the maverick minister and (later) politician, Ian Paisley (b.1926), provided a focus for disaffected Presbyterians, concerned at the implications of ecumenism and liberalism.

Nevertheless, the Protestant churches in Ireland have been deeply involved with practical initiatives to foster reconciliation, such as the Corrymeela Community (founded in 1965) in the north and the Glencree Reconciliation Centre (founded 1994) in the south, and the Irish School of Ecumenics, with bases in both Belfast and Dublin. Though the Good Friday Agreement of 10 April 1998 formally brought to an end the paramilitary violence, it left Irish Protestantism with the continuing challenge of dealing with sectarian attitudes and assumptions.

By the end of the twentieth century, the largest religious grouping in Northern Ireland remained the Presbyterian Church – in the 1991 census 337,000 people (21.4% of the population) gave their religion as Presbyterian. The two other main denominations were the Church of Ireland, with 279,000 members (17.7%), and the Methodists with 60,000 (3.8%).

Conclusion

The linkage between religion and political, cultural and even racial identity in Ireland makes understanding Irish Protestantism particularly complex and fascinating. Presbyterians can be politically liberal and theologically conservative; firm Unionists can be fiercely proud of the Irish origins of the Church of Ireland; 'Anglicans' can be committed Irish speakers. Disentangling these various strands is not just difficult – it is impossible, for they have become intertwined in markedly different ways, depending upon time, circumstance and Protestant denomination. What is clear is that religion still serves as a major force in defining identity, especially in Northern Ireland. The close association between political power and Protestantism, and the sense of being an embattled minority, has decisively shaped the Protestant outlook that, historically, has combined a sense of religious and cultural superiority, and mystification at the hold which 'popery' has maintained on the Irish people, with an Old Testament sense of being a chosen people. As a result, despite the markedly different tenor of the Protestant churches in the south, and for all the middle-class interest in ecumenism and commitment to reconciliation, the obdurate and unyielding Northern loyalist remains to this day emblematic of the Irish Protestant spirit, with its twin poles: hatred (and fear) of Catholicism; and a firm fundamentalist evangelicalism.

Further Reading

Akenson, D. H. (1971). *The Church of Ireland: Ecclesiastical Reform and Revolution, 1800–1885*. New Haven, CT: Yale University Press.

Bolton, F. R. (1958). *The Caroline Tradition of the Church of Ireland with Particular Reference to Bishop Jeremy Taylor*. London: SPCK.

Bowen, Desmond (1978). *The Protestant Crusade in Ireland, 1800–70: A Study Of Protestant–Catholic Relations Between the Act of Union and Disestablishment*. Montreal: Gill & Macmillan.

Brooke, Peter (1987). *Ulster Presbyterianism. The Historical Perspective 1610–1970*. Dublin: Athol Books.

Connolly, S. J. (1992). *Religion, Law and Power: The Making of Protestant Ireland 1660–1760*. Oxford: Oxford University Press.

Ford, Alan (1997). *The Protestant Reformation in Ireland*, 2nd edn. Dublin: Irish Academic Press.

Ford, Alan, McGuire, James and Milne, Kenneth (eds.) (1995). *As by Law Established. The Church of Ireland since the Reformation*. Dublin: Lilliput Press.

Greaves, R. L. (1997). *God's Other Children. Protestant Nonconformists and the Emergence of Denominational Churches in Ireland, 1660–1700*. Stanford, CA: Stanford University Press.

Hempton, David and Hill, Myrtle (1992). *Evangelical Protestantism in Ulster Society, 1740–1890*. London: Routledge.

Holmes, Finlay (2000) *The Presbyterian Church in Ireland: A Popular History*. Blackrock, Ireland: Columba Press.

McDowell, R. B. (1975). *The Church of Ireland 1869–1969*. London: Routledge & Kegan Paul.

Megahey, Alan (2000). *The Irish Protestant Churches in the Twentieth Century*. London: Macmillan.

Phillips, W. A. (ed.) (1933). *History of the Church of Ireland from the Earliest Times to the Present Day*, 3 vols. Oxford: Oxford University Press.

CHAPTER 10

Nordic Protestantism to the Present Day

Aasulv Lande

The great Reformation which took place in Western Christendom half a millennium ago swept into the Nordic countries over a period of 30 years from the 1520s, and followed a generally similar pattern in all Nordic countries. Two new Nordic states emerged in the 1520s: West Scandinavia centred in Denmark, and East Scandinavia centred in Sweden. Both states formed Lutheran state churches. During the five following centuries the number of Nordic national units increased from the original two blocks to five independent countries, all with Lutheran state churches. Forced by ideas of religious plurality from inside and secularization from outside, the established alliance between state and church has become increasingly questioned and a Protestant variety has emerged amid the ideologies and religious alternatives of late modernity.

The Sixteenth Century: From Reform to Reformation

Nordic reaction to the economic and political power of the Hansa covenant had inspired the Danish-led Nordic Kalmar Union, uniting Denmark, Sweden and Norway under a single monarch, from 1397. There were, however, movements in Sweden and Norway working for independence. The appearance of Protestantism had different effects under these circumstances. Whereas it inspired an independent Swedish state in the East, it confirmed Danish authority in Western Scandinavia. After an early period of inspiration through biblical humanism, largely mediated through the German city of Rostock, Lutheran influence from Wittenberg became the dominating ideological power in both kingdoms.

Denmark, Norway and Iceland

Building on a basis laid by biblical humanism, Reformation ideas spread in middle-class Malmö (which was then part of Denmark) and Copenhagen. The preacher Hans Tausen (1494–1561), who had studied in Wittenberg, was the first Dane to put a definite evangelical stamp on the growing reform movement. The Lutheran Reformation was politically secured in Denmark by the rule of Christian III (1536–59). In 1537 a national church assembly adopted a Church Ordinance based on the Lutheran teaching of the two kingdoms. While a specific Lutheran doctrine was not adopted, church ministers were nevertheless instructed to possess and use the Bible, Luther's *Sunday Postilla*, *Confession Augustana* and *Small Cathechism*, Melanchthon's *Loci Communis*, *Saxon Visitations* and the Danish *Church Ordinance*. Johannes Bugenhagen cooperated closely from Wittenberg, and visited Copenhagen where he ordained seven Bishops, six from Denmark and one from Norway. A Bible translation named after Christian III appeared in 1550 and Hans Thommison's Hymnal in 1569.

In Norway, biblical humanism and Reformation thought gained ground in Oslo, but even more so in the Hansa city of Bergen, where the first Norwegian Lutheran Bishop, Geble Pederssøn, took office. Norwegian strategies for national independence rested, however, with the Roman Catholic Archbishop in Nidaros (Trondheim), Olav Engelbrektsson. His defeat and departure in 1537 meant that the Reformation confirmed Norwegian subordination to Danish administration. The Danish *Church Ordinance* was adopted, and Danish replaced Norwegian nationally as the administrative and religious language. The Bible of Christian III also shared the Norwegian religious language.

Iceland demonstrated a sharper resistance to reform. A violent uprising, led by the Holar Bishop Jon Arason, was crushed and the bishop was executed. Thereafter Icelandic resistance was broken and the Danish *Church Ordinance* implemented. The linguistic tradition of Icelandic was, however, retained. An Icelandic translation of the Bible appeared in 1584.

Sweden and Finland

The leading reformer in Sweden was Olaus Petri (1493–1552) who studied in Uppsala, Leipzig and Wittenberg. Insisting on the authority of the Bible, he stressed the spiritual essence of the church. Gustav Vasa had emerged a victorious king in Sweden and Finland in the 1520s, breaking out of the Danish-dominated Kalmar union. At the 1527 national congress in Västerås he gained support from the Swedish nobility in dissolving church property. Canon law and dependence on Rome were discontinued. Advised by Olaus Petri, the national congress stated that the Word of God should be preached purely and clearly. An unsuccessful attempt at Roman Catholic restoration led to the Uppsala Assembly in 1593. The immediate occasion was the possibility of a Polish king inheriting the Swedish throne. Fearing a political union with Catholic Poland, a

Swedish Church Council confirmed its national and Lutheran character as a *conditio sine qua non* for any union with Poland. Protestantism in Sweden thus strongly manifested its national character.

In the emerging new church structure episcopacy was given a prominent role. Cathedral chapters remained centres for education of Protestant ministers. In 1571 a national *Church Law* was adopted. Like the Danish Norwegian *Church Ordinance* it was based on the Lutheran two-kingdom doctrine. Luther's *Smaller Catechism*, a Swedish liturgy, hymnal and handbook were published and circulated around 1530. Liturgical reforms were moderate, and elements that might be given an evangelical interpretation were retained in the new Swedish mass. The Gustav Vasa Bible was published in 1541.

The Finnish Reformation, likewise, emerged under the royal leadership of Gustav Vasa. Swedish-speaking congregations in Finland closely followed the reformatory procedures of central Sweden. Finnish-speaking congregations experienced the Reformation by different channels. In 1520s reformational ideas spread from Turku/Åbo. The outstanding Finnish reformer Mikael Agricola (1508–57), later Bishop in Turku/Åbo, was educated in Wittenberg and particularly influenced by Philip Melanchthon. Agricola was a pioneer of Finnish language use in society and church, and produced a basic reader in the Finnish language, followed by a prayerbook and a translation of the New Testament (1548). The development of the Finnish language in church continued – a Finnish hymnal appeared in 1580. Although Finland politically remained a unit under Sweden, the Reformation inspired a popular and national renewal in Finnish culture and religion.

The Seventeenth Century: Lutheran Orthodoxy Emerges

The seventeenth century was characterized by the struggle between Denmark and Sweden for Nordic supremacy and increasing Swedish engagement on the European continent. Denmark suffered several setbacks in wars with Sweden and Germany, most notably the loss of Skåne to Sweden in 1658. The religious hinterland of contemporary political turmoil showed, however, a socially supportive attitude. Lutheran orthodoxy not only worked as a stage of affirming reformatory belief – it also provided religious comfort in a time of political confusion and social discomfort. The spirit of the age was expressed artistically by contemporary hymnwriters. The witch-hunt that took place during this century in Nordic countries – showing a cruel religious answer to turmoil and uncertainty – will not be treated in this outline.

Denmark, Norway and Iceland

Famines, epidemics, cold winters and rainy summers further plagued an already defeated Denmark, and the population's health deteriorated. As a result of political developments, the degree of religious uniformity increased. In the spirit of the century, King Christian IV chose for his national slogan *Regna firmat pietas*, a motif which actually made proper religion a condition for progress. In 1660 Denmark-Norway became an autocratic royal state. The Royal Law (*kongeloven*) of 1665 declared that the king was the supreme authority and only responsible to God. Although Christ was recognized as the spiritual head of the church, the external order of the church lay firmly in royal hands.

Penitence became a theme of ecclesiastical thought and teaching. Several educational institutions were established, culminating in university reform and a compulsory university exam in 1629. The continued use (for a century) of the textbook (1633) by Jesper Brochmand, *Universæ Systema Theologiae*, testified to the stability of orthodox Lutheranism. But even orthodoxy had a plural character. For example, Holger Rosenkrantz argued for an anthropocentric theology in the line of Philip Melanchthon and Catholic traditions. Mysticism, in the wake of Johann Arndt and Paul Gerhard, also reached Denmark in the first decades of the century. Puritan and conformist devotional literature from England spread as well.

Spiritual trends of the age were expressed by Thomas Kingo (1634–1703), the first great Danish hymnwriter. His masterly baroque language gave a poetic twist to a bold Lutheran faith: repentance, sin, guilt and awareness of personal calling. The Kingo hymnal was officially approved in 1699, serving the church in Denmark-Norway for a century to come.

By introducing autocratic rule in 1660, Norway was further subjected to Danish rule. In contrast to the Danish economy, the Norwegian economy progressed steadily during the century. Thanks to forests, fishing and related industries Norway became more of an equal partner to Denmark; Norwegian self-confidence was on the rise, and the wider Norwegian experience entered the religious sphere. In Bergen Dorothe Engelbrektsdatter (1634–1716) wrote hymns on the transience of life in a popular Lutheran vein (e.g. *Dagen viker og går bort* and *Når verden med sin glede sviker*). Hymns by Peter Dass (1647–1707) from Alstadhaug in Nordland prefecture radiated a paternal warmth and toughness that reflected his close contact with fishing communities in Northern Norway. His courageous and outspoken description of the living conditions in the region remains legendary. Theologically inspired by Jesper Brochmand, his hymn *Herre Gud dit dyre Navn og Ære* has become a treasure of international hymnody.

Iceland also fostered outstanding hymnwriters during the time of Lutheran orthodoxy. Especially influential was Hallgrimur Petursson (d.1674) who published *Fifty Lenten Hymns*. These hymns combined objectivist orthodoxy with deep personal piety. The pietistic flavour of these church hymns is considered a reason why the pietist movements never challenged the ecclesiastical structure of Islandic Lutheranism.

Sweden and Finland

For Sweden the seventeenth century was a period of expansive wars, whereby Sweden ascended as a European power. The dominating royal figure was Gustav

II Adolf who ruled from 1611 to 1648. Together with Fieldmarshal Axel Oxenstierna (1583–1654), he led the Swedish expansion into Eastern Europe – involving the country in the Thirty Years' War (1618–48). The war with Denmark was bitter, but Skåne went to Sweden in the peace treaty of 1658. The last two decades of the century were, however, peaceful.

The Lutheran Church in Sweden and Finland retained the characteristic diocesan structure, inside which autocratic bishops ruled their sees. Church ministers were organized as a special class, *consistorium regni*, conflicting regularly with the desires of royals and patrons. Autocratic pressure upon church bodies was strengthened after the conversion to Catholicism by Queen Christina (1654). The fact of her conversion, however, demonstrated a pluralist capacity of Lutheran orthodoxy. The Bishop in Strängnäs, Johannes Matthiae, thus expressed an ecumenical spirit approving of a confessional plurality. Disputes led in 1663 to a consolidation around the Lutheran *Formula of Concord*. As in Denmark-Norway, theological education was now the business of universities. A new university, besides Uppsala, was established in 1666 in Lund. Cartesian philosophy, which had been defended in the Swedish centre of learning in Uppsala, initiated debate, which concluded by declaring Cartesianism a heresy in the theological field, but allowing its use in other sciences. A new Swedish hymnal appeared in 1695 prepared by Jesper Svedberg, a preacher at the royal court. There are similarities to the Danish hymnal by Kingo. It was in use for more than a century and provided orthodox Lutheranism with a poetic image. The Gustav Adolf Church Bible came in 1618 and reappeared in a revised version in 1703 as the Bible of Karl XII.

In Finland, a university – Åbo Akademi – was established in 1640, powerfully informing the theology of the Finnish church. The prelate, Isak Rothovius, led orthodoxy to dominance in accordance with Swedish models. However, as in Sweden, in Finland the line of orthodoxy was not left undisputed. Professor Terserus in Turku/Åbo defended an ecumenically tolerant attitude to differences of confessions in a 1662 catechism. For a period he was discharged from his office as bishop, but eventually reinstated. Lutheran concern for Finnish culture and language continued. Orthodox professors at Åbo Akademi promoted Finnish language and a policy of general education. A Finnish hymnal and a collection of hymns for Swedish-speaking congregations were also published.

The Eighteenth Century: Orthodoxy, Enlightenment and Pietism

During the eighteenth century, Nordic societies remained involved in wars in the rest of Europe and conflicts between themselves. The hereditary social structure, however, was in the process of breaking up, replaced by class structures based on industrial production. A wave of pietist revival spread and tensions with the established church became the order of the day. Enlightenment ideas also swept over European Christendom and left their marks on Nordic Protestantism. As Lutheran orthodoxy also remained prominent throughout this period, a complex pattern of alliances and interactions developed.

Denmark and Norway

State pietism was a special feature of Denmark in the eighteenth century. While pietism was given special legal status, it was at the same time forced into a form of state submission. The supervision of pietists rested with church officials (based on the 1741 *Danish Conventicles Act*). Accordingly, lay gatherings, which were characteristic of pietism, were to be led by the official minister of the local church – a heritage of orthodoxy. The leaders of the pietist movement in Denmark-Norway were Bishop Eric Pontoppidan (1698–1764) who published a pietist catechism, and the hymnist Hans Adof Brorson (1694–1764). His collection of hymns, *The Costly Clenod of Faith* (*Troens Rare Klenodie*), gave moving literary expressions to the idea of renouncing the world.

The spirituality of the time contained a demand for a living Christianity. The Danish-Halle mission to Tranquebar in India began in 1705. During the reign of Fredrik IV (1699–1730), a Mission Collegium was founded in Copenhagen (1714). Christian VI (1730–46) was the most prominent representative of state pietism, as he surrounded himself with pietist advisors. Subsequently, he promoted Christian education. In 1739 a new educational law opened the first elementary schools in the double kingdom and reformed the university system.

Other strands of pietism possessed a nonconformist potentiality and led to tensions over religious authority. In such instances wider Enlightenment ideas such as tolerance and religious freedom advanced the position of pietism. For example, a colony of Moravians in Christiansfeld in Denmark was recognized in 1771.

Nonetheless, pietist and Enlightenment ideas were mostly in conflict. Enlightenment freedom extended beyond the borderlines of Protestantism and various universities started to free themselves of theological control. New rationalist ideas by Christian Wolff (1679–1754) influenced Danish-Norwegian theology and the Norwegian-born writer and historian Ludvig Holberg fought both superstition and metaphysics. In tune with rationalist thinking he emphasized Christianity as an ethical system. The official theology of the universities embraced the rationalist and ethical interpretation of faith.

The pietist movement inspired Norwegian missionary initiatives. The Sami mission developed from a group of seven ministers in Western Norway naming themselves 'The Pleiad' (*syvstjernen*). Their leader, Thomas von Westen (1682–1727), was appointed by the *Missionscollegium* in 1716 to work among the Sami in North Norway, and made several journeys to the North. The *Seminarium Lapponicum* was established in Trondheim (1717) to educate missionaries to the Sami. Another minister, Hans Egede (1686–1758) experienced a calling to preach to the 'poor Greenlanders', whom he believed to be descendants of Norwegian Viking settlers. The Norwegians had, however, disappeared, and Egede decided to work as a pioneer missionary among the Inuit of Greenland.

Johan Ernst Gunnerus, Bishop of Trondheim 1758–73, promoted Enlightenment ideas in Norway. He wrote on dogmatics and in 1760 founded *Det Kongelige Norske Videnskabers Selskab*, a scientific society. Ordinary Norwegian believers did not receive Enlightenment ideas easily. Erik Pontoppidan's pietistic catechism, for example, remained in the schools whereas the *Evangelisk-Christelig Psalmebog* – an Enlightenment hymnal – met strong opposition from congregations.

Sweden and Finland

Karl XII died in 1718, and with him died the royal autocracy and Swedish status as a European power. Swedish administration, in contrast to Denmark, was quickly dominated by Enlightenment ideas. After Karl XII's death there followed a 50-years long 'Age of Freedom' and from 1771 to 1792 Sweden was subjected to the aesthetic concerns of King Gustav III. Nonetheless, there were pietistic movements. A pietist revival spread around 1700 from the coastal city of Karlskrona and found a wide response. The movement was, however, opposed by both Lutheran orthodox and Enlightenment groups. In 1726, again in contradistinction to Denmark, the *Conventicle Act* forbade religious gatherings of lay people.

Pietism in Sweden was a combination of ethical radicalism and spiritual contemplation. The former movement was largely inspired by Halle – the radical pietist Joseph Konrad Dippel (1673–1734) also belonged to this general tendency. He visited Sweden in 1726–9 and his teaching of a subjective and ethical atonement was widely received, but split the pietist movement. Radical pietism developed chiliastic features and a critical attitude towards the church. As the state actively intervened, radical pietism actually disappeared as an organized movement around 1740. Moravian spirituality inspired by Zinzendorf (1700–60) then began to dominate pietism. In the 1740s a difference between radical pietism (largely related to Halle) and the spirituality of the Moravians became evident. In the end, the Moravians exerted a strong influence for a century. The writing *Nådens ordning til saligheten* and the collection of songs *Sions sånger* are devotional expressions of Swedish Moravianism.

Wolffian rationalism influenced Sweden from the 1730s onwards, even spreading among clergy, and tensions with Lutheran orthodoxy occurred. Two different examples of this incursion are significant. The great natural scientist Carl von Linné (1707–78) mediated between Lutheran orthodoxy and Enlightenment ideas. To him natural science verified religious belief and led to true knowledge about the divine majesty, omnipotence, omniscience and mercy.

Emanuel Swedenborg (1688–1772), son of Bishop Jesper Svedberg, came closer to the radical pietists. He combined speculative vision with insights from natural science, neoplatonic mysticism and Enlightenment ideas. Inspired by Dippel, he developed a doctrine of justification based on experience and ethical concerns. His ideas spread in England – and have maintained their appeal as a unique combination of Enlightenment ideas and mystical thought. Without doubt, Enlightenment ideas led to increased religious tolerance. As a result, religious freedom for non-Swedes was legally confirmed in 1781. However, when combined with orthodoxy, it also undergirded the uniformity and validity of the Church of Sweden for Swedes.

Even before 1700 Finland was influenced by pietist revivals. Orthodox professors and church leaders such as Gezelius the Younger were in close contact with the German pietist leader Spener and published devotional literature in a conservative, pietist spirit. Some Finnish pietists attacked the church sharply. A remarkable example is the minister Achrenius who, for a period, came to support separatist thought. Embracing apocalyptic ideas, he left his profession but later returned as a church-loyal pietist. Moravianism broke through after the 1741–43 war with Russia and spread throughout Finland. Other forms of pietism are also found, including a penance movement with ecstatic and psychopathologic features which appeared in the Swedish Tornedalen revival in the 1770s. In 1796 a related revival movement broke into Savolaks in Finland and inspired numerous Finnish revival movements.

Contrasting with the different types of revivals, Enlightenment ideas were promoted by Finnish intellectuals. Professors like Johan Brovallius and Carl Fredrik Mennander, both natural scientists who were later appointed bishops, broadly worked for Enlightenment-derived and educational reforms.

The Nineteenth Century: Revivals, Confessionalism and Liberation

The Nordic national structure changed as Finland and Norway emerged as separate, national units. Through democratic reforms power was transferred to the people and autocratic government crumbled. Lutheranism suffered the same fate and lost its monopoly within Nordic religious life. The patriarchal church structure followed suit and gave in to lay power, and revival movements were crucial promoters of democratization. There was also a growing pluralism that challenged Christian traditions. Liberation was a great theme of the nineteenth century.

Denmark and Iceland

The official Danish church and their ministers were largely informed by Enlightenment ideas by the dawn of the nineteenth century. Among these – but retaining a conservative and dogmatic orientation – was Bishop Jakob Peter Mynster (1775–1854) who became the leading figure in the church. Bishop Hans Martensen (1808–84) was in dialogue with Hegelian thought and tried to mediate between church and culture. He disagreed with emerging Gruntvigian ideas as well as with the individualism of Søren Kierkegaard and the pietist individualists. However, the latter stood for the new theme: liberation, that had been introduced by the ideas in the new constitution of 1849, which emphasized religious freedom. A priority was, however, given to the Evangelical Lutheran Church, which was seen as the Danish folk-church and supported by the state as such. The right to establish a free congregation with its own pastor was approved in 1868.

The subject of freedom was pursued in different ways by the two great theological personalities of the century: Søren Kierkegaard (1813–55) and N. F. S. Grundtvig (1783–1872). Kierkegaard spoke for Christian decisiveness – the freedom of absoluteness – in pronounced conflict with the compromising nature of church Christianity, in his view exemplified by Martensen. In his later works Kierkegaard developed an uncompromising critique of the church. Grundtvig started his career by radically attacking rationalist-influenced Christianity. Inspired by Lutheranism and experiences from English Christianity, he developed a church-centred freedom focusing on 'the living Word'. By this he meant the preached word and, furthermore, the apostolic confession which he saw as prior to biblical texts. He envisaged a unity of culture and faith and formulated the slogan 'First human then Christian' (*Menneske først, kristen så*). In numerous hymns he praised creation, ordinary human life and fellowship in the Spirit. Danish folk high schools were inspired by Grundtvig and brought his ideas of Christian joy in creation to farming towns and fishing communities.

Iceland remained as a part of the Danish kingdom during the nineteenth century. However, neither Grundtvig or other Danish movements influenced Iceland's Protestantism, as the Icelandic cultural creativity continued in its own context. For example, a new liturgical handbook was created and a hymnal was again published in 1886.

Norway

Norway separated from Denmark, only to be united with Sweden in 1814 in accordance with the peace treaty concluding the Napoleonic wars. The national liberation of Norway, inspired by the French Revolution, was expressed in the constitution of 1814. The evangelical Lutheran State church remained, and so did the *Conventicle Act*. But in 1842 a law permitting dissidents' free practice of their faith replaced the *Conventicle Act*. Previously Norwegian ministers had studied at Copenhagen University, but after 1813 theological teaching began at Kongelig Fredriks Universitet in Christiania (Oslo). Its biblically based teaching was inspired by the early Grundtvig, but when in 1825 Grundtvig gave tradition priority over the Bible some Norwegian professors parted from their earlier teacher.

Moravian thought constituted a background of the revival movement initiated by Hans Nielsen Hauge (1771–1824). After a mystical experience of calling on 5 April 1796 he started as a preacher, holding gatherings and also promoting the country's industrial development. Fears of Norwegian independence movements aggravated the persecution of Hauge. He was imprisoned for activities contrary to the *Conventicle Act*, but released in 1814 after 10 years. The Hauge revival was particularly strong among farmers and in rural settings, and paved the way for other revivals. A mission movement was organized by *Norsk Misjonsselskap* in 1842. Its pioneer missionary H. P. S. Schroeder (1817–82) worked in South Africa, for the last year in a separate organization. His ideas of a church mission contradicted the ideas of the pietist administration.

Towards the end of the century several respected Norwegian authors broke with church-based Christianity. Originally a Grundtvigian, Bjørnstjerne Bjørnson (1832–1910) embraced atheistic Darwinism in the 1880s. Arne Garborg (1851–1921) saw the religious question as his main literary challenge.

National and pietist renewal inspired Norwegian hymn writing. The hymnal of Magnus Brostrup Landstad appeared in 1869. Professor Elias Blix (1836–1902) wrote hymns in the new Norwegian language, combining Hebrew and Norwegian images. His collection *Nokre Salmar* (1892) introduced a liberating voice to Norwegian congregations.

Sweden

From 1809 Swedish life and politics were founded on ideas of the Enlightenment and espoused religious freedom. The state church model remained in Sweden, although gravely altered. The loss of Finland to Russia in 1809 led to a national grief – but also to a national revival.

Swedish thinkers were innovative in their dual commitments and reactions. For example, the philosopher E. G. Gejer, in a treatise about the Enlightenment, declared himself a Christian in a 'personal fashion'. He came to represent a religious liberalism with emphasis on freedom of conscience. Another example, S. Ödmann (a disciple of the natural scientist Carl von Linné), combined a Bible-oriented and contemporary rational spirituality. Henrik Schartau (1757–1825) worked in Lund from 1785. He represented an understanding of freedom quite different from the moods of rational liberalism. He emphasized Lutheran teaching on ministry and considered lay gatherings to be misguided enthusiasm. Confronting Moravian subjectivism he preached and held large catechistic sessions in Lund. His influence in Sweden is still seen after two centuries. Rather than extolling freedom, Schartau pointed to its limitations.

Two types of revivals had a more evangelical, inner character. North Swedish revivals differed in their stronger Moravianism and focus on lay people. Swedish 'readers' (läsare) from the North studied the Bible as well as Pontoppidan and

Luther. Devotional literature was a constitutive feature of their piety. Karl Olof Rosenius (1816–68) was influenced by Anglo-American contacts, especially George Scott, a Methodist preacher in Stockholm. Rosenius preached an evangelical doctrine but liberation from guilt was one of his favourite themes. He was a founding father of *Evangeliska Fosterlandstiftelsen* (1856), an organization which remained inside the Swedish Lutheran church.

In Karesuando, the northernmost congregation in Sweden, Lars Levi Lästadius (1800–61) worked from 1825 onwards. He preached orthodox Lutheranism, emphasizing confession of sin and absolution. But ideas of liberation were also apparent in the contextual and Sami element of the Lästadian movement. It spread among the Sami, increasing their self-confidence and self-esteem. Lästadius's role among the Sami might be compared to the role of Grundtvig among Danish farmers.

A conflict had built up between the Swedish revival movements and the established church, especially the high church movement in Lund. Professor (later Bishop and Archbishop) Henrik Reuterdahl (1795–1870) considered church and state in Sweden to be an insoluble unity. As Minister for Church Affairs he revived the *Conventicle Act* to stop uncontrolled lay gatherings. The action led to a polarization between the Church of Sweden and the free churches. The sharp legal reaction was later modified and the *Conventicle Act* was dissolved in 1858.

Internal problems in the revival movements meant that schisms were unavoidable. A follower of Rosenius, P. P. Waldenström (1838–1917), preached the love of Christ in the tradition of Dippel, but rejected the necessity of an objective atonement, claiming 'Atonement is not needed for the sake of God but for the sake of human beings'. His ideas led to a break with *Evangeliska Fosterland-stiftelsen*. In 1878 the Swedish Covenant Church (*Svenska missionsförbundet*) was established as a separate church.

Revival movements kindled an interest in overseas mission. Peter Fjellstedt was a Swedish pioneer for the cause. Inspired by Anglican missionary initiatives he worked with the Swiss Basel Mission. While the Swedish Mission Society had begun in 1835, Fjellstedt was instrumental in the foundation of Lund's *missionssällskap* in 1845, which later merged with Swedish Mission Society to become a Lutheran Church Mission.

Religious themes were central to Swedish literature in the 1890s – examples are Verner von Heidenstam, Gustaf Fröding and not least Selma Lagerlöf.

Finland

Inspired by Swedish revivals, Paavo Ruotsalainen (1777–1852) arose as a pietist leader in Finland. His great concern was certainty of salvation. But, with Hans Nielsen Hauge, he mediated between the church and revival, wanting to remain in the church. Other revivals occurred in Österbotten (Western Finland) and Karelen. Eventually Ruotsalainen's theology of assurance was attacked and became a source of schism in the movement.

The Rosenius-inspired preacher F. G. Hedberg followed a more evangelical orientation than Ruotsalainen, and an organization, *Lutherska evangeliförsamlingen*, was established in 1873. The organization remained inside the Finnish church.

The Twentieth Century: Democratization

Two processes run parallel in the twentieth century. Unified and monopolist Lutheran Christianity gave way to a religious plurality and a secularist environment. The resulting social change promoted an ecumenical outlook, opening the church to new relationships outside the national and cultural borders. This pluralist situation led into a basic discussion on theological identity, and different answers were given by 'orthodox' and 'liberal' theology. In relation to democracy the question was on polity: 'is the church to be governed from above or from below?' and 'are ordinary believers or ordained office holders to govern the future of the church bodies?'

Denmark

In Denmark the democratization process and its subsequent effect on church polity has been stronger and more marked than the identity debate on liberal or orthodox theology. A result of democratization – led by the Danish Liberal party – was the establishment of congregational boards (*menighedsråd*) in 1903. All rituals were revised around 1900 and the Grundtvigian influence was particularly visible. The Danish church retained its basically congregational character, and might rightly be characterized, as argued by the distinguished church historian Hal Koch, as 'well-ordered anarchy'. When, in 1946, a congregation wanted a woman minister a theological confrontation came to the surface which serves as the Danish model. Amid protests from Internal Mission and the majority of clergy, ordination of the first woman took place in 1948.

After a liberal and humanist theology prevailing in Denmark before the First World War, a Barthian or dialectical theology trend appeared. In the 1920s a group of angry young church leaders attacked liberal theology and other factions in the Danish folk church. They took their name from the periodical *Tidehverv* and have remained a unique radical and objectivist presence in Danish theology and church life. Danish theology, subsequently, has basically followed German traditions. The influence of Grundtvig and Kierkegaard remain powerful (at least in the churches) but not central. The position of Grundtvig is confirmed after celebration of the second centenary of his birth in 1983. Interest in Kierkegaard has also increased – a centre for Kierkegaard studies in Copenhagen was established in 1993. Kaj Munck, who was killed by the Nazis during the war, was a disciple of Kierkegaard and interpreted Christianity as martyrdom in his spirit.

Barthian thought was strong in the 1950s and 1960s, the ethical theology of Niels Hansen Søe (1895–1978) providing an illustration. During the 1960s and 1970s ecumenism was well represented by Kristen Skydsgaard (1902–90) and Leif Grane (1918–). The theological faculty of Århus University (founded 1942) has provided fresh Danish contributions to theology. K. E. Løgstrup has argued for an ethics based on a universal awareness while Regin Prenter and his colleague Johannes Aagaard emerged as original Danish missiologists. Prenter was one of the first Scandinavian theologians to give interreligious dialogue a theological rationale. Aagaard has been a committed critic of neoreligious 'guruism'. A group devoted to interreligious dialogue, 'Ikon', emerged from the circle around Johannes Aagaard in 1992.

Non-Lutheran Protestants are still a minority in Denmark. The largest group is the Danish Baptist Fellowship with 6,000 members.

Norway

The general transition to a democratic church government in Norway has not been smooth. The war situation from 1940 to 1945 was an exception to the normal church order. Bishop Bergreav emerged as the ecumenical church leader in the confrontation with Nazism. The 1942 document *Kirkens grunn* expressed the right of a church to protest against state autocracy (albeit in the context of the war) and yet the state church system was maintained to the turn of the millennium. The government appoints bishops and provosts. Appointment of priests, however, is now left with diocesan councils (*bispedømmeråd*). The responsibilities of congregational councils, established in 1920, has increased. Since 1969 Norway has had an independent Church Council (*kyrkjeråd*). A further move away from the state, a Church Assembly (*kyrkjemøte*) with the final decision in spiritual matters and ecclesiastical policies, was established in 1984. The positions of bishops as well as of the government are thus weakened parallel to the growing importance of democratic organs.

The first decades of the century, however, were marked by questions of a theological nature. As a protest against the instalment of a liberal professor in dogmatics at Oslo University, the private Lutheran School of Theology (*Det teologiske menighetsfakultet*) was established in 1908. Professor Ole Hallesby, whose background was the conservative Erlängen theology, became its dominant teacher. As a church politician he worked to exclude liberals from positions in the church. A confrontation took place in 1953 when Bishop Schelderup attacked Hallesby for preaching the doctrine of hell in a radio broadcast. The discussion flared and was formally brought to a conclusion by a decision in the Norwegian parliament admitting room for different interpretations of the doctrine. This, however, was eclipsed by the issue of the ordination of women. Schelderup ordained the first woman to the priesthood in 1961.

Norway has fostered a few theologians of outstanding quality, such as the Old Testament scholar Sigmund Movinckel, who developed a cultic interpretation of the *Psalms*. The missionary Karl Ludvig Reichelt (1877–1952) contributed towards a Christian understanding of Buddhism by his writings and work among Buddhist monks in China.

During the twentieth century Bible translations appeared in the Norwegian language for the first time since the Reformation. The Orientalist Alexander Seippel (1851–1938) produced unique New Norwegian translations utilizing ideas later found in theologies of liberation. Hymnody has continued in the tradition of Magnus Brostup Landstad and Elias Blix. Among noted contributors are Anders Hovden, Svein Ellingsen and Arve Brunvoll.

The Norwegian Mission Society and the Norwegian Lutheran Mission are the strongest mission organizations with church-founding work in Africa and Asia. The two organizations have a critical attitude to the World Council of Churches. The Christian Mission to Buddhists has provided a special Nordic contribution in the field of interreligious dialogue.

In 1992 the membership of the state church was 88 per cent of the total population (4.2 million). Although only about 3 per cent attend church every Sunday, 80 per cent of the population are baptized and confirmed and about 55 per cent are married in the church. The church cares for 95 per cent of funerals. The figures demonstrate the varied influence of secularization on church traditions. Other Protestant churches are markedly of a minority character: the Lutheran Free Church has about 50,000 members, Pentecostals about 40,000, Methodists about 18,000 and Baptists about 12,000.

Iceland

In 1918 Iceland became an independent republic. The former Danish-Icelandic Lutheran state church model was initially governed by the Icelandic Department of Religion. However, a Church Council was established in 1931 and from 1957 a Church Assembly, with certain administrative authority, was formed. Iceland has one diocese with its bishop residing in Reykjavik. There are extra bishops for Skálholt and Hólar. The bishop is chosen by a body consisting of church ministers and lay people. The first woman priest was ordained in 1974.

Liberal theology came to Iceland in the beginning of the twentieth century, represented by the learned Bishop Jon Helgason. Icelandic liberal theology was open to spiritism during and after the Second World War, and Professor Haraldur Nielsson was a dynamic spokesman for spiritualist theology. Critical views of this Icelandic theological tradition have been expressed, influenced by the Danish Internal Mission. The YMCA and YWCA movements came early to Iceland and constitute a large lay organization in cooperation with the Norwegian Lutheran Mission. Membership of the Icelandic national church includes 92.4 per cent of Icelanders, while the majority of nonmembers belong to the Lutheran Free Church.

Sweden

The Church of Sweden was the first Nordic church to disestablish the state church system. Various church councils (*kyrkomötet*) have central authority within the church. The Bishops' Council convenes annually and has a role in preparing the church assembly. The role of bishops has been diminished by the democratic election of congregational councils, cathedral chapters and the church assembly. Political parties, in turn, present lists of candidates for election to the national church boards. The church has three boards of national significance: the Mission Board, the Board of Diakonia and the Board for Swedish Church Overseas. A majority of representatives to the church boards are selected on lists presented by ordinary political parties. But at times nonpolitical groups successfully present lists of candidates for election.

A high church faction opposed the 1958 decision to admit women for ministry. The first woman to be ordained in the Church of Sweden was Margit Sahlin (1960). Ministers who refuse to recognize women as ministers in the church are currently barred from ordination in the Church of Sweden.

A dominating personality in the Swedish church during the last century has been Professor and later Archbishop Nathan Söderblom (1866–1931). Influenced by Ritschl and Harnack, he fought uncompromisingly for the freedom of research. Noted contributions to theology are his 1903 work *Uppenbarelsereligion* (Revealed Religion) and his struggle for ecumenical unity, as manifested in the first Universal Conference on Life and Work which met in Stockholm in 1925. The 1925 meeting, in turn, reflects the 1895 initiation of the Student Christian Movement in Vadstena. The Church of Sweden has consistently promoted ecumenical work. In 1968 an ecumenical congress was arranged in Uppsala. The relationship to the Anglican Church has been especially notable.

Einar Billing was a representative of the so-called 'young church' movement (*ungkyrkorörelsen*) and he emphasized the religious dimensions of the folk church. A breakthrough of a more doctrinally conservative ecclesiastical theology was originated by Bo Giertz, Bishop in Western Sweden (Göteborg 1949–70).

The Lund theologians exerted a strong influence, and Anders Nygren was a dominating figure. Dialectical in character, Nygren contrasted the Christian idea of *agape* with the Greek concept of *eros*. Gustav Wingren promoted a creation-oriented theology reminiscent of the Grundtvigian Dane Løgstrup. Wingren, in particular, opposed the objectivist methodology of the Uppsala philosopher Ingemar Hedenius. The Pentecostal expansion in Sweden, led by the charismatic preacher Lewi Pethrus (1884–1974), has been exceptional. The Word of Life movement (*Livets ord*), with its centre in Uppsala, saw a dynamic period under the leadership of Ulf Ekman in the 1980s and 1990s. The movement has an international network and is especially committed to mission in the previous Soviet Union.

In 1997 85.3 per cent of Swedes were members of the Lutheran Church of Sweden, 78.4 per cent of newborn babies were baptized and 49.7 per cent confirmed. In the same year 91,939 Swedes were registered as Pentecostals, the largest Protestant group outside the Swedish Church. There are 70,000 members of Swedish Covenant Mission.

Finland

The question of church and state was first raised by the Social Democrats in 1903, but was soon removed from the political agenda. After Finnish independence (1917) state tensions between the conservative political right and revolutionary left were reflected in the church. Generally, the church sided with the right in the civil war that occurred at the time of independence. A religious freedom act in 1922 extended the right to establish independent churches and also the right for individuals to declare themselves as having no religious affiliation. Self-governance for Finnish folk churches was granted only in 1973 with the establishment of a central supreme Church Council. The members of the Church Council are selected democratically.

The Finnish tension between folk church spirituality and evangelical revivalism remains. During the Second World War Finland became isolated from other Nordic countries due to its comradeship with Germany in fighting the Sovjet Union. The Finnish Lutheran Church, likewise, had supported the patriotic struggle against Bolshevik Russia. Nonetheless, Christian concern for social issues were confirmed by the war experience and continued to be a source of contention after the war. The military chaplain Erki Niinivaara (1907–85) developed a theology of social concern related to the teaching of Gustav Wingren. Internal mission organizations took a critical stand against this type of theology. The Evangelical Lutheran Internal Mission Society, led by Urko Muromaa (1890–1966), and neorevivalist movements such as The Evangelical Lutheran Folk Mission of Finland (1967) expressed criticism of such a socially and culturally open theology. A sharp opponent of Niinivaara was Osmo Tiililä (1904–1972), a Professor of Systematic Theology. Eventually Tiililä left the Lutheran Church of Finland. Finally, after 30 years of controversy, in 1986 the Supreme Church Council allowed ordination of women in the Lutheran Folk Church.

During the twentieth century, Finland has produced some remarkable church architecture. Examples include the postfunctionalist Chapel of Resurrection in Turku (1940), the 'formless church' in Vuoksenniska (1958) and the Tampere Kaleva Church (1966). Another Finnish modern contribution is the *Thomas Mass* – engaging new groups of people in an active and participatory church liturgy. A new hymnal was produced in 1984 and a new translation of the Bible in 1992.

Finnish theologians have developed a Lutheran-based research dialogue in close contact with Orthodox theology. As such, broad contacts with Russian Orthodoxy have emerged and are noteworthy. For example, Professor Seppo Teinonen (1924–95) pioneered a method of systematic theological concern for ecumenism and missiology, which has been continued by Professor Mannermaa at Helsinki University. A substantial ecumenical achievement took place in the Finnish diocese of Porvoo in 1992, with the issue of the *Porvoo Common Statement* (Council for Christian Unity, 1993). It expressed the visible unity of Anglican churches in the UK and the Nordic and Baltic Lutheran churches.

About 85 per cent of Finns are members of the Evangelical Lutheran Church. Among the minority Protestant churches Pentecostals are the largest group with 50,000 members.

References

The Council for Christian Unity of the General Synod of the Church of England (1993). *The Porvoo Common Statement Conversations between the British and Irish Anglican Churches and the Nordic and Baltic Lutheran Churches & Essays on Church and Ministry in Northern Europe*, Occasional Paper 3. London: Church House Publishing.

Further Reading

Brohed, Ingmar (ed.) (1996). *Church and People in Britain and Scandinavia*. Biblioteca Historico-Ecclesiastica Lundnsis 36. Lund: Lund University Press.

Grell, Ole Peter (1995). *The Scandinavian Reformation from Evangelical Movements to Institutionalisation of Reform*. Cambridge, UK: Cambridge University Press.

Hope, Nicholas (1995). *German and Scandinavian Protestantism 1700–1918*. Oxford: Oxford University Press.

Österlin, Lars (1995). *Churches of Northern Europe in Profile. A Thousand Years of Anglo-Nordic Relations*. Norwich, UK: The Canterbury Press.

CHAPTER 11

Protestantism in the Netherlands to the Present Day

Peter van Rooden

The present-day Netherlands emerged as a political entity in the last quarter of the sixteenth century. The new state was the haphazard result of internal political upheavals and the fortunes of international war. Religion was deeply involved with the crisis that shattered the unity of the territories north of France and west of the Empire that the Habsburg family had patiently gathered during the fifteenth and the first half of the sixteenth centuries. Conversely, the political outcome of what became known as 'the Revolt' determined not only the religious settlement of the Dutch Republic but also the religious identities of the people living in the shattered Habsburg Netherlands. This close relation between political and religious developments has endured to the present.

Early Protestants and the Dutch Revolt

When the Revolt broke out, Protestantism in the Netherlands had been fairly effectively kept at bay for 50 years. Whatever compromises Charles V was willing to make with Protestants in the Empire, he was not prepared to accept religious dissent in the territories he had inherited. It was not that there was little interest in reform or rebellion. Erasmian and Lutheran conceptions had, from an early date, been absorbed by clergy, schoolteachers and artisans. These dissidents met in small groups to discuss the Bible and its interpretation. They were supported by a flood of heterodox books, mostly published in Antwerp.

Anabaptism, a much more popular movement, had emerged in the wake of Melchior Hoffman's preaching in 1530. Dutch Anabaptists were deeply involved in the Münster revolution. In the Netherlands too, they engaged in direct political acts: for instance, attacking the city hall of Amsterdam in 1535. They were fiercely persecuted and effectively suppressed. It was only in the 1550s that

Anabaptist circles re-emerged, most of them influenced by the pacifist message of Menno Simons. In these same years the Reformed movement started to build churches in the south. Their churches had consistories and, from the early 1560s onwards, there were attempts at a synodal organization modelled on the French Huguenots. The Reformed church was strongly influenced by Calvinism, but other Reformed influences were important as well: the Heidelberger Catechism was translated into Dutch in 1563 and reprinted at least 60 times before 1585.

In the 1560s a general revolt broke out against the centralizing policies of the Brussels government of the Habsburg Netherlands. Twenty years later, political and military vicissitudes had resulted in a new and independent political entity in the North, which had introduced the Reformation in its Reformed variety, standing over against the southern provinces of the Habsburg Netherlands – which had been reconquered by Spanish troops and where Protestantism had effectively been wiped out by a militant counter-Reformation. The now Protestant Dutch Republic would remain at war with Spain and the Southern Netherlands till 1648.

The Dutch Republic as a Confessional State

The fundamentals of the religious geography of the Netherlands were determined between 1600 and 1625. In a 20 to 40 mile wide belt right behind the front lines, stretching from the south-west to the north-east through the middle of the present-day Netherlands, no attempts at Catholic reorganization were tolerated. The Reformed church in these areas was closely allied with public authority, and subject to an almost completely Erastian regime. All inhabitants of this area were reckoned to belong to the Reformed church, and over time it became homogeneously Protestant. The areas to the south and east of this Protestant belt that were conquered by the armies of the Dutch Republic after 1625 – Twente, Brabant and Limburg – have remained solidly Catholic to the present day. Confessional identity in these areas had been strengthened over two generations, and the Republic was never able to suppress all Catholic organization there.

A highly original religious order developed in a third area, north and west of the 'Protestant belt', in the provinces of Holland, Utrecht and part of Friesland. Here, from a very early date, political authorities had allowed the re-establishing of Catholicism. The Mennonites, the peaceful successors to the violent Anabaptists of the 1530s, also found most of their adherents here. Following the phenomenal economic expansion of the Dutch Republic, this was the area where Lutheran churches and Jewish synagogues were established, organizing immigrants from the Iberian peninsula, Germany, Scandinavia and eastern Europe.

In this core area of the Dutch Republic the Reformed Church, too, enjoyed the most liberty. It could engage in various conflicts about its confession and public status. Theologically, these conflicts have been interpreted as a process by which conceptions stemming from other centres of Reformed Protestantism, such as Heidelberg and Zürich, were slowly excluded in favour of the strict Calvinism as taught in Geneva. The process culminated in a fierce conflict about predestination between two Leiden professors of theology, Jacobus Arminius and Franciscus Gomarus. In the second decade of the seventeenth century, during a truce in the war with Spain, all of the many political conflicts within the young Republic became clustered around this theological debate and the Republic was brought to the brink of civil war. In 1618–19, after the victory of their political allies, the followers of Gomarus used the Synod of Dordrecht to commit the public church of the Republic to a mitigated version of the doctrine of double predestination, which henceforth would remain a hallmark of orthodox Calvinism, distinguishing it from Arminianism.

In the course of the seventeenth century, the religious order of the Dutch Republic stabilized into a peculiar form of the confessional state. The Reformed Church had a monopoly on public expressions and manifestations of religion. It was supported by political authority, and was financed from public funds. Public office could not be held by those who were members of other religious groups. On the other hand, no laws forced people to attend the services of the public church or to take part in its rituals. Marriages could legitimately be contracted before the civil magistrate. Baptism was not obligatory, although it seems to have been generally sought. With some misgivings, the Reformed Church generally baptized all children, but it accepted as full members only those who were willing to make a public confession of faith and to submit to its discipline. Over time, all those who did not explicitly belong to other religious groups were considered to be Reformed. The confessional nature of the Dutch Republic rested upon the toleration of other religious groups, who were always accorded a lower social status.

Organizationally, religious groups were among the main building blocks of the local worlds of the Dutch Republic. In cities such as Amsterdam or Leiden, Reformed, Lutherans, Jews, Mennonites, Arminians and Catholics were important elements of the local political economy. Socially, religion in the mature Dutch Republic tended to be produced in the form of a public order, accommodating the hierarchical nature of these local political worlds. Both in word and deed, discursively and practically, creating and sustaining early-modern Dutch Christianity boiled down to strengthening social hierarchies. The existence of different religious groups, the famous 'toleration' of the Dutch Republic, was part and parcel of this social production of Christianity in the form of a public order. The Reformed Church was most visible and 'public', with the 'tolerated' Dissenters much less so, and the 'conniving' Catholics not allowed to show themselves at all. Ideologically, the public Reformed Church rested upon a massively detailed intellectual orthodoxy, defined at the Synod of Dordrecht, and defended by university-based theologians, jealously guarding the public sphere they represented. There were vigorous theological debates in the seventeenth- and eighteenth-century Netherlands, but they all took the form of a judicial-like determination of the borders of the legitimate public sphere, deeply intertwined with political power.

The Protestant Nation

This Dutch confessional state was challenged by the emergence of an enlightened sociability and the rise of cultural nationalism from the 1750s onwards. Both developments tended to stress the importance of moral individuals over against social and political hierarchies, and could easily integrate pietistic notions. An indigenous revolution in the 1780s was suppressed, but in 1795 French armies installed these defeated revolutionaries as caretakers of a satellite state. They overhauled the decentralized Dutch Republic and made it into a modern nation state on the French model. The Kingdom of the Netherlands, installed after the fall of Napoleon, inherited the new national bureaucracy of the revolutionaries and immediately reorganized all churches to involve them in the task of nation building and creating citizens. As this fitted in quite nicely with several evangelical and liturgical initiatives aimed at creating Christian individuals that the churches had undertaken during the revolutionary years, there was very little opposition to this political project.

Socially, religion in the new Kingdom of the Netherlands was produced in the form of individual believers, members of the moral community of the nation. The state and the churches invested heavily in religious mass education. Ideologically, Christianity was depicted as a simple moral conviction, which every individual could attain, and which was to be propagated in a public sphere open to all. This notion had already been used to justify the revolutionary separation of church and state, undertaken in 1796: all religious groups are equal, as they all attempt to inculcate the inner piety that is the core of the moral life of the responsible citizen.

This new notion of the function of Protestantism also justified the way in which the Dutch state treated the overwhelming mass of its citizens as objects to be improved and transformed. Religion was the most important means by which this educational relation between the state and its citizens was expressed. This legitimization of political inequality was based as much upon practice as upon ideology. During the first three-quarters of the nineteenth century, the Dutch Protestant churches, supported by the state-sponsored primary education system, engaged in an unprecedented process of religious education, even as it confirmed the processes of cultural class formation which formed the basis of the new Dutch nation state. The ideal of the nation as a community of moral individuals was considered to be the true expression of Protestantism.

Protestantism, Mass Politics and the Welfare State

In 1834, secession (*Afscheiding*) took place within the former unified 'public' church. Six (of almost 1,500) ministers, five of them quite young, set up a new organization. They harked back to the Calvinist doctrine upheld by the public church of the Republic, yet it is also clear that they gained adherents by tapping into popular discursive notions about ministers not being really pious, but only learned. The contemporary character of the secessionist movement becomes clearer in light of the fierce reactions it provoked. The secessionists unequivocally threw into question the close links between citizenship, knowledge and piety that formed the basis of the order of the new Dutch kingdom. In response the Dutch government quartered troops with families that had seceded, dismissed schoolteachers and other public servants who joined the movement, and in general did its utmost to make their lives miserable. Many, as a result, emigrated to the USA. Still, the movement grew at an amazing rate, gaining the adherence of 4–5 per cent of all Dutch people in the 1880s.

During the 1870s and 1880s, with the emergence of modern mass politics in the Netherlands, the higher levels of Dutch Protestantism – the universities, the main cities and the higher organizational levels of the church – polarized both ecclesiastically and politically. Ecclesiastically, the conflicts involved the emergence, from the early 1860s, of modernist theological notions developed at Leiden University, denying miracles and the doctrine that the Scriptures are inspired. The nature of religious education in the primary school system became a politically divisive issue from 1857. This ongoing polarization in the second half of the nineteenth century resulted in a new geographical structure, opposing orthodox and liberal Protestant areas, superimposed upon the much older contrast between Protestant and Catholic areas, and enduring to the present day.

Abraham Kuyper (1837–1920), a Leiden-trained theologian who became an orthodox minister and later a journalist and national politician, decisively influenced the nature of both these conflicts. Kuyper was a superb agitator and mobilizer, and a natural-born mass politician. Better than anyone else in the Netherlands he understood both the strength of mass politics and the necessity of dramatic political stances to engender mass support. The most important way in which he convinced his followers of the importance of their struggle was by presenting them with a new view of history. He described Dutch history as an ongoing struggle between three principles: Catholicism, Calvinism and liberal humanism. The essential element of this historical view was its dramatic appeal. Dutch national life was depicted as a struggle between radically different principles. Kuyper's movement, true to its modern nature, was very vague about its ultimate ends, shifting them according to short-term political successes or failures. It is clear that for some time the neo-Calvinist movement was considered to be a possible alternative way to organize Dutch Protestantism in its entirety, taking over the former public church and driving out the liberals. At the end of the 1880s, however, it became clear that this would not happen. Instead, Kuyper led his followers out of the former public church, joining with the larger part of the churches that had issued from the *Afscheiding* and setting up the new, neo-Calvinist *Gereformeerde Kerken in Nederland*. This decisively shattered the unity of the Protestant nation.

From the beginning, Kuyper had resolutely decided to forego any attempt at reforming the public school system in an orthodox Protestant direction. Instead, he opted for confessional schools to be established apart from the public school system. His concentration on this issue conferred a supreme strategic advantage. It made possible an alliance with the Catholics, who wanted confessional schools of their own, the basis of the emancipation from their status as second-class citizens. Kuyper's interpretation of the Dutch nation as made up of three different groups offered an excellent justification for this strategy. Although it was a huge slap in the face for all those Protestants – liberal and orthodox – who had identified the nation with Protestantism, it made possible the devaluation of the public school as no more than an instrument of a particular group and interest. At the same time it justified the alliance of Catholics and orthodox Protestants, whose wishes for separate schools accorded with the divided nature of the nation.

Elsewhere in Europe, such ideological ghettos had emerged as well, for example the Socialist and Catholic movements in Germany. In the Netherlands, these ghettos took over the nation, almost eclipsing the notion of a common citizenship. What elsewhere were minority movements and subcultures, in the Netherlands became 'pillars' (*zuilen*). The term, although fairly late (post-Second World War), perfectly expresses the notion that the Netherlands was made up of several distinctive ideological groups, which together supported the nation, and that one belonged to the nation by belonging to one of these groups.

The 'pacification' of 1917 which ended the political struggles between liberal and confessional parties was, in reality, a clear-cut confessional victory. It rested upon the introduction of universal suffrage and the equal public financing of public, Catholic and Protestant primary schools. The introduction of universal suffrage introduced a period of more than 50 years in which Christian political parties would poll more than half of the vote. During the better part of the twentieth century, religion was a more important aspect of social identity in the Netherlands than class or region. Organizationally, Christianity was promoted by means of all the elements of modern social life: schools and universities, journals and magazines, mass political parties, associations and cultural organizations, organized sports and cultural activities, trade unions and employers' organizations. Socially, twentieth-century Dutch Christianity was thoroughly ethnicized. Being an orthodox Protestant or Catholic was a matter of birth, and over time both identities were physically inscribed: for example, by the 1950s the Dutch could ascertain each other's religious' identity at a glance or by a person's speech. Intellectually, Christianity had become an ideology, a total conception of the whole world and of all history from a self-conscious partisan viewpoint, meant to engage people in a social movement.

The former public church had been badly shaken by the Kuyperian secession of the 1880s and even more by the emergence of the pillarized society, which shattered its pretentions to be the national (*vaderlandse*) church. After the Second World War, there was a sudden surge for renewal, which allied itself with the new welfare state and, though less explicitly, with the Socialists, who had shed their German orientation and looked instead towards the modernizing British Labour Party. In a dizzying surge of renewal, social engineering by the state and modern American management techniques were enthusiastically embraced as a way to overcome the inefficient and non-Christian pillarized society. The not-so-secret hope was to put the Catholics and neo-Calvinists in their place.

The modern Dutch welfare state, established in the 1960s, did indeed break the power of the pillars, but it did not fulfil the hopes of the former public church. The restored social and moral unity of the nation resulted in a period of acute dechristianization. More than half of Dutch people living at the end of the twentieth century did not reckon themselves to belong to any church. Those who did were less involved with their churches than ever before. The main Dutch Protestant churches, the former national church, the Kuyperian neo-Calvinists, and the Lutherans were in an interminable process of reunion, all the while suffering a massive haemorrhage of members. Orthodox Calvinists, descendants of those followers of the 1834 *Afscheiding* who had not joined up with Kuyper, had since the 1970s built up their own organizational world, in the wake of the collapse of the Protestant pillar. Yet this new Protestant world was no longer a pillar. It was not one of several building blocks of the Dutch nation, but a ghetto. Many of its children are escaping this sect by joining the Evangelical movement in the Netherlands, which holds out a promise of a warm piety that is not linked with a total social world and a particular and restrictive lifestyle. Dutch Evangelicalism and Pentecostalism finds it hard, though, to attract members from outside this fairly limited market of the youth of reorganized orthodox Protestantism.

Bibliographical Information

Augustijn's (1994) article "Niederlande" describes the history of Christianity in the territory of the modern Netherlands from the early Middle Ages to the present day. His interpretation of the early Dutch Reformation and the events leading up to the Synod of Dordrecht is still authoritative. The article offers an extensive bibliography. Jonathan Israel's massive *The Dutch Republic* (1995) is very good on day-to-day politics and religion, especially during the seventeenth century. R. Po-Chia Hsia and Henk van Nierop (2002) offers the most recent work on the religious diversity of the Republic. No English language book on the social history of Dutch religion in the eighteenth century exists, but there is a marvellous intellectual history of the period in Joris van Eijnatten's *Liberty and Concord in the United Provinces* (2003). Michael Wintle's (1985) *Pillars of Piety* offers a competent interpretation of nineteenth century Dutch church history, while van Rooden (2003) contains a more political interpretation.

References

Augustijn, Cees (1994). Niederlande. In Gerhard Krause & Gerhrad Müller (eds.), *Theologische Realenzyklopädie*, vol. 24. Berlin: Walter de Gruyter, pp. 474–502.

Israel, Jonathan (1995). *The Dutch Republic: Its Rise, Greatness and Fall, 1477–1806*. Oxford: Clarendon Press.

Po-Chia Hsia, R. and van Nierop, Henk (eds.) (2002). *Calvinism and Religious Toleration in the Dutch Golden Age*. Cambridge, UK: Cambridge University Press.

van Eijnatten, Joris (2003). *Liberty and Concord in the United Provinces: Religious Toleration and the Public in the Eighteenth-Century Netherlands*. Leiden: Brill.

van Rooden, Peter (2003). Long-term Religious Developments in the Netherlands, 1750–2000. In Hugh McLeod & W. Ustorf (eds.), *The Decline of Christendom in Western Europe, 1750–2000*. Cambridge, UK: Cambridge University Press, pp. 113–29.

Wintle, Michael (1985). *Pillars of Piety: Religion in the Netherlands in the Nineteenth Century, 1813–1901*. Hull, UK: Hull University Press.

CHAPTER 12

Protestantism in Eastern Europe to the Present Day

Parush Parushev and Toivo Pilli

Any researcher addressing the issue of the development of Protestantism in Eastern Europe is faced with at least two difficulties. The first is to define 'Eastern Europe' and the second is to decide how Protestantism is to be understood.

The area that is called Eastern Europe in geopolitical terms today has quite a complex historical development and this is reflected in its Protestant history and development. In the context of Protestantism, the Baltic countries of Estonia, Latvia, and Lithuania had long-standing cultural and religious contacts with the Nordic countries, specifically Sweden. In the seventeenth and eighteenth centuries, the Baltic region also experienced the robust presence of both Prussia and imperial Russia. The traditional Central-Eastern European peoples of present-day Poland, Czech Republic, Slovakia, Hungary, the Transylvanian area of Romania, Croatia, and Slovenia are part of Western European development as dominated by the Austro-Hungarian Empire and its history. Roman Catholicism and its opposition are dominant themes here. The cultural and religious life of Russia, Belarus, Ukraine, Bessarabia, and the Caucasian peoples in the last two centuries has been inseparably tied to the historical development of Russia. Part of this history is the interaction with the Orthodox Church. Finally, Protestantism in the so-called Balkan states of Romania, Bulgaria, Bosnia and Herzegovina, Serbia and Montenegro, Macedonia, Albania, Greece, and Turkey took root and developed under the dominance of the Islamic Ottoman Empire.

The term 'Protestant' itself also has diverse content. In the Eastern European context it includes Lutheran and Reformed Church traditions (the usual definition), but also the Hussite Church and the Evangelical Church of Czech Brethren. Moreover, the Anabaptists, through German Mennonite and Herrnhuter communities in Russia, Estonia and old Livonia, had a formative influence for the indigenous Protestant movements. Neo-Protestants such as Baptists, Pentecostalists and Seventh Day Adventists made their way to Eastern European countries in the second half of the nineteenth century and during the first decades of the twentieth century. The list is far from complete: one could add pockets of Unitarians in Hungary and Romania; Methodists in the Baltics and the Balkans; Congregationalists in Bulgaria; and a Nazarene presence in Romania, Bulgaria and former Yugoslavia. At the end of the twentieth century an influx of missionary and charismatic movements added a further flavour to an already complex recipe.

The mosaic becomes even more colourful if one attempts to trace the development of Protestantism through the centuries. By the end of the Council of Trent in 1563 the majority in Poland, Lithuania, Bohemia and Hungary professed Protestant faith, but after the Counter-Reformation Catholicism regained its dominance. In countries such as Russia, Ukraine and Belarus Protestantism has always been a minority religion. Nevertheless, indigenous attempts at the reformation of church life in Orthodox communities in the eighteenth century resembled similar attempts in the Western part of Europe undertaken in the sixteenth century. In what follows, we will trace some of the chronological and cultural trajectories of Eastern European Protestantism.

The Beginning of Protestantism

The traditional view of the beginning of Protestantism ties it to the sixteenth-century Reformation movements. The new thinking spread rapidly into the east of Europe in the 1520s. Andreas Knopken, who had come to Livonia with a commendatory letter from Philip Melanchthon, preached reformational ideas in Riga (Latvia) as early as in 1521. The magisterial Reformation, particularly Calvinism, had a remarkable impact in (present-day) Poland, which was already influenced by humanistic and Hussite views. Königsberg University was founded in 1544, for example, in East Prussia for the training of Protestant preachers. In Hungary, Protestantism had direct ties with Martin Luther through personal contact with a prominent Reformation leader Matthias Dévai Biró (d. 1545). Even in Russia there were signs of early Protestant presence. In the mid-sixteenth century, Matthew Bashkin, probably influenced by some Lithuanian Protestants living in Moscow, was imprisoned in Volokamsk monastery for his non-Orthodox views (which also seem to have been Unitarian).

The Spread in Largely Roman Catholic Countries

Because of the Roman Catholic opposition encountered, Protestant expansion in Eastern Europe was far from smooth. The Catholic Counter-Reformation weakened Protestantism in many Central-Eastern European countries. Except for some minor remnants, the Counter-Reformation almost wiped out Protestantism in Slovenia and Croatia and certainly paralysed Protestant development in Poland. Similar histories occur in Hungary and in Bohemia and Moravia, where up to 90 per cent of the population were Protestant by the end of the sixteenth century, but this was dramatically, permanently and rapidly reversed. As a result, in present day Hungary a quarter of the population belongs to Protestant churches (primarily Lutheran and Reformed) while the majority population is Roman Catholic. Today approximately 40 per cent of Czechs are Roman Catholic and only 10 per cent belong to non-Catholic denominations (Hussite, Evangelical Church of the Czech Brethren, and others). In Poland and Lithuania, only a very small minority of the population is Protestant.

Several factors contributed to the resilience of Protestantism in certain regions. The steady growth of the German-speaking Protestant population in some areas prepared the ground for the renewal and the later growth of Protestantism in the 1800s – which was already anticipated by the previous century's pietistic influences. The renewal came when several so-called neo-Protestant, or evangelical, movements (Baptists, Seventh Day Adventists, proto-Pentecostals and others) reached Eastern Europe. In other cases the policies of tolerance (usually by 'Enlightenment' monarchs) helped to strengthen the Protestant cause in the areas with a strong Roman Catholic presence. Such was the effect of the Edict of Toleration issued by Joseph II in the Austro-Hungarian Empire in 1781.

In the nineteenth century, the migration of Hungarian, Czech, Slovak and German Protestants into the northern areas of the southern Slavs (now Slovenia, Croatia, Vojvodina), after the Ottomans were forced to withdraw, significantly contributed to the advance and later renewal of Protestantism in South-East Europe. The colporteurs of the British and Foreign Bible Society who distributed biblical literature and parts of the Bible also added to the growth of Protestantism in Poland, the Balkans and other areas.

Through American missionary activity in the first half of the nineteenth century (first launched in Beirut in 1819), Protestantism slowly penetrated the territories of south-east Europe and the Ottoman-controlled Middle East among the present peoples of Turkey, Greece, Bulgaria, Macedonia, Albania, Lebanon, Syria, Armenia, and Kurdistan. The first Protestant community (predominantly Armenian) in the Ottoman Empire was officially established by a Sultan's charter on 1 June 1840. A Protestant liberal arts college (Robert College) was founded in Istanbul in 1863, itself the product of a previous Congregational Bible school established in 1840.

The Spread in Largely Orthodox Countries

Protestant history in Eastern Europe is both well and poorly documented. While the story of Protestantism in Central-Eastern Europe is known to a certain extent, the development of Protestantism among the eastern Slavs, and the Orthodox reaction to it, is relatively unsurveyed. Lutheran and Reformed beliefs penetrated the Russian Empire through peasants, traders and craftsmen of German, Swiss or Scandinavian origin as early as the seventeenth century, but they almost never put down roots among the indigenous people. As a result, their history is left unknown and their effect unclear. After the establishment of the Moscow Duchy and the formation of the independent Russian Orthodox Church and Patriarchate (in the sixteenth century), Orthodox Christianity became the only legal form of Christianity in the vast region of Russia and Ukraine (as well as later in Belorussia and Bessarabia). Eventually there emerged groups – the Dukhobors (Spirit wrestlers) and the Molokany (milk drinkers) – who can be considered 'Protestant' in their thinking and against whom the Orthodox Church reacted. Their histories are, consequently, better documented.

The Dukhobors emphasized the role of the Holy Spirit in their theology. This, combined with their belief in nonviolence and refusal of military service, the specific grounds of persecution, have led some scholars to relate their emergence to nearby immigrant Quakers. The Molokany (most probably named for drinking milk during fasting times or the refusal of alcoholic beverages) had a strict ethical biblicism organized around the Ten Commandments and the Sermon on the Mount. Molokany spread in the Imperial lands, including Siberia, Ukraine and the Caucasus, and even emigrated to North America. By the end of the nineteenth century, most Molokany had merged with the Baptists. It is worth noting that many early Russian Evangelical Christian and Baptist leaders had Molokany backgrounds.

In the nineteenth century, some Protestant groups – pietists, Stundists and Baptists – stood out because of their moral standards, and made significant impact in aristocratic society. Protestant pietistic forms (personal conversion and devotional life), through Bible study and prayer meetings, were common in some circles of influence. One of the far-reaching results of the pietistic movement in Russia was the founding of the Russian Bible Society (1812–14), though the translation of the Bible into contemporary Russian was completed only in 1876. It should also be mentioned that the first decades of the nineteenth century saw a re-emergence of the pietistic Herrnhuter movement in some other parts of Tsarist Russia, such as the Baltic region.

In the twentieth century Baptists became the largest Protestant group in Russia and Ukraine. Baptists emerged from three sources: Pashkovism (in St Petersburg), the Stundist movement (in Ukraine), and a separate beginning in the Transcaucasus region.

Pashkovism is a result of the evangelistic meetings of 1874 held by Lord Radstock (a British nobleman who had joined the Plymouth Brethren) in St Petersburg in which some Russian nobility were converted. Most notable of the converts was Colonel V. A. Pashkov, whose advocacy of Radstockism was such that the whole movement was named after him. In their organization, at least initially, Pashkovites did not ordain leaders or baptize, but they were solely engaged in Christian literature distribution and emphasized spiritual renewal. In 1908 one Pashkovite, Ivan Prokhanov (of St Petersburg), founded the Union of Evangelical Christians. By 1922 it had grown up to 250,000 members. In its confession and its principles the Union was Baptist and it was accepted into the Baptist World Alliance.

Ukrainian Stundism, first seen in Kherson province in the early 1850s, has its roots in the pietism of German Mennonite and Lutheran colonists. The German Protestant colonists were allowed to exercise their own faith but were prohibited from proselytizing among the Orthodox. Nonetheless, their influence through Bible hours (*Stunden*) reached beyond their own community. Their doctrines and church organization as expected paralleled western Protestants in that they believed that the Bible was the only basis for faith and rejected Orthodox liturgical elements. Specifically pietistic inclinations can be seen in their abstaining from strong drink and dancing. The powerful nineteenth-century German Baptist leader Johann Gerhard Oncken (1800–84) visited Stundist communities and persuaded them to accept believer's baptism. Oncken also affected many key Mennonite leaders in Ukraine.

The third cradle of Slavonic Baptist life was the Transcaucasus area. Martin Kalweit, a German Baptist from Lithuania, founded a small Baptist community in Tiflis (now Tbilisi) in the 1860s among the Molokany. From this group Ivan Kargel (1849–1937) and Vassili Pavlov (1854–1924) emerged as two of the most influential Russian Evangelical Christian and Baptist leaders. Caucasian Baptists formed the Russian Baptist Union in 1884.

Surprisingly, at the beginning of the Bolshevik regime, the Baptist and Evangelical Christian movements saw tremendous growth. By 1929 there were approximately 500,000 adult members in both Unions of Baptists and Evangelical Christians. Adding children and family members, the figure could easily increase up to three million. However, at the end of the 1920s the favourable attitude of the Soviet government turned into severe persecution. Membership diminished drastically and wartime devastations accelerated the process. Furthermore, while Evangelical Christians and Baptists had a similar theology, attempts to join the two movements had failed until 1944 when the officially atheist government forcefully united the two groups for the purpose of effective control. The amalgamation was called the All-Union Council of Evangelical Christians-Baptists. In August 1945 Pentecostals were added to the All-Union, and in the 1960s the majority of Mennonite Brethren followed. The post-war period in the Soviet Union is characterized by Soviet government policy to allow only the Orthodox Church and one organized Protestant community to operate legally (although with some exceptions, such as Catholics, Lutherans, and Methodists). Those Protestant groups who were not willing to join the All-Union remained illegal and formed underground structures. Those who professed their legal Protestant (All-Union Churches) beliefs had severe strictures placed on their public and personal lives, including access to education and choice of career. Underground church members faced far worse.

The Future of Eastern European Protestantism

After 1945 the Communist governments of Eastern Europe largely dominated the life of Eastern European Protestant communities. That dominance is over now, but its legacy is there, reflected in the uneasy relationship between the secular state and the churches, the absence of mature structures of theological education, and a strained relationship between the Protestant groups and culturally dominant religions. At the beginning of the twenty-first century, in the widely secularized and rapidly changing Eastern European societies, a major challenge that the diverse Protestant groups face is to establish a network of cooperation and a sense of unity in mission.

Further Reading

Basse, O. and Stricker, S. (eds.) (1989). *Religionen in der UdSSR*. Zollikon, Switzerland, G2W Verlag.

Brandenburg, H. (1977). *The Meek and the Mighty: The Emergence of the Evangelical Movement in Russia*. New York: Oxford University Press.

Buscay, M. (1959). *Geschichte des Protestantismus in Ungarn*. Stuttgart: Evangelisches Verlagswerk.

Otter, J. (1970). *The Witness of Czech Protestantism*. Prague: Kalich.

Ramet, S. P. (ed.) (1992). *Protestantism and Politics in Eastern Europe and Russia: The Communist and Postcommunist Eras*. Durham, NC: Duke University Press.

Ramet, S. P. (ed.) (1993). *Religious Policy in the Soviet Union*. Cambridge, UK: Cambridge University Press.

Reshetnikov, Yu and Sannikov, S. (2000). *Obzor Istorii Evangel'skogo-Baptistkogo Bratstva na Ukraine*.Odessa: Bogomyslie.

Sannikov, S. (2001). *Dvadtsat' Vekov Hristianstva. Vtoroe Tysjacheletie, Tom II*. Odessa and St Petersburg: Bogomyslie.

Savinskii, S. N. (1999–01). *Istorija Evangel'skih Hristian-Baptistov Ukrainy, Rossii and Belorussii, Tom I (1867–1917), Tom II (1917–1967)*. St Petersburg: Biblia dlja Vseh.

Savinskii, S. N., Dyck, J. P., and Savchenko, P. D. (eds.) (1989). *Istoriia Evangel'skih Khristian-Baptistov v SSSR*. Moscow: AUCECB.

Sawatsky, W. (1981). *Soviet Evangelicals Since World War II*. Kitchener, Ontario: Herald Press.

Sawatsky, W (1986). Evangelicals in Eastern Europe Compared. *Occasional Papers on Religion in Eastern Europe* 6, 4 (August), Princeton, NJ: Princeton University Press.

Schmidt, C. (2000). *Auf Felsen gesagt: die Reformation in Polen und Livland*. Göttingen: Vandenhoeck.

CHAPTER 13

French Protestantism to the Present Day

Alister E. McGrath

The origins of Protestantism in France can be traced back to the 1520s. There is evidence of growing interest in Lutheranism around this time, particularly within the University of Paris and within sections of the royal family. John Calvin, whose family came from the Noyon area, is thought to have been influenced in the late 1520s and early 1530s, at least to some extent, by the emergent evangelical groupings in Paris and Orléans.

Significant growth took place within the French Protestant movement during the late 1550s, helped to no small extent by Calvin's patronage from Geneva. French Protestant pastors were trained in Geneva, under Calvin's guidance and protection, and smuggled into France in order to establish and develop local congregations. The origins of the term 'Huguenot', regularly used to designate French Protestants around this time, remains unclear. Rapid growth within the movement led to tensions with traditional Catholics, which exploded in the Wars of Religion. The origins of this protracted struggle date to 1562, when the Duke of Guise's supporters opened fire on Hugenots. Protestant rhetoric became increasingly revolutionary in the late 1560s, with its leading representatives advocating that Christians did not have the obligation to obey leaders who themselves defied God. Calvin himself, after advocating for many years that obedience to the civil authorities was a Christian duty, came to the conclusion that a prince who persecuted the church had forfeited his right to be obeyed. A new phase of hostility was opened up with the St Bartholomew's Day Massacre (1572), in which an entire generation of Huguenot leaders were massacred. This event prompted the predominantly Protestant town of La Rochelle to refuse to pay taxes to the French crown, provoking further hostilities. Eventually, the Edict of Nantes (1598) offered a degree of security to French Protestants, establishing certain centres as 'safe havens' for Huguenots. The revocation of this edict in 1685 by Louis XIV brought an end to this period of toleration, and caused many Huguenots to seek refuge abroad, especially in England.

Protestantism now became a minority faith within France, characterized by the watchword *savoir resister*. Although the suspension of persecution in 1763 offered Protestants relative security, this proved short-lived. The French Revolution (1789) brought new hostility to all forms of Christianity within France, including Protestantism. The subsequent restoration of Roman Catholicism (1801) brought few tangible benefits to Protestants. The increasingly secular attitude of the French republic after 1905 led to a reduction in tension between Protestants and Catholics. Although making up only 2 per cent of the population in the year 2000, French Protestants such as Lionel Jospin and Jacques Ellul have distinguished themselves in the fields of political life and theological engagement.

Further Reading

Ligou, Daniel (1968). *Le protestantisme en France, 1598–1715*. Paris: Société d'Edition d'Enseignement Superieur.

Poland, Burdette C. (1957). *French Protestantism and the French Revolution: A Study in Church and State, Thought and Religion, 1685–1815*. Princeton, NJ: Princeton University Press.

Van Kley, Dale K. (1996). *The Religious Origins of the French Revolution: From Calvin to the Civil Constitution, 1560–1791*. New Haven, CT: Yale University Press.

CHAPTER 14

Italian Protestantism to the Present Day

Alister E. McGrath

Evangelical attitudes were widespread within the Italian church of the 1520s and 1530s, with a number of leading Italian churchmen reflecting various degrees of sympathy towards the reforming agenda of Martin Luther. However, the increasingly politicization of Italian church life in the 1540s led to a growing perception that any degree of sympathy with Protestantism was tantamount to disloyalty to Rome, and a corresponding disinclination to engage with the Protestant agenda. By 1565, Protestantism had virtually been eliminated from Italy as a serious threat to Roman Catholicism. It was only in 1848 that Protestants were finally given their religious freedom, along with Jews. This critical development led to a revival within Italian Protestantism. New congregations were established, both within traditional indigenous Protestant communities (especially the Waldenses) and churches whose origins are to be traced to Anglo-American influence, such as the Methodists and Baptists. The Facoltà Valdese di Teologia was founded in 1855 near Turin, and in 1920 transferred to a site in Rome close to the Vatican.

Today, Protestants account for less than 1 per cent of the Italian population, predominantly consisting of Pentecostal and charismatic groupings, existing uneasily alongside the older traditional denominations. In recent years, complex patterns of immigration from Eastern Europe has led to a modest expansion in the Protestant population, with an increasing number of Protestants being of non-Italian origin. The authoritative *Enciclopedia delle religioni in Italia* (2001) distinguishes nearly one hundred different strands within modern Italian Protestantism, leading to the conclusion that the movement is at present both fragmented and inherently fissiparous.

References

Introvigno, Massimo (ed.) (2001). *Enciclopedia delle religioni in Italia*. Turin: Elledici.

Further Reading

End, Thomas van den (1969). *Paolo Geymonat e il movimento evangelico in Italia nella seconda metà del secolo XIX*. Turin: Editrice Claudiana.

Comba, Emilio (1950). *Storia dei Valdesi*. Torre Pellice: Claudiana.

Tedeschi, John A. (1999). *The Protestant Reformation in Sixteenth-Century Italy*. Kirksville, MO: Thomas Jefferson University Press.

CHAPTER 15

Protestantism in the United States of America to the Present Day

John Corrigan

Protestantism Comes to America

Protestantism arrived in America a century after Roman Catholicism, but to a region of the New World that had been left largely unexplored by the Spanish and French. The strings of missions established by the enterprising friars in the borderlands of New Spain from Florida to California, and the French explorations of the St Lawrence valley, Great Lakes, and Mississippi River valley framed the English (and other nations') colonial ventures on the eastern seaboard, but did not immediately challenge them. Accordingly, the seventeenth-century growth of Protestantism in America was largely unimpeded by Roman Catholic interests, and in the eighteenth century, when frictions between French and English colonies became more pronounced, they were brought decisively to a halt by the French cession to England of all territories east of the Mississippi (excluding New Orleans) in the Treaty of Paris (1763). Protestantism, in short, rooted easily in an American soil that was a world apart from the religious strife in Europe, from the monumental bloodletting of the sixteenth- and seventeenth-century religious wars between Catholics and Protestants.

The Puritan settlement of New England, which began in 1620 and produced relatively stable sustainable communities by the mid-1630s, was grounded in a lively and committed Protestantism. Opting for the Atlantic crossing in order to escape persecution in England, Puritans brought with them a devotion to the Bible, respect for the clergy, the cultivation of modesty and simplicity in every-day life, and an emphasis on spiritual rebirth, or conversion. They also imagined their migration to America as a commission from God. Casting their relationship with God in terms of a covenant, they pledged themselves to the ideal of pure religious communities, "holy commonwealths," and they surmised that God would protect and strengthen those communities inasmuch as Puritans were diligent in cultivating piety and policing morality.

John Cotton, a Cambridge-trained minister whose preaching led to many conversions among the early English settlers of New England, took the lead in articulating the theology of the Puritan communities, particularly with regard to pressing questions about baptism, clerical authority, church government, and the moral life (e.g., *The Way of the Churches of Christ in New England*, 1645). A coauthor of the defining document of the New England Way, the Cambridge Platform of 1649, Cotton stressed faith in God as the key to salvation. He was not the only minister in New England, however, and his was not the only voice. Debate frequently broke out among laypeople and clerics alike over some of the central theological themes of Puritanism. In one of these cases, Anne Hutchinson, a highly educated and theologically informed follower of Cotton who arrived in New England shortly after him in 1634, publicly protested against what she believed to be religious doctrine that valued good deeds, or "works," over faith in God. Labeled an antinomian (i.e., "against" the "laws of moral conduct") for her insistence that only God knows the elect and that good works were no sure indication of salvation, she was summoned to a court of ministers to explain her theological views. Unsuccessful in defending herself, she was excommunicated by her church in 1638, and she left the colony for Rhode Island.

Rhode Island, where Hutchinson lived briefly before removing herself to Long Island Sound, had been founded in 1636 by Roger Williams, who had also fallen foul of the Massachusetts authorities for his unorthodox views, in his case regarding the relation between the civil and ecclesiastical authorities. Williams, like Cotton and a large number of other New England clergy, was educated in England at Cambridge, became an Anglican minister, and, after embracing Puritanism, came to America in 1631. He believed that the Bible taught that church and state should be kept separate – so, for example, the civil authority should not enforce the first four of the Ten Commandments, as was the case in Massachusetts. The legislature rejected his views, and banished him to England. With his family and some friends, he fled south instead, founding the city of Providence. He eventually obtained from England a charter for the colony of Rhode Island that granted religious liberty to all who lived there. Quakers were among the first groups to take advantage of that religious freedom, settling there at mid-century after having been badly treated by the authorities in Massachusetts (including the hanging of four Quakers there between 1659 and 1661).

Population growth in New England, the diversification of religious viewpoints, social stratification and frictions that came with the escalation of the Atlantic trade, and the fact of less vigorous piety in the second generation of Puritans led to other problems for the holy commonwealths. Church membership slipped. The ministers predicted woe, but many laity remained unconcerned. Some people worried that New England had drifted from its obligations under the covenant. Others encouraged that drift in their work and social life. One of the defining moments in this transition from one kind of Protestantism to another – from Puritanism to Congregationalism, in a sense – was the Salem witch-hunt of 1692. That hysteria, which was centered in Salem village, led to the deaths of at least 25 people, 19 by hanging. Social change in Salem, reinforced by personal grudges in the community, set the stage for the accusations and subsequent inquisition. The authority of the clergy was briefly and dramatically reasserted in Salem, but after Governor Phips put an end to the witchcraft court, a stream of recantations and apologies followed, including admissions of error from the clergy, whose stature in New England was significantly diminished.

In the southern colonies, religious life did not preoccupy the population as it did in New England. The so-called "Southern religious ethic" was not grounded in any sense of covenant with God, and the Protestant settlements in the southern tidewater – from Delaware to Georgia – were much less ambitious than their northern counterparts in supervising everyday morality. Conceived as a trading enterprise, the initial colonization of Virginia developed as an economic venture, not a religious experiment. The Anglican clergy who came in small numbers to Virginia were confined within a lay trustee system of church administration that limited and manipulated their power to affect the social world of the planters. The Anglican Church was formally established by law in Virginia, but piety was unimpressive. Church organization was weak and there were no bishops. Anglican preaching in the South, which tended to focus on issues of obedience, decorum, and manners, underscored the differences between the planting class (and their clergy) and the have-nots, and in the process fostered class conflict.

Located geographically between the lax South and the holy commonwealths of New England, the various Protestant groups that settled the middle colonies represented an assortment of national backgrounds and religious points of view. Many of the groups that came to the middle colonies were schismatic or sectarian. The Dutch who established the colony of New Netherlands at the mouth of the Hudson River had little ambition for religion in the New World, but the Reformed faith of the Dutch took root in New Jersey, especially after the English acquired the Dutch colony and renamed it New York in 1664. Also in New Jersey, in the Philadelphia area, and along the Delaware and Hudson Rivers – which had been settled by Finns and Swedes in the 1640s – Lutherans established small communities beginning in the 1620s. Puritans settled in New Jersey as well. Pennsylvania, founded by the Quaker William Penn in 1681, attracted not only Quakers but numerous other groups seeking refuge from religious persecutions and wars in Europe. Mennonites came to Germantown, Pennsylvania in 1683, where they shared a meeting-house with Quakers. Amish and Hutterites arrived, and in the first part of the eighteenth century, Dunkers, Moravians, and Schwenckfelders followed. Lutheran congregations, Dutch Reformed, and Quakers succeeded in organizing themselves into societies, and Luther's German Bible was published in 1743 (followed in 1771 by the first American printing of the King James Bible). Henry Muhlenberg, who came to Philadelphia in 1742, was especially effective in drawing Lutheran congregations throughout the middle colonies into association. Muhlenberg, who strongly opposed

Quakers, Mennonites, and several other groups in the middle colonies, also represents something of the complexity of religious life in that region before the Revolution. In spite of the fact of numerous examples of cooperation among religious groups there – the middle Atlantic was religiously diverse in a way unknown in New England or the South – Protestants fought frequently with each other, over issues of doctrine and local influence.

Patterns of Revival and Reform

Scotch-Irish Presbyterians also settled the middle colonies, Philadelphia becoming a presbytery by the early eighteenth century – and they were present in New England and the South as well. The fledgling seminary established by Gilbert Tennent, known as the "Log College" of New Jersey, trained Presbyterian clergy who played key roles in launching and sustaining the mid-eighteenth-century religious revivals that swept through the colonies in the 1720–50s. Collectively known as the Great Awakening, the revivals were characterized by conversions on a scale previously unseen in America. Fueled by the emotional preaching of itinerant ministers, and engaging people from a wide range of denominations, the various local outbreaks of piety that began in New Jersey under the preaching of Tennent and the Dutch Reformed minister Theodore Frelinghuysen coalesced into a recognizable pattern of mass conversions and unprecedented emotional display during the visit of the charismatic preacher George Whitefield. A deacon in the Church of England, Whitefield toured the colonies in the early 1740s, arousing his audiences with extempore preaching that was so elegant and poignant, said Benjamin Franklin, that merely the manner in which he pronounced the word "Mesopotamia" would cause people to weep.

Jonathan Edwards, the other leading figure of the revival, likewise preached effectively to his congregation in Northhampton, Massachusetts, witnessing a flurry of conversions there. Edwards, however, made his main mark as the theologian of the revival. His attempts to understand the revival issued in a number of treatises that profoundly shaped the religious culture of New England and contributed substantially to the development of the following two centuries of American Protestantism. Defending the revival against critics such as Charles Chauncy of Boston, who labeled it an undisciplined outburst of "heat" that produced no "light," Edwards, in *The Distinguishing Marks* (1741), and especially, the *Treatise on Religious Affections* (1746), linked revival piety to moral regeneration. Two subsequent works, *Freedom of the Will* (1754) and *Original Sin* (1758), developed nuanced and complex understandings of human nature that incorporated some of the arguments of Enlightenment *philosophes* as well as Christian doctrines.

In the years leading up to the revolution, the so-called "black regiment" of Protestant clergy (a reference to the color of clerical dress) helped to articulate American frustration with British colonial policies. Charles Chauncy, Jonathan

Mayhew, Samuel Cooper, and other New England ministers, together with colleagues from New York and Philadelphia, criticized the British from their pulpits, a sermon of Mayhew's on one occasion leading directly to mob violence. Most important for Protestantism, however, in terms of its relationship to the Revolution, was the formal separation of church and state that came in the wake of independence. Thomas Jefferson's *Virginia Statute for Religious Freedom* (1786) was supported by evangelicals such as Baptists and Methodists who had grown more vocal since the Great Awakening in the southern Piedmont (the revival there having been promoted by itinerant graduates of the Log College). The statute separated church and state and ended legal oversight of religious belief. Protestant groups such as Baptists who had fought against the established Anglican Church in Virginia (which in most cases became the Episcopal Church after 1784) supported it. Passage of the statute set the stage for the ratification of the first amendment to the US Constitution, which guaranteed freedom of religion and ended the formal establishment of religion, that is, the support of a religion through public revenues. Many of the states continued their traditions of public support for religion, however, because of ambiguity about the applicability of federal statutes to the individual states. By this means, Congregationalism was kept secure in Connecticut and Massachusetts well into the nineteenth century.

Among the several currents that shaped Protestantism at the beginning of the nineteenth century, the two most important were the emergence of camp meetings, and other forms of religious revival, and the efforts of Protestant churches to reform society through the organization of voluntary associations. The camp meeting, which was a feature of religious life in frontier areas, had a precursor in the open-air revivals that were a part of the Great Awakening. Developed in frontier Kentucky by Presbyterian preachers and "circuit riders" – itinerant ministers on horseback who rode a circuit of assignments through sparsely settled areas – camp meetings were held outdoors over the course of several weeks. They were characterized by highly animated expressions of religious faith, sometimes referred to as "exercises," as in the "jerking exercise," "fainting exercise," and "barking exercise." The Cane Ridge, Kentucky revival of 1801, which attracted as many as 25,000 people, was supervised by Barton W. Stone, who, with his followers, joined with Alexander Campbell to form the Christian Church (Disciples of Christ) 30 years later. The days-long format of the meetings, and the uninhibited performance of emotionality among the participants, remained key features of the revivalism of the Second Great Awakening, which unfolded in various ways north and south, east and west.

The Second Great Awakening featured several styles of piety. A revival that began at Yale College under President Timothy Dwight served as a model for Dwight's student, Lyman Beecher, in the latter's revival preaching in New England in the early nineteenth century. That revival, in the northeast, was characterized by a view of conversion as a more gradual process and one imbedded in the usual means of preaching, church attendance, prayer, Bible reading, and study. In upstate New York, in communities that were developing rapidly along the Erie Canal, the effervescent emotionality associated with frontier revivals was more visible. Charles Grandison Finney's program there of "new measures" included the "anxious bench" beside the preacher for people whose conversions were near and who might benefit by proximity to him, and the protracted meeting, which could last several days. Differences of style between Beecher and Finney were never entirely settled (although Beecher eventually embraced some of Finney's ideas and approach) and the awakening never had the kind of theological center – common ideas and practices – that characterized the revival in the previous century. However, the 1820s and 1830s gave birth to a vast number of voluntary associations in virtually every part of the country where the revival took place. Those associations typically crossed denominational lines, incorporating a number of Protestant groups. Frequently they were focused on social reform, in causes ranging from temperance and crusades against prostitution to the organization of resources for the support of widows, care of orphans, or construction of hospitals. They also included mission enterprises, religious publications projects, and moral improvement societies. Of particular importance in antebellum America were the abolitionist movements, which were organized through church associations. The American Colonization Society, which was organized in 1817, raised money to remunerate masters for their slaves, and then sent the former slaves back to Africa (Liberia). The fervor of the awakening was more typically manifest in movements such as those associated with the Quaker sisters Sarah and Angelina Grimke, Theodore Weld, Frederic Douglass, William Lloyd Garrison, and others who called for the immediate emancipation of slaves.

New Ventures

The emergence of African-American denominations took place against the backdrop of the Second Great Awakening. Just as the nation pursued various pathways towards a new self-understanding in the wake of the break with England, individual groups (e.g., frontier Methodists, upper-class Congregationalists, American Episcopalians) carved out more stable identities for themselves within the dominant Protestant population. African Americans established their own frameworks for collective religious life through various means but especially in the forming of the African Methodist Episcopal Church (AME) and the African Methodist Episcopal Zion Church (AMEZ) in the early nineteenth century. In both cases the new denominations grew out of black dissatisfaction with their treatment in the white churches – being forced to sit apart from whites, noninclusion in parts of the service, nonrepresentation in church government, and other forms of discrimination. The AME evolved from Richard Allen's leading a group of people out of St George's Church in Philadelphia in 1787. The denomination was established in 1816 when Francis Asbury consecrated Allen as its first bishop. The AMEZ came about as a result of protests by Peter Williams, James Varick, and several other African Americans at the John's Street Church in New York City in 1796. The AMEZ was officially chartered in 1801. The majority of blacks remained within the Baptist and Methodist churches, but after the formation of the black denominations many of those who chose to stay within the major Protestant denominations pursued more ambitious agendas of protest and social reform.

Some American Protestants elected to remove themselves from the debates and the cooperative ventures of the urban and seaboard congregations in order to pursue community experiments in religious innovation. The assortment of utopian and communal movements that subsequently sprang up in the first half-century or so of the new nation featured a range of theologies and styles of everyday devotion. Shakers, who had settled in New York (having emigrated from England under the supervision of Mother Ann Lee) established a string of over 20 communities by 1825. They embraced a notion of God as Father-Mother and a ritual style that featured dancing and emotional "shaking." John Humphrey Noyes's Oneida Community, established in upstate New York in the 1840s, arranged relations between the sexes according to a scheme of "complex marriage" and perfectionist theological views. The Mormons, who gathered around Joseph Smith after his publication of the *Book of Mormon* in 1830, believed in ongoing divine revelation to the church, through its leaders, and sought the "New Jerusalem" on the western frontier. Known as the Church of Jesus Christ of Latter Day Saints, its members practiced polygamy ("plural marriage") and fought frequent battles, both in print and in military engagement, with critics throughout the nineteenth century.

Debate over slavery and anticipation of civil war resulted in schisms in the Protestant churches. Southern denominations that were formed out of disagreements with church members in northern states included the Southern Baptist Convention (1845), Presbyterian Church in the US (originally 1857), Methodist Episcopal Church, South (1844), and a southern faction of the Episcopal Church. The last of these, the Episcopal Church in the South, reunited with the northern branch immediately after the Civil War. The other denominations that had split into northern and southern factions took longer to re-establish common ground, and some, such as the Southern Baptist Convention, continue to stand alone.

Just before the Civil War, in 1858, the Businessman's Revival, a widespread revival distinguished by its heavily male participation, reinforced the themes of conversion and personal regeneration. Especially manifest in cities such as New York, Boston, and Philadelphia, but also visible in rural areas, in southern cities such as Wilmington, and as far west as San Francisco, it was characterized by lay leadership, prayer meetings, and noon-hour services for businessmen. Following on the heels of the severe economic crash of 1857, it demonstrated the ongoing appeal of Protestant evangelical notions of sin, repentance, and the action of divine grace. Its most important contribution to American Protestantism was its popularization of the notion of prayerful requests to God as a sign of faith and a necessary exercise in the spiritual life of Protestants.

Liberal Protestantism began to emerge in force after the Civil War, the way having been prepared by various antebellum writers and religious leaders. William Ellery Channing's explication of "Unitarian Christianity" (a profession that would lead to emphasis on Jesus as human exemplar rather than divine savior) to an audience in Baltimore in 1819 served to identify liberalism as a distinct strand of American Protestantism. Ralph Waldo Emerson's "Divinity School Address," preached at Harvard in 1836, urged a rejection of the myths of Christianity in favor of intuition. And Horace Bushnell's *Christian Nurture* (1847), which questioned the notion of human depravity and challenged revivalism, promoted Sunday school education (which was developing rapidly at that time) and encouraged people to recognize the possibilities for spiritual improvement through activities in the world. One of the consequences of theological innovations such as these was the increased toleration among Protestants, in the period after the Civil War, for doctrinal looseness and a reorientation towards the world – which was envisioned as a potential fountainhead of possibilities for redemption.

Liberal theology was less known for its constructive theology than for its styles of worship and its accommodation to social theories of *laissez-faire*, social Darwinism, and self-reliance. Protestant preaching turned decisively from the centuries-old model of Word/explication/application to a format influenced by the lively and extemporaneous preaching of revivalists, whose style had been increasingly influential over the course of the eighteenth and nineteenth centuries. The Bible remained key to Protestant religious life, but there was a growing tendency to approach it from another angle, less as a record of the historical development of Christianity and a proof text for doctrinal authority, and more as an expression of wisdom and a means of inspiration. One of the consequences of the changes wrought by liberal theology was the emergence of a gospel of wealth that linked worldly success through diligent striving with spiritual status and prospects for the afterlife. The extreme statements of this thinking, which were manifest in ministers' pulpit declarations of wealth as an indication that a person was saved, were challenged by a range of other leaders, both secular and clerical, who stressed benevolence and stewardship as the hallmarks of the Christian life. The middle ground was defined by "Wealth," an article published by the industrial monopolist Andrew Carnegie in 1889, which turned the meaning of the phrase to a defense of the importance of sharing one's wealth with others, of charity as the necessary final step in the unfolding of a good life. Carnegie, like the nineteenth-century "princes of the pulpit," Phillips Brooks, Henry Ward Beecher, Russell Conwell, and others, nevertheless continued to promote the notion that wealth was an indicator of a person's moral status, that wealth came, as William Lawrence, Brooks's successor as Episcopal bishop of Massachusetts said in 1900, "only to the man of morality."

Revivalism, in the form of highly orchestrated urban gatherings, rose to national prominence in the latter part of the nineteenth century through the efforts of Dwight L. Moody, an unordained, nondenominational, and sentimental preacher, and founder of the Moody Bible Institute in Chicago. In the early twentieth century, the leading revivalist was Billy Sunday, an ex-professional baseball player, who presented himself as a "rube of the rubes," a man of rural Iowa origins and old-fashioned upbringing. His athletic emotional performances on revivalist stages across America gained him a broad following. When his popularity peaked on the eve of World War I, he was renowned not only for his ability to coax conversions from revival attendees, but for his successes in inspiring social reform, particularly in temperance and antiprostitution campaigns.

Social reform was addressed more directly by the leaders of the Social Gospel movement in America. Reacting to liberal theology's accommodation to classist social theory, the proponents of the Social Gospel endeavored to craft a more precise theological statement regarding the place of the person in society. Walter Rauschenbusch, a Baptist minister who served time early in his career in an impoverished New York City neighborhood, and Washington Gladden, a Congregationalist minister and prolific author, were at the forefront of the movement. Calling for the Christianizing of society through reform, social justice, and cooperation, Rauschenbusch, Gladden and others looked forward to the historical realization of a social "Kingdom of God" characterized by harmony. Their influence – particularly through Rauschenbusch's *Christianity and the Social Crisis* (1907) – was felt across the Protestant denominations, and led to the formation of the Federal Council of the Churches of Christ in America in 1908. The FCC, through merger with other church agencies, became the National Council of Churches in 1950.

The Challenges of Modernity

Early in the twentieth century the issue of gender came to a head with the Men and Religion Forward Movement, an interdenominational effort to draw men back into the churches. The movement was partly a reaction to gains made by women, partly a representation of the "muscular Christianity" and imperialistic nationalism of the period, and partly an outgrowth of the well-established Young Men's Christian Association (the American branch of which had been established in Boston in 1851). It featured a traveling program of lectures and workshops, and recruited boys and young men into the Boys Brigades of America, the forerunner of the Boy Scouts. This impulse found expression in twentieth-century organizations such as the Fellowship of Christian Athletes and the Promise Keepers movement.

For a century, women had been intensifying their efforts to gain social equality as American citizens (a campaign culminating in the passage of women's suffrage in 1920) and to enlarge their role in the Protestant churches. Membership
of Protestant churches has always been characterized by a "female majority"
who provide audiences for sermons, participants for rituals, and financial
support for the churches. Women felt themselves called to preach virtually from
the beginning of the English settlement of North America, but very few had
been ordained into the ministry. The first of these, Antoinette Brown, was fully
ordained in the Congregational Church in Butler, New York, in 1853. It was not
until 1889 that Anna Howard Shaw was ordained by the Methodist Protestant
Church. Nearly a hundred years passed after that before Marjorie Matthews
became the first woman bishop in the United Methodist church. Along the way
there were many female preachers, in the larger evangelical churches and
among groups such as the Quakers and the nineteenth-century Christian Connection. Women established and sustained a host of reform societies, leading
national campaigns for such causes as temperance (i.e., Frances Willard's
Women's Christian Temperance Union), abolitionism, religious education, and
female suffrage. Debate about religion and women's roles became pronounced
with the publication of Elizabeth Cady Stanton's provocative *The Woman's Bible*
in 1895–98. Against this background, the movement to boost male involvement
in the churches, as well as the promotion of "muscular Christianity" by Billy
Sunday, Josiah Strong, and others, represented something of the anxiety Protestant church leaders were experiencing about their own roles *vis à vis* the demands
of women.

Protestants also had difficulty coming to terms with the influx of Roman
Catholics and Jews, which dramatically changed the demographic makeup of
the nation between 1880 and 1925. Protestants previously had indulged their
suspicion of such groups in various nativist campaigns, fomented by reactionary
periodicals such as *The Protestant*, and marked by violence against non-
Protestants in the form of church burnings, vandalism, and assault. By the
1920s Protestant fears had contributed to a revived and powerful Ku Klux Klan
that carried out terrorist attacks on Catholics and Jews in many states.

Protestants were challenged theologically in their attempts to come to terms
with the demands of women, and to reconcile themselves to the fact of a rapidly
increasing population of Catholics and Jews. Their theological efforts were complicated by the growing prestige and authority of science. Whether in the area
of Biblical studies, geology, astronomy, economics, or the cluster of areas that
together comprised the business of "evolution," the capability of science to force
wholesale reconsideration of cherished notions of cosmic and social order was
inescapable by the early twentieth century. The problem was not entirely new to
the churches, as during the course of the nineteenth century some denominations had begun to explore ways in which to incorporate the most pressing scientific conclusions into their views of the world. Liberals had the least trouble
accommodating science, and though evangelicals had to try harder, many were
able to come to some rapprochement with the new theories. Some, however,

sought in the Bible a standpoint for resistance. They drew on the interpretations of mid-nineteenth century Princeton seminary theologians Benjamin Warfield and Charles Hodge, who, in the issues of the *Princeton Review*, had made a case for biblical inerrancy. Beginning as a series of Bible conferences in the 1860–80s, the movement came to be associated with Niagara, New York, where it flourished during the 1890s. The ideas that developed from this background eventually took shape as *The Fundamentals* (1910–15). The essays collected in that publication attacked Catholics, Mormons and others, opposed the demands of women, rejected new forms of biblical criticism such as the German "higher criticism," and strenuously resisted evolution and other scientific theories. Insisting on the inerrancy of Scripture, they affirmed the necessity of organizing personal life and social life according to biblical models. The term "fundamentalism" appeared in Curtis Lee Laws's *Baptist Watchman-Examiner* in 1920. The movement took root in Northern Baptist and Presbyterian seminaries, and conservatives distilled their ideas in short series of statements about doctrine. Liberals answered with the Auburn Declaration of 1924, setting the stage for the "monkey trial" of 1925, which took shape as a battle of fundamentalists against liberals. The trial in Dayton, Tennessee of John Scopes for teaching evolution in a public school ended in the humiliation of the Presbyterian antievolution spokesman, William Jennings Bryan, and led to the stagnation of the fundamentalist movement in the 1930s. Fundamentalists renewed their campaign against modernity, however, in the 1950s, under the leadership of the Baptist revivalist and anticommunist Billy Graham, and in the 1970s, when they focused their criticisms on a set of issues that included feminism, homosexuality, abortion, parental authority, and religion in public life.

Fundamentalism became a major theme among Protestants in the twentieth century, influencing debate in virtually all of the denominations and furnishing an easily recognizable public profile to conservative Protestantism. Alongside it another influential movement developed from its beginnings in the early twentieth century – Pentecostalism – which emerged out of various healing and holiness movements of the late nineteenth century and through the promotion of "Spirit baptism" at C. F. Parham's Topeka Bible College. The most distinctive feature of Pentecostalism, *glossolalia*, or "speaking in tongues," is associated with worship at the Azusa Street Church in Los Angeles in the spring of 1906. *Glossolalia* as practiced by the worshipers there was taken as a sign of the presence of the Holy Spirit in that community, and specifically as an indication of individuals being "baptized" or "filled" with the Holy Spirit.

Pentecostals sought to restore practice of the primitive Christian religion, so as to form a religious community uncomplicated by church history and the various sediments of sacramental, clerical, and doctrinal tradition that had accumulated over the centuries. For Pentecostals, the vitality and authority of the primitive church rested above all in the events of Pentecost, when followers of Jesus who gathered for prayer shortly after his death experienced the "gifts" of the Holy Spirit. Those gifts, sometimes called the "latter rain," included healing, prophecy, miracles, and various other capabilities in addition to speaking in tongues. For many Pentecostals, the yearning for the experience of regeneration was intensified by their belief that the end of the world and the coming of Christ were imminent. Those who were not baptized in the Holy Spirit would suffer the terrible tribulations of the end times while the saved escaped them through the miracle of the "rapture."

Pentecostals organized themselves into denominations such as the mostly African-American Church of God in Christ, which was nurtured by Charles H. Mason. Also important were the Church of God, which probably began in 1902 on the heels of the Camp Creek, North Carolina Holiness revival, and the Assemblies of God, which, after several false starts, settled its headquarters in Springfield, Missouri in 1918. Healing has played a major role in the movement since its beginnings. Aimee Semple McPherson, founder of the Church of the Foursquare Gospel in Los Angeles, has been a model for Pentecostalist healers since the 1920s. Pentecostalist religious life, as it developed in the twentieth century, created a popular religious culture that included counterparts of the secular culture such as television programs, concerts, musical recordings, business manuals and self-help books, diet programs, sporting events, fashion, and so forth, all massaged in such a way as to reflect a Christian viewpoint. Pentecostalism by the late twentieth century firmly embraced the culture of the Protestant middle class. It was one of the largest and fastest growing movements within American Protestantism, had exercised extensive influence on Christianity outside of North America, and was represented in Roman Catholicism in the devotions of "charismatic Catholics."

Evangelical Protestant missionizing was rapidly accelerated at the beginning of the twentieth century. Missionary enterprises had been fostered during the nineteenth century by the so-called "mainstream" Protestant denominations – usually identified in the mid-twentieth century as the Presbyterian Church in the USA, Reformed Church in America, Episcopal Church, American Baptist Convention, United Presbyterian Church, United Methodist Church, United Church of Christ, the Southern Baptist Convention, The Lutheran Church-Missouri Synod, American Lutheran Church, Disciples of Christ (Christians), and the Unitarian-Universalists. Particularly in the aftermath of the Businessman's Revival of 1858 (sometimes called the Prayer Union Revival), those churches (or their precursors) mounted ambitious missions to Africa, Latin America, and Asia, with missions to China becoming the leading initiative by 1900. Evangelical initiatives within and outside of those denominations built upon this background of mission activity so that by the mid-1920s there were as many as 15,000 American and Canadian missionaries in the field. The number of missionaries grew steadily throughout the twentieth century, particularly in connection with evangelical groups (which joined forces under umbrella organizations such as the Evangelical Foreign Missions Association) and Pentecostal groups such as the Assemblies of God. Premillennialism, a focus on demonology, and a strong aversion to cultural relativism characterize the efforts of many Protestant missionary groups, and have contributed substantially to gains in Africa and South America.

During the Depression, regional religious movements emerged within Protestantism. Led by clergy from a wide range of denominations, they deployed martial imagery to rally Protestants to conservative agendas, blaming the nation's economic trauma and human suffering on Jews, Catholics, and other non-Protestant groups. Coinciding with the revival of the Klu Klux Klan, these movements – such as Lutheran pastor Frank Buchman's Moral Re-armament, the Kansas Baptist Gerald B. Winrod's Defenders of the Christian Faith, and North Carolinian William Dudley Pelley's Legion of Silver Shirts – were largely fundamentalist reactions to modernity. Protesting against the teaching of evolution, the New Deal, and other seemingly liberal causes, they began to unravel as the nation went to war in the 1940s, but their legacy was apparent in later twentieth-century movements such as the Christian Coalition.

In the aftermath of World War II, the Protestant denominations experienced a surge in membership, new church construction, and public involvement. Presbyterian layman John Foster Dulles, who served as the Secretary of State under Dwight D. Eisenhower (1952–9), was the "priest of nationalism" who brought a strongly ecumenical Protestant influence to the shaping of policy. The ecumenical efforts on the part of virtually all of the Protestant churches during the 1950s-60s in fact marked the decades as a hothouse of aspirations and plans for Protestant theological consensus. The reunions of denominations that have been divided since the Civil War – the joining of North and South Methodist churches in 1939, for example – set the stage for broader cooperation as represented in the Consultation on Church Union, which, during the 1960s–80s brokered theological agreements among Methodist, Episcopal, Presbyterian, and UCC denominations.

Conservatives and Liberals

Alongside ecumenicalism, postwar revivalism characterized the religious mood of the nation. That revivalism was manifest not only in increased churchgoing, but especially in the re-emergence of revival preaching and evangelical conversion ritual. The Baptist revivalist Billy Graham, who became a national figure following a successful crusade in Los Angeles in 1949, set the tone for much of the revival religion of the time. Premillennialist, deeply anticommunist, and wary of demonic forces (but secure in the belief that angels were "God's secret agents"), Graham offered a religious vision that was well suited to the Cold War atmosphere of the 1950s and 1960s. Preaching the evils of sin and the necessity for spiritual regeneration, Graham drew large crowds to his urban revivals, and he eventually became a religious consultant to American presidents.

Graham's revival crusades, which were lavishly detailed and finely orchestrated events, were broadcast on radio and television. Those broadcasts found a large and responsive audience. Just as Graham had built upon the religious broadcasting modeled by the Catholic Depression-era "radio priest" Father

Coughlin and the Catholic television pioneer Bishop Fulton J. Sheen, subsequent Protestant preachers built upon Graham's successes. Televangelism, which captured the attention of Protestants in the 1970s and 1980s, beamed evangelical Protestant messages into homes across the nation, and, indeed, the world. Marion Gordon "Pat" Robertson founded the Christian Broadcasting Network (CBN) in 1965 as a vehicle for charismatic Protestantism. Focusing on prayer and healing – physical as well as spiritual – Robertson cultivated a large and loyal audience through transmission of "The 700 Club" program, and eventually mobilized that audience as a political force. His political organization, the Christian Coalition, in the late twentieth century sought to influence national, state, and local policy on the issues of interest to most conservative evangelicals (e.g., opposing evolution, abortion, and homosexual rights) and eventually served as a base for the failed campaign of its founder for President. The televangelism ministry of Pentecostals Jim and Tammy Bakker began at CBN, but acquired a stronger national profile after they began broadcasting their "Praise the Lord" (PTL Club) show in 1974. Their cable television program reached 13 million households before the organization broke up in the late 1980s following revelations of Jim's affair with a church secretary and massive financial fraud (for which Jim originally was sentenced to a jail term of 45 years). Assemblies of God evangelist Jimmy Swaggart, whose televangelism ministry reached almost two million households by the late 1980s, likewise lost his authority when his activities with a prostitute became public. Jerry Falwell, a Baptist Fundamentalist pastor in Lynchburg, Virginia, began broadcasting his "Old-Time Gospel Hour" in 1968. Drawing on the support of his viewers, he established a college (Liberty University) and a national political organization, the Moral Majority (1979). Like other prominent Protestant televangelists, Falwell was conservative, and tended to broach his agenda for social action in terms of his opposition to modernity.

Liberal Protestantism has also been active in various causes since the middle of the twentieth century. Protestant denominations played a pivotal role in the Civil Rights movement (1954–66) that sought to end discrimination against African Americans, particularly in the South. The Southern Christian Leadership Conference, which was founded in 1957 and led for a time by Baptist pastor Dr Martin Luther King, Jr, was at the forefront of that movement. Individual denominations also developed means by which to address racism, for example, the Commission on Religion and Race created by Presbyterians in 1963 and the Episcopalian Society for Cultural and Racial Unity. The churches likewise provided a foundation for protest against the Vietnam War and nuclear escalation. By the end of the twentieth century, Protestant churches – together with Jewish and Catholic groups – had developed a theological basis for criticism of human spoliation of the environment. The Evangelical Environmental Network, which includes several dozen evangelical organizations and conferences (some of which are conservative on other matters), has been active in promoting an interpretation of the Bible as care for creation. Individual denominations have issued their own statements as well, as in the case of the Evangelical Lutheran Church in America, which adopted a statement on environmental care in 1993.

Protestant campaigns for female ordination have resulted in much discussion, some action, and some reaction since the mid-twentieth century. The Presbyterian Church (USA) began ordaining women in 1956. Since that time, the numbers of female ministers in Protestant denominations has greatly increased, especially during the period 1977–97, when, for example, female ordinations in the American Baptist Church rose from 157 to 712; in the Episcopal Churches in the USA from 94 to 1,394; and in the United Methodist Church from 319 to 3,003. By the late 1990s, over 50 percent of Unitarian-Universalist clergy were women. Southern Baptists have ordained hundreds of women as well, but the strongly conservative turn taken by that denomination in the late 1990s, and especially a commitment to the authority of men over women that was announced in 2000, undermined or curtailed pastoral opportunities for women.

Gay rights became a live issue within the Protestant churches in 1964, with the founding of the Consultation of the Church and the Homosexual, a series of meetings organized by gay groups and Methodist agencies in San Francisco. The Universal Fellowship of Metropolitan Community Churches, founded in 1969 by Troy D. Perry, who had been a minister in the Church of God, grew to over 100,000 members by 1990. Some denominations became active in outreach to the gay community during this time, while others continued to characterize homosexuality as sinful. Most official Protestant positions on homosexuality fell between the approach of the Unitarian-Universalist Association, which allows same-sex marriage, to Southern Baptist condemnation of homosexuality: most support gay rights but oppose homosexual practice, and welcome gays into their churches but refuse to ordain or marry them.

At the beginning of the twenty-first century, Protestantism in America was enormously more complex than it was in the nineteenth century. The proliferation of denominations has been profound: some came about through theological innovation, others through schism, others as a result of racial and ethnic difference, and yet others because of re-emergent regional emphases. The complexity of Protestantism is equally manifest in its fluidity, in the way that Americans move from one congregation to another, one denomination to another, bringing with them expectations and tastes that influence the congregations that they join or rejoin. Protestants have also complicated their religious life through popular devotions, and through their embrace of or flirtation with ideas and practices – reincarnation, astrology, healing arts, goddess-worship – not historically linked to Protestant institutions. Pentecostals increasingly represent their religious life with reference to popular culture in all of its forms, from motorcar racing to dieting. The dynamic aspect of American Protestantism is visible in all such developments. While sharing a past grounded in the Reformation of the sixteenth century, American Protestants in the twenty-first century identify themselves in a myriad of ways.

Further Reading

Allen, Leonard, Hughes, Richard T., and Bellah, Robert (1988). *Illusions of Innocence: Protestant Primitivism in America, 1630–1875*. Chicago: University of Chicago Press.

Hammond, Phillip E. (1992), *The Protestant Presence in Twentieth-Century America: Religion and Political Culture*. Albany, NY: SUNY Press.

Hall, David D. (1989). *Worlds of Wonder, Days of Judgment: Popular Religious Belief in Early New England*. New York: Knopf.

Hatch, Nathan O. (1989). *The Democratization of American Christianity*. New Haven, CT: Yale University Press.

Heyrman, Christine (1997). *Southern Cross: The Beginnings of the Bible Belt*. Chapel Hill: University of North Carolina Press.

Hutchinson, William R. (ed.) (1989). *Between the Times: The Travail of the Protestant Establishment in America, 1900–1960*. Cambridge, UK: Cambridge University Press.

Jenkins, Thomas E. (1997). *The Character of God: Recovering the Lost Literary Power of American Protestantism*. New York: Oxford University Press.

Mathews, Donald G. (1979). *Religion in the Old South*. Chicago: University of Chicago Press.

May, Henry Farnham (1991). *The Divided Heart: Essays on Protestantism and the Enlightenment in America*. New York: Oxford University Press.

Ostrander, Richard (2000). *The Life of Prayer in a World of Science: Protestants, Prayer, and American Culture, 1870–1930*. New York: Oxford University Press.

Rubin, Julius H. (1994). *Religious Melancholy and Protestant Experience in America*. New York: Oxford University Press.

Schmidt, Leigh Eric (2000). *Hearing Things: Religion, Illusion, and the American Enlightenment*. Cambridge, MA: Harvard University Press.

Thuesen, Peter Johannes (1999). *In Discordance with the Scriptures: American Protestant Battles over Translating the Bible*. New York: Oxford University Press.

Wacker, Grant (2001). *Heaven Below: Early Pentecostals and American Culture*. Cambridge, MA: Harvard University Press.

Winner, Lauren F. and Balmer, R. H. (2002). *Protestantism in America*. New York: Columbia University Press.

CHAPTER 16
Shapers of Protestantism: Jonathan Edwards

Stephen R. Holmes

Jonathan Edwards (1703–58) is routinely described as the greatest theologian to have been born on American soil. It was not always thus. His star has risen over the past 50 years or so for a variety of reasons, and the scholarly attention paid to him has increased correspondingly. The year 2003 sees the tercentenary of his birth, and will no doubt witness another flurry of publications. What is it that makes this American Puritan so particularly interesting in our day?

It has been said of Crick and Watson, the discoverers of the double helix shape of the DNA molecule, that they were no cleverer than many other people of their generation in different disciplines in British universities, but that they had the good fortune to have something to be clever about. Their discipline presented them with a major issue that needed solving, and that was capable of solution at that moment. I have no wish to cast aspersions on the intellect of these fine scholars, or indeed on that of Jonathan Edwards, but I suspect that his continuing interest lies not just in his undoubted genius, but in a similarly fruitful location. As Edwards was born, the philosophical discussions of John Locke, and the implications of the scientific theories of Isaac Newton, were changing the intellectual world, among English-speaking peoples at least, beyond recognition. If the great vision of true Christianity that the Puritans had lived and breathed was to survive into this new age of modernity, there was a need for a theological demonstration that it was not incompatible with the coming ways of thought. At the heart of Edwards's genius, perhaps, was his attempt to offer such a demonstration.

Today the announcement that we are now all 'post-modern' echoes in our ears: whatever this may mean, it at least indicates that we are collectively beginning to realize that the ways of thinking we have inherited are not necessary, and even perhaps that they are not adequate. The writings of one who analysed these ways of thought from the perspective of the gospel of Christ, and whose thought was as brilliant as it was pious, must be of interest to Christian thinkers seeking to make sense of our own times. Jonathan Edwards was marginalized in his own lifetime, misunderstood in the century that followed his death, and mocked in the century that followed that. Finally, perhaps, he is being appreciated as the devout and profound Christian thinker he is.

Edwards's Life

Edwards was born in 1703. He was the fifth child, and only son among 10 daughters, of Timothy Edwards, himself a minister, and Esther, daughter of Solomon 'Pope' Stoddard, the minister of Northampton church in Massachusetts, and a significant figure of the times as his epithet indicates. The beginnings of Edwards's own ministry came in a small New York Presbyterian congregation, which however soon reunited with its parent church. After a brief period as a tutor at Yale, and some illness, Edwards accepted a call to assist his grandfather, now 83, in the ministry in Northampton. When the great man died in 1729, Edwards succeeded to the pulpit he was to occupy for the next 21 years, a period encompassing the events of the 'Great Awakening' (a revival, parallel to the British 'Evangelical Revival' and led by some of the same people, notably George Whitefield), in which he was heavily involved. His ministry in Northampton also saw significant controversy: Edwards sought to shore up the New England Calvinist settlement as the first cracks began to appear, and argued with his congregation over admission to the Lord's Table, and matters of church discipline.

These pastoral disagreements led to Edwards's removal from his pulpit. He and his family settled in Stockbridge, Massachusetts. The (not quite) seven years they spent there were remarkable: Edwards lived in poverty, far from any seat of learning or library; endured conflict with the leading merchant family of the town (who wanted to exploit the Native Americans); gave himself in ministry to teaching, befriending and defending his Native American flock; and produced a flow of writings which are the basis of his present reputation. From that unlikely frontier post flowed *The Freedom of the Will*, *Original Sin*, *True Virtue* and a number of other works.

Edwards's genius was recognized, and he was invited to the presidency of Princeton. As the town was then ravaged by smallpox, he was given the new vaccine. The science, however, was in its infancy, and he contracted the disease from the vaccine and died in March 1758, at the age of 54. He had in mind greater works, which, we must assume, would have flowed even more freely from the context of an academic appointment; what he had written is ample testimony to his industry, his piety, and his ability.

Edwards's Theology

The substance of Edwards's theology is built on the great achievements of European Reformed orthodoxy; his recommendation (in a letter) of François Turretin and Peter van Mastricht as the theologians he had learnt most from is indicative of the origins of his thought. The mode of his theology is that of the Puritan pastor-scholar, who studied for the benefit of his congregation, and wrote mostly on those occasional themes that his pastoral duties demanded. The heart of his theological vision was a conception of God's glory, which borrows from, but goes beyond, Mastricht. God's own eternal life as Father, Son and Spirit is perfectly happy and complete. Just so, God does not need the world; there is nothing lacking in God's life that the world can make up. However, the perfection of God's life is infinitely beautiful, and the perception of beauty by intelligent beings is a moral good, and so it is better that this recognition should happen than not. The ultimate reason for creation, then, is for intelligent creatures (angels and human beings) to exist and behold God's glory, the shining beauty of his perfection. In all that he does, God acts that the perception of his glory, and so the enjoyment of his beauty, may be maximized. God does not gain anything by being thus glorified: how can perfection be improved? It is, however, a moral good that this should happen, and so he acts to make it happen. (This, in summary, is the argument of the *Dissertation Concerning the End for Which God Created the World*.)

It is clearly not appropriate, under such a scheme, to assume that God left the discernment of his glory to chance. Every part of creation must be so ordered by God that his creatures' understanding of, and delight in, his glory is maximized. The essence of God's self-glorification is the salvation won in Jesus Christ, the incarnate Son, and so the creation in whole and in part is ordered to increase the visibility to intelligent creatures of the grand narrative of the gospel (fall, incarnation, passion, resurrection, Pentecost and the time of the church, the return of Christ and final consummation). What seem to the modern reader the most alien, or possibly most medieval, features of Edwards's corpus reflect this point: his endless typologizing of creation, finding 'images or shadows of divine things' in every part of the created order, is merely a necessary concomitant of this prior understanding. The world and its history are indeed a vast network of symbols and correspondences, providentially ordered by God so that the glory of the gospel may be discerned. Not just the eternal fate of human beings (predestination), but every 'incidental' detail of the created order must be decreed by God in the way that will most promote his glory. One of Edwards's earliest writings, 'On Insects', dating from his teenage years, offers not just a natural history of flying insects, but an improvement of the same, discussing how the ordering of their lives images forth the gospel story. Such a coda may have been standard for the day, but for Edwards it becomes vital, and his notebook of *Images or Shadows* demonstrates the breadths and lengths he will go to in finding correspondences. The 'filth' in which newborn children are covered is a representation of their guilty state before God as a result of original sin; the unfading colour of the sky represents the undiminishing joys of heaven, and so on.

It is not just natural history, however: Edwards's sustained attempts to map the political events of his day to the images of the book of Revelation (which are again likely to be merely incomprehensible to the modern reader) indicate a belief that God providentially orders the events of world history to display the truth of the gospel narrative, and so his own glory, just as much as he does the objects in the created world. Edwards believed (for various reasons) that the Puritan polities of America would be the source of a worldwide revival of religion, and that recent events in history confirmed and illustrated this. The discovery and production of immense natural and agricultural riches in the Americas was an image of the vast riches of the gospel that would be discovered in the 'new' world; their export to Europe was a precursor of the same thing happening in spiritual terms. Again, the invention of the telescope, which made heavenly objects appear so much clearer, and indeed nearer, was a type of the coming revival of religion – when heavenly things would indeed become nearer and plainer. Edwards scoured the newspapers of the day looking for events that could be used to map the unfolding of God's providential plan with the description of that plan in the Apocalypse; the loss of Spanish merchant ships was a part of the coming fall of antichrist. (Edwards, in common with most Puritans, identified the papacy with the antichrist.)

Nor, finally, is it credible that God would allow the accidental waste of some of his creatures. Rather, if perdition is to be the fate of some, it must be a fate decided on by God to further display his perfections to those creatures who shall finally be found rejoicing in his presence. Edwards's (notorious) preaching of hell often emphasizes the utility of eternal punishment in demonstrating the infinite justice of God, the magnitude of his holiness, and the depths of the mercy and grace he displays in the gift of redemption. The saints in heaven will be able to see the sufferings of the damned in hell, and the sight will increase their understanding of God's perfection, and so their joy in God, and the worship they offer.

Given this, Edwards is compelled to teach (the traditional Reformed doctrine of) double predestination, and indeed wrote two significant works in defence of Calvinism, which was coming under sustained attack in his day. *Original Sin* was the first, asserting the imputation of Adam's guilt to all his descendants. The second, generally considered to be the more significant of the two, was *The Freedom of the Will*. This is an argument for what in philosophical terms is called 'compatiblism', the idea that a deterministic, or in this case predestinarian, doctrine is not incompatible with a robust account of human freedom. Edwards's position is built on the assertion that to be free is to be able to choose one's course of action, without any interference from external constraints. So it is not implausible to assume that all our choices are predictable, if only we know enough about our motives and preferences. Nor is it inappropriate to describe choices as freely made even though we can explain their roots in terms of chemical reactions in the brain, or the divine arrangements of the created order. Edwards defends this with an impressive barrage of philosophical and theological arguments.

Edwards's particular interest, however, is not in a philosophical nicety, but in an ethical objection to Calvinism. It had been argued that a choice that was determined could not be ethically significant. That is, if I cannot but do such-

and-such, whether because of my genetic makeup or the predestining activity of God's Spirit, I should not be blamed for so doing. This argument is intuitively attractive, but (as Edwards demonstrates) devastating, not just to traditional Calvinism, but to almost all forms of ethical discourse. One implication of this position, for instance, is to absolve from any blame someone who is so used to violence that it has become habitual: his violent reaction to his wife's failure to respond to his drunken advances was a reflex result of alcoholism and habit, and thus entirely predictable and unavoidable. The very fact, then, that should compound the guilt of his action, becomes under this alternative scheme that which absolves it. For Edwards, the decisive case is divine: God's goodness and holiness is a necessary result of who he is, and yet clearly it is praiseworthy and so morally relevant. Edwards's way through the argument is to analyse the concept of necessity. There are certain forms of necessity – factors which are external to me – which do remove my moral culpability: if I act in a particular way because someone is holding a gun to my head, or because I have unwittingly taken a hallucinogenic drug, I cannot be held fully responsible for my actions. Other forms of necessity – those internal to me – establish my moral culpability: actions that are so habitual that I cannot avoid them, for instance.

With this defence in place, Edwards can assert Calvinist double predestination: my choice to accept or reject the gospel of Christ is freely made, and morally significant, although predetermined by God. Thus Edwards can teach that God preordains that certain of his creatures should finally suffer his severity, so that the advancement of his glory can be fully realized, without any infringement of the 'rights' of his creatures. This argument, historically, was perhaps doomed to failure, inasmuch as the coming Enlightenment with its celebration of human dignity and responsibility would find such themes utterly alien; whether it has yet been effectively answered (as opposed to merely mocked or ignored) is a moot point.

The works thus far described are, in my judgement, those that were central to Edwards's theological project. He also published several controversial works which are consonant with the main thrust of his thought, but not central to it. This category includes perhaps his most famous writing, *The Religious Affections*, and the other writings on revival that led up to it.

The Great Awakening began in Northampton in 1734, after Edwards preached a series of doctrinal sermons on Calvinist themes. It lasted in waves across colonial America for 15 years or so, but Edwards's congregation was only powerfully affected for the first two years, and then again under the ministry of George Whitefield in 1740. Many church leaders saw dangers of 'enthusiasm' in the revival (in the eighteenth century, 'enthusiasm' meant fanaticism – an unreasoned and unreasonable religious attitude), compounded by the habits of some of the itinerant revival preachers, who would denounce unsupportive ministers as 'unconverted'. Among other things, these opponents objected to the extremes of emotional display that took place in revival services (including screaming, weeping, uncontrolled laughter, and physical symptoms such as falling or jerking), claiming that true religion was a matter of believing certain intellectual propositions, and that such emotionalism was a distraction, if not a demonic deception.

Edwards was initially simply supportive of the revival, and his earliest revival writing, *The Narrative of Surprising Conversions* (1736) was merely descriptive of what God was doing among his people. As the controversy matured, Edwards attempted to analyse the revival experiences, and to steer a careful middle course between a rejection of what God was really doing, and an uncritical celebration of all that went on, no matter how bizarre. He developed this position theologically in *The Distinguishing Marks of the Spirit of God* (1741), and further, with narrative examples, in *Some Thoughts Concerning the Revival* (1742). *The Religious Affections* (1746) was his mature statement of his thoughts.

'Affections' are, roughly, strong emotions. They are central to true piety, according to Edwards, who cites the biblical commendations of love for God, the fear of God, and so on. To suggest that real faith is unemotional, then, is simply false. However, it is equally erroneous to suggest that all emotion is evidence of the work of the Spirit in a person's life. Edwards's key contribution, perhaps, is the concept of a 'negative sign' – something that, while either spectacular or frightening, proves nothing, either way. To begin with, Edwards's point was simply that to take physical, vocal or emotional manifestations as adequate evidence either for or against conversion is not acceptable. A person worked on by the Spirit of God might very well respond in such ways; so might someone deluded, insane or possessed. A humble devotion in religion and an unostentatious holiness of life was the only admissible evidence for this conclusion, whether accompanied by the most astonishing displays, or whether achieved quietly and without fuss.

By the time he came to write the *Affections*, however, Edwards's thought had become more pessimistic. The long list of negative signs, each with attached Scripture proofs, becomes so comprehensive that one is tempted to wonder if anyone may have assurance of their salvation. The positive signs, designed to give assurance, speak of such imponderables as 'balance', and culminate in a lengthy and impassioned account of persistence in Christian practice until death as the decisive proof. It is tempting, psychologically, to see the fact that those who he had hoped converted in the revival were now hounding him from his pulpit as the decisive element in this, and no doubt there is a measure of truth in the idea. Edwards's youthful optimism about transformed Christian lives had proved unfounded, and this cannot but have influenced his thinking. He was too good a theologian, however, for this to be his only consideration; this introduces an important Edwardsean concept, the 'sense of the heart'.

To understand this, some background is necessary. The Puritan tradition that Edwards had inherited had struggled with the psychological description of conversion. This was largely due to a prevailing understanding of human psychology that believed discrete 'faculties' existed, notably a thinking faculty (the 'mind') and a volitional faculty (the 'will'). Conversion obviously involved both faculties, in that the gospel is to be believed, and decisions of faith and repentance are to be taken, but one must have the prior role. So was conversion

fundamentally a matter of knowing, with volitional consequences, or fundamentally a decision, with intellectual concomitants? Neither was adequate, but
arguments persisted about which was more so. The new psychological theories
of John Locke, however, offered a way through the impasse, in their refusal to
divide the mind up into such discrete entities. Edwards seized on this possibility,
and developed the concept of a psychological event that was at once intellectual
and volitional. This he called the sense of the heart.

In an important sermon, 'A Divine and Supernatural Light', on Mt 16:17,
Edwards described the way in which conversion comes to one who has previously known the gospel story, and even believed it to be factually accurate. The
new feature is a perception of the beauty, the harmony, the perfect justice
and fittingness, of what God has done. This is an experiential understanding,
equivalent to tasting a food one had only heard about, and so really compre-
hending what before now was only report. Conversion is not just about knowing
and believing the gospel, but about being overwhelmed with awe and joy at the
rightness of what God has done.

At the heart of Edwards's account of the psychology of conversion, then, is
this new experiential knowledge, but how can anyone be sure that they have this
particular experience? The problem goes back to Calvin himself, who spoke of a
temporary faith, that mimics the signs of true piety. The pastor must attempt to
discern the truth (the burden of Edwards's writings on the issue of qualifications
for communion), but certainty is unobtainable. In this connection it is also
important to remember the different social situation Edwards experienced:
where today a person in search of selfish religious gratification would find it in
any one of the variety of new religious movements available, in Edwards's day
such a person might well appear faithful in Christian practice. The possibility of
an apparent piety which was false, because not growing from a true sense of the
heart, was obvious and serious, and so the lack of assurance that seems to be
the result of the tests in *The Religious Affections* is inevitable.

The Significance of Edwards's Theology

These, then, in too-brief outline, are the major themes of Edwards's theology.
Why might he matter today? There are arguments or ideas that Edwards
advanced that we might borrow to address issues in our own context: gaining
wisdom on distinguishing a true work of the Spirit of God from *The Religious
Affections*, perhaps, or defending Calvinism with the arguments in *The Freedom
of the Will*. Such borrowings are significant, and not inappropriate, but I want
to suggest something deeper. Edwards was a theologian of modernity – perhaps
the first such. He wrote with a profound grasp of what Newton and Locke had
to say, and offered response after response to the Deists who, in the spirit of the
nascent Enlightenment, used such new ideas to attack Christian orthodoxy.
In an age that describes itself as post-modern, that is finally, in its intellectual

pursuits and its popular cultures, repudiating the totalizing claims of the modernistic synthesis that was built on Newton and Locke, Edwards has something profound to say. He saw through the deceptions and half-truths of the Enlightenment with startlingly penetrative vision, and critiqued them in the name of the gospel of Christ. He offered a way to think Christianly that was able to accept what was true, wholesome and edifying in the new ways of thinking, and to deal with what needed repudiation. No doubt he was wrong about many things. No doubt he had his own blind spots and distortions. His attempts to render Reformed orthodoxy credible, relevant and life-giving in the language of modernity, and in the face of the Enlighteners remains, nonetheless, powerful and astonishingly relevant for the reinvigoration of Reformed Christianity in our own day.

Bibliographic Information

At the time of writing, 18 volumes of a complete edition have been published by Yale University Press, under the general editorship of Harry S. Stout; this will be the definitive edition for many years when complete. The old two-volume S. E. Dwight and E. Hickman edition is still in print from various sources, and contains most of the significant works.

Further Reading

Cherry, Conrad (1993). *The Theology of Jonathan Edwards: A Reappraisal*. Bloomington: Indiana University Press.

Holmes, Stephen R. (2000). *God of Grace and God of Glory: An Account of the Theology of Jonathan Edwards*. Edinburgh: T & T Clark.

Jenson, Robert W. (1988), *America's Theologian: A Recommendation of Jonathan Edwards*. Oxford: Oxford University Press.

Marsden, George M. (2003). *Jonathan Edwards: A Life*. New Haven, CT: Yale University Press.

Pauw, Amy Plantinga (2002). *The Supreme Harmony of All: The Trinitarian Theology of Jonathan Edwards*. Grand Rapids, MI: Eerdmans.

CHAPTER 17

Canadian Protestantism to the Present Day

Darren C. Marks

The quest for a Canadian identity has become a national obsession, borne out of the history, location, and geography of Canada. Its development from an "ad hoc" colonial outpost to nationhood, its proximity to the United States of America, and its vast geography indelibly mark Canadian identity as a whole, and its Protestantism specifically. Canada is still consciously involved in a very lively debate on *what* Canada should be. The "prolonged adolescence" (Grant 1977: 18) of Canada appears, at the beginning of the twenty-first century, to have turned full circle to its seventeenth century origins of a novel cultural mosaic. The comfort of Canada in no longer being a British colony has given way to a new discomfort about being a "cultural colony" of the United States.

An Accidental Mosaic

English-speaking Canada, unlike French interest in New France,[1] was, until the mid-eighteenth century and the beginnings of unrest in New England, of little interest to the British crown. Early British interest in present-day Canada was divided between exploiting natural resources and containing French expansion. The earliest Protestant settlers in Canada were mainly a mixture of British Anglicans and Presbyterians and American Congregationalists, whose business interests, not religious commitments, saw them active in "Canada." Any clerical work was haphazard and almost entirely directed towards military garrisons and the nearby settlers, but a form of early religious tolerance can be detected with Protestant military chaplains crossing denominational lines to meet demand. By 1700 new immigrants to English Canada expanded the Protestant mix to include English Puritans, Baptists, and Quakers (including two women missionaries, Hester Biddle and Mary Fisher). Mission activity began modestly with the 1703 appointment of John Jackson by the Society for the Propagation of the Gospel to the settlement of St John's, Newfoundland. Post-1750 economic migrants, both English-speaking and non-English-speaking, bring Moravian pietism, German Lutheranism, and English Methodism into the Protestant mosaic. The 1755 expulsion of the French-speaking Acadians allowed a new American-derived migration of Free Churches into the then largely French Maritimes. Finally, the decades around the American Revolution (1775–83) doubled English Canada's population as Loyalists resettled in Ontario and the Maritimes from New England. Of note in this migration were freed and escaped African slaves whose predominant Protestant affiliation was Baptist. Two important early leaders were the black American David George (1742–92) and the white Britain John Burton, whose apprentice Richard Preston (1790–1861) later formed the African Baptist Chapel in Halifax.

With the 1791 creation of Upper Canada (Ontario) and Lower Canada (Quebec and the Maritimes), the mosaic looked as follows. Lower Canada was primarily composed of Anglicans, Methodists, Congregationalists, and Presbyterians, although there were pockets of other traditionally nonconformist communities. French-speaking Lower Canada was staunchly Roman Catholic. Upper Canada was initially more diverse, having the non-English-speaking Lutherans, Mennonites, and Moravians and the English Quakers form communities alongside British settlements. Following the Loyalist influx, which by 1812 composed nearly 80 percent of Upper Canada's population, "distinctly American forms of particular denominations" (Murphy, 1996: 113) ran alongside British Protestants and rurally based non-English-derived pockets of Protestant identity.

Unlike New France or New England, the lack of a formal or subscribed plan of colonization meant that British North America was haphazardly organized. There was no initial overarching vision or consensus of what kind of colony Canada was to be, only *that* it be. For each Protestant denomination or sect a centralized vision of identity – as nation and denomination – seemed secondary to the ordinary business of life itself. The vast geography meant that resources were critically short, especially spiritual resources in the form of clergy and buildings. The typical template was that only the larger urban settlements could afford to build churches, call clergy, and run churches. Smaller rural centers were left largely alone or had to share any resources. This isolationalism and spiritual vacuum would later help explain the growth of revivalism in the rural and native populations and the success of American Methodist circuit riders (beginning 1786 in Lower Canada and 1794 in Upper Canada). Three markers of Canadian Protestant identity flow out of this initial mosaic pattern. The first is that paucity of resources often meant that limited forms of "religious tolerance" were dictated by circumstances. Specific denominations could afford neither buildings nor hired clergy, and therefore often shared with proximate denominational cousins. Second, larger towns began to have a different religious character in that they could afford to replicate European and

American Protestant denominational competition as they could afford to build, call, and equip. Finally, the center of gravity for ecclesiastical institutions was to be located with the laity. Any form of ecclesiastical establishment or centralized control (especially from abroad or America) was met with resistance and suspicion.

By the 1800s the mosaic begins to crack, with the two competing forces in Canadian Protestantism straining against each other. The urban-based and politically elite re-creation of British society, an Anglican-Presbyterian-British (Wesleyan) Methodist coalition, begins to try to assert a "British" identity and hegemony, but runs counter to the nonconformist rural and mercantile-based Loyalist-influenced (and financed) Protestant traditions. This period is also the zenith of limited positive relations towards Catholicism, who shared the British distrust of evangelical – meaning American – enthusiasts who advocated republicanism. Centralization and uniformity played out against quasi-republicanism (later federalism) and nonconformity. The next century sees the playing out of these two polar opposites.

"Mindful of Duties as Christians in Wilderness Lands"[2]

Two histories begin to merge in the late 1700s. The first is the "outer history" of powerful institutions, church leaders, and politics, while the second is the "inner history" of popular religion or smaller groups such as revivalists or evangelicals. Both are necessary to understand Canadian Protestant identity. While both histories stress the Canadian shift from colony to Christian nation in ethos, the rationale as to how this "Christianized" nation should emerge varies. For the mainstream, largely urban-based, British-derived Protestant elite, to be Christian and Protestant was a cultural replication of Britain, complete with an established Anglican church. For the nonmainstream Protestants – Baptists, Congregationalists, American Methodists[3] – influenced by New England piety and Wesleyan theology, to be Christian and Protestant was to experience new birth and to live with the hope of a new kingdom divorced from worldly political concerns (Stewart & Rawlyk, 1972: 88). Radical individualism and a focus on winning souls, the answer to spiritual decay and rationalism, declared that involvement in the nation-creation was of secondary importance to the business of the kingdom. As long as the state permitted religious freedom, often granted by sheer isolation alone, and promoted virtuous society, the Christian had little interest in political squabbles – particularly of the kind seen in the American colonies.

The transformation from wilderness outpost to "Christian garden" on a macro-level can be understood as a move to counter American rebellion and influence in British North America. The 1787 appointment of Charles Inglis (1734–1816) as bishop of Nova Scotia, and by extension all of British North America, followed by the 1791 Canada Act granting one-seventh of all crown land grants to be given to Protestant churches – that is, Anglican churches – effectively created a *de facto* established church. Inglis's appointment signaled the intention of the British crown to privilege Anglicanism. Inglis's own equivocation between the "duty owed God" and the "duty owed the king" (Murphy 1996: 126) marks the effort of Anglicanism as a means to secure allegiance to the crown and to offset the agitating influence of American religious sectarianism replete with ideas of the Enlightenment. The double threat of French-derived Enlightenment "atheism" and American-derived religious dissent bred a pestilent cocktail of democracy and social unrest for which one vaccine was the presence of a strong, centralized, and crown-loyal Anglican church (Rawlyk, 1994: 102).

Several factors, however, resisted the attempt to establish the Anglican Church. The first is the sheer diversity of non-Anglican Protestant and Roman Catholic settlers. Many Protestants – Presbyterians, Wesleyan Methodists, and Congregationalists – were quite happy to resist the tide of Enlightenment free thinking and American-style democracy by stressing a society based on British Christian values, but not at the expense of a *de facto* established church (Moir, 1959: xii). From 1812 until the 1840s these voices, joined by an increasingly political Free Church movement and in particular Methodism under Egerton Ryerson, would consistently resist any formal attempt to grant Anglicanism preferred status. A measure of religious freedom, in principle, was granted outside Anglicanism but advantageous laws, imperial and colonial, such as the initial 1791 Canada Act and subsequent additional clergy reserves land grants and restrictions on education for non-Anglicans, effectively created a church–state alliance that excluded the proffered religious tolerance. In Upper Canada contention centered on land grants while in Lower Canada-Maritimes the contention centered on education. By 1840 compromises restricted Anglican control of education and gave Presbyterians, Methodists, and Roman Catholics a share of the lucrative clergy reserves.

A second factor is the "inner history" of early Canada, divorced from the urban corridors of power but equally committed, for different reasons, to the creation of a "Christian garden" out of the Canadian wilderness. While much of the battle between establishment and an embryonic nationalism was fought in public via newspapers (such as Egerton Ryerson's (1803–82) *Christian Guardian* and John Strachan's (1778–1867) *The Church*) and tracts by the powerful few, the Methodist circuit riders in Upper Canada and the evangelical preachers of the Maritimes had another vision of Canadian identity as a "people highly favored of God." To understand why, despite having a vast influx of Loyalists and voluntarists, British North America was not prone to join the American Revolution or subscribe to American political structure, and why Canada in the nineteenth century had a mollified liberalism in its Protestant churches, one needs to understand the role of evangelical pietists.

Anglican preferment meant that many other Protestant identities (excluding British Methodists and the Church of Scotland) were dependent on American support for much of the 1700s and early 1800s. Surprisingly the "contagion of (American) disaffection" met with an unexpected quietness in transplanted Loyalists to the political struggles of their fostering American brethren. Certainly geography plays a part: the lack of a truly centralized and powerful government except in the urban centers made governmental intervention haphazard and minimal for rural communities. The dispersion of settlements also made it relatively easy for a small military presence to isolate the few dissenting centers and individuals. Nonetheless, the fact remains that, despite widespread contact and dependence, Loyalists remained largely "apolitical" towards the struggles of the American Revolution. This apolitical perspective is a benchmark of a great revivalism that swept through the rural populations of Lower Canada and the Maritimes in the 1770s and up to 1783 (Stewart & Rawlyk, 1972: 93).

The expulsion of the French Acadians was understood by Loyalists as an opportunity to transform a Roman Catholic and pagan wilderness into a Christian garden granted a providential imprimatur. This vision of a "Christian utopia" merged with a revivalism that blended Anglican moralism and proto-Methodist mysticism (in William Law's *Serious Call to a Devout and Holy Life*) with American-developed evangelicalism in such a manner as to minimize the political overtones of democratic egalitarianism and the principle of voluntary association in favor of a preoccupation with one's spiritual state. As seen in the preaching of Henry Alline (1748–84) and the "New Light Movement," a renewal of New England Puritanism (moralism) without its essential Calvinism, the cooperative providential role of the individual before God above and beyond mere politics was essential. The Christian was to reject interest in politics (except where it hindered the gospel) and to concentrate on conversion, piety, and the cocreation of a Christian society. Alline argued for a cooperative place in Christian history for the individual but not in a political form as found in American revivalism. For the Loyalist revivalists their commitment to God was purer than that of their American kin in that they could rise above the petty politics that consumed the Americans and focus, instead, on "spiritual" truths. Unlike their American parents, they were "God's pure people," who though sharing forms of American utilitarianism, were essentially apolitical.

The evangelical awakening explains the lack of resonance to American interests outside of British circles in British North America. However, it also contributes with its intrinsic voluntarism to a post-1812 foundation for dissent against establishment and a movement towards nationalistic federalism in Methodist, Baptist, and other Free Church traditions.[4] It represents a counterbalance to the continued rehabilitation of British values in what is increasingly thought of as a separate nation. The evangelical tradition also brings another theological marker to the fore in that it is one parent, itself already a hybrid of British Loyalist and American interests, of the coming hybrid of American and British theological interests into a unique Canadian theological voice.[5]

"A Sense of Proportion": Sedimentation, Mission, and Modernity[6]

Beginning with the *de jure* closure of establishment in 1854, through to the 1930s, Canadian Protestants were engaged with a growing tide of secularism and urban change. Canada, confederated in 1867, grew into its identity as a "middle power." This period of sedimentation and reaction is also the great age of Canadian mission.[7] What galvanized Protestants across Canada was a sense of continuing a form of Christian Protestant society under threat from Roman Catholicism via the new non-British immigrants,[8] Anglo-Catholicism via the Tractarian movement, and modernity itself.[9] For the urban-based denominations the primary expression of Christian society was the equivocation of "Victorian values and progressiveness" – or British Protestantism. Mission in the city was a mission to the urban dispossessed and the non-Protestant. Great philanthropic societies and movements such as the Sunday School and temperance movements were formed to meet the challenges of the new cities. For the rural communities and the evangelical denominations the primary expression of a Christian society was a general resistance against modernity itself, particularly ideological in regard to Darwinianism and the "new theology." Mission in this instance is the creation of independent theological colleges and mission to the indigenous peoples. In both instances, for mainline and free churches, the sedimentation of a national denominational identity became increasingly important. Intradenominational ecumenism worked to create national bodies to shore up funding and resource management problems derived from the previous ad hoc dependence on American and British parents.

The initial conflation between the secular/sacred and nation/establishment prepared the way for denominational schools. The initial charters of Canada's earliest universities were largely church-based and had their charters, complete with modified religious testing of faculty and students, contested by a prosecular movement in an alliance with the Free Churches.[10] The formation of a single nondenominational university, for example, was posited as a solution in the University Act of 1849. The University of Toronto was to be a secular institution, without religious testing, lacking theological training, and not permitting clergy to serve as either Chancellor or President. As long as secular education promoted "a sane and tactful course" in regard to civic responsibility, most Protestant leaders were happy to allow a separation of theological-religious training from wider higher education.[11] The effect of the closure on the education debate was twofold. First, it drove denominational schools into an ossification of their particular identities. Second, it signaled the isolating of Canadian Protestantism from an increasingly secular wider society, except in the promotion of a common societal good. Late Victorian Canada *was* church-oriented and Protestant but its relevancy took forms that became the Social Gospel movements of the 1920s. By the 1960s even this point of contact was eroded and Protestantism, especially mainstream forms, seemed anachronistic.

The late 1800s marks the struggle with Darwinism and higher criticism. In almost all denominational schools, debate over higher criticism in particular, and the role of wider modernity, flared. The vast majority of faculty, trained in either Europe or America, found the "grassroots" boards to be resistant to new teaching on the Bible and the new speculative theologies (Moir, 1982: 19–57). Until the 1930s the radical programs of German and American theology could only find forms sympathetic to the sense of Canadian propriety and Canadian evangelical roots, both guarded by nonacademic powerful lay leaders.[12]

Propriety meant that scholarship could continue unencumbered with religious connotations unless it directly challenged societal norms. In the case of the Darwinian debate, as long as Darwin's theories remained scientific (in the Baconian sense of empirical and not speculative) and applied (in the Reid "Common Sense" of appropriate range of application to the material and not the moral world) they found acceptance from Protestant thinkers (McKillop, 1987a: 44–53). In fact, the study of the book of nature, as in William Paley and largely replicated in Canada's James Bovell's (1817–80) 1859 work *Outlines of Natural Theology*, could lead to a wonderment at the Christian God. The Scottish Enlightenment's position of reason, guided and circumscribed by revelation, as directed toward moral improvement, held a powerful influence in Canadian Protestant circles. The threefold erosion of a Baconian scientism (method over speculation), a stress on Scottish "Common Sense" philosophy, and a static but divinely ordered Newtonian–Paleyan world by the turn of the century in favor of idealism and process rekindled the metaphysical debate on Darwinianism (McKillop, 1987b). Modernity was welcome as long as it remembered it was a guest in the Protestant house.

Ironically, Canada's eighteenth-century revivalist tradition also contributed to the rapid rise of secularism in Canada, particularly in Methodist and low-church Anglicanism. Although older revivalist tradition was not so much a formal set of doctrines but a loose set of assumptions, these assumptions allowed a dialogue with modernity that paralleled the wider secular conversation. These assumptions included belief in the fallen nature of human reason, in a providential God, and the subsequent relevancy of the Bible as a blueprint for a society. These parallel the secular trinity of Bacon–Paley–Reid. The "wounded reason" of sinners meant that science, useful in itself as technique, could not address the true needs of human society and must be confined to technical solutions. This is a form of Baconism. The activity of a providential God mimics the Paleyan belief in an ordered universe, so that Protestant evangelical society – voluntarist and democratic – is the best manner forward (and blessed) for a culture. Finally, it is only proper that God's inerrant or inspired Word, the Bible, should be the guidebook, limiting but still in dialogue with reason and science, towards such a society and mission (Gauvereau, 1991). A curious hybrid occurs in the evangelical mind, largely divorced from either European-American speculative attempts of synthesis (mainly idealism) and the extreme American fundamentalist hostility towards modernity. This hybrid holds the primacy of revelation and the need for a dialogue with secular society but values theology only to the extent that it serves assumptions already committed to. Furthermore, it also kept modernity (and theology) largely uncritiqued as long as modernity kept to its own sphere of knowledge and it remained, at worst, neutral or, at best, cooperative to the vision of a revived society. The end result, for both Canadian mainline Protestants and Canadian evangelicals, was a form of unsophisticated biblicalism and a historist progressivism that conflated Canadian Protestant, mainly Anglo-Saxon, society with civilization and Christianity.

Post-1918 Canadian evangelicals and mainline denominations simply did not have the academic resources to counter the disillusionment of Western society and the rise of the sciences that it initially encouraged. Tethered to an ideological historicism, and to a promotion of science as neutral technique or method, it was vulnerable to the failure of the former and the sheer explanatory power of the latter. The only permissible point of contact between the secular and sacred was a stress on the sociological good inherent in thoughtful religion.[13] Protestantism in Canada splintered into either a reactive position similar to American fundamentalism or positioned itself as a vehicle for the promotion of a wider cultural liberalism. The sharp rise of Bible schools and colleges from 1919 to 1939 is evidence of reaction[14] and one interpretation of the Presbyterian–Methodist Church Union (United Church) is as a movement towards this functional interpretation of Protestant mission heavily committed to social reform and relevance over theological distinction (Keith, 1985).

Fragmented Gods and a Return to Mosaic

The last 50 years has seen Canada change in many significant ways. Immigration patterns have made Anglo-Saxon Canada a minority as other cultures add to the ethnic and religious mosaic. No longer is Canada even nominally a Christian nation. Religious Studies departments are, by and large, divorced from faith-based study of religion in favor of scientific study. Wilfred C Smith (1916–2000) was McGill's first purpose-appointed (1949) Professor of Comparative Religion. Feminist scholars have reminded Canadian Protestants that one can never return to the marriage of culture and Christianity without marginalization and of the need for a Christian experience that includes the feminine and the "other."[15] Non-European-based Protestant forms (and mission) and the rapid rise of Pentecostalism and American evangelicalism have sharply affected traditional Protestantism. Mainline denominations, when growth occurs, often finds it in non-European variants while American evangelicalism (and fundamentalism) attracts historical Canadian evangelical churches, especially in low-church Anglican and Free Church forms.[16] Assisting this last tendency is the mass exportation of American church resources to Canadian laity. Finally, the dream of the "Lord's dominion" or "Christian garden" seems now more than ever a chimera as Protestant and Catholic institutions struggle with their own history of institutional abuse, particularly in regard to the indigenous peoples. Canadian Protestantism, for good or evil, has turned full circle. It remains a laity-centered, geographically or linguistically influenced phenomenon that struggles towards a coherent identity, still thinks itself a theological colony, and wonders how it can be relevant.

One Attempt for Identity: Douglas John Hall

With the exception of George P. Grant's (1918–88) *Lament for a Nation* (1963) there has been little attention paid to a philosophical or theological interpretation of Canadian identity. One notable recent voice, however, has been McGill's Douglas John Hall. Hall's work, heavily influenced by Grant,[17] argues that Canadian identity, including that of the church, suffers under a "cultural malaise" derived from its history and placement. Canada's history, its colonial adolescence, and linkage to wider American values such as optimistic and scientific-economic progress, and its geography as an isolated "Northern" nation, combine to lend Canada a "skepticism" in spite of its proximity to the United States. "Nordicity," for Hall, a geographical and climate-derived isolationism, means that "true belief," the American alliance of nationalism and religion (via Calvinistic providentialism), never truly took root in Canadian Protestant church forms, providing a way forward for Canadian theologians and churches to manifest the Christian gospel in the West (Hall, 1993: 110–11).

Although Canadian Protestant churches have followed the largely Western position in holding to a form of liberalism, it did and does so in a manner that is political rather than merely the "academic humanism" of American liberalism or the "religiously simple" and reactionary personalistic American pietism. Canadians, Hall argues, have always understood, borne out of "survival" (Atwood, 1972), that *stewardship* – in critique of and by life-affirming action in the modern world – is a *leitmotif* of Christian life. For Canadian Protestants in an age of pluralism, nuclearism, and at the end of an American Constantinianism (*theologia gloria*) the task is a rediscovery of the "meaningfulness of existence" divorced from the ills of America's covert nihilism (Hall, 1993: 290). The means to do this is an embracement of "Christian distinctiveness" and a recovery of "Christian theology and preaching" as a locus of God's action in the world (Hall, 1996: 462). This means a "thinking renewal" of the "*theologia crucis*," a critical alliance with the oppressed and marginalized and a mission of stewardship towards the "spiritual demands of the ordinary," found within the very core of Protestantism (Hall, 1996: 460). Canadian "values" such as "tolerance," "difference," and "otherness" are given theological approval. Hall, while arguing for a distinctly Canadian voice, largely turns to the resources of German theology and European origins. However, he seems reluctant to argue for the Christian exclusiveness found in the ecclesiological theologies of his Germanic heroes. Nonetheless, Hall appears to support the thesis that whatever Canadian Protestantism is, it is shaped by its dual relationship to America and Europe.

Notes

1   The province of Quebec (New France to 1763 and Lower Canada after 1791) quickly shifted its vision from being a location of exploited resources to a Roman Catholic society and mission field with the charter of New France (1627). The key difference from New England (American) and then British North American English settlers at this early stage of colonization is the French commitment towards *les bons sauvages*, whose conversion to Christianity would, in turn, spur on European Catholics towards greater faith.

2   Stewart and Rawlyk (1972: 28).

3   "British" Wesleyans were active in the 1830s, supported by the Colonial Office, to eradicate the American Wesleyan republican influences.

4   Much of the early revivalist movements, including Alline's New Light movement, were translated into Baptist churches. Much of the early American Methodist flavor of Upper Canada is mitigated post-1812 due to widespread British immigration. What remained, however, is the intrinsic sense of voluntarism that even British forms contained, despite competing political conservativism.

5   Examples of this include S. F. Wise's thesis that American evangelicalism, and sense of providence in particular, combines with a Burke-influenced British conservativism that immobilized any sense of nationalism in favor of traditionalism. Carl Berger argued that Canadian nationalism is inherently a fusion of American notions of juridical freedoms with British traditionalism, allowing diversity to be valued and protected by law but in such a manner as to give preeminence to British values as the norm. See McKillop (1987).

6   Moir, 1982.

7   See Moir and McIntire (1988). Indigenous missions were largely the activity of Methodists whose missions included education and centralization, but by 1840 racist policies undermined cooperation with the first nations as reservations became limiting to the promised program of land ownership and independence. After 1840 centralization was coercive and understood as a negative by the first peoples.

8   Protestantism in Quebec remained largely influenced by its decided alliance with (and dependence on) English-speaking Canada rather than French Canada, even in education and culture.

9   Roman Catholic support for the Metis rebellion of 1869–70 also added much fuel to the anti-Catholic sentiment.

10   Dalhousie University (1817), although Church of Scotland, did not in principle exclude other denominations. However, it did remain staunchly Presbyterian and by the 1830s this caused Baptists and Methodists to establish their own colleges.

11   Moir (1982: 23). Religious education persisted into the 1980s in Canadian public schools.

12   A few examples suffice: Toronto stalwart S. H. Blake's 1909 successful challenge to University College's perceived conflation of religious studies with Christian doctrine; and, one of many dismissals for heterodoxy in all institutions, Victoria College's firing of George C. Workman.

13   For example, the neo-orthodoxy movement never thrived in Canada (Moir, 1982: 73).

14   There were over 100 in Canada by 1980, half of which were formed between 1919 and 1939 (Moir, 1982: 96).

15   Dorcas Gordon (1995) notes that Canadian feminist scholarship does not vary from other national counterparts in its themes. Marilyn Legge (1992) counters this in a small measure by asserting that Canadian literature can provide a blueprint for a Canadian feminist theology.

16   Most notably Thomas T. Shields of the Jarvis Street Baptist Church.

17   He borrows heavily Grant's critique of the West as being a failed "technocracy" with its belief in a progressivism that will solve or absolve human suffering. In fact, Grant argues that such a technological progressivism must end up, as argued by Nietzsche, in the culture of the amoral superman. See, famously, Grant (1969) and also Hall (1987: 37–44, 1993: 84, 1996: 461).

References

Atwood, Margaret (1972). *Survival: A Thematic Guide to Canadian Literature.* Toronto: Anasis.

Gauvereau, Michael (1991). *The Evangelical Century: College and Creed in English Canada from the Great Revival to the Great Depression.* Kingston, ON: McGill-Queen's University Press.

Gordon, Dorcas (1995). Feminist Theology in Canada. In Ofelia Ortega (ed.), *Women's Views, Theological Reflection, Celebration and Action.* Geneva: WCC Press, pp. 127–37.

Grant, George P. (1963). *Lament for a Nation.* Toronto: McClelland and Stewart.

Grant, George P. (1969). *Time as History.* Toronto: University of Toronto Press.

Grant, J. W. (1977). Religion and the Quest for National Identity. In Peter Slater (ed.), *Religion and Culture in Canada.* Waterloo, ON: Canadian Corporation for Studies in Religion, pp. 7–22.

Hall, Douglas John (1987). *Thinking the Faith: Christian Theology in a North American Context.* Minneapolis: Fortress.

Hall, Douglas John (1993), *Professing the Faith: Christian Theology in a North American Context.* Minneapolis: Fortress.

Hall, Douglas John (1996) The Future of Protestantism in North America. *Theology Today* 52(4): 458–66.

Keith, C. N. (1985). *The Resistance to Church Union in Canada 1904–1939.* Vancouver, UBC Press.

Legge, Marilyn (1992). Colourful Differences: "Otherness" and the Image of God for Canadian Feminist Theologies. *Studies in Religion* 21(1): 67–80.

McKillop, A. B. (1987a). Nationalism, Identity and Canadian Intellectual History. In A. B. McKillop (ed.), *Contours of Canadian Thought.* Toronto: University of Toronto Press.

McKillop, A. B. (1987b). Caliban: The Missing Link (Daniel Wilson). In A. B. McKillop (ed.), *Contours of Canadian Thought.* Toronto: University of Toronto Press, pp. 61–98.

Moir, John S. (1959). *Church and State in Canada West.* Toronto: University of Toronto Press.

Moir, John S. (1982). *A History of Biblical Studies in Canada: A Sense of Proportion.* Chico, CA: Scholar's Press.

Moir, John S. and McIntire, C. T. (1988). *Canadian Protestant and Catholic Missions 1820s–1960s.* New York: Lang.

Murphy, T. (1996). English Speaking Colonies to 1854. In T. Murphy and R. Perin (eds.), *Concise History of Christianity in Canada.* Toronto: Oxford University Press, pp. 108–89.

Rawlyk, G. (1994). *The Canada Fire: Radical Evangelicalism in British North America*. Kingston, ON: McGill-Queen's University Press.

Stewart, G. and Rawlyk, G. (1972). *A People Highly Favoured of God: The Nova Scotia Yankees and the American Revolution*. Toronto: Archon.

Further Reading

Grant, J. W., Moir, J. S., and Walsh, H. H. (eds.) (1966–72), *History of the Christian Church in Canada* (3 vols). Toronto: Ryerson Press.

Murphy, T. and Perin, R. (eds.) (1996). *Concise History of Christianity in Canada*. Toronto: Oxford University Press.

Stackhouse, John G. (1993). *Canadian Evangelicalism in the Twentieth Century: An Introduction to its Character*. Toronto: University of Toronto Press.

CHAPTER 18

Indian Protestantism to the Present Day

Ivan Morris Satyavrata

The Beginnings of Protestant Mission in India to 1858

Protestant influence in India had inconspicuous beginnings, with the establishment of British, Dutch and Danish trading stations in the first half of the seventeenth century. An Anglican chaplain of the East India Company, Patrick Copeland, was responsible for the conversion of the first Indian Protestant, baptized in England in 1616, and other chaplains likewise engaged in the occasional mission activity. Later evangelical-minded chaplains, such as Claudius Buchanan and Henry Martyn, would be much more active in their missionary activities. The European trading companies were, however, generally opposed to missionary work in the territories under their control.

The first organized Protestant mission in India began with the arrival in 1706 of two German Lutherans, Bartholomew Ziegenbalg and Henry Plutschau, at Tranquebar, 150 miles south of Madras on the East coast of India. The Tranquebar Mission began with the patronage of King Frederick IV of Denmark, and subsequently earned the support of Anglican mission associations such as the Society for Promoting Christian Knowledge (SPCK) and the Society for the Propagation of the Gospel (SPG). The most significant contribution of this mission was the first translation of the Bible into an Indian vernacular, with the publication of the Tamil Bible in 1792. A leading figure in the Tranquebar Mission was C. F. Schwartz, whose personal integrity and Christian statesmanship greatly enhanced the credibility of the Protestant missionary enterprise in India.

Protestant mission in North India began with the arrival of the first missionary for the British Baptist Missionary Society (BMS), William Carey, in 1793. Carey established a mission station at Serampore near Calcutta. Although the Serampore mission primarily devoted itself to conversion, significant contributions were also made in the fields of education, journalism and social reform.

The mission's most important contribution was in the area of Bible translation: by the end of Carey's life, he had facilitated the translation of portions of the Bible into 34 indigenous languages. The arrival of the Scottish missionary, Alexander Duff, in Calcutta in 1830 marked the introduction of a new phase in Protestant missions, in which liberal English education began to be used as a tool in mission. Duff's approach succeeded in drawing high caste Hindus to Christianity and gained popularity, but also would become the focus of much debate in subsequent years.

The evangelical awakening in Britain in the late eighteenth and early nineteenth century saw the emergence and arrival in India of a number of other mission agencies, including the London Missionary Society (LMS) and the Church Missionary Society (CMS). A key figure for the LMS was W. T. Ringeltaube, the first Protestant missionary to Travancore, whose work saw mass conversions among the *Shanars* or *Nadars*, a section of low caste Hindus in south India. The CMS, under the leadership of a German Lutheran, C. T. E. Rhenius, also saw large numbers of converts in the Tirunelveli district.

The Basel Mission worked in South Kanara on the west coast and other missions such as the Gossner Evangelical Lutheran Mission and the Leipzig Lutheran Mission soon followed. The first American Mission was the American Board of Commissioners for Foreign Missions. Other American missions to arrive in India during the first half of the nineteenth century included Presbyterians, Baptists and Lutherans.

The achievements of the first 150 years of the Protestant missionary presence in India included 331 churches, 130,500 Protestant Christians, over 2,000 boarding and day schools, 48 ordained Indian Christian workers and 700 catechists (Menachery, 1982: 41). Protestant missions had also helped initiate a number of social and moral reforms against the practices of *sati* (the Hindu widow's self-immolation on her husband's funeral pyre), infanticide and oppression of Hindu widows. Unfortunately the cultural imperialism that was implicit in the predominant missionary attitude towards Indian culture and religion resulted in intense mid-century conflict between the Christian missionary and Hindu communities. A growing perception that Christianity was a denationalizing force intensified and hardened Hindu resistance to Christian missionary work.

This provided the context within which the struggle for an authentic Indian Christian identity began to be expressed in the work of some early pioneers of indigenous Christianity. These include Krishna Mohan Banerjea (1813–85), a Bengali high caste convert, whose contributions as a priest, scholar, social reformer, national civil rights leader and statesman earned him both an honorary Doctor of Law from Calcutta University and a title of honour from the British Government. Lal Behari Day (1824–94), another Bengali convert who became a pastor-evangelist and nationalist, was the first to propose the concept of an Indian national church based on the Apostles Creed, inclusive of Roman Catholics and free from foreign control. Nehemiah Goreh (1825–95), a high caste Brahmin by birth and reputable Sanskrit scholar, became an effective and renowned Christian apologist. These represent a class of Indian Christians who remained passionately Christian and deeply Indian at the same time, thus earning the respect of fellow Indians of other faiths.

Widespread dissatisfaction with British rule led to the 1857 'Sepoy mutiny', an uprising by Indian military personnel in north India. Although the revolt was anti-British rather than anti-Christian, both missionaries and Indian Christians suffered persecution because of their proximity to the Europeans. The event became a watershed in the history of Indian Christianity, as its immediate cause was the rumour of forced conversions. As such, whatever the true cause, it was inevitable that religious persecution of Christians accompanied it. The result was that the British Government issued an edict disclaiming any interest in proselytization, and effectively distanced colonial politics from Christian mission.

Protestant Christianity in India Since 1858

In 1958 the government of India passed from the British East India Company to the British Government, and its policy of religious neutrality provided a favourable atmosphere for missionary activity. Protestant missions in India thus experienced their most vigorous growth in the second half of the nineteenth century. While the older missionary societies consolidated and extended into new territories, a number of new American and European missionary societies began work in different areas.

Most growth during this period was through group or mass conversions from the oppressed classes (or 'Dalits'). These occurred in the wake of a series of severe famines and plagues between 1870 and 1920, during which Christians were active in organizing relief work. Consequently, between 1870 and 1900, the number of Protestant Christians in India quadrupled. By 1930 it was estimated that 80 percent of Protestants were the products of mass conversions. While the motives of mass converts to Christianity have been suspect, the liberation and empowerment of the Dalits may be Protestantism's most significant contribution to India.

Protestantism also experienced rapid growth among aboriginal tribal groups during this period, through programs of economic aid, education and medical services. These, again, contributed to both a social liberation and a spiritual emancipation. For instance, the first Protestant mission among the Naga tribe in northeast India was established in 1886, and by 1950 there were about 50,000 Naga Christians. Churches in the north-eastern states of Nagaland, Mizoram and Meghalaya have continued to grow rapidly since India's independence. Following 1858, Protestant social projects added to their mandate of nation building, with a renewed emphasis on educational and medical work. The establishment of orphanages, widows' homes, leper asylums and agricultural and industrial training institutions became important components of rural developmental programmes.

The Indian Protestant search for identity in the twentieth century was largely shaped by the independence struggle and the birth of the Indian nation in 1947. Although most Christians saw British rule in India as providential, since it provided freedom for missionary activity, missionary and Indian Christian leaders such as C. F. Andrews, K. T. Paul, V. S. Azariah, S. K. Datta and S. K. Rudra encouraged active Christian participation in the national struggle. During the drafting of the Indian constitution these leaders, with maturity and foresight, rejected the suggestion of a separate electorate for Christians.

The nationalist spirit expressed itself as the impulse towards indigenization, contextualization and the aspiration for a national church. The missionary attitude to Indian culture had, in general, always been decidedly negative. Conversion to Christianity usually meant that the convert broke with the cultural and social traditions of the community and embraced a Western way of life. A growing awareness of their rich cultural heritage helped Indian Christians to develop a positive attitude to indigenous culture and pursue indigenization of worship, church architecture and evangelism while working towards self-government and support. Likewise concern for the need of using thought forms and constructs shaped within the distinctly Indian religious and sociopolitical context has occupied many Indian Protestant minds over the past 150 years. Creative Indian thinkers include Sadhu Sundar Singh, A. J. Appasamy, N. V. Tilak, P. Chenchiah, V. Chakkarai, P. D. Devanandan, M. M. Thomas, S. J. Samartha and V. K. Samuel.

Part of the ethos of a national Indian identity was the establishment of church union movements. K. C. Banerjea's Christo Samaj (1887), Parani Andi's National Church in India (1886) and the Western India Native Christian Alliance (1871) were nineteenth-century precursors of later national and indigenous church union movements. The two most important of these unions were the formation of the Church of South India (CSI) in 1947, and the Church of North India (CNI) in 1970. The CSI brought together the south Indian Anglican dioceses, the South Indian United Church (Presbyterian and Congregational) and the south Indian districts of the Methodist Church (British). The constituents of the CNI were the north Indian Anglican dioceses, the United Church of North India (Presbyterian and Congregational), the Council of Baptist Churches in North India, the Disciples of Christ, the Church of the Brethren and the Methodist Church (British and Australian). At present negotiations for an even wider national union of churches are being carried out. Two other ecumenical organizations are important to note. The National Christian Council of India (NCCI), formed in 1914, is an ecumenical agency that coordinates common concerns of churches and Christian institutions, providing a forum for interdenominational consultation and concerted action. A parallel body in the Evangelical Fellowship of India (EFI) – although theologically more conservative – was formed in 1951. It networks over a hundred denominations and parachurch agencies.

The twentieth century saw the arrival of some younger Western evangelical and Pentecostal missions in India, and a number of new indigenous church and mission movements. Many of these largely independent evangelical or charismatic church movements continue to experience phenomenal growth and, together with the older Protestant denominations, constitute about 60 per cent of India's approximately 30 million Christian population (Johnstone & Mandryk, 2001: 310). Indigenous Protestant missions began with the formation of the Indian Missionary Society (IMS) in 1903, and the National Missionary Society (NMS) in 1906, but in the last few decades the indigenous missionary movement has burgeoned to over 44,000 workers in about 450 mission agencies (Johnstone & Mandryk, 2001: 311).

Although some sections of the Protestant Church in India are experiencing decline due to corruption and nominalism, there is ample evidence of vitality and growth. The future of Protestantism in India hinges largely on how effectively it succeeds in resolving the issue of self-identity: whether it is able to affirm continuity with historic and global Protestantism, and yet remain authentically Indian – culturally integrated within Indian society.

References

Johnstone, P. and Mandryk, J. (2001). *Operation World: 21st Century Edition*. Carlisle, UK: Paternoster.
Menachery, G. (ed.) (1982). *The St. Thomas Christian Encyclopaedia of India*. Trichur: The St. Thomas Christian Encyclopaedia of India.

Further Reading

Baago, K. (1969). *Pioneers of Indigenous Christianity*. Madras: CLS.
Firth, C. B. (1976). *An Introduction to Indian Church History*. Madras: CLS.
Mundadan, A. M. (1984). *Indian Christians: Search for Identity & Struggle for Autonomy*. Bangalore: Dharmaram Publications.
Neill, S. (1984). *A History of Christianity in India: Beginnings to AD 1707*. Cambridge, UK: Cambridge University Press.
Neill, S. (1985). *A History of Christianity in India: 1707–1858*. Cambridge, UK: Cambridge University Press.
Perumalil, H. C. and Hambye, E. R. (eds.) (1972). *Christianity in India: A History in Ecumenical Perspective*. Alleppey: Prakasam Publications.
Richter, J. (1908). *A History of Protestant Missions in India*. London.

CHAPTER 19

South-East Asian Protestantism to the Present Day

Yung Hwa

South-East Asia consists of 11 nations: Brunei, Cambodia, Indonesia, Laos, Malaysia, Myanmar, the Philippines, Singapore, Thailand, Timor and Vietnam. It is ethnically diverse with hundreds of languages and a melting pot of all the great Asian religions and folk beliefs. The population was 518 million in 2000, with Christians forming 21.2 per cent, of which 8.8 per cent are Protestants, including all mainline denominations, Pentecostals and independent churches. The Philippines has the highest proportion of Protestants (24.1%), followed by Indonesia (9.7%) and Singapore (7.2%), with the lowest in Cambodia (0.9%). Given that only around 8 per cent of Asia's entire population is Christian, these figures show that Christianity is particularly vibrant in the region, although the church remains relatively weak in Cambodia, Laos and Thailand.

History and Identity

Protestant history may be best separated into two historical epochs, each with differing emphases and resultant identities. The two epochs are the sixteenth to the nineteenth centuries and the twentieth century.

Sixteenth to nineteenth centuries

Curiously, the origins of Protestantism in the region is linked to early Roman Catholic missions (1534) to the Moluccas islands. Dutch takeover of the East Indies in 1605 from the Portuguese resulted in the Dutch United East India Company forcing all Catholics to embrace Reformed Christianity. Thus the oldest Protestant church in Indonesia today, the Moluccan Protestant Church, is considered to date either from 1534 or 1605, depending on its Catholic or Protestant origin. Over the next two centuries, there was little European action to advance the indigenous church. However, despite this missionary lethargy, the first complete translation of the Bible in an indigenous language was published in Malay in 1733.

The nineteenth century brought fresh impetus to the growth of Protestantism to the region. American Baptists began work in Myanmar (Burma) in 1813. The London Missionary Society sent William Milne, a Presbyterian, to Malacca in 1814. In the same year, the Netherlands Missionary Society began sending missionaries to Java and the Moluccas. Anglicans came as military and settlement chaplains to Myanmar in 1813 and Singapore in 1826, with missionaries to indigenous peoples arriving later. Other groups and denominations followed in quick succession, including Rhenish missionaries, German Lutherans, Plymouth Brethren, and American and British Methodists. From 1840 onwards, indigenous churches began emerging in the Philippines. Many, such as the five million strong Philippines Independent Church today, originated in part as a protest against colonialism and as independence movements against Spanish Catholicism.

The twentieth century

Protestant denominations and missions from the West continued to impact the whole region throughout the twentieth century. Until the outbreak of the Second World War, except for the Filipino independent churches and some overseas Chinese churches, church leadership was largely in the hands of Western missionaries. With few exceptions, little emphasis was given to the training of indigenous leaders in the region. During this period, Protestant identities were largely, though not exclusively, rooted in those of Western denominations.

The end of the war ushered in a period of immense change. In tandem with nationalistic independence movements, mission-founded churches likewise moved towards independence, at least organizationally if not always financially. Leadership increasingly passed into indigenous hands. This period also saw rapid institutional growth of seminaries, parachurch organizations, and denominational and interdenominational structures.

Protestant churches have had a significant social impact in the region. In countries where Christian presence was relatively strong, mission schools made major contributions to education before national independence, after which governments increasingly took over this responsibility. Protestant-founded universities continue to play significant roles in Indonesia and the Philippines. Protestant churches have contributed significantly to social outreach in the region through ministries such as running orphanages and recently in drug rehabilitation work. Individual Protestants have also significantly impacted national politics in countries like Indonesia, where some such as Johannes Leimena played key roles in the independence movement, and the Philippines, where Jovito Salonga was Senate President (1987–92) and Fidel Ramos the President (1992–8).

Protestantism has experienced steady growth throughout the last century. Particularly following the Second World War many indigenous independent or free churches began emerging throughout the region. But unlike the earlier indigenous movement in the Philippines, these came out of Protestant free-church traditions or newer charismatic models, and are not necessarily tied up with nationalistic concerns. In general, the majority of Protestants in the region are theologically conservative in doctrine and often, but not numerically, Pentecostal-charismatic in spirituality. Indeed most of the large churches, some with over 10,000 members, in Bangkok, Jakarta, Kuala Lumpur, Manila and Singapore are Pentecostal-charismatic. But it is questionable whether all this growth has also been marked by the emergence of true indigeneity in theology, spirituality and pastoral practice.

The Future

There is no doubt that Protestantism as a whole is growing rapidly in the region, except for a small minority of churches caught in traditionalism or overly influenced by Western liberal theology. Moreover, churches in Singapore, Malaysia and the Philippines are sending missionaries overseas, including to the West, in increasing numbers. All indications point to continuing rapid growth and an increasing impact on world Christianity in the coming years.

However, Protestant churches in Southeast Asia face three crucial challenges. First, the churches must learn to overcome the growing pressures of restrictions on religious freedom, especially in Muslim dominant countries. In general, where Christianity is in the minority, relationship between Catholics and various Protestant groups are cordial because of the need to band together to deal with state restrictions. It would probably be correct to say that only in the Philippines, where Christianity is dominant, are there any overt tensions between Protestants and Catholics. At the same time, within Protestantism, there are continuing tensions between ecumenical, evangelical and Pentecostal-charismatic churches, although the lines between these grouping are often blurred.

Second, the emergence of an increasingly post-denominational and independent Protestant mindset in the region threatens to lead to growing divisiveness instead of opening the way for the development of a deeper ecumenism based on the gospel.

Finally, Protestantism in the region and Asia in general has, in the past, been built on a Western identity and thus described as 'culturally deformed' for many Asians. An indigenous identity rooted firmly in both the biblical faith and the region's contextual and cultural distinctiveness is desperately needed if the present growth is to be both sustained and nurtured.

Further Reading

Athyal, Saphir (ed.) (1998). *Church in Asia Today: Challenges and Opportunities*. Singapore: Asia Lausanne Committee for World Evangelization.

Freston, Paul (2001). *Evangelicals and Politics in Asia, Africa and Latin America*. Cambridge, UK: Cambridge University Press.

Hwa, Yung (1997). *Mangoes or Bananas? The Quest for an Authentic Asian Christian Theology*. Oxford: Regnum.

Roxbrough, John (1995). Context and Continuity: Regional Patterns in the History of Southeast Asian Christianity. *Asian Journal of Theology* 9: 30–46.

Sunquist, Scott (ed.) (2001). *A Dictionary of Asian Christianity*. Grand Rapids, MI: Eerdmans.

CHAPTER 20

Japanese Protestantism to the Present Day

Nozomo Miyahira

Origins (c.1850–80s)

Protestant Christianity in Japan essentially dates back to the mid-nineteenth century, when Western European powers launched into treaties of commerce and amity with Japan. In 1859 American and English missionaries reintroduced Protestant Christianity to Japan, although Christianity was still under an official ban until 1873. The first Japanese Protestant Christian was baptized in 1865 by James H. Ballagh (1832–1920) of the Reformed Church in America, and in 1872 Christians baptized by him established the first Protestant church in Yokohama. These Christians, the Yokohama Group, sought an evangelical, non-denominational and self-governing character.

Protestant churches, called *Kirisuto Kokai* (Church of Christ), quickly emerged in Tokyo, Kobe and Osaka. Missionaries from the American Reformed and Presbyterian Churches, along with the American Board, held a joint conference in 1872 to help existing Protestant churches to unite as one church on the basis of a Japanese identity, but in fact, due to missionary intransigence, the union did not materialize as hoped.

In 1877 the Reformed and the Presbyterian missions united to form *Nihon Kirisuto Icchi Kyokai* (The Union Church of Christ in Japan) with a highly denominational character, whereas in 1886 the American Board organized *Nihon Kumiai Kyokai* (the Associated Churches in Japan) characterized by congregationalism and an independent spirit. After 1886 the Union Church and the Associated Churches attempted unification, but this was in vain due to the strong objection raised by Niijima Jo (1843–90), a Japanese Missionary of the American Board and a founder of the *Doshisha Ei Gakko* (Doshisha English School, 1875, later Doshisha University). Japanese Christians taught by an American educationalist, Leroy L. Janes (1837–1909) at the *Kumamoto Yo Gakko*

(Kumamoto Western School) or the Kumamoto Group, would make a deep impact on later generations in the Associated Churches.

In 1887 the *Nihon Sei Ko Kai* (Japan Holy Catholic Church) was founded, funded by the American Episcopal Church, the Society for the Propagation of the Gospel and the Church Missionary Society. This church adopted the Lambeth Quadrilateral of 1888. In 1907 the *Nihon Mesojisuto Kyokai* (Japan Methodist Church) was built as a collaboration by three American Methodist churches. The latter half of the nineteenth century saw Baptist, Lutheran and other Protestant missionaries from the USA landing in Japan to plant respective churches, but efforts for self-support by the Japanese laity proved problematic across the board.

The *Mukyokai* (Non-Church Movement), led by Uchimura Kanzo (1861–1930), steered a different course. Uchimura was a member of the Sapporo Group, a group of students influenced by the American agronomist, William S. Clark (1826–86) at the *Sapporo No Gakko* (Sapporo Agricultural School, later Hokkaido University). In 1891 Uchimura had to resign his teaching post at the *Daiichi Koto Chugakko* (The First High School, later part of Tokyo University), as his faith prevented him from bowing to a document containing the Imperial Precept on Education signed by the Emperor. From 1900, he took the initiative in creating *Mukyokai* groups engaged mainly in Bible study, while regarding the clergy and the sacraments as hindrances to the Christian faith.

Theological and Social Issues (1880–1939)

From the late 1880s liberal theology, known as *Shin Shingaku* (new theology) began to become popular through the influence of the American Unitarian Association and the *Allgemeiner evangelisch-Protestantischer Missionsverein*. In 1901 a heated theological controversy over the doctrine of the Trinity and Christology broke out between Uemura Masahisa (1858–1925) from the Yokohama Group, later a founder of the Tokyo Shingakusha (Tokyo Theological Seminary, 1904) and Ebina Danjo (1856–1937) from the Kumamoto Group, later Chancellor of Doshisha University. Uemura supported the divinity of Christ and the doctrine of substitutionary atonement as the basis of historic Protestantism, while Ebina thought of Christianity as an ultimate realization of religious consciousness, universal to all human beings, and therefore also relating to Confucianism and Shintoism. The conference of the *Fukuin Domeikai* (Evangelical Alliance in Japan) held in 1902 approved a view closer to Uemura's, but Ebina remained influential in the Japanese Christian community. Ebina's more general liberal understanding of human progress later guided Yoshino Sakuzo (1878–1933), Professor at Tokyo Imperial University (later Tokyo University), to champion democracy in the imperialistic polity in the second decade of the twentieth century.

In the 1930s Kagawa Toyohiko (1888–1960), a Christian social reformer, proposed a nationwide evangelistic movement called *Kami No Kuni Undo* (the Kingdom of God Movement). The American social gospel stimulated not merely Kagawa but also Nakajima Shigeru (1888–1946), Professor at Doshisha University when Ebina was Chancellor there, to develop a 'social Christianity' invested in a practical social ethic. Opposing this 'social Christianity', Takakura Tokutaro (1885–1934), one of the followers of Uemura and a devotee of Peter T. Forsyth, insisted upon an evangelical Christianity that stressed the human need for redemption against human progressivism.

Many Japanese theologians in the 1930s converted to the theology of Karl Barth, but they catered to the wider Japanese nationalism without appreciating Barth's criticism of Nazism in the Japanese context. In 1937 Yanaihara Tadao (1893–1961), one of the disciples of Uchimura, was forced to resign his professorship of economics at Tokyo Imperial University, because of his severe criticism of aggressive Japanese foreign policies in Asia. It is not surprising that after the war, in 1951, when the anti-Christian social structure had already been overturned, he became the Chancellor of Tokyo University.

The United Church of Christ in Japan and the Second World War (1939–45)

The Imperial Diet passed the *Shukyo Dantai Ho* (Religious Organizations Act) in 1939 with a view to controlling all religious organizations, including Christian churches. In 1941 more than 30 Protestant denominations were incorporated into *Nihon Kirisuto Kyodan* (The United Church of Christ in Japan) and their leaders were instructed to keep the churches under the aegis of the government. This was a rejection of the headship of Christ in favour of one mandated by the government. Their mandate was to support the Japanese wartime regime and to suppress Asian Christians by coercing them into worshipping the Japanese Shinto shrines, while propaganda argued that the United Church was the ideal form of Japanese Christianity to replace Western-derived Christianity in Asia.

Japan unconditionally surrendered in 1945, and the United Church followed this by stating that the United Church must follow the Emperor's holy will and now contribute to the formation of the New Japan. Within a few years, unsurprisingly, many churches including Korean churches in Japan seceded from the United Church to return to older denominational roots or to form new denominations.

Through dialogues with other Asian churches and a gradual admission of a destructive Japanese nationalism in the wider Japanese culture, in 1967 Protestant denominations began to admit responsibility for their wartime collaboration while members of the United Church. The United Church is still active in Japan and remains for many, including other Asian churches, a challenge because of its role in the war and the post-war period. World War Two and its aftermath have left indelible marks on Japanese Protestantism, not only in terms of its collaboration but also in terms of its theological and ideological commitments.

Post-war Protestant Theology (1945 to the present)

The defeat in 1945 left the Japanese utterly dejected and from within this painful emotional climate emerged *Theology of the Pain of God* (1946) by Kazo Kitamori (1916–98), later Professor of Systematic Theology at Tokyo Union Theological Seminary (which itself belongs to the theological tradition of the Yokohama Group). For Kitamori the concept of the pain of God is not a kind of Sabellian Patripassianism that claims that the suffering of the Son on the Cross reveals the suffering of the Father himself. Instead, the pain of God consists essentially in the fact that the Father not only begets the Son but also leads him to suffer and die on the Cross, and that God forgives unforgivable sinners. In this sense the pain of God is not a substantial or ontological concept, but rather a concept of the relation between the Father and the Son, God and sinners.

As a follower of Nishida Kitaro (1870–1945), who was the representative Japanese philosopher before the defeat, and also as the first Japanese student of Karl Barth, Takizawa Katsumi (1909–84) developed a theology of Immanuel. Nishida set forth a theory that contradictory concepts such as transcendence and immanence are mutually complementary to each other. Takizawa found in the reality of Immanuel – God being with us in Christ – which Barth emphasized, a dialectic relationship between God and humanity, transcendence and immanence. In dialogue with Takizawa, who took a favourable view of Buddhism, Yagi Seiichi has continued to elaborate on a point of contact between Christianity and Buddhism. Yagi's study (Yagi and Ulbrich, 1973) is also based on a parallel phenomenon he discerned between his conversion to Christianity and his enlightenment in Zen Buddhism. Yagi argues that both experiences set human beings free from something conceptual. Furuya Yasuo, who taught at the International Christian University founded in 1949 by both American and Japanese Christians, has also endeavoured to relativize Christianity and instead develops a pluralistic Christian theology open to other religions including Buddhism (Furuya, 1997).

Attempts to indigenize Christian theology into an Asian or a Japanese context have been made by Takenaka Masao (Doshisha University). He has also been active in the study of indigenous Christian art and ethics. Takenaka has maintained active dialogues with Asian theologians and shares the Asian understanding of God as the 'rice of life', not Christ as the 'bread of life' (Takenaka, 1986). More recently, Miyahira Nozomo (2000) has commenced unfolding a Theology of the Concord of God by reformulating the doctrine of the Trinity as 'three betweennesses' and 'one concord' in a Japanese cultural climate.

Future Tasks

Japanese Protestantism has contributed immensely to modernization in Japanese education, welfare and politics, but the Protestant Christian population is still under 1 percent. This disproportionate relation in Japan presents the following tasks.

First, Protestant Christians need to collaborate in pursuing an integration of learning and faith applicable to teaching in each academic discipline. Early in its history Japanese Protestant Christianity was quick to embrace new ideas and show remarkable adaptation, at least theoretically, to Japanese society. It is equally clear, however, that these movements, whether liberal or conservative, have also fallen into a gap in execution between theologians and Japanese Christians. 'Taught' Christianity, highly prized by Japanese theologians, must be practised as a living Christian faith able to concretize those ideas.

Second, and related to the first, 'evangelical' and 'liberal' Protestantism should not be viewed as separate or competing lines of thought within the expression of Japanese Protestantism. Rather, serious explorations, breaking away from the sectarian schisms and inheritances of its mission roots, must be made in order to establish a Japanese Christian social praxis based on the traditional Christian doctrines but able to meet the challenge of Japan today.

Third, Protestant Christianity, far from a monolithic religion itself, can stimulate indigenous Japanese theology in various ways, while tapping Japanese cultural and philosophical tradition and exercising vigilance against negatives inherent in Japanese society, such as exclusionary nationalism. In this respect the work of two theologians are of note and value. Miyata Mitsuo's comparative work of wartime nationalism and its interpenetration in the church in Germany and Japan is a masterful analysis of the perils of church and state relation. Dohi Akio, as a historian, has made massive contributions with his analysis of Japanese Protestant thought, on Christian response to the Emperor system and problems of discrimination. It is to the work of individuals such as this that the future of Japanese Protestantism must look if it is to remove the dross of its past while recovering the genius of its identity in the global church.

References

Furuya, Y. (ed.) (1997). *A History of Japanese Theology*. Grand Rapids, MI: Eerdmans.
Kitamori, K. (1946). *Theology of the Pain of God*. London: SCM Press.
Miyahira, N. (2000). *Towards a Theology of the Concord of God: A Japanese Perspective on the Trinity*. Carlisle, UK: Paternoster Press.
Takenaka, M. (1986). *God is Rice: Asian Culture and Christian Faith*. Geneva: World Council of Churches.
Yagi, S. & Ulbrich, L. (eds.) (1973). *Gott in Japan*. Munich: Kaiser.

Further Reading

Dohi, A. (1979). Christianity in Japan. In T. K. Thomas (ed.), *Christianity in Asia: North-East Asia*. Singapore: Christian Conference of Asia.

Drummond, R. H. (1971). *A History of Christianity in Japan*. Grand Rapids, MI: Eerdmans.

Ikado, F. & McGovern, J. R. (eds.) (1966). *A Bibliography of Christianity in Japanese Protestantism in English Sources (1859–1959)*. Tokyo: International Christian University Press.

Lee, R. (1967). *Stranger in the Land: A Study of the Church in Japan*. London: Lutterworth.

Michelson, C. (1959). *Japanese Contributions to Christian Theology*. Philadelphia: Westminster Press.

Miyata, M. (1963). *Der politische Auftrag des Protestantismus in Japan*. Hamburg: Herbert Reich Verlag.

Mullins, M. R. (1998). *Christianity Made in Japan: A Study of Indigenous Movements*. Honolulu: University of Hawaii Press.

Phillips, J. M. (1981). *From the Rising of the Sun: Christians and Society in Contemporary Japan*. Maryknoll, NY: Orbis.

Takizawa, K. (1987). *Das Heil im Heute Texte einer japanischen Theologie*. Göttingen: Vandenhoeck & Ruprecht.

CHAPTER 21

Korean Protestantism to the Present Day

Young-Gi Hong

One of the distinctive characteristics of the Christian map in the twentieth century is that the center of gravity of Christianity moved away from the West. In the development of non-Western Christianity the rapid growth of Korean Christianity is a noticeable phenomenon. Korean Protestantism in its short history has come to constitute about 20 percent of the whole population (about 46 million) and has become a major religion today, alongside the more traditional Buddhism (24%) and Catholicism (7%), whose Korean mission was much earlier. Korean Protestantism is best understood from the perspective of three epochs: from its introduction (1884) to the liberation from Japanese rule (1945), from the liberation to 1987, and from 1987 to the present.

Introduction (1884) to the Liberation (1945)

The trajectory of Korean Protestantism and the subsequent acceptance of Western values is unique for an Asian country. Protestantism was introduced to Korea in 1884, after a century of Catholicism. The major source for the new-found missionary impetus came from the United States. Dr. Horace Allen, the first Western missionary to Korea, was sent by the Presbyterian Church. Over the next decade, missionaries from several mission organizations and denominations arrived in Korea: Methodist Episcopalians in 1885, Canadian Baptists in 1889, English Anglicans in 1890, and Southern American Presbyterians in 1892.

Part of the rapid success of the growth of missionary-planted Protestantism is related to the cultural and political decline of the Chosôn dynasty (1392–1910) and then, during the Japanese occupation, the political pressures from Japan. Young and progressive Koreans were yearning for new solutions to age-old problems: Western technology and knowledge offered hope and progress to them while the ordinary Korean was simply disenfranchised as one political system replaced another without any real change. The profound despair and discontent prompted by national political and social crises meant that Protestant Christianity came to be regarded as an attractive alternative to the corrupt bureaucracy of the Chosôn dynasty and the forced identity of Japanese occupation.

Protestant Christianity in Korea then is ineluctably linked to modernization. Protestantism has been coupled with the values of modernity – education, technology, and industrialization – and political sensibilities such as equality, freedom, and eventually democracy. The simple equation is that Korean modernization meant Westernization, and Protestant Christianity was accepted as an enlightened ideology that brought modernization (Park, 1992: 345–71). It is not surprising that many of the "indirect methods" of mission adopted by the first Protestant missionaries (e.g., the establishment of schools, hospitals, and publishing houses) were quickly embraced and formed substantial institutional and ideological structures that now seem to be part of a modern Korean ethos.

During the Japanese colonial period (1910–45), many Koreans expressed their hostility to the Japanese by becoming Christians, which was seen as being both a rejection of Japanese values, and also a movement towards political emancipation and even, in a curious fashion, an assertion of a uniquely Korean self-identity (Ro, 1983: 163). Protestantism could be accepted for its support of the much-needed movement towards modernization without a collision with a pre-existent nationalism, as the dominant *colonial* nationalism was that of Japan, not of Korea (Min, 1992). Korean Christianity therefore forged a strong link with a new emerging Korean nationalism, one that had already rejected its own political and cultural structures of the 600-year-old Chosôn dynasty and now had an alien ideology forced on it. The active role of the Protestant churches in the Independence Movement in 1919 is an example of this interrelationship between a growing nationalism and Protestant forms. In 1920 the Protestant population was 323,574, about 1.4 percent of the population, but by the end of the occupation this had increased to 507,922. Put in theological terms, "eschatological hope" in the context of suffering reinforced the development of the movement.

From Liberation to Democratic Transition (1987)

Following liberation, the outbreak of the Korean War (1950–3) left deep emotional and mental scars on Korea. The trauma of the war ushered in another period of expansion, widespread evangelization, and further cultural openness to Western ideology. Korean Protestantism during this period was characterized by rapid church growth (mainly through evangelical or later charismatic

Protestants who came in large numbers) and marked by its contribution to the democratization movement (mainly through progressive Protestants).

In 1960 the Protestant population was 623,072, but by 1985 it had strikingly increased to 6,489,282, or 16.1 percent of the population. Concomitantly there was an explosion of churches (5,011 in 1960 to 35,869 in 1995) and a variety of denominations. Presently there are nearly 200 Protestant denominations within Korea. By far the most important denominations are the evangelical (mainly Presbyterian and Methodist) or charismatic-derived ones as they quickly prioritized nationals in the leadership of local congregations (Ro, 1996: 40). Their conservative theology, which the first Western missionaries brought, has largely been replicated in the majority of Protestant churches and one finds an emphasis on evangelism, a congregational church polity, the Bible, and a vibrant spirituality, with a particularly Korean stress on prayer (Hong, 1997: 206–16).

To date Korean churches are influenced by American church growth theology praxis and have adapted it into their context (Yi, 1994: 180–201). This has encouraged the use of technology and strategies of church growth that lead many church leaders and Koreans to believe that the megachurch is preferred. David Martin has identified the Korean Protestant scene as "a spiritual enterprise culture" that requires "in the top echelon, a kind of international manager of the Spirit" (Martin, 1990: 143). As a result, large congregations are interpreted as a sign of religious prosperity and market success. This enterprise culture has also brought about a negative effect in that the effectiveness of evangelical strategy is often judged on the quantity of "results." This phenomenon of megachurches may be understood, on a positive note, as not only the product of a combination of cultural and contextual factors (e.g., modern large-scale and rapid urbanization) and benefits from modernity (e.g., the use of technologies, resources, and the mass media), but also the use of lay leadership in well-functioning small group systems, and strong pastoral leadership that elicits passionate spirituality from church members (Hong, 2000).

There are over 400 large churches with more than 1,000 adult attending members in Sunday services, and 15 megachurches with more than 10,000. Some of the largest congregations in the world are in Korea. The Yoido Full Gospel Church, an Assemblies of God church led by Rev. Cho Yong-Gi, is the largest congregation with over 230,000 attending members. The Kumran Church, the largest Methodist congregation, has an attending membership of 30,000.

While the majority of Korean Protestants focused on church growth, progressive historical Protestants played a leading role in the democratization movement against the military dictatorship from the 1960s to the 1980s. Christian churches and cathedrals frequently served as sites of meetings, prayers, and demonstrations, as police were much more hesitant about breaking up antigovernment activities taking place on sanctified ground (Chang, 1998: 42). *Minjung theology*, developed in the mid-1970s, provided a norm and basis for democratic activism and was decidedly influenced by the liberation theology of Latin

America. *Minjung*, meaning "the people," is a political interpretation of Korean Christian experiences (Suh, 1981: 19) following paradigms found in the Bible. It tried to contextualize Korean theology by applying the biblical message of the alleviation of the suffering of the marginalized to Koreans suffering under political and social oppression (cf. So, 1983; Na, 1988) during the military occupation. Minjung theology rationalized Christian participation in secular politics in support of democracy against the military rulers, and also against the injustice and inequality suffered by many Koreans adrift in the cultural move towards modernization. Minjung theology, although much esteemed in rarified progressive church circles, and despite its hope of political impact, was finally an elite project and marginalized itself – inevitably colliding with the "critically conservative" political thinking of evangelicals (that is, of the vast majority of Korean Christians) For them, the Korean church needed a new theological framework, not derived from Protestant liberalism or Latin American theology to undergird its social action and critique. Despite the Minjung movement and the ever-increasing growth of evangelical and charismatic Protestants, Korea remained under military dictatorship from 1960 to 1987. This period marked rapid industrialization, urbanization, and political and social oppression until 1987 when unprecedented demonstrations forced the hand of the military government and democratic elections were called.

From Democratic Transition (1987) to the Present

This period does not mark a great deal of numerical growth for Korean Protestantism. But Korean Protestantism entered a new maturity in that it began its own missionary expansion and saw the emergence of a political stress in the previously seemingly apolitical evangelical and charismatic Protestants. In 1979, the number of countries to which the Korean church sent missionaries was 26, but it increased to 138 in 1996 and to 145 in 2002. In 1979 there were 93 missionaries sent from Korea; now there are over 10,000, with the expectation of more each year. Korean churches, originally the product of mission activity, are now one of the largest missionary providers to the rest of the world, including the West.

The period after 1987 also marks evangelical-charismatic Protestant participation in civil society movements. Korean evangelicals and charismatics began to campaign for political justice in elections and to found a number of civil movement groups, such as the Citizens' Coalition for Economic Justice and the Christian Ethics Movement. Such Protestant-based groups constitute nearly 70 percent of about 1,150 nongovernmental organizations and related groups operating in Korea. Given the large numbers of evangelical-charismatic Protestants it is not surprising that there is a large representation in politics. Declared Christian congresspersons (Protestant and Catholic) comprise 177 members, nearly 65 percent of all congresspersons in the 16th National Assembly. This percentage is above that of Christians in the population (around 28%) and raises the question of how their subsequent political "theologies" or interests actually reflect, or will collide with, a much wider Korean society.

The Future of Korean Protestantism

Korean churches have been blessed with amazing growth throughout turbulent times, and are expected to gain greater political and social significance in Korean society. This raises the question of whether Korean churches will keep their vitality in Korean society as a whole and continue to grow in the same manner as in their earlier history. Korean Protestantism, especially in its more conservative forms, is suffering from its own success in that it now faces the problem of stagnation in membership, nominal Christians, and an ever-increasing gap of social credibility (Hong, 1999). Korean churches must retain and develop their spiritual vitality by renewed commitment to prayer and evangelism in an age of modernity, economic affluence, and spiritual-numerical success. Korean churches must also upgrade their social credibility in the eyes of the Korean people. Although at present Christians enjoy an important position within Korean society, this alone does not guarantee that they will not become irrelevant both to a wider Korean society and to the Christian gospel in its Korean ministry. The future of Korean Protestantism will depend on its developing and integrating new social concerns that presently face Korea with its historically successful missionary zeal.

Finally, Korean churches are expected to gain more influence in World Christianity in the future. In order for the Korean churches to exercise Christian leadership in the world, they need to embody a sacrificial spirit in order to share their spiritual and material blessings, and also their personnel, with developing countries and to build an effective network with the other world churches in sincere dialogue (Hong, 2000). The Korean church needs Christian leaders who can preach, lecture, and write in English to enlarge its impact on the world churches. The Korean church also needs Kingdom leaders who can think and act in terms of Kingdom growth rather than mere institutional growth. Church growth in Korea should not be limited to Korean society but should have a positive impact on the world churches. The future lies open for the Korean churches, if only they remain faithful to the gospel.

References

Chang, Yun-Sik (1998). The Progressive Christian Church and Democracy in South Korea. *Journal of Church and State* Spring, 40, 2: 437–65.

Hong, Sung-wook (1997). Theological Conceptualization of the Concept of God in Korea. Ph.D. thesis, The Oxford Centre for Mission Studies (with Wales University).

Hong, Young-gi (1999). Nominalism in Korean Protestantism. *Transformation: An International Evangelical Dialogue on Mission and Ethics* 16, 4: 136–41.

Hong, Young-gi (2000). Revisiting Church Growth in Korean Protestantism. *International Review of Mission* 353: 190–202.

Martin, David (1990). *Tongues of Fire*. Oxford: Blackwell.

Min, Kyong-bae (1992). *Hanguk Kidok Kyohoesa* (The History of the Korean Christian Church). Seoul: Taehan Kidokyo Ch'ulp'ansa.

Na, Yong-Wha (1988). A Theological Assessment of Korean Minjung Theology. *Concordia Journal* 14, April: 138–49.

Park, Young-sin (1992). Kidokgyo wa Sahoe Byôndong (Christianity and Social Change). In *Yôksawa Sahoe Byôndong* (History and Social Change). Seoul: Min Young Sa, pp. 56–88.

Ro, Bong-rin (1983). Non-spiritual Factors in Church Growth. In Bong-rin Ro and Marlin L. Nelson (eds.), *Korean Church Growth Explosion*. Seoul: Word of Life Press & Asia Theological Association, pp. 159–70.

Ro, Chi-jun (1996). Hanguk Kyohoe Ûi Kaegyohoizuui (The Emphasis on Local Congregations in the Korean Church). In Won-kyu Yi (ed.), *Hanguk Kyohoe wa Sahoi* (Korean Church and Society), 3rd edn. Seoul: Nathan, pp. 39–73.

So, Nam-dong (1983). *Minchung Sinhak Tamku* (An Exploration of Minjung Theology). Seoul: Hangilsa.

Suh, David Kwang-Sun (1981). A Biographical Sketch of an Asian Theological Consultation. In Kim Yong Bock (ed.), *Minjung Theology: People as the Subject of History*. Singapore: Commission on Theological Concerns, pp. 17–42.

Yi, Wôn-gyu (1994). *Han'guk Kyohoe-ui Hyônsil-kwa Chônmang* (The Reality and Prospect of the Korean Church). Seoul: Sôngsô Yôngu (Bible Study) Press.

Further Reading

Grayson, James Huntley (1985). *Early Buddhism and Christianity in Korea: A Study in the Implantation of Religion*. Leiden: E. J. Brill.

Grayson, James Huntley (1989). *Korea: A Religious History*. Oxford: Oxford University Press.

Kim, Andrew E. (1995). A History of Christianity in Korea: From its Troubled Beginning to its Contemporary Success. *Korea Journal* 35, 2: 34–53.

Kim, Andrew Byung-Yoon (1999). Rethinking of Korean Missions. *Journal of Asian Mission* 1, 1: 101–19.

CHAPTER 22

Chinese Protestantism to the Present Day

Carver T. Yu

Chinese Protestants have struggled for their identity in a context of unprecedented social-political turmoil and cultural transformation in China from the
Opium War (1839–42) to the Communist Cultural Revolution of 1949. The
backdrop of hostile nationalistic reaction against Christianity (as a foreign religion), the general perception of the complicity of the Christian mission with
Western imperialism and colonialism, and the reality of denominational and
theological divisions in the package of the Christian faith brought into China
by missionaries have created and challenged Chinese Protestant identity. The
Taiping Rebellion (1851–64), which clothed political intent with an indigenous
but syncretistic form of the Christian religion, complicated earlier issues in
Chinese Protestant history. Likewise, the "New China" and its communist commitments have exacerbated many systemic problems. Each epoch of Chinese
history seems to build on its predecessor's inability to found a coherent identity.
China's missionary heritage, its rejection (or suspicion) of Western cultural
forms (in all China's political identities) and its own unique attempts at syncretism or indigenization are the themes that interweave in the tapestry of
Chinese Protestantism and play out in the very real and concrete situation of its
people.

Origins of the Chinese Protestant Church

Robert Morrison (1782–1834) arrived in China in 1807. He baptized the first
Chinese convert, Cai Gao (1788–1846), after seven year's labor. In terms of
number, his success was meager. However, over 12 years, with the help of
William Milne (1785–1822), he completed the translation of the Bible into
Chinese. He also composed numerous hymns in Chinese and wrote several books
on basic doctrines and church organization. Morrison's (and Milne's) main
contribution was this massive effort of translation. Milne arrived in 1813, and

moved to Malacca in 1815 with the vision of converting and training Chinese for the task of evangelizing China. For that purpose, the Anglo-Chinese College was founded in 1818. The second Chinese convert, Liang Ah Fa (1789–1855), was baptized by Milne in 1816, trained by him, and later ordained by Morrison in 1827 to become the first Chinese minister. Milne's other contribution for Chinese Protestant identity is in a gospel tract he wrote, *Zhang Yuan Liang You Xianglun* (Dialogues Between Two Friends, Chang and Yuan), which set a model for indigenous evangelism.

Liang marks the beginning of "Chinese" Protestantism. His first convert was his wife, who became the first Chinese female baptized into the Protestant Church. In 1828, he performed his first baptism as a Chinese minister for a young Chinese convert Gu Tian Qing. Later, another of his converts, Qu Ang, baptized and subsequently ordained by him, became a significant leader in the development of Protestantism in Hong Kong. Liang's significance is not only as a pastor; he was also the first indigenous Christian writer. Though relatively uneducated, he produced in 1819 his first gospel tract, *Jiushilu Cuoyao Luejie* (A Brief Exposition of the Summary Record of Salvation). In 1828, he wrote another tract, *Shuxue Shengjing Luelun* (A Brief Discourse on the Understanding of the Bible), which was basically a testimony of why he believed despite persecution. A year later, he wrote a simple exposition on Christian life, *ZhenDao Wenti Qianjie* (A Simple Exposition of Questions Concerning Truth). Due to Liang's effort, the first Chinese *Qidaowen Zanshensi* (Book of Prayer and Hymns) was produced in 1833. Perhaps the most significant of his writings was a tract titled *Quan Shi Liangyan* (Good Words for Admonishing the Age). It integrated Confucian ethics with the Christian idea of a heavenly kingdom of righteousness and equality and represented the first serious attempt of indigenous theology. The emphasis was on moral transformation of the person through repentance. The tract made a great impact on Hong Xiuquan (1814–64), who was subsequently converted, and started the God-worshiping Society, which later became the base for the Taiping Rebellion.

Another important figure in the beginning of the Chinese Church was Ho Tsun Sheen (1817–71). Accompanying James Legge (1814–97) from Malacca to Hong Kong in 1843 and working closely with him, Ho became the first Chinese minister in Hong Kong. Through him, the indigenous Chinese church in Hong Kong came into being. Liang Ah Fa, Qu Ang, Ho Tsun Sheen, and Hong Xiuquan provided the trajectories from which Chinese Protestants would follow, namely the poles of reliance or sympathy towards Western missions and ideology, and a movement, sometimes extreme, towards indigeneous leadership, worship-praxis, and theology.

The burden of imperialism

Chinese Protestant identity emerged steadily, though slowly. The Opium Wars, however, dealt a heavy blow to the young fragile church. Missionaries were widely suspected of collaborating with Western imperialists. The charge was not unmerited. Robert Morrison, for example, served as translator for the East India Company, and later accompanied Lord Amherst in his diplomatic endeavors in China. His son, John Robert Morrison (1814–43), both served as the British Consulate in Guangzhou and was actively involved in missionary work. The Christian church, particularly missions, was accused of a grave moral failure in condoning and even exploiting the opium trade for furthering the cause of spreading the gospel. Indeed, Charles Gutzlaff (1803–51) would travel on an opium trading ship along the Chinese coast to distribute gospel tracts. To further fuel resentment, humiliating treaties and edicts of toleration imposed on the Chinese contained advantageous terms and rights for missionaries and their Chinese converts. Protestant missionaries – such as Gutzlaff, Peter Parker (1804–88) and Elijah C Bridgman (1801–51) – were involved not only as interpreters but also as secretaries in the negotiation of treaties. Missionaries appeared to the Chinese all too ready to exploit China's defeat in order to further their religious invasion. Only the Anglican Church made a feeble protest against the war. Christianity was thus perceived by the Chinese as a foreign religion forced onto China by gunboats as part of the Western scheme of cultural invasion. David Urquhart (1805–77) was the lone voice in Britain to condemn the introduction of Christianity into China by force.

The 1858 Tianjing Treaty and the subsequent Convention in 1860 gave missionaries greater freedom than ever before to spread the gospel in all parts of China. Hostile Chinese reactions spread at the same time. By the end of 1860, a highly influential anti-Christian tract *Pixie Jishi* (A Record of Facts for Warding off Heterodoxy) was widely distributed. Outbreaks of sporadic violence resulted in the killing of missionaries and Chinese converts and the burning of churches. These incidents were preludes to the Boxer Uprising of 1900, in which hundreds of missionaries and Chinese converts were killed. The young Chinese church was caught between the upsurge of nationalism and its dependence on Western churches. The "foreignness" of their religion was a serious stigma. A few Chinese Christian leaders, such as Chen Mengnan and Chen Dao Ren, demanded the formation of an indigenous Chinese Church independent of foreign control. Chen Mengnan organized independent Chinese churches in the Guangdong province in 1873, while Chen Dao Ren expressed the need for an indigenous church in 1879 in his *Reformation of the Mission Enterprise in China*. Some missionaries began to recognize the urgency for the Chinese church to become indigenous and independent. John Campbell Gibson (1849–1919) advocated the idea of a "self-supporting, self-governing and self-propagating" Native Church. In 1881 he put the idea into practice by organizing a "three self" presbytery in Shantou in the Guangdong province. However, the concept of a fully independent indigenous Chinese church had not yet been seriously considered by missionary societies. In fact the process of indigenization proved to be too slow and too late for the church in China to cope with the rapid sociocultural transformation and political upheaval in China in the early part of the twentieth century, and Chinese Christians had to pay a heavy price for that failure.

At the turn of the twentieth century, defeated in the Sino-Japanese War (1895) and by an allied Western force in the Boxer Uprising, China was on the brink of being divided and colonized by foreign powers. A crippling indemnity imposed in 1901, and the scramble for concessions to Western powers, brought patriotism and xenophobia to a new height. The Church in China was categorically perceived as foreign and thus met with strong emotional rejection. From the May Fourth Movement of 1919 onward, there was an intense anti-Christian movement among intellectuals and at the popular level. At the same time, while the whole nation embarked feverishly on a course of cultural transformation for the sake of national salvation, Chinese Protestants remained uncertain in regard to faith and culture as well as their divided identity. The question of how they could identify with their compatriots in national reconstruction while holding a foreign religion rejected by them never abated. Chinese Christian leaders – Cheng Jianye (1881–1939), Zhao Zichen (1888–1979), and Liu Tingfeng (1891–1947) – worked to indigenize the Christian faith on the one hand, and sought to participate in cultural transformation based on Christian values on the other.

For a truly indigenous Chinese Church to emerge, the biggest obstacles were not only its Western dependence or origin but also the confusing variety of denominations compounded by differences in national origin, theological persuasions, church organization, and liturgy. Conflicting approaches, competition, and even rivalries were not uncommon with more than 130 missionary societies from six countries. Cooperation, when it manifested at all, merely meant avoidance of competition. The so-called *Comity Agreements* merely defined which mission would work within what territory, usually organized around the national origin of the mission agency. The church was thus highly fragmented.

This problem was discussed at the World Missionary Conference held in Edinburgh in 1910. Organic union of mission bodies of similar doctrines, and federation of groups by geographic location, were proposed. The China Continuation Committee was set up to facilitate such unification. In 1917, steps for unity were proposed: uniting churches of similar ecclesiastical order, intercommunion between churches in particular areas, and finally the formation of the Chinese Council of Churches. Denominational union within Chinese missions of differing national origin led the way. In 1922, for example, the Presbyterian Churches of Britain, Canada, New Zealand and the United States, together with churches belonging to the London Missionary Society and American Board of Commissioners for Foreign Missions, united as the General Assembly of Presbyterian Churches in China. Likewise, Anglicans united as the *Zhonghua Sheng Gong Hui*. Congregationalists later united with the Presbyterians. In short order, Lutherans, Baptists and Methodists each united. The next step would be interdenominational union. After much effort in 1927 six major denominational bodies joined together as the Church of Christ in China. While this was a notable step forward, only about one-third of Protestant churches in China were represented.

Indigenization also moved in a different direction from attempts to found national churches with revivalist evangelists like Watchman Nee (1902–62),

Wang Mingdao (1900–91), Wang Zhai, and John Sung (1901–44) leading the way. This form of indigenization was more grassroots-based and therefore more idiosyncratic in composition. Watchman Nee, for example, separated himself from the Methodist Church over the issue of baptism and ordination. Deeply influenced by the Brethren polity, he started the "Local Church Movement" with the idea of one church for each locality. His church grew rapidly and spread from Shanghai to Shandong, Jiansu, Zhejiang and Fukien, and was later widely known as "the Little Flock." Wang Mingdao separated himself from the Presbyterian Church (over infant baptism), and became an independent evangelist preaching personal salvation and the transformation of society through personal repentance and spiritual renewal. His preaching tours generated a huge following. In 1936, he founded a church, "the Christian Tabernacle," that called for strict spiritual discipline, removal of corrupt leaders, and a separation from foreigners. It was estimated that by 1949 independent churches founded through these itinerant evangelists alone accounted for one-fourth of the total number of Chinese Christians. In many ways, these are the forerunners of the "house churches."

The eradication of Protestantism

After the establishment of New China under the Communist Party in 1949, anticapitalist and anti-imperialist ethos forced the church to review its relations with foreign missions. The "three-self" principle of complete independence from foreign control was adopted and indigenization took on a new political meaning. "Three-self" and nationalistic patriotism, which meant unquestioning support of the Communist Party, became intertwined. Under the leadership of Wu Yaozong (1893–1979), the Three Self Patriotic Movement (TSPM) was founded in 1950 so that the Christian Church in China could become "China's Christian Church." Foreign links were severed and denominationalism purged. Chinese churches were brought within the TSPM, coordinated by the governmental Religious Affairs Bureau. By 1958, many churches were closed and congregations were coalesced into a few state-approved churches. During the Cultural Revolution even those few churches were closed. The only churches that would survive were the underground "house churches." House churches, locally run and organized, are often regarded as the truest or most genuine forms of indigenous church in China bred in isolation.

Creating a Truly Chinese Church and Theology

Church organization and the establishment of indigenous leadership were certainly significant in the quest for Protestant identity in China, but the real test of authentic indigenous identity lay somewhere deeper. Several questions remained and were asked across all epochs of Chinese Protestant history: "Was the gospel brought to the Chinese truly the Word that became flesh and made its dwelling among them, full of truth yet also full of grace?"; "Were Chinese Christians able to show the relevance of the Christian faith to their struggle for national salvation and cultural reconstruction?"; "Did the Christian faith empower Chinese Christians to become active participants rather than alienated observers in determining the future of China?" Chinese missions and theologians, across China's history, have had to address both the problems of indigenization and contextualiztion. The following are some of the more notable attempts, and the critiques of such attempts.

William Milne was the first Protestant missionary to tackle the question of indigenization. In his gospel tract *Dialogues Between Two Friends, Chang and Yuan*, he addressed the Confucian ideal of attaining inner saintly personhood expressed in sagely statesmanship. He affirmed the ideal, yet questioned the comprehensiveness of such a vision of life, pointing to the reality of sin in human nature and to the wonder of the Creator's love manifested in Jesus Christ. Milne's colleague, James Legge, took a similar approach. He attempted to clear misunderstandings of the Chinese humanistic tradition prevalent in the West. As a result, he undertook the task of translating Chinese "classics" into English as a way to affirm the value of the tradition. American missionary W. A. P. Martin (1827–1916) likewise affirmed the spiritual and scientific insights of the Chinese humanistic tradition. However, he thought that those insights needed to be extended further in order to reach the ultimate truth. In his book *Tiandao Xaoyuan* (Pursuing the Source of the Way of Heaven), he used two Confucian concepts, *Gewu* (investigation and understanding of things in accordance with their own nature) and *Zhizhi* (comprehensive and ultimate knowing), to show that the Chinese had contributed profound insights into the understanding of the nature of things. To arrive at comprehensive and ultimate knowledge, the Christian faith could add illumination to insights. So he proposed the formula of "adding Confucius and Jesus together." Many missionaries, however, were much less optimistic about the value of the Chinese humanistic tradition.

It is much more interesting to see how *Chinese* Christians dealt with the problem of Chinese culture. In the second half of the nineteenth century, there were indigenous theological reflections of considerable depth. Meng Juezi, a Chinese Christian of the Basel Mission (his name means "awakened dreamer") addressed the common Chinese dream of attaining saintliness through self-cultivation but added that the dream seemed ever unattainable. The human will, due to weakness, was inadequate to deal with its uncontrollable desires and insurmountable selfishness. Thus he showed adeptness in adapting Christian Protestant notions such as the "unfreedom" of the will (and sin) to the Chinese mindset. Others – Chang Ding, Yuan Ang Bong, and Lee Ang Fu – also testified to their aspiration yet disappointment at attaining authentic and saintly personhood. The realization of the reality of sin (and therefore the need of salvation) through self-reflection was the key to their spiritual awakening. The Confucian ideal was affirmed, but something more than self-cultivation needed to be done. The issue of whether "salvation" could be attained through the self or through the "power" of an "Other" (Christ) was raised.

Zhao Zichen brought an ontological dimension to the Confucian–Christian dialogue started in the early part of the twentieth century. Affirming Confucian personalism and its cosmic dimension, he added that "Christianity is a personalism in which the Absolute is a person that comes into relation with His creatures" (Zhao Zichen, 1918: 371). The cosmos, grounded on and infused with God's personhood, is God's continual outflowing and the unfolding of God's immediate self-consciousness, self-transcendence, and self-direction in love. Jesus Christ, then, is the true manifestation of perfect personhood and the expression of God in love. He alone is the true attainment of what Confucius aspired to. Christ's immediate awareness of his unity with God, the source of creation, is the common point for both divine self-expression of love and human aspiration in the image of God.

These various attempts at indigenous dialogues have one thing in common: they all tried to maintain continuity with their cultural tradition (dominantly Confucianism) while aiming to bring it to a new height of achievement through the Christian faith. Zhao, unlike his predecessors and those who would follow, betrays an optimism characteristic of liberal Protestantism before World War II. The Cultural Revolution would retrieve awareness of human depravity, but find echoes of it in both Chinese and Christian traditions. Confucianism, Neo-Confucianism in particular, had consistently ignored the thread of human depravity, and found the Christian concept of sin repugnant. However, contemporary Neo-Confucianist philosophers are more ready to talk about "the awareness of the darkness in humanity."

In addition to finding a compatible dialogue with Chinese philosophy, indigenization would also need to address the much more difficult issue of "ancestor worship." Missionaries such as Martin pleaded for toleration, pointing to the fact that kneeing and prostration before what symbolized the presence of ancestors should not be understood as worship, as these postures were commonly practiced in the family context as respect toward one's parents. Other missionaries of pietist or fundamentalist orientation would object to such toleration and see the practice as idolatry. This divide between tolerance and objection pretty much dictates the forms of the present conversation in Chinese Protestant churches in regard to ancestor worship.

The Effect and Future of Chinese Protestantism

Catalyst – critique and fragmentation

While the issue and history of contextualization caused considerable tension among missionaries as well as Chinese Christians before 1949, the contribution of Protestant churches to Chinese society was substantial, if not sustained, in terms of medical, educational, and political reform. Mission societies such as the China Inland Mission, while concentrating on evangelism, used medical and educational services as means to propagate the gospel. Many missionaries – Martin, Timothy Richard (1845–1919), and Young J. Allen (1836–1907) – advocated reform of the Chinese society through education as well as the Christian message. Instead of just "saving heathens from the suffering of hell," the responsibility of Christians "to save heathens from the hell of suffering in the world" was equally important. 1844 saw the founding of the Ningbo Mission School, and in short order numerous primary and secondary schools and 13 universities were established through mission and church effort. In 1875, Allen started a news magazine, *Wan Guo Gung Bao* (Global News), that by 1878 (under William Muirhead 1822–1900) actively called for reform of many social ills and corruptions in China. Together with Richard, Martin, and Alexander Williamson (1829–90), Allen and Muirhead established the Society for the Diffusion of Knowledge (*Guan Xue Hui*). This society, and Richard in particular, was most active in promoting social, cultural, and political reform. Richard's proposals for the modernization of China were highly regarded by government officials. He later became deeply involved in the "Hundred Day Reform" headed by Kang Youwei (1858–27), and was invited to serve as advisor to the Emperor.

Richard and Allen set an example to Chinese Christians in working out the social implications of the gospel. They were, however, criticized by many of their peers for what seemed to be a preoccupation with what would be known as a "social gospel." However, their vision was a vision of the Kingdom of God being unfolded in history. The debate between those who exclusively preached a gospel for personal salvation and those who saw political reform and cultural transformation as part and parcel of the gospel intensified after the May Fourth Movement. Wang Mingdao is representative of the camp advocating personal salvation. Wu Leiquan (1870–1944), Zhao Zichen, and later Wu Yaozong, who saw the Christian message as highly relevant to the social reconstruction in China largely adopted a more integrative approach. Tensions intensified when Communist ideology and its antireligion rhetoric became the dominant force in sociopolitical reform. Some saw Communism as consonant with the previous "social" teaching of many Chinese theologians and leaders and warmed to it despite the antireligion posture. Others saw Communism as a force of destruction, especially in terms of its uncompromising antireligion posture and rejected it and its confluence with social reform initiated and earlier proposed by many Christians. Thus many reject what Richard, Allen, Wu Leiquan, Zhao Zichen, and Wu Yaozong saw as integral (but not exclusive) to the Christian Gospel – a critique of social structures from the vantage of the gospel.

A new humanity in China?

It is interesting to note that at the height of the Cultural Revolution, when China was thrown into chaos and its people into intense suffering, Western Christian theologians mythologized the Maoist "New Humanity" in China. In the early 1970s, ecumenical seminars and conferences were held to discuss the "theological meaning of New China." In the Båstad Seminar, C. S. Song suggested that Christians should see "New China" as a secularized version of salvation history. Donald E MacInnis, similarly, referred to the "new humanity in China" as ushered in by Mao. The only dissenting voice was that of Philip Shen who cautioned against the Maoist–Christian euphoria and called for a theological critique of power (Lutheran World Federation, 1976). In many ways, the largely Western conversation about Maoist–Christian dialogue is an academic rehearsal of China's own history. In it there are voices calling for accommodation and dialogue and a hope of finding a theory that allows an indigenous Chinese voice but somehow this theory seems disjointed from the praxis and situation of the Chinese people.

The Protestant church in China is experiencing phenomenal growth. A relatively conservative estimation puts it at 20 million. Nevertheless, the Protestant Church is again in an intense search for identity in a new era of rapid economic reform oriented toward a market-driven economy. Beneath the surface of conformity under the TSPM and Christian Council, diversity is emerging in response to the various challenges. Theological exploration, however, remains hesitant. Fragmentation once more remains a threat.

Further Reading

Barnett, S. W. and Fairbank, J. K. (eds.) (1985). *Christianity and China – Early Protestant Missionary Writings*. Cambridge, MA: Harvard University Press.

Bays, Daniel H. (1996). *Christianity in China: From the Eighteenth Century to the Present*. Stanford, CA: Stanford University Press.

Cohen, Paul (1963). *China and Christianity – The Missionary Movement and the Growth of Chinese Anti-foreignism 1860–70*. Cambridge, MA: Harvard University Press.

Hsü, Immanuel C. Y. (1990). *The Rise of Modern China*. New York: Oxford University Press.

Hunter, A. and Chan, K. K. (1993). *Protestantism in Contemporary China*. Cambridge, UK: Cambridge University Press.

Fairbank, John K. (ed.) (1973). *Missionary Enterprise in China and America*. Cambridge, MA: Harvard University Press.

Lam, Wing-hung (1983). *Chinese Theology in Construction*. Pasadena, CA: William Carey Library.

Latourette, Kenneth S (1929). *A History of Christian Mission in China*. New York: Macmillan.

Lutheran World Federation/Pro Mundi Vita (1976). *Christianity and the New China*. South Pasadena, CA: Ecclesia Publications.

Lutz, Jessie G. (1965). *Christian Mission in China: Evangelist of What?* Boston: Heath.

Lutz, Jessie G. (1988). *Chinese Politics and Christian Missions: The Anti-Christian Movement of 1920–28*. Notre Dame, IN: Cross Cultural Publications.

Whyte, Bob (1988). *Unfinished Encounter: China and Christianity*. London: Fount.

Ying Fuk-tsang (1995). *Cultural Accommodation and Chinese Christians (1860–1911)*. Hong Kong: China Alliance Press.

Zhao Zichen (1918). The Appeal of Christianity to the Chinese Mind. *Chinese Recorder*, 49.

CHAPTER 23

Protestantism in Australia, New Zealand and Oceania to the Present Day

Ian Breward

Protestantism in Australia and New Zealand has been predominantly British in ethos, with significant variants in Oceania. American impact has grown since the 1950s. Civic, confessional and evangelical variants must be noted.

British occupation of New South Wales in 1788 saw the beginnings of Protestantism in chaplaincies to convicts, officials and settlers. Despite differences, Protestants combined in educational, evangelistic and philanthropic activities, united by evangelicalism, hostility to Rome (a dominant theme in Protestantism until the 1970s) and optimism about missions to the peoples of the Pacific and Asia. Samuel Marsden planted Church Missionary Society workers in New Zealand in 1814, followed by Wesleyans who also worked in Tonga, Samoa and Fiji. Polynesian Protestants outnumbered British migrants until the 1850s, providing hundreds of missionaries to other parts of the Pacific and establishing strong village theocracies. Settler churches depended heavily on Britain for ministers and money, when mineral discoveries and availability of land fuelled migration, and expanded the need for expansion of government. The Treaty of Waitangi (1840) attempted to balance Maori interests and colonization in New Zealand. Aborigines were less fortunate. Many settlers regarded indigenous religion and culture with contempt, as obstacles to Christian civilization. Protestant missionary methods failed, as did attempts to establish the Church of England. Other denominations attacked the privileges of Anglicans. Governor Bourke recommended government subsidies for all churches in 1836. The Anglican majority were the main beneficiaries, but Presbyterians and Wesleyans were also assisted in keeping pace with the expansion of settlement. Such grants lasted until the 1890s in Western Australia, but were abolished in 1855 in New Zealand, because Bishop Selwyn wanted the church to have spiritual independence. Aid to church schools continued in most colonies until the 1870s, when a free, compulsory and secular public system was established. Many Protestants welcomed this change, believing that the God-given tasks of church and state should not be confused, without in any way limiting the churches' responsibility to work for a new model Christian society.

Protestant demography remained relatively stable until the 1970s, with regional variations due to Roman Catholic numbers, which were lowest in New Zealand, South Australia and Tasmania. Elsewhere, they were over 20 per cent and a challenge to Protestants used to dominating a much smaller minority, suspect about their allegiance to the crown or liberal and democratic values. Universal male suffrage and responsible government from the 1850s diminished these doubts, for Catholics were soon active in politics, the professions and philanthropy. Neighbourly co-operation could not be avoided in isolated settlements, though Freemasons and Orange Lodges kept Protestant sentiment alive among those whose religious commitment was slight. Protestant political parties never took, despite the passions roused by *Ne Temere*, the papal decree of 1908 stipulating that the children of mixed marriages must be brought up as Catholics, and what seemed seditious utterances by Roman bishops, such as Liston in Auckland who was acquitted of a charge of sedition in 1922 after a Protestant-inspired trial. Anglicans were the dominant shapers of civic Protestantism, supported by Congregationalists, Presbyterians and Wesleyans. Confessional and evangelical identity was found not only in the major churches, but also among Lutherans, Baptists, Churches of Christ and the Salvation Army. Ethnic identity was an important component of Protestantism, but Welsh and Gaelic rarely lasted beyond the second generation of migrants. Worship and publication in German ceased because of the intensity of anti-German feeling in the First World War among some British Protestants, who behaved disgracefully against fellow Australians. Internal migration, intermarriage and the absence of smaller denominations in country towns and rural districts weakened denominational identity and underlined Protestant commonalities.

Defining Protestant boundaries is complicated by the fervent repudiation of Protestantism by some Anglo-Catholic Anglicans, who came to control a number of rural and metropolitan dioceses. Sydney and Melbourne were the exceptions. The latter developed a comprehensive ethos, but with many evangelical parishes and Ridley College – an Anglican theological college with an evangelical tradition – but Sydney remains unequivocally Protestant and evangelical. New Zealand Anglicans were less polarized by party networks, but like their Australian counterparts were often dismissive of other Protestants and saw themselves as an unofficial established church. Roman Catholics, however, were never in doubt that Anglo-Catholics were Protestants, even if some sectarian groups repudiated them and other major churches attacked their ritualism and theology.

While Protestants differed markedly on polity, worship and aspects of morality, it was Anglicans, Lutherans, some Baptists and Churches of Christ who rejected intercommunion and interchange of pulpits. Despite this, Protestants shared many deep convictions and greatly influenced the social construction of their societies. They were convinced that God providentially ordained their colonies for colonization and the development of Christian nations. The supreme authority of the Bible, liberty of conscience, the right of private judgement, justification by faith alone, honouring the Sabbath and behaving with integrity in one's vocation were widely recognized as Protestant fundamentals, even if exegesis led to different doctrinal conclusions and sharp polemic.

Protestants valued education highly. When they lost subsidies for their schools, they energetically fostered Sunday schools, which in some colonies reached almost 80 per cent of the juvenile population. They provided libraries and religious nurture, trained leaders and offered many cultural and sporting activities. Their anniversaries and picnics were major social events, and many had a strong evangelistic emphasis, which was an important barrier to the diffusion of theologically liberal ideas. Anglicans, Presbyterians and Wesleyans established secondary schools and residential university colleges, which powerfully shaped Protestant elites and community leaders. They valued capitalism and suspected socialism, contributing significantly to the economic growth of the colonies by the foundation of both large and small businesses, as well as agricultural and pastoral industries.

The foundation and support of a plethora of improving societies was an expression of Protestant activism for the well-being of their neighbours. Savings banks, libraries, temperance societies, orphanages and homes for the blind, aged, disabled and mentally ill, were all part of embodying the Kingdom of God. Protestants lobbied their parliamentarians on Sabbath observance, regulation of gambling, family law, prostitution and alcohol abuse, as well as protection of missionaries and ending the labour trade on Queensland sugar plantations. Legislatures opened with prayer and all the major churches actively encouraged the foundation of public hospitals. Methodists and the Salvation Army combined effective evangelism with wide-ranging social compassion, making imaginative use of the pastoral gifts of Bible women (precursors of deaconesses, involved in Bible teaching, pastoral work and education), deaconesses and evangelists in urban mission. Protestants played an important part in the pioneering social legislation of the 1890s and 1900s. Some were active in trade unions and the formation of Labour parties, but most preferred the political style of liberalism, seeing free trade as applied Christianity.

Newspapers exerted considerable social leverage, whether they were small rural papers or metropolitan dailies with circulations larger than influential British papers. Many editors were convinced Protestants and welcomed articles and editorials by leading clergy. Denominations had their own journals, with robust commentary. Large number of books, booklets, sermons and tracts were published in all the colonies, along with British and American publications which informed colonists of the latest religious intelligence and theological trends. While the Australian and New Zealand colonies were provincial, the quality of theological discussion was high and quite the equal of that in major British and American cities.

By the end of the nineteenth century, difficult theological issues were widely discussed, not only because of freethinkers' attacks, but also because of fiery debates in the colonies, and the attraction of theological liberalism over against narrowly constructed confessionalism. The 1880s controversy over Charles Strong of Scots Church, Melbourne about how to interpret the atonement and other traditional doctrines to changing contemporary culture was symptomatic of difficulties in all the churches, but especially for Presbyterians. Regular visits of international evangelists reinforced the appeal of evangelical varieties of Protestantism, and inspired many to offer for missionary service in the Pacific, Asia, Africa and Latin America, though that was also encouraged by the Student Volunteer Movement and Student Christian Movement which grew out of the visits of the missionary statesman John Mott to Australian and New Zealand universities. Home missions were also important, growing rapidly in the twentieth century, and developing into service for those living within the vast distances of the Australian outback. Presbyterians, Anglicans and Methodists ministered to all, not just to their own flock, imaginatively using aeroplanes and radio to provide medical services.

Implicitly racist attitudes about the limitations of indigenous peoples and cultures and Chinese miners encouraged paternalistic policies of denominational and faith missions. Distinction between culture and gospel was not an issue, for the spiritual superiority of British Christianity was still axiomatic for many Protestants. Missions to Aborigines were a dismal failure in the nineteenth century, except for Lutheran work in Central Australia. Frontier conflicts, dispossession, murder and deadly European diseases dramatically reduced the Aboriginal population, although strong Maori churches had emerged in New Zealand by the 1860s. Land wars and unjust confiscations convinced many Maori that British Christianity was not for them. Prophetic leaders with deep scriptural knowledge created very durable versions of Maori Protestantism. Remnants of Anglican and Methodist communities survived and grew slowly in the twentieth century, though weakened by the emergence of the Ratana Church in the 1920s, and the failure of church leaders to give real authority to Maori clergy and lay leaders.

Similar problems surfaced in Melanesian churches and in the Aboriginal missions which resumed in the twentieth century. Aborigines remained locked into a paternalistic system of governance until the 1970s, reinforced by racist public attitudes and destructive government policies which removed children from their families until the 1960s. Missionaries with anthropological training pioneered changes of attitude to indigenous culture, which were invaluable when huge new populations were found in the New Guinea Highlands in the 1920s and 1930s. Missions and the Australian Government had to find new models of partnership. When the twentieth century began, many Protestants looked forward optimistically to further religious and social progress. The worst of the depression of the 1890s was over, and Australians were excited by the formation of the Commonwealth in 1901. Attempts to unite Protestant churches on both sides of the Tasman failed in the first decade; but hope remained despite many setbacks. Finally, Congregationalists, Methodists and Presbyterians united in Australia in 1977, with some Presbyterians staying out of the Uniting Church. A wider scheme in New Zealand included Anglicans and the Churches of Christ, but was finally rejected by Anglicans in 1976. Comity agreements in Melanesia, the formation of mission councils in the 1920s, cooperation in religious teaching in state schools, the founding of the Melbourne College of Divinity in 1910, Bible colleges and combined theological teaching in Sydney and Dunedin were examples of practical ecumenism. Key clergy were involved in the partnerships which led to the formation of the World Council of Churches, and in the formation of national councils of churches in both Australia and New Zealand. Evangelical ecumenism was expressed in parachurch groups, missionary cooperation and evangelism, notably in the influential Billy Graham campaigns.

Theological disagreements between evangelicals and Liberals strained Protestant unity, but only Presbyterians resorted to heresy trials. Professors Samuel Angus and Lloyd Geering, and Dr Peter Cameron attracted huge public interest for their expositions of contemporary faith. Defenders of historic Protestantism were typecast as defensive, mean-spirited and backward-looking. Anglican evangelicals in Melbourne and Sydney reacted differently, developing scholarship and spirituality, as well as potent lay networks, some of which fell into super-holiness and antinomianism.

By the 1980s, regional theological scholarship had expanded and matured, with fruitful interaction with Roman Catholics and Orthodox colleagues that gave fresh impetus to contextual theology, indigenous issues, and the boundaries between science and religion. Mainstream churches wrestled with the challenge of rapidly growing Pentecostal churches and charismatic groups, and the separatism they engendered.

Protestant churches grew dramatically after 1945, but attendance in the major denominations peaked in the 1960s and then went into serious decline, especially among the under-30s, when commitment to institutions generally diminished during the watershed years of the 1960s and 1970s, a time when leisure options grew, television relativized morality and dissent took forms which left Protestantism uncertain about which directions to follow. New forms of mass entertainment, changed musical styles, and the emergence of articulate feminism were not effectively countered by revised liturgies; contemporary music, songs and hymns; or by attempts at theological relevance. Asian religions, new age ideas and skilfully marketed self-help spiritualities left Protestantism looking vulnerable, compared with Orthodoxy and Roman Catholicism. Complicity in male domestic violence and aberrant sexuality has been very costly in credibility and compensation payments. Acceptance of inclusive liturgical language has been patchy, as has recognition of women's potential for leadership and the importance of feminist theological perspectives. Lutherans, Pentecostals and Presbyterians, with some Anglicans, have rejected the ordination of women in the name of fidelity to Scripture, but most Anglicans, New Zealand Presbyterians and the Uniting Church reached the opposite conclusion. Polynesians and Melanesians have, for cultural reasons, been very resistant to changes in gender boundaries.

Paradoxically, some forms of institutional decline have been more than matched by new forms of recognition. Both Australia and New Zealand have had

Anglican archbishops appointed as governor-general. Pacific Protestants have provided many clergy to assist in government after independence. Church schools, chaplaincies and social welfare services have expanded because of generous government subsidies, so that churches are now major employers, and increasingly constrained by governmental priorities, despite generous giving by members and skilful investment of capital. Though Protestantism is decreasingly influential politically, its values and priorities still influence many parliamentarians, even if the number of public theologians and advocates with national stature have diminished. Though Protestants used radio very creatively from the 1920s to the 1970s, their influence through television has declined in prime time. They have been as bewildered as other agencies by the power of electronic data transmission that has made censorship almost impossible. Yet possibilities for cultural connection with themes explored in television, film and video are very real, even if it is hard to reach consensus on the priorities of Christian witness.

The growth of aid and development agencies with Christian bases since the 1960s underlines how powerfully Protestant styles of compassion run. Numbers of coalitions have emerged to recall Protestants to the historic foundations of their faith, but without agreed criteria for resolving deep theological divisions, Protestants are vulnerable to the powerful forces of cultural change. Many of the foundations on which they relied for identity have weakened, even disappeared.

Exclusion of Asian migrants has gone. Britishness has been replaced by multiculturalism. Roman Catholics are the largest body of regular worshippers. Other religions challenge Christian hegemony. Migration has modified Protestantism, with strong Korean, Indonesian, Chinese and Pacific Island churches standing outside mainline networks, or challenging denominational priorities. Aboriginal, Maori and Islander Christians have rejected the normative character of the British and European heritage and demanded that their own cultural heritage be given due weight. That has had divisive political consequences when it has involved claims to land and sacred sites that threaten miners' and pastoralists' power, and challenge the secular religion of development.

Some Protestant leaders have been captivated by post-modernism and political correctness, or selective historical reconstructions. Many members and their children have dropped out of census allegiance into the categories of 'No religion' or 'Object to state', the numbers of which have grown in striking similarity to the decline of denominational allegiance. Almost 39 per cent of the population now use civil celebrants rather than clergy for rites of passage.

Residual Protestantism survives in the search for authenticity and freedom in spirituality, rejection of ecclesiastical authority, dissent and individualism, none of which require commitment to any external religious community, or to the sacrificial community service which characterized earlier generations of civic Protestants. Civic, confessional and evangelical Protestantism has shown remarkable ability to adapt contextually when in vital connection with its biblical and experiential foundations. That can be seen most clearly in the Pacific

Islands, where traditional culture and village Christianity are closely integrated. That synthesis has come close to collapse with military coups in Fiji, destructive civil wars in Bougainville and in the Solomon Islands, and the near collapse of civil society in parts of Papua New Guinea, amid a welter of violent competing corruptions.

In Australia and New Zealand, Protestantism still retains strong missionary outreach, capacity for practical service, scepticism about pretentious claims to piety and virtue, and ability to innovate. Its networks and values are still influential, but fragile, unless renewed by major recommitment from a younger generation. Theological and ethical issues are still divisive, for the balance between unity and diversity is always elusive. Issues of gender, sexuality, ecology, social justice and ethnicity are the context in which witness to divine grace seen in the crucified and risen Lord, and experience of transformation by the Spirit in the Christian community might remake evangelism and the capacity for hope-filled activism which energized regional Protestantism for two centuries.

Further Reading

Breward, I. (2001). *A History of the Churches in Australasia*. Oxford: Clarendon Press.

Carey, H. M., Breward, I., Doumanis N., Frappell, R., Hilliard, D., Massam, K., O'Brien, A., Rutland, S. D., Thompson, R. (2001). Australian Religion Review. *Journal of Religious Studies* 24.3–25.1.

Davidson, A. K. (1997). *Christianity in Aotearoa*. Wellington: NZEFM.

Hutchinson, M. (2001). *Iron in our Blood*. Sydney: Ferguson.

Kaye, B. (ed) (2002). *Anglicanism in Australia*. Melbourne: Melbourne University Press.

Piggin, S. (1996). *Evangelical Christianity in Australia*. Melbourne: Oxford University Press.

Thompson, R. (2002). *Religion in Australia*. Melbourne: Oxford University Press.

CHAPTER 24

African Protestantism to the Present Day

John S. Pobee

Africa, the second largest continent, covering an area of just under 12 million square miles, encompasses many and diverse peoples, races, cultures, religions, histories and temperaments in about 52 sovereign and independent nations. It may be divided into two major regions: Africa north of the Sahara and Africa south of the Sahara. The former is largely Hamitic, Arabic-speaking and Muslim. Africa south of the Sahara is peopled by aboriginal Bushmen of the Kalahari region, the Khoikhoi or Hottentots of the south-west, Pigmies of the Congo forest, Hamitic peoples of north-eastern and east-central Africa, Blacks and Caucasians. The Caucasians, mainly Dutch and English, have lived in Southern Africa since 1653 and 1820 respectively and have no other home than Southern Africa.

Africa used to be described as the sleeping giant. Today constant news and reports of wars, excruciating and abject poverty, sickness especially the AIDS epidemic, genocide and political instability constitute evidence of a continent very much alive, if not a continent in turmoil. Alongside much negative reporting stands the story of rich mineral and other natural resources. Today the continent bears the marks of slavery, European colonialism (Neill, 1966: 284–411), missionary movements and now globalization.

A study of such a large continent can only be variegated, in broad strokes and almost a silhouette. But pluralism – religious, cultural, ethnic and racial – characterizes the continent and constitutes the context in which Christianity as a whole lives its life.

Homo Africanus, Homo Religiosus Radicaliter

African traditional religions, Christianity and Islam are evident in different countries, in varying mixes, percentages and degree of influence. Africa has become the heartland of world Christianity (Walls, 1976: 180), with Christian predominance in Ghana (c.62%), Kenya (c.73%), Uganda (c.78.3%), Republic of South Africa (c.79.2%) and Namibia (c.96.3%). Likewise, Islam is very strong and making continued advances, predominately in North Africa since the military conquest by Muslim Arabs in 647, as well as in Senegal (91%), Mali (80%), Sudan (73%) and Gambia (84%). It is also growing in Kenya, Tanzania, Uganda, Malawi, Mozambique and South Africa. Islam is an ever-increasing challenge for African Christians.

The history of the Crusades has determined that Christians and Muslim in Africa look at each other with suspicion. Islamic religion tends to become a state religion and its teachings and practices permeate all economic, social and political institutions and policies. Hence sharia has become a *causus belli* between Christians and Muslim in the Sudan and Nigeria where Protestants and Roman Catholics have been at a social disadvantage and under persecution. As early as 1910, Islam was judged sufficiently strong to evoke a call for establishing a 'Christian belt' across sub-Saharan Africa as a strategy for halting Islamic southern advance. There is also heightened concern for all kinds of religious fundamentalism, Islamic in Algeria, Egypt and Sudan, and in South Africa Afrikaaner fundamentalism led by the Reformed Church of South Africa.

Protestantism in an African Context

Protestantism, a product and legacy of the sixteenth-century schism in the Latin Church, came to Africa bearing the marks of its founding schism and division. The sundering of the *Una Sancta*, not only Protestant churches from Catholicism but also from each other, was transplanted to Africa. Later still, Protestant traditions from North America also came to Africa. The Protestant missionary enterprise was, in part, an attempt to undermine Roman Catholicism, established in Africa in the fifteenth century. Relationships were far from easy and often competitive and vicious. For example, Portuguese and Spanish missionaries considered the Reformed-Presbyterian faith of the Dutch on the coast 'Calvin's poison' (de Marees, 1605) while Catholics felt similar disgust for Protestants where both were active.

Eighteenth-century Protestant missionary work in Africa was the outgrowth of the evangelical revival. Its marks included a literal interpretation of the Scriptures, the offer of forgiveness and grace, a serious sense of accountability to God, belief in the love and judgement of God, a Puritan ethic, and an emphasis on personal religion. This revival spawned missionary societies such as the Baptist Missionary Society which arrived at Baviaanskloof, South Africa in 1792; the Society for the Propagation of the Gospel (Anglican), which worked in the Gold Coast and South Africa in the eighteenth century; the Denmark-based Trankebar Mission; the Moravian Mission from Herrnhut who operated in Genadendal South Africa; the Church Missionary Society which worked in

Sierra Leone, Uganda, Nigeria and Kenya; the Evangelical Missionary Society or more commonly the Basel Mission in Ghana and Cameroon; the North German Missionary Society of Bremen (Ustorf, 2002) in Ghana and Togo; the Paris Evangelical Mission Society which worked in Lesotho in 1833 to set up a mission which became the Church of Basutoland; and the London Missionary Society. Thus Protestant denominationalism was introduced into Africa as mission societies emerged, by and large, under the auspices of specific denominations, each carving a piece of Africa as its own and stamping regions with individual Protestant emphases.

Complicating the story further is the linking of mission with European trade and later European colonialism. The Society of the Propagation of the Gospel, for example, came to the Gold Coast at the invitation of the Company of Merchants (later the Royal Africa Company). The Rev. Thomas Thompson became the first Anglican missionary to Cape Coast, Gold Coast, 1751–6, as a chaplain to the British in the castle. Pieter de Marees, a trader from Holland, introduced the Reformed tradition to Moree in Ghana in 1600. Similarly, the Basel Mission came to Osu, Ghana under the auspices of the Danish governor. In South Africa Robert Moffat served as Cecil Rhodes' interpreter in Matabele. Christian missions were projected as yet another face of European colonial life in Africa. Adventure, study, politics, trade and evangelism came in one package, namely Protestant missions writ large. This mix implied an anthropology by which Africans were defined in terms of Western values, and especially an assumed European superiority.

Mission outposts in Africa were often styled 'daughter churches' of the parent church in Europe. Thus a paternalistic relationship existed between the founding churches and the African churches. Church structure as a consequence was very hierarchical. For example, in Lesotho, church leadership was in the form of the *Seboka* (Assembly), composed of 16 missionaries and nine local or African ministers, which looks reasonably egalitarian. However and crucially, the *Sekoba* had no authority to deal with the administration of overseas funds, secondary or industrial education because the *Seboka* had African representation. Such matters were the sole responsibility of the conference of European missionaries. This paternalism, widespread throughout most of Africa, particularly in Southern Africa, is seen by Africans as a technique of white domination through guardianship.

Consequently churches have become the targets of African politicians and nationalists. Churches, according to such rhetoric, prepared the way for eventual enslavement by the political compatriots of the missionary. Kwame Nkrumah of Ghana makes the classic statement that 'the stage opens with the appearance of missionaries and anthropologists, traders, concessionaires and administrators. While the missionaries with "Christianity" implore the colonial subject to lay up "treasures in heaven where neither moth nor rust doth corrupt", the traders, concessionaires acquire his mineral and land resources, destroy his arts, crafts and home industries' (Nkrumah, 1958; cf. Pobee, 1975: 217–37).

As mentioned earlier, the denominational demography of Africa has been determined by the balkanization of Africa by colonialists. Missionaries often went where they could enjoy colonial protection. The Society for the Propagation of the Gospel (SPG), the Universities Mission to Central Africa and the Church Missionary Society (CMS) went to the Gold Coast (Ghana), Tanganyika (Tanzania), South Africa, Nigeria and Southern Rhodesia (Zimbabwe) where the English governed. This rather arbitrary balkanization has been a continued problem for Africa, as it ignores historic African cultural and ethnic boundaries in favour of one borne out of European expediency.

Despite being denominationally and nationally biased, missions were seen as outposts of churches in Europe, never churches in their own right. Thus the CMS was not called a church but CMS Mission. Anglicanism in Ghana was successively called SPG and the English Church Mission. Presbyterianism in Ghana was styled the Basel Mission. This was not only a question of nomenclature; those churches were *governed* from overseas even if there were representatives of the mission board locally. This has been problematic for many obvious and lamentable reasons – too many to recount.

African Protestant churches, thus, have been in a 'North Atlantic captivity'. Given the North Atlantic provenance of the missions and missionaries, 'it was inevitable that African churches should at first be extensions of "home churches" abroad' (Nketia, 1962: 112). African churches were transplants and replicas in respect of their theology, worship, structures and so on. Even the spiritualities and élan of the Protestant churches have been in North Atlantic captivity: 'In the first excess of evangelistic zeal little or no attempt was made to understand the African way of life' (Dike, 1957). The reasons for this scenario were varied. Obviously the missionaries could only bring what they had. But there was also a *theological* mindset as articulated by Rev. Richard Sibbes (cited by Rooy, 1965: 30). In a seventeenth century sermon, *Lydia's Conversion*, he argued that 'God in preparation for the most part civilizeth people, and then christianizeth them'. Needless to say, civility was judged by European standards and culture.

However, some missionary theorists such as Henry Venn, secretary of CMS (1842–72), touted the idea of a *euthanasia of mission* by which missions aimed at establishing a self-supporting, self-governing and self-propagating church. This movement was often thwarted: for example, in 1864 when the CMS attempted to appoint Samuel Ajayi Crowther as Bishop of the Niger Mission, the Rev. Hinderer (a CMS missionary in Nigeria) argued that if 'they [the Africans] hear that a black man is our master, they will question our respectability' (D. Hinderer to H. Venn, 15 November 1864, CMS CA2/049).

The nineteenth-century movement of Ethiopianism in southern Africa and Nigeria spearheaded the resistance to the ideology of white Christian domination. The movement was a motley group (Shepperson, 1968; Ayandele, 1966; Pobee, 1992). Ayandele quoting Agbebi, for example, writes of the classic agenda of Ethiopianism: 'to render Christianity indigenous to Africa, it must be watered by native hands, turned by native hatchet, and tended with native earth.

It is a curse if we intend for ever to hold the apron strings of foreign teachers doing the baby for aye' (Ayandele, 1966: 200). However real the bigotry and paternalism of the missionaries, a distinction between European colonialism, which often reduced Africa to brute and raw creation and the missionaries, who treated Africa and Africans humanely, is important, taking into account their own biases (Ayandele, 1966: 12).

Despite the presence of Western missionaries, the true agent of Protestant mission in Africa is the peculiar African creation of the local catechist. The unsung hero of African church history prepared the ground for the missionary/priest, nursed the congregation, won souls for the church, and stayed with the people at the grassroots. He was the holy man on whom the African Christian community was focused. He is an African leader for Africans.

The Protestant churches in Africa made their mark in two ways. The first was by introducing and fostering formal education in most African countries, responding to the African's overwhelming desire for knowledge and the power to read and write like white people. Schools were pioneered by the missionaries and in most countries, particularly Anglophone Africa, in partnership with the colonial administration. Though the church's educational work was originally designed to be a handmaid for missions and a training ground for Christian life, it soon became more secular by fitting people for places in a Western-style society and the civil service. Second, because Africa was plagued by malaria, yellow fever, diphtheria and dysentery, churches took medical work to be an important aspect of their ministry and mission. Thus the churches demonstrated their concern not only for heaven but also with earthly and human welfare. Another important contribution, often ignored, of the Christian mission churches is the work of producing written forms of African languages for the first time. This has contributed, in subtle ways, to developing the consciousness, pride and identity of Africans.

The Post-Independence Period

Before independence, in most former African colonies, Christian churches appeared to be the only heavyweight institutions, for good or evil, in society that could stand up to the African nationalist movements and governments. There was inevitably an initial, and in some cases a continual, struggle between church and state. African nationalists often tried to paint churches as colonial lackeys who were out of tune with true African aspirations. The nationalists, often mouthing socialist rhetoric, have tried to edge churches out of keystone areas such as education and health (e.g. Ghana under Kwame Nkrumah). However, in almost all cases, churches were left to continue in those ministries, which is perhaps more evidence that the church continues to be a heavyweight player in African societies.

African Theologies

Today African Protestant churches are trying to shape themselves according to an African ethos, so that Christ may become truly African too. Two pieces of evidence are worth reviewing here. First is the emergence of African theology. Missionary Christianity peddled what used to be called 'classical theology', contextually minted in Europe and largely a product of Enlightenment culture. This was characterized by a stress on rationality, absolute individualism, and a literate academic approach to Christianity. Such an approach in Africa, where the majority are not literate, is not exactly helpful.

Four types of African theology are emerging which seek liberation from North Atlantic constructs of theologizing. The first is an African narrative theology. The non-literate and barely educated are also called to give account of their faith. Here, the theologian becomes an articulate individual in the midst of such a community who captures their way of thinking. Such theology is found in song and dance, art, story telling, and lastly sermons. It is communitarian in that it starts from the African's communitarian epistemology and ontology, not from metaphysics but from the experience of Christian life of Africans. It is sometimes called 'theology-by-the-people' (Amirtham & Pobee, 1986).

The second African theology is the product of African theologians who, though trained in the North and West, are endeavouring to hold dialogue between the eternal non-negotiable Word of God and the African reality and context, especially the African culture that hitherto had been discounted. Its Protestant pundits include Christian G. Baeta (evangelical Presbyterian, Ghana), Harry Sawyerr (Anglican, Sierra Leone), Bolaji Idowu (Methodist, Nigeria), John Mbiti (Anglican, Kenya), and Kwesi A. Dickson (Methodist, Ghana). These dialogical theologians are a bridge between North–South and East–West theologies and heritages.

The third African theology is the liberation theology, primarily from Southern Africa, that tries to let the Word of God engage the socio-economic and political realities of their context. An important catalyst in its evolution was the racist ideology that previously operated in Southern Africa. Among such Protestants theologians, all from South Africa, are Desmond Tutu (Anglican), Manas Buthelezi (Lutheran), Allan Boesak (Reformed) and John de Gruchy (Congregationalist).

Finally, the emerging African Feminist-Womanist theologies have developed from the continent-wide Circle of African Women in Theology. Two of its leading voices are Mercy Amba Oduyoye (Methodist, Ghana) and Musimbi R. A. Kanyoro (Lutheran, Kenya). They argue that the truth about the reign of God will remain hidden until all take on board the views and participation of women. In Katie Cannon's Foreword to Oduyoye and Kanyoro (1992), she writes: 'African women theologians have turned once-invisible words into reflective, critical insights, so that concepts knowable only to sound and hearing are now viable and available to an infinite range of readers' (Cannon, 1992: viii).

These four strands of theology in Africa agree on certain points. First, theology is a wisdom by which members of the church live; it is not only knowledge. As wisdom it must have the capacity to engage the emotions without which change and renewal are impossible. This theology has three constituencies in the church, the academy and the world – not just the academy. Second, the ecumenical vision must be a catalyst for a theology that will renew church and society. African Protestantism has rejected the arbitrary separations of its founding missions and instead embraces movements that are ecumenical and respectful of African identities and heritages. Finally, theology must be incarnational in the sense of meeting the needs of Africans in the situation of a fallen world that is yet in the process of redemption. To be both wise and ecumenical, African theology must be incarnational, addressing African society with the timeless gospel of Jesus Christ, not a gospel of its 'North Atlantic Captivity'.

African Initiatives in Christianity

The most important offshoot of the Protestant tradition in Africa, evidenced by rapid and vibrant growth, is African Initiatives in Christianity (AIC). These churches represent a protest against the 'North Atlantic captivity' of the gospel and the church. Their various designations – some self-definitions and some labels from outside – indicate their varied emphases and critique of the historic Protestant churches. They have been called a *syncretistic movement*, a designation originating in Bengt Sundkler's description of them, which he later retracted, as 'the bridge over which Africans are brought back into heathenism' (Sundkler, 1948). This identifies their tendency to mix received Christianity with African traditional religions and practices such as polygamy. AICs are also *separatist churches* meaning that they are schismatic offshoots from the historic Protestant churches. Thus the Church of the Lord or *Aladura* separated itself from the CMS-founded Anglican Church in Lagos, Nigeria. The Church of Christ in Africa (Kenya) broke away in 1959 from the Anglican mission in Kenya.

Two related forms of AICs are prophetic and messianic-based churches. Some AICs are popular *prophetic movements*, centring on a charismatic teacher, which echoes what has been said above about the holy person in African Christianity. The *Apostolwo Fe Dede Fia Hiabo Nuntimya* (Apostle Revelation Society) was established in 1939 by Prophet Wovenu, himself once a member of the Evangelical Presbyterian Church. *Messianic movements* (e.g. Zion Christian Church and the Nazarene Baptist Church of South Africa) emphasize messianic aspirations, especially in apartheid South Africa. There has been some confusion about the term 'messianic' and it has been proposed to replace messianic with 'iconic', by which is signalled that a prophet is identified as the reflection and concretization of Christ, without necessarily usurping Christ's unique place (Sundkler, 1976: 193, 310).

Finally, some AICs are *spiritual* or *Pentecostal* or *charismatic* churches. Regardless of whatever connections they may have with North American Pentecostal movements, in Africa they represent dissatisfaction with the type of Protestant Christianity that had become very cerebral and did not manifest acts of power in the Spirit. An example of this tradition is the Musama Disco Christo Church of Ghana and its emphasis on prophecy, healing, prayer, holiness and a concern for inner renewal and not on institutional structure or administrative form. Of course, AICs may be a mixture of all the above in some form.

AICs play varied socio-political, economic and religious roles in rural and urban environments. They represent the search of African peoples, particularly within the Protestant tradition for 'a place to feel at home and where they have a sense of belonging' (Pobee, 1998: 35).

Protestantism has existed on the African Continent for over 200 years. For much of that period it was driven by a missionary impetus, but Africa's missions have metamorphosed into African churches. This change corresponds to an evident vitality of the African Protestant churches, calling for new relationships in response to the shifting of political and economic power from northern metropolises and multinationals to the developing world. African churches, and particularly the AICs, lead the critique on the very cultures that spawned them and argue for an African Protestantism and Christianity.

An important aspect of this change in relationships is the change from traditional patterns of North–South relationships to churches engaging one another on the continent itself. In this regard, as mentioned earlier, the ecumenical movement has been an important catalyst. The formation of the All Africa Conference of Churches (AACC) in 1963, an assembly of Protestant churches in Africa, has been the catalyst in this new development. And, of course, it is not unrelated to the wider ecumenical development that radiated from the 1910 Edinburgh Conference.

Local circumstances have also forced ecumenical collaboration. Churches have needed to join ranks to face up to dictatorships by African governments. The cruel apartheid situation in South Africa forced the churches in Southern Africa to work together as a united voice in the South African Council of Churches to counter the situation. Protestant churches in Zaire, forced by President Mobutu, became one state-recognized united Protestant church. Similarly, the AACC has been intervening in war-torn Sudan, where the Muslim-Arabic government was oppressing non-Muslims. There are also in-country issues such as recurring natural disasters that have forced Protestants into ecumenical cooperation.

The striking aspect of the post-missionary era is focused by the debate on a missionary moratorium. Many African Christians think the continuing preponderance of foreign missionaries is a hindrance to the 'self-hood' of the African church. The moratorium aims to exclude anything that negatively affects the effective development of African spiritual resources. This includes easy acceptance of traditional mission practices of the equivocation of the 'Bible with the plough' and 'Christianity with commerce and development'. AICs regard three components to be essential for an African church and mission: self-motivation, self-contextualization and self-critique. While willing to work with traditional missions in the development of a truly African church, AICs are not willing to return to a missionary 'North Atlantic captivity', however implicit the relations between mission and development.

The moratorium raises another important theological point and the challenge for Africa. As Africa becomes the heartland of world Christianity, world Christianity is becoming more truly universal (Walls, 1987) as its core message of the incarnation demands. The Protestant churches of Africa are part of this unfolding globally incarnated body of Christ, and are a voice that, by focusing on the African Christ, refuses to be subsumed into a new form of colonial dependence.

References

Amirtham, S. A. and Pobee, J. S. (1986). *Theology by the People*. Geneva: WCC.

Ayandele, E. A. (1996). *Missionary Impact on Modern Nigeria*. London: Longmans.

Cannon, Katie (1992). Foreword. In Mercy Oduyoye and Musimbi Kanyoro (eds.), *The Will to Arise*. Maryknoll, NY: Orbis.

De Marees, P. (1605). *Description et récit historique du riche royanne d'or de Guinea*. Amsterdam: Cornille Claesson.

Dike, K. N. (1957). *Origins of Niger Mission*. Ibadan: Ibadan University Press.

Neill, S. (1966). *Colonialism and Christian Missions*. London: Lutterworth.

Nketia, J. H. (1962). The Contribution of African Culture to Christian Worship. In Ram Desai (ed.), *Christianity in Africa as Seen by the Africans*. Denver, CO: Swallow.

Nkrumah, K. N. (1958). Speech at the Conference of Independent African States in Accra. 18 April. In William V. S. Tubman and Kwame Nkrumah, *Speeches Delivered at the Inaugural Session, Parliament House, Accra, Ghana*. Accra: Government Printer.

Pobee, J. S. (1975). Church and State in the Gold Coast. *Journal of Church and State* 17: 217–37.

Pobee, J. S. (1992). *Skenosis: Christian Faith in an African Context*. Gweru, Zimbabwe: Mambo.

Pobee J. S. (1998). *African Initiatives in Christianity*. Geneva: WCC.

Rooy, S. H. (1965). *The Theology of Missions in the Puritan Tradition*. Delft: J. W. D. Meinema.

Shepperson, G. (1968). Ethiopianism Past and Present. In C. G. Baeta (ed.), *Christianity in Tropical Africa*. London: Oxford University Press.

Sundkler, B. G. M. (1948). *Bantu Prophets in Southern Africa*. London: Oxford University Press.

Sundkler, B. G. M. (1976). *Zulu Zion and Some Swazi Zionists*. Uppsala: Gleerup.

Ustorf, W. (2002). *Bremen Missionaries in Togo and Ghana 1847–1900*. Accra: Asempa.

Walls, A. F. (1976). Towards Understanding Africa's Place in Christian History. In J. S. Pobee (ed.), *Religion in a Pluralistic Society*. Leiden: Brill.

Walls, A. F. (1987). The Christian Tradition in Today's World. In Frank Whaling (ed.), *Religious Situation of the World from 1945 to the Present Day*. Edinburgh: T & T Clark.

Further Reading

Hastings, A. (1974). *Wiriyamu*. London: Search Press.

Hastings, A. (1994). *The Church in Africa 1450–1950*. Oxford: Clarendon Press.

Pobee, J. S. (1983). African Spirituality. In G. S. Wakefield (ed.), *Dictionary of Spirituality*. London: SCM.

Pobee, J. S. (1988). *Kwame Nkrumah and the Church in Ghana 1949–1966*. Accra: Asempa Press.

PART II
Protestantism and Present Identity: Relations and Influence

Protestantism and its Relations

25 Protestantism and the Bible   251

26 Protestantism and the Arts   268

27 Protestantism and Politics, Economics, and Sociology   287

28 Protestantism, Law and Legal Thought   298

29 Protestantism and the Sciences   306

Protestantism and its Influence

30 Protestantism and Liberalism   322

31 Protestantism and Feminism   332

32 Protestantism and Fundamentalism   344

33 Protestantism and Racism   357

34 Protestantism and Judaism   372

35 Protestantism and Spirituality   382

36 Protestantism and Missions   392

CHAPTER 25

Protestantism and the Bible

R. Kendall Soulen

Protestant Christians today use and interpret the Bible in a bewildering variety of ways. Time has shown that the Reformation principle *sola scriptura* (scripture alone) possesses a messy fecundity, giving rise generation after generation to overlapping but often clashing communities of biblical interpretation. Indeed, one thing Protestants today often share is a tendency to deplore the ways many of their fellow Protestants use and interpret the Bible.

Nevertheless, many Protestants do in fact relate to the Bible in broadly similar ways, ways that unite them not only with each other but also with Catholic and Orthodox Christians. There are at least two reasons for this.

One reason is rooted in what the ecumenical church bequeathed to Protestants at the time of the Reformation, namely, liturgical and theological traditions that go back to the church's origins. When Protestant Christians today gather for worship, they praise God in the words of the Bible, they offer prayers and sing hymns filled with biblical allusions, they study the Bible and teach it to their youth. Most notably, perhaps, they listen to a congregational leader read and interpret the Scriptures aloud, and they do so with the expectation that God will use the interpreted Scripture to speak afresh to the gathered community. All of these uses of the Bible are rooted in the life of the ancient church and synagogue, and they unite Protestants not only with each other but also with Catholic and Orthodox Christians, and even with Jews.

The other reason has its roots in what the Protestant movement has bequeathed to the ecumenical church over the last two and a half centuries, namely, the possibility of adopting a modern, critical perspective on the Bible, the church's sacred Scriptures. Protestants were not the only early pioneers of modern biblical criticism, nor have all Protestants ever accepted biblical criticism. But Protestants and Protestant institutions were the first to embrace the critical study of the Bible in a programmatic way, and they were the first to insist that future clergy be taught to understand and be able to use the results of biblical criticism. Today a vast fund of scholarship concerning the Bible's historical origins and literary composition exists that was inconceivable to Christians of an earlier age. Make of it what one will, this fund of scholarship is now an inescapable fact, one that confronts Protestant, Catholic, and Orthodox Christians alike, and, to that extent at least, places them all in a common situation.

Unfortunately, these two sources of unity among Protestants and other Christians also contain seeds of division. For Protestants not only inherited ancient ways of using the Bible to worship God, but they modified them as well, thereby contributing first to the rupture of the Western church, and then to the ongoing rupture of the Protestant movement itself. Similarly, Protestants helped create modern biblical criticism, but from the outset they have disagreed bitterly about its truth and implications for Christian living.

If, therefore, we are to tell the story of Protestantism and the Bible, however briefly, we must spend some time looking at how early Protestants received and modified ancient approaches to the Bible, and thereby created a family of overlapping but also conflicting approaches to the Bible. And we must take a look at the rise of modern biblical criticism, and take account of some of the ways contemporary Protestants have sought to come to terms with it.

Reformation Trajectories and Challenges

The sixteenth-century Protestant Reformers inherited most of their basic convictions about the Bible, even as they modified them in light of a powerful experience of the Bible as the living Word of God. We can examine the result by looking at how the Reformation generation typically understood the Bible's *central content and purpose*, its *authority*, and its *proper interpretation*. In each case, we will see that the Reformers set fruitful trajectories for later Protestants to explore, and simultaneously created lasting problems that Protestants still wrestle with today.

The content and purpose of the Bible: Christ alone – by faith alone

Since ancient times, Christians have used the Bible to worship God on the supposition that the Bible represents some kind of unity. To some extent, Christians have supposed that this unity flows from the fact that the Bible is inspired, that is, that God authored it through many human authors. More significantly, however, Christians have understood the Bible's unity to flow from the fact that it was all about one great thing, and that it had been given by God to the church for one great purpose. What the Bible was *about*, they assumed, was the inexhaustible truth and wisdom of God, as reliably spelled out by church councils dealing with the Trinity, the incarnation, and, in the Western tradition influenced by St Augustine (354–430), salvation by grace rather than by works. What the Bible was *for*, they thought, was to provide instruction and enlightenment to Christians of every age in matters of faith and obedience.

The Reformers generally accepted these tacit understandings about the Bible's content and purpose. Their contribution was to bring both points into vividly sharper focus. They could do this, in part, because they belonged to the first generation of theologians to reap the benefits of Christian humanism. Luther studied the New Testament in the original Greek, thanks to a new edition prepared in 1516 by Desiderius Erasmus (1466–1536), a priest and cosmopolitan humanist who was the most famous scholar of his day. Yet while the Reformers were indebted to the humanist revival for fresh editions, grammars, and so on, they did not achieve their insights by linguistic skill alone. Instead, they arrived at their convictions about the Bible's content and purpose in the course of teaching, preaching, praying, and working to reform the church.

The heart of the Reformer's discovery was that Bible was not a book about doctrine and instruction, no matter how helpful or divine, but a book about *news*, something that *had happened*, and something altogether wonderful at that. The good news at the Bible's heart was that God out of sheer overwhelming love and mercy had turned to save wicked men and women through the obedience of one man, Jesus Christ, who took their wickedness upon himself so that they in turn might share in his righteousness and life through faith. For the Reformers, this news of salvation in Christ alone (*solus Christus*) was the central theme of all the prophets and the apostles. It was the infinitely precious treasure for the sake of which the Bible also was precious. As Luther put it, the Scriptures are "the swaddling cloths and the manger in which Christ lies . . . Simple and lowly are these swaddling cloths, but dear is the treasure, Christ, who lies in them" (Luther, 1960: 236). Or in Calvin's words, "This is what we should in short seek in the whole of Scripture: truly to know Jesus Christ, and the infinite riches that are comprised in him and are offered to us by him from God the Father" (Calvin, 1958: 70).

This understanding of what the Bible was about led the Reformers to a corresponding understanding of what the Bible was for, as surely as thunder follows lightening. If the Bible is about the news of Christ, then it exists in order to be *proclaimed*, so that people can hear the news and believe it. For the Reformers, faith in the gospel was not adjunct to salvation, but was salvation itself, the way that God put wicked people right (hence justification by faith alone – *sola fide*). The Reformers would have been amazed by the idea that the Bible can be rightly studied and understood in a neutral or uncommitted way, as later proposed by historical criticism. For them, the Bible can be rightly understood only by those who read it hoping and expecting to be addressed by the living Word of God, and who are eager to respond to that word with faith and obedience.

The Reformers' sharpened vision of the Bible's content and proper use has proven to be fantastically fruitful. It has unleashed wave upon wave of Christian revival and inspired tenacious missionary efforts that have gradually spread Christian faith around the globe. It has given birth to new ways of doing Christian theology that have expressed the contents of the Bible in dialogical and interpersonal terms rather than in the categories of Platonic and Aristotelian philosophy. And it has provided spiritual grist for influential intellectual movements that have profoundly shaped modern culture, from the German idealism of Hegel and Fichte to the existentialism of Heidegger and Sartre and beyond.

At the same time, the Reformers' account of the Bible's content and purpose contains the seeds of future problems. For the underlying dynamic of their vision is as fragile as it is rich. On one side, the whole Bible must stay in contact with what the Bible is about, namely, God's living Word of salvation, the gospel of Jesus Christ. On the other side, the whole Bible must be read in ways that stay in contact with what the Bible is for, creating and sustaining faith. But these elements can easily fall apart. One way this can happen is when the interpreter becomes preoccupied with the Bible in its own right, unconnected to the Word of God that speaks through it and the church that hears it. This threatens to happen in Protestant Scholasticism, and almost certainly occurs in many forms of modern biblical criticism. But the breakdown can also happen when Christians try to link God and the church apart from the Bible altogether. This danger was already evident in radical Reformers like Thomas Müntzer (c.1489–1525), a German Anabaptist who held that the Holy Spirit spoke directly to him in fresh revelations apart from Scripture. Arguably, it is present again in some forms of liberal theology as well.

The authority of the Bible – sola scriptura

Prior to the Reformation, Christians tended to think of the Scriptures as one element in a large constellation of divine institutions in the church, alongside the sacraments, the priesthood, and doctrine. All of these served in various ways to mediate God's saving grace to the faithful, and so all of them together enjoyed a claim to divine authority.

The Reformation changed this picture dramatically by offering a radically simplified picture of how God's favor toward us in Christ (what Protestants typically mean by grace) is communicated to the church: through Scripture alone. The Reformers demote the rest of the constellation. Its elements no longer have independent significance, but are now simply signs and servants of the Bible's message. This implies a new conception of priesthood, for example, which is now understood to mean that all believers are called by the Word and empowered by the Spirit to minister to one another in the church. Above all, it implies a new understanding of scriptural authority. If Scripture alone is the medium of God's saving Word, then Scripture alone must be judge over all matters of belief, conduct, and worship in the church.

Sola scriptura simplifies and concentrates divine authority in a way that has had huge consequences for the church and Western culture generally. The principle confers dignity on voices of dissent by establishing a court of appeal that towers above all mere human authority, whether of pope, emperor or king. It offers a lofty vantage from which to survey and judge inherited tradition. Finally, it offers all this to everyone, or at least everyone who can read the Bible. While this last may not have been Luther's intention, it was the inference many drew from his example.

But *sola scriptura* also creates problems that have bedeviled Protestants from the outset. Exactly what portions of previous tradition does the Bible authorize? Luther himself adopted a largely conservative position. While he trimmed back the number of sacraments, for example, he held fast to the ancient church councils. But others soon took a more radical view. Michael Servetus (1511–53), a physician and early enthusiast of the Reformation, concluded after lengthy study that the Bible did not teach the Trinity or the divinity of Christ, views that eventually led to his arrest, trial, and execution in Calvin's Geneva. A related problem is this: what attitude should Protestants take on issues where Scripture is silent? Does the Bible permit what it does not explicitly prohibit, for example, organ music in worship? Lutherans and many Anglicans have tended to answer "yes," holding that such customs are neutral or indifferent (*adiaphora*), that is, permissible so long as they are not required for salvation. But Puritans and many pietists have tended toward the opposite view: what the Bible does not explicitly allow it prohibits. In sum, the Reformation program of *sola scriptura* has had a paradoxical result. It unites Protestants by differentiating them from Catholics and Orthodox Christians. But it has proven to be a continual source of fragmentation within the Protestant movement itself.

The interpretation of the Bible: the literal sense and the clarity of Scripture

The Reformers inherited an approach to biblical interpretation known as the *Quadriga* (originally a four-horse chariot). The *Quadriga* distinguished four *senses* or levels of meaning in a biblical text: a literal or historical level, and three spiritual levels – the tropological (concerned with morals), the allegorical (concerned with doctrine), and the anagogical (concerned with the world to come). The point of the system was to direct the reader beneath the letter of the text to discover hidden truths considered richer and more spiritually valuable. This approach was thought to be especially necessary for the Old Testament, whose literal sense was often deemed particularly unnourishing, but it was also permitted when interpreting the New Testament too.

Although Luther made use of the *Quadriga* in his early years, he and other sixteenth-century Reformers gradually found this system to be cumbersome, artificial, and above all unnecessary. For them, the gospel was not hidden below the surface of the Bible, but was present in the literal sense of Scripture itself. They held this to be true not only of the New Testament, but of the Old Testament too, for they interpreted the literal sense of the Old Testament in a strongly prophetic fashion, as intrinsically oriented by God toward the coming

Messiah. Thus Calvin can write, "If one were to sift thoroughly the Law and the Prophets, he would not find a single word which would not draw and bring us to [Jesus Christ]" (Calvin, 1958: 70). At the same time, the Reformers did not simply reject the idea that Scripture has a *spiritual* sense. Instead, they reinterpreted it to refer to the *use* that the Holy Spirit makes of the letter of Scripture to awaken faith in the heart of the reader. According to this view, the spiritual sense refers not to a secret meaning hidden beneath the letter, but to the literal sense itself as the means by which God speaks to the believer.

Another feature of Reformation hermeneutics is the rule that Scripture is its own interpreter (*scriptura sui ipsius interpres*). Opponents of the Reformation argued that the Bible contained too many obscure passages to stand alone as supreme authority in the church: it needed an equally authoritative interpreter to stand alongside it. The Reformers insisted that the Bible's main message was perfectly clear to the unprejudiced reader, and that the Bible's clearest passages provided all the light necessary to illuminate more obscure verses. In this way, they sought to ensure that church tradition remained subservient to the letter of Scripture, not its master or equal.

The Reformation emphasis on the literal sense of Scripture helped to create a new form of popular Christian piety centered in preaching, reading, and studying the Bible. As a result, Protestant populations between the sixteenth and early twentieth centuries probably commanded a higher level of biblical literacy across a broader cross-section of occupations than ever before in Christendom. Today, similar kinds of Bible piety are taking root among peoples throughout Asia, Africa, and Indonesia.

But the Protestant approach to interpretation has created lasting problems, too. Above all, the notion of "the literal sense" of Scripture has proven to be remarkably slippery. Time has shown that a person's understanding of the Bible's literal sense depends a great deal on the context in which one reads a given passage, and the purpose for which one reads it. The Reformers read each verse in the light of every other, and they saw the whole centered in Christ. With the rise of historical criticism, however, Protestants increasingly understood the literal sense of Scripture to refer to what a given passage once meant in its original historical setting, rather than what it means in its current literary place within the Bible. As this shift occurred, it became vastly more difficult to see the Bible's literal sense as the vehicle of the Spirit's contemporary work. And it also became more difficult to read the Old Testament as a prophetic voice that points to Christ.

Post-Reformation Trajectories and Challenges

Protestant approaches to the Bible today reflect not only trajectories and problems of the sixteenth century, but also of religious movements and perspectives that sprouted chiefly in the seventeenth and eighteenth centuries. Here we note three such movements that developed characteristic approaches to the Bible

whose impulses continue to be felt today, in a variety of overlapping and mutually influencing ways.

Protestant scholasticism

A university-based movement that flourished chiefly in German-speaking lands
from 1550 to 1750, Protestant scholasticism sought to be a loyal guardian of
the Reformation, but gradually developed an approach to the Bible that differed
markedly from that of the Reformers. In place of the Reformers' emphasis on
what the Bible was *about* (the gospel) and what it was *for* (awakening faith), the
Scholastics became preoccupied with the Bible itself, and above all, with establishing its supreme authority over against Roman Catholic claims on behalf of
the pope. In the process, they gave a whole new prominence to the doctrine
of biblical inspiration. They held that since God directly dictated every word of
Scripture (verbal inspiration), the Bible mirrored God's own perfect truthfulness,
and was free from error in every respect (plenary inspiration). In the words
of Johannes Quenstedt (1617–88), professor of theology at the University of
Wittenberg, "each and everything presented to us in Scripture is absolutely
true whether it pertains to doctrine, ethics, history, chronology, topography, or
onomastics" (*Systema*, P. 1, C. 4, S. 2, q. 5, quoted in Preus, 1970: 346).

The Scholastics also shifted the Reformers' emphasis from the Bible as *news*
to the Bible as *doctrine*. To describe that doctrine as accurately as possible, they
reintroduced the vocabulary of medieval scholasticism that the Reformers had
generally avoided (hence the movement's name). And while the Scholastics
never lost touch with the importance of repentance, faith, and obedience, they
increasingly interpreted all this in terms of giving intellectual assent to the
propositional content of faith.

Scholasticism stands at the head of a stream of Protestantism that seeks
to combine belief in the Bible as the Word of God with the highest standards of
academic rigor. The weakness of this tradition has proved to be its rigid doctrine
of inspiration, which tends to make the Bible rather than the Bible's message
the focus of attention, and leaves little room for acknowledging the humanity of
the biblical authors.

Pietism

Arising as a reaction against Scholasticism in late seventeenth-century
Germany, Pietism quickly spread to England, Holland, and the New World, and
today is a major force in global Christianity. Philip Jacob Spener (1635–1705),
a founder of the pietist movement, sought to reform theological education by
reclaiming the Bible for the ordinary life of faith. He and other piestists insisted
that the proper use of the Bible was to lead to faith in Christ. They affirmed the
doctrine of inspiration but were uninterested in trying to prove it by rational
argument, pointing instead to inward assurance created by the Holy Spirit. For
them, the Bible's drama of salvation was to be played out within the believer's

heart. John Wesley (1703–91), Anglican priest and founder of Methodism, emphasized studying the Bible in small groups in conjunction with practices of prayer, exhortation, and confession. From the beginning, pietists have embraced popular Christian education, founding numerous Bible societies that print and distribute cheap Bibles, and producing huge volumes of devotional literature, including poetry, hymns, and calendars.

A strength of Pietism has been to keep alive the Reformers' concern that Christians read the Bible for the sake of Christ, even as it pitches that conviction in a new key, emphasizing personal experience and intense devotion. A weakness of Pietism, however, has been a tendency to emphasize the heart's engagement with Scripture at the cost of the mind's, and to sidestep the most difficult challenges to faith.

Millenarianism

Protestants have often shown an intense interest in the parts of the Bible that are concerned with the end of this world and the beginning of the world to come. Among the radical Reformers this interest sometimes took millenarian form, that is, the belief that Christ will return to reign upon earth for one thousand years before ushering in the world to come. Explicitly condemned by early Protestant confessions as a Judaizing heresy (cf. *Augsburg Confession*, art. 17), millenarian ideas nevertheless took hold again among some seventeenth-century Puritans and Anglicans, and have reappeared in forms of popular Protestantism ever since. Millenarian outlooks are characterized by intense interest in biblical chronology and contemporary events, interpreted in light of the book of Daniel and of Revelation (especially chapter 20). They also typically assign the Jewish people a significant place in God's contemporary dealings with the world, in contrast to the many other forms of Protestantism that regarded Judaism as obsolete. An influential variation of millenarian ideas appears in the work of J. N. Darby (1800–82) and C. I. Scofield (1843–1921), who taught that Christ would rescue all true Christians before a final period of tribulation befalls the earth.

At its best, millenarianism nourishes hope in God's this-worldly promises and pricks the conscience of domesticated churches. It is surely not coincidental that eschatological themes play a prominent role in the hymnody of enslaved blacks in nineteenth-century America, helping them to endure and ultimately prevail. But at its worst, millenarianism treats the Bible as a codebook and fosters credulous escapist forms of Christian faith.

The Rise of Modern Historical Criticism

Starting in the late seventeenth century, a new approach to reading the Bible began to appear that was less interested in the Bible as the unique medium of the Word of God than as the product of human authors, basically similar to other ancient and modern writings. Now known as historical criticism, the approach was initially represented only by a few mavericks such as the Dutch Jewish philosopher and rationalist Benedict Spinoza (1632–77). Spinoza held that the interpreter must not approach the Bible assuming its truth from the outset, and that the Bible in fact contained numerous contradictions and errors, views that led to his expulsion from the synagogue. From the late eighteenth century onward, however, historical criticism gained an ever-sturdier foothold at German Protestant universities. By the mid-twentieth century, the historical critical approach to the Bible enjoyed a virtual monopoly on intellectual respectability at Protestant seminaries and universities throughout Europe and North America.

The reasons for the steady rise of historical criticism are complex. One factor was the Enlightenment's spirit of emancipation, which sought to break the church's authority over religious, academic, and political spheres of life. Another was budding empiricism, which inspired defenders and opponents of biblical authority alike to concentrate on sifting *evidence* for the Bible's credibility. But historical critics have also consistently justified their approach by appealing to principles of the Reformation. Their aim, as they have seen it, has been to clear away the dogmatic overlay of church tradition (now including Protestant church tradition), so that the Bible's original literal message can speak for itself once again.

In reality, historical critics actually created a new conception of what it means to understand the Bible. The goal of historical criticism has been to determine what a biblical passage *meant* in its original historical context (the *sensus literalis historicus*), not what (if anything) it *means* to people today. The Reformers, in contrast, assumed that the literal sense of a biblical passage naturally encompasses both past and present meaning, and that the interpreter's job was to clarify both. Furthermore, historical criticism holds that to understand the Bible rightly, the interpreter must conscientiously set aside all of his or her prior theological commitments, and apply only the same criteria of judgment applicable to ordinary life. In contrast, the Reformers believed one should approach the Bible in faith and attentive humility, expecting to be addressed by the living Word of God. Finally, historical criticism holds that the main prerequisites for successful interpretation are extensive training in languages and historical methods. To these, the Reformers would have added spiritual disciplines such as prayer, meditation, and participation in the church's life and worship.

Despite these differences, or rather because of them, historical criticism gradually painted a new picture of the Bible shockingly different from previous tradition. We can explore this new picture by looking at three issues.

Source criticism and the composition of the Pentateuch

Traditionally, Christians (and Jews) believed that Moses was the author of the Pentateuch (the first five books of the Bible). Early historical critics, however, noted that these books contain numerous contradictions, repetitions, changes in literary style and so on. Whereas previous Christians tried to reconcile or "harmonize" such passages, early historical critics offered a different solution: the Pentateuch was a composite made up of originally separate traditions. In the 1870s, Karl Heinrich Graf and Julius Wellhausen proposed an influential form of this hypothesis, according to which the Pentateuch was composed of four sources of substantially different origins and outlooks (known as J, E, P, and D), originating from 850 to 450 BCE. Their hypothesis helped create the subdiscipline known as source criticism (study of literary sources), which was eventually joined by form criticism (study of popular genres), redaction criticism (study of editorial composition), and numerous others. The upshot was the creation of a new picture of the Bible as a loose conglomoration of written and oral traditions that originated in vastly different circumstances and were edited and recombined over the course of time.

The quest for the historical Jesus

Traditionally, Christians regarded the four Gospels as different but equally reliable reports about Jesus. Early on, however, historical critics such as Samuel Reimarus (1694–1768) drew a sharp distinction between what the Gospels *report* that Jesus said and did and what he *actually* said and did. Ever since, historical critics tried to get behind Gospel traditions that originated after Jesus's death (e.g., reports of his resurrection, miracles, miraculous birth) to Jesus himself. In the second half of the nineteenth century, historians produced dozens of biographies of Jesus, believing they could construct an objective portrait of Jesus's personality and aims by using historical methods to separate fact from fiction in the Gospels. The scholar, organist, and physician Albert Schweitzer (1875–1965) crushed this hope in his book, *The Quest for the Historical Jesus* ([1906] 1998). The book demonstrated that the nineteenth-century portraits of Jesus simply mirrored their authors' liberal ideals. Since then, scholars have differed about the merits of renewed quests for the historical Jesus. Many argue that such portraits are thinly conjectural, while others argue that more sophisticated methods will produce better results. In either case, however, scholars now accept a new verdict about the Gospels: they are not neutral, unprejudiced reports, but testimonies saturated throughout with the theological perspectives of the early church.

The Religionsgeschichtliche Schule *and the uniqueness of Christianity*

Toward the end of the nineteenth century, scholars began to notice surprising similarities between ancient Israel and other ancient peoples of the Middle East, and between early Christianity and other religions of the time. Eventually a movement was born known as the *Religionsgeschichtliche Schule* (history of religions school) whose goal was to describe the origin and development of Judaism and Christianity against the backdrop of Near Eastern religion generally. Ernst Troeltsch (1865–1930), professor at the University of Berlin and the movement's primary theologian, argued that the new historical perspectives ruled out supernaturalistic faith entirely, and required Christians to accept the historically relative and conditioned nature of the Bible and Christianity. Many theologians and biblical scholars have refused to accept Troeltsch's consistent historicism, arguing that it does not take the Christian tradition's theological claims seriously enough. Nevertheless, the *Religionsgeschichtliche Schule* has helped demonstrate that ancient Judaism and Christianity are not as exceptional as traditional readers of the Bible had assumed, but are parts of a broad interconnected fabric of human culture and religion.

Contemporary Approaches to Biblical Interpretation

Historical criticism has brought genuine gains to the Protestant understanding of the Bible. It has brought many biblical writings into sharply finer focus and increased sensitivity for the Bible's literary and theological diversity. More importantly, perhaps, they have given many modern readers of the Bible an unprecedented appreciation for what one might call the Bible's *humanity*. The Bible did not fall from the sky but was born from a deeply human and enormously intricate history. This knowledge enables many Protestants to view the biblical writings as human works with which it is at times possible and even necessary to disagree, for example, on moral matters pertaining to the treatment of slaves, women, or homosexuals, or on cosmological issues pertaining to the origins of the universe. At the same time, however, historical criticism also has a negative side. Above all, it has made it more difficult for many Protestants to *use* the Bible in the ways that the Reformers held that it should be used: to promote knowledge of and communion with God.

One common way Protestants manage the resulting challenge is by ignoring it. Critical perspectives on the Bible are confined to the academy, while churches continue to use and interpret the Bible in more or less traditional ways. In addition to mutual indifference, however, Protestants have developed several strategies for responding to the challenge of historical criticism. Three such strategies are outlined here, which together map a broad terrain within which many Protestants today navigate, moving at times closer to one strategy, at times closer to another.

Conservative approaches

Conservative approaches to biblical interpretation reaffirm the character of the Bible as the inspired Word of God and on that basis deny the validity of many or most of modern historical criticism's findings and methods. The roots of this strategy go back to Protestant Scholasticism and, to a lesser degree, Pietism. In nineteenth-century America, the strategy was ably represented by several generations of gifted Presbyterians associated with Princeton Theological Seminary, such as Archibald Alexander (1772–1851) and Charles Hodge (1797–1878). Today, the approach is common among conservative Protestants such as evangelicals, fundamentalists, Pentecostals, and others.

A conservative approach to the Bible typically emphasizes the inseparability of faith in the inerrancy of Scripture and faith in Christ. If the former falls, so does the latter. In the words of Charles Hodge, "Faith . . . in Christ involves faith in the Scriptures as the Word of God, and faith in the Scriptures as the Word of God is faith in their plenary inspiration. That is, it is the persuasion that they are not the product of the fallible intellect of man but of the infallible intellect of God" (Hodge, 1983: 137). From this starting point, a conservative approach typically goes on to reaffirm the harmonious and noncontradictory unity of the Bible, its essential freedom from error, and so. Wherever the findings and methods of historical criticism appear to challenge these views, they are rejected.

Sophisticated advocates of a conservative approach argue that historical criticism rests on a number of tenets that cannot be demonstrated by historical investigation alone and that are finally philosophical or theological in character. The historical critic approaches the text having decided in advance to evaluate it according to criteria that are secular in character. Naturally this approach yields unsatisfactory results, for it gives unwarranted normativity to the interpreter's experience and beliefs. In the name of objectivity, historical criticism substitutes a human-centered worldview for a God-centered one. Instead, the conservative approach insists, one must read the Bible with unreserved trust in its truthfulness and authority.

Yet despite its hostility toward modern historical criticism, conservative approaches to the Bible are often modern in unwitting ways. They share historical criticism's preoccupation with questions of evidence and historical factuality. Moreover, they are arguably no less prone to imposing external criteria on the Bible's message, if only by being selective in the texts they emphasize. For example, many contemporary conservatives give great weight to the New Testament's few injunctions against homosexual activity, while passing quickly over Jesus's more extensive teachings on nonviolence.

Liberal approaches

Liberal approaches to biblical interpretation typically hold that Christians are morally and intellectually bound to accept biblical criticism's verdict regarding the Bible's human origins and historically conditioned character. This demands in turn, they believe, a substantially new account of how Christians understand the Bible's authority and significance for Christian life today.

An important progenitor of this strategy was the German theologian Friederich Schleiermacher (1768–1834). Raised in the Pietist tradition, and later professor of theology at the University of Berlin, Schleiermacher saw the biblical interpretation of his day locked in fruitless battle between moralistic rationalism on the one side and defensive supernaturalism on the other. He tried to transcend the conflict by arguing (with the rationalists) that Christians must read the Bible like any other book, while holding (with the supernaturalists) that it contained something of supreme religious significance. This, for Schleiermacher, was the New Testament's memory of Jesus's religious personality, which continued to exercise historical influence that shaped and enlarged the church's fellowship with God. He de-emphasized other traditional claims, such as miracles, the significance of the Old Testament, and the inspiration of the whole canon.

Schleiermacher stands at the head of a family of liberal strategies that continue to locate the *source* and *norm* for Christian life in some aspect of the biblical witness, such as its portrait of Jesus, or its prophetic concern for justice and liberation. However qualified, the strategy's continued affirmation of biblical authority put it in a line of descent from the magisterial Reformers. In contrast, another family of liberal approaches rejects the idea that the Bible can properly serve as a norm for Christian life today. Since all religious inheritances from the past are historically conditioned and imperfect, Christians are justified in using the Bible only as a *source* of valuable memories, symbols, images, and so forth. Meanwhile, Christians must seek the *norm* for religious life in their contemporary experience of God, and future Christians will have to do the same. This strategy draws inspiration from the radical historicism of Ernst Troeltsch, theologian of the *Religionsgeschichtliche Schule*, and arguably from the radical Reformers, who sought guidance directly from the Holy Spirit apart from God's Word in the Bible.

The second strategy in particular has been adopted by a number of contemporary movements that interpret Scripture in light of the history, contemporary circumstances, and aspirations of a particular historically oppressed group, such as feminist interpretation, womanist interpretation, gay/lesbian interpretation, and so on. Generally speaking, these movements see the modern interpreter as standing on the same level as the biblical text, and view the relation between them as one of dialogue, or, more realistically, struggle. The reader should take the biblical text seriously enough to be open to its influence, especially insofar as it can inspire Christians today to seek greater justice, human flourishing, and so on. On the other hand, these approaches caution that the church has often used the Bible to justify the subjugation of women and the mistreatment of minorities and dissenters. Therefore the reader must approach the Bible with suspicion and be prepared to reject its claims whenever they seem to legitimate oppressive interests.

Despite differences in strategy and emphasis, liberal approaches to the Bible generally agree that it is imperative to liberate the Bible's genuine message from the historically conditioned thought forms – not merely of accumulated tradition – but of the Bible itself. One contemporary fruit of this insistence is the preparation of new inclusive-language translations of the Bible, which use gender-neutral terms in place of masculine ones that are deemed to reflect the Bible's patriarchal origins. A moderate example of this is the New Revised Standard Version (1989), which retains the masculine pronoun for God, but elsewhere uses paraphrases, for example "brothers" is rendered as "brothers and sisters" (cf. Rom 15:14). Liberal advocates regard such modifications as in keeping with the Bible's central message, while conservative critics reject them as attempts to impose contemporary standards on the unchanging Word of God.

Postcritical approaches

A third family, known as postcritical interpretation, reaffirms the Bible's character as the living Word of God but declines to uncritically accept or reject the validity of historical critical perspectives on the Bible. Instead, the postcritical perspective holds that Christians should cultivate the church's own indigenous ways of using and interpreting the Bible, while drawing selectively on a variety of modern and premodern insights to help them in this task.

The postcritical approach draws inspiration from the Swiss Reformed theologian Karl Barth (1886–1968). Trained by liberal theology and historical criticism to understand and accept the Bible's *humanity*, Barth nevertheless came to believe that these approaches shortchanged the Bible's *divinity*. Without rejecting the validity of historical criticism, Barth gave renewed prominence to the Reformers' belief that the Bible is the Word of God, the unique medium of God's living speech to the church. However, Barth did not understand this to mean that the Bible possesses some inherent quality that directly mirrors God's perfection, such as infalliblity, as the Protestant Scholastics and their conservative heirs had long assumed. Rather, for Barth, the Bible's deity consists in the free and gracious *use* that God makes of the Bible to reveal something that transcends its human authors, namely, God's Word made flesh, Jesus Christ.

Postcritical theologians such as Hans Frei (1922–88) have stimulated interest in new literary approaches to the Bible such as narrative interpretation. In his book *The Eclipse of Biblical Narrative*, Frei (1975) argued that the rise of historical criticism brought about a great loss of sensitivity to one central way the Bible speaks of God, namely, through its literary qualities, and above all, through its extended stories and realistic narratives. Precritical theologians such as Luther and Calvin read biblical narratives with unsurpassed literary sensitivity, in part because they took their historical veracity for granted. Once this veracity was called into question, however, critics and defenders of the Bible alike began to pay less attention to the stories themselves than to the historical events thought to lie behind the text. In the process, Frei held, theologians actually lost touch with the way the biblical narratives communicate knowledge of God. Frei's recommendation was that Christians relearn how to read the Bible's narratives *as narratives* without immediately pressing them into service as historical reports. The biblical narratives portray the truth about God's identity and character more after the fashion of an oil portrait than a photograph, distorting surface features to make accessible a deeper truth incommunicable by other means.

Another important postcritical scholar is Brevard Childs (1923-) who has proposed what he calls a canonical approach to biblical interpretation. Traditional historical critical methods assume that the earliest form of the biblical text is the most important. They therefore aim to dissolve the biblical text into its antecedent kernels, just as Graf and Wellhausen dissolved the Pentateuch into the strands known as J, E, P, and D. But, Childs (1992) objects, this whole project runs counter to the logic that gave rise to the Bible in the first place. Jews and Christians deliberately put older traditions into new contexts, thereby creating new literary wholes that are irreducible to their previous components. This process continued until it ultimately culminated in the formation of the biblical canon. The canon itself is a text in its own right in which all discernible units large and small take on new hues and connotations within the whole. It therefore deserves to be taken seriously as a framework of interpretation in its own right, especially for interpreters who regard the Bible as sacred Scripture, rather than as documents of ancient Near Eastern religion.

Proponents of postcritical biblical interpretation hold that it draws on the strengths of liberal and conservative approaches while avoiding their tendency to pit the humanity and divinity of the Bible against each other. But postcritical approaches are also vulnerable to criticism, for example, for being unclear about whether and to what degree that truth of the Bible is tied to the reliability of its historical statements.

The Future of Protestantism and the Bible

Protestantism was born as a reform movement within the universal church. Yet for five hundred years, Protestantism's relation to the Bible has helped to make it something more akin to the great uncontrolled laboratory of Christianity, where it seems every experiment is permitted its season, with predictably wide-ranging results. As the Protestant movement nears its sixth century, the future of Protestantism and the Bible seems likely to be marked by the following trends.

Protestants today adopt modern critical perspectives on the Bible as a supplement to ancient uses of the Bible rooted in liturgical and theological tradition (e.g., prayer, preaching, praise), not as a replacement for them. This trend is likely to continue as modern biblical criticism loses some of its former luster of intellectual superiority. Protestant scholars are more aware than they once were that the Bible can be interpreted rationally from a variety of perspectives. The Enlightenment goal of applying neutral criteria of judgment to the Bible has largely given way to the goal of becoming critically aware of the premises (theological, philosophical, methodological, and cultural) that different communities bring to the study of the Bible.

Contemporary Protestant communities use and interpret the Bible through the lens of cultural heritages other than those of Europe and North America. This trend will certainly continue as the Protestant movement grows exponentially in Africa and the Far East while struggling in the lands of its origins. For the foreseeable future, non-Western Protestants are likely to sift the heritage of Western biblical scholarship with increasingly critical eyes. Today many Protestants in Asia and Africa believe it is necessary to liberate the Bible from the legacy of Western colonialism, and find new ways to express Christian faith in terms indigenous to their own cultures. Tomorrow, these new experiments in biblical faith may help to revitalize Protestant churches in Europe and North America.

Finally, Protestants today are perhaps more aware than in the past of the relative strengths of Catholic and Orthodox approaches to the Bible, which emphasize tradition and continuity above constant experimentation. Even when Protestant experiments bear good fruit, the communities that enjoy them are often small and prone to fracture. If Protestants are to preserve what is worth preserving in the Protestant relation to the Bible, therefore, they may do well to learn more from their Catholic and Orthodox brothers and sisters than they have in the past.

References

Calvin, John (1958). Preface to Olivétan's New Testament (1535/43). In Joseph Haroutunian (ed.), *Calvin's Commentaries*, Library of Christian Classics, vol. 23. Philadelphia: Westminster Press.

Childs, B. S. (1992). *Biblical Theology of the Old and New Testaments*. Minneapolis: Fortress Press.

Frei, Hans (1975). *The Eclipse of Biblical Narrative: A Study of Eighteenth and Nineteenth Century Hermeneutics*. New Haven, CT: Yale University Press.

Hodge, Charles (1983). The Inspiration of Holy Scripture, its Nature and Proof. In Mark. A. Noll (ed.), *The Princeton Theology, 1812–1921*. Phillipsburg, NJ: Presbyterian and Reformed Publishing Co.

Luther, Martin (1960). Preface to the Old Testament. In E. Theodore Bachmann (ed.), *Luther's Works*, vol. 35. Philadelphia: Fortress Press.

Preus, Robert (1970). *The Theology of Post-Reformation Lutheranism*. St. Louis: Concordia Publishing House.

Schweizer, Albert ([1906] 1998). *The Quest for the Historical Jesus*. Baltimore: Johns Hopkins University Press.

Further Reading

Abraham, W. J. (1998). *Canon and Criterion in Christian Theology*. Oxford: Clarendon Press.

Felder, C. H. (ed.) (1991). *Stony the Road We Trod: African American Biblical Interpretation.* Minneapolis: Fortress Press.

Gerrish, Brian A. (1982). *The Old Protestantism and the New: Essays on the Reformation Heritage.* Chicago: University of Chicago Press.

Lindsell, Harold (1976). *The Battle for the Bible.* Grand Rapids, MI: Zondervan.

Pelikan, Jaroslav (1959). *Luther the Expositor.* St. Louis: Concordia Publishing House.

Preus, James (1969). *From Shadow to Promise: Old Testament Interpretation from Augustine to the Young Luther.* Cambridge, MA: Harvard University Press.

Reventlow, H. G. (1985). *The Authority of the Bible and the Rise of the Modern World*, trans J. Bowden. Philadelphia: Fortress Press.

Rogers, Jack and McKim, Donald (eds.) (1979). *The Authority and Interpretation of the Bible.* San Francisco: Harper and Row.

Schüssler Fiorenza, Elizabeth (1990). *Bread Not Stone: The Challenge of Feminist Biblical Interpretation.* Edinburgh: T & T Clark.

Soulen, Richard N. and Soulen, R. Kendall (2001). *Handbook of Biblical Criticism*, 3rd edn. Louisville, KY: Westminster/John Knox Press.

Steinmetz, David (ed.) (1990). *The Bible in the Sixteenth Century.* Durham, NC: Duke University.

Wood, Charles M. 1981. *The Formation of Christian Understanding: An Essay in Theological Hermeneutics.* Philadelphia: Westminster Press.

Yeo, Khiok-khng (1998). *What has Jerusalem to do with Beijing? Biblical Interpretation from a Chinese Perspective.* Harrisburg, PA: Trinity Press International.

CHAPTER 26
Protestantism and the Arts

Trevor Hart

> Protestantism – the adroit castrator
> Of art; the bitter negation
> Of song and dance and the heart's innocent joy –
> You have botched our flesh and left us only the soul's
> Terrible impotence in a warm world.
> *(Thomas, 1995)*

Bitter Negation

The subject of this chapter is altogether more complex and ambiguous than is sometimes supposed, and the attempt to address it helpfully in a brief compass behoves us to draw some careful distinctions early on. R. S. Thomas's poetic complaint (see above) cannot be denied its legitimacy, and it finds many echoes and resonances in the literature. That the Reformation had immediate, substantial and negative implications for Christian attitudes to the arts is clear and is reflected, for example, in the barbed observation of the humanist Erasmus as early as 1526 (explaining the departure of Hans Holbein the Younger from Basel for the Netherlands) that 'here the arts are freezing' (Christensen, 1996: 74; see also Michalski, 1993: 192). The popular perception of Protestantism as characterized at best by frigid Philistinism, lacking in sensibility or serious interest in beauty, and at worst by a determination to clamp down upon, if not stamp out, artistic endeavour and enjoyment wherever possible, is not without foundation. One only has to dwell (as many treatments of our theme do) on the outbursts of iconoclastic frenzy which accompanied the Reformation's spread across Europe (see, e.g. Christensen, 1979, esp. chs 3 and 5; Duffy, 1992: 390ff.; Freedberg, 1988; Gutmann, 1977: 75–63; Michalski, 1993, esp. ch. 3). And yet, of course, such caricature misses far more than it apprehends.

The particular polemical context of the Reformation gave a prominence and urgency to specific aesthetic questions. This led to a rash of acts of over-zealous hooliganism which were supported and encouraged by some Reformers just as surely as they were eschewed and condemned by others. For, while the overall disposition of the Reformation towards art may be argued to have had a nega- tive impact upon art's immediate well-being,[1] the attitudes of the Reformation's major theologians were far from uniform, let alone consistently negative. Nor, of course, was the Reformation itself concerned with 'the arts' in any broad- brush manner. Indeed, we should note early in this chapter that our use of this category 'the arts' reflects a peculiarly modern way of thinking, and despite our given title we should avoid the distorting anachronism involved in reading a modern conception of 'the arts' back into the period prior to the eighteenth century (Wolterstorff, 1997: 6ff.). The Reformers' concerns were directed towards what they saw as the dangerous (i.e. idolatrous) misuse of particular artistic objects and practices in that late-medieval Christianity which was their wider target. In practice this meant the visual and plastic arts (chiefly painting and sculpture) as deployed in liturgical and other religious contexts (Hardy, 1999). As we shall see, while some Protestants allowed this critical reaction to taint their disposition toward human artistry more broadly, others distinguished clearly between sacred and secular uses of and subjects for art, and saw the latter as worthy human responses to God's gift of an orderly and beautiful creation. So art, creative imagination as such, was not the issue at the Reformation, but the way certain themes had been and were being deployed in visual art in the religious culture of Catholicism.

The Reformation may certainly be said to have rediscovered and reinstated an ancient theological concern (reaching back through the centuries to the Hebraic cast of mind of the Old Testament prophets) with the limits and legitimacy of human attempts to represent God's mysterious reality in material form.[2] Yet, as we shall see, it was the specific theological, socio-economic and cultural cir- cumstances of the day that gave rise to the particularly vigorous (and at times pathologically vicious) responses which ensued. We shall not understand its significance or the fervour that drove it unless and until we appreciate that those who wielded the sharpened instruments believed they were performing life-saving surgery on a cancer, not capricious castration.

This leads us to the obvious but important observation that what Reforma- tion attitudes and practices with respect to the visual arts amounted to at that particular moment of history is not the whole story of Protestantism's rela- tionship with the arts as such, nor the index of its capacities. It may be that deep and persisting patterns of an unnecessary and unhelpful sort were etched on the very soul of Protestantism by the vigour with which these battles were originally fought, resulting in a more dispersed suspicion of the creative arts (what John McIntyre, 1987: 7 dubs Protestant 'iconophobia'), especially in any context which juxtaposes them directly with Christian faith. So, for example, in seventeenth-century England we find John Bunyan prefacing his classic The Pilgrim's Progress with an apology aimed at Puritan readers for whom divinely revealed truth should never be sullied by association with the 'dark figures' and allegories thrown up by human imagining (see Bunyan, 1954: 1–7). Others in other ages have doubtless felt a similar need to justify their endeavour to bring faith and artistry together in one way or another. But the history of Protestantism nonetheless manifests a wide variety of different attitudes to, and accommodations of, art in relation to life, faith and theology. In identifying some of these, a question which may helpfully be kept in view is how far Protestantism, with its distinctive theological emphases, possesses resources for a positive evaluation of human artistry, and how far it may be supposed to have benefited (or to possess resources capable of benefiting) the arts.

Such a wider perspective must not, though, lose sight of the critical concerns of the Reformers. For, however precisely focused and overstated these may sometimes have been, and however morally problematic the actions to which they sometimes led may appear, they arose from insights that are of abiding and wider aesthetic and theological significance. Indeed, in an age where, for many, aesthetic experience has effectively substituted itself for religious faith as a perceived window onto 'spiritual' realities (see Pattison, 1999, esp. ch. 1), we may find that Reformation perspectives possess a curious freshness, reminding us of things which some theological approaches to art (not least some in the Protestant tradition) appear to have forgotten or broken faith with. In what follows, while concentrating chiefly on the historical context out of which distinctively Protestant attitudes to human artistry were born, I shall suggest that Protestantism is indeed capable of developing a positive theological account of and engagement with the arts which, precisely in its affirmation of them, constrains and criticizes as it locates human creativity in relation to God's own. In John de Gruchy's words, it proves to be 'iconic and aniconic at the same time', the challenge being to maintain that tension faithfully and creatively (de Gruchy, 2001: 27).

'Goodly Sights': On the Eve of Iconoclasm

Concern about the appropriate use of images in 'the nonverbal mediation of religious belief' (Hardy, 1999: 6) did not suddenly emerge fully fledged in the early sixteenth century. Its history is as ancient as Christianity itself, and those Reformers who chose to do so were able to draw upon a long tradition of theological reflection on the subject. The substantive theological issue, as we have already noted, was that of the capacity of creaturely (and, more specifically, material) reality to represent, and thereby mediate, the reality of God; or, perhaps, the capacity of God to be known through such things. For Christians this issue was, and is heightened by, the core claim that God, while wholly other than the created world, has actually appropriated creaturely form, chiefly in the incarnation, but also through the physicality of baptism and the Eucharist, and more broadly in engaging directly with the life and history of his creatures. The modes of presence and activity posited are different in each case; but each involves the relationship between God and the creature being mediated by physical things.

None of this was lost on exponents of icons in the Byzantine debate which rumbled on from the seventh to the ninth centuries.[3] So, for example, John of Damascus (c.665–749) argued directly from the incarnation that veneration of images of Jesus could not be judged idolatrous, since God himself had rendered himself in human form. It could not be breaking the second commandment to honour a picture of God's own self-imaging in the flesh. Opponents of icons, though, held that this defence was specious, and simply proved the idolatrous nature of such worship. What was pictured in such images was precisely the *humanitas*, the 'flesh' of Christ, and not his deity (which by definition could never be pictured). So those who venerated them were not worshipping God, but only a creaturely physical reality behind which the invisible and mysterious reality of God remained hidden. Both parties were agreed that the image as such was not to be confused with God. Where they differed was on its capacity to refer beyond itself to God, and to direct human worship appropriately. Those who advocated the use of images thus developed a sophisticated theology of iconic transparency, insisting that in worship the mind's eye was naturally directed *through* the visual symbol to terminate on the mysterious reality beyond it. To collapse these two levels of reference, or to separate them from one another, so that attention was directed onto the image *as such* was to fall into a crass literalism, untrue to their proper understanding and use.

Similar arguments can be found among Western writers of the later medieval period concerning religious art. Images, they insist, without being God are nonetheless capable of figuring or signifying God in such a way as to inform the mind and move the affections in worship. William Durandus (in his *Rationale Divinorum Officiorum* of 1286) cites approvingly some verses inscribed on an altar frontal in Bergen, reminding worshippers of the fundamental distinction between that which they see with their eyes *corporaliter*, and that which their hearts and minds are meant to discern *spiritualiter* (Camille, 1989: 203). It is the transcendent referent which is the proper object of worship, and not the physical image itself. The same careful insistence is found in Thomas Aquinas (c.1224/5–74) who, typically, cites Aristotle in support of his view:

> As the Philosopher says (*De Memor. et Remin.* i) there is a twofold movement of the mind towards an image: one indeed towards the image itself as a certain thing; another, towards the image in so far as it is the image of something else. . . . Thus therefore we must say that no reverence is shown to Christ's image, as a thing – for instance, carved or painted wood. . . . It follows therefore that reverence should be shown to it, in so far only as it is an image. (*Summa Theologica* 3, Q. 25, Art. 3, cited in Camille, 1989: 207)

Given this circumspect understanding, Bonaventure (1217–74) confidently identifies three vital functions of the religious image: to educate the illiterate masses concerning core doctrinal and narrative tenets of the faith (he refers to images as 'more open Scriptures'), to arouse due devotion and inculcate a worshipful disposition since 'our emotion is aroused more by what is seen than by what is heard', and to imprint certain vital truths on our memory (*Liber III Sententiarum*, IX, a. 1, q. 11, cited in Jones, 1977: 84). In each of these regards visible images were observed to be more efficient than the written or spoken word, and a higher value came to be placed upon them.[4]

This practical exaltation of image over word in medieval piety reminds us, though, that iconoclasm can never escape the image per se, since the word functions by its capacity to evoke or generate mental images of one sort or another, and nowhere is this more apparent than in the Christian Scriptures. To speak and think of God as Lord, or father, or shepherd, or rock is just as surely to trade in images as to paint or sculpt him as such. But Bonaventura's observation about the superior efficacy of the physical image for certain devotional purposes draws attention helpfully to an important distinction between physical and mental images which may hold particular significance in liturgical and devotional contexts. The very solidity and sensuousness of the painting or sculpture impresses itself upon us with a degree of inflexibility and permanence, drawing our attention to the image itself and as such.

As Immanuel Kant was to observe much later, judgments about beauty are always judgments about particular manifestations of it, and questions such as 'what is it meant to be?' are irrelevant to the case.[5] An object may well be 'an image of X', but in so far as we judge it to be beautiful, we are looking at it with all such considerations bracketed out, and allowing it to impress itself upon us in all its sheer particularity. Beauty, we might say, is by nature opaque. In the case of the mental image, though, the opposite appears to be the case. As philosophers in the twentieth-century phenomenological tradition observed, if we strip away the reference 'is an image of' then nothing whatever remains to look at, and we realize that a mental image has no existence in and of itself; it is inherently transparent, has its existence precisely as a vehicle for directing us to something else; is, in fact, 'a way of thinking about' something else.[6] It is, we might say, anhypostatic, having its proper meaning and force only in its vital relation to something else. This leads us to ask whether the mental image (evoked or painted in our mind's eye through the word) may be more naturally suited to the careful distinction between image and prototype which the religious context demands? Or, put negatively, is it likely that the physical image with all its sensuous affect will be more prone to collapsing these two levels with idolatrous outcomes? The Reformation, we should observe, was more a response to the grass roots popular religion of the late medieval period than to the highest thoughts of its theologians. The masses had not read Aquinas and, as Michael Camille (1989: 207) notes, the need for constant reiteration of a sophisticated 'visual code' during the period indicates at least the ever-present danger of popular misunderstanding.

In practice, as Camille's study shows, this danger was realized in all manner of ways. From the late thirteenth century onwards there can be traced an erosion of any popular awareness that images were to be looked *through* rather than looked *at*. Instead, there was to be found an increasing attention and devotion to the image itself and as such, and the investment of it with powers and status unbefitting its reality as, in itself, a mere aesthetic object. A frankly superstitious preoccupation with the tangible paraphernalia of religion captured the public imagination and, in due course, spawned an entire economy as a veritable 'image explosion' (Camille, 1989: 219) ensued. As William Jones notes, 'Popular piety filled the churches of Europe with a diversity of sacred art – rood screens, wall-paintings, stained-glass windows, crucifixes, statuaries, reliquaries and monstrances' (Jones, 1977: 83). To patronize the production of such devotional objects (whether for use in churches or domestically) came to be viewed as, in itself, an act of pious 'good works,' and Europe's artistic community rapidly adapted itself to this growing market (Jones, 1977: 86–7; Camille, 1989: 214).

Spiritual, economic and wider political concerns became mixed up in this development, and thus iconoclasm, when it arrived, was laying an axe to the root of an entire social status quo in which the wider populace was heavily invested. Its chief focus remained, though, a theological and spiritual one. Statues and paintings (not just of Christ, but depicting God the father and – most frequently – the Virgin and other saints) had become the focus of individual middle-class cultic guilds established to maintain them, and were regularly invested with miraculous powers and associated with profound (and often bizarre) visionary experiences (Camille, 1989: 223–4). Such objects – increasingly realistic rather than abstract in their depiction (Camille, 1989: 213–14; Hardy, 1999: 7) – were used in liturgical drama and festival processions and, as one study observes, readily acquired 'an aura of peculiar sanctity as divine personalities or presences' (Forsyth, 1972: 49, cited in Camille, 1989: 223). This popular fascination with cultic physicality was further stimulated and seemingly underwritten, as Camille notes, by the religious establishment when, in 1215, the Fourth Lateran Council promulgated the eucharistic doctrine of transubstantiation (in which the creaturely realities of bread and wine were held to 'become' – rather than simply 'figuring' or referring the worshipper through themselves to – the body and blood of Christ), a development further reinforced by the instigation of the Feast of Corpus Christi in 1264 (Camille, 1989: 215). Nobody was formally suggesting that religious images were to be afforded analogous treatment, but popular imagination had been decisively encouraged to identify rather than to disentangle signifier and signified. If the result did not amount to 'idolatry', then it was hard to see what ever would.

'Unseemly Representations': Reformation Responses

This centrality of the cult of the image to the web of late medieval religion helps us to understand the otherwise seemingly odd attention granted to aesthetic concerns at the Reformation. One recent study has suggested that 'The Reformation may even be regarded as a contest over the meaning and control of images, their power to save and to damn, and the legitimate authority or tyranny they represented' (de Gruchy, 2001: 38). Like modern studies in the sociology of knowledge, the Reformers in their own way recognized the powerful hold which image-based media may have upon the human spirit, and their capacity to shape and control religious, political and moral identity for good or ill (Freedberg, 1989). However, while the major Reformers were agreed in their opposition to the idolatry which they perceived in the Roman church, they differed as regards the practical implications of suppressing or correcting it.

Among the earliest and most radical responses was that of Andreas Bodenstein von Karlstadt (1486–1541) (see Zorzin, 2002). When Martin Luther fled for the relative safety of the Wartburg, in the wake of his condemnation by the Diet of Worms in 1521, Karlstadt implemented a rigorous reform of worship at Wittenberg, including the abandonment of clerical vestments and the removal from churches and destruction of all religious images. In writings such as his 1522 treatise, 'On the Removal of Images', Karlstadt advocated the use of Mosaic law in the civic sphere, deprecated the role of scholarly learning in interpreting Scripture (and, indeed, the value of the arts and humanities for Christians), and urged all Christians to follow the immediate dictates of the Holy Spirit (see Dillenberger, 1990: 90; Sider, 1978). In response to such urgings by Karlstadt and others, many clearly judged themselves led by the Spirit to implement without further delay the apparently clear and relevant injunction of the second commandment (Exodus 20: 4–5a), regardless of official ecclesiastical or civil jurisdiction, and a spate of disorderly and illegal ransackings of churches ensued. Civic authorities were placed under huge pressure, and some were forced effectively to authorize in retrospect actions of violent iconoclasm for fear of the unrest and destruction getting completely out of hand. Others managed to effect a gradual and staged process while they weighed the possible political and economic consequences of their actions (Christensen, 1979: 107–48). There can be little doubt that it was widespread public support that led to the spread, both unofficial and official, of rigorous iconoclasm where it occurred. As so often, though, democracy proved to be an unreliable index of truth, and the groundswell was theologically unsophisticated and often at the mercy of educated extremism.

More moderate than Karlstadt, but nonetheless unrelenting in his insistence that visual and plastic art be banished from liturgical and devotional contexts, was Ulrich Zwingli (1484–1531) whose influence among people and city magistrates alike in Zurich resulted in 1524 in 'an orderly but thorough destruction of virtually all material accessories to worship' (Christensen, 1979: 107). Zwingli had no time for illegal acts of iconoclasm (see, e.g. Potter, 1976: 130–1). Nor (unlike some in the Radical Reformation) was he an opponent of the arts as such. Trained as a humanist, he retained respect for the cultural products of antiquity, and valued the highest achievements of the human spirit in any sphere (see Klauber, 2000) so long as they did not engender attitudes or practices incompatible with a Christian piety and hope properly focused on God alone through faith (Potter, 1976: 114–15). False bearings here were, he believed, by definition idolatrous and the essence of Godlessness.[7] Even artistry with a religious theme was tolerable for Zwingli, so long as it did not intrude on devotional contexts where it might give rise to inappropriate feelings of reverence.[8]

Thus, what Bonaventure had celebrated as the image's positive gain (its capacity to arouse and direct the emotions in worship) Zwingli eschewed as its chief weakness since, he held, fallen human beings are naturally prone to false worship and, despite the careful distinctions of scholastic theologians, images in church or other devotional situations inevitably become the occasion of idolatry and rob God of the worship due to him alone. Images of Jesus are especially inappropriate and dangerous (though purely 'historical' representations of him in depictions of gospel scenes are acceptable outside churches and for non-devotional use), dealing only at the level of the sensuous and unable to communicate the true Christ to us (Stephens, 1986: 174) – a clear echo of the ancient iconoclasts' insistence that images could not show forth the deity but only the 'flesh' of the Saviour. For Zwingli, too, the religious image was spiritually opaque, rendered such by human sinfulness rather than its own incapacities or anything in the nature and capacities of God. His insistence that religious subjects in art must be purely 'historical', though, indicates resistance to any pictorial depiction of God even for non-devotional ends. The second commandment, therefore, Zwingli held to be binding on Christians as a prescription against the deployment of the visual arts inside places of worship, a divine strategy for the avoidance of an otherwise inevitable idolatry.

Martin Luther's (1483–1546) attitude to religious images was more ambiguous.[9] For Luther the Reformation was always first and foremost about another theological issue altogether; namely, the doctrine of justification by grace through faith rather than works. Compared to this, he considered the matter of paintings and sculpture in church *adiaphora* – a matter of relative unimportance. Indeed, he insisted, no amount of smashing and burning could get rid of superstitious idolatry, since this was lodged deep in the sinful human heart and was likely to be established even more firmly there by any external attempt to dislodge it; whereas, once the heart was liberated by faith from the snares of works-righteousness, the ritual abuse of wood and stone in an attempt to court favour with God would be bound to cease, having no further motive force.[10] Luther's stated opposition to the religious image, therefore, centred primarily on its appropriation within and bolstering of a false understanding of how to stand justified before God. He also objected strongly to the huge amounts of money consequently invested in producing and venerating such images, money which could and should have been spent in alleviating poverty and human distress.[11]

Luther certainly never resorted to the somewhat crude 'because the Bible says so' warrant for iconoclasm (the more violent manifestations of which he considered to be a triumph for the devil rather than Christ).[12] Indeed, he interpreted the second commandment explicitly as a gloss on the first, a proscription of the making and use of plastic 'gods' as such, and not a prohibition on representative artistry more widely, even for use in church.[13] More broadly, Luther resisted the idea that Judaic ceremonial law is binding on Christians, it being part of what has been abrogated by the New Covenant. Possession of images, therefore, he considered to be a matter of Christian freedom, though the superstitious veneration of them was clearly sinful and to be abandoned. Luther's thought on the matter evolved, though, from critical and cautious tolerance to recognition of the value of the image as a device for shaping religious identity in positive, rather than negative, ways. Human beings, he insisted, cannot help forming images of the objects of their attention and reflection. The religious image is merely an extension of the mental image. If, therefore, 'it is not a sin but good to have the image of Christ in my heart, why,' Luther inquires, 'should it be a sin to have it in my eyes?'[14] We have suggested above one reason why to do so might be more likely to furnish the occasion for sin, but Luther follows Bonaventura in advocating the benefits of religious art. For Luther, though, these benefits lie solely in pedagogy, 'for the sake of remembrance and better understanding' among the faithful.[15] Prioritizing of the Word was not, therefore, exclusive of the image since the 'Word' could, ironically, be faithfully painted and etched just as surely as it had been made flesh. As we shall see, this concession was to provide a new impulse for established art forms, and the development of entire new forms and media.

Iconoclasm had been adopted and implemented as official policy in Geneva in 1535 (Michalski, 1993: 59). When John Calvin (1504–64) arrived in the city a year later, therefore, he had no need to engage in the sort of urgent polemics designed to shape immediate praxis, and his eventual published reflections on the question of religious art betray the advantages of careful systematic reflection over impulse and rhetorical overstatement. Calvin is often listed together with Karlstadt, Zwingli and others as, at heart, an iconophobe (Michalski, 1993, ch. 2), and the theological tradition associated with him has frequently been named as the chief perpetrator of art's adroit castration.[16] The 1559 edition of the *Institutes of the Christian Religion* reveals, though, a more complex and subtle understanding than we might expect to find. Calvin, unlike Luther, is certainly emphatic in his rejection of images in liturgical and devotional contexts. His criticism is directed chiefly towards visual representations of God as such (rather than portrayals of Christ or the saints) and reflects the tenor of his wider doctrine of God. While he appeals to the abiding force of the Mosaic law, therefore, the foundation for Calvin's rejection of such art is his insistence that God so transcends the creaturely order that any attempt at visual depiction amounts to a denigration of his glory and majesty (see *Inst.* I.xi). 'Unseemly representations' are, that is to say, not only *inadequate* to bear the weight of transcendence but contradict God's very being and profane his name. Since the chief end of human beings is to know God truly and to offer him due worship (*Inst.* I.iii.3) it follows that all figurations of deity must be prohibited absolutely, in church and elsewhere.

Calvin also banishes all images of other sorts from the sanctuary, rejecting their alleged pedagogical value on the grounds that the human soul inclines naturally to idolatry wherever the opportunity for it arises (*Inst.* I.xi.9), that many of the likenesses (of virgins, martyrs etc.) to be found in medieval churches were actually morally dubious ('examples of the most abandoned lust and obscenity', *Inst.* I.xi.7), and that there would be far fewer 'unlearned' Christians in the first place if the Church took seriously its responsibility to preach the Gospel and teach basic doctrine (ibid). Interestingly, this unstinting iconoclasm in the sacral sphere was not carried through in its domestic counterpart where – recognizing that the context in which an image is viewed has everything to do with its meaning – Calvin was content for believers to keep visual depictions of biblical narratives (Michalski, 1993: 70).

This distinction between sacral and secular spheres of life forms an important part of the Renaissance background to Calvin's thinking, and emerges in his attitude towards the arts in particular (Ramsay, 1938: 12–17). Despite the admittedly damning comments that he makes about the presumption and dangers of the visual arts in church, it is misleading to suggest that Calvin had 'a negative attitude towards human creativity and imagination' more widely.[17] While he inevitably insists that true creativity belongs to God alone, Calvin celebrates the second-order powers of imagination and invention ('the mother of so many marvellous devices') with which God has invested the human soul (see *Inst.* I.v.5, I.xv.6) and identifies artistic vision and skill as among those things which the Holy Spirit 'distributes to whomever he wills for the common good of mankind' (*Inst.* II.ii.16). These gifts, he notes, are distributed 'indiscriminately upon pious and impious' (*Inst.* II.ii.14), being part of that common grace which is nonetheless to be acknowledged and admired by believers (together, for example, with the great learning of philosophers and scientists) lest, 'by holding the gifts of the Spirit in slight esteem, we contemn and reproach the Spirit himself' (*Inst.* II.ii.15).

Indiscriminate rejection or belittling of the arts, therefore, is an affront to God just as surely as is their misuse in the sacral sphere. God, Calvin insists elsewhere – in a passage which shows him to be anything but aesthetically frigid – has provided for his creatures things which 'seem to serve delight rather than necessity' (*Inst.* III.x.1), and we should enjoy them as he intended us to. A purely utilitarian philosophy denigrates God's beneficence, 'robs a man of all his senses and degrades him into a block' (*Inst.* III.x.3). Of course, Calvin steers carefully away from any apparent condoning of unbridled sensory excess. The key principle is that things should be enjoyed in accordance with their divinely intended end. Hence, painting and sculpture are to be enjoyed as gifts of God, 'conferred upon us for his glory and our good'. In the hands of fallen creatures they can and have been abused (not least in the sacral context), but there is 'a pure and legitimate use' of them to be enjoyed (*Inst.* I.xi.12). The artist, Calvin suggests, should depict only that 'which the eyes are capable in principle of seeing', whether 'histories and events' or 'images and forms of bodies' (ibid.). We may take 'capable of' as meaning in principle rather than in fact, and read this as permissive of a degree of imaginative invention and licence. But it is clear that Calvin, following upon his absolute resistance to the visual figuration of God, is uncomfortable with figurative depiction more broadly. It is in this particular sense that he emits negative signals about the imaginative (which functions on the basis of tracing and constructing analogies and metaphors) and fails to appreciate the more than mimetic capacities of art in engaging with the wonders of God's creation. As John de Gruchy (2001: 41) has noted, it is a pity that Calvin did not allow his commitment to Chalcedonian Christology to inform him more directly at this point. The relationship between the two 'natures' of the Son of God, while admitting of no confusion whatever, must yet be capable of figuration if the humanity is truly to inform our understanding of God, as Calvin insists it does (e.g. *Inst.* II.xiv.3). Indeed, the logical structure of the incarnation as Chalcedon presents it comes tantalizingly close to that of metaphorical predication, in which both unity and distinction must be maintained without loss, which always contain(s) the whisper, "it is *and it is not*" (McFague, 1982: 13), but in which one reality accommodates itself in giving another, strikingly different, reality to be known.[18] The accommodation involved in incarnation, in other words, might have afforded Calvin both a model for a more adequate account of poetic vision, and, perhaps, a basis for reckoning with the possibility that God might lay hold of human artistry and render it capable of illuminating his way of working in the world and its history.

Refocusing the Eyes of Faith?

Given the variety and complexity of Reformation responses to 'aesthetic' questions, we should expect the progeny to be mixed, and history does not disappoint the expectation. As Paul Tillich (himself a Protestant theologian for whom positive engagement with the arts was vital to the substance of theological reflection and construction) observes, the broad pattern reflects directly the Reformation preoccupation with the Word, and reveals a relative 'lack of the arts of the eye' in Protestant life (Tillich, 1964: 214). Those art forms where the ear is privileged – music and literature (the latter effectively baptized into this category by virtue of its oral roots and the practice of reading Scripture aloud) – have increased while other forms (including drama whose significant oral aspect is eclipsed by its visual and concrete nature) have decreased. This, Tillich holds, is theologically unfortunate since 'the very nature of the Spirit stands against the exclusion of the eye from the experience of its presence' (ibid). We have seen that there are Christological reasons for supporting this claim, though the concerns about idolatry which haunted the Reformers should not be lightly pushed aside in a rush to rediscover the role of 'the eyes of faith'.

The roots of the Reformation in the Renaissance protected the arts from any wholesale destruction or neglect, and secured instead a reorientation of sensibility and a redistribution of energy within Protestant artistry.

As a religion of the Word it would be surprising if Protestantism had not made some positive contribution to the literary arts. A theological emphasis placed on the appropriation of the message of Scripture by the individual believer led to the production and sale of large numbers of small-format Bibles, prayer books and collections of sermons in vernacular translations and, while it is difficult to correlate the evidence precisely (not everyone who purchased such books could necessarily read them!), a recent study concludes that there can be little doubt that the Reformation was at least one strong impulse among a number leading to a demonstrable increase in literacy during the sixteenth century in Europe (Maag, 2000: 543). It has been noted that John Calvin, himself a product of a solid humanist education, made a substantial contribution to the adaptation of the French vernacular for the purposes of philosophical and theological discourse (in the past these 'high' matters had been the preserve of Latin) at a time when its use by artists such as Rabelais was in its vulnerable infancy (Ramsay, 1938: 15). In broad terms, then, Protestantism may be said to have encouraged both the development and popular appreciation of literature. More specifically, it has been argued that this 'bookish' impulse, together with a deepened appreciation of individual perspective and the everyday concerns of the 'ordinary' believer, fed directly into the emergence of the novel as a literary form in the eighteenth century (see e.g. Watt, 1987: 74–85).

The most obvious 'art of the ear' is music, and although some Protestant traditions have retained the caution shown by certain Reformers about music's capacity to shape human feeling and thereby detract from the intellectual and spiritual purity of the Word in worship (see Wilson-Dickson, 1992: 64ff), most have enthusiastically sung their faith as well as reading and speaking about it. For Martin Luther, himself a musician of considerable gifts, music was second only to theology in its importance for faith; this was due both to its role as a natural vehicle for the promulgation of the Word, and its capacity, in unison with the poetic articulation of faith, to dispose the heart and the spirit appropriately toward God (see Stewart, 1914: 57). As well as composing hymns, Luther was an enthusiastic plagiarizer of popular melodies, borrowing folk tunes, children's songs and the like, and replacing profane with religious lyrics. This policy of 'redeeming' melody from popular culture (continued by others since, including the renowned eighteenth-century hymn writers Isaac Watts and John and Charles Wesley) (see Westermeyer, 1998: 203ff) has succeeded in enabling congregations to participate fully in the musical elements of worship. While it may not itself constitute high culture, it has undoubtedly been effective in inculcating a basic musical awareness and appreciation among the gathered faithful. In any case, we ought not to underestimate the musical worth of much popular hymnody over the centuries, and from Luther's German Mass onwards vulgar forms have generally been juxtaposed with more aesthetically refined elements in worship. We should not forget that, before the advent of recording technology, church was one of relatively few places where an opportunity regularly to hear and participate in music was available to most people. In the development of the Western musical tradition, therefore, Protestantism may be supposed to have played at least two distinct roles: first, in drawing otherwise uncultured people into a positive relationship with music through congregational singing, and second as patron to musicians and composers who, both alongside and through their regular liturgical duties, were able to pursue their artistry to the full. An obvious (if somewhat exceptional) example is the Lutheran J. S. Bach (1685–1750) who composed more than three hundred cantatas for liturgical use (many of which may only have been intended for use once) but also took the use of the keyboard as a solo instrument to hitherto unknown heights (see Stewart, 1914: ch.VI) and thereby placed his stamp decisively upon musical history.

Although Tillich is correct to suggest that 'the arts of the eye' have been relatively disadvantaged in Protestant spheres of influence, it is important not to overstate what is indeed a matter of relativity. Here, too, the story is a mixed one. In the immediate wake of the Reformation many painters, sculptors and woodcarvers certainly found themselves effectively robbed of a market, and to the economic hardship which this produced must be added the forced interruption of living traditions which should have handed on both skills and a body of interpretation to the next generation (Christensen, 1979: 164–80). Where one branch of artistic opportunity was pruned, though, others quickly sprouted and grew. Highly decorated shrines and crucifixes were no longer wanted, but appropriately decorated pulpits and altar surrounds were. The burgeoning technology of the woodcut, initially developed within the monastery but largely secularized during the Renaissance, was now drawn back into the church's sphere of influence for both pedagogical and propagandist purposes. Illustrated Bibles and prayer books abounded, and single-sheet broadsheets attacking the Catholic Church hierarchy were mass produced and circulated (see Pettegree, 2000: 468; Christensen, 1979: 170). Recognition of the political power of the image (especially the mass-produced image) also led to some of the Reformers permitting their portraits to be painted or sketched. Lucas Cranach the Elder's (b.1472) famous woodcut depictions of Martin Luther were not born of vanity or adulation, but from a deliberate political desire to depict the reformer 'as man of God, and, later, as statesman of the church, in counterbalance to the hostile propaganda of his adversaries' (Pettegree, 2000: 472).

Nonetheless, a century or so later in the solidly Reformed Netherlands, as Simon Schama notes, even 'Impeccable Calvinists were not averse to sitting for their portraits' (Schama, 1999: 211) and for considerations of a rather different sort! Portraiture, indeed, remained one obvious source of patronage for the painter, and as a subject of artistic concern undoubtedly received a boost from the secularizing impulse of the Reformation, its theological emphasis on the importance of the individual, and its affirmation of humanity as created in (albeit fallen from) the image and likeness of God, while never to be confused with its Creator. So, too, the early development of rich traditions of landscape and 'still life' painting may be traced in significant part to what from one perspective must be viewed as the liberation of the medium from subservience to the church and its concerns, and the growing interest (for example in Calvinism) in 'what the eye can see', namely, the created order in all its complex glory (Kuyper, 2000: 147, 167; Ramsay, 1938: 85ff.). In numerous ways, therefore, in the visual as well as other arts, we see that what the culture of Protestantism has led to is not a dark and forbidding sky against which the brilliant course of occasional artistic meteors may be traced, but a reorienting and refocusing of the artistic 'gaze', including a secularizing and humanizing impulse (Macmillan, 1990: 8). And this is not in spite of its theology, but a direct reflection of its convictions about how God is properly to be understood as related to the world he has made.

While painting discovered many new secular subjects for its gaze, though, religious ones remained important. Works by Dürer (1471–1528), Cranach the Elder and Holbein the Younger (b.1498) all reveal a vibrant Protestant (mostly Lutheran) religious imagery in the early sixteenth century, though it is one in which a profound shift of theological and practical emphasis may be discerned, away from the needs of religious devotion, and towards pedagogy.[19] Theological themes (e.g., the Lutheran polarity of law and gospel) and realistic scenes from scriptural narrative dominated this emergent tradition of religious art in a bid to exploit the benefits of the visual, 'showing' the Word, without collapsing back into the perceived failings of medieval visual piety (see Christensen, 1996: 76–7).

A century later, in the Dutch Republic ultra-Protestantism held politics and culture firmly in its sway. The young Rembrandt van Rijn (1606/7–69) was born and raised in Leiden, also the birthplace of the growing religious conflict between the 'Remonstrants' and 'Counter-Remonstrants' which would eventually engulf the whole Republic with its aftershocks. Its 'resolution' at the Synod of Dort in 1619, when Rembrandt was just 12 or 13 years old, imposed a strict Calvinist government upon his homeland, and one which represented the more iconoclast end of the spectrum of Protestant sympathies. Even in this religiously highly sensitized city – a 'temple of the Word' as Schama (1999: 209) dubs it – inventories of the personal effects of the deceased reveal the existence of a healthy market not just for images of secular subjects, but also for paintings of Christian 'religious history', narrative scenes from both testaments of the Bible, now purposed for domestic rather than cultic use (Schama, 1999: 196–215). Rembrandt himself was to serve both markets, though in his hands the distinction between secular and sacred rather breaks down as his attention to ordinary everyday scenes assume a distinctly 'theological' dimension, all things being bathed in the light radiated by a sense of God's justice and mercy as Tim Gorringe (1995) suggests, while his explicitly 'religious' images often concentrate our gaze more on the human and this-worldly aspects of the story depicted than on the interventions of a supposed remote transcendence. In as much as Rembrandt evokes a theology, that is to say, it is one which, without any loss of sense of mystery, nonetheless sees that mystery as present in the midst of every human circumstance, and transfiguring it. It is not just a theology of 'common grace', but one that eschews the very distinctions which this category presupposes, and sees instead the redemptive presence of God in Christ 'taking flesh' again in the midst of the general, the ordinary and the everyday.

Getting the Relationship Right

As the great Calvinist writer Abraham Kuyper (1837–1920) observed in his 1898 Stone lectures, the key problem by then was once again that of carefully disentangling the religious from a damaging conflation of it with the aesthetic, and it was Protestant rather than Catholic perspectives which he now had in mind as perpetrating a new and virulent mode of idolatry (Kuyper, 2000: 142ff.). The rush of romantic voices to fill the spiritual vacuum left by rationalism at the end of the eighteenth century had had a profound impact on Protestant theologians, and nowhere more so than in relation to their views on the religious or 'spiritual' significances of art. The radical immanentalism of the philosopher Schelling (1775–1854), according to whom art was a vital means by which human spirit (and thereby the divine Spirit of which it is a direct manifestation) comes to self-expression (Berlin, 2000: 98), is closely related to Feuerbach's (1804–72) understanding of religion itself as a symbolic projection of an unconscious self-awareness onto the clouds. The perception of the entire physical, biological and historical 'process' as a bid for self-consciousness and self-expression by the mysterious forces of 'Spirit' led naturally to an association of human culture with 'the religious', and of art or 'high culture' in particular with the most fully realized forms of this bid. For many thinkers, not least those who had become disenchanted with the old theological dogmas so effectively 'deconstructed' by rationalist accounts, the aesthetic gaze (for art was understood here precisely as the occasion for contemplation) seemed now to provide a privileged alternative route of access to knowledge of 'the divine'. It was not that art was once again being conscripted into ecclesiastical service. This time the imperialistic intent was in the opposite direction entirely; 'nature', 'culture' and 'art' were lodging a bid for the territory of faith as their own, and claiming the prerogatives of the divine for this world. The Christian doctrine of the incarnation, Hegel (1770–1831) had suggested, was a symbolic expression of the idea that God and humanity were essentially already one. Incarnation was a cosmic principle rather than a unique interruption of historical continuities by God's particular kenotic 'becoming'. Art, with its careful attention to the world, was thus viewed by many as already a site of 'religious' or spiritual concern. The aesthetic gaze was equivalent to worship (see Pattison, 1999: 22).

We are back here with the very issues that so haunted the Reformers, and which provoked their ire, not least the effective loss of the vital distinction between created and uncreated, God and the world, and the consequent misdirection of the human 'religious' impulse. As in the sixteenth, so too in the nineteenth and early twentieth centuries there followed responses which tended unhelpfully in the direction of immediate suspicion if not denigration of the arts and their place. There was, we might say drawing on a familiar Christological analogy, a swing from a 'monophysite' to a 'Nestorian' tendency in the perception of the relationship between the two. At the beginning of the twenty-first century, though, we find ourselves back with monophysitism. A sudden rush from arid secularism to embrace some form of 'spiritual' reality, combined with a conviction that it is unlikely to be found within the mainstream religious traditions, promote art and artistry once again as prime candidates for alternative sources of 'spiritual' satisfaction.

As Kuyper realized in his day, the most fruitful response from the churches will likely be one which neither baptizes the arts as surrogate sacraments, nor one which rejects them, or seeks to sideline or stifle their contribution to the rich complexity of human living; but rather one which locates them with their own distinctive integrity within a theologically informed vision of humanity, and of God's purposes for and ways of dealing with the world. Kuyper's own attempt to do this had its problems, but the attempt itself was well conceived, and has been continued by others within the Neo-Calvinist tradition (see, e.g. Rookmaaker, 1970; Seerveld, 1980; Wolterstorff, 1997). It is an attempt which, whatever the particular theological problems raised by different versions of it,[20] succeeds in putting paid to the prejudice with which we opened this chapter. Protestantism, far from being incapable of accommodating the arts within its distinctive vision, and no matter how many times it has, in Thomas's words, 'botched our flesh', is nonetheless a tradition or set of traditions possessed of rich theological resources for rediscovering the true value of human artistry and its significance for us as God's creatures, firmly embodied in the physical processes of nature, equally firmly embedded in those webs of cultural forms (including 'religious' ones) which point to our transcendence of mere physicality, and called by God to a distinctive vocation and end (see Wolterstorff, 1997: 67–90).

Notes

1   See, for example, on the decline of German art tradition in the late sixteenth century, Christensen, (1979: 164–80).
2   See de Gruchy (2001: 36). See further and more generally pp. 17–49.
3   For a thorough account of the history and issues see Cameron (1992). More concisely see Parry (2000).
4   See Jones (1977) drawing on the testimony of Durandus.
5   See Kant (1987: 64): '*Beautiful* is what, without a concept, is liked universally'. See further, §9: 61–4.
6   So, for example, Ryle (1963, ch. VIII) and Sartre (1972). For a full critical account see Warnock (1976, Part IV).
7   See Stephens (1986: 154–5). Zwingli writes 'Whoever has sought help and confidence from a creature which the believer ought to seek only with God, has made a foreign god for himself' ([1523] 1984: 69).
8   'Outside church as a representation of historical events without instruction for veneration, they may be tolerated.' (Zwingli, ([1523] 1984: 71).
9   What follows in this paragraph is based largely on the helpful overview provided in Christensen (1979: 43–65).
10   See sermon preached on 11 March 1522 (*LW*, vol. 51: 83). Also 'Against the Heavenly Prophets' (1525) in *LW* (vol. 40: 84–5).

11 See sermon preached on 12 March 1522 (*LW*, vol. 51: 86).
12 See *LW* 40:105.
13 See *LW* 40:86.
14 See *LW* 40:100.
15 *LW* 40:99. See also *LW* 43:43.
16 Cf, for example, the observation of P. T. Forsyth (1905: 145) that 'If our spirits habitually think of Nature as cursed and God-forsaken we can have no more Art than Calvinism has left to Scotland.'
17 De Gruchy (2001: 41–2), drawing on a fleeting and unsubstantiated assertion in Bouwsma (1988: 80).
18 Janet Martin Soskice (1985: 49–51, 64–6) describes metaphor as possessed of unity of subject and plurality of associative networks (one hypostasis, two natures?), and as involving the positing of some striking or *prima facie* strained conjunction.
19 On these three figures in particular see Pettegree (2000: 462–83).
20 For a critical analysis of some key thinkers in the Neo-Calvinist tradition, and an attempt to build constructively on their insights see Begbie (1991), esp. pp. 142–258.

References

Begbie, Jeremy (1991). *Voicing Creation's Praise: Towards a Theology of the Arts*. Edinburgh: T & T Clark.

Berlin, Isaiah (2000). *The Roots of Romanticism*. London: Pimlico.

Bouwsma, William (1988). *John Calvin: A Sixteenth-Century Portrait*. Oxford: Oxford University Press.

Bunyan, John (1954). *The Pilgrim's Progress*. London: J. M. Dent & Sons.

Calvin, John (1960). *Calvin: Institutes of the Christian Religion*, ed. John McNeill, trans. Ford Lewis Battles. Philadelphia: Westminster Press.

Cameron, Averil (1992). The Language of Images: The Rise of Icons and Christian Representation. In Diana Wood (ed.), *The Church and the Arts* (Studies in Church History, xxviii). Oxford, Blackwell, pp. 1–42.

Camille, Michael (1989). *The Gothic Idol: Ideology and Image-making in Medieval Art*. Cambridge, UK: Cambridge University Press.

Christensen, Carl C. (1979). *Art and the Reformation in Germany*. Athens, OH: Ohio University Press.

Christensen, Carl C. (1996). Art. In Hans J. Hillerbrand (ed.), *The Oxford Encyclopedia of the Reformation*. Oxford: Oxford University Press, pp. 74–80.

de Gruchy, John (2001). *Christianity, Art and Transformation*. Cambridge, UK: Cambridge University Press.

Dillenberger, John (1990). *Images and Relics: Theological Perceptions and Visual Images in Sixteenth-Century Europe*. Oxford: Oxford University Press.

Duffy, Eamon (1992). *The Stripping of the Altars*. New Haven, CT: Yale University Press.

Forsyth, Ilene (1972). *The Throne of Wisdom: Wood Sculptures of the Madonna in Romanesque France*. Princeton, NJ: Princeton University Press.

Forsyth, P. T. (1905). *Religion in Recent Art*. London: Hodder and Stoughton.

Freedberg, David (1988). *Iconoclasm and Painting in the Revolt of the Netherlands 1566–1609*. New York and London: Garland Publishing.

Freedberg, David (1989). *The Power of Images: Studies in the History and Theory of Response*. Chicago: University of Chicago Press.

Gorringe, Tim (1995). Rembrandt's Religious Art. *Theology* 98: 15–19.

Gutmann, Joseph (ed.) (1977). *The Image and the Word: Confrontations in Judaism, Christianity and Islam*. Missoula, MT: Scholars Press.

Hardy, Daniel W. (1999). Calvinism and the Visual Arts: A Theological Introduction. In Paul Corby Finney (ed.), *Seeing Beyond the Word: Visual Arts and the Calvinist Tradition*. Grand Rapids, MI: Eerdmans, pp. 1–16.

Jones, William R. (1977). Art and Christian Piety: Iconoclasm in Medieval Europe. In Joseph Gutmann (ed.), *The Image and the Word*. Missoula, MT: Scholars Press, pp. 75–105.

Kant, Immanuel (1987). *Critique of Judgment*, trans. Werner S. Pluhar. Indianapolis: Hackett.

Klauber, Martin (2000). Zwingli. In Trevor A. Hart (ed.), *The Dictionary of Historical Theology*. Carlisle, UK: Paternoster Press, pp. 576–7.

Kuyper, Abraham (2000). *Lectures on Calvinism*. Grand Rapids, MI: Eerdmans.

Luther, Martin (1955–86). *Luther's Works* [LW], American edn., Jaroslov Pelikan and Helmut T. Lehmann (eds.), 55 volumes. St. Louis and Minneapolis: Concordia and Fortress.

Maag, Karin (2000). Education and Literacy. In Andrew Pettegree (ed.), *The Reformation World*. London: Routledge, pp. 535–44.

McFague, Sallie (1982). *Metaphorical Theology: Models of God in Religious Language*. Philadelphia: Fortress Press.

McIntyre, John (1987). *Faith, Theology and Imagination*. Edinburgh: Handsel Press.

Macmillan, Duncan (1990). *Scottish Art 1460–1990*. Edinburgh: Mainstream.

Michalski, Sergiusz (1993). *The Reformation and the Visual Arts*. London, Routledge.

Parry, Ken (2000). Iconoclast Controversy. In Trevor A. Hart (ed.), *The Dictionary of Historical Theology*. Carlisle, UK: Paternoster Press, pp. 268–70

Pattison, George (1999). *Art, Modernity and Faith*, 2nd edn. London: SCM Press.

Pettegree, Andrew (ed.) (2000). *The Reformation World*. London: Routledge.

Potter, G. R. (1976). *Zwingli*. Cambridge, UK: Cambridge University Press.

Ramsay, M. P. (1938). *Calvin and Art Considered in Relation to Scotland*. Edinburgh: Moray Press.

Rookmaaker, H. (1970). *Modern Art and the Death of a Culture*. Downers Grove, IL: Inter Varsity Press.

Ryle, Gilbert (1963). *The Concept of Mind*. London: Penguin.

Sartre, Jean-Paul (1972). *The Psychology of Imagination*. London: Methuen.

Schama, Simon (1999). *Rembrandt's Eyes*. London: Penguin.

Seerveld, Calvin (1980). *Rainbows for the Fallen World: Aesthetic Life and Artistic Task*. Toronto: Tuppence Press.

Sider, Ronald J. (ed.) (1978). *Karlstadt's Battle with Luther: Documents in a Liberal-Radical Debate*. Philadelphia: Fortress Press.

Soskice, Janet Martin (1985). *Metaphor and Religious Language*. Oxford: Clarendon Press.

Stephens, W. P. (1986). *The Theology of Huldrych Zwingli*. Oxford: Oxford University Press.

Stewart, G. Wauchope (1914). *Music in the Church*. London: A & C Black.

Thomas, R. S. (1995). The Minister. In *Collected Poems 1945–1990*. London: Phoenix, p. 54.

Tillich, Paul (1964). *Systematic Theology*, vol. 3. Welwyn, UK: Nisbet.

Warnock, Mary (1976). *Imagination*. London: Faber.

Watt, Ian (1987). *The Rise of the Novel: Studies in Defoe, Richardson and Fielding*. London: The Hogarth Press.

Westermeyer, Paul (1998). *Te Deum: The Church and Music*. Minneapolis: Fortress Press.

Wilson-Dickson, A. (1992). *The Story of Christian Music*. Oxford: Lion.

Wolterstorff, Nicholas (1997). *Art in Action: Toward a Christian Aesthetic*. Carlisle, UK: Solway.

Zorzin, Alejandro (2002). Andreas Bodenstein von Karlstadt. In Carter Lindberg (ed.), *The Reformation Theologians: An Introduction to Theology in the Early Modern Period*. Oxford: Blackwell, pp. 327–37.

Zwingli, Ulrich ([1523] 1984). A Short Christian Instruction. In H. Wayne Pipkin (ed.), *Huldrych Zwingli Writings*, vol. 2. Allison Park, PA: Pickwick Publications.

CHAPTER 27

Protestantism and Politics, Economics, and Sociology

J. Philip Wogaman

In relating Protestantism to sociopolitical thought and development, one is
struck by a paradox: Protestant churches, movements, and thinkers have played
and continue to play important roles on all sides of most issues. Protestantism
was a significant influence in the development of modern capitalism, but was
also important in the evolution of socialist thought. Protestantism has been a
major force in the struggle against racism, but it also helped provide legitimation for racial segregation and apartheid. Protestantism has been a principal
support for pacifism, but it has also been in league with nationalistic movements
and war efforts of one kind or another. Protestantism has encouraged human
rights and political democracy, but it has in some instances been a factor in the
emergence of totalitarianism. Protestantism has been on both sides in the great
debates over abortion and homosexuality that have troubled Western societies
in recent years.

Why the paradox? As a preliminary observation, the very fact that Protestantism was a movement toward religious *freedom* made it also a force toward
religious and social *pluralism*. Roman Catholicism was never as monolithic as
often supposed, but as a revolt against the authoritarian tendencies in that faith
tradition, Protestantism could be expected to produce a rich variety of ecclesial
styles and teachings.

It may be a mistake to attribute the Enlightenment to Protestantism, but it is
also worth noting that Protestantism was much more receptive to its influences,
including those bearing directly upon sociopolitical and economic thought.
Does that suggest that Protestantism has had a greater tendency toward cultural
accommodation, taking on the coloration of dominant secular cultural forces
in particular settings? Possibly so, but the lines of influence can flow in both
directions: just as secular culture has influenced Protestant faith and life, so
Protestantism has influenced secular culture. H. Richard Niebuhr's classic work,
Christ and Culture (Niebuhr, 1951) explores several sharply divergent types of

relationship between spiritual commitments and cultural realities. Niebuhr (1894–1962) – who was incidentally brother of Reinhold Niebuhr – devoted early attention to sociology of religion, focusing later on theology and ethics. His *Christ and Culture* is at the intersection between these two emphases. Richard Niebuhr's work is also an illustration of how profoundly Ernst Troeltsch's classic study of the relationships between church and society (Troeltsch [1911] 1931) influenced both sociology of religion and Christian social ethics. Troeltsch's magisterial survey of 19 centuries of Christian history well illustrates that Christians and their churches have sought to relate their faith to social issues in every age. That may be especially true in the decades following publication of Troeltsch's work, and despite the paradox, it is certainly true of Protestantism.

Protestantism and Politics

If politics can be understood as a community when it acts as a whole,[1] special attention must be paid to attitudes toward the power that is thus focused to achieve social purposes. Specifically, attention must be given to power as coercion. Protestantism has exhibited three contrasting tendencies in addressing questions of coercive power.

The first of these, often taking its cue from the Sermon on the Mount (esp. Matthew 5–6), rejects the use of force, either by sectarian withdrawal from the political sphere[2] or by engagements with public life through solely nonviolent forms of influence. The latter has been well illustrated by the Society of Friends (Quakers), whose pacifist witness has been remarkably consistent for more than three centuries. This approach to power was exemplified by the Russian novelist/philosopher Leo Tolstoy, who taught that human nature is essentially good. If the coercive instruments of state, such as police, armies, and prisons, could be removed, that innate human goodness could be expected to flourish (see especially Tolstoy, 1885 and [1905] 1961). While Tolstoy was not himself a Protestant, his pacifist and anarchist views were largely derived from New England Quakers (especially Adin Ballou). One of the best exemplars of recent Protestant pacifism was the Mennonite theologian John Howard Yoder (see Yoder, 1972). Yoder's views are especially significant because he has largely avoided the more sectarian tendencies of Mennonite Christianity, expressing that community's typical pacifism in more sophisticated theological form. Yoder, unlike Tolstoy, had few illusions concerning the perfectability of human nature. Sin is a real and persisting tendency in all human beings. And yet, Jesus has shown the way. Jesus's way of nonviolence – as expressed in the Sermon on the Mount – is politically effective. If it had not been, he never would have been crucified! By following the way of Jesus, we can also be effective, though not always in the foreseeable future. Jesus, too, was temporarily defeated through his crucifixion. But, through the resurrection, God confirmed the way of Jesus. It is not our responsibility to seek to manage the course of history. We are to be faithful to Jesus's way, and we can trust God to take care of the end results.

In what way can such pacifist tendencies be regarded as specifically Protestant? While pacifism also has ancient Christian roots – indeed, earliest Christianity may have been predominantly pacifist – the Protestant recovery of an emphasis upon the political relevance of the Bible may be very important here. The widespread use of the Bible among Protestants, commencing with Luther, invited fresh reading, especially of the Gospel narratives and teachings of Jesus.

The second Protestant political tendency is more covenantal. It is to understand the state as an expression of the social contract among the participants in society. The basic idea has very ancient roots, the germ of which can be found in Socrates (as related by Plato) and the early Stoic tradition. The Enlightenment social contract theorists, especially Hobbes, Locke, and Rousseau, projected it into the modern world. Of these, Locke was most distinctively a Protestant Christian, but it is debatable whether his ideas were more theological or philosophical in origin. The contract tradition is the basic source of democratic thought in the modern world. So far as Protestantism is concerned, it was expressed most distinctively in the Calvinists, notwithstanding some of John Calvin's own authoritarian tendencies.

What was it about Calvinism that proved especially receptive to those more ancient and more philosophical expressions of democratic thought? It can be argued that it was Calvinism's emphasis upon the sovereignty of God, transcending every human expression or authority. If God is greater than all human beings and if, as the Calvinists also emphasized, all humanity is flawed by original sin, then it follows that no human being or elite oligarchy can be entrusted with unqualified power. Power, broadly distributed through the body politic, is responsible and self-correcting. All must be free to participate since all can also, at least potentially, be responsive to the transcending will of God.

Mainline Protestant denominations have generally provided broad support for democracy, including those human rights that are basic to participation by all of the people. The World Council of Churches' early (1948) formulation of the "Responsible Society" is a good illustration:

> Man is created and called to be a free being, responsible to God and his neighbour. Any tendencies in State and society depriving man of the possibility of acting responsibly are a denial of God's intention for man and His work of salvation. A responsible society is one where freedom is the freedom of men who acknowledge responsibility to justice and public order, and where those who hold political authority or economic power are responsible for its exercise to God and the people whose welfare is affected by it. Man must never be made a mere means for political or economic ends. Man is not made for the State but the State for man. . . . For a society to be responsible under modern conditions it is required that the people have freedom to control, to criticise and to change their governments, that power be made responsible by law and tradition, and be distributed as widely as possible through the whole community.[3]

That statement well summarizes the increasingly dominant Protestant attitude toward democracy, including the linkage between responsibility to God and to the community, and with an underlying realism about political power.

The latter point had been anticipated by Reinhold Niebuhr's familiar aphorism, "Man's capacity for justice makes democracy possible; but man's inclination to injustice makes democracy necessary" (Niebuhr, 1944: xiii). Niebuhr himself, while a pacifist in his earlier career, became a strong proponent of American entry into World War II. His "Christian realism" can be contrasted with Yoder's position, at least in that Niebuhr considers it imperative for Christians to take responsibility for their actions and to do whatever they can to achieve actual results that express their social convictions. His opposition to the Vietnam War, which surprised many, was therefore not a return to his earlier pacifist leanings; rather, it was based upon his assessment of the realities of that war.

In the latter part of the twentieth century a more conservative evangelical movement found its voice in American politics. Under the leadership of figures like Jerry Falwell, Pat Robertson, and Ralph Reed, movements like the Moral Majority and the Christian Coalition sought to achieve dominance in American politics on behalf of conservative positions on cultural issues like abortion and homosexuality and on economic issues such as, especially, the economic role of government. While not all of the evangelicals could be described as fundamentalists, their political movements often sought support from chosen scriptural texts, taken literally. The most literalistic of the conservative movements was undoubtedly Reconstructionism, founded by the American fundantalist Rousas Rushdoony, whose objectives included the structuring of public life exactly along biblical lines, including the Levitical Code with all of its legalisms and severe punishments. While such an extremist is an embarrassment to the more moderate political views of most evangelicals, the latter have generally exhibited intolerant attitudes toward non-Christians as equal participants in public life. Further complicating the picture, some evangelical Protestants have taken the view that they should not participate in politics at all. (That would include the Amish and the Hutterians, among others.)

Protestants thus have presented widely divergent approaches to politics. Over time, the main weight of Protestant opinion has probably been best represented by the ecumenically minded churches and their theologians. While these Protestants can disagree on major issues – such as the question of war – they are united in their commitments to democracy and equal human rights for all.

Protestantism and Economics

Early in the twentieth century, the German sociologist Max Weber contributed a seminal work on the influence of Protestantism on the development of modern capitalism (Weber, [1904–5] 1930). While he did not (as commonly supposed) consider Protestantism to have *caused* capitalism to emerge in Western society, he did attribute the peculiar cultural form of Western capitalism to Protestant influence. Weber was especially impressed by the Protestant doctrine of vocation, especially in its Calvinist form. We are all "called" by God to service in the world. In that Protestant form, the word "vocation" is not limited to those who are called to a priestly role in the church; it includes all useful employment. In economic life, that doctrine translated into an activist work ethic, thus into a strong impetus toward productive enterprise. We should not be content with things as they are; we should improve them, to the greater glory of God.

As Weber sees it, this not only contributed religious fervor to the acquisitive instinct associated with capitalism, it added a certain almost ascetic dimension. We should act to increase the sum total of wealth, but we should be good stewards of that wealth, devoting it not so much to our own selfish consumption as to other good works. Weber takes the principal founder of Methodism, John Wesley, to exemplify something of that spirit. In his writings on economic matters, that eighteenth-century British leader summarized Christian responsibility in three parts: gain all you can, save all you can, and give all you can. Evidently the early Methodists were more receptive to the first two of these than to the third, for Wesley bemoans the effects of Methodist economic prosperity upon Methodist spirituality:

> I fear, wherever riches have increased, the essence of religion has decreased in the same proportion. Therefore I do not see how it is possible, in the nature of things, for any revival of true religion to continue long. For religion must necessarily produce both industry and frugality, and these cannot but produce riches. But as riches increase, so will pride, anger, and the love of the world in all its branches. . . . We ought not to prevent people from being diligent and frugal; we must exhort all Christians to gain all they can, and to save all they can; that is, in effect, to grow rich. (quoted in Weber, 1930: 175)

That dilemma suggests the complexity of understanding how Protestantism has influenced economic life. Clearly, Protestantism has often been supportive of capitalism. Indeed, as Weber has reminded us, Western capitalism has flourished most in precisely those places that have been most receptive to Protestantism, particularly in its Calvinist or Reformed expressions: Switzerland, Scotland, England, the United States. In such places, the captains of industry and commerce have been, at least historically, more visibly Protestant than anything else. But it remains a nice question whether, as Wesley remarked, economic success has contributed to or diminished the ardor of their religious commitments. In some cases, indeed, economic success allied with Protestant spirituality may give rise to self-righteousness: I have worked hard, I have been diligent, I have played by the rules, therefore God has rewarded me with success. People who are less well-off than I may be poor because they have not been as diligent and responsible as I have. Periodically, even today, the attitude surfaces in visible form that spiritual piety is rewarded with economic success. The late nineteenth-/early twentieth-century American Bishop William Lawrence preached that "in the long run, it is only to the man of morality that wealth comes. . . . Godliness is in league with riches." The speech, frequently repeated before appreciative audiences of people in an economic position to feel reassured by such words, reinforced a persisting tendency among many Protestants to affirm capitalism as a divinely ordained economic order. A twentieth-century journal, *Christian Economics*, was sent free of charge to Protestant clergy throughout the United States through the kindly generosity of a very wealthy Presbyterian layman. Every page of the publication made clear that a Christian economics is one altogether committed to *laissez faire* capitalism.[4]

It is striking that much of the reaction against unrestrained capitalism also had Protestant roots. The Christian Socialism of mid-nineteenth-century England is a case in point. While the leading figures of this movement, especially the English theologian F. D. Maurice, may have been vague about the economic implications, they were clear that economic competition should be subordinated to economic cooperation. We are all a part of the same human community, divinely intended to become the "Kingdom of Christ." Maurice criticized, equally, the "unsocial Christians and the un-Christian socialists" (Maurice, 1884: 35).

A more clearly socialist alternative among Protestants was supplied by the German Christoph Friedrich Blumhardt (1842–1919) and the American leader of the Social Gospel movement, Walter Rauschenbusch (1861–1918). Blumhardt confronted the spiritual consequences of the greed inspired by Capitalism:

> And now, when Socialism sets up the goal that every person have an equal right *to bread*, that matters of ownership be so arranged that neither money nor property but the life of man become the highest value, why should that be seen as a reprehensible, revolutionary demand? . . . Resistance will be of no avail, because it is God's will that all men in every respect should be regarded equal. (Eller, 1980: 23)

On economic matters, Rauschenbusch was also essentially socialist. While not all of the leading figures in the Social Gospel movement were clearly socialist, the movement was characteristically critical of unrestrained capitalism and the greed that it seemed to foster. The Social Gospel movement itself is generally dated from 1865 to the outset of World War I (1914), but its influence continued throughout the twentieth century in various ways. The Liberation Theologians of the 1970s and 1980s, both Protestant and Catholic, were even more clearly socialist, often discernibly influenced by Marxism.

As the twenty-first century began, Protestant economic thinking continued to be expressed in diverse ways. If anything, however, Protestants had become less ideologically definable. After the ending of the Cold War and the virtual collapse of Marxism as a world movement, global economic relationships had become more clearly defined by free market institutions. Protestant thinkers, while not uncritical of excesses and inequalities fostered by those patterns, have yet to articulate clear alternatives.[5]

Protestantism and Sociology

It would be difficult to establish a meaningful relationship between Protestantism, as such, and sociology as an academic discipline. However, if "sociology" is understood to mean thought about society in more general terms, much more can be said. Are there discernible patterns of Protestant thought regarding race relations, the family, sexual relations, gender, cultural values, and so forth? There definitely are, although again Protestantism exhibits diversity of thinking.

In respect to race relations, Protestants were numbered both among the stoutest defenders and most resolute critics of racism and racial segregation (or *apartheid*). Much racism in the modern world was projected out of the seventeenth- to nineteenth-century institution of slavery (especially in America). While slavery has a history reaching to prehistoric times, the reinforcement of slavery by racism is a product of more recent history. The slavery practiced in recent centuries was mostly through the enslavement of dark-skinned Africans. In the slavery controversies of nineteenth-century America, Protestants (mostly Southern) supported the institution by questionable biblical exegesis purporting to represent divine judgment of persons of color. The cause of slavery itself was defeated, first through the British abolition of the slave trade and then through the freeing of American slaves following the Civil War. Nevertheless, the racist ideologies used to justify slavery persisted in the support of racial segregation (and in the support of South African *apartheid*).

Even comparatively liberal Protestant thinkers often either shared the ideology or were silent. (Interestingly, the Social Creed adopted by the newly formed Federal Council of Churches of the United States in 1908 was silent on race relations, despite the passing of laws enforcing segregation in Southern states during that period and the many incidents of lynching.) As late as 1936 a prominent, and otherwise quite liberal, Methodist theologian, Albert C. Knudson, spoke at the General Conference of the (then named) Methodist Episcopal Church in support of racial segregation in the church. God had, in his view, created the races separate and intended to keep them that way![6]

Such a perspective was to shift dramatically after World War II. This was partly as a result of greater wartime racial intermingling, partly influenced by careful studies by social scientists demonstrating the inherent equality of persons of different racial groups and the social causes of perceived inferiority, and partly due to more careful theological analysis. The major Protestant impetus toward racial equality and integration was, however, from African American Protestant leaders, most notably Martin Luther King, Jr. Dr King energized the Civil Rights Movement and captivated the imagination of the nation.

By the end of the twentieth century racism and racial segregation were thoroughly repudiated in virtually all Protestant churches.

On two sociocultural issues, abortion and homosexuality, Protestantism has yet to achieve any kind of consensus. Protestants are to be found on both sides of the battle lines over abortion, in both the "prolife" and "prochoice" camps. Complicating matters further, some Protestants take the view that abortion should be a legal option but in most instances morally disapproved. Former President William J. Clinton remarked, somewhat in this vein, that abortion should be safe, legal, and rare. But other Protestants, including especially the evangelicals, have sought legal prohibitions. Yet others support freedom of choice and feel that a range of circumstances warrant moral as well as legal approval.

Among American Protestants the homosexuality issue proved especially divisive during the last quarter of the twentieth century. Major Protestant denominations, such as the Presbyterians, Methodists, United Church of Christ, Disciples, Episcopalians, and Lutherans were driven by conflict over this issue. Should homosexual persons be allowed to exercise pastoral ministry? Should pastors be allowed to officiate at services solemnizing marriage-like relationships between persons of the same gender? Negative responses to such questions tended to dominate in the major denominations, but with very substantial dissent.

Similar conflict has concerned the relative status of men and women. From about the middle of the twentieth century, most of the major Protestant denominations became advocates of equal status in society. Increasingly, they applied the same principle to their own life, most notably with the ordination of women as clergy. By the end of the century, that had become quite routine in a number of the principal denominations – with Southern Baptists being the main exception in that, although they do ordain women, their ministry is hedged about with significant restrictions. In similar vein, the language used in liturgies and hymns became more inclusive. Generic male language was changed and, with increasing frequency, the use of exclusively male language in referring to God was avoided.[7]

Reflections

In surveying this somewhat confusing picture, one is struck by the sheer diversity of Protestant views and practices. On some matters (such as the condemnation of racism) Protestantism seems to have arrived at consensus. On other issues, the differences among Protestants (even within the same denomination) can be quite as great as the differences between Protestants and other Christians. Moreover, one observes considerable changes of viewpoint over time.

Why the diversity? Why the conflicts? Why the changes? Some might say it is because Protestantism lacks central agreed-upon sources of authority for its views. In one sense that may be so. Even the common appeal among Protestants to the Bible is as much a source of conflict as of consensus. The Bible is itself a battleground between fundamentalist Protestants and those who make less literalistic uses of Scripture. Those who look for authoritative answers to political, economic, and social questions, either in a written scripture or in ecclesial authority, are courting disillusionment.

But that does not mean that Protestants lack authoritative bases for their response to such questions nor that they are dependent upon the shifting perceptions and values of a given cultural milieu. Rather, I think, it is that Protestantism – at least at its best – is responding to a more transcendent and spiritual source of authority. If one believes that God is infinitely greater than we are, the implication is that all questions must remain open to fresh insight. "New occasions teach new duties, time makes ancient good uncouth," as the Protestant nineteenth-century poet James Russell Lowell reminds us. Protestantism could reverse itself on the issue of slavery and could embrace democracy and human rights in general because of an underlying conviction that the eternal God is not to be identified absolutely with any social order or system. Democracy could find support among Protestants because that political tendency is, in principle, most open to self-correction and the empowerment of all citizens.

But Protestantism has also responded most readily to an expansive understanding of God's grace – that is, the love of God for all people, despite their imperfections. Such doctrine is an affirmation, at the root, of the inclusive bonds of community. It is a caution against the ever-recurring tendencies among the religious toward self-righteousness. We are all sinners standing in the need of God's grace. Hence, the impetus toward love of people who are very different is reinforced by fundamental religious doctrine. Translated into, say, economic policy this undergirds a drive toward overcoming poverty. Economic ideology must be subordinate to the practical questions of what really does benefit people and what does minimize the effects of status divisions within society.

We can note finally that there has been a persisting endeavor among Protestants to harmonize their attitudes toward society in general with their ecclesiologies – their views and practices in the structuring of their churches. To be sure, some Protestants have retreated into sectarian isolation, regarding the world as totally corrupt and beyond reform. And some Protestants have relegated their churches to secondary status. But for those taking both church and world seriously, the drive toward the integrity of ecclesiology and social doctrine is much more consistently expressed. The social pronouncements of many Protestant denominations and of the modern ecumenical movements in which they supply principal leadership are often a reflection of that integrity. Those who criticize Protestant practice often do so on the basis of Protestant assumptions.

Notes

1 The definition is elaborated in Wogaman (2000: 11–32).
2 A tendency well illustrated by the Bruderhof communities, cf. the writings of Eberhard Arnold or J. Heinrich Arnold (Farmington, PA: Plough Publishing House).
3 World Council of Churches (1948: 200–1). The use of generic male language, culturally typical of the period, can be noted with regret.
4 One's impression, upon reading many issues of that publication, is that the message was essentially that of the Austrian school of economics and figures like Ludwig von Mises, and that the original Protestant emphases upon the sovereignty of God and doctrines of vocation and stewardship were subordinated to that.
5 Daniel Finn's volume *Just Trading* (1996) is an illustration of thoughtful analysis. While Finn is Roman Catholic, his work was developed out of ecumenical dialogue involving both Protestants and Catholics sponsored by the Churches' Center for Theology and Public Policy. By the twenty-first century it had become difficult to distinguish the work of Protestant from Roman Catholic ethicists and theologians on economic questions.
6 It should be noted that some Protestant theologians, such as Reinhold Niebuhr, took a diametrically opposed view. Niebuhr's 1932 classic, *Moral Man and Immoral Society*, includes a section speculating on how African Americans could attain completely equal status in American society.
7 The popular hymns of Brian Wren are an especially good illustration. University-related divinity schools and the seminaries of "mainline" Protestant denominations gave increasing support to these trends.

References

Eller, Vernard (ed.) (1980). *Thy Kingdom Come: A Blumhardt Reader*. Grand Rapids, MI: Eerdmans.

Finn, Daniel (1996). *Just Trading: On the Ethics and Economics of Internationl Trade*. Nashville, TN: Abingdon.

Maurice, Frederick (ed.) (1884). *The Life of Frederick Denison Maurice: Chiefly Told in his Own Letters*. New York: Scribner.

Niebuhr, H. Richard (1951). *Christ and Culture*. San Francisco: Harper and Row.

Niebuhr, Reinhold (1932). *Moral Man and Immoral Society*. New York: Scribner.

Niebuhr, Reinhold (1944). *The Children of Light and the Children of Darkness*. New York: Scribner.

Tolstoy, Leo (1885). *My Religion*. New York: Crowell.

Tolstoy, Leo ([1905] 1961). *The Kingdom of God is Within You*. New York: Farrar, Straus.

Troeltsch, Ernst ([1911] 1931). *The Social Teaching of the Christian Churches*, 2 vols. New York and London: Macmillan.

Weber, Max ([1904–5] 1930). *The Protestant Ethic and the Spirit of Capitalism*, trans. Talcott Parsons. New York: Scribner.

Wogaman, J. Philip (2000). *Christian Perspectives on Politics*, rev. edn. Louisville, KY: Westminster/John Knox.

World Council of Churches (1948). *Man's Disorder and God's Design*, vol. 3. New York: Harper & Bros.

Yoder, John Howard (1972). *The Politics of Jesus*. Grand Rapids, MI: Eerdmans.

Further Reading

Rauschenbusch, Walter (1907). *Christianity and the Social Crisis*. New York and London: Macmillan.

Wogaman, J. Philip (1993). *Christian Ethics: A Historical Introduction*. Louisville, KY: Westminster/John Knox.

CHAPTER 28

Protestantism, Law and Legal Thought

John Witte Jr.

Most Western nations today are dedicated to the rule of law and have constitutions that define the powers and provinces of political authorities and the rights and duties of their political subjects. Most nations make formal distinctions among the executive, legislative and judicial powers of government and functions of law, and distinguish among bodies of public law, private law, and criminal law, each with its own forms and norms of due process of law. Most have sophisticated rules and procedures to facilitate the legal transactions and interactions of their citizens and subjects and to resolve disputes between and among citizens and the government. Most recognize multiple sources of law – international treaties and conventions, national constitutions, statutes, regulations, judicial precedents, customary practices and so forth. Protestantism has made significant contributions to a number of these Western legal ideas and institutions – particularly during the Protestant Reformation era in Europe and in later Reformed and evangelical movements on both sides of the Atlantic.

Reformation Era

The sixteenth-century Protestant Reformation was, in part, an attack upon the legal power and political structure of the medieval Catholic Church. Since the twelfth century, the Western Christian church had been organized as an autonomous political authority in Western Christendom holding the legal power of the spiritual sword. The medieval church claimed a vast jurisdiction – power to make and enforce laws governing doctrine, liturgy, clergy, church property and polity, marriage, family, inheritance, trusts, education, charity, contracts, moral crimes and more. The church developed a system of canon laws that was enforced by a hierarchy of church courts and clerical officials spread from Italy to Ireland, from Portugal to Poland.

The Protestant Reformation began as a call for freedom from this regime – freedom of the individual conscience from canon laws, freedom of political officials from clerical power and privilege, freedom of local clergy from centralized papal and conciliar rule. "Freedom of the Christian" was the rallying cry of the early Reformation. Catalyzed by Martin Luther's posting of the Ninety-Five Theses in 1517 and his burning of the canon law books in 1520, Protestant leaders denounced canon law and clerical authority with unprecedented alacrity and urged radical legal and political reforms on the strength of the new Protestant theology.

All the early Protestant leaders – Martin Luther, John Calvin, Thomas Cranmer, Menno Simons and others – taught that salvation comes through faith in the gospel, not by works of the Law. Each individual was to stand directly before God, to seek God's gracious forgiveness of sin, and to conduct life in accordance with the Bible and Christian conscience. To the Reformers, the Catholic canon law administrated by the clergy obstructed the individual's relationship with God and obscured simple biblical norms for right living.

The early Reformers further taught that the church was at heart a community of saints, not a corporation of law. Its cardinal signs and callings were to preach the Word, to administer the sacraments, to catechize the young and to care for the needy. The Catholic clergy's legal rule in Christendom obstructed the church's divine mission and usurped the state's role as God's vice-regent called to appropriate and apply divine and natural law in the earthly kingdom. To be sure, the church needed internal rules of order to govern its own polity, teaching, and discipline. Church officials and councils needed to oppose legal injustice and combat political illegitimacy. But, for most Protestants, law was primarily the province of the state rather than the church, of the magistrate rather than the minister.

These new Protestant teachings helped to transform Western law in the sixteenth and seventeenth centuries. The Protestant Reformation broke the international rule of the Catholic Church and the canon law, permanently splintering Western Christendom into competing nations and regions, each with its own religious and political rulers. The Protestant Reformation triggered a massive shift of power and property from the church to the state. State rulers now assumed jurisdiction over numerous subjects previously governed by the church and its canon law, such as marriage and family life, property and testamentary matters, charity and poor relief, contracts and oaths, moral and ideological crimes.

In Lutheran and Anglican polities, the state also came to exercise considerable control over the clergy, polity, and property of the church, forcibly divesting the Catholic Church and its clergy of huge property holdings and periodically subjecting Catholic and Protestant dissenters to severe repression. In Calvinist polities, church and state officials shared power and property more evenly, though often with no less severe consequences to traditional Catholic institutions or to new Protestant nonconformists. Most Anabaptist communities withdrew from civic life into small self-sufficient communities that were governed internally by biblical principles of discipleship, simplicity, charity, and nonresistance and that set their own standards of worship, discipline, and education.

These massive shifts in legal power and property from church to state in Protestant lands did not break the ties between law and Christianity. For all of the Reformation's early anticanonicalism, many Protestant magistrates and jurists eventually transplanted Catholic canon law rules and procedures directly into their new state laws. Protestant authorities trimmed these canon laws of Catholic theological accretions that they found obsolete or offensive. But they retained many canon law norms and forms that were grounded in Scripture and Christian tradition, applying them in many of the new civil statutes and court decisions.

Moreover, Protestant leaders brought some of the new Protestant theology to direct and dramatic legal expression. For example, Protestant theologians replaced the traditional Catholic idea of marriage as a sacrament of the church with new ideas of the marital household as a social estate, covenantal bond, or little commonwealth of the earthly kingdom. On that basis, Protestant jurists developed a new state law of marriage, featuring requirements of parental consent, state registration, church consecration, and peer presence for valid marital formation, and introducing absolute divorce on grounds of adultery, desertion, and other faults, with subsequent rights to remarry at least for the innocent party.

Protestant theologians replaced the traditional understanding of education as a teaching office of the church with a new understanding of the public school as a "civic seminary" for all persons to prepare for their Christian vocations. On that basis, Protestant magistrates replaced clerics as the chief rulers of education, state law replaced church law as the principal law of education, and the general callings of all Christians replaced the special calling of the clergy as the *raison d'être* of education.

Protestant theologians introduced a new theology of the "three uses" of the moral law set out in the Bible, particularly the Ten Commandments. On that basis, Protestant jurists developed arresting new biblical theories of natural law and equity; introduced sweeping changes in civil laws of social welfare and moral discipline; and developed an integrated theory of the retributive, deterrent, and rehabilitative functions of criminal law and of ecclesiastical and domestic discipline.

Protestant theologians, particularly Anabaptists, emphasized the voluntary qualities of the Christian faith – that an adult individual must make a conscientious choice to accept Christ, to scale the wall of separation between the fallen world, and to enter into the garden of religion. Though initially rejected, this idea eventually became an important cornerstone for later Western legal theories of liberty of conscience and free exercise of religion.

Later Reformed Accents

While each of the four main branches of the Reformation, and the sundry denominations that grew from them, continued to influence discrete legal and political institutions in the following centuries, it was the Reformed and evangelical movements that eventually translated these early Protestant teachings into the most influential legal and political reforms in the West.

Various Reformed writers converted Martin Luther's famous doctrine that a person is at once sinner and saint (*simul iustus et peccator*) into a firm anthropological foundation for later Western theories of democracy and human rights. On the one hand, these Reformed Protestants argued, every person is created in the image of God and justified by faith in God. Every person is called to a distinct vocation, which stands equal in dignity and sanctity to all others. Each is a prophet, priest, and king and responsible to exhort, to minister, and to rule in the community. All thus stand equal before God and before their neighbors. Every person is vested with a natural liberty to live, to believe, to love and serve God and neighbor, and is entitled to the vernacular Scripture, to education, to work in a vocation. On the other hand, these Reformed Protestants argued, every person is sinful and prone to evil and egoism. All need the restraint of the law to deter them from evil and to drive them to repentance. Every person needs the association of others to exhort, minister, and rule him or her with law and with love. Each individual, therefore, is inherently a communal creature, and belongs to a family, a church, a political community.

These social institutions of family, church, and state are divine in origin and human in organization. They are created by God and governed by godly ordinances. They stand equal before God and are called to discharge distinctive godly functions in the community. The family is called to rear and nurture children, to educate and discipline them, to exemplify love and cooperation. The church is called to preach the word, administer the sacraments, educate the young, and aid the needy. The state is called to protect order, punish crime, and promote community. Though divine in origin, these institutions are formed through human covenants. Such covenants confirm the divine functions, the created offices, of these institutions. They also organize these offices so that they are protected from the sinful excesses of officials who occupy them. Family, church, and state are thus organized as public institutions, accessible and accountable to each other and to their members. Particularly the church is to be organized as a democratic congregational polity, with a separation of ecclesiastical powers among pastors, elders, and deacons; election of officers to limited tenures of office; and ready participation of the congregation in the life and leadership of the church.

From the later sixteenth to the later eighteenth centuries, various Reformed groups recast these theological doctrines into democratic norms and forms. Protestant doctrines of the person and society were cast into democratic social forms. As all people stand equal before God, they must stand equal before God's political agents in the state. As God has vested all people with natural liberties of life and belief, the state must ensure them of similar civil liberties. As God has called all to be prophets, priests, and kings, the state must protect their constitutional freedoms to speak, to preach, and to rule in the community. As God has created people as social creatures, the state must promote and protect a plurality of social institutions, particularly the church and the family.

Protestant doctrines of sin, in turn, were cast into democratic political forms. The political office must be protected against the sinfulness of the political official. Political power, like ecclesiastical power, must be distributed among self-checking executive, legislative, and judicial branches. Officials must be elected to limited terms of office. Laws must be clearly codified and discretion closely guarded. If officials abuse their office, they must be disobeyed. If they persist in their abuse, they must be removed, even if by revolutionary force or regicide. These Protestant teachings were among the driving ideological forces behind the revolts of the French Huguenots, Dutch Pietists, and Scottish Presbyterians against their monarchical oppressors in the later sixteenth and seventeenth centuries. They were crucial weapons in the arsenal of the Puritan revolutionaries in seventeenth-century England and eighteenth-century America. They remained important sources of inspiration and instruction during the great modern age of democratic construction on both sides of the Atlantic.

New Evangelical Accents

While Reformed legal and political thought continued to influence the Western tradition until the twentieth century, evangelical accents became increasingly prominent in the nineteenth and early twentieth century, particularly in America.

The rise of American evangelical legal and political influence was, in part, a function of simple demography. American evangelicals had their roots in small colonial Baptist and Anabaptist communities, many clustered in Roger Williams's Rhode Island. Their small size and separatist leanings kept them from exercising much political influence at first. The First Great Awakening (c.1720–70), however, divided many Protestant denominations into traditional Old Light and evangelical New Light groups. It also sparked the rise of Baptist and Methodist churches, whose leaders joined others to secure constitutional guarantees of religious liberty for all. The Second Great Awakening (c.1810–60) splintered and stunted traditional Reformed, Anglican, and Lutheran denominations still further and led to the explosive growth of Baptists and Methodists.

The rise of evangelical legal and political influence was also, in part, a function of theological innovation. While nineteenth-century American evangelicals did not work out a detailed new political theology or theological jurisprudence, they added accents to the Protestant inheritance that helped shape American law and politics until well into the twentieth century. For example, evangelicals emphasized Christian conversion, the necessary spiritual rebirth of each sinful individual. On that basis, they strongly advocated the liberty of conscience of each individual, free speech, and the rights and duties of the missionary to proselytize, both on the American frontier and abroad. Evangelicals had a high view of the Christian Bible as the infallible textbook for human living. On that basis, they celebrated the use of the Bible in public school classrooms, the military, prisons, and elsewhere, while they castigated Jews, Catholics, Mormons and others for their use of partial, apocryphal, or surrogate Scriptures. Evangelicals emphasized sanctification, the process of each individual becoming holier before God, neighbor, and self. On that basis, they underscored a robust ethic of spiritual and moral progress, education and improvement of all.

Many evangelicals coupled this emphasis on personal conversion and sanctification with a concern for social reform and moral improvement of the community. Great numbers of evangelicals eventually joined the national campaign and Civil War to end slavery – though this issue permanently divided Methodists and Baptists, as well as Presbyterians and Lutherans. Nineteenth-century evangelicals were more united in their support for successive, and sometimes successful, campaigns for new laws against dueling, freemasonry, reservations for native Americans, lotteries, drunkenness, Sunday mails, and Sabbath-breaking. In the later nineteenth century, many evangelical leaders also joined the struggle for the rights of emancipated blacks, poor workers, women suffragists, and labor union organizers – none more forcefully and successfully than Walter Rauschenbusch, the leader of the Social Gospel Movement. But on these issues, too, evangelical camps were often bitterly divided.

On occasion, nineteenth-century evangelicals became actively involved in national party politics, such as in the three unsuccessful presidential campaigns of William Jennings Bryant at the turn of the twentieth century. Most American evangelical groups, however, were suspicious of the national government and were staunch believers in the virtues of federalism and the prerogatives of state and local government. Many evangelicals further believed that the individual congregation and the voluntary association were the most essential sources of governance and improvement. They regarded churches, schools, clubs, charities, businesses, unions, corporations, learned societies, and other voluntary associations as essential buffers between the individual and state, essential curbs upon state power, and essential instruments of law and authority in their own right.

Modern Pathways

After World War II, Reformed and evangelical Protestantism diminished as a legal and political force in America, though individual Protestant luminaries such as Reinhold and Richard Niebuhr charted provocative new pathways, and various Protestant ethicists and theologians continued to develop important new themes, particularly relating to just war theory, the environment, and biotechnology. But modern American Protestantism did not develop an authentic political model or program of legal reform on the order of Roman Catholicism after the Second Vatican Council. Some Protestants repeated old legal and political formulas, often nostalgically (and selectively) recounting Protestant progress and prowess in American history. Other Protestants focused their attention on single political issues – the restoration of prayer in public schools, the eradication of abortion, the protection of the traditional family – often mobilizing ample political support and securing occasional legal victories for these causes. Still others, particularly in the World and National Council of Churches, threw their support behind ecumenical and interreligious programs. But a comprehensive Protestant political and legal platform, faithful to the cardinal convictions of historical Protestantism and responsive to the needs of an intensely pluralistic modern polity, did not emerge in the twentieth century.

A notable exception to the recent pattern of Protestant political and legal quietism in America was the civil rights movement of the 1950s–60s that helped to bring greater political and civil equality to African Americans in a series of landmark statutes and cases. Another exception was the rise of the Moral Majority and Christian Coalition in the 1980s and early 1990s as a broad political and cultural campaign to revitalize public religion, restore families, reform schools, reclaim unsafe neighborhoods, and support faith-based charities. A still further exception has been the very recent coalition of Protestant and other religious academics who have led campaigns for the greater protection of religious freedom in the world and the cultivation of the interdisciplinary field of law and religion. Whether these movements are signposts for a vibrant new Protestant mission and ministry to law and politics remains to be seen.

Further Reading

Berman, H. J. (1983). *Law and Revolution: The Formation of the Western Legal Tradition.* Cambridge, MA: Harvard University Press.

Helmholz, R. H. (1996). *The Spirit of the Classical Canon Law.* Athens, GA: University of Georgia Press.

Hutson, James H. (ed.) (2000). *Religion and the New Republic: Faith in the Founding of America.* Lanham, MD: Rowman & Littlefield.

Klaasen, Walter (1981). *Anabaptism in Outline: Selected Primary Sources.* Scottdale, PA: Herald Press.

Marty, Martin E. (1987). *Religion and Republic: The American Circumstance.* Boston: Beacon Press.

McLoughlin, William C. (1971). *New England Dissent, 1630–1833,* 2 vols. Cambridge, MA: Harvard University Press.

Noll, Mark A. (1988). *One Nation Under God? Christian Faith and Political Action in America.* San Francisco: Harper & Row.

Skinner, Quentin (1978). *The Foundations of Modern Political Thought*, 2 vols. Cambridge, UK: Cambridge University Press.

Stokes, Anson P. (1950). *Church and State in the United States*, 3 vols. New York: Harper and Bros.

Vallauri, Luigi and Dilcher, Gerhard (1981). *Christentum, Säkularisation und Modernes Recht*, 2 vols. Baden-Baden: Nomos Verlagsgesellschaft.

Walzer, Michael (1965). *The Revolution of the Saints: Study in the Origins of Radical Politics*. Cambridge, MA: Harvard University Press.

Witte, John, Jr. (2000). *Religion and the American Constitutional Experiment*. Boulder, CO, New York, and Oxford: Westview Press.

Witte, John, Jr. (2002). *Law and Protestantism: The Legal Teachings of the Lutheran Reformation*. Cambridge, UK: Cambridge University Press.

CHAPTER 29

Protestantism and the Sciences

Ted Peters

Like twins reared separately, Protestant Christianity and modern science were born at the same time into the same family of Western European lineage. They both inherited the same ancestry: a biblical belief in a God who creates a world distinct from divinity and therefore a contingent creation; plus a Hellenistic philosophical belief that both the human mind and the natural world are organized rationally and represented by mathematical structures. Both Protestantism and science were educated by the disciplined thinking of medieval Roman Catholic scholasticism. They both rebelled against hierarchical authority over what the individual heart should believe and over what the individual mind should think. They both took stands against superstition, magic, and human manipulation of alleged supernatural powers.

The overlapping biographies of these twins can be organized into three broad periods: the Copernican, the Kantian, and the contemporary. The first period, the Copernican revolution, has three internal stages: Copernicus himself at stage one in the sixteenth century, with Galileo and Newton marking stages two and three in the seventeenth century. This period concludes with a mechanistic worldview, according to which nature follows a course dictated by laws that never go on a holiday and never need divine intervention or action. The Kantian period, our second, tells how some Protestants developed two languages, one for science and one for faith, untranslatable into one another. The two languages permitted peaceful coexistence between science and theology. Finally, in the contemporary period the Kantian two languages are still widely spoken, but many Protestants are pressing for consonance, for harmony to be gained through dialogue and perhaps even through mutual interaction.

Though the modern period is described by some in terms of a warfare between science and religion, this does not seem to fit the actual history. John Hedley Brooke, an Oxford historian of science, argues, "the image of perennial conflict between science and religion is inappropriate as a guiding principle" (Brooke,

1991: 33). The other extreme, to describe this period as a history of peace and tranquility, would also be misleading. Rather, Protestant history from the Reformation to the present day records a mixture of exploration and threat, advance and withdrawal, enthusiasm and doubt.

The Copernican Revolution and the Protestant Reformation

Although the Copernican revolution and the Protestant Reformation shared the same century, the sixteenth, they traveled in separate orbits with only occasional intersecting. The first subject of what would become *modern* science was astronomy, and what we now think of as the Copernican revolution took three stages to convince Europe. Nicholas Copernicus (1473–1543) at the University of Cracow, Poland, initiated the first stage. Copernicus determined he needed to reform the worldview he had inherited, namely the Ptolemaic worldview of ancient Greece. The Ptolemaic (*geocentric*) understanding held that the earth is immovable and that the sun and the other planets orbit the earth. Relying upon his own observations (without a telescope) plus his own mathematical calculations, in *De revolutionibus orbisum caelestium* (1543) Copernicus advanced the hypothesis that the sun, not the earth, stood at the center of the universe, and the earth – like the other planets – revolves around the sun. This *heliocentric* view of the universe could not be substantiated empirically, so during the sixteenth century it stood as a mere philosophical David against the Goliath of Hellenistic Ptolemaic tradition. Copernicus's argument was not yet compelling.

Turning to the other twin, Protestantism, we observe that Martin Luther (1483–1546) heard tales of Copernicus's new thought but apparently had no serious engagement. One offhand remark appears in 1539 – four years prior to the astronomer's major book – in Luther's *Table Talk* (*LW*, 54: 358) where he ponders a rumor that Copernicus believes the earth moves rather than the sun and the sky: "This would be as if somebody were riding on a cart or in a ship and imagined that he was standing still while the earth and the trees were moving. . . . This is what that fellow does who wishes to turn the whole of astronomy upside down." Luther added that it was the sun that stood still, not the earth, in the biblical description of Joshua fighting at Jericho (Joshua 10: 12). This remark did not come from Luther's own authored writing but from students who took notes. Spoken in jest, it ought not be interpreted as indicating any general opposition to science.

Central to Luther and to the other Reformers was the role played by Holy Scripture in formulating theological commitments. Although they were literalists, they were neither uncritical nor were they rigid. Luther described the Bible as the "cradle of Christ," thereby ranking scriptural texts according to their relative value for teaching a God of grace and salvation. This hermeneutic indirectly opened scriptural interpretation to new developments in science as they describe God's created order. "The astronomers are the experts from whom it is most convenient to get what may be discussed about these subjects [sun, moon, and stars]. For me it is enough that in those bodies, which are so elegant and necessary for our life, we recognize both the goodness of God and His power" (LW, 1: 41).

John Calvin (1509–64) opened the door even further by suggesting that the biblical authors could tailor their renderings to fit the mind of the reader. In his *Commentary on Genesis* he reports that Moses adapts his discourse to common usage. When common usage changes, as it does with scientific development, such a hermeneutical insight permits and encourages expanded interpretation. The overriding concern of Luther and Calvin was to see the glory and grace of God in the beauty of creation, so any hesitancy toward science was due to a fear that dispassionate research may render invisible the divine authorship.

Both Luther and Calvin could distinguish between astrology and astronomy, and both rejected astrology as idolatry while celebrating astronomy as science. Luther was both amused and annoyed by the interest in astrology exhibited by his colleague, Philip Melanchthon (1497–1560). The science of astronomy that measures the stars, as valuable as this is, cannot measure the divine creator of the stars. Beyond the aims to which "astronomy, medicine, and all natural science are intended," wrote Calvin, our "mind must rise to a somewhat higher level to look upon his glory" (*Institutes*: I.V.2).

Evidence of this nonadversarial relationship is that near the end of Luther's life, Wittenberg became a podium for Copernicanism. Lutheran Reformer Andreas Osiander (1496–1552) wrote an anonymous preface to the first edition of Copernicus's major work, *De revolutionibus*, for its 1543 publication. This preface includes the infamous line: "it is not necessary that these hypotheses should be true, or even probable; but it is enough if they provide a calculus which fits the observations." Two things are significant to note. First is the acceptance of hypothesis as a component to developing new ideas. Second, that this work has scientific value even if not true. Osiander supported the book's publication, to be sure; yet it appears he feared dogmatic rejection from church authorities. As an outspoken Reformer writing the preface, he may have sought to make it easier for Roman Catholics to adopt by deleting his own name. Just the previous year, 1542, the Inquisition had been reestablished to stamp out Lutheran influence, so by his feeble attempt at anonymity Osiander might have sought to avoid contaminating Copernicus's science with a Lutheran association. Historians debate whether Copernicus himself was aware or approving of the notorious preface.

In summary, Copernican thinking within its own century awaited further scientific confirmation before it could attain the status of irrefutable truth that it presently enjoys in modern society. The Reformers, though dimly aware and moderately interested, were preoccupied with other theological agendas, especially scriptural interpretation and the struggle with Roman Catholicism. For both Protestants and Catholics, the Reformation and Counter-Reformation became the primary lens through which any new developments could be viewed. Catholics were poised to see new developments in science as a variant on Protestant deviancy from church authority; whereas Protestants, somewhat more poised to welcome new developments, had their eyes directed toward holy writ with only furtive glances toward the starry heavens.

Galilean Copernicanism

The century following the history-shaking events of the Reformation witnessed a period of Protestant consolidation and the establishing of foundations. Aristotelian metaphysics was retrieved, and scholasticism returned to the Reformation church bodies. Within this approach theological claims became propositional. The Reformation's *sola scriptura* metamorphosed into a new emphasis on verbal inspiration and biblical inerrancy. The Bible became the source of revealed information articulated in propositional form. Even though Luther and Calvin had never questioned the Bible's divine status, seventeenth-century Protestants developed a vigorous defense of biblical authority, claiming its dictation by the Holy Spirit. By implication, not only does the Bible cradle Christ and the message of salvation, it also becomes the divinely appointed authority on matters of astronomy and the other sciences. Even though Copernican astronomy had found a home in Protestant universities, the clouds of a coming storm were beginning to form. The new science would rebel against both Ptolemy's physics and Aristotle's metaphysics; and for those who interpreted Scripture through the logic of Aristotle in conjunction with the cosmology of Ptolemy, a conflict could not be avoided.

The cultural storm approached as the Copernican revolution inserted a distance between God and the world, making it more difficult to perceive the presence of the Creator within the creation. Despite the advances in mathematical support for heliocentrism as offered by the German astronomer Johannes Kepler (1571–1630), the second stage actually begins with the Italian mathematician Galileo Galilei (1546–1642). Galileo adapted the telescope to astronomy (and in doing so discovered moons orbiting Jupiter among other fascinating things) and more importantly provided the observational evidence on behalf of Copernican heliocentrism. Galileo revived otherwise dormant attention to Copernicus with the result that Copernicus's book (*De revolutionibus*) was finally put on the index of banned books by the Catholic Church in 1616. This was followed in 1632 by an order from Pope Urban VII through the Inquisition to compel Galileo to recant, and the Italian scientist remained under house arrest until his death, the year Newton was born.

Kepler and Galileo buttressed the mathematical evidence for heliocentrism and both affirmed that God organizes the creation mathematically and that the human mind is capable of understanding divine reason. Both rejected Aristotle's notion of final causality – that is, both considered science to be the study of efficient causation in nature and not the study of final ends or purposes. Both altered the Aristotelian concept of change; no longer did change refer to transition from potentiality to actuality but rather the rearrangement of particles in time and space. Both of these Copernicans sought to reconcile Scripture with science.

However, a slight difference became historically decisive. Kepler, following Plato and rejecting Aristotle, had a mystical temperament and emphasized how God's mathematical thoughts daily structure the natural world. Galileo's temperament was more rationalistic, emphasizing how mathematics functions in a lawlike way as a mechanism for nature. For Galileo, the scientist could describe nature without reference to the divine. Natural laws provide exhaustive explanations. Though Galileo was a devout Roman Catholic believer, he set the stage for a description of nature devoid of providential action.

Galileo supported Copernican heliocentrism with telescopic observations in his major work of 1632, *Dialogo sopra i Due Massimi Sistemi del Mundo*. For him, the glorious natural world (and our world) was created by God. However, and crucially, God is the first cause only; thereafter the laws of nature describe the cause and effect relations. Although Galileo was a theist, in relegating God to first cause and removing God from active intervention, the seeds were sewn for the rise of deism.

For *sola scriptura* Protestants, as well as the Vatican hierarchy, Galileo posed a challenge with his declaration of independence on behalf of the scientific interpretation of nature. In a letter to Castelli in 1613, Galileo wrote:

> The Holy Bible and the phenomena of nature proceed alike from the divine Word, the former as the dictate of the Holy Spirit and the latter as the observant executrix of God's commands . . . Nothing physical which sense-experience sets before our eyes, or which necessary demonstrations prove to us, ought to be called in question (much less condemned) upon the testimony of biblical passages. (Dillenberger, 1960: 88)

With Galileo, the "Book of Nature" suddenly appeared on the same level as the "Book of Scripture." Nature gained an independent status to which other truth must conform.

De-centering Earth

It is frequently said that the Copernican revolution shocked European Christianity by de-centering the planet Earth and thereby de-centering the focal status of the human being within nature. There is little or no evidence to support the claim that change in cosmic geography shocked either Protestants or Roman Catholics. Far more serious than heliocentrism was the emerging empirical epistemology that would rely upon independent experimental knowledge and reject biblical authority; and still more important yet was the emerging ontology of a natural world operating mechanistically without divine participation or intervention.

Somewhat disconcerting to the religious psyche, however, was a battle internal to theology regarding many worlds. A question raised centuries prior to

Copernicus was this: did God make only one world or many? Some, arguing from an Aristotelian commitment to oneness as perfection, argued for a single world. Others looked to the stars and wondered if each might support a living world similar to Earth. Although the science of Copernicus and Galileo did not deal directly with extraterrestrial life, its impetus to deviate from Aristotle seemed to support the many worlds alternative. Toward the end of the seventeenth century books appeared in France and England espousing the "many worlds" view. They argued that the vastness of the universe dwarfs planet Earth in size and the possible existence of extraterrestrial civilizations blunts the human sense of self-importance. Yet they also retained the earlier sense of human centrality in their contention that human minds are responsible for the contemplation of this possibility and the celebration of the human mind makes it all bearable.

Despite the drama over cosmic centrality, the theological debates were themselves oriented around the contest between biblical and extrabiblical knowledge. No mention of extraterrestrial life appears in the Bible, so some Protestant extremists sought to deny the possibility. Opposing parties used speculation on other worlds as leverage for establishing the independence of scientific research in developing new knowledge. This contributed to advances in natural theology as it advocated knowledge testifying to God apart from scriptural authority. The net impact doctrinally was that creation – because the scope of our understanding of creation could now be expanded by science beyond what the Bible has bequeathed us – took center stage and sent strict biblically revealed redemption to the wings. The domain of nature became divorced from its Christological center.

Newtonian mechanism

The theater of activity moves in the latter half of the seventeenth century from the Continent to England and to the metaphor of the clock. The father of chemistry, Oxford scientist Robert Boyle (1627–91), sought to demonstrate divine design in the natural realm. Science is a religious task, Boyle argued, disclosing the admirable workmanship that God displays in the universe. Boyle likened the natural world to a clock (the cathedral clock in Strasbourg is the specific clock on Boyle's mind) with a finely engineered mechanism. The clock metaphor emphasized the orderly course of the world, an autonomous machine, with which God would occasionally tinker when performing a miracle. Miracles would not, however, call into question the normal dependable order discernible to the scientist as the laws of nature.

The revolutionary forces set in motion by Copernicus attained full victory in the work of Cambridge mathematician and physicist Sir Isaac Newton (1642–1727). Author of scientific works such as *Philosophia Naturalis Principia Mathematica* (1687), *Optics* (1704), and *Arithmetica Universalis* (1707), Newton is remembered and applauded for unifying the heavens with earth in a single mathematical concept of nature united by the laws of mechanics and the law of gravity. By invoking the idea that all bodies everywhere operate with mutual gravitation, he ascertained that the forces that keep the planets in their orbits must be reciprocally the squares of their distances from their centers. Newton applied what was known about terrestrial mechanics to the heavenly bodies and thereby erased any previously presumed gulf of difference. Derivation of such knowledge is experimental, mechanical, and mathematical.

Although likening the natural world to a well-designed clock, Newton emphasized that it needs God as the clock maker – that is, as the first cause. Further, the world clock also needs God for frequent adjustment and repair. Newton was again a theist, believing in an active God whose *concursus* with nature performed necessary tasks such as determining the actual paths of planets in their orbits. Historians of science view this as a mistake on Newton's part, as later research would provide a scientific explanation for actions he had thought to be divine. When asked by Napoleon (in an alleged conversation) about God's intervention into planetary orbits Pierre Simon, Marquis de Laplace answered, "I have no need of that hypothesis." What subsequent scientific history would carry beyond Newton is the image of nature as a universal and mathematizable mechanism, dependable and discernible, with no need for divine intervention. "Given the mechanical world and his religious faith, Newton had creatively related the two," judges John Dillenberger, "But Newton's successors saw that the two did not necessarily imply each other" (Dillenberger, 1960: 125).

In terms of the number of pages, Newton wrote more on theology than on science. Much of his theological work remains unpublished. Yet, even in his published theological treatises, Newton asserted that space in the natural world is the divine sensorium; God is present to the world while allowing the world to operate according to natural law. "The true God is a living, intelligent, and powerful Being," he writes in *Principia Mathematica*; "In him are all things contained and moved; yet neither affects the other: God suffers nothing from the motion of bodies; bodies find no resistance from the omnipresence of God. It is allowed by all that the Supreme God exists necessarily; and by the same necessity he exists always and everywhere" (Dillenberger, 1960: 123). Rather than ask how Protestants react to such science, it is better to think that this *is* Protestantism *as* science. Alexander Pope put it this way in his *Epitaph on Newton*:

> Nature and Nature's laws were hid in night;
> God said, Let Newton be! and all was Light.

Protestants share with Roman Catholics and Orthodox Christians a number of theological commitments that have fertilized the growth of natural science in the modern world. First, the monotheistic commitment implies a unity and universality to principles ordering the world. Second, the doctrine of Creation, understood as a contingent divine act – God is free and did not need to make the world the way it is let alone make the world at all – implies that we cannot deduce the nature of the world from abstract principles; rather, we can understand this world only by observation. Third, nature is positively affirmed not only because it is a witness to the marvel and wonder of its divine creator but also because it is beloved by God and therefore we human beings must treasure nature. Fourth, by affirming that secular vocations are as divine as religious vocations, Luther and Calvin indirectly inspired later Puritans and others to actively pursue scientific study as a sanctified this-worldly enterprise (Barbour, 1966: 46–9).

What was missing or inadequate in astronomy and cosmology and physics, from the Protestant point of view, was the moral dimension of human existence. Methodist champion John Wesley (1703–91) could write two treatises on the practical value of modern science, one on medicine and one on electricity, plus *A Survey of the Wisdom of God in the Creation; or a Compendium of Natural Philosophy* (1777). On the one hand, Wesley saw signs of a divine designer in the design of nature. On the other hand, Wesley voiced impatience with science when it seemed to divert attention from what is really important to human life and welfare. What really is important is to see that God created us with a moral capacity to love one another.

Miracles

The eighteenth century witnessed a battle over the theological significance of miracles. Seventeenth-century science had increased confidence in the exhaustive order of cause and effect in the natural world, and the essence of miracle came to be understood as a divine intervention that temporarily disrupted the order. In a miracle God inserts a divine cause into the otherwise autonomous nexus of secondary causes. The first cause that created the order of nature *ex nihilo* in the first place returns in a miracle to disrupt it for a providential end.

John Locke (1632–1704), the English philosopher who authored *Essay Concerning Human Understanding* (1690) and other political works influential on the development of American democracy, was a contemporary of Newton. In *The Reasonableness of Christianity as Delivered in the Scriptures* (1695) and *A Discourse on Miracles* (1704), Locke analyzed miracles and marshaled biblical accounts into a rational defense that Jesus is the messiah. Eyewitness testimony, in particular, to Jesus's miracle-working power was subjected to review and found reliable. Miracles, in short, testify to the credibility of Christian faith.

In his *A Short and Easy Method with the Deists* (1698), Charles Leslie (1650–1722) offered three rules to establish the credibility of witnesses to miracles: first, the event must be subject to outward senses such as seeing and hearing; second, a miracle must be public if it is to be considered verifiable; and third, the miracle must result in new customs or practices to demonstrate its social impact. Later Protestants added a fourth rule: the miracle must lead to a willingness on the part of Christian believers to suffer persecution for the faith. These remain in usage even today.

Theologians of this era believed miracles were rare. Some Protestants were willing to limit the miracle-working era to the biblical period, whereas Roman

Catholics extended it to contemporary times through the miracle-working powers of the saints. Of significance here is that Protestants presumed that testimonies of miracles contributed to the rational credibility of Christianity; and by limiting miracles to rare events that disrupt the natural order, they could rely upon that order as well for testimony to God's creative design.

A philosophical revolution prosecuted by David Hume (1711–76) reversed the meaning of what it meant to be rational. To be rational, from Hume forward, is to affirm that the order of nature remains exhaustively intact and further to deny, by definition, miracles. In his "Essay on Miracles" within the larger work, *Philosophical Essays Concerning Human Understanding* (1751), Hume delimits the concept of experience to experience of what is lawful in nature: "It is experience only, which gives authority to testimony; and it is the same experience, which assures us of the laws of nature . . . We may establish it as a maxim, that no human testimony can have such force as to prove a miracle, and make it a just foundation for any such system of religion" (Hume, 1962: 132–3). In other words, we use experience to establish the laws of nature – how could we then use experience to establish the violation of those laws? Due to this tie between experience and the ubiquity of natural law, we must eliminate miracles as something rationally knowable. Without miracles, post-Hume theologians were left with only the world's original design as testimony to the divine responsibility toward nature.

From Kant to the Two Languages

There are two kinds of reason, not one, said German philosopher Immanuel Kant (1724–1804), namely reason applying to the starry heavens above and reason applying to the moral law within. What we know as the causal law in nature (every natural event has a natural cause) is not constrained by the objective world, he says in *Kritik der reinen Vernunft* (*The Critique of Pure Reason*, 1781); rather, human consciousness is so constituted that it must interpret empirical observations in terms of cause and effect. Human reasoning, in short, results from the synthesis of experience with the external world plus *a priori* structures such as space and time that come from the human mind. Because cause and effect reasoning is limited to our understanding of the external *physical* (phenomenal) world, Kant concludes that we cannot have knowledge *of the same type* for three *theological* (and therefore noumenal) ideas: God, freedom, and immortality. Decisive to note is that Kant splits human knowing. Disciples of Kant could no longer speak of noumenal realities such as God on the same plane with phenomenal realities as observed by scientific research.

Even though divine matters could no longer be known as we know physical objects, Kant could justify speaking of God, freedom, and immortality by turning to the moral law within human awareness. The stern universal (if rational) voice of conscience, he argued, bespeaks a transcendent source. The sense of duty implies that we are free (else fated and not able to fulfill conscience) and that immortality is promised (else why bother?). In his *Religion innerhalb der Grenzen der blossen Vernunft* (*Religion Within the Limits of Reason Alone*) (1793), Kant stressed that shouldering moral responsibility is an end in itself, even if it needed the noumenal for its initial foundation. Kant relied upon the moral sense within, not the testimony of miracles from without.

Kant marks a fork in the rivers, one flowing toward Liberal Protestantism and the other toward Conservative Protestantism. The liberal stream took a turn to human subjectivity with Friedrich Schleiermacher (1768–1834) and Albrecht Ritschl (1822–89) leading to the nineteenth-century cultivation of a morally conscious Christianity bent on transforming society into the kingdom of God. The roles of faith and reason were reversed. Whereas, for Locke, reason provided the basis for faith, liberal Protestant faith gave rise to its own reasoning. Instead of miracles producing faith, faith produced miracles as a form of interpretation of otherwise natural physical events. The religious language of liberal Protestants shied away from speaking of the objective world studied by science and instead turned to the subjective sphere of consciousness, faith, and values. What we know as the distinction between right and wrong, good and evil, faith and nonfaith, became a subjective overlay superimposed on an otherwise valueless nature studied by a value-free science.

Conservative Protestants were left to hold on to a divine design objectively manifested in the natural realm and discoverable by science. Nonetheless, conservatives also feared that the direction being taken by modern science buttressed by Kantian philosophy would lead to atheism. "They were remarkably right," says Dillenberger, "But their own course of action was more shrouded in defensive and rear-guard ways of thinking than in any creative advance through the problems" (Dillenberger, 1960: 186).

The language of fact versus the language of meaning

The Kantian divide between two types of reason marks the next stage in this history, not only for Protestantism but also virtually for all of Western culture. Many commentators liken the divide to speaking two separate languages, with science speaking the "language of fact" and religion speaking the "language of meaning." Science deals with objective reality, whereas religion deals with subjective interpretations of reality. Science is concerned with the physical, whereas religion is concerned with the spiritual. Science asks questions about penultimate reality, whereas religion asks about ultimate reality. The most prominent scientists, such as Albert Einstein, have held to the two-language view: science speaks of objective facts whereas religion speaks of subjective values, and society needs both.

Even belligerent advocates of atheism (based upon scientific materialism or secular humanism) hold to the two-language scheme. This includes Marxists and Maoists. Science and religion speak separate languages, contend spokespersons such as mathematician Bertrand Russell, astronomer Carl Sagan, and biologist Richard Dawkins, and though science speaks truthfully about reality, religious language speaks only of imaginary fictions, of pseudo-knowledge. To be authentic and democratic, society should live exclusively according to the language of science and according to humanistic values based upon the materialist worldview.

Twentieth-century neo-orthodox Protestant theologians such as Karl Barth, Paul Tillich, Rudolf Bultmann, Reinhold Niebuhr, and Langdon Gilkey have vociferously defended the two-language view. Gilkey spoke for the era while taking the stand in a 1981 courtroom in Little Rock, Arkansas, as expert witness against the teaching of creation as a scientific subject in the public schools. He testified that science asks "how?" while religion asks "why?" Science deals with objective or public knowing of *proximate* origins, whereas religion and its theological articulation deals with existential or personal knowing of *ultimate* origins (Gilkey, 1985: 49–52, 108–13). What Gilkey advocates is that a healthy society speaks both languages.

It is important to note that the two-language view emerges as a modern cultural phenomenon, fully embraced by the liberal Protestant tradition and its progeny, the neo-orthodox and related schools of thought. Conservative Protestants have also absorbed the two-language view from culture and render it limited support, but conservative theologians are still more likely to think of theology as speaking about objective reality. Hence, conservatives are more likely to see scientific and theological languages as commensurate (Murphy, 1996: 58).

It is always a mistake to presume that liberal Protestantism is proscience and conservative Protestantism is antiscience. The distinction lies rather in whether or not one can speak of God, moral freedom, and immortality along with miracles in objective terms, in the same kind of language that science speaks.

Evolution versus fundamentalism, creationism, and intelligent design

With the publication of the *Origin of the Species* in 1859, the match was lit for a fiery controversy that has been burning down to the present. To explain variation and change in species, Charles Darwin (1809–82) enunciated the key principle of evolution: "natural selection" or "survival of the fittest." Natural selection explains *post hoc* the evolutionary success of those species now in existence compared to those species that have become extinct. When the wide variety of individual differences within a species becomes a factor in adapting to changing environmental circumstances, and when some adaptations are selected for and others selected against, large-scale Malthusian selection occurs with the surviving remainder determining the heritable traits of a new species. The last half of the twentieth century added the concept of genetic mutation to explain heredity with greater precision, resulting in the neo-Darwinian synthesis of natural selection with genetic mutation. The DNA that survives is considered a competitive success, the victor in nature's relentless and impersonal struggle to determine who will be more fit.

Darwinism has received mixed reviews among Protestants. Fundamentalists and evangelicals, for whom science and religion still speak the same language, are quite likely to see conflict. Liberal Protestants following the Kantian tradition of two languages see no conflict; they are more likely to either ignore evolutionary theory or in some rare cases incorporate evolution into Christian anthropology.

Evolution appeared to be a challenge to fundamentalists for whom authority, if not inerrancy, of Scripture is paramount. Bishop Samuel Wilberforce (1805–73) of Oxford is remembered for saying that Darwin was guilty of limiting God's glory in creation and that "the principle of natural selection is absolutely incompatible with the word of God" (White, 1896: I, 70). At the John T. Scopes "monkey trial" in Dayton, Tennessee, July 10–21, 1925, William Jennings Bryan (1860–1925) defended the authority of the Genesis account of creation against biological Darwinism, and defended Christian values and democracy against social Darwinism. Much less absolutely, American fundamentalist Reuben A. Torrey (1856–1928) conceded that a person could "believe thoroughly in the absolute infallibility of the Bible and still be an evolutionist of a certain type" (Numbers, 1992: 39).

Fundamentalists are not alone in providing a Protestant response to Darwinism. Scientific creationists and advocates of "intelligent design" oppose Darwinian theory; other Protestants have embraced Darwinian theory and even see themselves as evolutionary theists. Whereas fundamentalism appeals to the authority and even inerrancy of the Bible, scientific creationism and intelligent design appeal to scientific arguments against the common descent of humanity from prehuman life forms and for restricting natural explanations to natural factors. "Young Earth Creationists" at the Institute for Creation Research in El Cajon, California, for example, hold that the earth was created pretty much as we find it less than 10,000 years ago, and that at the moment of creation God fixed the species. Creationists can accept microevolution within a species, but they reject macroevolution from one species to another.

Intelligent design advocates are less concerned about the age of the earth and more concerned about explaining how one species surpasses another in macroevolution. They emphasize that emergent life forms are irreducibly complex – that is, complex life forms could not result merely from incremental change through natural selection. What is required for new evolutionary developments, they say, is "intelligent design" by a transcendent intelligent designer. The struggle between Darwinism and intelligent design is the struggle between a strictly natural explanation and a theological explanation, and both are claimed to be scientific. Fundamentalists, creationists, and intelligent design proponents all agree that naturalistic ethics based upon Darwinian principles such as survival of the fittest corrupt social morals by approving brute selfishness, *laissez faire* capitalism, and "might makes right" nationalism.

Other contemporary Protestants of the hypothetical consonance mind (discussed below) work to incorporate the anthropology of evolutionary theory into their theology. Arthur Peacocke adds *creatio continua* to *creatio ex nihilo* in his doctrine of creation, and argues that God has established a dialectic between law and chance by which the world operates. Evolution is the history resulting from God's gifts of law and chance. "God is the Immanent Creator creating in and through the processes of the natural order" (Peacocke, 1993: 104).

The Contemporary Question of Consonance

Speaking two languages has become less than intellectually satisfying for many contemporary Protestants and their Roman Catholic colleagues. If there is only one God and one world, then there must be only one truth. Science at its best and theology at its best seek only one thing, the honest truth about reality. Furthermore, both science and theology are realistic – that is, both presume the existence of a reality to which their propositions refer. To be sure, neither advocates a *naive realism*, wherein what you see is what you get; but both operate with variants of *critical realism*, according to which some things cannot be known directly but can be pursued indirectly. Neither God nor electrons can be known directly, yet critical realism asserts that they are "there." Even though some criticize critical realism for its alleged foundationalism (Murphy), others believe "critical realism offers considerable potential as a theoretical bridge between the two disciplines" (McGrath, 1998: 164). With such things in mind, many scholars are looking beyond warfare and even beyond the two-language model to dialogue. "The imagery of 'dialogue' is thus vastly to be preferred to the unhelpful (and frankly rather outdated) image of 'warfare'" (McGrath, 1998: 28).

In the final quarter of the twentieth century the Notre Dame University historian of science Ernan McMullin began asking if we might be ready for exploring greater consonance between scientific and theological claims about the world. What has developed among many Protestant theologians is a methodological agenda of *hypothetical consonance*. It is hypothetical, as it seeks to test the waters of both science and faith, to see if they are the right temperature for some degree of mixing.

The term "consonance" in the strong sense means accord or harmony. Full accord or harmony between scientific and theological claims does not yet exist; they still sing different melodies. Yet consonance in a weak sense appears to be progressive and fruitful. In the weak sense consonance is put forth hypothetically, identifying common domains of "question-asking." Recent discoveries and theoretical advances in fields such as quantum physics, Big Bang cosmology, and thermodynamics, for example, have raised questions within science of transcendence, about a divine ground to the physical universe. The God-question rises up out of scientific reasoning itself (Davies, 1983: ix). Many theologians are readying themselves for dialogue, for conversation with scientists on the hypothesis that in the future further consonance may be uncovered (Peters, 1998: 18–19).

Robert John Russell (b. 1946), an ordained minister in the United Church of Christ who holds a doctorate in physics, founded the Center for Theology and the Natural Sciences at the Graduate Theological Union in 1981. Russell has proposed that whenever we discover consonance between a theological and a scientific claim, we will also find an element of dissonance closely related. For example, the finite age of the universe according to Big Bang cosmology (the theory that the entire universe began with a bang some 15 billion years ago) is consonant with the theological claim that creation is temporally finite. Yet the open Big Bang model pictures the universe as infinite in size, making it dissonant with the theological assumption that creation is spatially finite. Russell has further proposed that the presence of dissonance and its relation to consonance should drive the discussion further in creative ways; in this case, by expanding the concept of finitude scientifically and theologically.

This agenda reflects the central tenet of Russell's program: to promote the creative mutual interaction of science and theology. He advocates a "two way interaction between scientific and theological research programs" (Russell, Clayton, Wegter-McNelly, and Polkinhorne, 2001: ii), meaning that when research is taken up by theology it takes science into consideration; and it means that at some point we should expect theology to suggest fruitful areas of research for science to pursue. Nancey Murphy, who teaches Christian Philosophy at Fuller Theological Seminary in Pasadena, California, measures both science and theology on the basis of whether or not they foster progressive research programs – that is, do they yield fruitful new knowledge or expanded understanding? (Murphy, 1990: 85–7).

At the beginning of the third millennium, we find a number of leaders in the growing dialogue between science and faith to be hybrids, individuals with advanced accomplishments in both Christian theology and natural science. John Polkinghorne of Cambridge University is an ordained Anglican priest with a widely respected reputation as a researcher in physics. Recently retired Oxford University professor Arthur R. Peacocke, also an Anglican priest, is a trained biologist. Peacocke has organized the Society for Ordained Scientists. Celia E. Deane-Drummond has degrees in both genetics and theology as credentials for her position as Professor in Theology and the Biological Sciences at Chester College of Higher Education. Alister E. McGrath, Professor of Historical Theology at the University of Oxford, holds a doctorate in molecular biology. Physicist and theologian Ian G. Barbour, now emeritus Professor at Carleton College in Minnesota, is widely known for classifying patterns of interaction between science and religion and for proposing two-way traffic on a bridge of Whiteheadian metaphysics. Philip Hefner, a systematic theologian and former director of the Zygon Center for Science and Religion in Chicago, though not a hybrid, has pioneered an extensive integration of Christian anthropology with biological and cultural evolution.

At least two theologians in the dialogue would like to see theology considered as scientific. Wolfhart Pannenberg, emeritus Professor of Systematic Theology at Munich, contends that theological statements are constructed as hypotheses. Because they cannot be confirmed directly by examination of the subject matter to which they refer, namely God, theological assertions must be confirmed only indirectly according to their ability to illuminate reality. This renders theological commitments provisional, subject to further confirmation. The ultimate confirmation of our beliefs about God, then, will come eschatologically when we, as St Paul says, see God face to face.

Thomas Forsyth Torrance, who taught Systematic Theology at the University of Edinburgh from 1952 until 1979, argues that theology is scientific (actually meta-scientific) because it is objective due to its subject "God." Just as scientists must remain humble before the truths of nature as they are revealed through experimentation, and be willing to change their mind, so also must theologians render themselves humble and obedient before the revelation of God. Like Karl Barth (his teacher), Torrance begins with God's self-revelation to us; and this constitutes God's objectivity. Human subjectivity does not manufacture belief in God; rather, it responds to God as God comes to us in revelation. "Scientific theology is active engagement in that cognitive relation to God in obedience to the demands of His reality and self-giving" (Torrance, 1969: v).

Turning to the evangelicals, the American Scientific Affiliation (ASA) was founded in 1941 to serve practicing scientists in the evangelical Christian community. Its membership consists of people with degrees in one or another natural science, and it seeks to wrestle with the intellectual problems posed by the dialogue between science and faith. These members pledge "as stewards of God's creation, to use science and technology for the good of humanity and the whole world" (Hearn, 1997: 21).

References

Barbour, Ian G. (1966). *Issues in Science and Religion*. New York: Harper.
Brooke, John Hedley (1991). *Science and Religion: Some Historical Perspectives*. Cambridge, UK: Cambridge University Press.
Calvin, John (1960). *Institutes of the Christian Religion*, trans. Ford Lewis Battles, ed. John T. McNeill, 2 vols. Louisville, KY: Westminster/John Knox Press.
Davies, Paul (1983). *God and the New Physics*. New York: Simon and Schuster.
Dillenberger, John (1960). *Protestant Thought and Natural Science*. New York: Doubleday.
Gilkey, Langdon (1985). *Creationism on Trial: Evolution and God at Little Rock*. San Francisco: Harper.
Hearn, Walter R. (1997). *Being a Christian in Science*. Downers Grove, IL: InterVarsity Press.
Hume, David (1962). *On Human Nature and the Understanding*, ed. Antony Flew. London: Collier Macmillan.
Luther, Martin (1955–86). *Luther's Works (LW)*, American edn, ed. Jaroslav Pelikan and Helmut T. Lehmann, 55 vols. St. Louis and Minneapolis: Concordia and Fortress.

McGrath, Alister E. (1998). *The Foundations of Dialogue in Science and Religion*. Oxford: Blackwell.

Murphy, Nancey (1990). *Theology in the Age of Scientific Reasoning*. Ithaca, NY: Cornell.

Murphy, Nancey (1996). *Beyond Liberalism and Fundamentalism: How Modern and Postmodern Philosophy Set the Agenda*. Valley Forge, PA: Trinity.

Numbers, Ronald L. (1992). *The Creationists*. Berkeley: University of California Press.

Peacocke, Arthur R. (1993). *Theology for a Scientific Age*. Minneapolis: Fortress.

Peters, Ted (ed.) (1998). *Science and Theology: The New Consonance*. Boulder, CO: Westview.

Russell, Robert John, Clayton, Philip, Wegter-McNelly, Kirk, and Polkinghorne, John (eds.) (2001). *Quantum Mechanics: Scientific Perspectives on Divine Action*, vol. 5. Vatican City State and Berkeley, CA: Vatican Observatory and CTNS.

Torrance, Thomas F. (1969). *Theological Science*. Oxford: Oxford University Press.

White, Andrew Dickson (1896). *A History of the Warfare of Science with Theology*, 2 vols. New York: Dover.

Further Reading

Barbour, Ian G. (1990). *Religion in an Age of Science*. San Francisco: Harper.

Deanne-Drummond, Celia E. (2001). *Biology and Theology Today*. London: SCM Press.

Hefner, Philip (1993). *The Human Factor*. Minneapolis: Fortress.

Pannenberg, Wolfhart (1976). *Theology and the Philosophy of Science*. Louisville, KY: Westminster/John Knox.

Pannenberg, Wolfhart (1993). *Toward a Theology of Nature*, ed. Ted Peters. Louisville, KY: Westminster/John Knox.

Peters, Ted (2003). *Science, Theology, and Ethics*. Aldershot, UK: Ashgate.

Polkinghorne, John (1998). *Science and Theology*. London: SPCK.

CHAPTER 30

Protestantism and Liberalism

Mark D. Chapman

The primary focus of liberalism is simply the supreme importance of liberty: 'by definition a liberal is a man who believes in liberty' (Cranston, 1967: 459). There are obvious comparisons to be made with the defining moment of Protestantism in Luther's *The Freedom of a Christian* of 1520: 'A Christian is a perfectly free Lord of all, subject to none' (Dillenberger, 1961: 53). Yet, for Luther, liberty was conferred from God for a life of faith and action, but rooted solely in God and in no capacity of the human being. Against Erasmus, Luther could write: 'There can be no "free-will" in man, or angel or in any creature' (Dillenberger, 1961: 203). Just as in Luther the freedom of the individual is a complex idea, so 'Because different men at different times have meant different things by liberty, "liberalism" is correspondingly ambiguous' (Cranston, 1967: 459).

Negative Liberalism

In his classic defence of liberalism John Stuart Mill saw liberty as resting in the sovereignty of the individual: any restriction on human freedom is at the very least questionable. Liberalism thus came to emphasize the liberties of individuals against the authority of the state (Mill, 1962: 135). The state functioned solely to preserve such liberties, often against the tyranny of the majority. The self is thus prior to any conception of society: 'Each person is to have an equal right to the most extensive total system of equal basic liberties compatible with a similar system for all' (Rawls, 1971: 302). Liberalism in this sense is primarily a *negative* concept which questions all forms of governmental action except those which ensure the possibility of liberty (Berlin, 1969). The word 'liberalism' was first used in 1810 of a Spanish political party modelling itself on the British tradition of tolerance which emerged from the British Glorious Revolution of

1688. John Locke's philosophical defence of this settlement (together with Montesquieu's defence of the separation of powers) was later a major influence on the American Constitution, with its legal protection of individual rights and democratic authority against monarchy and oligarchy.

The Enlightenment

The background to these political developments lies in the Enlightenment, with its challenge to inherited ideas of authority in all spheres of life, including the religious. No institution, however hallowed, was completely beyond the scope of criticism. In his classic formulation Immanuel Kant wrote: 'Our age is . . . an age of criticism, and to criticism everything must submit' (Kant, 1929: 9). It was primarily on account of his critical understanding of freedom and the importance of the self-legislating individual that philosophers and theologians came to see Kant as the 'philosopher of Protestantism' *par excellence* (Paulsen, 1899). This model of liberalism was associated with the notion of a 'civil society', where a critical public sphere was acknowledged quite distinct from the state (Habermas, 1962). Throughout eighteenth-century Europe, but particularly in Britain and in parts of Germany, a dynamic process of communication developed which resulted in the proliferation of organizations devoted to critical thought, together with ever increasing levels of personal correspondence: liberalism was identified with open communication and dialogue (Bödeker, 1988; van Dülmen, 1992; Porter, 2000). Some saw this critical process as closely bound up with the Protestant idea of freedom: the liberty of the individual was Luther's great triumph. For instance, the theologian L. T. Spittler wrote in 1782: 'on the whole we have achieved an extraordinary amount through this revolution of the last thirty years, and it will probably one day be characterised as one of the most radiant periods of the history of the Lutheran church' (cited in Vierhaus, 1985: 18, my translation). In contrast to France, where the Roman Catholic church was resistant to liberty, in England, and to a lesser extent in Germany, liberal ideas were often conveyed by the clergy. In turn, a great deal of literature motivated by religious concerns and often in the vernacular was produced for an educated non-specialist public (Möller, 1986: 268–80; Wehler, 1987: 303–12; Porter, 2000: 96–129).

In the eighteenth century the effects of this critical 'negative' liberalism were strongly felt in theology with the so-called 'Neology' which originated in Halle, a centre of the German Enlightenment. Johann Salomo Semler used the term *liberalis theologia* as early as 1774 to describe the historical investigation of the New Testament unconstrained by dogmatic presuppositions (Graf, 2002). As with Kant, Semler looked to a gradual emancipation from the tutelage of the past towards the glorious liberty of the rational kingdom in contrast to the dominant ecclesiasticism of the past. The political currents of such a theology, with its threats to the confessionalist state, made some critical liberal theologians, among them W. M. L. de Wette (1780–1849), into champions of the freedom of speech against the repressive measures of the Restoration period which followed the defeat of Napoleon.

This German example indicates the close connections between religious and political authority in the Protestant states of Europe. Where there was a widespread acceptance of liberalism in the political sphere, as in England, there was frequently a toleration of liberal ideas in the church and in theology. For the most part, however, Protestant churches and theologians in Germany were opposed to enlightened ideas, seeing themselves as defenders of a supernaturally based absolutism in both church and state. Among Protestants, although critical liberalism was occasionally regarded as a development towards the flourishing of free individuals, it was more often understood as seditious and revolutionary.

The German Idea of Freedom

Liberalism was not solely restricted, however, to such a critical negative understanding. As with Luther, many thinkers saw an inherent problem of anarchy and antinomianism in the unbridled liberty of the individual. The long memory of the Thirty Years' War, and the suspicion of political anarchy and terror which emerged in the French Revolution, meant that individual liberty itself was a decidedly questionable ideal in the German states. In this context, the figure of F. D. E. Schleiermacher (1768–1834) is pivotal, although he never used the word 'liberal' to refer to his theology: if he was a liberal at all, his liberalism was of a very different kind from that of the earlier negative liberals of the Enlightenment. Schleiermacher, like many of his contemporaries (most obviously Hegel), developed a more 'positive' understanding of the relationships between the individual and society: to flourish or to be authentically free the individual needed to be integrated into a concrete social whole. Such an idea of freedom was later called the 'German Idea of Freedom' (Troeltsch, 1925: 80–107), although it has analogues elsewhere. Furthermore, especially in his later writings, Schleiermacher displayed a greater respect for the ecclesiastical tradition than many of his enlightened predecessors: not unreasonably his followers used the term 'mediating theology' to describe their position. Methodological criticism was far from the heart of Schleiermacher's mature theological system.

After the failure of the liberal revolutions of 1848–9 a group of prominent theologians founded the German Protestant Union in 1863, which again exemplifies this more positive understanding of liberalism: true liberty for the individual required realization in a social universal. One of the principal theologians of this movement was Richard Rothe (1799–1867), who, while criticizing the alliance of Lutheran orthodoxy and the police state, sought at the same time to establish a culturally homogeneous national liberalism in both church and state. While he endeavoured to make Christianity attractive to those who had been alienated from the church, he was no defender of pluralism. 'Protestant freedom' (where Luther was regarded as a national hero) was often developed in opposition to the internationalism of Roman Catholicism and the cosmopolitanism of Judaism. Other theologians adopted a similar model: for instance, the post-Hegelian theologian, Otto Pfleiderer demanded a 'Germanization of Christianity'. At the beginning of the twentieth century, as liberal theologians began to analyse the crisis of modernity in terms of the fragmentation and the relativization of values, so some moved towards ideologies of a 'cultural synthesis'. Indeed 'liberal theology' often functioned as the religious counterpart to a nationalist ideology. 'Individualism' was often little more than a term of abuse: the quest for community following the collapse of traditional patterns of social organization was often made at the expense of individuality (Tönnies, 1988).

In German academic theology in the imperial period after 1870 the relationships between liberalism and Protestantism are equally complex: although he refused the term 'liberal', Albrecht Ritschl (1822–89), professor of theology at Göttingen from 1864, adopted a Kantian epistemology, but also tried to show how God and the world were to be combined in an all-embracing system. Post-Ritschlian theologians, misleadingly labelled by their detractors as 'culture Protestants' (Graf, 1986; Hübinger, 1994; Rupp, 1977), were often divided over the nature of freedom. Wilhelm Herrmann (1846–1922), for instance, moved towards a position of extreme dualism, where the freedom of faith seemed to exert no influence over the world, whereas Ernst Troeltsch (1865–1923) continued in the Kantian tradition, displaying a critical engagement with modernity and also retaining a sense of the importance of the autonomous individual (Chapman, 2001a).

Despite the obvious failure of conceptions of positive liberty during the First World War, when many 'liberal theologians' associated themselves with the national cause, many of the leading culture Protestants during the 1920s were explicitly prepared to identify themselves as political liberals, defending a more negative view of liberty, primarily on account of the hostility shown towards pluralism from many different quarters, and a belated recognition of the dangers of the German Idea of Freedom. Leading figures such as Martin Rade and Adolf von Harnack defended human rights, autonomy, and freedom of conscience and their political expression in the Weimar Constitution. Some, including Troeltsch, even participated in the Weimar system as active politicians.

Karl Barth's vigorous post-war polemic failed to distinguish between types of liberty, regarding culture Protestantism as an ideological legitimation of an anti-religious secularism with its origins in the Enlightenment (Barth, 1961: 15). This caricature overlooks many of the subtleties and the differences between pre-First World War scholars, and has also meant that the history of liberal theology in the later part of the twentieth century is only just beginning to receive critical attention (Wolfes, 1999). What is important to stress is that both positive and negative forms of liberalism were defended by 'liberal theologians'. Although they were all interested in the possibilities for Christianity within the constraints of modernity, this did not necessarily make them 'liberals' in the negative or critical sense: Troeltsch remained the exception. Other 'liberal theologians' were very far from liberal, failing to defend human rights, individualism and pluralism. Similarly 'historical relativism' was often seen simply as something which needed to be 'overcome' in a vision of 'the whole'. 'Liberal theology' was thus often just as anti-pluralist as the German state. The critical theories of the Enlightenment dissolved into theologies and philosophies of total visions (whether 'positive liberal' or confessionalist), where autonomy was quickly absorbed into an anti-pluralist nationalism. With only a few exceptions (see Rendtorff, 1982) a critical Kantian form of liberalism has been virtually absent from the German theological scene since the First World War. For the most part, however, the Protestant churches have been more willing to accept the liberal values enshrined in the Federal Republic.

England

In England the fate of liberalism was very different from that of Germany: most importantly, there was a far greater degree of pluralism and toleration than in most of the rest of Europe. The values of negative liberalism presented less of a political threat. Despite a strong deist and free-thinking tradition which maintained an ambivalent relationship with the established church, the Church of England (which was usually regarded as Protestant), like the governments it served, displayed a limited degree of acceptance of Enlightenment ideas. The 'latitudinarian' tradition of the Cambridge Platonists continued into the eighteenth century, allowing for ecclesiastical support of scientific and critical activity. The study of theology was far less professionalized than its counterpart in Germany, which allowed clergy to become involved in many other activities and to associate with other thinkers. The 'Broad Church' tradition which dominated the Anglican establishment in the nineteenth century was thus more inclined towards a defence of a negative view of liberty (although most religious thinkers attacked Benthamite utilitarianism) (Reardon, 1995). Through the nineteenth century, political liberalism also found its defenders among the many branches of Protestant non-conformity (Cowling, 2001).

Central to the Broad Church understanding of liberty was the thought of Samuel Taylor Coleridge (1772–1834), particularly his *Aids to Reflection* (1825) which associated religion with the rights of critical self-government animated by a sense of 'manly energy' (aretē). The autonomy of the individual was combined with the notion of education into truth. Following this lead, in the early years of the nineteenth century there was a great respect for an educated self-regulation in all affairs: positive freedom was established by a process of critical education which moderated aimless individualism. Most of the leading figures of the Broad Church shared with Kant the view that 'human beings can only become human beings by education' (Kant, 1963: 17). Coleridge left his mark on a whole generation of scholars in Cambridge, and through figures like Julius Hare (1795–1855) he was deeply influential on F. D. Maurice (1805–72). For Maurice, the comprehensive national church existed to 'tell the world of its true Centre, . . . to maintain the order of the nation and the order of the family' (Maurice, 1891: I, 251). Both national church and national education functioned as a check on the selfishness of the prevalent individualism. Thomas Arnold (1795–1842) propagated a similar method through his influential reforms at Rugby School and in his ideal of a national church made up of critical thinkers: 'The "Idea" of my life [is] . . . constructing a truly national and Christian Church, and a truly national and Christian system of education' (Stanley, 1844: II, 12). Under Arnold's influence theological liberalism again came to be associated, through educational reformers and theologians like Benjamin Jowett (1817–93) and Frederick Temple (1821–1902), with the enlightened pedagogical ideal of growth into human maturity. There was no right 'in all exercise of the intellectual powers . . . to stop short of any limit but that which nature, that is, the decree of the Creator, has imposed on us. . . . If we have made mistakes . . . the enlightenment of the understanding is the best means to show us our folly' (Temple, 1860: 57–8).

Christian truth was thus no special knowledge apprehended through God's direct communication, but was known in the same way as anything else, and open to the same means of verification. Critical study posed no great threat to the Christian religion, which meant that many English liberals sought to reconcile the claims of the natural sciences with those of religion (see Temple, 1884). The critical method was also applied to the study of history, which marks one of the major achievements of English scholarship in the nineteenth century, but also displays a nationalist positive form of freedom. Latent within the liberal Anglican idea of history pioneered by Arnold, H. H. Milman, and A. P. Stanley (Burrow, 1981) was a tension between a strong sense of cultural superiority and a defence of pluralism and tolerance (see Creighton, 1985). Not surprisingly, many conservative critics, most prominently John Henry Newman, regarded Anglican liberalism as a nationalist heresy (Thomas, 1991).

In the early twentieth century, as Victorian complacency began to be questioned, so many liberals under the influence of T. H. Green developed a more philosophically refined understanding of positive freedom, which frequently resorted to Hegelian idealism to defend the integration of the personality in the social whole (Bosanquet, 1923). The New Liberalism of J. A. Hobson and L. T. Hobhouse sought to replace the old liberalism, which they saw as increasingly individualistic, with the positive freedoms of a strong state (see Hobson, 1909; Chapman, 2001b). A strange hybrid of the educational optimism stemming from Thomas Arnold combined with the positive freedoms of New Liberalism in the theology of William Temple (Nicholls, 1989: 61–87), which remained dominant in the English theological and political scene until the rise of economic neo-liberalism in the 1980s. Such positive liberalism, however, was frequently aligned with the socialism of the British Labour Party. In recent years the negative liberalism of the post-war human rights legislation has been questioned by the positive freedoms associated with the communitarianism and paternalism of some recent political theory (Chapman, 2000).

The USA

The relationships between liberalism and protestantism are different still in the United States. The official political ideology of the founders embraced constitutionalism and human rights, promoting a rigid separation of church and state: negative liberty was enshrined in a Bill of Rights. This meant that the dominant Protestant religion tended to be regarded as a private matter (Marty, 1970). Nevertheless, through the nineteenth century many theologians, initially those working in parish ministry rather than teaching in seminaries, were influenced by European liberal thought (Dorrien, 2001). Horace Bushnell (1802–76), like his English counterparts, was deeply influenced by Coleridge, focusing both on the metaphorical character of religious language as well as the nurture and growth of the Christian life. Although he provoked much controversy, his theology is more akin to Schleiermacher's mediating theology than to the rigorous criticism of Kantian liberalism: he nevertheless sought to make connections between theology and the politics of civil rights.

Despite frequent controversy, a moderate liberalism, which sought to embrace human reason and a scientific study of history, spread throughout the country after the 1880s. It gradually moved into the seminaries, including Andover in Massachusetts, which saw the rise of 'progressive orthodoxy' from 1885, and Union in New York under A. C. McGiffert (1861–1933) and William Adams Brown (1865–1943). This period also saw the development, under Washington Gladden of Columbus, Ohio (1836–1918), of more political understandings of theological liberalism: the language of negative liberalism began to enter theological discourse, although many theologians shared the dominant cultural and national superiority of the time (Dorrien, 2001: 409–12).

The Chicago Divinity School was founded in 1895 on the principle of a close interaction between sociology, ethics and theology in the attempt to ameliorate social problems: social and political progress became central to the curriculum. The leading figure, Shailer Mathews (1865–1941) claimed to derive his ethical ideal of social individuality from the teachings of a Christ who legitimized the fraternal (and evolutionary) goals of the Christian idea of positive freedom, against the individualism of much American Protestantism: 'The expanding Christian society . . . will consist of groups of individuals each possessed of the same spirit and method of life as that taught by their Master' (Mathews, 1895–6: 424–5). Moving in a similar direction, Walter Rauschenbusch (1861–1918), professor at Rochester Theological Seminary, formulated an explicitly Social Gospel which focused on the Kingdom of God 'as a great synthesis in which the regeneration of the spirit, the enlightenment of the intellect, the development of the body, the reform of the political life, the sanctification of industrial life and all that concerns the redemption of humanity shall be embraced' (Rauschenbusch, 1984: 76). Like other liberals, Rauschenbusch, who was prepared to engage in the detailed study of economics and sociology, sought after the unity of thought and action in a synthesis aimed at social and political regeneration (Minus, 1988). In the United States such liberal solutions were often marked by a naïve progressive optimism and were subjected to critique during the 1920s and 1930s, particularly after the Depression. Partly under the influence of European dialectical theologians, many erstwhile liberals, most importantly the Niebuhr brothers, re-invigorated orthodox teaching on sin, questioning the Social Gospel and its idealization of the American Progressivist ideology: 'A God without wrath, brought men without sin, into a kingdom without judgment through the ministrations of a Christ without a cross' (Niebuhr, 1937: 173).

Prospects

The relationships between liberalism and Protestantism are so closely bound up with developments in political theory that it is difficult to make any predictions for the future. On the one hand, political globalization has seen the rapid spread of liberal democracies and human rights legislation throughout the world, which embody many of the values of classic negative liberalism. On the other hand, however, many philosophers and theologians are becoming increasingly aware of the complex ideologies that rest beneath the rhetoric of freedom (Song, 1997: 126; Milbank, 1990). Nevertheless it is important to note that the disastrous experience of some 'positive' forms of liberty in the twentieth century, which have been used to justify the totalitarian ideologies of the 'age of extremes', should make Protestants wary of siding too quickly with those who are ready to dismiss the critical negative liberalism of the Kantian tradition (Graf, 2002: 36–8).

References

Barth, Karl (1961). Evangelical Theology in the Nineteenth Century. In *The Humanity of God*. London: Collins, pp. 11–33.

Berlin, Isaiah (1969). *Four Essays on Liberty*. Oxford: Oxford University Press.

Bödeker, H.-E. (1988) Aufklärung als Kommunikationsprozeß. In R. Vierhaus (ed.), *Aufklärung als Prozeß*. Hamburg: Meiner, pp. 89–111.

Bosanquet, Bernard (1923). *The Philosophical Theory of the State*. London: Macmillan.

Burrow, J. W. (1981). *A Liberal Descent: Victorian Historians and the English Past*. Cambridge, UK: Cambridge University Press.

Chapman, Mark D. (2000). Pluralism, Welfare and the 'Common Good'. *Political Theology* 2: 33–56.

Chapman, Mark D. (2001a). *Ernst Troeltsch and Liberal Theology*. Oxford: Oxford University Press.

Chapman, Mark D. (2001b). *The Coming Crisis*. Sheffield, UK: Sheffield Academic Press.

Cowling, Maurice (2001). *Religion and Public Doctrine in Modern England. III. Accommodations*. Cambridge, UK: Cambridge University Press.

Cranston, Maurice (1967). Liberalism. In Paul Edwards (ed.), *Encyclopedia of Philosophy*. London: Macmillan, vol. III, pp. 459–61.

Creighton, Mandell (1985). *Persecution and Tolerance*. London: Longmans.

Dillenberger, John (1961). *Martin Luther. Selections from his Writings*. Garden City, NY: Doubleday.

Dorrien, Gary (2001). *The Making of American Liberal Theology*. Louisville, KY: Westminster/John Knox.

Graf, Friedrich Wilhelm (1986). Kulturprotestantismus. *Archiv für Begriffsgeschichte* 28: 214–68.

Graf, Friedrich Wilhelm (2002). What has London to do with Augsburg? In Mark D. Chapman (ed.), *The Future of Liberal Theology*, Aldershot, UK: Ashgate, pp. 18–38.

Habermas, Jürgen (1962). *Strukturwandel der Öffentlichkeit*. Berlin: Leuchterhand.

Hobson, J. A. (1909). *The Crisis of Liberalism*. London: King.

Hübinger, Gangolf (1994). *Kulturprotestantismus und Politik*. Tübingen: J. C. B. Mohr.

Kant, Immanuel (1929). *Critique of Pure Reason*. London: Macmillan.

Kant, Immanuel (1963). Universal History. In L. W. Beck (ed.), *On History*. Indianapolis: Bobbs-Merrill, pp. 11–26.

Marty, Martin E. (1970). *Religious Empire: The Protestant Experience in America*. New York: Dial Press.

Mathews, Shailer (1895–6). Christian Sociology. *American Journal of Sociology* 1: 69–78, 359–80, 457–72, 604–17, 771–84.

Maurice, F. D. (1891). *Lincoln's Inn Sermons*, 6 vols, London: Longmans.

Milbank, John (1990). *Theology and Social Theology*. Oxford: Blackwell.

Mill, John Stuart (1962). *Utilitarianism and Other Essays*. London: Fontana.

Minus, Paul M. (1988). *Walter Rauschenbusch: American Reformer*. New York: Macmillan.

Möller, Horst (1986). *Vernunft und Kritik*. Frankfurt: Suhrkamp.

Nicholls, David (1989). *Deity and Domination*. London: Routledge.

Niebuhr, H. Richard (1937). *The Kingdom of God in America*. Chicago: Willett Clarke.

Paulsen, Friedrich (1899). *Kant, Der Philosoph des Glaubens*. Berlin: Reuther und Reichard.

Porter, Roy (2000). *Enlightenment*. London: Penguin.

Rauschenbusch, Walter (1984). *Selected Writings*. New York: Paulist Press.

John Rawls (1971). *A Theory of Justice*. Cambridge, MA: Harvard University Press.

Reardon, Bernard M. G. (1995). *Religious Thought in the Victorian Age*. London: Longman.

Rendtorff, Trutz (ed.) (1982). *Glaube und Toleranz*. Gütersloh: Gerd Mohn.

Rupp, George (1977). *Culture Protestantism*. Atlanta, GA: Scholars Press.

Song, Robert (1997). *Christianity and Liberalism*. Oxford: Clarendon Press.

Stanley, A. P. (1844). *Life and Correspondence of Thomas Arnold*. London: Fellowes.

Temple, Frederick (1860). The Education of the World. In *Essays and Reviews*. London: Longmans, pp. 1–58.

Temple, Frederick (1884). *The Relations Between Religion and Science*. London: Macmillan.

Thomas, Stephen (1991). *Newman and Heresy. The Anglican Years.* Cambridge, UK: Cambridge University Press.

Tönnies, Ferdinand (1988). *Community and Society.* New Brunswick, NJ: Transaction Books.

Troeltsch, Ernst (1925). *Deutscher Geist und Westeuropa.* Tübingen: J. C. B. Mohr.

van Dülmen, Richard (1992). *The Society of the Enlightenment.* Cambridge, UK: Polity.

Vierhaus, R. (ed.) (1985). *Wissenschaften im Zeitalter der Aufklärung im 18. Jahrhundert in Deutschland.* Göttingen: Vandenhoeck und Ruprecht.

Wolfes, Matthias (1999). *Protestantische Theologie und moderne Welt.* Berlin: de Gruyter.

Wehler, H.-U. (1987). *Deutsche Sozialgeschichte.* Munich: Beck.

CHAPTER 31

Protestantism and Feminism

Cynthia L. Rigby

Since the time of the Reformation, feminist thinkers have raised their voices from among the Protestant ranks. As disciplined Christian believers, they have drawn from Protestant doctrine in arguing for the full inclusion of women in every sphere of life. They have loved the tradition, they have critiqued it, and they have contributed to shaping it. This chapter will explore the relationship of feminism to Protestantism first by offering an historical overview; then by surveying current contexts, issues, and figures; and finally by envisioning the future.

Historical Overview

While the term "feminist" did not emerge until the nineteenth century, feminist scholars generally identify certain figures and lines of thought as "feminist" prior to this time. Broadly put, to speak of feminism in relation to the history of Protestantism is to reflect on those movements and persons whose aim was to promote the full humanity of women, or women's "flourishing."[1] Protestant feminists hold that women can thrive only when their equal creation in the image of God is affirmed practically as well as theoretically, becoming manifest in actual, physical, this-worldly reality. Efforts to win women's acceptance as preachers, voters, and ordained members of the clergy are grounded, historically and theologically, in Protestant convictions about the character of God's creative work.

Feminism and the Reformation

The theologies of the Reformation have been both praised for nurturing, and criticized for impeding, feminist aims. Commonly decried are Reformation teachings concerning the "orders of creation," used to justify the superiority of men over women. Both Calvin and Luther argue that, while women are equally created in the image of God, Eve's creation after that of Adam signifies that her relationship to him is one of subordination.[2] In our prefallen condition, Luther and Calvin assure us, the submission of female to male would have been painless. Women's struggles to submit to their husbands and accept their more limited role in church and society are not endemic to their subordination as God originally intended it, they argue, but are consequences of the Fall. Because Eve violated her subordinate role in offering the fruit to Adam, the relationship between men and women is ever afterwards strained. In light of this reading of the creation story, Luther and Calvin counseled women to remember that their role is divinely ordained and to bear any suffering associated with it with humility, accepting it as a consequence of their sin.[3]

Protestant feminists through the centuries have rejected the Reformers' teaching that women's subordination is God's intention, for at least four reasons. First, they see a fundamental equality between Adam and Eve in the first creation story (Genesis 1). Second, they believe that Christ has come to redeem us from the consequences of the Fall, including the tyranny of men over women. Third, they believe it is nonsensical to argue that women are subordinate to men because Eve was created after Adam. By this logic, Adam would be subordinate to all other mammals created before him. Finally, Protestant feminists reject women's subordination as a divinely ordained good or a divinely ordained punishment because they believe such assertions both misrepresent the character of God and undermine the full equality of human beings created in God's image. In the words of African theologian Louise Tappa, liberation is not possible "as long as our view of God is nourished by, or reflects, the belief that it is God who from the beginning has created one human category inferior to the other" (Tappa, 1988: 31).

These arguments manifest clear and conscious opposition to Luther and Calvin's teachings regarding women's subordination. Significantly, however, Protestant feminist thinkers have not rejected all Reformation teachings outright, but have drawn upon many of the Reformers' insights in developing their critiques of Reformation anthropology. In addition to nurturing the transformation of women's roles in church and society *via* appeal to the Reformation notion that "the church is always in the process of being reformed" (*ecclesia reformata, semper reformanda*), feminist thinkers lay claim, in their work, to Reformation emphases regarding the priesthood of all believers, the vocation of marriage, and *sola scriptura*.

The priesthood of all believers   The Protestant emphasis on "the priesthood of all believers" supports the conviction that women are full participants in Christ's church. At the heart of the message of the Protestant Reformers was a critique of the clericalism of the papal church. Luther's Ninety-five Theses were devoted, in large part, to condemning the church's bureaucracy. It was not the case, the Reformers believed, that people of faith needed the mediation of a cleric or of an institution in order to stand in a right relationship to God. In the context of the Christian community, Luther taught, each of us acts as priest to the other as we bear Christ to one another. Calvin, similarly, urged all Christians to embrace their calling as priests by interceding in prayer for one another, testifying that Jesus Christ is the one Mediator between God and humanity, and engaging in works of love.

Contrary to the notion that the ordained priest occupied a privileged position in relation to God, Luther and Calvin understood Scripture to teach that every person is equally claimed and called to his or her particular vocation by God. A pastor preaching to a congregation, a laborer planting in a field, a father diapering his child: all are called to glorify God in their work.[4] Feminists are among those who recognize that the doctrine of vocation has too often been misused, by those in power, as a means for coercing women and minority persons into "joyfully" embracing menial tasks. But it has also been appropriately used to affirm men and women of faith in their day-to-day lives. According to Blaisdell, the doctrine of Christian vocation "appealed to urban middle class women" of the sixteenth century because it "supported . . . and lent dignity to . . . their already active lives in business, artisan specialties, and the home" (Blaisdell, 1985: 34).

Marriage as a vocation   In the context of this inclusive priesthood, marriage grew to be accepted as a vocation equally worthy, in the eyes of God, to celibacy. Luther's and Calvin's treatment of marriage, when compared with earlier theological understandings, left room for reflection on the relationship between husband and wife as a partnership – an unequal partnership, but a partnership nonetheless.

The rising status of marriage was a mixed blessing. As Rosemary Radford Ruether explains, the Reformers on the one hand emphasized that the primary purpose of marriage was companionship, not procreation. On the other hand, however, Protestant glorification of marriage meant that "women lost the option of a religious vocation distinct from marriage" (Ruether, 1998: 116). They were left with only one acceptable calling, from the standpoint of social expectation: "to be wife and mother," living in subordinate relationship to their husbands (ibid.). And yet many women, such as Elizabeth of Leeuwarden, an Anabaptist, "appointed themselves to places of leadership" in their zeal to spread the message of the Gospel. Women left their proscribed sphere at great cost to themselves: Leeuwarden, for example, was martyred in 1549 (Sprunger, 1985).

Sola scriptura   As priests bearing Christ, women as well as men were encouraged to read, study, and test the Scriptures for themselves. Consistent with the idea that all believers are priests, the Reformers insisted that the reading of Scripture should not be confined to the clergy. While they certainly did not advocate self-reliant readings, recommending guidance from the scholars of the church and hermeneutical accountability to the communion of saints, Luther and Calvin exhorted believers habitually to engage in first-hand study of Scripture. In his preface to *The Institutes of the Christian Religion*, for example, Calvin explains that the purpose of the volume is to "lend [his readers] a hand" in their reading of Scripture, "in order to guide them and help them to find the sum of what God meant to teach us in [God's] Word" (Calvin, 1960: 6). He ends his prefatory remarks by "urging" his readers to test his work by the Scriptures themselves (ibid.: 8).

Protestant feminist thinking was born and nurtured in a context where this principle of *sola scriptura* was in play. With Protestant emphasis on reading Scripture in the vernacular and teaching children the Bible and catechism at home, there was both opportunity and incentive for women to study and rehearse Scripture (see Blaisdell, 1985: 21–8). While the earliest Protestant feminist thinkers rarely offered direct challenges to patriarchal interpretations of Scripture, they began circumventing their prescribed silence and subordination by appeal to alternative biblical and theological teachings.[5] Argula von Grumbach, for example, admitted in a 1523 letter that the Apostle Paul's mandate that a woman remain silent did not allow her to advocate for a faculty member at the University of Ingolstadt whom she believed was being mistreated. She argued, however, that "when no man will or can speak, I am driven by the word of the Lord when he said, 'He who confesses me on earth, him will I deny.'" Buttressing her case further, she says she "takes comfort in the words of the prophet Isaiah . . . , 'I will send you children to be your princes and women to be your rulers.'" Finally, she insists that her appeal is not a case of "a woman's ranting, but the Word of God" (Douglass, 1985: 97).

Another example of a woman who was led to engage in nonconformist behaviour by her reading of Scripture is Marie Dentière, who lived in Geneva at the same time as Calvin. Douglass explains that Dentière "feels called to write and speak, knowing full well that these roles are neither ecclesiastically nor culturally approved for women" because "she has so internalized the Reformed teaching of the freedom of the Christian and has so situated herself in the biblical view of God's liberating work in history" (Douglass, 1985: 102). In Dentière's words: "If God then has given graces to some good women, revealing to them by his Holy Scriptures something holy and good, will they not dare to write, speak, or declare it one to another?" (p. 104).

As women read and interpreted Scripture for themselves, many became convinced that patriarchal paradigms that subordinated women to men were unbiblical. Invited by the Reformers to read with a critical eye, feminists in centuries following went on not only to assess patriarchal interpretations of Scripture, but the patriarchal character of the biblical text itself. An ongoing question for Protestant feminists who embrace *sola scriptura* is: how do we read the Bible *as women*, simultaneously recognizing both the ways it liberates us and the ways it oppresses us?[6]

The seventeenth and eighteenth centuries

By the mid-seventeenth century, many English women active in the Nonconformist movement were engaged in "printing, writing, and translating religious works" (Greaves, 1985: 83). Where they were not permitted to teach or to preach, and rarely allowed to participate in the government of the church in any way,[7] working with written texts served as a surreptitious vehicle for women's ministerial service and contribution to theological discourse.

Though society scorned, ridiculed, and feared women who spoke publicly (Ludlow, 1985: 99), a number of women became "petticoat preachers" (ibid.: 93). The most famous among them was Anne Hutchinson (ibid.: 95). Born in England, Hutchinson immigrated to colonial New England and was eventually banished from Massachusetts, both because her teaching was considered to be heretical and because she taught as a woman. "You have rather bine a Husband than a Wife and a Preacher than a Hearer; and a Magistrate than a Subject," she was told (Bednarowski, 1993: 68, citing Hall, 1968: 382–3). Back in England, women's activities (including public speaking, prophesying, and petitioning against "the traditional collection of tithes") provoked a request to Parliament "for repressive action" (Ludlow, 1985: 93–4). Some historians speculate that the surge of women's revolutionary activities during this period was a direct result of the teachings and spirit of the Reformation, which welcomed them into the public sphere indirectly, by valuing them as wives and mothers (ibid.: 94).

The eighteenth century saw the birth of voluntary associations in New England. Through their involvement in these societies, Protestant women planned revivals and were acknowledged as spiritual leaders (Moran, 1985: 126; Scott, 1993). Over time, "feminine piety" came to be seen as crucial for the well-being of the church. According to common wisdom, however, feminine piety could be nurtured only when women kept to their proper sphere, keeping in check their "darker" Eve-like character that was prone to deception (Moran, 1985: 129).

The suffrage movement of the nineteenth century

Nineteenth-century American feminism has been appropriately described as "witty" (Huber, 1993: 173). Certainly, those who opposed women's suffrage were taken off guard by creative arguments made by Elizabeth Cady Stanton, Sarah Grimké, and Sojourner Truth. Women *are* more spiritual than men, they agreed – and this is exactly why they should get the vote. Truth was among those who reconstrued the popular view that women, like Eve, were inherently deceptive. "If the first woman God ever made was strong enough to turn the world upside down all alone," she proclaimed, "these women together ought to be able to turn it back, and get it right side up again!"[8]

While there is a concern often raised (by some Protestant leaders) that feminist theology represents a coopting of secular feminism, the nineteenth-century suffrage movement reveals that the feminist movement was actually launched and galvanized by feminist theology. Protestant women and men working for women's suffrage (as well as other reforms, including abolition and temperance) offered compelling interpretations of Scripture to support their convictions. Jesus was speaking to women as well as men when he said, "don't hide your light under a bushel," Sarah Grimké insists; to withhold the vote from women is clearly to impede them from following Christ's mandate.[9] Yet Protestant feminists of the nineteenth century did not draw upon religious themes simply because they served the causes of suffrage, abolition, and temperance. On the contrary, these women worked for what they believed in because "religious motivation" was at the "core of their existence" (Gifford, 1993: 183).

One of the most significant developments at the interface of Protestantism and feminism in this period was the publication of *The Woman's Bible*. Edited by Elizabeth Cady Stanton, *The Women's Bible* offered critical interpretations of biblical passages dealing with women and women's roles. The appendix to the book includes diverse answers to two questions posed by Stanton: (1) "Have the teachings of the Bible advanced or retarded the emancipation of women?" and (2) "Have they dignified or degraded the Mothers of the race?" (Stanton [1895] 1993: 185). Stanton's intention was to invite women to reflect on the ways in which Protestant Christianity had inhibited them by engaging in focused biblical study.

Into the twentieth century

Less than a half a decade after women got the vote (in 1918) came another important period in the relationship between Protestantism and feminism in the United States. After World War II, there was a strong societal push for women to leave the workforce they had successfully negotiated during wartime and return to the domestic sphere. Protestant churches generally encouraged women to understand themselves primarily as wives and mothers. And yet, by the 1950s, many mainline Protestant churches had recognized the gifts and callings of women and begun actively ordaining them as ministers of Word and Sacrament. In order to do this without compromising on the Protestant conviction that Scripture is the "norming norm" of the Christian faith, Protestants frequently argued for contextualizing the most prohibitive passages regarding women's roles. While critiques of the patriarchal character of the biblical text were rarely as trenchant as Stanton's, many twentieth-century Protestants shared in Stanton's quest for new interpretations that allow women fuller participation.

In 1960 Jewish feminist theologian Valerie Saiving published an article that continues to have a profound effect on how Protestant feminist thinkers understand sin. In "The Human Situation: A Feminine View," Saiving (1979) argues that sin, like all theological concepts, has been described and addressed from the vantage point of male experience. Men are commonly guilty of the sin of "pride," Saiving explains; pride is remedied when one does not think of oneself more highly than one ought. The difficulty is that women are generally not guilty of pride as much as self-deprecation, or devaluing themselves. The correction to the "feminine sin" of self-deprecation is not to lower one's estimation of oneself, but to recognize one's value. Protestant feminists since Saiving have since done a great deal of work addressing "feminine sin," encouraging women to live with the consciousness of their "original righteousness,"[10] their creation in the image of God.

Present Context, Issues, and Figures

The last quarter of the twentieth century was marked by exponential growth in literature written by both Roman Catholic and Protestant feminists. By the mid-1980s, there were enough feminist theological works to support a semester class in feminist theology. Courses often featured, in the discipline of theology, Mary Daly's *Beyond God the Father* (1973), Letty Russell's *Human Liberation in a Feminist Perspective* (1974), and Rosemary Radford Ruether's *Sexism and God-Talk* (1983); in biblical studies they included Phyllis Trible's *God and the Rhetoric of Sexuality* (1978) and Elizabeth Schüssler Fiorenza's *In Memory of Her* (1993). By the mid-1990s, works in feminist theology were so plentiful that it was difficult for instructors to decide which books to choose![11] Feminist reconstruals of the liturgical tradition (see, e.g., Proctor-Smith, 1990), of the structure of theological education (see, e.g., Chopp, 1995), and even of feminist trajectories themselves (see, e.g., Keller, 1986) were by now prominent in the literature.

Strikingly, the growth in Protestant feminist literature includes numerous works by scholars who are not satisfied with self-identifying as "feminist." Womanist scholars including Katie Geneva Cannon (*Black Womanist Ethics*, 1988) and Delores Williams (*Sisters in the Wilderness*, 1993) work to address issues related to race and class disparities, as well as to sexism. Womanist thinkers have challenged white feminists to recognize the ways in which they participate in the system as oppressed oppressors, as Sarah in relation to Hagar (see Williams, 1993). Latina feminists (sometimes self-identified as "*mujerista* theologians") such as Protestant theologian Elsa Tamez (*The Amnesty of Grace*, 2002) and Roman Catholic theologian Ada Maria Isasi-Díaz (*En la lucha*, 1993) emphasize that they differ from many Caucasian feminists with their emphasis on community and family life. Around the world, Protestant feminists from a wide variety of contexts and with a wide range of perspectives have entered into the conversation, sharing their insights into how the full humanity of women may be more effectively promoted. These voices include, for example, African theologian Mercy Oduyoye (*Daughters of Anowa*, 1995) and Asian theologian Chung Hyun Kyung (*Struggle to Be the Sun Again*, 1990).

The drive for greater inclusivity, in recent feminist theologies, extends beyond the sphere of humanity to include all creatures, even the earth itself. Rosemary Radford Ruether's *Gaia and God* (1992) and Sallie McFague's *The Body of God* (1993) argue that Jewish and Christian theologies need to reconceive their understandings of stewardship and the incarnation. Stewardship does not give us license to dominate the earth, but the responsibility to care for it; in the incarnation, God entered not only into the human condition, but into the heart of the creation.

Future Relationship of Protestantism and Feminism

In 1983, the Presbyterian Church (USA) added to their *Book of Confessions* the "Brief Statement of Faith." In exegeting the third article of the Apostle's Creed, this statement affirms, "The same Spirit who inspired the prophets and apostles . . . calls women and men to all ministries of the church" (*Book of Confessions*, 1994: 276). While many Protestant denominations today do ordain women, the majority worldwide do not. While many Protestants reject women's subordination to men in favor of mutual submission, a significant number still adhere to the Reformation argument that women can simultaneously be both companions to men and their subordinates.[12] Protestant feminists, rejecting such arguments as inconsistent with the "priesthood of all believers," continue to work toward full equality. In the future, feminists hope that growing commitment to the realization of this equality will compel Protestant leaders to uphold women's ordination as *status confessionis*. Protestant feminists look forward to the day when all Protestants join hands in protesting injustices against women including domestic violence, clitoridectomies, female infanticide, and women making less money than men for the same work.

Protestant feminists will, in the future, continue to press Protestantism toward greater inclusivity. While marriage and the subsequent nurturing of children will always be upheld as a vocation, marriage may not always be seen as preferable to other vocations or family structures. Models for family which are today developing, and will continue to take shape in the future, include unions between homosexual persons and adoption of children by homosexual couples, living singly, living with members of one's first family, living together with friends, and parents living with children but without a spouse or partner. Most Protestant feminists will be among those who insist on the full inclusion of homosexual persons, of persons of other faiths, and of all creatures – human and nonhuman alike – created by God. Many other Protestants will resist the feminist drive for full inclusion, struggling with biblical texts that seem to argue that Christian identity requires a modicum of exclusivity. As they work to include all, Protestant feminists will – as they always have – engage in rereading, and reinterpreting, the biblical texts.

Future discussion of the relationship between Protestantism and feminism will focus not only on the inspiration feminist thinkers receive from the Protestant tradition and the critiques feminists have made of Protestantism. It will also consider how Protestantism has been shaped by feminist thinking. Already, feminist theological reflection has had an impact on the character of Protestant worship, broadening the range of ways we refer to and think about God. Feminist theologians have raised questions that have made their way into mainline Protestant conversation, including: "Is Christian life characterized, primarily, by self-denial?", "Are there nonviolent approaches to understanding the cross?" (see, e.g., Brock & Parker, 2001), and "What is the character of power-relations, in the context of a Christian community reflecting the image of the triune, egalitarian, God?"

Someday, articulating the relationship between Protestantism and feminism, as it stands in that moment, will no longer be necessary. The hope is that Protestantism will take on the aims of feminism to such a degree that it would be redundant to refer to oneself as a "Protestant feminist." This does not mean, of course, that all Protestants will suddenly agree on every controversial issue. It does mean, however, that Protestants will share the recognition that working for the full humanity of all is not optional, from the standpoint of the gospel mandate.

In the meantime, it is a step to think of "feminism" not as an outsider to Protestantism that critiques it from afar. Rather, Protestant feminists stand at the heart of Protestant traditions, working alongside their Protestant brothers and sisters in the struggle to discern and to realize what it means to be Christian believers.

Notes

1   For more on this, see Rosemary Radford Ruether (1983).
2   See, for example, Calvin's commentary on I Corinthians 11:8 and I Timothy 2:13–14 in Calvin (1988). The volumes in question are: *The First Epistle of St. Paul to the Corinthians*, trans. J. W. Fraser and *Second Corinthians, Timothy, Titus, Philemon*, trans. T. A. Smail.
3   For a more detailed feminist reading of the theological anthropology of Luther and Calvin, see Rosemary Radford Ruether (1998: 117–26).
4   Nancy J. Duff (1997: 69–81) explains this beautifully.
5   This point is made and compellingly argued by Jane Dempsey Douglass (1985).
6   For more on this, see Mary Ann Tolbert (1989).
7   Greaves (1985: 83) notes that, even in the Nonconformist churches, women were excluded from activities such as selecting a pastor or excommunicating "wayward members."
8   Sojourner Truth, "Ain't I A Woman?" reproduced in Schneir (1972: 95, citing from *History of Woman Suffrage*, vol 1, Rochester, NY: 1881).
9   Sarah M Grimké, "Letters on the Equality of the Sexes and the Condition of Women," reproduced in Schneir (1972: 40, citing from *Letters on the Equality of the Sexes and the Condition of Women*, New York: Burt Franklin, 1970).
10   This is a term used by Rita Nakashima Brock (1988).
11   Published in 1996, the *Dictionary of Feminist Theologies*, edited by Letty M. Russell and Shannon Clarkson, includes a comprehensive bibliography of Roman Catholic and Protestant feminist works.

12   The Southern Baptist Convention in the United States holds, for example, that women are equal to their husbands even as they submit to them.

References

Bednarowski, Mary Farrell (1993). Outside the Mainstream: Women's Religion and Women Religious Leaders in Nineteenth-Century America. In Martin Marty (ed.), *Modern American Protestantism and its World: Historical Articles on Protestantism in American Religious Life, 12: Women and Women's Issues*. Munich: Saur, pp. 68–91.

Blaisdell, Charmarie Jenkins (1985). The Matrix of Reform: Women in the Lutheran and Calvinist Movements. In Richard Graves (ed.), *Triumph Over Silence: Women in Protestant History*. Westport, CT: Greenwood Press, pp. 13–44.

Book of Confessions (1994). In *The Constitution of the Presbyterian Church (USA)*. Louisville, KY: Office of the General Assembly.

Brock, Rita Nakashima (1988). *Journeys By Heart: A Christology of Erotic Power*. New York: Crossroad.

Brock, Rita Nakashima and Parker, Rebecca Ann (2001). *Proverbs of Ashes: Violence, Redemptive Suffering, and the Search for What Saves Us*. Boston: Beacon Press.

Calvin, John (1960). *Institutes of the Christian Religion*, ed. John T. McNeill, trans. Ford Lewis Battles, vol. XX of the Library of Christian Classics. Philadelphia: The Westminster Press.

Calvin, John (1988). *Calvin's New Testament Commentaries: A New Translation*, David W. Torrance and Thomas F. Torrance (eds.). Grand Rapids, MI: Eerdmans.

Cannon, Katie Geneva (1988). *Black Womanist Ethics*. Atlanta, GA: Scholars Press.

Chopp, Rebecca (1995). *Saving Work: Feminist Practices of Theological Education*. Louisville, KY: Westminster/John Knox Press.

Chung, Hyun Kyung (1990). *Struggle to Be the Sun Again: Introducing Asian Women's Theology*. Maryknoll, NY: Orbis.

Daly, Mary (1973). *Beyond God the Father: Toward a Philosophy of Women's Liberation*. Boston: Beacon Press.

Douglass, Jane Dempsey (1985). *Women, Freedom, and Calvin*. Philadelphia: Westminster Press.

Duff, Nancy J. (1997). Vocation, Motherhood, and Marriage. In Jane Dempsey Douglass and James F. Kay (eds.), *Women, Gender, and Christian Community*. Louisville, KY: Westminster/John Knox Press.

Gifford, Carolyn DeSwarte (1993). Sisterhoods of Service and Reform: Organized Methodist Women in the Late Nineteenth Century. An Essay on the State of the Research. In Martin Marty (ed.), *Modern American Protestantism and its World: Historical Articles on Protestantism in American Religious Life, 12: Women and Women's Issues*. Munich: Saur, pp. 174–89.

Greaves, Richard L. (ed.) (1985). Women in Early English Nonconformity. In Richard L. Greaves (ed.), *Triumph Over Silence: Women in Protestant History*. London: Greenwood Press, pp. 3–12.

David Hall (ed.) (1968). *The Antinomian Controversy, 1636–1638: A Documentary History*. Middletown, CT: Greenwood Press.

Huber, Elaine C. (1993). They Weren't Prepared to Hear: A Closer Look at *The Women's Bible*. In Martin Marty (ed.), *Modern American Protestantism and its World: Historical*

Articles on Protestantism in American Religious Life, 12: Women and Women's Issues. Munich: Saur, pp. 168–73.

Isasi-Díaz, Ada Maria (1993). *En la lucha/In The Struggle: A Hispanic Women's Liberation Theology.* Minneapolis: Fortress Press.

Keller, Catherine (1986). *From a Broken Web: Separation, Sexism and Self.* Boston: Beacon Press.

Ludlow, Dorothy P. (1985). Sectarian Women in England, 1641–1700. In Richard L. Greaves (ed.), *Triumph Over Silence: Women in Protestant History.* London: Greenwood Press, pp. 93–123.

McFague, Sallie (1993). *The Body of God: An Ecological Theology.* Minneapolis: Fortress Press.

Moran, Gerald F. (1985). "The Hidden Ones": Women and Religion in Puritan New England. In Richard L. Greaves (ed.), *Triumph Over Silence: Women in Protestant History.* London: Greenwood Press, pp. 125–49.

Oduyoye, Mercy (1995). *Daughters of Anowa: African Women and Patriarchy.* Maryknoll, NY: Orbis.

Procter-Smith, Marjorie (1990). *In Her Own Rite: Constructing Feminist Liturgical Tradition.* Nashville: Abingdon Press.

Ruether, Rosemary Radford (1983). *Sexism and God-Talk: Toward a Feminist Theology.* Boston: Beacon Press.

Ruether, Rosemary Radford (1992). *Gaia and God: An Ecofeminist Theology of Earth Healing.* San Francisco: HarperCollins.

Ruether, Rosemary Radford (1998). *Women and Redemption: A Theological History.* Minneapolis: Fortress Press.

Russell, Letty (1974). *Human Liberation in a Feminist Perspective – A Theology.* Philadelphia: Westminster Press.

Russell, Letty and Clarkson, Shannon (eds.) (1996). *Dictionary of Feminist Theologies.* Louisville, KY: Westminster/John Knox Press.

Saiving, Valerie (1979). The Human Situation: A Feminine View. In Carol P. Christ and Judith Plaskow (eds.), *Womanspirit Rising: A Feminist Reader in Religion.* New York: Harper & Row, pp. 25–42.

Schneir, Miriam (ed.) (1972). *Feminism: The Essential Historical Writings.* New York: Random House.

Schüssler Fiorenza, Elizabeth (1993). *In Memory of Her: A Feminist Theological Reconstruction of Christian Origins.* New York: Crossroad.

Scott, Anne Firor (1993). On Seeing and Not Seeing: A Case of Historical Invisibility. In Martin Marty (ed.), *Modern American Protestantism and its World: Historical Articles on Protestantism in American Religious Life, 12: Women and Women's Issues.* Munich: Saur, pp. 18–32.

Sprunger, Keith L. (1985). God's Powerful Army of the Weak: Anabaptist Women of the Radical Reformation. In Richard L. Greaves (ed.), *Triumph Over Silence: Women in Protestant History.* London: Greenwood Press, pp. 45–74.

Stanton, Elizabeth Cady ([1895] 1993), *The Women's Bible.* Boston: Northeastern University Press.

Tamez, Elsa (2002). *The Amnesty of Grace: Justification by Faith from a Latin American Perspective.* Eugene, OR: Wipf & Stock.

Tappa, Louise (1988). The Christ-Event: A Protestant Perspective. In Virgina Fabella and M. A. Oduyoye (eds.), *With Passion and Compassion: Third World Women Doing Theology.* Maryknoll, NY: Orbis, pp. 30–4.

Tolbert, Mary Ann (1989). Protestant Feminists and the Bible: On the Horns of a Dilemma. *Union Seminary Quarterly Review* 43 (1–4): 1–17.

Trible, Phyllis (1978). *God and the Rhetoric of Sexuality*. Philadelphia: Fortress Press.

Williams, Delores (1993). *Sisters in the Wilderness: The Challenge of Womanist God-Talk*. Maryknoll, NY: Orbis.

Further Reading

Dowell, Susan and Hurcombe, Linda (1987). *Dispossessed Daughters of Eve: Faith and Feminism*. London: SCM Press.

Jin, Yong Ting (1988). New Ways of Being Church: A Protestant Perspective. In Virginia Fabella and Mercy Amba Oduyoye (eds.), *With Passion and Compassion: Third World Women Doing Theology*. Maryknoll: Orbis, pp. 100–7.

Marty, Martin (ed.) (1993), *Modern American Protestantism and its World: Historical Articles on Protestantism in American Religious Life, 12: Women and Women's Issues*. Munich: K.G. Saur.

MacHaffie, Barbara J. (1986). *Her Story: Women in Christian Tradition*. Philadelphia: Fortress Press.

MacHaffie, Barbara J. (ed.) (1992). *Readings in Her Story: Women in Christian Tradition*. Minneapolis: Fortress Press.

Oden, Amy (ed.) (1994). *In Her Words: Women's Writings in the History of Christian Thought*. Nashville: Abingdon.

Tucker, Ruth A. and Liefeld, Walter (1987). *Daughters of the Church: Women and Ministry from New Testament Times to the Present*. Grand Rapids, MI: Zondervan.

CHAPTER 32

Protestantism and Fundamentalism

William V. Trollinger, Jr.

Definition and Theology

The term "fundamentalism" has been used to describe a host of religious movements across the globe that are militantly antimodernist, aggressively patriarchal, literalist in their reading of sacred texts, and assiduous in their efforts to draw boundaries between themselves and outsiders. While "Islamic fundamentalism" has received the most attention, particularly after the September 11, 2001 terrorist attacks, scholars and journalists have also applied the term to movements within such disparate traditions as Judaism, Sikhism, and Hinduism, as well as to various Christian groups.[1]

There are benefits to understanding fundamentalism as a global movement that grows out of deep-seated and intense opposition to (aspects of) modernity, and that is found in a wide array of religious traditions. Among other things, such an approach allows for interesting and often insightful comparative analysis. But there are problems with defining fundamentalism generically and applying it globally. Not only does such an approach not lend itself to definitional precision, it can devolve into derogatory shorthand for reactionary religious groups.

As a result, and for the purposes of this chapter, it is best to understand fundamentalism where it started, as a *religious movement within Protestantism*.[2] Fundamentalism had its origins in late nineteenth and early twentieth-century Anglo-American evangelicalism, and it blossomed into a full-fledged religious movement in the years immediately after World War I. To a great degree fundamentalism has been an American phenomenon, with its origins and greatest strength in the United States, although it has had a limited presence in Canada (and although, as George Marsden (1980: 221) has observed, it has often been "successfully propagated overseas by its vigorous missions.") While there are a multitude of evangelical connections between the United States and the remainder of the Anglo-American world, for a variety of reasons – including a greater commitment to established churches and to ecumenism – the fundamentalist movement never had the impact in England or even in Canada that it had in the USA.[3]

Of course, all this leads to matters of definition. The term "fundamentalism" was coined in 1920 by a Baptist periodical editor, Curtis Lee Laws, to refer to conservative evangelicals in the Northern Baptist Convention who were willing to engage in "battle royal for the Fundamentals" of the faith (Laws, 1920). Fundamentalists shared and share with other evangelicals a commitment to the authority of the Bible, the necessity of a conversion experience for salvation, and the importance of sharing the good news of the gospel with others. What distinguishes fundamentalists from other evangelicals – and the line here is admittedly quite blurred – is that they are stridently opposed to "modernism," including theological liberalism, Darwinism, and secularism.[4]

It would be a mistake, however, to view fundamentalists merely as conservative traditionalists committed to resisting change and repelling error. In their zeal to combat modernism these contentious evangelicals latched onto two relatively new theological doctrines, both of which reflected their intense antimodernism. Most important is biblical inerrancy, the cornerstone of fundamentalist theology. The modern doctrine of inerrancy was most fully developed in the late nineteenth century by Presbyterian conservatives at Princeton Seminary, including Charles Hodge, A. A. Hodge, and Benjamin Warfield. It was an antimodernist response to "higher criticism," a sociohistorical approach to the Scriptures that was championed by theological liberals, and that raised serious questions about the supernatural character and literal authenticity of the biblical record. In stark opposition, the doctrine of Biblical inerrancy emphasized that the original "autographs" are the infallible product of the Holy Spirit's guidance. As such, they contain no errors of any sort; they are accurate in all that they have to say, including when they speak on matters of history, science, and the like.[5]

Joel Carpenter has cogently observed that the Princeton theologians "defended biblical authority and inerrancy with a carefully nuanced balancing of the Bible's divine and human character." But in their war on modernism the fundamentalists have jettisoned nuance, a point that pertains to their understanding and use of inerrancy. Attacking those who have emphasized the Bible as a human and historical product, fundamentalists have focused almost exclusively on the Bible's supernatural character. It is thus difficult to distinguish between the fundamentalist doctrine of inerrancy – with its emphasis that the Bible must be read "literally" – and the dictation theory of Scripture, in which human beings simply served as recorders of God's words (Carpenter, 1997: 69–75, quote p. 72).

Biblical inerrancy is crucial to dispensational premillennialism, an eschatological system which, for some scholars, is the distinguishing characteristic of fundamentalist theology. Premillennialism holds that the millennium – the thousand-year reign of God's kingdom on earth – will not occur until Christ returns to earth to establish it; it is in stark contrast with postmillennialism, an optimistic view of history that holds that the Spirit-led church will usher in the millennium, followed by Christ's return. While premillennialism has an ancient lineage, dispensational premillennialism – or, simply, dispensationalism – was developed by Plymouth Brethren founder John Nelson Darby in Great Britain in the mid-nineteenth century. Darby traveled to the United States to make the case for his ideas; his disciples quite successfully promoted dispensationalism in a series of prophecy conferences in the United States in the late nineteenth century. But it was Cyrus Scofield's Reference Bible, a dispensational gloss which first appeared in 1909, that cemented the popularity of dispensationalism among conservative evangelicals.

According to dispensationalism, history is controlled by supernatural forces; if read literally – hence the importance of inerrancy – the Bible (particularly the books of Daniel and Revelation) provides a sure guide to the past, present, and future of human history. History is divided into (generally seven) separate segments, or dispensations; in each dispensation God tests human beings, humans fail, and the era ends with a divine judgment on humans (e.g., the Genesis flood). The current dispensation, the "church age," is marked by the increasing apostasy of the institutional church and the increasing decadence of modern civilization. But at the end of the church age – which will be preceded by the return of Jews to Palestine and the re-establishment of the state of Israel – Christ will return in the air (the "rapture") to retrieve faithful believers from the world. The world will then endure seven years of "tribulation," which will include the reign of the antichrist and the persecution of Jews who have converted to Christianity. This time of tribulation will end with the return of Christ and the saints, who will defeat the enemy and establish the millennial kingdom headquartered in Israel.[6]

Fundamentalist Movement, 1910s–1950s

Many North American evangelicals in the late nineteenth and early twentieth centuries accepted both biblical inerrancy and dispensational premillennialism. These protofundamentalists were concerned – but not surprised, given that dispensationalism had warned them of the increasingly apostate church – by the spread of theological liberalism in the major Protestant denominations and seminaries. In response, Lyman and Milton Stewart, wealthy California oilmen who were evangelicals, funded the publication of *The Fundamentals*, a 12-volume series of essays that appeared between 1909 and 1915, and that made the case for conservative Protestant theology. While the Stewarts and the editors – A. C. Dixon, Louis Meyer, and Reuben Torrey – were dispensationalists, not much was made of dispensationalism or other controversial ideas. Instead, editors and essayists sought to present a united front in defense of the "fundamentals of the faith" (Marsden, 1980: 118–23).

Despite the fact that these 12 volumes contributed to the coining of the term "fundamentalist," it would be a mistake to view these books, with their relatively irenic tone, as signaling the beginning of fundamentalism. The fundamentalist movement did not come into being until a few years later, out of the cultural crisis engendered by World War I. Woodrow Wilson's holy war against German barbarism convinced many Americans that the very survival of Western civilization and Christian morality were at stake. Conservative evangelicals were caught up in this spirit of alarm, but they had a ready explanation for Germany's devolution, namely its widespread acceptance of higher criticism, theological liberalism, and Darwinian evolutionism. And this explanation carried with it a warning: as Germany went, so would the USA, if it did not change its ways.

In this atmosphere – further charged by the 1918 British capture of Jerusalem from the Turks, which thrilled dispensationalists as evidence that the last days were at hand – many conservative evangelicals in the United States were transformed into militant antimodernists. Six months after the war ended, and with the Red Scare gaining momentum, these radicalized evangelicals gathered in Philadelphia to create the World's Christian Fundamentals Association (WCFA), an event hyperbolically described by the organization's first president, William Bell Riley, as "of more historic moment than the nailing up, at Wittenberg, of Martin Luther's *Ninety-five Theses*" (Riley, 1919: 3). The interdenominational WCFA set for itself two primary goals: to promote its understanding of Christian orthodoxy, including inerrancy and dispensational premillennialism, and to aggressively fight the modernist menace. Toward these ends the WCFA concluded its May 1919 convention by dispatching its leaders on a well-publicized campaign throughout the United States and Canada.[7]

The fundamentalist forces began their antimodernist campaign by targeting the spread of theological liberalism in major denominations. While most denominations in the United States were touched by fundamentalism and endured some sort of fundamentalist controversy, the fiercest battles took place among the Northern Baptists (NBC) and the Northern Presbyterians (PC-USA). There were good reasons for this. Both denominations had Calvinist roots, and hence there was a heritage of emphasizing the importance of affirming correct doctrine – that is, conditions were conducive for a movement that emphasized "fundamentals of the faith." Moreover, and unlike their counterparts in the South, liberalism had made significant inroads among Northern Baptists and Presbyterians – that is, there was an enemy for the fundamentalists to fight. Led by Riley in the NBC and J. Gresham Machen and William Jennings Bryan in the PC-USA, the fundamentalists sought to rid the seminaries and mission fields of theological liberals and to commit their respective denominations to fundamentalist creedal statements.

While large numbers of Northern Baptists and Presbyterians were theologically conservative, many of them were also denominational loyalists who were unwilling to engage in the militant action demanded by fundamentalists. Frustrated by these "fearful compromisers," William Bell Riley in 1922 joined with other militants to create the Baptist Bible Union, which sought to unite all Baptist fundamentalists in North America in the war on modernism. Joining Riley from the South was J. Frank Norris, the firebrand pastor of Fort Worth's First Baptist Church who tirelessly blasted the Southern Baptist Convention for its laxity on modernism. From the North came Canada's most visible fundamentalist, T. T. Shields, pastor of Toronto's Jarvis Street Baptist Church and leader of an aggressive campaign in the early 1920s to rid McMaster Divinity College of modernism. Not only was Shields chosen as the BBU's first president, but he served as president of the organization's short-lived and controversy-ridden Des Moines University (Elliott, 1995: 364–9; Stackhouse, 1993: 23–34).

The Baptist Bible Union notwithstanding, it was clear by 1925 that fundamentalists had failed to capture control of either the NBC or the PC-USA.[8] But the WCFA had already turned its attention from ridding denominations of modernist theology to ridding America's schools of Darwinian evolutionism. With a commonsensical understanding of science as limited to observable facts and demonstrable laws, fundamentalists considered evolution to be a speculative "unscientific" theory. Moreover, fundamentalists viewed Darwinism, with its rejection of the Genesis creation account and its emphasis on natural processes, as inimical to orthodox Christianity. Finally, Darwinian evolutionism, with its emphasis on human beings as but highly developed animals, was a grave threat to the moral foundations of Western civilization; again, the obvious example was the World War, caused and fueled by a Germany inspired to dastardly aggression by its acceptance of the Darwinian "survival of the fittest."

In response to this deadly threat, the WCFA and other fundamentalists – most prominently William Jennings Bryan – embarked on a campaign designed to pressure state lawmakers to ban the teaching of evolution in the public schools. One state to pass such legislation was Tennessee, which in 1925 made it illegal "to teach any theory that denies the Story of Divine Creation of man as taught in the Bible, and to teach instead that man has descended from a lower order of animal." When schoolteacher John Thomas Scopes and the American Civil Liberties Union challenged the law, William Jennings Bryan volunteered his services to the prosecution. The result was the famous Scopes Trial, conducted in July 1925 in Dayton, Tennessee to great media fanfare, including a live broadcast on a Chicago radio station. While Scopes was ruled guilty of violating Tennessee's antievolution statute (a judgment that was eventually reversed on a technicality), ACLU attorney Clarence Darrow and reporter H. L. Mencken successfully portrayed Bryan and his fundamentalist supporters as rural hicks who were woefully ignorant of modern science and ridiculously out of touch with modern urban culture.

The Scopes trial and William Jennings Bryan's death one week later took the steam out of the antievolution crusade. While some southern state legislatures proceeded to pass bills banning the teaching of Darwinism, there was little enthusiasm for such legislation in the North, a point emphatically driven home in 1928, when an antievolution law pushed by William Bell Riley in his home state of Minnesota suffered an ignominious defeat.[9] The national fundamentalist crusade had collapsed, having failed to cleanse the public schools of Darwinian evolutionism, and Protestant denominations of theological modernism. Contemporary commentators and scholars over the next half-century were convinced that this failure signaled the death of fundamentalism. While this reactionary movement might survive for a while in benighted pockets of the North American landscape, the march of progress ensured that modernity would triumph, and fundamentalism would disappear.[10]

The experts could not have been more wrong. Fundamentalism proved to be a remarkably resilient and dynamic force. Despite the failed crusades of the 1920s and the attendant negative publicity, fundamentalists successfully regrouped at the local level in the United States and Canada. Some fundamentalists formed independent (often "Bible" or "independent Baptist") churches. Some controlled churches that were, at least nominally, affiliated with a mainline denomination. Others brought churches together to create fundamentalist denominations, including the Orthodox Presbyterian Church, the Bible Presbyterian Church, the General Association of Regular Baptist Churches (which emerged from the Baptist Bible Union), the World Baptist Fellowship and Baptist Bible Fellowship (both of which grew out of the J. Frank Norris empire), and the Conservative Baptist Association. In Canada, there was T. T. Shields' Union of Regular Baptist Churches, the Fellowship of Independent Baptist Churches, and the Convention of Regular Baptists of British Columbia, all of which eventually merged. In all these forms – independent, nominally mainline, or part of a fundamentalist denomination – fundamentalist churches flourished. Their success was due in great part to a rapidly expanding web of nondenominational organizations, including publishing houses, mission agencies, and, most important, Bible institutes. The numerous Bible schools scattered across the United States and Canada, Chicago's Moody Bible Institute being the most prominent, provided churches in their region with fundamentalist ministers, secretaries, Vacation Bible School workers, Bible conferences, and Sunday School materials, as well as home and foreign missionaries.

By the 1940s fundamentalists began to move beyond the local level, seeking – as good evangelicals – to bring the gospel to the masses. They proved to be quite adept at making use of radio, evinced by Charles Fuller's "Old-Fashioned Revival Hour" and the various programs broadcast over Moody's WMBI. They also conducted evangelistic campaigns and created evangelistic organizations such as Youth for Christ, out of which came such future luminaries as Billy Graham. In the years immediately after World War II, when Americans and others in the West were anxious about the spread of Communism and the possibility of nuclear war, the fundamentalist message proved quite appealing.[11]

This emphasis on revival, as opposed to antimodernist crusades, aggravated tensions that existed just below the surface in the fundamentalist movement. In response to the 1920s debacle some fundamentalists committed themselves to "separation," adding as a doctrinal requirement the refusal to cooperate with those who did not fully share their theological commitments (some went further by insisting on noncooperation with those who shared their theology but who did not fully separate from those who did not). But in the 1940s and 1950s a group of less militant (and often younger) fundamentalists emerged who rejected this extreme separatism while also de-emphasizing dispensational premillennialism. The separatists were appalled by such compromises. The first crack in the movement appeared in the early 1940s, with the creation of two competing fundamentalist organizations: the American Council of Christian Churches, established by the militant Presbyterian Carl McIntire, who insisted that fundamentalists separate completely from denominations affiliated with the World Council of Churches; and the National Association of Evangelicals, organized by moderate fundamentalists, including J. Elwin Wright and Harold J. Ockenga, who emphasized "positive outreach" more than negative attacks (Carpenter, 1997: 141–232). But the real explosion in the fundamentalist ranks came in the 1950s, with the evangelist Billy Graham as the focal point. Graham's willingness to cooperate with mainline Protestants in his revival campaigns infuriated McIntire, Bob Jones, Jr., and other separatist leaders, and they began to turn on Graham and his supporters as traitors to the faith.

When the dust had settled by the end of the decade, the fundamentalist movement had split into two groups: the neo-evangelicals, who were the much larger group, and who over time simply came to call themselves "evangelicals," and the much smaller group of separatists, who boldly retained the label "fundamentalist."[12] While our focus here is the fundamentalist side of this division, it seems important here to point out that a significant and influential segment of contemporary evangelicalism, particularly in the United States, has its roots in fundamentalism and has been shaped by its fundamentalist heritage. This becomes clear when one observes, as Harriet Harris has pointed out, the "ongoing preoccupation with inerrancy" on the part of many evangelicals; it is also clear when one compares evangelical and fundamentalist institutions of higher education in the USA, given that both generally require faculty members to sign (often similar) faith statements, and both often engage in boundary maintenance, removing faculty members who have strayed in their theology or their lifestyle (Harris, 1998: 43; Trollinger, 1996). While there are whole segments of evangelicalism that were not greatly affected by the fundamentalist controversies of the 1920s, and while many evangelicals have worked very hard to distance themselves from the opprobrious label "fundamentalist," there is no question that contemporary evangelicalism, especially in the North American context, has been greatly influenced by fundamentalism.[13]

Politicized Fundamentalism: 1960s to the Present

In the years after the movement divided, separatist fundamentalists once again concentrated their efforts at the grass-roots level, establishing and growing churches (some of which became quite large), supporting fundamentalist "faith" missions, building up their colleges (most prominently, Bob Jones University and Tennessee Temple University), and engaging in revival work. While the media occasionally noticed the fundamentalists, most of the time they were beneath the cultural radar. But in the late 1970s fundamentalists surprisingly returned to the spotlight. Appalled by the dramatic social changes that had taken place in the United States – including the sexual revolution; the feminist, antiwar, and civil rights movements; and the increasing secularization of American life – many fundamentalists became politically mobilized, driven to restore "Christian America." Fundamentalism had always been associated with militarism, market economics, and patriotism; such ideas were popular in post-Vietnam, post-Watergate America, and politically energized fundamentalists played a central role in what became known as the Religious Right.

In fact, it was a fundamentalist Baptist minister and radio preacher, Jerry Falwell, who in 1979 established the first important Religious Right organization. Describing itself as "prolife, profamily, promoral and pro-America," the Moral Majority played an important role in the election and re-election of President Ronald Reagan, a fundamentalist icon even though he was only nominally religious. While the Moral Majority collapsed in the mid-1980s, primarily because it lacked a grass-roots base, fundamentalists played an active role in televangelist Pat Robertson's 1988 presidential campaign (the candidate's arch-conservative political ideology and moral rhetoric allowing fundamentalists to overlook the fact that he was a charismatic). Out of this failed campaign came the most important Religious Right organization to date, the Christian Coalition. Led by right-wing wunderkind Ralph Reed, the Christian Coalition reported one million members in the early 1990s, and played a crucial role in the 1990 re-election of North Carolina's Jesse Helms to the Senate, the 1991 confirmation of Clarence Thomas to the Supreme Court, and the 1994 Republican takeover of Congress. While the Christian Coalition, too, faded away by the end of the decade, fundamentalists have continued to be very aggressive politically, having established themselves as an essential and very active part of the Republican coalition.[14]

It is a point of pride for many Canadians that they have not seen anything comparable to the Moral Majority and Christian Coalition. But there are some interesting historical precedents in Canada, and there are indications at the beginning of the twenty-first century that a Canadian version of the Religious Right may be emerging. In the 1930s, "Bible Bill" Aberhart, dispensationalist preacher and founder of the Calgary Prophetic Bible Institute, was elected premier of Alberta as head of the Social Credit party, which Aberhart founded, and which unsuccessfully sought – as a response to the Depression – to reorganize the province's credit system and to give each resident $25 a month.[15] At his death in 1943 Aberhart was succeeded as premier by Ernest Manning, a graduate of Aberhart's Bible Institute who moved the Social Credit party toward mainstream conservatism (and who also took over Manning's "Back to the Bible Hour" radio show). Manning's son, Preston, an evangelical, founded the federal Reform Party, which in 2000 evolved into the Canadian Alliance. Lay Pentecostal preacher and independent Christian school principal Stockwell Day – also from Alberta – was chosen to lead the new organization; in a moderate version of Religious Right campaigns in the United States, Day pushed a socially conservative, "prolife, profamily" agenda that resonated with some Canadians but frightened many others. Responding to the furor, in 2002 the Alliance replaced Day with a fiscal conservative who has evinced less interest in politicizing social issues (Hoover, 2000; Spendlove, 2002).

In the States, fundamentalists have not just voted for "prolife, profamily" candidates; they have also actively worked against the Equal Rights Amendment, gay rights, and, most important, abortion rights.[16] Regarding the latter, it is remarkable that once politically quiescent fundamentalists are now engaging in lobbying, picketing, civil disobedience, and, at the movement's edges, violence. Fundamentalists have also become quite involved in the campaign to halt what they see as the rapid and dangerous spread of immorality, socialism, and secularism in the public schools; they have hence worked to eliminate or restrict sex education classes, to remove material critical of America and capitalism from textbooks, and to re-establish officially sanctioned prayer (ruled unconstitutional by the American Supreme Court in 1962). Returning to an old issue, contemporary fundamentalists have also fought the spread of Darwinian evolutionism; this time, they have sought to force public schools to give equal time for "creation science," which propounds that all life appeared on earth less than 10,000 years ago, and that all life was created in six 24-hour days.[17]

More in keeping with their separatist heritage, American fundamentalists have established thousands of fundamentalist primary and secondary schools; in the 1990s they also became prime movers in the "home schooling" movement. Still, militant fundamentalists such as Bob Jones III have criticized politically active fundamentalists for violating the premise of strict separation. Of course, the critics are correct: politicized fundamentalists have worked with nonfundamentalists, including Catholics and evangelicals. The latter cooperation points to a narrowing of the gap between activist fundamentalists and conservative evangelicals that has taken place with the emergence of the Religious Right in the USA. One indication of this can be found within the Southern Baptist Convention, where fundamentalists and conservative evangelicals joined to capture the levers of denominational power, the result by the 1990s being a purge of SBC agencies and seminaries of noninerrantists. As in the 1920s, fundamentalism has sparked controversy and conflict in a major Protestant denomination; by the 1990s SBC agencies and seminaries had been essentially purged of noninerrantists.[18]

Fundamentalist theology, with its commitments to inerrancy and dispensational premillennialism, and the fundamentalist movement, in both its separatist and its politicized forms, will not be disappearing from Protestantism any time in the near future. In fact, as fundamentalists remain more committed to the traditional missionary enterprise than almost any other group within Protestantism, its influence will continue to spread across the globe. That fundamentalism survives and thrives will continue to baffle many nonfundamentalists. But its success is really not that surprising. Fundamentalism – and here we can move beyond Protestantism to the host of other groups who have been labeled "fundamentalist" – has successfully tapped into the deep reservoir of discontent with modernity, offering to its adherents certainty, community, and, of course, salvation.

Notes

1   The Fundamentalism Project, administered by Martin E. Marty and R. Scott Appleby, has produced the most important scholarship involving fundamentalism in a variety of religious traditions. See Marty and Appleby (1991, 1993a, 1993b, 1994, 1995). For a valuable discussion of comparative fundamentalism, see Harris (1998: 325–6).

2   See Virginia Lieson Brereton (1990: 165–70); Joel Carpenter (1997: 3–12).

3   Regarding fundamentalism (or lack thereof) in Great Britain, see Marsden (1980: 221–7; 1977); Bebbington (1989); Rennie (1994, esp. pp. 336–42). Regarding Canada, the notion of Canadian fundamentalism has provoked a fascinating academic conversation, focused on two questions: To what degree did/does fundamentalism exist in Canada? To what degree is fundamentalism in Canada simply an American export? For our purposes here, it is enough to say that fundamentalism has had a limited impact on Canadian religious life, and that – particularly in the early movement – there were some very interesting connections between Canadian fundamentalists and American fundamentalists. For an introduction to this discussion, see Elliott (1995); Lipset (1990, esp. p. 16); Rennie (1994: 342–5); Stackhouse (1993, esp. pp. 11–12, 21–3, 33–4).

4   Marsden (1988). While I contend that Marsden's "militant antimodernism" remains the best way to understand fundamentalism, I am also quite aware that this definition lacks precision. See Trollinger (2001: 264–8, 280–1).

5   For a classic discussion of the Princeton Theology and its connection with fundamentalism, see Sandeen (1970, esp. pp. 103–31). See also Noll (1988). For a discussion of how the discussion of inerrancy operates in contemporary fundamentalism, see Kathleen Boone (1989).

6   For dispensationalism and fundamentalism, see Boyer (1992); Marsden (1980, esp. pp. 48–71); Weber (1987).

7   For more on the World's Christian Fundamentals Association and the origins of the fundamentalist movement, see Trollinger (1990: 33–44).

8   For more on the denominational crusades, see Marsden (1980: 164–85); Trollinger (1990: 52–9).

9   For more on the antievolution crusade, see Larson (1985); Trollinger (1995).

10   For examples of this interpretation, see Cole (1931: 35–40, 336–7); Hofstadter (1962: 117–36); Furniss (1954: vii, 177–9); McLoughlin (1967: 45).

11   For fundamentalism in the 1930s and 1940s, see Carpenter (1997). For the role of Bible Schools in fundamentalism, see Brereton (1990). For fundamentalist Baptists in Canada and their organizations, see Burkinshaw (1995, esp. pp. 91–9, 131–5, 165–9); Stackhouse (1993: 29–31).

12   For a look at a key "neo-evangelical" institution as a window into the fundamentalist split, see Marsden (1987).

13 There is an ongoing argument over the degree to which fundamentalism has shaped and is central to twentieth-century evangelicalism in the United States. Donald Dayton, in particular, has criticized George Marsden and others for overemphasizing the importance of fundamentalism and de-emphasizing the importance of the holiness and Pentecostal traditions. See Dayton (1993). In that same issue Marsden and others respond to Dayton. See also Carpenter (1997: 236–8).

14 Much has been written on the Religious Right, but most important is William Martin (1996). For more on Jerry Falwell, see Susan Friend Harding (2000) and Frances FitzGerald (1981).

15 John Stackhouse (1993: 22, 35–45) convincingly argues that by the time Aberhart had become premier he was moving – in theology and practice – "beyond fundamentalism, and out of evangelical leadership" (p. 22). See also Elliott and Miller (1987).

16 The question of women's role is crucial to the religious right; for a historical treatment see Margaret Lamberts Bendroth (1993).

17 For a comprehensive study of creationism in the United States, see Numbers (1992). As Numbers points out, the early fundamentalist movement contained a great variety of creationist theories, the most popular of which allowed for an ancient earth: the day–age theory, in which each day of creation was actually a great expanse of time; and the gap theory, in which a vast amount of time separated the original creation and the six days of Genesis. But in modern fundamentalism creationism has become virtually synonymous with "young earth" theories of creation.

18 For the fundamentalist controversies in the Southern Baptist Convention see Ammerman (1990); Hankins (2002); Leonard (1990).

References

Ammerman, Nancy (1990). *Baptist Battles: Social Change and Religious Conflict in the Southern Baptist Convention*. New Brunswick NJ: Rutgers University Press.

Bebbington, David W. (1989). *Evangelicalism in Modern Britain: A History from the 1730s to the 1980s*. London: Unwin.

Boone, Kathleen (1989). *The Bible Tells Them So: The Discourse of Protestant Fundamentalism*. Albany: State University of New York Press.

Bendroth, Margaret Lamberts (1993). *Fundamentalism and Gender: 1875 to the Present*. New Haven, CT: Yale University Press.

Boyer, Paul (1992). *When Time Shall Be No More: Prophecy Belief in Modern American Culture*. Cambridge, MA: Harvard University Press.

Brereton, Virginia Lieson (1990). *Training God's Army: The American Bible School, 1880–1940*. Bloomington: Indiana University Press.

Burkinshaw, Robert (1995). *Pilgrims in Lotus Land: Conservative Protestantism in British Columbia, 1917–1981*. Montreal: McGill-Queen's University Press.

Carpenter, Joel (1997). *Revive Us Again: The Reawakening of American Fundamentalism*. New York: Oxford University Press.

Cole, Stewart (1931). *The History of Fundamentalism*. New York: Richard Smith.

Dayton, Donald (1993). The Search for the Historical Evangelicalism: George Marsden's History of Fuller Seminary as a Case Study. *Christian Scholar's Review*, 23: 12–33.

Elliott, David R. (1995). Knowing No Borders: Canadian Contributions to American Fundamentalism. In George A. Rawlyk and Mark A. Noll (eds.), *Amazing Grace: Evangelicalism in Australia, Britain, Canada, and the United States*. Montreal: McGill-Queen's University Press, pp. 349–74.

Elliott, David R. and Miller, Iris (1987). *Bible Bill: A Biography of William Aberhart*. Edmonton: Reidmore.

FitzGerald, Frances (1981). A Disciplined, Charging Army. *New Yorker*, May 18: 53–141.

Furniss, Norman (1954). *The Fundamentalist Controversy, 1918–1931*. New Haven, CT: Yale University Press.

Hankins, Barry (2002). *Uneasy in Babylon: Southern Baptist Conservatives and American Culture*. Tuscaloosa: University of Alabama.

Harding, Susan Friend (2000). *The Book of Jerry Falwell: Fundamentalist Language and Politics*. Princeton, NJ: Princeton University Press.

Harris, Harriet A. (1998). *Fundamentalism and Evangelicals*. Oxford: Clarendon Press.

Hofstadter, Richard (1962). *Anti-Intellectualism in American Life*. New York: Random House.

Hoover, Dennis (2000). A Religious Right Arrives in Canada. *Religion in the News*, 3, online at ⟨www.trincoll.edu/depts/csrpl⟩.

Larson, Edward (1985). *Trial and Error: the American Controversy over Creation and Evolution*. New York: Oxford University Press.

Larson, Edward (1997). *Summer for the Gods: The Scopes Trial and America's Continuing Debate over Science and Religion*. New York: Basic.

Laws, Curtis Lee (1920). Convention Side Lights. *The Watchman-Examiner*, 1 July: 834–5.

Leonard, Bill (1990). *God's Last and Only Hope: The Fragmentation of the Southern Baptist Convention*. Grand Rapids, MI: Eerdmans.

Lipset, Seymour Martin (1990). *Continental Divide: The Values and Institutions of the United States and Canada*. New York: Routledge.

McLoughlin, William (1967). Is There a Third Force in Christendom? *Daedalus* 96: 43–68.

Marsden, George M. (1977). Fundamentalism as an American Phenomenon, a Comparison with English Evangelicalism. *Church History* 46: 215–32.

Marsden, George M. (1980). *Fundamentalism and American Culture: The Shaping of Twentieth-Century Evangelicalism, 1870–1925*. New York: Oxford University Press.

Marsden, George M. (1987). *Reforming Fundamentalism: Fuller Seminary and the New Evangelicalism*. Grand Rapids, MI: Eerdmans.

Marsden, George M. (1988). Fundamentalism. In Charles Lippy and Peter Williams (eds.), *Encyclopedia of the American Religious Experience: Studies of Traditions and Movements*, 3 vols. New York: Scribner, vol. II, pp. 947–8.

Martin, William (1996). *With God on Our Side: The Rise of the Religious Right in America*. New York: Broadway.

Marty, M. E. and Appleby, R. Scott (eds.) (1991). *Fundamentalisms Observed*. Chicago: University of Chicago Press.

Marty, M. E. and Appleby, R. Scott (eds.) (1993a). *Fundamentalisms and Society: Reclaiming the Sciences, The Family, and Education*. Chicago: University of Chicago Press.

Marty, M. E. and Appleby, R. Scott (eds.) (1993b). *Fundamentalisms and the State: Remaking Politics, Economics, and Militance*. Chicago: University of Chicago Press.

Marty, M. E. and Appleby, R. Scott (eds.) (1994). *Accounting for Fundamentalism: The Dynamic Character of Movements*. Chicago: University of Chicago Press.

Marty, M. E. and Appleby, R. Scott (eds.) (1995). *Fundamentalisms Comprehended*. Chicago: University of Chicago Press.

Noll, Mark A (ed.) (1988). *The Princeton Defense of Plenary Verbal Inspiration*. New York: Garland.

Numbers, Ronald (1992). *The Creationists*. New York: Knopf.

Rennie, Ian S. (1994). Fundamentalism and the Varieties of North Atlantic Evangelicalism. In *Evangelicalism: Comparative Studies of Popular Protestantism in North America, the British Isles, and Beyond, 1700–1990*. New York: Oxford University Press, pp. 333–50.

Riley, William Bell (1919). *The Great Divide; or, Christ and the Present Crisis*. Philadephia: Bible Conference Committee.

Sandeen, Ernest (1970). *The Roots of Fundamentalism: British and American Millenarianism, 1800–1930*. Chicago: University of Chicago Press.

Spendlove, Paul (2002). After Party Election, Canadians Have Less Faith in Politics. *Christian Science Monitor*, April 11: 7.

Stackhouse, John S. Jr. (1993). *Canadian Evangelicalism in the Twentieth Century: An Introduction to Its Character*. Toronto: University of Toronto Press.

Trollinger, William Vance Jr. (1990). *God's Empire: William Bell Riley and Midwestern Fundamentalism (Religious Higher Education in the United States)*. Madison: University of Wisconsin Press.

Trollinger, William Vance Jr. (1995). Introduction. In *The Antievolution Pamphlets of William Bell Riley*. New York: Garland, pp. xii–xviii.

Trollinger, William Vance Jr. (1996). Independent Christian Colleges. In Thomas Hunt and James Carper (eds.), *Religious Higher Education in the United States*. New York: Garland, pp. 519–42.

Trollinger, William Vance Jr. (2001). How John Nelson Darby Went Visiting: Dispensational Premillennialism in the Believers Church Tradition and the Historiography of Fundamentalism. In Loren Johns (ed.), *Apocalypticism and Millennialism: Shaping a Believers Church Eschatology for the 21st Century*. Scottdale, PA: Herald, pp. 264–81.

Weber, Timothy (1987). *Living in the Shadow of the Second Coming: American Premillennialism, 1875–1982*. Chicago: University of Chicago Press.

CHAPTER 33
Protestantism and Racism

Paul R. Griffin

The question this chapter answers is: what has been the influence of Protestant theological ideas on racism, specifically on the antiblack attitudes that have dominated in America since the rise of Protestantism in the sixteenth century? My thesis is straightforward. Protestant theological ideas played a major role in shaping the ideas of race that sustained slavery in the past. Those same ideas continue to define and support racism today. To trace out the history of this influence, the chapter first revisits John Calvin's Reformed theology and looks at the ways in which Puritan heirs of that theology corrupted it into a Protestant theological defense for their racist claim that whites were created superior to blacks. Following a discussion of how the Puritan ideas of race influenced racist views of theologians, physicians, and scientists from the post-Colonial years through the Civil War decades, the chapter looks at their impact on the thoughts of two celebrated late nineteenth and early twentieth-century theologians – Josiah Strong and Walter Rauschenbusch. The chapter then moves to the present and looks at the ways in which Protestantism, specifically its liberal side, continue the racial legacy of the Puritans today. The discussion focuses on the liberal side because the racial attitudes of the conservative side – represented by the Jerry Falwells and Pat Robertsons – have already been well documented.

In visiting libraries to study what has already been written in answer to this question, one is quickly struck by how the scholarly world has all but ignored it. Apart from my recent study – *Seeds of Racism in the Soul of America* (Griffin, 1999/2000) – that examines the theological ideas behind race hate, there is only one other book that attempts to provide detailed answers to this question, namely Forest G. Wood's (1990) *The Arrogance of Faith: Christianity and Race in America from the Colonial Era to the Twentieth Century*. One can point to several reasons why scholars have not searched out answers to this question. Much of the scholarship on racism traditionally has comes from social scientists who focus on the ways in which concrete realties such as economics, class, geographic areas, and other kinds of demographics have shaped race prejudice. Although these studies present useful and exciting information, their interest is simply not in how ideas – especially theological ones – have influenced racial bigotry. A second explanation is that many religion scholars who do study this question concentrate their analyses on antebellum Protestant churches and the ways in which they endorsed and participated in slaveholding. While these writings provide important insight into Protestantism's support of slavery, they fail us in two other crucial ways. First, they offer no clue as to whether slaveholding Christians turned to theological ideas to help them justify that un-Christian activity. Second, they give no insight into whether theological ideas continue to influence present-day patterns of racism. A final reason is that some scholars are so closely connected to the Protestant tradition, either as personal confessors or as college, university, or seminary professors, and therefore they lack the distance – or in some cases the freedom – necessary for discussion of Protestantism's theological relationship with racism.

Because the scholarly world has virtually ignored writing about the influence of Protestant theological ideas on racism, many today – both inside and outside the academy – are either ignorant of, or misguided about, that impact. An example of this is found in the thoughts of Ellen Goodman (noted American syndicated newspaper columnist). Goodman recently wrote about President George W. Bush's efforts to promote tolerance for the Islamic religion in the aftermath of the terrorist attack on the World Trade Center in New York City. Critiquing America's record on religious tolerance, Goodman (2001) says that although diversity has long been a part of the country's religious landscape, "this was by no means preordained. Many Europeans first settled here in search of religious freedom – for themselves. The early Boston Puritans 'warned out' a Jewish merchant, passed an anti-Catholic law, hanged four Quakers and regarded Native Americans as heathens."

On the surface, Goodman's critique would seem fair in the light of what history books and monographs have lulled us into believing about the Puritans. But probing more deeply, one finds a serious omission in her analysis. It fails to include any mention of how the Puritans mistreated black people. One has to ponder how Goodman can so accurately recite the history of the Puritans' mistreatment of Jews, Catholics, Quakers, and Native Americans and not make a single reference to their racist attitudes toward black people. This neglect suggests that she either does not know or has purposefully avoided noting that Puritan Christians were among the first people in the New World to enslave Africans and declare them heathens. Moreover, these devout men and women hold the distinction of being the very first Protestant Christians anywhere to use theological notions to define and defend their racism. Although Goodman is not an academic, her slight of the Puritan's degradation of black people is typical of the way scholars have neglected analysis of the history of Protestantism's involvement in the shaping of racist beliefs and practices. Let's be straightforward and honest here. In searching library books, one finds that some writings have so glorified the Puritans as holy men and women that their evil hands in the shaping of American racism appear as absolutely clean and saintly. This was not the case.

From the moment the Puritans first settled in America in the 1630s to this very day, Protestant theological ideas have been the foundation of the notion that black people are inferior to whites and that God preordained them to be this way. Although scholars have often intentionally ignored it, the historical record shows that hardcore racists and social conservatives have not been the only ones to advance this notion. Many liberals, from the Colonial era to the present, who claim to be the "friends" of black people have also asserted and promoted these racist ideas. As impolite as it might be to raise it, even some radical white feminists over the centuries have pushed this idea of a God-ordained black inferiority (Griffin, 2000: 104–22).

In *Seeds of Racism in the Soul of America*, one of my goals is to demonstrate that knowledge of the religious history of racism is crucial for two prominent reasons. First, if we are ever to acquire a true grasp of racism's real nature, we must first understand that, whatever else it might be, racism is a religion. It is a religion because it was Christians – not crude and unlettered southern plantation owners, as most of our history books are prone to tell us – who first cast racial bigotry into a system of twisted theological ideas. Over the past five centuries this theologically informed racism has become an orthodox confession, not only in the churches but also in secular society. This brings us to the second reason why the knowledge of religion's role in racism is so critical. Ever since antiblackness first became normative in America during the colonial era, efforts to not only understand but also to eradicate it have concentrated on visible realities such as slavery, economic and social discrimination, and segregation. But history, in the form of the antislavery/abolitionist crusades, the Civil War, the Reconstruction, the recent black civil rights movements and the federal laws that resulted from them, has painfully and repeatedly demonstrated that while each of these efforts has had some immediate measurable impact on racism, not one of them has been successful in ending racial prejudice. The failure of these sincere and powerful efforts to end racism affirms that antiblackness is more than the racist practices that can be readily seen by the naked eye. Racism in America, as well as throughout Western societies and South Africa, has always been just as much a matter of evil thoughts in the mind and heart as it has been of concrete deeds of the hand.

Scholarly neglect to research and write about the powerful role Protestant theology has played in constructing and promoting these "sinful thoughts" helps keep the masses ignorant of this "bad side" of the Protestant faith. But as Dr. Martin Luther King, Jr. warned in 1958, if we are ever to be successful in the struggle to understand and combat racism, the churches and their members must first "try to get to the ideational roots of race hate, something that the law [and other material efforts] cannot accomplish." According to King, "the church must face its historic obligation in this crisis [because] in the final analysis the problem of race is not a political but a moral issue" that was created by the racist twisting of Protestant theological ideas (1958: 167). To unpack those theological ideas and to understand how Protestant Christians were the first to turn them into a theology of race let us turn briefly to the Reformed theology of John Calvin.

Puritans and the Legacy of Calvinism

Calvin's Reformed theology was ripe for subsequent Calvinists to corrupt into a theological defense of white supremacy over black people as God-ordained (despite the fact that Calvin himself never intended it this way). Rooted in a literal biblicism, especially of the Hebrew Scriptures, this theology supported two historic Christian teachings that could easily be twisted to defend the claim that blacks are inferior to whites and hence only fit for slavery and segregation outside the mainstream. These two theological pillars were the doctrines of sin and predestination (also called divine election.) Following the tradition of Paul and Augustine, Calvin taught that sin is hereditary and that every human being born after Adam and Eve is an absolutely depraved sinner with no ability to alter that state. Salvation, according to Calvin, is strictly the work of an all-sovereign God who also wills the extent to which evil will afflict some people through others. Concerning predestination, he taught that it is God who predetermines who will be redeemed and receive eternal life and who will be condemned and receive eternal damnation.[1]

Puritans blended Calvin's views of sin and predestination with their own understandings of two other historic Christian teachings in creation and covenant. Giving their own unique spin to the doctrine of creation, Puritans argued that God had not created humanity equal. Instead, God created a hierarchy of humanity ranging from the highest to the lowest. Puritan John Winthrop, the first governor of the Massachusetts Bay colony, put it this way: "God almighty in His most holy and wise providence hath so disposed of the condition of mankind as in all times some must be rich, some poor, some high and eminent in power and dignity, others mean and in subjection" (Winthrop, 1931: 282).

The Puritans' understanding of covenant was just as narrow as their understanding of creation. Driven by a strict biblical literalism, they argued for a federal or full covenant – modeled after the Mosaic covenant – in which they claimed God had made them the new chosen people, replacing the ancient Hebrews. Self-proclaimed to be God's new chosen race, Puritans insisted on the requirement that only those who could give visible proof of their divine election by living an absolutely pure and holy life could be members of their full covenant.

Coming to America, Puritans wasted no time in twisting these four doctrines (sin, predestination, creation, and covenant) into a theology of racism that they could use to define and defend their degradation of black people. For example, as early as 1634, a mere four years after the Puritans first began settling in America en masse, Theophilus Eaton, Puritan governor of the Connecticut colony, is reported to have boasted that he had been holding blacks in slavery for some time and would continue that practice "forever or during his pleasure." Drawing on the ancient Israelite law codes in Leviticus (specifically 25: 44–6), Eaton argued that as God's new chosen and covenanted people Puritans were placed under a divine duty to enslave or otherwise segregate black people from the elect, lest they somehow defile the righteous as the infidels are claimed to have done in biblical times.[2]

In 1641, less than a decade after Eaton's historic boast, the Massachusetts Bay Colony passed the first act legalizing slavery anywhere in the land (Whitmore, 1890). Both of these events predated the rise of slavery as a legal institution in any southern colony. Although scholars have given broad discussion to these two events in other contexts, they have disregarded their relationship to Protestantism. This neglect speaks again to how scholars have consistently avoided critiquing the Puritan faith's influence on racial bigotry.[3]

Eaton was not the only Puritan molding Protestant biblical and theological ideas to support race prejudice. Reading through the literature of the more celebrated Puritans – those whom scholars have rushed to hail as among the world's greatest, but have not rushed to challenge for their racism – one finds a virulent racism against black people that is informed by these same ideas. Even the writings of Cotton Mather, who scholars have praised as one of America's greatest Christian theologians, reflect a theologically grounded racism. Speaking about black people, Mather commonly referred to them as "the miserable children of Adam and Noah" who are "the Blackest Instances of Blindness and baseness" and "the most brutish of Creatures upon Earth." Further distorting the four doctrines into a theological defense of Puritan antiblackness, Mather argued that the Puritans were not being un-Christian toward black people because "it is God who caused black people [to] fall into a dreadful condition [of slavery] because [God] created them the vassals of Satan" (Mather, 1706: 2–3; see also Mather, 1940).

In the historical progression of Protestantism's promulgation of racist theological ideas, Judge John Saffin – another well-regarded Puritan leader – surpassed Mather. Saffin, in a vitriolic response to an antislavery pamphlet published and circulated by one of his colleagues (Judge Samuel Sewall), published the first systematic defense of slavery in America in 1701. His *A Brief and Candid Answer to a Late Printed Sheet, Entitled, The Selling of Joseph* pushed the doctrines of creation, sin, predestination, and covenant to their utmost extreme. He argues that blacks have no legal or divine "right to liberty and all outward comforts of this life" because God "hath ordained different degrees and orders of men, some to be High and Honourable, some to be Low and Despicable . . . yea, some to be born slaves, and so to remain during their lives"[4]

Imposing a clearly racist slant on Paul's discussion of the various members of the body in 1 Corinthians 12:12–26, Saffin warns Christians that they "must dare not to think" that God created black people "equal and of like dignity" with whites, lest they desecrate "all the sacred rules, precepts and commands the Almighty hath given the sons of men to observe and keep in their respective places, orders, and degrees" (Moore, 1866: 252). He poetically contrasts blacks with Joseph and says that the enslavement of black people must not be equated with the selling of Joseph because "cowardly and cruel are those blacks innate, Prone to Revenge, Imp of inveterate hate, . . . Mischief and Murderous . . . Libidinous, Deceitful, False, and Rude . . . The Spume Issue of Ingratitude. The Premises consider'd all may tell, How near good Joseph they are parallel" (Moore, 1866: 256).

The question here is: how could Puritans give Christian doctrines such a racist bend and still claim themselves to be God's people? For Saffin, Mather, Eaton, Winthrop, and other Puritans the answer was easy. They were convinced that when God elected them the "chosen race" and ordained them to turn America into the "new Jerusalem," God gave them the same commandments that God gave the ancient Hebrews – let no "heathen" run free in the "holy land" of the elect.

Unlike southern slaveholders, who argued that they enslaved Africans because they needed an "abundant and cheap labor force," Puritans never sought to justify their racism in this fashion. Instead, they were quite honest in confessing that their racism was tied to their theology. According to their own words, they believed that the elect had to enslave and ostracize black people in order to avoid being guilty of "invert[ing] the order that God hath set in the world" (Moore, 1866: 252). For Puritans, domination and degradation of black people was not a mere economic or social necessity. Racial supremacy was a divine mandate that whites had to constantly practice, less they violate their covenant with God.

While some might say that this assessment of the Puritans is unfairly harsh, consider that Winthrop D. Jordan, a noted scholar of racial attitudes in America, could only say that the Puritans' racist conduct was done "rather mindlessly." However, Professor Jordan quickly adds these words as a caveat, that acting without serious forethought and prayerful introspection "was not their way" (Jordan, 1969: 66). The Puritans never acted without serious deliberation and prayer because everything they did had to conform to what they understood to be God's will. This is the reason they spent so much time twisting the doctrines of creation, sin, predestination, and covenant into a systematic theology of race and racism.

From the colonial era to the Reconstruction, the racist distortions these pious Protestants placed on the four doctrines attracted widespread and open assent all across the American religious landscape. Every denomination and every religious body endorsed them in some way or other. Southern clerics regularly lifted up the idea of white supremacy over blacks from their pulpits, while their trained colleagues in the seminaries and colleges put it forth as both historical facts and divine truths in their classrooms. Examples can be found in the volumes of publications that were written in support of slavery and white supremacy between the 1700s and the Civil War. Among these were Richard Nisbet's *Slavery Not*

Forbidden by Scripture (1773), Leander Ker's *Slavery Consistent With Christianity* (1840), Samuel B. How's *Slaveholding Not Sinful* and *Slavery the Punishment of Man's Sin, Its Remedy, the Gospel of Christ* (1855), John B. Thrasher's *Slavery a Divine Institution: A Speech made before the Breckinridge and Lane Club* (November 5, 1860).

Although historians have avoided discussing it, the same kind of sweeping support of the four doctrines could be found in northern pulpits, seminaries, and colleges. For example, the Reverend Wilbur Fisk, a prominent Methodist clergyman and president of Wesleyan University in Connecticut during the 1830s, was a staunch defender of slavery and white supremacy. Citing 1 Corinthians 7:20–2 ("Let each of you remain in the condition in which you were called"), Fisk insisted that "the general rule of Christianity not only permits but enjoins a continuance of the master's authority" to enslave black people forever (cited in Barnes, 1855: 29).

While the Civil War brought an end to legal slavery and thus exploded the claim of a God-ordained black inferiority, the old Puritan theologies of racism continued to thrive during the decades after the Civil War. But this time, those ideas did not just bear fruit among Christians. They also yielded great harvests among scientists and physicians. With the ubiquitous and thunderous voices of both southern and northern preachers and trained theologians proclaiming a God-ordained black inferiority, scientists such as the renowned Jean-Louis Rodolphe Agassiz quickly connected scientific theories to those theological ones. In an essay entitled "The Diversity of the Origin of the Human Race," Agassiz used ethnological differences to assert that black people are innately inferior to whites and although Africans have been "in constant intercourse with the white race, there has never been a regulated society of black men developed on the [African] continent." According to Agassiz, white people must dominate black people because they are "naturally" incapable of high civilization (Agassiz, 1850).

Sharing what had become the national belief in innate black inferiority, some physicians began vigorous campaigns to portray black people as medical threats to the physical well-being of the white race. New York physician Dr. Robert W. Shufeldt argued, "It is a thoroughly proven fact that the negro in the United States is among other things, a constant menace to the health of the white race by reason of his being a pronounced disseminator of some five or six of the most dreaded diseases known to man" (Shufeldt, 1915: 249). Not content with declaring blacks "health hazards," Schufeldt insisted, "the truth is that the negro today, untrammeled and free from control, is rapidly showing atavistic tendencies. He is returning to a state of savagery, and in his frequent attacks of sexual madness, his religious emotionalism, superstition, and indolence, is himself again – a savage" (Shufedt, 1907: 115). Shufeldt's racist ideas so closely emulate arguments made by the Puritans that if one did not know better one might conclude that the Puritan Judge John Saffin had resurrected from his grave and was uttering them. This again shows Protestantism's commanding influence on racism.

As expected, Christian clerics and lay people were not silent about promoting white supremacy during the post-Civil War decades. Driven by the reality that their whole way of living had crumbled, southern slaveholders sought to recover that "great white past" by becoming even more aggressive in advancing racist theological ideas. To a large degree, this aggression was fueled by fear. Since the Europeans first traveled to Africa and laid eyes on black people, some whites have feared them. The color, physiognomy, culture, religion, and intelligence of Africans appeared to these whites to be undeniable proof that blacks were not only innately different and inferior to all other races, but also to be feared as "beasts." I am convinced, said Charles Carroll, that God has not created black people human beings "but apes" Carroll (1900: 87). Carroll so strongly believed blacks were subhuman that in 1900 he wrote what has become the most extreme and vicious book ever written about black people, "*The Negro a beast;*" *or, "In the Image of God": The reasoner of the age, the revelator of the century! The Bible as it is! The negro and his relation to the human family! . . . The negro not the son of Ham. . . .*

Josiah Strong and Walter Rauschenbusch

Although scholars have slighted it, the post-Civil War decades through the first 50 years of the twentieth century were ones in which some of America's most celebrated clergy became leaders in the teaching of antiblack sentiments. Topping the list of these clergy were Josiah Strong (1846–1916) and Walter Rauschenbusch (1861–1918). Strong was the general secretary of the American branch of the Evangelical Alliance and one of the most influential religious leaders of the late nineteenth and early twentieth centuries. Although an evangelical religionist, he was an avid supporter of Darwinism. Following in the footsteps of his Puritan progenitors, Strong was certain that America was predestined to become God's "New Jerusalem." He also was just as certain that black people were intellectually and spiritually "less than whites" and hence could play no part in helping America move toward that divine destiny. To defend his position, Strong added Darwinian evolutionism to Puritan ideas of race. He then claimed that black people could not participate in America's ascension to God's dominion on earth because they had come from "a lower barbarism than any [found] in Asia [or throughout the world]" (Strong, 1893: 3–4).

Scholars have ignored the racism in Walter Rauschenbusch's thoughts. But as much as it may pain some and embarrass others, the thoughts of this highly celebrated theologian and champion of social equality and justice for the white poor clearly show the stain of racist ideas. Like Strong, Rauschenbusch supported Darwinian evolutionism and he used this scientific approach to buttress his belief that America was evolving into God's earthly domain. Wrapped in sophisticated rhetoric, the racist views of this heralded theologian-pastor regarding black people and their role in America's progression toward God are not glaringly open. But looking carefully at three statements he made about slavery, those beliefs readily become manifest. These statements are: "one reason why the South broke down in our Civil War was that its slave labor kept it industrially incompetent"; "slavery has disappeared not simply because it contradicted the moral convictions of mankind, but because it was inefficient labor and unable to stand against the competition of the free man working for his own good"; and "the slave could be trusted only with the crudest tools and employed at the coarsest forms of agriculture [since] the higher motives that give the perpetual spring and keenness of edge to our work – the hope of economic advancement, the desire for honor, the sense of duty, and the love of work for its own sake – scarcely touched him" (Rauschenbusch, 1912: 195–6).

Let's cut to the quick here. Rauschenbusch's three statements represent a view of black humanity that is almost a carbon copy of the old Puritan idea of a God-ordained black inferiority. For example, to say that the "slaves could be trusted only with the crudest tools and employed at the coarsest forms of agriculture" because they had not been "touched by higher motives" is a broad racist stroke that falsifies the truth about the integrity and trustworthiness of slaves. If slaves, as Rauschenbusch claims, could only be trusted "with the crudest tools" and, if the "higher motives" that encourage decency and industry had not "touched them," then how do we account for the fact that there is no documented evidence that slave women, whose slavemasters and slavemistresses commanded them to be nannies for their babies, ever murdered those infants, even though they had every opportunity to do so? If slaves were such untrustworthy and ruthless people, then how do we account for the fact that slave women who were raped and forced to bear the offspring of their rapists never turned on their violators and murdered them? If slaves were such "inefficient laborers," then how did the South have a prospering economy until the War? One has to wonder whether Rauschenbusch gave any thought to these questions as he was depicting slaves in a way that, although not as truculent as Judge Saffin, nonetheless duplicates the racist characterization of blacks made nearly three centuries earlier.

That Rauschenbusch shared the old Puritan racialism is further evidenced by the way he understood and treated the white men and women whose cause he defended. Although these whites were largely in the same condition as most blacks – semiliterate, poor, and socially ostracized – there is no indication that Rauschenbusch ever questioned their abilities to contribute to the advancement of the society. On the contrary, this is what his social gospel was all about – uplifting the oppressed so that they could become participants in America's move toward God's earthly kingdom. Unfortunately, this elevation neglected human beings whose skin color was dark. Thus, the only difference between Rauschenbusch's racist views and Saffin's was that his rhetoric was more sophisticated. Cutting through his cultured racism, Rauschenbusch's thoughts clearly show him endorsing the accepted theologically informed belief of his age; namely that "the negro is a different being from the white man, and therefore, of necessity, was designed by the Almighty Creator to live a different life" under the dominion of the master (Van Evrie, 1868: 312).

Seemingly nothing could bring an end to this old Puritan idea. It had, as Plato had taught about ideas in general, taken on the ability to lie dormant in the mind until a real-life need incites it into concrete expression.[5] Moreover, because it was rooted in four doctrinal teachings that are central across Protestant denominations and churches, it was able to find zealous defenders not only among hardcore Calvinists, but also among members of every other denomination and religious group from Episcopalians to Methodists to Unitarians and from conservatives to liberals. Thus, the religion of antiblackness marched all across America from Rauschenbusch's age to the black civil rights decades of the 1950s, 1960s, and 1970s.

Liberal Protestantism Since the 1950s

It was during these decades that something "miraculous" appeared to be developing within Protestantism, specifically within the liberal part of this tradition. The "bad theology" of race that this faith had been authoring and sowing for over four centuries at last seemed headed for its deathbed. Although there were a myriad of factors involved, the seeming demise of these racist ideas also reflected to an important degree Protestantism's response in 1963 to the violence that racists in Birmingham, Alabama had openly and defiantly inflicted upon marchers as they followed Dr. Martin Luther King, Jr. in protest against race bigotry in that city. Caught on national and international television cameras, the brutality of that violence – whips, dogs, clubs, fists, fire hoses – galvanized sympathizers for the black struggle from all across the world. Spurred on by this widespread support, liberal Protestantism joined the battle. Indeed, northern progressive churches as well as some southern ones sprang into action to help defend black humanity.

The *National Council of Churches* (NCC) assumed a leadership role in that defense. Responding in 1963 to the brutality perpetrated against black people in Birmingham, the NCC formed a Commission on Religion and Race. The task of this commission was to bring the nation's mainstream Protestant churches together in a united front against racial discrimination. As a sign of the churches' commitment to this goal, the commission devoted its energies and resources to helping convince Christians, especially in the Midwestern states, to vote for passage of both the Civil Rights Bill of 1964 and the Voting Rights Bill of 1965. Without the efforts of the commission and liberal Protestants, it is unlikely that either of these bills would have been passed.[6]

The passage of the two bills brought a legal end to the racist practices that had kept African Americans locked out from working and participating in the various public arenas. For the first time in America's history, black men and women now had a legal right to participate in marketplace venues that in the past had been segregated and slammed shut to them. African Americans now were a part of the very "manifest destiny" movement that Puritans and their theological successors over the years had fought to ban blacks from, through twisted, racist, theological arguments. Liberal Protestantism finally appeared to have begun living up to one of its central confessions, "in God all people are equal." Major denominations such as the United Methodist Church, the Episcopal Church, the United Presbyterian Church, the United Church of Christ, and the American Baptist Church all seemed to be supporting this teaching in varying ways and degrees. One of the foremost strategies these denominations employed here was the creation of special programs designed to attract African Americans to become ordained in their ministries. It was not uncommon to find local churches inviting black preachers to speak from their pulpits on Sunday mornings or at special programs.

Protestant churches were not the only ones appearing to be embracing that confession. Church-related schools, especially seminaries, also now began to witness to it. For example, Union Theological Seminary in New York City invested $500,0000 of its endowment to projects of racial elevation. Seminaries at Yale and Harvard Universities began unprecedented efforts to recruit black students and also to employ black professors to develop and direct African American Studies programs (see, e.g., Findlay, 1993: 218).

Liberal Protestantism during the 1960s gave the appearance that it was dedicated to ending its racist past and helping spread racial equality and justice all across America. But Protestantism's embrace of this principle died almost as quickly as it began. By the close of the 1960s, liberal Protestant churches and their leaders had all but abandoned the black quest for humanity and justice.

The question that rises here is why did liberal Protestants so quickly desert the black struggle? One does not have to search deeply for an answer. Although scholars have left it unexamined, there has always been an unspoken racial boundary beyond which many liberal Christians have never been able to go, despite their support of black social equality. Bluntly put, although they were stirred into action by the brutalities inflicted on blacks during the civil rights era, many liberal Protestants never were able to move beyond the level of "compensating desegregationists" on the issue of race and racism. Compensating desegregationists are convinced that the only responsibility they have as alleged racial egalitarians is to support black societal liberation through mandated social, economic, and political desegregation. Their minds still poisoned by the old Puritan ideas of race, they see no reason for taking the additional and more difficult step of affirming blacks as their human equals. As *Christian* compensating desegregationists, some white liberals during the 1960s had no difficulty in supporting and defending the right of African Americans to vote and enjoy certain kinds of opportunities in the workplace. But they had serious problems in taking the additional step of affirming the equal humanity of black people with all other races.

Although Urban Studies scholars have not been forthright about it, it was liberal compensating desegregationists who helped lead the "white flight" from the urban cities during the late 1950s and early 1960s. Although these progressives fought for desegregation of institutions, and although they showed no fear about African Americans working alongside, they were absolutely horrified at the prospect of black people living next door to them in their all-white neighborhoods. Here enters the chicanery of liberals in attempting to hide their racism. During the 1960s and 1970s, they joined with conservatives and hardcore racists in putting forth the explanation that they had to flee to the suburbs because lower-class African Americans were causing the decay that was beginning to consume urban cities. Common sense tells us that powerless poor blacks could not have been the source of urban decline. They were not that source because they were not the first black men and women to move into all-white urban neighborhoods. Poor blacks possessed neither the money nor the inclination to move into all-white neighborhoods. It was African Americans who came from the ranks of the black middle and upper class who first moved into previously all-white city neighborhoods. So who were these African Americans that white Christian liberals claimed to be destroying their neighborhoods? They could only have been these black men and women who possessed the educational, economic, and social means and graces not to have caused urban decay. These blacks had the same human aspirations as white liberals. Thus, contrary to what liberals have said, the reason they fled from the lofty Victorian houses, the quality schools, the manicured lawns, and the downtown conveniences with which they had once been so satisfied was because they simply could not accept blacks, even those from middle- and upper-class ranks, as their equals. Their minds were still contaminated by the racist ideas sown by their ancestors. So while they could affirm desegregation, they simply could not bring themselves to admit the equality of black humanity with white. In this, they show themselves no different from some racist conservatives and extremists. In their hearts and minds these liberals accept the arguments of their Puritan ancestors that black people are different from and less than all other races.

Because their acts of racism often have been so violent and blatant, discussions of racism over the years have centered on conservatives and hardcore racists. But as these few paragraphs have attempted to show, although they have not been publicly associated with acts of physical violence acts, Christian liberals are little different than their conservative counterparts when it comes to embracing the twisted Protestant theological ideas first planted by the Puritans.

The one glaring difference between the two groups is that liberals throughout American history have learned to be more sophisticated with their antiblackness. From the Puritan era to the present, their sophistication often has been in the form of an eerie silence regarding the matter of race and racism. For example, the writings of heralded American theologians stretching from Jonathan Edwards through H. Richard Niebuhr, Rheinhold Niebuhr, and Paul

Tillich are conspicuously empty of any critical analysis of the interplay between Christian ideas and racism. While all of these "giants" wrote volumes analyzing the finer points of theology and showing how theology relates to human enterprises, none raised a question about how Protestants repeatedly have corrupted theology in order to justify antiblackness as God-ordained.

As we seek to not only understand but also to find solutions to the persistent problem of racism, the silence of these revered liberal Protestant thinkers is most troubling. Troubling because their writings – void of any critique of Protestantism's racist history – are the very ones that seminaries and graduate schools of religion continue to lift up as standard reading for all who would learn and embrace the Protestant faith. Free of any critique of Protestant history in shaping racist attitudes, these writings give the false illusion that this faith is colorblind. But as these pages have attempted to demonstrate, skin color has always been one of the key emphases of many who embrace this tradition. Indeed, as Kyle Haselden said, Protestantism in the hands of bigoted Christians has long been the "mother of racial patterns, the purveyor of arrant sedatives, and the teacher of immoral moralities" as it relates to black people (Haselden, 1964: 14).

Rarely does a historian venture solutions. But I offer one here. In an era when some are asking again what can we do to bring an end to race prejudice, we must once more insist that Protestant churches are one, if not the, starting point. The churches hold this status because they still have not confessed and repented of their sins in making racism a cornerstone of this society. If there is any hope of a day when antiblackness will no longer be a hallmark of the society, Christians must rise up and be the first to confess the mighty roles Protestantism has played in shaping that bigotry. Such a confession has been difficult for a variety of reasons. But the neglect of scholars to tell the story of how Protestantism and its theologians, from the Puritan era to the present, often have been leaders in planting, resowing, and resowing again and again the evil seeds of race hate into the very soul of America stands large. Hopefully, this chapter is a step in making at least a small bit of that history known.

Notes

1   John Calvin's theology is detailed in his *Institutes of the Christian Religion: Instruction in Faith*.
2   The quotation comes from Eaton's daughter, so the precise date when he made his announcement is debatable. See Baldwin (1908: 31).
3   Forest G. Wood (1990: 254) says that this neglect "has been reflected in the writings of some of the most influential students of New England history."
4   John Saffin (1866), *A Brief and Candid Answer to a Late Printed Sheet, Entitled, The Selling of Joseph*, reprinted in an appendix in Moore (1866: 251–6).
5   Plato's discussion of the eternality of ideas can be found in his *Timaeus, and the Critias, or Atlanticus*.
6   My position differs from that of Findlay (1993: 62 ff).

References

Agassiz, Jean Louis Rodolphe (1850). The Diversity of the Origin of the Human Race. *Christian Examiner and Religious Miscellany* 49: 142–3.

Baldwin, Simeon E. (ed.) (1908). *Papers of the New Haven Colony, Historical Society*, vol. 7. New Haven, CT: New Haven Historical Society.

Barnes, Albert (1855). *An Inquiry into the Scriptural Views of Slavery*. Philadelphia: Parry and McMillan.

Carroll, Charles (1900). *"The Negro a Beast;" or, "In the Image of God": The Reasoner of the Age, the Revelator of theCcentury! The Bible as it is! TheNegro and his Relation to the Human Family! . . . The Negro not the Son of Ham. . . .* Salem, NH: Ayer.

Findlay, James Jr. (1993). *Church People in the Struggle: The National Council of Churches and the Black Freedom Movement, 1950–1970*. New York: Oxford University Press.

Goodman, E. (2001). Diversity Doesn't Prevent Atrocities. *Dayton Daily News*, December 26, p. 10A.

Griffin, Paul R. (1999) *Seeds of Racism in the Soul of America*, Cleveland, OH: Pilgrim Press; paperback (2000) Naperville, IL: Sourcebooks.

Haselden, Kyle (1964). *The Racial Problem In Christian Perspective*. New York: Harper Torchbook.

Jordan, Winthrop D. (1969). *White Over Black: American Attitudes Toward the Negro, 1550–1812*. Baltimore: Penguin Books.

King, Martin Luther Jr. (1958). *Stride Toward Freedom: The Montgomery Story*. New York: Ballantine Books.

Mather, Cotton (1706). *The Negro Christianized: An Essay to Excite and Assist That Good Work, the Instruction of Negro Servants in Christianity*. Boston: B. Green.

Mather, Cotton (1940). *Rules for the Society of Negroes*. In Thomas J. Holmes (ed.) *Cotton Mather: A Bibliography of His Works*, vol. 3. Cambridge, MA: Harvard University Press.

Moore, George H. (1866). *Notes on the History of Slavery in Massachusetts*. New York: Appleton.

Rauschenbusch, Walter (1912). *Christianizing the Social Order*. New York: Macmillan.

Shufeldt, Robert W. (1907). *The Negro A Menace to American Civilization*. Boston: Gorman Press.

Shufeldt, Robert W. (1915). *America' Greatest Problem: The Negro*. Philadelphia: F A Davis.

Strong, Josiah (1893). *The New Era; or, The Coming Kingdom*. New York: Baker and Taylor.

Van Evrie, John H. (1868). *White Supremacy and Negro Subordination; or, Negroes a Subordinate Race, and (So-Called) Slavery Its Normal Condition*. New York: Van Evrie and Horton.

Whitmore, William H. (1890). *The Colonial Laws of Massachusetts*. Boston: Rockwell and Churchill.

Winthrop, John (1931). A Model of Christian Charity. In Stewart Mitchell (ed.), *Winthrop Papers 1623–30*. New York: Russell and Russell, pp. 282–93.

Wood, Forrest G. (1990). *The Arrogance of Faith: Christianity and Race in America from the Colonial Era to the Twentieth Century*. New York: Knopf.

Further Reading

Bell, Derrick (1987). *And We Are Not Saved: The Elusive Quest for Racial Justice*. New York: Basic Books.

Hacker, Andrew (1992). *Two Nations: Black And White, Separate, Hostile, Unequal.* New York: Charles Scribner's Sons.

Kelsey, George D. (1965). *Racism and the Christian Understanding of Man.* New York: Charles Scribner's Sons.

Ruchames, Louis (1969). *Racial Thought in America, Vol. 1, From the Puritans to Abraham Lincoln.* Amherst: University of Massachusetts Press.

Sharp, Douglas R. (2002). *No Partiality: The Idolatry of Race and The New Humanity.* Downers Grove, IL: InterVarsity Press.

CHAPTER 34
Protestantism and Judaism

Clark M. Williamson

Martin Luther

An account of the relationship of Protestantism to Judaism must begin at the beginning, with Martin Luther (1483–1546) whose tracts and sermons expressed his view of Judaism. In 1523, Luther wrote "That Jesus Christ Was Born a Jew" (*LW* 45). In it Luther discloses his familiarity with the church's abuse of Jews: "Our fools, the popes, bishops, sophists and monks – the crude asses' heads – have hitherto so treated the Jews that anyone who wished to be a good Christian would almost have had to become a Jew" (200). This tract is devoted to suggesting methods to argue with Jews from the Scripture. After having surveyed a host of passages which he interprets as pointing to Jesus Christ, he asks: "Where will one find a prince, or messiah, or king, with whom all this accords so perfectly, as with our Lord Jesus Christ?" (228).

Twenty years later, Luther wrote "On The Jews and Their Lies" (*LW* 47). Contradicting his earlier argument, Luther now contends for precisely that mistreatment of Jews against which he had protested. Luther denounces "the false lying boasts of the Jews," by which he means claims about the covenant between God and the people Israel, the law, circumcision, and being children of Abraham. Luther engages in a scriptural argument with Jews of the "we're right/you're wrong" variety. He regarded his Christological interpretation of Old Testament passages as the "literal" interpretation. He called the contradictory, Jewish interpretation of the same passages as "confused lies and tomfoolery" (243). He recited anti-Jewish medieval superstitions, such as the blood libel and well-poisoning, and turned to his recommendations as to how Jews should be treated.

"What shall we Christians do," he asks, "with this rejected and condemned people, the Jews" (268)? He answers: "First, to set fire to their synagogues or schools and to bury and cover with dirt whatever will not burn . . ." (ibid.). "Second, I advise that their houses also be razed and destroyed . . . Third, I advise that all their prayer books and Talmudic writings, in which such idolatry, lies, cursing, and blasphemy are taught, be taken from them . . . Fourth, . . . that their rabbis be forbidden to teach henceforth on pain of loss of life and limb" (269). "Fifth, . . . that safe-conduct on the highways be abolished completely for the Jews" [so that they cannot do business] . . . "Sixth, . . . that usury be prohibited to them, and that all cash and treasure of silver and gold be taken from them and put aside for safekeeping" (270). "Seventh, I recommend putting a flail, an ax, a hoe, a spade, a distaff, or a spindle into the hands of young, strong Jews and Jewesses and letting them eat their bread in the sweat of their brow" (272).

Luther recommends, lastly, "let us emulate the common sense of other nations such as France, Spain, Bohemia, etc., compute with them how much their usury has extorted from us, divide this amicably, but then eject them forever from the country" (272). Some of Luther's Protestant colleagues (Melancthon and Bullinger) were appalled by this tract and Luther's later *On Schem Hamphoras*, which was, if anything, worse. Yet Luther's views were typical of medieval Christians. John Eck, Luther's nemesis, did not oppose Luther on the topic of anti-Judaism, boiling over as he could against the "cunning, false, perjured, thievish, vindictive, and traitorous Jews" (cited in *LW* 47: 129). Twentieth-century anti-Semites would republish these tracts.

Jaroslav Pelikan commented "that the time has come for those who study Luther and admire him to acknowledge, more unequivocally and less pugnaciously than they have, that on this issue Luther's thought and language are simply beyond defense" (cited in Littell, 1979: 105). In this spirit, the Church Council of the Evangelical Lutheran Church in America on 18 April, 1994, declared:

> As did many of Luther's own companions in the sixteenth century, we reject this violent invective, and yet more do we express our deep and abiding sorrow over its tragic effects on subsequent generations. In concert with the Lutheran World Federation, we particularly deplore the appropriation of Luther's words by modern anti-Semites for the teaching of hatred toward Judaism or toward the Jewish people in our day. (Church Council of the Evangelical Lutheran Church in America, 1994)

John Calvin

John Calvin (1509–64), the Geneva reformer, had little first-hand contact with Jews in that city. Jews had been expelled from Geneva in 1491. Calvin's attitude toward Jews and Judaism is "maddeningly complex" (Engel, 1990: 123). He claims "all men adopted by God into the company of his people since the beginning of the world were covenanted to him by the same law and by the same doctrine as obtains among us" (Calvin, *Institutes*, I: 428). The difference between the "old" covenant with the people Israel and the "new" covenant with the church are differences of form, not substance; "the two are actually one and the same." They differ in the "mode of dispensation."

The Israelites are "equal to us not only in the grace of the covenant, but also in the signification of the sacraments" (*Institutes*, I: 431). In principle, Calvin breaks with the traditional anti-Jewish arguments that the church replaces the people Israel in God's grace as well as with the invidious distinctions that claim, for example, that Christianity is a religion of grace whereas Judaism is one of works-righteousness. No, says Calvin, rather, it is we Christians who "must be reckoned as members of his [Abraham's] tribe (Genesis 12: 3)" (*Institutes*, I: 437). Calvin had a hard time staying true to his remarkable insight. When he delineated the differences between the two "modes of dispensation" he argued that the old covenant provided "types," whereas the church receives the "reality." God's covenant to Israel was "veiled"; that in the New Testament "reveals the very substance of truth as present." The former covenant was "temporary," the latter permanent. "The former is the preaching of death, the latter of life" (*Institutes*, I: 453–4).

Had Calvin followed through coherently on his fundamental insight, that Jews and Christians alike stand on nothing but God's unconditional justification of the ungodly, that Christians are therefore also children of Abraham, he would have made good on his theological breakthrough. That development, however, largely happened much, much later, only after the *Shoah* (Hebrew for "catastrophe," referring to the destruction of six million Jews by the Nazis).

Exactly this breakthrough was made in 1970 by the General Synod of the Netherlands Reformed Church. It affirmed that Christian faith is "built" on the faith of the people Israel and claimed that Israel's faith was "exclusively based on God's election" ("Israel: People, Land and State," World Council of Churches, 1988: 51). The very existence of the people Israel is a gift of grace. What was true prior to the time of Christ remains true today: Jewish faith and worship gives voice to an awesome gratitude about being loved by God and given the gift of Torah (the "way" in which God wants Israel to walk).

Similarly the General Assembly of the Presbyterian Church (USA) affirmed that the church "has been engrafted into the people of God established by the covenant with Abraham" and that the relationship of the Jewish people and the church to each other "is based on that gracious and irrevocable election of both" ("A Theological Understanding of the Relationship between Christians and Jews," World Council of Churches, 1988: 109–10).

Friedrich Schleiermacher

Friedrich Schleiermacher (1768–1834) was a German theologian whose influence on Protestant theology has been massive. He regarded all religions as different ways of giving expression to one fundamental, prereflective feeling, that of our "absolute (utter) dependence" on God. The various religions are related to each other "as different stages of development, and as different kinds" (Schleiermacher, 1928: 31). Judaism, Christianity, and Islam exist on the "highest plane" of development, religions of the monotheistic type. The limitation of Judaism, according to Schleiermacher, is that "by its limitation of the love of Jehovah to the race of Abraham, [it] betrays a lingering affinity with Fetishism . . ." (1928: 37). Because Christianity is free from this weakness (and comparable weaknesses in Islam), it "takes its place as the purest form of Monotheism which has appeared in history" (38).

Schleiermacher concedes that Christianity has an historical connection with Judaism, but he argues "as far as concerns its historical existence and its aim, its relations to Judaism and Heathenism are the same" (Schleiermacher, 1928: 60). Schleiermacher contends that "Christian piety, in its original form, cannot be explained by means of the Jewish piety of that or an earlier time, and so Christianity cannot in any wise be regarded as a remodeling or a renewal and continuation of Judaism" (ibid.: 61). Schleiermacher's view of the Scriptures follows from this. According to him, "the rule may be set up that almost everything in the Old Testament is for our Christian usage, but the husk or wrapping of its prophecy, and that whatever is most Jewish in it has the least value" (ibid.: 62). Consequently, "the Old Testament appears simply a superfluous authority for dogmatics [Christian theology]" (ibid.: 115).

Thus, as R. Kendall Soulen has argued, Schleiermacher sharpened Christianity's tendency to "render God's identity as the God of Israel irrelevant for shaping conclusions about God's enduring purposes for creation. Indeed, . . . Schleiermacher explicitly refuse[s] to identify the God of Christian faith with the God of Israel" (Soulen, 1996: 19); ". . . the Israelite dimension of Christian faith is cut away altogether" (ibid.: 68). Thus Schleiermacher "exacerbate[s] the standard model's supersessionism and flight from history" (ibid.: 79).

Adolf von Harnack

Adolf von Harnack (1851–1930) was a German church historian and a strong proponent of liberal Protestant theology. Harnack was fascinated by the second century heretic Marcion, one of the first to propose that the church adopt a "new" testament. Given the claim that the new covenant succeeds and displaces the old covenant, as Christianity usurps the place of Judaism in God's favor, it is not surprising that someone would try to rid the church of the Scriptures of Israel. This is what Marcion proposed.

Although Marcion's attempt to rid the church of the "old" testament in favor of the new was defeated, he caused the church to adopt a new policy. Prior to Marcion, Christians formed the Scriptures simply by adding new books to the

Scriptures of Israel. 2 Peter 3:15–16 mentions that the letters of Paul had been added to the "other Scriptures." Marcion radically altered this procedure. The church kept the Scriptures but separated the "Old Testament" from the "New Testament." The "very concept of a New Testament as distinct from the Old may well go back to Marcion's repudiation of the Jewish scriptures" (Perrin, 1974: 331).

Harnack contended:

> the rejection of the Old Testament in the second century was a mistake which the great church rightly refused to make. That it was retained in the sixteenth century was due to a fatal legacy which the Reformation was not able to overcome. However, for Protestantism since the nineteenth century to cherish it as a canonical document is the result of a religious and ecclesiastical paralysis. (Harnack, 1921: 248–9).

When we turn to Harnack's understanding of the historical figure of Jesus, we find the point at which he has had his most massive influence on subsequent scholars and theologians. His influence on how we understand the historical Jesus has outlived the career of theological liberalism.

In his *The Mission and Expansion of Christianity*, Harnack observed that Jesus addressed "his fellow countrymen. He preached only to Jews." His message arose from the heart of Judaism: "Not a syllable shows that he detached this message from its national soil, or set aside the traditional religion as of no value. Upon the contrary, his preaching could be taken as the most powerful corroboration of that religion." Jesus "took his stand upon the soil of Jewish rights, i.e., of the piety maintained by Pharisaism." Yet the Pharisees, says Harnack, not only preserved the best in Judaism; they also debased it. Against their "selfish, self-righteous temper" Jesus "waged war." In battling the "loveless and godless" Pharisees, he broke "with the national religion, for the Pharisaic position passed for that of the nation; indeed it represented the national religion." Harnack argued that the church's universalism was based on the universalism of Jesus's message, evident in his prediction of "the rejection of the nation and the overthrow of the temple." Jesus "shattered Judaism, and brought out the kernel of the religion of Israel. Thereby – i.e., by his preaching of God as the Father, *and by his own death* – he founded the universal religion, which at the same time was the religion of the Son" (Harnack, 1961: 36, 43).

The paradox here is that Harnack was well aware of the church's tradition of anti-Judaism. He saw that Paul's view that the "church did not abrogate the special promise made to the Jews" was nothing more than "a Pauline idiosyncrasy" in the ancient church. He characterized theological anti-Judaism as insisting that the Jews never were God's chosen people, that the Old Testament had nothing to do with the Jews but belonged from the outset to the church, and that Jews were punished by the burning of the Temple and the destruction of Jerusalem because they crucified Christ. Then he wrote a paragraph that is difficult to comprehend:

Such an injustice as that done by the Gentile church to Judaism is almost unprecedented in the annals of history. The Gentile church stripped it of everything; she took away its sacred book; herself but a transformation of Judaism, she cut off all connection with the parent religion. The daughter first robbed her mother, and then repudiated her! But, one may ask, is this view really correct? Undoubtedly it is, to some extent, and it is perhaps impossible to force anyone to give it up. But viewed from a higher standpoint, the facts acquire a different complexion. By their rejection of Jesus, the Jewish people disowned their calling and dealt the deathblow to their existence; their place was taken by Christians as the new People, who appropriated the whole tradition of Judaism, giving a fresh interpretation to any unserviceable materials in it, or else allowing them to drop . . . All that Gentile Christianity did was to complete a process which had in fact commenced long ago within Judaism itself, viz., the process by which the Jewish religion was being emancipated and transformed into a religion for the world. (Harnack, 1961: 66–7, 69–70)

In this way, Harnack justifies what he himself called one of the most unprecedented injustices in history.

Harnack acknowledged that the Pharisees were in possession of everything that Jesus proclaimed (Harnack, 1957: 47). But in his view they were a shabby lot:

As regards piety, the spring of holiness had, indeed, long been opened; but it was choked with sand and dirt, and its water was polluted. For rabbis and theologians to come afterwards and distill this water, even if they were successful, makes no difference. But now the spring broke forth afresh, and broke a new way for itself through the rubbish. (Harnack, 1957: 48)

Jesus's preaching of the Kingdom of God was a "definite signal for contradiction" of the prevailing religious system and brought him into conflict with the official leaders of Judaism, people who were aware of God's presence only in the law whereas Jesus "saw and felt Him everywhere" (ibid.: 50–1).

A more recent German scholar, Joachim Jeremias, refers to the "legalistic piety" of the Pharisees as the "cancer" of Judaism (Jeremias, 1971: 227). Christian scholars who have gone to the trouble to study Judaism in the time of Jesus, and who as a result know much more about the Torah (e.g., E. P. Sanders, Paula Fredriksen, James H. Charlesworth, and A. J. Levine), find no such conflict between Jesus and Judaism. Sanders' thorough study of early Judaism, *Judaism: Practice and Belief* (1992), provides an excellent antidote to the view of Judaism in Jesus's time as "rubbish."

Harnack died in 1930, three years before Hitler came to power in Germany. It is important to note that while Harnack held views of Judaism as an inferior religion, two facts are important. One is that he was an apostle of liberty and an opponent of authoritarianism (indeed, his dislike of Judaism stemmed from his view of it as authoritarian). The other is that to regard Judaism as an inferior religion, however wrongheaded that judgment is, does not make one who holds it a racist or a Nazi.

Gerhard Kittel

This distinction does not apply to the next thinker at whom we look. Gerhard Kittel (1888–1948), the first editor of the esteemed *Theological Dictionary of the New Testament*, was a "German Christian," that is, a member of one of the three "German Christian" groups that avidly supported Adolf Hitler. (Two excellent studies of German Christian theologians are Ericksen's (1985) *Theologians Under Hitler* and Jack Forstman's (1992) *Christian Faith in Dark Times*.) Large numbers of Protestant clergy became members of these groups (see Zabel, 1976: 229–32), including the noteworthy German scholars Paul Althaus, Heinrich Bornkamm, Walter Grundman, Emanuel Hirsch, and Heinrich Rendtorff. In 1933, after Hitler came to power, Kittel published *Die Judenfrage* (The Jewish Question). He took the standpoint of the National Socialist German Workers' Party (the Nazis) – that of a "positive Christianity." He argued that a positive Christianity could be achieved only by means of the struggle against Judaism. The "Jewish question" must be confronted as a religious question. Kittel's stated purpose was "to give the struggle against Judaism a Christian Meaning" (Kittel, 1933: 8).

The traditional theme of the "wandering Jew" was important to Kittel. Since the year 70, he claimed, Jews had been "a people destroyed across the face of the earth, having lost its home and living as a stranger among other peoples" (Kittel, 1933: 10). In such countries as Germany, Jews had increasingly assimilated into society. To Kittel, this was the problem. It led to intermarriage with Germans, a tendency that definitely had to stop. There were too many *Mischlinge* and *Halblinge*, "mixed breed or half-breed" people. "The baptism of a Jew does not touch his Jewish being . . . the converted Jew does not become a German, but a Jewish Christian" (ibid.: 70). Kittel fervently hoped that Hitler's new policies would put an end to the "innumerable half-breeds" in Germany and stop the *Rassenmischung* (race-mixing) that had gone on all too often. To achieve this end, Kittel argued that Jews in Germany should be utterly segregated in the manner of the medieval ghetto and allowed to play no role in the German state or culture. Jews should be barred from holding public office, from serving as judges or police, from the press, and from educating German youth. Because Jews were "overcrowding" the professions, they must be banned from them as well. Kittel argued against exterminating all Jews on the grounds that it would not be possible in the twentieth century (Kittel, 1933: 13,14). This is not a moral argument and he was factually wrong. Later, Kittel would agree with official policy.

Rethinking of Jewish–Christian Relations Since 1960

Beginning in the 1960s, chiefly with the Second Vatican Council of the Roman Catholic Church, churches, theologians, historians, and biblical scholars have produced many statements and studies of Jewish–Christian relations. A significant rethinking of Christian self-understanding in relation to Judaism and the Jewish people has taken place. Vatican II promulgated the document *Nostra Aetate* (In Our Time) in which it affirmed that the Church "draws sustenance from the root of that good olive tree onto which have been grafted the wild olive branches of the Gentiles (cf. Rom. 11: 17–24)" (Abbott, 1966: 664). The Council's statement initiated many other statements from National Catholic Bishops' Conferences in many countries as well as from local dioceses (see Helga Croner's two volumes of 1977 and 1985).

Protestant churches and ecumenical agencies have also issued numerous statements in which they increasingly rethought their relationships to Judaism and the Jewish people. Most of these statements can be found in *The Theology of the Churches and the Jewish People*, published by the World Council of Churches (1988). These statements become increasingly radical in their revisioning of Jewish–Christian relations. In 1980 the Synod of the Evangelical Church of West Berlin declared that the church's witness to the Jewish people "today means first all to live a Christian life that makes discernible God's Yes to the permanent election of Israel; thus the community of Jesus Christ can prove to be the one that is reconciled with the God who has elected Israel" (World Council of Churches, 1988: 103). Here the situation has been reversed. The question is now not that of the legitimacy of the people Israel but of the church: can the church "prove to be . . . reconciled with the God who elected Israel?"

Individual Protestant biblical scholars, historians, ethicists and theologians who have undertaken to reimagine Jewish–Christian relations are far too numerous to name. A nonexhaustive list of English-speaking theologians who have undertaken this includes Rosemary Ruether, Paul M. van Buren, R. Kendall Soulen, and Marvin Wilson.

Major church bodies and many scholars have been seared by the *Shoah*, the execution of six million Jews in the heart of Christian Europe, and have taken this as the occasion for a thorough re-examination of Christian thought and life. This effort has been sufficiently important to generate a response from a large number of Jewish scholars in the book *Christianity in Jewish Terms* (Frymer-Kensky, Novak, Ochs, Samuel and Signer, 2000). Other than further rethinking, which is always in order, the remaining question is: how much has changed in local Christian congregations?

References

Abbott, Walter M. (ed.) (1966). *The Documents of Vatican II*. New York: Guild Press.

Calvin, John (1960). *Calvin: Institutes of the Christian Religion*, ed. John McNeill, trans. Ford Lewis Battles. Philadelphia: Westminster Press.

Church Council of the Evangelical Lutheran Church in America (1994). *Declaration of the Evangelical Lutheran Church in America to the Jewish Community*. http://www.elca.org/ea/interfaith/jewish/declaration.html.

Croner, Helga (1977). *Stepping Stones to Further Jewish–Christian Relations*. London and New York: Stimulus Books.

Croner, Helga (1985). *More Stepping Stones to Jewish–Christian Relations*. New York: Paulist Press.

Engel, Mary Potter (1990). Calvin and the Jews: A Textual Puzzle. *Princeton Seminary Bulletin*, Supplementary Issue 1: 106–23.

Ericksen, Robert P. (1985). *Theologians Under Hitler*. New Haven, CT and London: Yale University Press.

Forstman, Jack (1992). *Christian Faith in Dark Times*. Louisville, KY: Westminster/John Knox Press.

Frymer-Kensky, Tikva, Novak, David, Ochs, Peter, Samuel, David Fox, and Signer, Michael A. (eds.) (2000). *Christianity in Jewish Terms*. Boulder, CO: Westview Press.

Harnack, Adolf (1921). *Marcion, das Evangelium von fremden Gott*. Leipzig: Hinrichs.

Harnack, Adolf (1957). *What Is Christianity?*, trans Thomas Bailey Saunders. New York: Harper & Row.

Harnack, Adolf (1961). *The Mission and Expansion of Christianity*, trans. and ed. James Moffatt. New York: Harper & Row.

Jeremias, Joachim (1971). *New Testament Theology: The Proclamation of Jesus*, trans. John Bowden. New York: Charles Scribner's Sons.

Kittel, Gerhard (1933). *Die Judenfrage*. Stuttgart: Kohlhammer.

Littell, Franklin H. (1979). *The Crucifixion of the Jews*. New York: Harper & Row.

Luther, Martin (1955–86). *Luther's Works* [LW], American edn., Jaroslov Pelikan and Helmut T. Lehmann (eds.), 55 volumes. St. Louis and Minneapolis: Concordia and Fortress.

Perrin, Norman (1974). *The New Testament: An Introduction*. New York: Harcourt Brace Jovanovich.

Sanders, E. P. (1992). *Judaism: Practice and Belief 63 BCE–66 CE*. London: SCM Press.

Schleiermacher, F (1928). *The Christian Faith*, eds. H. R. Mackintosh and J. Stewart. Edinburgh: T & T Clark.

Soulen, R. Kendall (1996). *The God of Israel and Christian Theology*. Minneapolis: Fortress Press.

World Council of Churches (1988). *The Theology of the Churches and the Jewish People: Statements by the World Council of Churches and its Member Churches*. Geneva: WCC Publications.

Zabel, James A (1976). *Nazism and the Pastors*. Missoula, MT: Scholars Press.

Further Reading

Charlesworth, James H. (ed.) (1991). *Jesus' Jewishness: Exploring the Place of Jesus in Early Judaism*. New York: Crossroad.

Fredriksen, Paula (1988). *From Jesus to Christ: The Origins of the New Testament Image of Jesus*. New Haven, CT and London: Yale University Press.

Fredriksen, Paula (1999). *Jesus of Nazareth: King of the Jews*. New York: Knopf.

Hilberg, Raul (1979). *The Destruction of the European Jews*. New York: Harper & Row.

Ruether, Rosemary (1974). *Faith and Fratricide*. New York: The Seabury Press.

Sanders, E. P. (1985). *Jesus and Judaism*. Philadelphia: Fortress Press.

Van Buren, Paul M. (1980–88). *A Theology of the Jewish–Christian Reality*, 3 vols. New York: The Seabury Press.

Williamson, Clark M. (1982). *Has God Rejected His People?* Nashville: Abingdon Press.

Williamson, Clark M. (1993). *A Guest in the House of Israel*. Louisville, KY: Westminster/John Knox Press.

Williamson, Clark M. (1999), *Way of Blessing, Way of Life: A Christian Theology*. St. Louis: Chalice Press.

Wilson, Marvin R. (1989). *Our Father Abraham*. Grand Rapids, MI: Eerdmans.

CHAPTER 35

Protestantism and Spirituality

Bradley P. Holt

Spirituality includes relationships to God, to the self, to other people, and to creation. It includes habitual practices that develop these relationships into deeper love. It is both lived experience and reflection on experience and, as a result, spirituality is increasingly recognized as a field of theological study.

This chapter will sketch Protestant spirituality first by noting some common themes and practices, then by an historical survey of five continents by describing general patterns and noting a few remarkable individuals and movements. Protestantism is found all over the globe.

Common Themes and Practices

When seeking to delineate what makes Protestant spirituality distinctive from Roman Catholic and Eastern Orthodox traditions, one is faced with a wide variety of beliefs and practices, but certain generalizations are possible.

Protestants insist on centering their spirituality on the Bible. Not only does Protestant *theology* aim to ground its concepts in the Scripture, but Christian *practice* as well focuses on the Bible. Protestants have emphasized literacy as an important skill for all Christians and worked hard to translate the Bible into vernacular languages. Literacy and translation are the basis for Bible study, a key component of Protestant spiritual practice anywhere in the world.

Protestant spirituality reflects its theology by placing justification by faith at the foundation of the Christian life. This belief about justification does not dictate any particular spiritual discipline, but gives a perspective on all of them. Protestants teach that no one can be made right before God by their spiritual practices, but only through God's gift of righteousness in the death and resurrection of Jesus Christ. Protestant theologians distinguish justification from sanctification.

Protestant worship services are also part of spiritual practice and reflect the high value given to community as a locus of spiritual formation. From Luther onwards, Protestants have emphasized the priesthood of all believers, and therefore the role of the laity in worship, especially in the singing of hymns and choruses. Much Protestant spirituality shines through the texts of its hymnody.

Protestant spirituality, at its best, is very "worldly" in the sense that it focuses on the daily lives of the laity. In reaction against Roman Catholic orders, pilgrimages, indulgences, celibacy, and sacraments, Protestants starting with Luther have insisted that the married life of ordinary Christians is just as honorable before God as the celibate life of a monastery. Family devotions have played an important role in Protestant spirituality, even though in recent decades in the West they have largely been neglected.

The use of extemporaneous prayers, as opposed to traditional set texts, is characteristic for many strands of Protestantism. Most Protestants would not repeat the Hail Mary nor use the rosary for prayer, but rather pray in their own words, silently or aloud, alone or in small groups. In some traditions, the minister at the Sunday service leads in a pastoral prayer of his or her own composition rather than using prayers composed for the whole church. Other Protestant traditions do repeat the Lord's Prayer and other historic or set prayers in their spiritual practice.

It may be noted that to a greater or lesser degree, Protestants have lost some valuable spiritual practices in their rejection of Catholicism. During the years since the Reformation, Protestants and Catholics often sought to distinguish themselves from the other just for the sake of being different. Some Protestants, consequently, have asked whether Catholic devotional practices should be reinstated or adapted for Protestant use. Among these are silent retreats, spiritual direction, pilgrimages, the sign of the cross, and various prayer forms. Along with these practices stands a huge literature of Catholic saints and devotion. The question here remains whether these are edifying for Protestants or misleading.

European Protestant Spirituality

Sixteenth and seventeenth century origins

It was a personal spiritual struggle that set off the most far-reaching of the movements to change the Christian Church. Luther's struggle to find a gracious God evolved into a religious and military conflict that divided the continent. The spiritual practices of the day did not satisfy Luther's conscience. When he had discovered Paul's revolutionary teaching about justification by faith, Luther began the long process of re-evaluating the whole panoply of Catholic devotions, sacraments, and merits. However, he was more conservative than some other Protestants would be as his judgment was that many of these should be kept or reformed instead of being discarded.

Five other distinctive characteristics of Luther's spirituality stand out. The first is his "theology of the cross," that has implications for spirituality. Secondly, Luther teaches that baptism is the model for daily Christian life. In his *Large Catechism* he describes "daily baptism," by which he means daily dying and rising with Christ, as the central spiritual discipline of the Christian life. Thirdly his own experience of *Anfechtung* or spiritual trial, together with his belief in justification, led him to assert that the Christian is simultaneously righteous and a sinner. Fourth, Luther's teaching about prayer is distinctive. He wrote a short essay for his barber on how to pray, in which he characteristically suggested using four types of prayer while meditating on the basic texts: the Lord's Prayer, the Apostles' Creed, and the Ten Commandments. Finally, one must take note of the spirit of freedom with which Luther approached spiritual disciplines. His most famous and succinct account of the Christian life is titled *The Freedom of a Christian*. In the course of this short book, Luther speaks of the paradoxes of life in Christ, especially of being both free and a servant.

In the century that followed Luther's death, most of his followers were engaged in working out the political and theological implications of his Reformation. The general tendency of Lutherans during this period was to seek purity of doctrine, which led them to emphasize the distinctiveness of Lutheranism in contrast to Catholic and Reformed positions, and in general to focus on the intellectual rather than the affective dimensions of Christian faith.

In reaction against these tendencies, some Lutherans began a reform movement called "Pietism," after its most notable platform, a book written by Philip Spener in 1675 called *Pia Desideria* (Pious Hopes). Spener called for a more intensive use of the Scriptures in the life of believers. He began to hold Bible study meetings in the middle of the week, and to center his preaching not on what would impress his audience but what would edify them. The division between Confessional and Pietist Lutherans was later to repeat itself many times in later history of other Protestants, and the dynamics of various kinds of renewal and resistance to them continue today. The Pietists influenced the Moravians and they in turn the English Evangelicals.

At about the same time as Luther was developing his form of spirituality in Germany, others in Switzerland were reforming the Catholic tradition in a more thorough way. The Reformed tradition sees Ulrich Zwingli as its earliest pioneer, but John Calvin in the second generation came to eclipse Zwingli, in recognition if not in influence. Zwingli was more radical than Luther, differing from Luther by stopping any practice he saw as unattested in Scripture or clearly commanded in the Bible. Thus, for example, he nailed shut the organ in his church, because the Bible does not command its use.

John Calvin was more moderate than Zwingli. For example, he wanted to continue the practice of weekly communion, whereas Zwingli saw the need for only four observances in a year. Calvin's doctrine of election, associated with double predestination, later became one touchstone of Reformed Orthodoxy, obscuring his contributions to spirituality. Calvin wrote of a *unio mystica* or mystical union between the believer and Christ. This was a form of mysticism not for the spiritual elite but for every believer, which was to be exercised by spiritual disciplines.

The Reformed tendency is to accept Luther's teaching of justification, but to develop it with a corresponding doctrine of sanctification. Sanctification came to mean the growth in holiness in the course of living as a member of the church. Luther loved to sing of freedom; Calvin, and the tradition following him, preferred to emphasize the disciplines of daily practice, fulfilling not only Christ's intentions for the individual, but also for society. Calvin gave much of his attention to the polity of Geneva.

The Church of England separated from Rome not on the grounds of doctrine or spirituality, but politics and economics. In the course of its turbulent development in the sixteenth and seventeenth centuries, the Church of England was influenced more by the Reformed than the Lutheran tradition. The Puritan movement within Anglicanism was a Reformed critique of Catholic practices deemed unbiblical.

The standard for worship in the Anglican Church, *The Book of Common Prayer*, became also its handbook for devotion and its foundation of unity. Written originally by Archbishop Cranmer, it was revised many times, but has always played a central role in Anglican spirituality. The prayer book condenses the seven monastic hours into two: Morning Prayer and Evening Prayer, to be prayed by the lay people in English. Among the great sixteenth- and seventeenth-century Anglican writers are Richard Hooker, Lancelot Andrewes, John Donne, George Herbert, John Milton, Jeremy Taylor, and Thomas Traherne. Their writings laid the foundations for an English- speaking tradition in which spirituality is clearly of central importance.

The final family of denominations stemming from early Protestant days, the Anabaptists, questioned even more of the Catholic tradition than the previous three. Their emphasis was on personal discipleship, a redeemed church membership, and radical separation from the world.

In Great Britain a parallel but different movement sprang up under the leadership of George Fox. The Society of Friends (Quakers) were pacifists, no respecters of persons and, like the Anabaptists, did not practice infant baptism. Their belief in the Spirit dwelling in every person made them socially egalitarian and offensive to those in power. John Bunyan's writings, especially *The Pilgrim's Progress*, were a major contribution to Protestant spirituality.

Eighteenth-century Europe

The rationalism characteristic of the 1700s was not friendly to traditional Christian spirituality, as it tended to discount the central teachings concerning the Trinity and incarnation, the death and resurrection of Jesus, the power of prayer, and the existence of miracles. The Enlightenment wanted to scrub Christianity clean of all superstition, but by doing so it scrubbed off the skin as well.

In the 1730s a renewal movement developed among the Anglicans. The emphasis on observed experience in the Enlightenment led John Wesley, the best known of the leaders of this movement, to observe his followers and to develop a distinctive doctrine of sanctification upon it. Wesley's eventual teaching about perfection and the "second blessing" of "entire sanctification" distinguished him from most other theologians.

He and his brother Charles had grown up very pious, forming a "Holy Club" at Oxford, and traveling to Georgia as missionaries. But his heart longed for assurance, especially after his contact with the Moravians. He later wrote famously that his heart was "strangely warmed" at a prayer meeting in Aldersgate Street, London, when he became assured that he did believe in Christ, and Christ's salvation was indeed his. The converts from his preaching were formed into small groups or "classes" where their Christian nurture took place. The Methodist societies eventually broke from the Anglican church, but only over John Wesley's dead body: he prevented the new denomination throughout his life. There were many Anglicans influenced by Wesley who did not become Methodist or join one of the other nonconformist denominations, but formed an evangelical wing of the Anglican Church that is widespread today.

Nineteenth-century Europe

Theological Liberalism emerged on the European continent alongside the artistic and cultural movement of Romanticism. Schleiermacher made feeling (*Gefühl*, although it is disputed what exactly this means), the standard of theological reflection and Christian life rather than Scripture or the rationalist standard in reason that had preceded him.

From Lutheran Denmark, however, a very different perspective emerged. Søren Kierkegaard, philosopher and theologian, was rebelling against the philosophical optimism of Hegel and the established church of his people. He profoundly challenged commonly held views of spirituality and invited his "dear reader" to break with the conventional view that it was easy to be Christian.

The Anglican Church was forever changed by a group of learned clerics centered in Oxford who called on the church to take most seriously the writers and practices of the early church. In effect, it was a call to the Catholic roots of the church. John Henry Newman, Edward Pusey, John Keble and others wanted a renewal of spiritual life by participation in the sacraments, attention to beauty, a renewal of monastic piety, a focus on union with God, and friendship with God. As in the evangelical movement, Anglo-Catholicism developed a wing of the church that is a spiritual characteristic of many Anglican parishes and institutions to this day.

The nineteenth century was decisive for the spread of Christianity to the rest of the world. In numbers greater than ever before, Europeans emigrated to the Americas, Africa, and Australasia. In this "great century of missions" indigenous churches were planted virtually throughout the world. The mission movement was based on a new spirituality. Europeans and North Americans in particular began to pray with the whole globe in mind, seeking discernment as to whether God was calling them to service overseas, and ordinary people began to take an interest in the welfare of other societies.

Twentieth-century Europe

Twentieth-century European spirituality has been much influenced by secular movements with their roots in Darwin, Freud, and Marx. In general terms the century saw a decline in the participation in communal and private devotion. Those Christians who did practice their faith became very conscious of making a choice to follow their practices and to gather with other people of faith.

The twentieth century was marked by wars and genocides. In the context of the rise of German Nazism, Dietrich Bonhoeffer's early book *Nachfolge* (translated as *The Cost of Discipleship*) not only made the phrase "cheap grace" part of the vocabulary, but pointed the way toward a revival of Lutheran spirituality. While teaching in an underground seminary Bonhoeffer wrote a perspective on *Life Together*, which included both the day together and the day alone. He advised pondering short Scripture passages in the tradition of monastic *lectio divina*.

C. S. Lewis, an adult convert to Christianity, had a widespread influence on Protestants through a prolific authorship. His influence was partly to make credible a worldview long discarded by theological liberals, which included the reality of demons and the significance of prayer. Lewis was a faithful Anglican, but he did not regard denominations as very important, favoring "mere Christianity."

Europe, the continent where Protestantism first appeared, produced spiritual movements and writers in the twentieth century in spite of a general decline in its Protestant churches. We turn now to other continents.

North American Protestant Spirituality

In the 1600s the Puritan frustration with life in England led to hopes for a new community in the wilderness far away. The dream was culturally very significant, but it could not endure. Only later in the 1700s would Jonathan Edwards, its most outstanding representative, appear. One of the initiators of the Great Awakening, Edwards was a brilliant scholar who was very conscious that relating to God was not only an intellectual matter. He is known for his vivid images in preaching, but also for his careful reflection on *Religious Affections* in the wake of the revival. Edwards had a deep sense of the beauty of God, an aesthetic dimension not often found among Protestant writers.

Native Americans, ruthlessly deprived of their land, nevertheless many times responded to calls for faith in Jesus. Later they were to contribute to new Protestant concerns for an ecological spirituality. African Americans, deprived of their African tribal communities, adopted the faith, and the suffering Jesus became the new friend of many a slave. After emancipation black churches grew apace and became the voice of the voiceless in a racist culture. In the context of a conservative evangelicalism, African Americans retained a spirituality of liberation. Their music is a major contribution to world spirituality.

It was from a mixed congregation of black and white members that there emerged onto the world scene a spirituality that would become the most rapidly growing element of Christianity during the twentieth century. The Azusa Street Revival of 1906 in Los Angeles is commonly regarded as the decisive event in the development of Pentecostal Christianity.

In addition to the usual marks of evangelical revivalist Protestantism, this movement had new teachings about the Holy Spirit. What John Wesley and the Holiness Movement called a "second blessing" or "entire sanctification," the Pentecostals identified with "baptism in the Holy Spirit." Further, they expected the gifts listed in 1 Corinthinas 12, notably the gifts of speaking in tongues, interpretation of tongues, and healing, to appear among them as in the primitive church. By the end of the century "Classical Pentecostals" had become more affluent, more educated, and in danger of losing some of their distinctiveness. Shortly after mid-century, Pentecostal spirituality began to spread among historic Protestant denominations attracted to the experiences reported by Pentecostals without the desire to leave their own church homes. This movement came to be called Charismatic Renewal. Late in the century a new form of Pentecostalism emerged: the independent charismatic congregation. They tended to attract young, upwardly mobile suburbanites who sought God's approval and blessing on their increasing affluence, and they did not find denominational loyalty important in their choice of a church. Many Protestants in North America have in fact gone far from the origins of Protestantism.

In quite a different direction others have been going back to Reformation and pre-Reformation traditions to enrich Protestant spirituality. More and more Protestants have been taking training in spiritual direction and attending retreats, often at Catholic centers, and sometimes in the practice of Ignatius of Loyola. In summary, the openness of Protestants to Roman Catholic spiritual traditions increased greatly in the late twentieth century.

Other notable individuals and movements in North America-derived Protestant spirituality include the Episcopalian Morton Kelsey, a leader in the use of Jungian psychology as a tool for spirituality, while on a popular level perhaps no single person has influenced Protestant spirituality more than Billy Graham. Many Protestants have been attracted to the so-called New Age Movement. Some of its ideas, including ecological concern, delight in exotic practices, and a search for integration of science and spirituality, have influenced many Protestants.

African Protestant Spirituality

In Africa, Protestant Churches grew in the twentieth century so much as to shift the "center of gravity" of the Christian world southwards. "African-initiated Churches" often serve now as models of this rethinking of the relation of gospel and culture. Their spirituality was not intended to be a mixing of traditional religion with Christianity, but their rejection of missionary leadership and their dependence on dreams and visions has meant a fresh interpretation of the faith in an African setting. If African spirituality is communal more than individualist; if it recognizes the powers of ancestors, spirits, and divinities more than empirical evidence; if it is guided by dreams and visions, with the expectation of miracles rather than the dry analysis of historical facts, these are all evidence that African culture is closer to that of biblical times than it is to post-Enlightenment Europe.

In South Africa, white Dutch Reformed Protestantism encouraged the development of apartheid while black Protestants endured and fought it. A kind of liberation spirituality and theology taught black pride while most whites were piously dug in for the defense of their race. Beyers Naude and other white Christians opposed the white majority at great cost. Desmond Tutu and others prayed and led nonviolent protests, becoming the voice of oppressed blacks.

In East Africa and Madagascar there were massive revival movements among people already nominally Christian. Church meetings at which there were sometimes dramatic demonstrations of the power of the Holy Spirit engendered a deep repentance and conversion of heart.

Asian Protestant Spirituality

Most Christians in Asia live as a small minority. This includes those Arab Christians in Southwest Asia who remain the last indigenous Christian believers in the land of Jesus. Christians live among majorities who practice Islam, Hinduism, Buddhism, and Shinto.

The diversity of the Asian continent is overwhelming. Thus Christian practice, in so far as it has grown away from European ways, is also diverse. Devotion and mysticism are central in India, while the secularity of industrialized Japan calls forth more pragmatism. The Burmese Baptists work under the oppression of a Buddhist military junta, while Thai Protestants are nominally free, but avoid any conflict with their Buddhist monarchy. China is a vast country with many underground Christians who have never seen a missionary. Other Chinese churches are recognized by the government and are flourishing at the price of muting their criticism. Only in Korea, the Philippines, and the South Pacific islands is there a substantial number of Protestant Christians. The spiritualities of these Asian Protestants engage themes of searching for indigenous ways to follow Jesus on the one hand and the anticolonial search for liberation on the other.

Latin American Protestant Spirituality

In the sixteenth century Central and South America came under the domination of Roman Catholic Spain and Portugal. It has only been recently that Protestants have grown to be significant minorities on this continent. Many Protestant churches have developed from North American missions, with a spectrum of views about the Catholic majority and the indigenous Indian religions, more or less incorporated into Catholic spirituality. On the far end of the spectrum are those conservative Protestants, many of them Pentecostals, who regard the Roman Catholic tradition with abhorrence and distinguish their spiritual practice sharply from that of the majority. Others would also find much to criticize in the tradition, but would sympathize with newer forms of Catholic devotion, especially base Christian communities, small Bible study groups in the Catholic church that emphasize social change. Denominations with longer histories in the North tend to fall into this group. It should also be noted that liberation theology, which grew out of spirituality, is led not only by Roman Catholic theologians but also by Protestants, such as Jon Sobrino.

Diversity and Unity

Protestantism is a family of churches of great variety. Some of the central themes of the first Protestants, however, have marked the spirituality of this movement permanently, so that there is a family resemblance among them throughout the world. A Burmese Baptist has similarities to a Chilean Pentecostal, a Nigerian Anglican, or a Norwegian Lutheran in such a way that will permit them to recognize one another. All center their spirituality on reading, praying, and preaching the Bible, in a context where Jesus is the central focus without competition with his mother. All will regard their spiritual practice not as the basis of their salvation but the fruit of the Spirit of Jesus, whose forgiveness is the basis for their life with God.

Further Reading

Abraham, K. C. and Mbuy-Beya, Bernadette (eds.) (1994). *Spirituality of the Third World: A Cry for Life*. Maryknoll, NY: Orbis.

Foster, Richard J. (1998). *Streams of Living Water: Celebrating the Great Traditions of Christian Faith*. San Francisco: Harper.

Hanson, Bradley (ed.) (1990). *Modern Christian Spirituality: Methodological and Historical Essays*. Atlanta, GA: Scholar's Press.

Hanson, Bradley (2000). *A Graceful Life: Lutheran Spirituality for Today*. Minneapolis: Augsburg.

Jones, Cheslyn, Wainright, Geoffrey, and Yarnold, Edward (eds.) (1986). *The Study of Spirituality*. Oxford: Oxford University Press.

McGrath, Alister (1991). *Roots that Refresh: A Celebration of Reformation Spirituality*. London: Hodder & Stoughton.

McGrath, Alister (1999). *Christian Spirituality*. Oxford: Blackwell.

Mursell, Gordon (ed.) (2001). *The Story of Christian Spirituality: Two Thousand Years, from East to West*. Minneapolis: Fortress.

Norris, Kathleen (1998). *Amazing Grace: A Vocabulary of Faith*. New York: Riverhead.

Peterson, Eugene (1997). *Subversive Spirituality*. Grand Rapids, MI: Eerdmans.

Senn, Frank C. (1986). *Protestant Spiritual Traditions*. New York: Paulist Press.

Thornton, Martin (1986). *English Spirituality*. Cambridge, MA: Cowley.

CHAPTER 36

Protestantism and Missions

Werner Ustorf

Christianity today is, in the main, non-Western, with a substantial proportion of its mission activities originating in the South. A recent biographical dictionary of the missionary movement clearly reflects this (Anderson, 1998). The generally accepted meaning of the word *mission* is, however, still shaped by the characteristics attributed to it during the Victorian period. The term indeed must hold together, rather precariously, what has always been a truly bewildering diversity of approaches, understandings and concepts. The first modern Protestant church of tropical Africa, for example, was not established by white missionaries but by freed African slaves led by David George who had migrated from Nova Scotia to Sierra Leone in 1792 (Sanneh, 1999), the same year that the first modern Protestant mission society was formed in Britain. Migration, emigration, the mass movements of refugees (now the presence of African churches in Europe) and the expansion of Christianity are quite different from mission, though they may all possess missionary implications (Latourette, 1937–45; McNeill, 1987; Gerloff, 1992; Walls, 1996); but this difference has not always been observed by the missionary propaganda. In this chapter I shall argue that missionary (in the Victorian sense of the term) Protestantism is a very particular phenomenon; that it was not born in the Reformation, but rather in the colonial encounter; that it was ambiguously inculturated in the European drive to unify the world through a twofold process involving modernization and Christianization; and that, with the collapse of this project, it was forced to radically reinvent itself (Funkschmidt, 2000).

Protestantism in the Sixteenth and Seventeenth Centuries – Was it Really Missionary?

The founding figure of modern missiology, Gustav Warneck (1834–1910), stated in his now famous verdict on fledgling Protestantism that not only did it lack any semblance of missionary activism, but also that it was devoid of even the slightest obligation to undertake missionary work: in his view, the Protestantism of this period – and in marked contrast to Catholicism – was simply non-missionary (Warneck, 1910: 6–23). Protestant mission historiography hastily scraped together what looked most promising for the construction of an *early* Protestant mission, and although some incidents and forerunners could indeed be found, they were historically marginal and did not challenge in principle Warneck's assessment. When, in the 1960s, participation in mission had become a sort of litmus test for ecclesiological authenticity – a test that within Protestantism perhaps only the small Moravian lay mission of 1732 and, later, some churches, mainly in Scandinavia and the United States, would have passed straight away – apologists of Luther, Calvin or the Anabaptists were quick to restore the damaged reputation of the heroes of the Reformation by discovering their specific forms of missionary thinking. These were the obligation of Christian governments (everywhere) to support (or, to be more accurate, to enforce!) Christian life, and the influence of the congregation on its own context, or in Luther's case the missionary impact of the *sola scriptura*, namely the dynamics of the word of God in the vernacular (Schäufele, 1966).

In this regard, it is perhaps possible to say that the Reformation had 'missionary potential' (Jongeneel, 1995: 223). However, these forms can be described equally as questions of pastoral or practical theology and would certainly not have convinced Warneck, for whom mission clearly meant the organized expedition overseas, the chief aims of which were the conventional ones of conversion, of preaching the gospel and of establishing the church. In other words, both views operate with quite different understandings of mission. Because of this, missionary attitudes could even be attributed to a man such as Luther (Gensichen, 1976: 6) who in his writings paid only scant regard to the fact that Christendom was expanding in the Americas, Africa and Asia and that whole nations there were fighting, not infrequently in the name of Christ, for their independence and even their mere survival. Luther was largely ignorant of other religions – apart from that of the Jews – and had hardly anything to say about those who were 'discovered', conquered, instrumentalized and redesigned in the image of Europe. Applicable to this revisionist interpretation is one of the old insights of the missionary movement: when everything is mission, nothing really is.

It is preferable then to return to Warneck; not because his definition is any closer to the essence of mission than that of others – a matter, incidentally, that continues to perplex missiologists (Bosch, 1991: 9) – but rather because his is a definition with which we can at least work without encountering the difficulty of having to decide, for example, whether or not the introduction of Bible colporteurs in the first half of the nineteenth century in Umeå, Sweden represents any sort of missionary agenda. We will focus therefore not on that which has been dubbed the area of *home missions*, but instead on the so-called foreign mission work of Protestantism. This work includes various aspects of the sending agencies, the historical and cultural parameters which gave rise to new directions in theological thinking, the methodologies duly applied, and the impact that all of this and the encounter with other cultures had on Protestantism itself. By the same token it is clear what is not included: as soon as indigenous Christian life is developing overseas the period of mission is over and that of local church history begins. Why then did Protestantism in the first hundred or so years of its history not develop the concept of foreign missions? Warneck believed he had detected the root of the problem in Reformation theology, and in particular in that of Luther and, later still, that of the Lutheran orthodoxy:

1   The assumption that the Great Commission (Matthew 28:19) related to the apostles, not to the church of today, and that the Christian message had already been carried to the ends of the earth – in 1590 both points had been refuted by the Anglican Adrianus Saravia (1532–1613), who unsuccessfully pleaded for foreign missions to be carried out by the church (he argued that bishops were the successors of the apostles. Beza, the successor of Calvin in Geneva, rejected Saravia's ideas).
2   The conviction that the reign of Christ was advancing, though hidden from human sight, and that Christ's return was imminent (with Melanchthon, Luther calculated that this would take place in the year 1558).
3   The theological speculation that the rejection of the gospel by Jews, Muslims and members of other religions was ultimately within the prerogative of God, who alone would know the elected ones, whether in or outside the church, and a prerogative not to be interfered with by human agency – missionary or otherwise.

The infamous report of the theological faculty of Wittenberg in 1651 (Raupp, 1990: 70f) is the continuation of this line of thought, and perhaps the climax of the anti-missionary tendency within Lutheran orthodoxy (and in much Calvinist thinking). In 1708 the same faculty tried to veto the Danish-Halle mission to Tranquebar, South India, by questioning the ordination of its missionaries. Here, as in the case of the German Justinian von Welz (1621–c.68; Laubach, 1989) with his plans to renew Christianity at home and establish an overseas mission society staffed by lay people (1644), it became clear that much Protestant anti-missionary resentment was based on the fear of the church authorities that the people – the lay men and women, the *viri saeculares*, religious enthusiasts and charismatics – would appropriate the gospel for themselves and run away with it, throwing into disarray those systems of theological and social control that Protestantism had erected only with some degree of difficulty. By the same token, as will be shown in the next section, the missionary Protestantism of the eighteenth and nineteenth centuries was the expression of a social and spiritual revolt from below, signifying deep dissatisfaction with mainline culture and a church inculturated in it, and hostile to what Isaiah Berlin (1980: 215) has called 'the shrivelling of the spirit by narrow and superficial systematizers'. This revolt was naïve enough to attempt the restoration of the church of the apostles on the mission field, and also to take the growth of the church overseas as evidence for the truth of Christianity vis-à-vis the humanist or secular view of the world. Institutionalized (inculturated) territorial Protestantism battled for centuries to contain this activist lay movement.

However, Warneck named another power that also worked in favour of foreign missions: he observed that the foreign mission activity of the Protestant nations increased as a direct relationship to their share in overseas trade and colonial possessions. Even in a post-colonial age, it seems, this observation still carries some force. A case in point is that represented by the more than 8,000 Presbyterian missionaries that (in 2000) one of the leading Asian export nations, the largely Protestant South Korea, sent abroad – only slightly less than the total number (all denominations) Britain produced at the height of its imperial power in 1899 (Goh, 2001; Porter, 1991: 3). Here, the meaning of the term *business* is distinctly double-edged. Colonialism and trade, irrespective of our feelings about it, provide the formative context for Protestant missions. Missionary awareness was therefore not to be found in the cradle of Protestantism; it first emerged in the course of the colonial encounter. Whether Protestantism is missionary by nature is, at least, questionable.

Neither the British Congregationalist John Eliot (1604–90), the so-called apostle to the Indians in Massachusetts, nor the Dutch Reformed theologian Georgius Candidius, Protestantism's first missionary to East Asia (in Taiwan, 1627), were sent out as *missionaries* (they were chaplains to the Europeans), nor did they have a conceptual understanding of mission. Eliot spoke of Israel (the Christian tribes of Europe) taking the Promised Land (the New World) where they had encountered the Canaanites (the American Indians). These enterprises were directly related to the colonial and merchant activities of Cromwell's New England Company (1649) and the Dutch United East Indies Company (1602) respectively – Christian organizations, and applying as a matter of course the *cuius regio eius religio* concept. Their chaplains, therefore, were the product not of mission but of migration, though Eliot and Candidius got involved in what were to become two of the first sustained missionary experiments undertaken by Protestantism. They form the first links in a long chain of government-funded attempts at the Christianization-cum-pacification of overseas territories – light-years away from the ideal of an independent indigenous church life. It is this colonial encounter that triggered practical and later theoretical steps in the direction of mission, such as the short-lived *Seminarium Indicum* that the East Indies Company had established in Leiden (1622–33). In principle, this also holds true for the royal Danish-Halle mission of 1705 in Tranquebar, though its best-known missionary, Bartholomäus Ziegenbalg (1682–1719), came to exemplify missionary solidarity with the poor, as well as becoming one of the ancestors of comparative religion.

The Enlightenment's Unruly Daughter: Protestant Missions in the Modern Era

The classics of Puritan literature, such as John Bunyan's *Pilgrim's Progress* of 1678, anticipated the ambivalent attitude that Protestant missions would later exhibit towards mainline European culture, the Enlightenment in particular (Stanley, 2001). This ambivalence is the result of the conflictive interaction of the powerful socio-economic and religio-cultural forces that formed the particular historical context of a new phase in the life of Protestantism, the modern missionary movement.

Based on transoceanic trade and the rationality of manufacture – later industrial production – an enterprising *bourgeoisie* had formed itself in many parts of western and central Europe and North America. In the spectacular revolutions of the seventeenth and eighteenth centuries this class had achieved its political emancipation from the *ancien régime*. Moreover, these circles, comprising (mainly Protestant) laypeople, had an interest in democracy and the emancipative push made by the Enlightenment. They had quickly come to dominate a public debate which they had promoted in countless associations and clubs, academic and otherwise. Different, for example, from the Society for the Propagation of the Gospel in Foreign Parts (1701), which had the full backing of the Anglican Church, these new associations were outside the control of the churches, and included the societies of foreign mission. In this period of cultural ferment, the Enlightenment, abolition, humanism, Christianity, Pietism, commerce, trade, and foreign mission went hand in hand, and the boards of the new private mission societies often reflected this particular mix of interests. The first of these modern agencies was the Baptist Missionary Society of 1792, a model for many others in the West (Stanley, 1992; Ward and Stanley, 2000). William Carey's (1761–1834) *Enquiry into the Obligations of Christians, to Use Means for the Conversion of the Heathens* of 1792 is a hybrid of the twofold European colonial project: to modernize the world; that is, to establish a global civilization of progress and Enlightenment in secular rationality, and to Christianize it by applying an equally universal religious rationality.

These private (and privately financed) societies were sovereign bodies: the gospel (not necessarily a particular creed) was their guide, and they worked vicariously on behalf of a cautious church. Strictly denominational mission agencies developed mainly in the nineteenth century (the Church Missionary Society of 1799 being the first). In supra-denominational or inter-denominational mission work it could happen that entrepreneurial laymen, such as bankers and merchants, became the corporate bishops, as it were, of the emerging churches in the South. Carey's Baptist mission work in and around Calcutta represents the break the Enlightenment, the religious revivals and also the missionary movement had made with the negative anthropology of the Reformation. It is based on the modern, almost messianic belief that people can be changed, indeed be reshaped or made anew as described in Daniel Defoe's *Robinson Crusoe* – trans-

formed culturally, intellectually and religiously, through *education*. The foundation of a college, the emphasis on philology, Bible translation, literacy and
publication (including texts of the Hindu classics) are characteristic of this
approach. Missionary attempts at raising literacy rates in the mission field were
sometimes more successful than those in the homelands. This period introduces
discipline into all areas of life – at home and abroad. In Protestantism, this not
only generates modern missions, but also prison reforms, such as the newly discovered educational 'advantages' of solitary confinement.

The eighteenth-century religious revivals in the West had developed in parallel with all of this, but also with some degree of tension. The new industrial
production and the collapse of the *orbis christianus* culture during the Enlightenment endangered not only the social position but also the ontological certainty of many believers; which is to say, their place in a world that was no longer
declared to be God's. Missionaries, such as David Livingstone (1813–73), were
often recruited from among the victims of modernization and prepared, on the
mission field, their re-entry to a respected position at home. The polemic against
materialism and secular culture in Methodism and much of the ninteenth-
century missionary literature and the consequent claim to have taken the 'biblical' high ground, which, it was then asserted, secured for them privileged
knowledge, points to the social unrest and also to the traumatic difficulty in
coming to terms with the Enlightenment. In general, however, the missionary
idea was constructed as the religious mirror image of the secular dream of a universal civilization, and it became as activist and bellicose in its critique of all
other religions and ideologies (Ustorf, 2000a).

Protestant missionary thought at the beginning of the nineteenth century
represents, on the one hand, the survival of a pre-modern worldview; on the
other, by focusing on the Bible in the same way as the scientists had on the laws
of science, and by emphasizing the subjectivity of religious experience, it affirms
the idea of the autonomy of the modern individual. The fundamentally modern
paradigms of equality and emancipation permeate this approach. One of the
most striking features of modern Protestant mission work is the liberation of
women. It offered women missionaries opportunities in the mission field the
like of which they could only dream of at home. This impulse had a direct
influence on the liberation of women in general (Bowie *et al.*, 1993; Robert,
1996). The freedom from religious control and the right of the individual to
make a religious choice were the necessary preconditions of Protestant mission
work – preconditions, moreover, that often had to be fought for in the face of
competition from the colonial and commercial interests that preferred not to
upset the indigenous populations. By combining all the elements, Protestant
missions in this period had repackaged the knowledge of God, putting it within
the safe confines of a *modern* interpretation of Christianity as an absolute religion, and came to see themselves as the executors of divine history. This divine
mandate included the conversion of anybody who might think differently,
including secularists and the Jews (to some degree also the Catholics) at home
and non-Christians elsewhere. At the centre stood a desire to tame any inde-

pendent or local designs for life and religion, and with this to take control of their social forms. The intention was to master the ambiguity and fuzziness of the world by applying a universal religious rationality. Through Christianization, the most ambitiously complete restructuring of humankind was attempted. In the words of Visser't Hooft (1959: 369), the first General Secretary of the World Council of Churches, mission had become a prisoner of modern Western civilization, not its prophetic reformer.

Protestant missions in this period, their publications in particular, have acquired a reputation for moral and intellectual inferiority: because of their schools and hospitals, there is the perception of a misuse of the need for education and healing as a missionary method; there is the habitual degrading, if not contempt, for cultures and religions in the non-Western world; the not infrequent collaboration with colonial and commercial interests (Stanley, 1990); and the glorification of the white missionary's role and the silencing of the local (African, Asian or other) contribution to the transmission of Christianity. It is a well-established fact that much of the missionary impact must be attributed not to white missionaries but to local men and women (Ustorf, 2002). This criticism is justified, but one should not overlook that the mission work of this particular period has resulted in four other, and major, processes of historical importance:

1   Much of Protestant mission work was (and increasingly is) decidedly international and supra-denominational (cf. the London Missionary Society of 1795, the oldest example of this type of agency; Thorogood, 1994). On the one hand, this relativized the cultural settings and also the historical roots of Protestantism; on the other, it enabled the indigenous variants of Christianity (Koschorke, 1998) that emerged abroad to develop within a broad ecumenical framework. Protestant mission work de-Protestantized the tradition.

2   In their educational activities in particular, Protestant missions released impulses that contributed to the subversion of colonialism and theological dominance. Graduates of the catechetical seminaries and high schools of the missions not only became leaders of the emerging local church; often they were leading figures of the anti-colonial discourse as well. Whether this quest for self-governance is an expression of the power of Christ or rather of the Enlightenment paradigm of equality (or of the meeting of both) is an important question.

3   Protestant missions, since the days of the Quaker linguist Hannah Kilham (1774–1832), tended to use the vernacular for the transmission of the faith. Thus the foundations had been laid for Christianity to break free from its Western cultural moorings and become a true world religion: that is, to move on with the help of maps and charts that were no longer defined by its occidental heritage, and, at the same time, to encourage an incredible diversification of ecclesiological models and theological approaches. Modern missions substantially transformed Christian identity

and contributed to the end of Christendom or of the European phase in the life of Christianity.

4   The missionary zeal of collecting, describing, analysing, and classifying non-Western knowledge – cultural, ethnological, and religious – led to a massive influx of alternative modes of thought into Western culture. Robert Morrison (1782–1834), the first Protestant missionary to China, did not only translate the Bible, he also produced a six-volume dictionary of the Chinese language (1815–22). This influx, however, worked like the 'cunning of history' in Hegel's *Philosophy of History*: it ran almost counter to world mission's efforts to universalize Christianity by undermining still further the collapsed monopoly of Christianity in Europe. The dream of Protestant missions was a religiously homogenized world; the outcome was the multiplication of religious approaches. Mission had become one of the strongest forces of pluralization.

Current Trends

The twentieth century witnessed tremendous efforts to overcome the burden and the divisions of the past and also to strive for unity. The great mission conferences from 1910 (Edinburgh) on, and the ecumenical movement, are the institutional expressions of this. Today, ecumenism is a mere shadow of its former self: there are around 34,000 organizationally distinct Christian denominations worldwide, and this tendency towards fragmentation is rising (Barrett, Kurian and Johnson, 2001). Meanwhile, the missionary movement is trying to distance itself from colonialism, Western culture and modernity, and the old unifying paradigm of 'Christocentric universalism' has been unceremoniously dumped. The concept of *missio Dei* has demythologized the church. In its place we now have a multitude of makeshift or pilgrim churches, many of them on the way towards a new identity, many now resolved to an accommodation with local culture, and all engaged in helping, criticizing, and reminding one another of their true purpose, while at the same time contesting the essential nature of Christianity. Concepts such as 'church', 'mission' and 'Christianity' have been called into question in the South, or the new homelands of this tradition. In the old territories of Christianity, Europe and the West in general, radical transformations in the understanding of mission have also occurred, mainly in the twentieth century: from the pioneering *Laymen's Inquiry* into foreign missions (Hocking, 1932), the discovery of Western culture as a missiological problem (e.g. the *Christian Message* project of the *International Missionary Council*, 1929–33, Ustorf, 2000b: 97–112, or the study *La France – Pays de Mission?*, Godin and Daniel, 1943), to the redrafting of the missionary agenda and the rewriting of Christian history in the period of decolonization, liberation theology and the pluralization of Christianity.

Luigi Pirandello once wrote a play about six actors who, while waiting for a playwright who would never arrive, discuss the script and the roles they have within it. This play may stand as an allegory for the state in which Protestantism finds itself today; similarly, such a process of self-reflection may lead us to the question whether there really is such a thing as Protestantism, or whether it is not in all of its characteristics more like a 'chameleon' (Hastings, 1999: 1). This consideration applies also to its impact on mission. One further trend now remains to be highlighted here.

Currently, the most significant process in Protestant mission work is the meteoric rise of the inter-denominational and predominantly US-based faith missions, the Pentecostal-charismatic presence, and the growth of local independent churches in what were previously mission fields. This trend, though already observable in the nineteenth century, has now reduced to insignificance the activities of the 'classical' or mainline missions (Fiedler, 1994; Barrett and Johnson, 2002). This process has reintroduced what enlightened theology and mission had excluded: signs and wonders, the middle world of spirits, and the immediacy of primal religious practices. In this perspective, the world – and its religions too – is pregnant with God's spirit, leading to an amalgamation of biblical and indigenous mythologies and to understandings of mission that have certainly not got the *nihil obstat* of occidental theological rationality, that is, the Christian syncretism of the North Atlantic tribes. Some label this a *second* or *African Reformation* (Anderson, 2001). Whatever we call it, it seems that for the majority of these Christians the first Reformation has little meaning. They are too busy recovering from what has been dubbed *occidentosis* (De Souza, 2001).

References

Anderson, A. H. (2001). *African Reformation. African Initiated Christianity in the 20th Century*. Trenton, NJ and Asmara: Africa World Press.

Anderson, G. H. (ed.) (1998). *Biographical Dictionary of Christian Missions*. Grand Rapids, MI: Eerdmans.

Barrett, D. B. and Johnson, T. M. (2002). Annual Statistical Table on Global Mission: 2002. *International Bulletin of Missionary Research* 26,1: 22–3.

Barrett, D. B., Kurian, G. T. and Johnson, T. M. (2001). *World Christian Encyclopedia. A Comparative Survey of Churches and Religions in the Modern World*, 2 vols, 2nd edn. New York: Oxford University Press.

Berlin, I. (1980). *Vico and Herder*. London: Chatto & Windus.

Bosch, D. (1991). *Transforming Mission*. Maryknoll, NY: Orbis.

Bowie, F., Kirkwood, D., Ardener, S., and Ardener, S. (eds.) (1993). *Women and Missions: Past and Present*. Providence, RI and Oxford: Berg.

De Souza, T. R. (2001). Orientalism, Occidentosis and other Viral Strains. Historical Objectivity and Social Responsibilities. In P. Malekandathil and T. J. Mohammed (eds.), *The Portuguese, Indian Ocean and European Bridgeheads*. Tellicherry, Kerala: Institute for

Research in Social Sciences and Humanities of MESHAR & Fundação Oriente, pp. 452–79.

Fiedler, K. (1994). *The Story of the Faith Missions. From Hudson Taylor to Present Day Africa.* Oxford: Regnum.

Funkschmidt, K. (2000). *Earthing the Vision. Strukturreformen in der Mission untersucht am Beispiel von CEVAA (Paris), CWM (London) und UEM (Wuppertal).* Frankfurt: O. Lembeck.

Gensichen, H.-W. (1976). *Missionsgeschichte der neueren Zeit,* 3rd edn. Göttingen: Vandenhoeck & Ruprecht.

Gerloff, R. I. H. (1992). *A Plea for British Black Theologies,* 2 vols. Frankfurt: P. Lang.

Godin, D. and Daniel, Y. (1943). *La France – Pays de Mission?* Lyon: Les Éditions de l'Abeille.

Goh, M. S. (2001). Koreanische Missionen. In Hans-Dieter Betz (ed.), *Religion in Geschichte und Gegenwart,* vol. IV, 4th edn. Tübingen: Mohr/Siebeck, p. 1687.

Hastings, A. (ed.) (1999). *A World History of Christianity.* London: Cassell.

Hocking, W. E. (ed.) (1932). *Re-Thinking Mission. A Laymen's Inquiry after One Hundred Years.* New York and London: Harper & Brothers.

Jongeneel, J. A. B. (1995). The Protestant Missionary Movement up to 1789. In F. J. Verstraelen, A. Camps, L. A. Hoedemaker, and M. R. Spindler (eds.), *Missiology. An Ecumenical Introduction.* Grand Rapids, MI: Eerdmans, pp. 222–8.

Koschorke, K. (1998). *Christen und Gewürze. Konfrontation und Interaktion kolonialer und indigener Christentumsvarianten.* Göttingen: Vandenhoeck & Ruprecht.

Latourette, K. S. (1937–45). *A History of the Expansion of Christianity,* 7 vols. New York: Harper.

Laubach, F. (1989). *Justinian von Welz.* Wuppertal, Germany: Brockhaus.

McNeill, W. H. (1987). Migration and Religion. In Mircea Eliade and Charles J. Adams (eds.), *Encyclopedia of Religion,* vol. 9. New York: Macmillan, pp. 515–19.

Porter, A. N. (1991). *Religion and Empire: British Expansion in the Long 19th Century, 1780–1914.* Inaugural Lecture, London, King's College, 20 November.

Raupp, W. (1990). *Mission in Quellentexten. Geschichte der deutschen evangelischen Mission von der Reformation bis zur Weltmissionskonferenz Edinburgh 1910.* Erlangen: Ev.-Luth. Mission.

Robert, D. L. (1996). *American Women in Mission.* Macon, GA: Mercer University Press.

Sanneh, L. (1999). *Abolitionists Abroad. American Blacks and the Making of Modern West Africa.* Cambridge, MA: Harvard University Press.

Schäufele, W. (1966). *Das missionarische Bewußtsein und Wirken der Täufer.* Neukirchen-Vluyn, Germany: Neukirchen.

Stanley, B. (1990). *The Bible and the Flag. Protestant Missions and British Imperialism.* London: Appolos.

Stanley, B. (1992). *The History of the BMS, 1792–1992.* Edinburgh: T & T Clark.

Stanley, B. (ed.) (2001). *Christian Missions and the Enlightenment.* Grand Rapids, MI: Eerdmans.

Thorogood, B. (ed.) (1994). *Gales of Change. Responding to a Shifting Missionary Context. The Story of the LMS, 1945–1977.* Geneva: WCC.

Ustorf, W. (2000a). What if the Light in you is Darkness? An Inquiry into the Shadow Side of the Missionary Self. In U. van der Heyden and J. Becher (eds.), *Mission und Gewalt.* Stuttgart: Steiner, pp. 139–52.

Ustorf, W. (2000b). *Sailing on the Next Tide. Missions, Missiology, and the Third Reich.* Frankfurt and New York: P. Lang.

Ustorf, W. (2002). *Bremen Missionaries in Togo and Ghana, 1847–1900*. Accra: Asempa.

Visser't Hooft, W. A. (1959). The Significance of the Asian Churches in the Ecumenical Movement. *The Ecumenical Review* 11: 365–76.

Walls, A. F. (1996). *The Missionary Movement in Christian History*. Maryknoll, NY: Orbis.

Ward, K. and Stanley, B. (eds.) (2000). *The CMS and World Christianity, 1799–1999*. Grand Rapids, MI: Eerdmans

Warneck, G. (1910). *Abriß einer Geschichte der protestantischen Missionen von der Reformation bis auf die Gegenwart. Mit einem Anhang über die katholischen Missionen*, 9th edn. Berlin: Warneck.

PART III

The Future of Protestantism

37 The Future of Protestantism: Ecumenism and the Mainline
    Denominations   405
38 The Future of Protestantism: Evangelicalism   421
39 The Future of Protestantism: The Rise of Pentecostalism   439
40 The Future of Protestantism: Postmodernity   453
41 The Future of Protestantism: The Non-Western Protestant World 468

CHAPTER 37

The Future of Protestantism: Ecumenism and the Mainline Denominations

Alan D. Falconer

The ecumenical movement, as William Temple once put it, 'is the great new fact of our era' (cited in Till, 1972: 176). In the course of the twentieth century, relations between churches of different Christian traditions have been radically transformed. After centuries of separations and hostilities, churches had entered configurations of co-operation, common commitment and communion. In this chapter, an attempt to account for this development will be made, the methods which have enabled churches to move from relationships of conflict to communion will be outlined, the main events in the story will be explored and some of the new challenges facing the mainline churches of the beginning of the new millennium will be identified.

Mission and Unity

The impulses for the contemporary ecumenical movement emerge, above all, from the missionary movement of the nineteenth century. Some attempts had been made to draw churches into unity on the basis of doctrinal agreement. In the 1830s, Samuel Schmucker, son of a German-born Lutheran pastor, issued a 'Fraternal Appeal to the American Churches. With a Plan for Catholic Union, on Apostolic Principles'. The appeal was based on a series of 12 articles formed from the principle articles of the Reformation Confessions of Faith. In the 1880s, Philip Schaff, the Reformed scholar, on the basis of historical study and his magisterial work on *The Creeds of Christendom* had come to the conclusion that central to the nature of the church was unity, and he suggested that there would be a coming together of Protestantism, Catholicism and Orthodoxy. He proposed unity by stages – individual, federal, organic. Schmucker, born in Maryland, and Schaff, who had settled in the United States, had been influenced by situations where there was a predominant church or only one church on the basis of *cuius regio eius religio*. In the United States, where no such political arrangement applied, it was clear that new relationships of co-operation and common witness were essential.

In the nineteenth century, revival movements that traversed denominational boundaries also helped to relativize denominationalism and point to a unity beyond church boundaries. The creation of the Evangelical Alliance (1846) was one such manifestation. To further the missionary task, the Young Men's Christian Association (YMCA, 1844), the Young Women's Christian Association (YWCA, 1855) and the World Student Christian Federation (WSCF, 1890) had been established. While those associations and movements sought to further missionary work across confessional boundaries, the different confessions began to form international associations to enable their member churches to bear witness at the international level. Thus in 1867, the Anglican bishops gathered for the so-called Lambeth Conference. The World Presbyterian Alliance and the International Congregational Council followed in 1875 and 1891 respectively. The Methodist churches formed a conference in 1881, and the World Baptist Union was founded in 1905. Fundamental to the existence of these confessional bodies was their desire to further the mission of the church.

Despite this extensive missionary endeavour, churches continued to divide. Most of the mainline churches in America split during the nineteenth century on the issue of slavery, thus reflecting the different sides of the American Civil War. In other places, division occurred over the question of church–state relations, as with the Disruption in Scotland. By the end of the nineteenth century two major tensions were evident in mainline Protestantism – missionary activity and a heightened confessional identity, and these could be countervailing forces.

On the basis of the missionary expansion of Christianity, international gatherings for the furtherance of mission were held from 1854 to 1900, in London and New York, the last of which was called the Ecumenical Missionary Conference, 'because the plan of campaign which it proposes covers the whole area of the inhabited world' (Latourette, 1967: 354). As Kenneth Scott Latourette notes in his official history of the ecumenical movement, 'on every continent and in almost every land there was a growing movement towards Christian unity' (ibid.).

It was as an outgrowth and climax of these missionary endeavours that a World Mission Conference was held in Edinburgh in 1910. Its membership and leadership was predominantly from the societies which had arisen from the religious awakenings within Protestantism in the preceding century. The two figures most associated with its organization were John R. Mott, a Methodist layman, and Joseph Oldham, who had been a secretary of the Student Christian Movement (SCM) of Great Britain and Ireland and of the YMCA in India. The conference, in addition to official delegates from missionary societies, included delegates from church mission boards and departments. This conference was a body that had more authority to speak on behalf of the churches than its predecessors.

From this International Missionary Conference in Edinburgh the contemporary ecumenical movement emerged. While there was great confidence that the world could be converted to the gospel, the existence of different and competing churches was seen to be a counter-witness to the gospel itself. How could the churches and the missionary societies seek to proclaim a gospel of reconciliation with integrity when they did not exhibit that same reconciliation in their own patterns of living and relationships? Why should non-Christians believe such a gospel? It was, above all, the situation where missionary societies were active that the call for integrity was made. The Indian Anglican delegate V. S. Azariah, for example, pointed to the counter-witness of divided churches. If the mission of the church was to be pursued, churches needed to co-operate and seek unity. Such a call for unity for the sake of mission challenged Protestant denominationalism and self-sufficiency, and in the pursuit of unity for the sake of mission a number of movements developed.

From Conflict to Communion

One of the delegates most exercised by the issue of division at Edinburgh 1910 was Bishop Charles Brent (American Protestant Episcopal Church). A missionary bishop in the Philippines, he realized that if churches were to be united for the sake of mission, they would need to overcome the questions of doctrine and of church polity that divided them. On his return from Edinburgh he proposed to his church that they call an international gathering of church representatives to discuss these issues. From the same Edinburgh conference, Dr Peter Ainslie (Disciples of Christ) returned to his church in the United States with the same idea. This happy coincidence began the process of establishing a World Conference on Faith and Order. There followed a long process of commendation and consultation. It was clear that this conference should not be an exclusively pan-Protestant event. Overtures were made to the Roman Catholic Church for their involvement. While there had been unofficial dialogues between Anglicans and Roman Catholics in the 1890s and again from 1922 to 1927 in the Malines Conversations, the Roman Catholic Church had asserted (in *Mortalium Animas*, 1927) that it was the only true church and therefore any unity would require the return of the other churches to Rome. However, the initiatives from Edinburgh 1910 received encouragement from two sources. In 1920 the Anglican Lambeth Conference issued an 'Appeal to all Christians' to seek moves towards unity. In the same year the Orthodox Ecumenical Patriarch issued an encyclical letter 'Unto the Churches of Christ Everywhere'. The latter, probably drafted by Archbishop Germanos of Thyateira, and approved by the Holy Synod, called for the establishment of a world league (*koinonia*) of churches. Clearly those initiatives had been born of the destruction of the First World War and the determination that nothing like it should happen again, and they reflected the secular call to establish a league of nations. The war showed the fragmentation of the church and its inability to proclaim a gospel of reconciliation. The gospel had been pressed into the service of competing nationalisms.

The First World Conference on Faith and Order took place in Lausanne in August 1927, where delegated representatives of Protestant and Orthodox Churches began to discuss the theological issues which held the churches apart. Throughout the twentieth century, these discussions were continued in a series of world conferences – Edinburgh (1937), Lund (1952), Montreal (1963) and Santiago de Compostela (1993). Between conferences the work was undertaken by a number of theological commissions and, since the foundation of the World Council of Churches in 1948, by the Faith and Order Commission. The principal questions which have been addressed in the attempt to assist churches as they move from conflict towards communion have been the sacraments, the different polities of the church (episcopal, presbyterial, congregational), grace and justification by grace through faith, the relation of Scripture to tradition and experience, the role of creeds and confessions of faith and the common confession of the apostolic faith through the Nicene-Constantinopolitan Creed, the apostolicity and the nature and purpose of the church, and the role and exercise of authority in the church.

While it is not possible in the scope of this chapter to indicate the results in each area of these dialogues, it is important to note the methodologies in evidence which have enabled the churches to move from conflict, competition or co-existence to co-operation and convergence, and finally to conversion and communion.

In the first period of theological dialogue – from 1910 to 1952 – a comparative methodology was employed. In this, churches that had not been in dialogue previously, or who had in an earlier age condemned the theological positions of others, patiently outlined their theological stance on the questions under review to each other. On the basis of their stated positions, a statement of what all the churches seemed able to accept was drawn up, and a list of the divisive points which needed to be resolved was noted. Those divisive points then formed the agenda for the subsequent discussions. Such a method was able to help the churches to overcome their prejudices about, and stereotypes of, each other, but was not capable of leading to communion. Indeed, the method is at root not dialogical but monological: I will accept you as long as and insofar as you agree with me.

At the Third World Conference on Faith and Order, therefore, a Christological and convergent methodology was enjoined. Perhaps it was because another devastating world war had sharpened the awareness of the urgency for the churches to seek unity that the inadequacy of the previous method was noted – or perhaps it was simply that the method had exhausted the possibilities – but in his address to the Lund Conference, Oliver Tomkins, later Bishop of Bristol but then associate general secretary of the World Council of Churches with responsibility for Faith and Order, proposed a radical change of direction. As is clear from the recent biography by the late Adrian Hastings, Tomkins, who had been born in China of LMS parents, educated in Cambridge and nurtured in the Student Christian Movement where he came under the influence of the evangelical Bishop Edwards Woods, played a decisive role in guiding the conference in four areas (Hastings, 2001). While President of the SCM in Cambridge and later on the SCM staff, Oliver Tomkins had been a colleague of a number of the most important British ecumenical figures – Kathleen Bliss, Lesslie Newbigin, Eric Fenn, Michael Ramsey and Robert Mackie. In these circles, the mode of engagement was a passionate wrestling with issues of the faith on the basis of Bible study and in the attempt to move beyond previously held positions. This experience he now brought to the Faith and Order movement when he encouraged articulating a common theological position on the basis of common sources of the faith and of common baptism in Christ. Secondly, Tomkins asked whether the churches should not do everything together except where differences of deep conviction compelled them to act separately. This question was incorporated into the Message of the Conference to the Churches and became known as the Lund Principle. In both these proposals there arose radical implications concerning the identity of the different churches. Both challenged the self-sufficiency and self-understanding of the different confessional traditions, Protestant and Orthodoxy, and emphasized a common bond in the Source and sources of the faith.

Oliver Tomkins was heavily engaged, along with Willem A. Visser't Hooft, another product of SCM and the first General Secretary of the World Council of Churches, in trying to secure the participation of the Roman Catholic Church in the ecumenical movement. While there were a number of dialogues between Protestant and Roman Catholic theologians in different countries of Europe, international involvement had been difficult to achieve. Thus Tomkins was involved in a series of consultations from 1949 to 1952, particularly with French Roman Catholics such as Yves Congar, and was finally able to secure the presence at Lund of the first officially appointed Roman Catholic observers. The final contribution of Tomkins to the Lund Conference was to highlight the importance of 'non-theological' factors in church division. While this had been the subject of an intervention at the Edinburgh 1937 conference by C. H. Dodd, this concern was in danger of getting lost. However, it was imperative that the churches face up to the fact that many divisions in the church had arisen from political, social, cultural and economic factors, and had then been justified by theological loci. To seek the unity of the church, therefore, involved more than the resolution of theological differences. It involved also the addressing of non-theological factors, as they were then designated – now they are more appropriately called 'non-doctrinal' factors.

After Lund, the Faith and Order Commission came to a common mind on the relation of scripture and tradition (Montreal), examined the different hermeneutical keys evident in different confessional traditions as they interpreted scripture and on the basis of this understanding of the sources of theology examined the issues of Baptism, Eucharist and Ministry (*Lima Report*, Faith and Order Plenary Commission, 1982) and have engaged in an exploration of the nature and purpose of the church, to name but two areas. The agreement on Baptism, Eucharist and Ministry emerged from a renewed attempt to go behind the differences of confessional understanding to their biblical roots. But what is the purpose of reaching such theological agreement? It became clear that a convergent methodology did not necessarily lead to communion. Another stage and methodology was and is required, namely conversion leading to communion.

The Lima agreement invited churches to consider their theology and practices, and to change in the light of the agreement reached. It was clear that churches needed to include other churches in their definition and understanding of what it meant to be church. This entails a radical change of perception and self-understanding.

In seeking to draw the churches through the stages from conflict, competition and co-existence, to comparative acceptance, co-operation and thence convergence and consensus to conversion and communion for the sake of enabling the gospel of reconciliation to be manifest with integrity churches have, through the Faith and Order movement, engaged in theological dialogue through the methodologies of comparison, convergence and communion. Initially such dialogue involved officially designated theologians from the Protestant and Orthodox Churches, but since 1968 has also included officially nominated Roman Catholic theologians.

From Identity-in-opposition Towards the 'Embrace of the Other'

The major division in the Western church was that which occurred in the sixteenth century. From that time a history of action, reaction and separation characterized the relationship between Protestant and Roman Catholic churches. Although in some places attempts over the centuries of rapprochement or mutual understanding – often with official approval – were made, the predominant attitude of antagonism prevailed. An identity-in-opposition emerged, where the self-definition of many Protestants was that they were not Roman Catholic – even to the extent of a different term to 'catholic' being substituted in the so-called ecumenical creeds. Characteristic theological positions took on the aspect not only of theological articulations of the faith, but of flags of identity. Thus many Protestant catechisms were crafted on the basis of denying or contradicting Roman Catholic positions, rather than presenting a cohesive and coherent account of church belief. Such identity-in-opposition was reinforced by the experience of communities, particularly in minority situations. For example, the dispersal of the Huguenots throughout Europe, particularly in the light of the Revocation of the Edict of Nantes, reinforced such oppositional positions.

Relatively little theological dialogue between Protestants and Roman Catholics had occurred since the sixteenth century. However, through the twentieth century a number of important initiatives and experiences began to create a new climate in some places. The Malines Conversations had led some Anglicans and Roman Catholics to see that they shared a common faith in the context of which a number of theological questions needed to be addressed. The work of Yves Congar and others initiated a theological dialogue, even although such did not engender a positive response from Roman Catholic authorities. Dialogue groups between Roman Catholic and Protestant theologians emerged in France and French-speaking Switzerland (Groupe des Dombes), the Netherlands, Germany and Ireland. The awareness of the common faith shared by Protestants and Roman Catholics was experienced in the prisoner of war camps during the Second World War, and the Week of Prayer for Christian Unity, developed by Abbé Paul Couturier, all helped to create a new climate. The experiments of the worker priest movement in France in the aftermath of the war also influenced pastors in other Christian traditions as they sought in their context to commend the faith in an increasingly secular situation. On the level of scholarship, liturgical and biblical scholars such as Cardinal Augustin Bea found themselves engaged in a common enterprise. These initiatives were not officially promoted nor recognized by the church authorities on the whole, but they did help to create a climate to appreciate the vast changes in the Roman Catholic Church when they occurred.

To the surprise of his own church, and of the Protestant and Orthodox churches, Pope John XXIII convened a council of his church with the intention of renewal. To prepare for this he also established what became the Secretariat for Promoting Christian Unity. At their urging, observers from the major confessional families were invited to attend this council. Invitations were sent to Christian World bodies such as the Lutheran World Federation (founded 1923 and 1947), the World Methodist Council, the World Council of Churches and the Ecumenical Patriarchate, and they all responded positively. The observers were consulted widely and many of their suggestions were incorporated in the conciliar texts (e.g. the impact of Oscar Cullmann on *Lumen Gentium*). The council itself approved a decree on ecumenism which impelled the Roman Catholic Church into participation in the ecumenical movement.

From the Second Vatican Council, a series of bilateral dialogues between officially appointed theologians of the Roman Catholic Church and of the different confessional families was initiated. The agenda was largely determined by previous relations between the Roman Catholic Church and the confessional tradition concerned (e.g. the Anglican–Roman Catholic International Commission, ARCIC). The dialogues helped the communities overcome their prejudices and stereotypes of each other. In some cases, they have enabled the two traditions to lift historic condemnations issued against each other. Most notably, this was evident in the signing of the *Joint Declaration on the Doctrine of Justification* between the Roman Catholic Church and the Lutheran World Federation (1999). However, while the results of this 30-year activity of bilateral dialogues have been widely disseminated (e.g. they are published in the two volumes of *Growth in Agreement*, Meyer and Vischer, 1984; Gros, Meyer, and Rusch, 2000), they have not yet led to communion.

The impact of the dialogues between Protestant and Roman Catholic representatives has been both positive and negative. It has led to a questioning of confessional identity by those bodies participating. But it also has led to a crisis of identity, particularly in those traditions that had defined themselves in opposition to the Roman Catholic Church. It is perhaps due to this dialogue above all that there has been a recurring concern with the issue of self-identity in specific Christian world communions – the Lutheran World Federation has undertaken a number of studies on this theme since 1970, though it is not alone in so doing. A second result of such dialogue has been the awareness that theological divisions are less determined by confessional boundaries and cut across the denominations. Thirdly, such dialogue with Roman Catholics has left some churches in a situation where they find themselves – particularly as minorities – unable to participate in dialogue because of the way they feel they have been treated by the Roman Catholic Church. In some situations they have withdrawn from ecumenical engagement.

United and Uniting

Decisions to change or to move towards communion do not reside with world confessional families or the multilateral dialogues of the Faith and Order movement. These bodies are simply instrumental in helping their member churches move towards unity. Their only authority, as William Temple put it, resides in the wisdom they offer. It is up to the individual churches to take appropriate action.

From Edinburgh in 1910, a number of churches in specific situations began to enter discussions with each other with the aim of entering union. Such negotiations began, not because of the icy blasts of secularism in creating a situation of numerical loss, thus inducing churches to huddle together for comfort and the sharing of limited resources, as Bryan Wilson (1964: 15) has suggested. Instead, church union negotiations began due to a passion for the mission of the church and to offer a credible witness to the gospel of reconciliation.

Some church unions emerged as the reconciliation of splits or estrangements within the one confessional tradition, for example the Church of Scotland in 1929. Others drew on a shared heritage of thought and piety, for example the United Church of Canada in 1925. Yet other church union negotiations drew together churches from different confessional traditions. Perhaps the best known of these are the Church of South India and the Church of North India. In both

cases, personalities associated with SCM were involved. Lesslie Newbigin played
a significant role in drafting the agreement and promoting the union of the
Church of South India, while the Irish Presbyterian David Kennedy played a
similar role in the Church of North India. Both church union negotiations drew
significantly on the multilateral results and insights of the Faith and Order Commission. The two union schemes, however, adopted different methodologies. In
the case of South India, they came to the conclusion that it was only as they
were united that it would be possible on the basis of shared experience to articulate the theological basis of the united church, while in North India a theological agreement was articulated and adopted prior to union. Both methods
continue to be applied in different situations. Of particular importance was that
they brought into union churches of Presbyterian, Methodist, Congregational
and Anglican polity. Here was a reconciliation of churches that had defined
themselves over against each other on the basis of polity. Unfortunately other
members of the Anglican family found it impossible to recognize this union or
reconciliation – at least not until all clergy had been ordained 'within the apostolic succession'. In India after patient dialogue and negotiation church union
brought together churches of different families into a new identity – for the sake
of the mission of the church.

Through the twentieth century, a number of other church unions were
consummated and a large number of negotiations continue.

Reconciled but not United

Another series of new relationships between churches of different communions
have been forged on the basis of bilateral and multilateral dialogues at the international level. Nonetheless, if the results of dialogues are really to be received,
then they should lead to changed relationships. In a recent paper to the Forum
on Bilateral Dialogues of the General Secretaries of the Christian World
Communions, Dr Mary Tanner charted the way in which the multilateral and
bilateral agreements – particularly the *Lima Report, Baptism, Eucharist, Ministry*
(1982) – had provided a basis for the reconciliation of churches. The new
relationship between Lutheran and Anglican Churches – Meissen (Germany),
Porvoo (Scandinavia and the Baltic), Common Mission (USA) and Waterloo
(Canada) – has changed the identity and brought these traditions into a new
shared ministry. Similar agreements between Lutheran and Reformed traditions
in Europe (Leuenberg 1973) and the Formula of Agreement (USA) have led to
a relationship characterized by 'affirmation and admonition' (Formula of Agreement), and have changed communities from oppositional postures to communal stances.

In the case of both united churches and the new relationships of reconciled
unity, however, it is clear that these involve only members of different *Protestant*
confessional families. Changing denominational profiles have so far been

confined to one broad tradition – Protestantism. Though there have been substantial changes of perception and commitment between Protestant, Orthodox and Roman Catholic traditions on the basis of dialogue, the different ecclesiologies and self-understandings of these three main traditions require further dialogue, and require to be placed in the context of how best one might be faithful and reflect God's mission in the twenty-first century.

Co-operating on Social-economic and Political Issues

Alongside the desire to engage in common mission and to overcome the theological questions which divide the church in the hope that the church could truly exhibit its gift in Christ and its calling to exhibit that community which God intends – a community reconciled and reconciling – another impulse towards unity emerged from the Edinburgh 1910 conference. While the patient work of theological dialogue was initiated, the need for the churches to address the contemporary problems of the world was evident.

The principal actor in bringing this need before the churches was Nathan Söderblom, Lutheran Archbishop of Uppsala and Primate of Sweden. Christian unity was, as Norman Goodall has noted in his history of the ecumenical movement, 'in his heart throughout a many-sided ministry and what, for him, gave special urgency to the matter was the need of a divided world for authentic witness to the unifying power of Christ' (Goodall, 1964: 57). As the First World War continued, he endeavoured to bring together Christian leaders from different sides of the conflict to a Christian conference. While this did not come about, Söderblom's project won the support of a number of leaders, particularly in England. Foremost amongst those was William Temple. The activities of Söderblom, Temple and others were born from the conviction that, while the kingdom of God can never be equated with any pattern of human society, Christ's gospel of the Kingdom carries with it guidance and peace for the better ordering of human relationships. This was the starting point of various movements that contributed to the formation of the Life and Work Movement. For example, in 1924, a gathering under the theme 'Conference on Christian Politics, Economics and Citizenship' (COPEC) was held under the chairmanship of William Temple. Out of these various national initiatives emerged the International Conference on Life and Work in Stockholm (1925).

Those participating in Stockholm were conscious of the need for mainline churches to give a common witness to the world – a witness which transcended national and denominational boundaries. While the movement received inspiration from significant figures of the Protestant world, it attracted the support also of prominent leaders of the Orthodox churches, particularly the Patriarchs of Alexandria and Jerusalem. The Stockholm conference was remarkable in encouraging the churches to make the attempt to reach agreement on the nature and main direction of Christian responsibility in national and international order. The slogan that came to be associated with Life and Work was

'Doctrine divides, service unites', though it has become apparent that this is, in fact, not such a clear characterization!

After the Stockholm conference, however, it became apparent that as churches sought to give a specifically Christian witness they were required to do so on the basis of theological insights. Just as the Faith and Order movement found itself constantly pushing towards the ethical and social implications of the gospel, so the Life and Work Movement found itself engaging in theological discourse. It became clear to both movements in the post-Stockholm and Lausanne period that they needed to work together, because of the interdependence of their concerns. Thus the second conference of both movements was held in the same year, in Edinburgh and in Oxford so that the proposal could be put to them that they merge to form what came to be known as the World Council of Churches. The Oxford Life and Work Conference participants list reads like a veritable *Who's Who* of leading churchmen, politicians, economists and figures from the arts and society. It directed its reflections on church, community, and state and, as with Faith and Order, agreed to form the World Council of Churches.

While the concern for joint witness on politics, social and economic matters was intended to bring the churches together, and whereas it involved the main Protestant denominations and the Orthodox Churches, it was not seen to be a factor which would necessarily change the identity of the denominations. Rather it led to the awareness of churches giving witness to the gospel beyond one's boundaries as churches began to act in solidarity with other churches in different parts of the world.

The concern to give common witness in an increasingly divided world has been continued in the World Council of Churches. Every Assembly has directed attention to these questions. In addition to these, two notable conferences have been held devoted to these issues. The first was the World Conference on Church and Society (Geneva, 1966) out of which emerged concerns for a theology of liberation arising from post-colonial churches participating in the reconstruction of their countries. The second major event was the World Convocation on Justice, Peace and the Integrity of Creation (Seoul 1990) that sought to encourage churches to commit themselves to a series of propositions on politics, social and economic matters. As with multilateral theological dialogue, these initiatives have again demonstrated that the attitude to such co-operation is not determined by traditional denominational boundaries, but cuts across the denominations. Such reflection and action, while it has undoubtedly brought the denominations together, has also been divisive within each mainline church. There are many who have difficulties with concerns on the political, social and economic agenda. Therefore, the World Council of Churches is perceived as being too political, while others draw different ethical and political conclusions from those of the World Council of Churches. Particularly controversial was the 1969 decision to establish a Programme to Combat Racism, and to act in solidarity with those seeking to overcome apartheid. In the light of this some churches, for example the Presbyterian Church in Ireland, withdrew their membership of the World Council of Churches.

Taking Counsel Together

As the churches have sought to reflect and give a common witness in society, they came together to form councils of churches, particularly at national level. Since most Protestant churches are specific to particular nations, these councils provided an opportunity for them to engage in transforming ways. Initially most councils engaged primarily in issues of common witness to society. On the whole they left the theological discussion of issues of faith and order to their participation in the Faith and Order Commission or their engagement in bilateral dialogues through their respective world confessional families. Since councils by definition are not decision-taking bodies, but places where common reflection takes place, the member churches themselves determine how far they will receive multilateral agreements and engage in common action. The members of councils of churches are churches themselves, and not ecumenically committed or driven individuals or groups. Initially these were largely Protestant in inspiration and organization, but of the 108 national councils of churches, the Roman Catholic Church is a member of 58. There are also seven regional councils, of which the Roman Catholic Church is a member of three. The Orthodox Churches are particularly prominent in the Middle East Council of Churches, the Conference of European Churches and the National Council of Churches of the USA. National and regional councils bring the churches together for common reflection and action, though many of these do not themselves have departments of theology or Faith and Order units. The common action and reflection has helped to increase trust between denominations but as churches have sought unity, they have created separate structures for church union negotiations.

Common Mission

It may seem perverse that having begun with the Edinburgh Missionary Conference of 1910, and with the call to unity for the sake of mission, to be returning to this theme only at this stage. However, this chapter is concerned with denominations and how they have developed and changed in the light of ecumenical encounter. After Edinburgh a continuation committee was established. Churches and mission agencies increasingly entered comity agreements through which they undertook not to impinge on the territory in which other agencies and churches were active. This was an attempt to move from competition to co-operation. Following the Edinburgh conference, a series of conferences were held in Jerusalem (1928), Tambaran, India (1938) and Whitby, Canada (1947).

All of these conferences were Protestant initiatives and they all took up and discussed issues at the cutting edge of missionary endeavour. One issue to which they returned again and again was that of dialogue with people of other living faiths. Intense debates centred on the tension between mission and dialogue. In those situations where Christians live as minorities they sought to engage in dialogue. Many missionary societies found this unacceptable. Throughout the history of the International Missionary Council and its successor body, the Commission on World Mission and Evangelism, this debate has continued, and has polarized churches. In particular, Hendrik Kraemer gave a spirited affirmation to mission and declared that on the basis of the work of Jesus Christ as Mediator, it was possible only to proclaim the self-sufficiency of Christ. As we shall see, this continuing debate led many evangelicals in the church to withdraw from participation in the Commission on World Mission and Evangelism.

A second feature of the discussion in the International Missionary Council was that of the emergence of churches in the developing world as independent churches. These churches grew in number after nations achieved independence, but it was clearly the hope in the nineteenth century that churches in Africa, Asia and Latin America would be self-supporting, self-financing and autonomous; this can be seen in the correspondence of the secretaries of the Church Missionary Society and the American Board of Missions at that time. This development changed the awareness of Protestant churches above all, and raised the question of how far denominational identity is shaped by belonging to and appropriating a confessional tradition and how far it is determined by contextual factors. The third major issue facing the International Missionary Council was whether they should join the World Council of Churches. A number of concerns dominated the discussion. By joining the World Council of Churches would the witness of the missionary societies be lost, as the World Council was a council of churches, not societies? Secondly, with its theological concerns and its work on political, economic and ethical concerns, would such a council pay attention to the missionary imperative? Did the council in fact have a strong theology of mission? Strong among the advocates was Lesslie Newbigin, who urged integration, and this was finally achieved in 1961. From that time, Orthodox – and later Roman Catholic – representatives have also been involved in the work of the Commission on World Mission and Evangelism. However, many evangelical Christians continue to be uneasy with these developments, and as with faith and order concerns and those of common witness, it was clear that such unease was not determined by denominational boundaries but cut across the denominations.

Lausanne 1974

Tension within the Protestant denominations increased during the 1960s. The WCC Assembly in Uppsala 1968 seemed to focus more on issues facing the world than on questions of theology or the mission of the church. There was unease within denominations, by evangelicals in particular, with the trends of liberation theology evident in some World Council of Churches discussions. There was opposition to the Programme to Combat Racism, and there was a suspicion that mission theology was not central enough to World Council of Churches concerns. There was deep concern that central aspects of Protestant thought were being compromised. The Tübingen professor Peter Beyerhaus and prominent evangelicals throughout the world articulated this. Thus in 1974 at Lausanne, some 2,540 evangelical leaders from over 150 nations gathered for the International Congress on World Evangelization. Under the leadership of the Anglican, John Stott, and of the evangelist, Billy Graham, a covenant was discussed and adopted. This covenant articulates the biblical basis of Christian world mission and emphasizes the uniqueness of Christ. It seeks to find a way of holding together evangelism and social witness while noting that evangelicals had tended to separate these, and noted the need at times for a missionary moratorium.

Those involved in the Lausanne Covenant formed a continuation committee, and many initiated a particular bilateral dialogue with the Vatican Secretariat for Promoting Christian Unity in which many of the concerns of the Lausanne Covenant were evident. The Evangelical–Roman Catholic Dialogue on Mission (ERCDOM) is unique in being a bilateral dialogue with representatives of different confessional traditions among the participants. The underlying commitment of those involved in the Lausanne Covenant is that they perceive through the action of Jesus Christ that they are one in Christ. They are therefore sharing in 'spiritual unity' and do not see the need to manifest that in church structure terms. However, this means that fundamental ecclesiological questions have not been addressed. Because of their impact, the concerns of the Lausanne Committee have continued to challenge all churches, even though those who attended Lausanne were not officially appointed delegates of their churches.

Protestant Identity in the Light of a Century of Ecumenism

This chapter has sought to chart the changing character of Protestant denominationalism as a result of ecumenical dialogue and encounter. Undoubtedly, Protestant churches and theologians shaped the ecumenical movement and its structures. Equally, Protestant churches themselves have been shaped by the movement. Through theological dialogue, Protestant churches have entered new relationship of unity, communion or co-operation with each other. They have moved from conflict and competition to theological agreement and shared ministry. In dialogue, they have moved away from identity-in-opposition to Roman Catholicism and have in some cases overturned the continuing validity of condemnations to initiate new relationships. Despite this involvement with Orthodox churches and the Roman Catholic Church the changing shape of the mainline churches has occurred within the wider Protestant family. It has also become evident that the division of the church is not only, perhaps not mainly, defined by confessional boundaries, but cuts through churches where people make common cause with like-minded members of other churches.

Presently mainline Protestants find themselves challenged by the surge of Pentecostal churches and of evangelical house churches. They find themselves in a situation where the majority of Christians live in the developing world, and are members of churches whose identity is increasingly shaped by contextual rather than confessional issues.

Mainline churches – Protestant, Orthodox and Roman Catholic – also need to keep wrestling with the nature and the vision of the unity being sought. Clearly, for theological reasons the vision of unity sought goes beyond the spiritual unity 'in Christ'. However two principal 'models of unity', while related, have been the subject of continuing wrestling. The first model has been evident in the discussions of the World Council of Churches and has inspired many church unions. This was well articulated at the New Delhi Assembly in 1961 on the basis of work undertaken by the Faith and Order Commission. One of its strongest advocates was Lesslie Newbigin. The unity envisaged is of a conciliar fellowship of local churches truly united. Such a model presupposes churches united for mission in each context, who are in constant dialogue with other churches truly united in the other contexts of the world.

The second model is that of reconciled diversity, which has emerged largely in the context of the bilateral dialogues, whose most articulate advocate was the Lutheran theologian Harding Meyer. Such a model seeks the goal of unity in communion, but does not necessarily presuppose a structural unity. After a period of tense debate between the proponents of each, reconciled diversity might well be a stage on the way towards a fuller manifestation of unity.

The challenge remains: how far are churches prepared to risk unity for the sake of participating in God's mission? How far are they able to let go that which has given comfort for the sake of the gospel? How far are churches prepared to act together in everything except those things where differences of deep convictions compel them to act separately? An increasingly divided world awaits the response of the churches as a body exhibiting the glimpsed alternative of the world as God intends it to be.

References

Faith and Order Plenary Commission (1982). *Baptism, Eucharist and Ministry (Lima Report; Faith and Order Paper no 111)*. Geneva: WCC.

Goodall, N. (1964). *The Ecumenical Movement*. London: Oxford University Press.

Gros, J., Meyer, H., and Rusch,W. (eds.) (2000). *Growth in Agreement II: Reports and Agreed Statements of Ecumenical Conversations 1982–1998 (Faith and Order Paper No. 187)*. Geneva: WCC.

Hastings, A. (2001). *Oliver Tomkins: The Ecumenical Enterprise*. London: SPCK.

Latourette, Kenneth Scott (1967). Ecumenical Bearings of the Missionary Movement and the International Missionary Council. In R. Rouse and S. Neill (eds.), *A History of the Ecumenical Movement 1517–1948*. London: SPCK.

Meyer, H. and Vischer, L. (eds.) (1984). *Growth in Agreement (Faith and Order Paper, No. 108)*. New York: Paulist Press and Geneva: WCC.

Till, Barry (1972). *The Churches Search for Unity*. Harmondsworth, UK: Penguin.

Wilson, Bryan (1964). *Religion in a Secular Society*. Harmondsworth, UK: Penguin.

Further Reading

Briggs, J., Oduyoye, M., and Tsetsis G. (eds.) (2003). *A History of the Ecumenical Movement 1968–2000*. Geneva: WCC.

Cope, J. and Kinnamon, M. (eds.) (1997). *The Ecumenical Movement: An Anthology of Key Texts and Voices*. Geneva: WCC.

Falconer, A. (ed.) (2002). *Eighth Forum on Bilateral Dialogues (Faith and Order Paper No. 190)*. Geneva: WCC.

Fey, H. (ed.) (1970). *A History of the Ecumenical Movement: The Ecumenical Advance 1948–1968*. London: SPCK.

Gassmann, G. (ed.) (1993). *A Documentary History of Faith and Order 1962–1993 (Faith and Order Paper No. 159)*. Geneva: WCC.

Lossky, N., Bonino, M., Pobee, J., Wainwright, G., and Webb, P. (eds.) (2003). *The Dictionary of the Ecumenical Movement*, 2nd edn. Geneva: WCC.

Newbigin, L. (1960). *The Reunion of the Church*. London: SCM.

Rouse, R. and Neill, S. (eds.) (1967). *A History of the Ecumenical Movement 1517–1948*. London: SPCK.

Vischer, L. (ed.) (1963). *A Documentary History of Faith and Order 1927–63*. St Louis: Bethany Press.

Vischer, L. (2002). World Communions, The World Council of Churches and the Ecumenical Movement. *The Ecumenical Review* 54, 1: 142–61.

Visser't Hooft, W. A. (1982). *The Genesis and Formation of the World Council of Churches*. Geneva: WCC.

CHAPTER 38

The Future of Protestantism: Evangelicalism

Mark A. Noll

At the start of the twenty-first century, evangelical Christianity constitutes the second largest worldwide grouping of Christian believers. Only the Roman Catholic Church enjoys more adherents in today's world Christianity than the evangelical churches. By comparison with other world religions, evangelical Christians – taken only by themselves – are more numerous than all non-Christian religions except for Muslims and Hindus. But of course to make such a claim, it is necessary to deal with the notoriously difficult question of how to define evangelicalism.

Definition

The word "evangelical" has several legitimate senses, all related to the etymological meaning of "good news." For Christians of many types throughout history the word has been used to describe God's redemption of sinners by the work of Christ. In the Reformation of the sixteenth century it became a rough synonym for "Protestant." That history explains why many Lutherans still employ the term for themselves (e.g., the Evangelical Lutheran Church in America or the Tamil Evangelical Lutheran Church in India). The most common use of the word today, however, stems from revival movements of the eighteenth century and from practitioners of evangelism and revival in the nineteenth and twentieth centuries. Among the most important of those public evangelical leaders have been the Cambridge pastor and preacher, Charles Simeon (1759–1836); the American teacher of Holiness, Phoebe Palmer (1807–74); the American pioneer of modern evangelistic techniques, Charles Grandison Finney (1792–1875); the English Baptist pulpiteer, Charles Haddon Spurgeon (1834–92); the first Anglican bishop in Africa, Samuel Ajayi Crowther (c.1806–91); the American lay evangelist, Dwight L. Moody (1837–99); the Indian Anglican bishop and church planter, V. S. Azariah (1874–1945); the London-based Bible expositor, John Stott (b. 1921); and the American globe-trotting evangelist, Billy Graham (b. 1918).

Whatever its other legitimate uses, "evangelical" describes the network of Protestant renewal movements arising during the eighteenth century in Great Britain and its colonies. Two complementary perspectives undergird this usage. "Evangelical" refers to the heirs of these Anglo-American religious revivals, but it also designates a consistent pattern of convictions and attitudes. In one of the most useful summaries of that pattern, the British historian David Bebbington (1989: 2–17) has identified four key ingredients of evangelicalism:

- Conversion: evangelicals are people who stress the need for a decisive turning away from self and sin to God in Jesus Christ;
- The Bible: evangelicals may respect church traditions to varying degrees and may use education, reason, and science to assist in talking about Christianity, but the ultimate authority for all matters of faith and religious practice remains the Christian Scriptures;
- Activism: evangelicals have historically been moved to action or to works of charity and sometimes to works of social reform, but above all to the work of spreading the message of salvation in Christ – all of which arise in response to their own experience of God's grace;
- The cross: evangelicals have also consistently stressed as the heart of Christian faith the death of Christ on the cross and then the resurrection of Christ as a triumphant seal for what was accomplished in that death (evangelicals regularly emphasize the substitutionary character of this atonement between God and sinful humans whereby Christ receives the punishment due to human sins and God gives spiritual life to those who stand "in Christ").

If evangelicals are marked by these four commitments, important questions of definition still remain, especially concerning relationships with fundamentalists, Pentecostals, charismatics, and members of "apostolic" churches in the southern hemisphere.

"Fundamentalism" is a term that arose in the United States during the early years of the twentieth century to designate conservative evangelicals who protested against the liberalization at work in some American denominations (Marsden, 1980). Fundamentalists insisted on holding to traditional Christian teachings for the infallibility of the Bible, the virgin birth of Christ, substitutionary atonement, and the return of Christ at the end of the world. In general, fundamentalists offered a militant defense of these supernatural elements of Christian belief. In more recent decades, self-described fundamentalists have been characterized by their desire to hold themselves separate from other forms of Christianity (including Roman Catholic, liberal Protestant, and some varieties of evangelicalism), and by their efforts at defining a strict view of the Bible's errorless character. In North America, fundamentalists have also contributed a moral urgency to politically conservative movements like the New Christian Right (Green, Guth, Smidt, and Kellstedt, 1996). Most evangelicals have not been fundamentalists, but many fundamentalists do fit within the traditional bounds of evangelicalism. It has recently become customary to define all religious movements that combine militancy with adherence to traditional religion as "fundamentalistic" (see Marty and Appleby, 1991–4). However, this extended use of the term is only occasionally helpful for understanding the relationship of fundamentalist Christians to evangelicalism.

"Pentecostalism" is a term that arose at the same general time as fundamentalism (Wacker, 2001; Synan, 2001; Martin, 2001). It describes evangelical believers who place fresh stress on the active work of the Holy Spirit and on the restoration of the direct experience of God witnessed in the New Testament. In its classic form, Pentecostals taught that "the baptism of the Holy Spirit" would be marked by "speaking in tongues" (an unlearned heavenly speech produced by the Spirit's direct agency) and also by miracles of healing and prophecy. Distinctly Pentecostal activity is usually traced to a revival in 1906 at a Holiness church on Azusa Street in Los Angeles, California, but similar phenomena were occurring at about the same time in Korea, Wales, South Africa, and other places. Today Pentecostal and Pentecostal-like churches make up the fastest growing segment of world Christianity. Pentecostalism grew directly from historical evangelical emphases, and most Pentecostals fit fairly well into the stream of historic evangelicalism.

"Charismatics" are Christians not associated with Pentecostal churches who nonetheless adopt some Pentecostal practices. During the second half of the twentieth century, charismatic movements appeared in many of the older, more traditional Protestant denominations, and also in the Roman Catholic Church. Like Pentecostals, charismatics stress the direct presence of God through the activity of the Holy Spirit, but do not necessarily organize entire churches, denominations, or agencies defined around this special work. Charismatic movements have been important in the shaping of recent evangelicalism, especially for making modified versions of historical Pentecostal practices much more common among evangelical churches in the West and in non-Western worlds alike. There is a strong charismatic influence in the affective new songs and contemporary forms of musical practice that are now common in world evangelicalism. Charismatics have also been one of the prime factors in promoting more self-conscious fellowship between Roman Catholics and evangelicals (Rausch, 2000).

The most difficult groups to categorize with respect to historic evangelicalism are the "Apostolic," "Zionist," and other indigenous Christian movements that have proliferated in the Southern hemisphere over the course of the twentieth century (Barrett, 1971; Daneel, 1987; Isichei, 1995). In Africa, these groups are sometimes known as "Aladura" churches, from a Yoruba word meaning "owners of prayer," or are called African Initiated Churches (AIC). Examples, from literally thousands of possibilities, include the Zion Christian Church of

Southern Africa and the Cherubim and Seraphim society of West Africa. But churches and movements with many similarities have also proliferated in other parts of the world, like the Universal Church of the Kingdom of God in Brazil, the house church movements in China, and many other rapidly developing church networks in India, the Philippines, Pacific Islands, Africa, and Latin America. As their names suggest, these Christian movements usually exercise a high degree of independence, they are usually well-adapted to the religious and social practices of their different regions, and they are as determined to recover the supernatural practices of New Testament Christianity as are Pentecostals. These indigenous groups are sometimes criticized by more traditional evangelicals for exalting the prophetic powers of their leaders or subordinating the work of Christ to the work of those same leaders. And some critics see too much ancestral religion surviving in these groups, as well as a penchant for promoting Christianity as a means to gain health and wealth in this life. A history of modern evangelical Christianity must pay considerable attention to such groups, for many of them originated from contact with evangelical missionaries from the West and most of them promote beliefs and practices that overlap with traditional evangelical emphases. Case-by-case analysis is the only way to discern whether such independent movements are best studied as merely another variant of evangelical Christianity or should be classified as something other than evangelical.

The evangelical traits have never by themselves yielded cohesive, institutionally compact, or clearly demarcated groups of Christians. Since its origins, evangelicalism has always been *diverse, flexible, adaptable*, and *multiform*. In particular, contextual settings have regularly colored the shape of evangelicalism (making, for example, some expressions very conservative politically and at least a few quite radical). Evangelical movements have sometimes been shapers of culture, for example, in the Scottish Highlands and throughout all of Wales in the nineteenth century; in wide areas of Canada, Britain, and the United States into the twentieth century; and more recently in some non-Western regions like South Korea, Singapore, East Africa, and several islands in the Pacific. Yet the degree to which evangelicals have adapted to local situations has also sometimes left evangelicals pervasively shaped by their particular cultures.

Evangelicalism has always been profoundly affected by its popular character. This reality is illustrated best in the United States where democratic forms of evangelicalism, chiefly Baptist and Methodist, were the great agents of national Christianization among both white and black populations during the first half of the nineteenth century (Hatch, 1989). At the same time, evangelical populism is often ambiguous in its appeals to authority. Sometimes evangelicals grant unusual influence to powerful leaders or organizational geniuses who, by means of populist rhetoric, replace traditional autocracy with their own iron discipline.

Despite this populist form and their characteristic concentration on practical goals in the present, evangelicals in the twentieth century have also numbered some of the leading theological defenders of traditional Christianity, especially the doctrines of the Reformation. Leaders like the British-born and Canadian-based J. I. Packer (b. 1926) and the American journalist, theologian, and editor Carl F. H. Henry (b. 1913) have been forthright advocates of historic Christian faith in works of careful yet passionate exposition (Henry, 1987; McGrath, 1997). The combination of democratic populism and persistent traditionalism means that evangelicalism partakes fully of both innovative and conservative elements.

Evangelicalism is not an organized religious movement as such, but rather represents an ever-diversifying series of local churches, parachurch agencies, national and international ministries, and interlocking networks of publications, preachers, and personal contacts. Mission agencies have always contributed substantially to the circulation and ligaments of the worldwide evangelical body. Today those agencies are more international than ever. Campus Crusade for Christ, International, for example, now employs over 15,000 workers around the world, with only about 1,000 from the United States. It is the same with Youth with a Mission, a church-planting agency with about 12,000 workers, of whom less than 2,000 are from the United States, and the Wycliffe Bible translators, less than half of whose staff members are Americans (Johnstone and Mandryk, 2001: 743–6).

Relief and development organizations like World Vision (US-based) and Tear Fund mobilize increasing evangelical expertise and funding for works of mercy in the non-Western world. World Vision by itself administers an annual budget many times larger than that of the World Council of Churches.

The evangelical presence in the standard denominations can be complicated. On the one hand, worldwide denominational connections among Anglicans, Assemblies of God, Baptists, some Lutherans, some Presbyterians, and in a few other traditional denominations do strengthen international evangelical networks. On the other hand, some churches and movements that were once staunchly evangelical have over the course of time lost the trademarks of evangelical religion.

The international ministries of leading preachers, Bible expositors, and evangelists also provide a measure of coherence for worldwide evangelicalism. Of such ministries in the second half of the twentieth century, those of the American evangelist Billy Graham and the Anglican minister John Stott were the most effective at propagating the Christian message and encouraging broad international contacts (Graham, 1997; Dudley-Smith, 1999, 2001).

A number of student ministries have also contributed greatly to the international circulation of evangelical personnel, ideas, and programs. Perhaps the greatest sense of international cooperation has arisen from the inter-related movements connected to the movement that began in Britain, Australia, Canada, and the United States as InterVarsity Christian Fellowship, but which has now evolved into a wide variety of local and regional organizations, like University and College Christian Fellowship (UK), Overseas Christian Fellowship (for Asia), Comunidad Internacional de Estudiantes Evangélicos (for Latin America), and the International Fellowship of Evangelical Students.

Situating evangelicalism has never been easy, but the absence of a quick and simple definition cannot obscure the importance of the movement over the course of the last three centuries.

History

The revivals of the eighteenth century that precipitated evangelicalism reflected the direct influence of three earlier Christian movements: an international Calvinist network in which English Puritanism occupied a central position, a Pietist revival on the European continent, and a High Church Anglican tradition of rigorous spirituality and innovative organization (Walsh, 1966).

In England and America, the Puritan movement of the seventeenth century featured many themes that later evangelicals would also promote, especially intense preaching about the need for a saving Christ and calculated opposition to the merely formal religion that Puritans saw infecting the Church of England. The prominence of the Bible, the focus on Christ as the means of salvation, and the emphasis on conversion are evangelical traits that once flourished among the Puritans. Similarly, evangelicals have continued to stress "true religion" over formal or merely notional faith in ways that were heralded by important figures of the Puritan era. These emphases were central, for example, in the nearly simultaneous writing in England of John Bunyan's *Pilgrim's Progress* (1678, 1684) and in late seventeenth-century colonial America of intricate poems by Edward Taylor (ca. 1645–1729), the Congregationalist minister of Westfield, Massachusetts, who composed them as preparation for the celebration of communion.

Yet there were also differences from Puritanism in the new evangelical movement. Where the Puritans worked for purified state–church establishments, most modern evangelicals have taken the separation of church and state for granted, or, as in England and Scotland, sat lightly to official state establishment. In addition, where Puritanism retained an exalted role for the clergy and great respect for formal learning, evangelicals since the eighteenth century have been powered by lay initiative and in the twentieth century have been wary of formal scholarship.

Almost as important in preparing the way for later evangelicalism were events in central Europe known as the Pietistic movement (Ward, 1992, 1999: 71–146). A great range of connections – literary, personal, pastoral and hymnic – linked the spirituality of Continental Pietism to almost every phase of early evangelical awakenings. The Pietists, who had themselves greatly benefited from the books of English Puritans, returned the favor many times over by pointing English-speaking evangelicals to ideals of true religion, models of organized philanthropy, a specific discourse regarding conversion, and a new focus on the assurance of salvation. This Pietist influence came through the books and students of the great early leaders at Frankfurt and Halle, P. J. Spener (1635–1705) and A. H. Francke (1663–1727), but even more from the Moravians under the leadership of Count von Zinzendorf (1700–60). In particular, Moravian pastors and missionaries brought to the English-speaking world a strong sense of the power of God to justify sinners freely by his grace and a renewed emphasis on the ability of repentant sinners to know with assurance that their sins are forgiven (Podmore, 1998).

A third important antecedent for full-scale evangelicalism came from High Church Anglicanism, which had suffered through many political-religious crises in the early years of the eighteenth century. Despite difficulties, however, a vigorous strand of High Church piety survived with special stress on "primitive Christianity," or the faith thought to have been practiced with great purity in the church's very first centuries (Duffy, 1977). Samuel and Susannah Wesley, the parents of John and Charles, were both diligent advocates of this High Church apostolic primitivism. Later evangelical movements would alter the terms of this emphasis, especially by turning to the Book of Acts as the model for primitive Christianity, but the primitivist urge remained a very important High Church bequest to nascent evangelicalism.

One of Samuel Wesley's other concerns also communicated a lasting bequest to evangelicalism, since he was a champion of the voluntary religious societies that High Church Anglicans had been establishing from the late 1670s (Walsh, 1986). These Anglican societies were set up to promote personal piety, to enforce morality in public, and to assist in spreading Christian literature and teaching abroad. While most evangelicals would have little to do with the exact shape of high Anglicanism, most of the main evangelical projects would be driven by principles of voluntary organization like those of their High Church predecessors.

Influences from Puritanism, continental Pietism, and High Church voluntary religion were the coals that revival winds blew into evangelical flame during the middle decades of the eighteenth century. When earnest protests against religious formalism gathered strength in London and English market towns, the Scottish Highlands and Lowlands, Wales, Ireland, and the North American colonies, and when this search for "a true religion of the heart" broadened and deepened, evangelicalism was the result (Noll, Bebbington, and Rawlyk, 1994). The first manifestation of the evangelical renewal of English-speaking Protestantism were revivals, intense religious "awakenings" that broke out simultaneously in England, Wales, and America, and only shortly thereafter in Scotland. The most visible human agents of these revivals were larger-than-life figures – the spell-binding preacher George Whitefield (1714–70), the indefatigable evangelist John Wesley (1703–91), and the brilliant theologian Jonathan Edwards (1703–58). But if these and other leaders, who were almost as well known in their day (like Howell Harris in Wales, John McLaurin in Scotland, or Gilbert Tennent in America), defined the revivals on a large canvass, experiences of countless ordinary men and women sustained the life of the evangelical Awakening.

From the start, news about evangelical experiences in particular places was passed on with great excitement to other interested parties in the North Atlantic region. In Scotland, Wales, Ireland, and England concerned Protestants read about the experiences of Abigail Hutchinson of Northampton, Massachusetts, who on a Monday morning in 1735 was turned from despair and alienation to God. As her minister explained the event, when "these words came to her mind, 'The blood of Christ cleanses from all sin' [they were] accompanied with a lively sense of the excellency of Christ, and his sufficiency to satisfy for the sins of the whole world. . . . By these things," Jonathan Edwards concluded, Abigail "was led into such contemplations and views of Christ, as filled her exceeding full of joy" (Edwards [1737] 1972: 193). Not long thereafter Protestants throughout the English-speaking world could read in the published journal of John Wesley what had befallen him at a small-group meeting in Aldersgate Street in London. It was on Wednesday, May 24, 1738, "where one was reading Luther's preface to the *Epistle to the Romans*. About a quarter before nine, while he was describing the change which God works in the heart through faith in Christ, I felt my heart strangely warmed. I felt I did trust in Christ, Christ alone for salvation; and an assurance was given me that He had taken away *my* sins, even *mine*, and saved *me* from the law of sin and death" (Wesley, 1988: 249–50). Many English-speaking Protestants followed just as closely the extraordinary revival at Cambuslang, near Glasgow in Scotland, which began in February 1742 and continued for several months, with special intensity at the highly ritualized communion seasons of the Scottish Kirk (Schmidt, 1989: 41–3).

Soon congregations and conventicles through the North Atlantic region were singing hymns describing such experiences. Most of evangelicalism's early hymn-writers wrote of what they had personally experienced, as did Charles Wesley (1707–88), who was nearly as important for the spread of early Methodism as his older brother John:

> O for a thousand tongues to sing
> My dear Redeemer's praise!
> The glories of my God and King,
> The triumphs of his grace! . . .
> He breaks the power of cancelled sin
> He sets the prisoner free;
> His blood can make the foulest clean –
> His blood availed for me.
>   (Wesley, 1983: 79–80)

Soon other writers were contributing to the hymnody that became the great engine of evangelical expansion and for more than two hundred years the most important means that evangelicals enjoyed for identifying each other as shared participants in the evangelical tradition. They included the Welsh Anglican deacon William Williams (1717–91, "Guide me, O thou great Jehovah"), the London Congregationalist Joseph Hart (1712–68, "Come, ye sinners, poor and wretched"), the Virginia Presbyterian Samuel Davies (1723–61, "Who is a pardoning God like Thee? Or who has grace so rich and free?"), and the slavetrader become Anglican priest John Newton (1725–1807, "Amazing Grace!"). Newton's influence was particularly great because it extended from hymnody to a wide-ranging work of mediation, networking, and constituency-building (Hindmarsh, 1996).

Along with the public preaching of repentance and free grace, new institutions arising to perpetuate that message, and hymns memorializing its effects, experiences like those of Abigail Hutchinson and John Wesley constituted the evangelical movement. Such experiences were not unique to English-speaking Protestants, for a general turn to inwardness characterized European religion of the eighteenth century among Roman Catholics as well as Protestants, Jews as well as Christians. Nor did these experiences constitute a new religion, for the individuals who were awakened in the evangelical revivals sustained many of the convictions, ecclesiastical practices, and moral expectations of earlier British Protestantism, especially as that tradition had passed through seventeenth-century Puritanism. If neither unique nor unprecedented, the eighteenth-century English-speaking evangelical awakening still created a distinct set of new emphases in the Christian world.

From the mid-eighteenth century evangelicals expanded their activities first in Britain and North America, but then soon also in other parts of the world. For much of the nineteenth century white evangelical Protestants constituted the largest and most influential body of religious adherents in the United States, as also in Britain and Canada. In the United States, Methodists, Baptists, Presbyterians, Congregationalists, and some Episcopalians shared broadly evangelical convictions, and evangelical elements were prominent among Lutherans, German and Dutch Reformed, and the Restorationist churches (Churches of Christ, Disciples of Christ) as well. In Britain, evangelicalism was strong in both established and dissenting churches, where it did a great deal to set the religious agenda of the Victorian era.

Although evangelicals often combated each other aggressively on the details of their convictions, in 1846 delegates from many churches in Britain and North America, as well as substantial representation from the European continent, created the Evangelical Alliance, a voluntary interdenominational organization whose doctrinal basis succinctly illustrated major points of mutual evangelical agreement. The founding convictions of the Alliance remain central to evangelical movements around the world to this day: (1) The divine inspiration, authority, and sufficiency of the Holy Scriptures; (2) The right and privacy of private judgment in the interpretation of the Holy Scriptures; (3) The unity of the Godhead and the Trinity of the Persons therein; (4) The utter depravity of human nature in consequence of the Fall; (5) The incarnation of the Son of God, his work of atonement for the sins of humankind, and his mediatorial intercession and reign; (6) The justification of the sinner by faith alone; (7) The work of the Holy Spirit in the conversion and sanctification of the sinner; (8) The immortality of the soul, the resurrection of the body, the judgment of the world by our Lord Jesus Christ, with the eternal blessedness of the righteous and the eternal punishment of the wicked; and (9) The divine institution of the Christian ministry, and the obligation and perpetuity of the ordinances of baptism and the Lord's Supper (Massie, 1847).

Well before 1846, evangelicals had also begun to take a growing interest in spreading Christianity to other parts of the world. In such efforts, English-speaking evangelicals lagged considerably behind their Continental Pietist colleagues who carried on active missionary efforts from the 1690s. Apart from a few efforts to reach native American Indians with the gospel, however, significant missionary labors by English speakers did not begin until the end of the century. The ex-American slave, David George, immigrated to Sierra Leone in 1792 as a dedicated preacher of revival just as that West African colony was being opened for outside settlement under the auspices of Anglican evangelicals. The next year, the English Baptist William Carey set out for India, shortly after he published a memorable appeal for missionary service, *An Enquiry into the Obligations of Christians to use means for the conversion of the Heathens*. Soon Carey's Baptist Missionary Society was joined by the Anglican Church Missionary Society, the interdenominational London Missionary Society, the American Board of Commissioners for Foreign Missions, and many other evangelical bodies in what would rapidly grow into great efforts of missionary proclamation (Stanley, 1992; Ward and Stanley, 2000). The missionary movement was a very important expression of evangelical zeal at work in English-speaking countries. It became even more important for planting seeds of Christianity in other parts of the world that would grow vigorously into strong indigenous churches.

The relationship of African-American Christianity to evangelicalism is complex. Blacks in America only began to accept Christianity in the mid-eighteenth century when the Christian message was presented to them by evangelists like Whitefield or the Virginia Presbyterian, Samuel Davies (Frey and Wood, 1998; Essig, 1982). To this day, most African-American denominations and independent congregations share many evangelical characteristics, including belief in the "new birth," trust in the Scriptures, and commitment to traditional morality. Some white evangelicals in the early years of the new United States, like the New England Congregational theologian Samuel Hopkins and the founder of American Methodism, Francis Asbury, were also early leaders in the fight against slavery. Yet other evangelicals, North as well as South, either tolerated or defended the institution. Throughout the nineteenth century almost all white evangelicals also frowned on elements of African ritual retained in the worship of black Christians. The fact that in the twentieth century white American evangelicals have mostly supported the social and political *status quo* that marginalized African Americans means that ties between black Protestants and white evangelicals are not as close as their shared religious beliefs might lead one to expect (Emerson, 2000).

The more general history of the twentieth century has witnessed a nearly unprecedented globalization of distinctly evangelical movements and of movements that share many evangelical features. To be sure, throughout the century, evangelicals remained important in the broader Christian histories of Britain and North America. The fundamentalist movement in the United States did preserve the essentials of supernatural Christianity but at the cost of increased sectarianism. American fundamentalism was driven by dispensational theology, a verse-by-verse approach to biblical teaching that made much of scriptural prophecy and the various dispensations that its advocates saw revealed in Scripture (Bass, 1960). The hermeneutics of dispensationalism has done much to influence later evangelicals in interpreting the first book of the Bible (Genesis) as a literal account of creation and the last (Revelation) as an equally literal account of the return of Christ. From the 1930s onwards, a growing number of American fundamentalists sought re-engagement with both culture and learning; increasingly they used the name "evangelical" to describe themselves (Carpenter, 1997). But evangelicalism in America was always broader than fundamentalism and dispensationalism, with widespread efforts in evangelism, church planting, social service, and education found in Holiness denominations like the Church of the Nazarenes, the Salvation Army, and the Christian and Missionary Alliance; with special contributions in peace making from Mennonites and other Anabaptists; and with educational leadership from the Christian Reformed and other traditional European denominations. At the close of the twentieth century, American evangelicals were growing in number, they were generous in supporting missionary and development work overseas, and they sponsored an untold number of educational, media, publishing, and social service organizations. Analysts differed on the spiritual and cultural health of the movement, but it remained a major part of American life (Marsden, 1984; Hunter, 1983; Wells, 1993; Smith, 1998; Noll, 2001).

The story in Britain differed from that in the United States because evangelicalism never lost its footing in the established churches of England and Scotland, even as it continued to shape the ongoing life of many of the dissenting denominations as well (Bebbington, 1989: 181–276; Hastings, 1991: 199–207, 453–8, 615–18; Tidball, 1994; Brady and Rowdon, 1996). Led by the powerful London preacher, Martyn Lloyd-Jones, some British evangelicals called for separation from establishment Anglicanism and Presbyterianism, but that call was countered by heightened evangelical contributions to both Scottish Presbyterianism and the Church of England. For the latter, two major national congresses at Keele (1967) and Nottingham (1977) testified to the evangelical willingness to play a larger role in the activities of the national church.

British evangelicals were not as successful at recruiting church members as their American counterparts, but they were spared some of the militant excesses of extreme fundamentalism. As had been the case since the nineteenth century, Ireland contributed more than its fair share of evangelical theologians, missionaries, and church leaders to the British evangelical cause (Hempton and Hill, 1992). British evangelicals were especially effective in reinaugurating serious academic scholarship in Scripture which had lagged since the middle of the nineteenth century (Noll, 1991: 62–90). In both Britain and America, it was a struggle to maintain vital evangelical life in connection with vigorous evangelical scholarship, but by the end of the century more and more voices could be heard with just that appeal (Noll, 1994; McGrath, 1996). And despite problems with communicating sophisticated theology to ordinary churchgoers, evangelical theology of several varieties was being published and discussed in quantities not seen since the nineteenth century (as samples only Fackre, 1993; McGrath, 1995).

In Canada, Australia, New Zealand, and South Africa, where vigorous evangelical communities had grown up in the nineteenth century as a reflection of evangelical strength in Scotland and Ireland, as well as England, the twentieth century witnessed many advances, but also registered significant retreat from previous national influence. Australian and New Zealand evangelicals were especially active as missionaries, but also witnessed their churches sharing in the gradual decline of Christian practice that affected their part of the world (Piggin, 1996; Davidson, 1991). In Canada, the evangelical cause was reinvigorated by fresh initiatives from Bible colleges, student ministries, the maturing of Pentecostal leaders, and effective interdenominational cooperation leading to the formation of the Evangelical Fellowship of Canada. But more like Britain, Australia, and New Zealand than the United States, evangelical adherence fell off from earlier levels in the broad secularization of Canadian life that took place after World War II (Stackhouse, 1993).

Whatever successes and failures may have marked the evangelical story in the West, the most remarkable evangelical developments of the recent past have been taking place in other parts of the world (Martin, 1990; Hutchinson and Kalu, 1998). Evangelicals from around the world continue to come to Britain, the United States, and Canada for training, but so now do missionaries from the Two-Thirds World arrive to spread the gospel among fellow immigrants in the West, and also to evangelize among Western pagans. To be sure, the newer evangelical churches of the world also face many difficulties of their own – instability, lack of wise leadership, shortage of educational materials, ethnic violence, numbing poverty, and more. But from these churches insights, practices, songs, and doctrinal emphases have also begun to flow back toward the original evangelical homelands. As one recent commentator has written with a focus on the Pacific: "New Zealand Maori, like other indigenous peoples, valued evangelical Christianity for its acknowledgment of the supernatural. . . . The results may put *pakeha* [New Zealanders of European descent] back into the beginners class of spiritual things" (Roxborogh, 2000).

According to the authoritative estimate of David Barrett, in 1900 well over 90 percent of the world's evangelical Christians lived in Europe or North America (Barrett, George, and Johnson, 2001, vol. 1: 13–14). But because of Western missionary activity, cooperative efforts at translating the Bible into local languages, the dedicated efforts of national Christians in many parts of the world, and developments in worldwide trade and communication – that earlier situation has been dramatically transformed. Today, at least by some definitions of the term, the number of evangelicals in each of Africa, Latin America, and Asia exceeds the total in Europe and North America combined.

Increasingly, the personnel that most effectively contribute to the spread of evangelical Christianity are recruited from the Southern rather than the Northern hemisphere.

The 2001 edition of Barrett et al.'s *World Christian Encyclopedia* presents even more dramatic evidence about the broader changes of recent decades. Using Barrett's narrowest definition of "evangelical," the *Encyclopedia* found that more "evangelicals" lived in the United States (40.6 million) than anywhere else in the world, but also that the next most populous "evangelical" countries were two where almost no evangelicals had existed 100 years ago: Brazil (27.7) and Nigeria (22.3). Of the next four countries where Barrett found the largest number of evangelicals, one was a historical center of evangelical strength (the United Kingdom, 11.6), but three had witnessed the growth of substantial evangelical populations mostly in the past century (India, 9.3; South Korea, 9.1; South Africa, 9.1). Of the remaining 24 countries where Barrett found at least one million evangelicals, only three were in Europe (Germany, Romania, Ukraine) and one in North America (Canada). Ten of these others were in Africa (Angola, Congo-Zaire, Ethiopia, Ghana, Kenya, Mozambique, Rwanda, Tanzania, Uganda, Zambia), five were in Asia or Australasia (China, Myanmar, Indonesia, Philippines, Australia), and five were in Latin America (Guatemala, Haiti, Mexico, Argentina, Peru).

If Barrett's more diffuse categories of "Pentecostal," "charismatic," and "neo-independent" are employed, the worldwide distribution of evangelical-like Christian movements is underscored even more dramatically. In the enumeration of these categories, Brazil leads all the rest (79.9 million), followed then by the United States (75.2), China (54.3), India (33.5), South Africa (21.2), the Philippines (20.0), Congo-Zaire (17.7), Mexico (13.0), and then many other countries from Asia, Latin America, and Africa, as well as Europe.

Of course all such efforts at counting things must be treated with caution. Evangelical Christians should be the first ones to agree with the recent assertion by Leigh Eric Schmidt: "Most of the things that count most about Christianity cannot be counted, like the warmth or coldness of prayer, the resonance or hollowness of scriptural words, the songs or silences of the saints in heaven, the presences or absences in the sacrament" (Schmidt, 1998: 640). Yet with proper cautions in place, research results such as provided by Barrett et al. testify to how extensive any worldwide account of evangelical Christianity must, at the start of the twenty-first century, actually be.

The Future

Contemporary efforts to describe the current course and the future of evangelicalism must be impressionistic, since the phenomenon designated by the word represents flexible beliefs and practices more than ordinary organizations. A recent survey in North America, for example, was intentionally constructed to probe the dimensions of evangelicalism in Canada and the United States (Noll,

2001: 30–8). It found that not all of those who called themselves "evangelicals" or a related term held to the traditional evangelical beliefs (although 74% in the USA did so and 51% in Canada). It also discovered that many people who did hold traditional evangelical beliefs were found in the Catholic Church (13% of the Americans and 25% of the Canadians who called themselves "evangelical"). And it found that only about half of those in the denominations descended from historical evangelical movements used terms like "evangelical" to describe themselves (44% in the USA, 57% in Canada). In other words, there is slippage in the use of evangelical terminology.

Yet if commonsensical distinctions are observed, much of the imprecision fades away. It is likely, moreover, that the patterns of the past will continue into the future. Relatively small numbers of individuals and agencies, often active in networks of voluntary societies or mission agencies, will self-consciously label themselves and their efforts as evangelical. Much larger numbers will be associated with churches and other institutions embedded securely in the historical evangelical movements. And still larger numbers from throughout the world, who may have only loose connections with original evangelical movements, will nonetheless continue to uphold the historic beliefs and practices of evangelicalism.

The challenges ahead differ considerably according to the local situation. For evangelicals in the former heartlands of Britain and North America, it will be a continuing labor to retain the historical evangelical combination of classical Protestant theology and effective popular outreach. A few evangelicals are tempted toward scholastic orthodoxies and are so alienated from contemporary culture as to become self-enclosed sectarian cliques. A more extensive danger is that the historic evangelical populism will degenerate into mere accommodation to culture, especially to the therapeutic demands of a consumer culture. More for American than British evangelicals, problems remain in maintaining some kind of intellectual vigor in an environment where evangelical subcultures easily run off into escapist literature (especially novels about the return of Christ), political extremism (usually of the Right), polemical science (especially scientific creationism), and affective anti-intellectualism (especially in some of the modern praise songs).

In Britain, the future health of evangelicalism depends on gaining a critical mass of adherents in order to build on the intellectual and organizational regrouping that has occurred over the last half of the twentieth century. In the lands of the former British Empire, the task is to revive indigenous reservoirs of evangelical vitality without being overcome by local secularism or by techniques borrowed from America. In various ways, moves are afoot in Canada, Australia, and New Zealand to shore up evangelical resources in the older established and mainline denominations while also making the most of fresh alliances involving Baptists, Mennonites, Reformed, Christian and Missionary Alliance, Pentecostals, and still more.

In the non-Western world, prospects for evangelical strengthening and for evangelical evacuation are both great. All throughout the southern hemisphere, the evangelical gospel message has worked wonders by providing hope and fellowship with God, but it is not yet clear that evangelicalism can be developed into profitable forms of interpersonal and social reconstruction. Evangelicals in Africa face enormous problems in health care, economic stimulation, and political collapse. The challenges are only slightly less in Latin America and the Pacific islands, where in different circumstances Pentecostal and Pentecostal-like evangelicals have made rapid strides in recent decades. But in these regions it remains unclear whether evangelicalism can serve as a replacement foundation for previous ways of life. In other areas of the world evangelicals clash violently with the forces of rampant Islam (Nigeria, Sudan, Indonesia, Pakistan) or militant Hinduism (India, Sri Lanka), and these violent outbursts are likely to continue. All throughout the Southern hemisphere evangelicals are also edging toward the exercise of political power, but with only some success at imitating the successes and avoiding the disasters that have marked evangelical politics in Britain and the United States (Freston, 2001).

For all evangelicals it remains a challenge to maintain the classical tradition of Trinitarian theological orthodoxy while absorbing the excitements of Pentecostal and charismatic faith. The ideal would be for traditional evangelicals to be quickened by movements of the Holy Spirit and devotees of the Spirit to learn balance and gravity from the traditionalists. But it could also happen that the traditional strengths of evangelical theology could be blown away by winds of the Spirit, and that new Pentecostal groups would come to imitate the deadening formalism and enervating moralism that have sometimes characterized the older evangelical movements.

Hope for the future of evangelicalism probably lies in whether its informal networks of communication can provide the discipline, the self-correction, and the connectedness that, at its best, has marked the history of the movement. Through the critical agents of transmission – voluntary associations (e.g., Bible societies and mission agencies); personal ties (e.g., linked to George Whitefield, Billy Graham, or John Stott); books (e.g., William Wilberforce's *Practical View of the Prevailing Religious System of Professed Christians* or J. I. Packer's *Knowing God*), periodicals (e.g., *The Christian History* of the 1740s or *Christianity Today* since the 1950s), hymns (by Charles Wesley, John Newton, and others) – evangelicalism has remained not only relatively cohesive, but relatively faithful to the Christian gospel. These agents and strategies of communication that once defined the character of evangelicalism in the regions of the North Atlantic, have now spread around the world. On their resilience would seem to hang the future of the movement.

References

Barrett, D. B. (1971). *African Initiatives in Religion: 21 Studies from Eastern and Central Africa*. Nairobi: East African Publishing House.

Barrett, D. B., George, T. K., and Johnson, T. M. (2001). *World Christian Encyclopedia*, 2 vols. New York: Oxford University Press.

Bass, C. B. (1960). *Backgrounds to Dispensationalism*. Grand Rapids, MI: Eerdmans.

Bebbington, D. W. (1989). *Evangelicalism in Modern Britain: A History from the 1730s to the 1980s*. London: Unwin Hyman.

Brady, S. and Rowdon, H. (eds.) (1996). *For Such a Time as This: Perspectives on Evangelicalism, Past, Present, and Future*. London: Evangelical Alliance.

Carpenter, J. C. (1997). *Revive Us Again: The Reawakening of American Fundamentalism*. New York: Oxford University Press.

Daneel, M. (1987). *Quest for Belonging: Introduction to a Study of African Independent Churches*. Gweru, Zimbabwe: Mambo Press.

Davidson, A. K. (1991). *Christianity in Aotearoa: A History of Church and Society in New Zealand*. Wellington: New Zealand Education for Ministry Board.

Dudley-Smith, T. (1999, 2001). *John Stott: A Biography*, 2 vols. Leicester, UK: Inter-Varsity Press.

Duffy, E. (1977). Primitive Christianity Revived: Religious Renewal in Augustan England. In D. Baker (ed.), *Renaissance and Renewal in Christian History*. Oxford: Blackwell, pp. 287–300.

Edwards, J. ([1737] 1972). A Faithful Narrative of the Surprizing Work of God in the Conversion of Many Hundred Souls in Northampton . . . New England. In C. C. Goen (ed.), *The Works of Jonathan Edwards, vol. 4: The Great Awakening*. New Haven: Yale University Press, pp. 128–211.

Emerson, M. O. (2000). *Divided by Faith: Evangelical Religion and the Power of Race in America*. New York: Oxford University Press.

Essig, J. (1982). *The Bonds of Wickedness: American Evangelicals Against Slavery, 1770–1808*. Philadelphia: Temple University Press.

Fackre, G. (1993). *Ecumenical Faith in Evangelical Perspective*. Grand Rapids, MI: Eerdmans.

Freston, P. (2001). *Evangelicals and Politics in Asia, Africa, and Latin America*. Cambridge, UK: Cambridge University Press.

Frey, S.,and Wood, B. (1998). *Come Shouting to Zion: African American Protestantism in the American South and British Caribbean to 1830*. Chapel Hill: University of North Carolina Press.

Graham, B. (1997). *Just As I Am: The Autobiography of Billy Graham*. San Francisco: Harper Collins.

Green, J. C., Guth, J. L., Smidt, C. E., and Kellstedt, L. A. (1996). *Religion and the Culture Wars: Dispatches from the Front*. Lanham, MD: Rowman and Littlefield.

Hastings, A. (1991). *A History of English Christianity, 1920–90*, 3rd edn. London: SCM.

Hatch, N. O. (1989). *The Democratization of American Christianity*. New Haven, CT: Yale University Press.

Hempton, D. and Hill, M. (1992). *Evangelical Protestantism in Ulster Society, 1740–1890*. London: Routledge.

Henry, C. F. H. (1987). *Confessions of a Theologian: An Autobiography*. Waco, TX: Word.

Hindmarsh, D. B. (1996). *John Newton and the English Evangelical Tradition*. New York: Oxford University Press.

Hunter, J. D. (1983). *American Evangelicalism: Conservative Religion and the Quandary of Modernity*. New Brunswick, NJ: Rutgers University Press.

Hutchinson, M. and Kalu, O. (eds.) (1998). *A Global Faith: Essays on Evangelicalism and Globalization*. Sydney: Center for the Study of Australian Christianity.

Isichei, E. (1995). *A History of Christianity in Africa*. London: SPCK, Grand Rapids, MI: Eerdmans.

Johnstone, P. and Mandryk, J. (2001). *Operation World: 21ˢᵗ Century Edition*. Carlisle, UK: Paternoster.

Marsden, G. M. (1980). *Fundamentalism and American Culture: The Shaping of Twentieth-Century Evangelicalism*. New York: Oxford University Press.

Marsden, G. M. (ed.) (1984). *Evangelicalism and Modern America*. Grand Rapids, MI: Eerdmans.

Martin, D. (1900). *Tongues of Fire: The Explosion of Protestantism in Latin America*. Oxford: Blackwell.

Martin, D. (2001). *Pentecostalism: The World Their Parish*. Oxford: Blackwell.

Marty, M. and Appleby, R. (eds.) (1991–4). *The Fundamentalism Project*, 4 vols. Chicago: University of Chicago Press.

Massie, J. W. (1847). *The Evangelical Alliance*. London: J. Snow.

McGrath, A. E. (1995). *Evangelicalism and the Future of Christianity*. Downers Grove, IL: InterVarsity Press.

McGrath, A. E. (1996). *A Passion for Truth: The Intellectual Coherence of Evangelicalism*. Downers Grove, IL: InterVarsity Press.

McGrath, A. E. (1997), *To Know and Serve God: A Life of James I. Packer*. London: Hodder & Stoughton.

Noll, M. A. (1991). *Between Faith and Criticism: Evangelicals, Scholarship, and the Bible*, 2nd edn. Grand Rapids, MI: Baker.

Noll, M. A. (1994). *The Scandal of the Evangelical Mind*. Grand Rapids, MI: Eerdmans.

Noll, M. A. (2001). *American Evangelical Christianity: An Introduction*. Oxford: Blackwell.

Noll, M. A., Bebbington, D. W., and Rawlyk, G. A. (eds.) (1994). *Evangelicalism: Comparative Studies of Popular Protestantism in North America, the British Isles, and Beyond, 1700–1990*. New York: Oxford University Press.

Piggin, S. (1996). *Evangelical Christianity in Australia: Spirit, Word, and World*. Sydney: Oxford University Press.

Podmore, C. (1998). *The Moravian Church in England, 1728–1760*. Oxford: Clarendon Press.

Rausch, T. P. (ed.) (2000). *Catholics and Evangelicals: Do They Share a Common Future?* Downers Grove, IL: InterVarsity Press.

Roxborogh, J. (2000). Mapping the Evangelical Landscape in New Zealand. In S. Emilsen and W. Emilsen (eds.), *Mapping the Landscape: Essays in Australian and New Zealand Christianity: Festschrift in Honor of Professor Ian Breward*. New York: Peter Lang, pp. 318–31.

Schmidt, L. E. (1989). *Holy Fairs: Scottish Communions and American Revivals in the Early Modern Period*. Princeton, NJ: Princeton University Press.

Schmidt, L. E. (1998). Mixed Blessings: Christianization and Secularization. *Reviews in American History* 26: 637–43.

Smith, C. (1998). *American Evangelicalism: Embattled and Thriving*. Chicago: University of Chicago Press.

Stackhouse, J. (1993). *Canadian Evangelicalism in the Twentieth Century*. Toronto: University of Toronto Press.

Stanley, B. (1992). *The History of the Baptist Missionary Society, 1792–1992*. Edinburgh: T & T Clark.

Synan, V. (2001). *The Century of the Holy Spirit: 100 Years of Pentecostal and Charismatic Renewal, 1901–2001*. Nashville: Thomas Nelson.

Tidball, D. J. (1994). *Who Are the Evangelicals?* London: Marshall Pickering.

Wacker, G. (2001). *Heaven Below: Early Pentecostals and American Culture.* Cambridge, MA: Harvard University Press.

Walsh, J. (1966). Origins of the Evangelical Revival. In G. V. Bennett and J. D. Walsh (eds.), *Essays in Modern English Church History: In Memory of Norman Sykes.* New York: Oxford University Press, pp. 132–62.

Walsh, J. (1986). Religious Societies: Methodist and Evangelical, 1738–1800. In W. J. Shiels and D. Woods (eds.), *Voluntary Religion.* Oxford: Blackwell, pp. 279–302.

Ward, K. and Stanley, B. (eds.) (2000). *The Church Missionary Society and World Christianity, 1799–1999.* Grand Rapids, MI: Eerdmans.

Ward, W. R. (1992). *The Protestant Evangelical Awakening.* Cambridge, UK: Cambridge University Press.

Ward, W. R. (1999). *Christianity under the Ancien Régime, 1648–1789.* Cambridge, UK: Cambridge University Press.

Wells, D. (1993). *No Place for Truth, or, Whatever Happened to Evangelical Theology?* Grand Rapids, MI: Eerdmans.

Wesley, J. (1983). Hymns. In F. Hildebrandt and O. Beckerlegge (eds.), *The Works of John Wesley, vol. 7: A Collection of Hymns for the Use of the People Called Methodists.* Nashville: Abingdon.

Wesley, J. (1988). Journal. In W. R. Ward and R. P. Heitzenrater (eds.), *The Works of John Wesley, vol. 18: Journals and Diaries I (1735–1738).* Nashville: Abingdon.

CHAPTER 39

The Future of Protestantism:
The Rise of Pentecostalism

Allan Anderson

Understanding Pentecostalism

Pentecostalism is the fourth and youngest major form of Christianity in the
world today after Orthodoxy, Catholicism, and Protestantism. Some would question whether it can rightly be called 'Protestant' at all, as it is so different from
historic Protestantism in many ways. Its traditions, however, do fall squarely
within the Protestant camp, as it arose within the radical arm of evangelical
Protestantism in the late nineteenth century. It has spread all over the world
within a remarkably short period of time, and in some parts of the world it is
now the dominant expression of Christianity. The foremost statisticians of world
Christianity, Barrett and Johnson, estimated that there were over 543 million
'Pentecostal/ charismatics/ neocharismatics' in the world in 2002 (Barrett and
Johnson, 2002: 23). These impressive figures are sometimes quoted to point to
Pentecostalism, constituting some 26 per cent of world Christianity, as the
largest force in world Christianity after Roman Catholicism (McGee, 1994: 276).
In spite of the common notion that Pentecostalism is a North American form of
Christianity, the 'Pentecostal/ charismatics' today are predominantly Africans,
Latin Americans and Asians. Their Christianity is not North American, despite
any links they might have with that continent through the process of globalization. The Third World continents are where the greatest expansion of Pentecostalism has occurred, although this does not preclude its obvious significance
in North America and parts of Europe.

Sociologists in particular have studied the rapid growth of Pentecostalism in
Latin America most extensively. An estimated 10 per cent of the continent's population are now Pentecostal; in Guatemala the figure might be as high as 30 per
cent, and in Chile and Brazil some 20 per cent (Martin, 1994: 74–5). Most of
this growth has occurred in the second half of the twentieth century. In Asia,

the fastest growing form of Christianity is a Pentecostal type, and here 'charismatic' Christianity so dominates the older churches that one can speak of the
'Pentecostalization' of Asian Christianity, particularly among Chinese, Korean,
Filipino, Indonesian and Indian churches. Observers who have tried to emphasize the 'American' nature of Pentecostalism throughout the world or the 'Americanization' of Christianity in Africa, Korea and elsewhere often miss the fact
that creative innovations and the selective transformation of 'foreign' symbols
are constantly occurring, and naturally, a synthesizing process takes place as
new religious forms interact with older ones (Anderson, 2000a: 115). The
important role of a rapidly growing new form of Pentecostalism has been recognized as one of the most significant expressions of Christianity in Africa, a
movement of revival and renewal that has arisen at the close of the twentieth
century, especially in the cities (Maxwell, 1995: 313; Gifford, 1998: 31; Anderson, 2000b: 237–55). Different forms of Pentecostalism have responded to the
existential needs of the worldviews of people throughout the Third World, all
offering a personal encounter with God through the power of the Spirit, healing
from sickness and deliverance from evil in all its appearances.

A limited, stereotyped and dogmatic understanding of 'Pentecostal' fails to
recognize the great variety of different Pentecostal movements in most of
the world, many of which arose quite independently of Western Pentecostalism.
Pentecostalism is better understood as multifarious movements concerned
primarily with the *experience* of the working of the Holy Spirit and the *practice*
of spiritual gifts. Barrett and Johnson's figures, at face value, illustrate the
point that Pentecostal and charismatic movements have many different shapes
and sizes all over the world. To accept these statistics means also accepting
the authors' inclusive definition of 'Pentecostal/charismatic'. That Barrett
and Johnson do not assume that the term is referring mainly to the denominational Pentecostals with roots in North America is clear. The majority group
included in this category is what they term a 'megabloc' of 394 million 'Independents', defined as having the 'synonymous alternate terms' of 'postdenominationalists' and 'neo-apostolics'. The statisticians explain that this new
'megabloc' includes the 'non-white indigenous' category in their earlier tables,
of which the majority consists of African and Chinese independent churches
(Barrett and Johnson: 24). Of course, there are difficulties with such a broad
classification, and understanding the terms 'Pentecostal/charismatic' is greatly
affected by it.

The several thousands of African independent church organizations go by
various names, and do not usually call themselves 'Pentecostal' or 'charismatic'.
In southern Africa, the majority of them are known as 'Zionist' and 'Apostolic'
churches; throughout Africa they refer to themselves as 'churches of the Spirit',
and in western Nigeria 'Aladura' ('people of prayer') churches. In addition to
these churches are a great number of rapidly growing independent charismatic
churches and 'ministries' throughout the continent, which are also 'African-
initiated' churches. In several countries in Africa these are becoming the dom-

inant form of Christianity, and in some nations, they form the majority of Christians – an extremely important component of world Christianity. There are similar forms of indigenous Christianity in other parts of the Third World, particularly in China, where independent non-registered churches abound that have created a form of Christianity often in opposition to the political order, but reflecting popular Chinese spirituality. Understandably, statistics of people in Chinese house churches are hard to come by, but one unofficial estimate put the number at 47 million in 1990, and many of these are rapidly growing Pentecostal groups. The differences between these indigenous and independent churches, and Western forms of Pentecostalism are considerable. Chinese independent churches have developed in isolation from the rest of Christianity for at least 50 years, and grew rapidly at a time when they faced severe opposition. Some of the largest of these churches, such as the True Jesus Church and the Jesus Family, may be considered Pentecostal (Anderson, 2000a: 116; see also the debate on Chinese Pentecostalism in Oblau, forthcoming; Deng, forthcoming; Tang, forthcoming).

All these forms of Pentecostalism practise gifts of the Spirit like healing, prophecy and speaking in tongues. Because of their 'Spirit' manifestations and pneumatic emphases and experiences, most of the earlier studies of these churches considered them 'syncretistic', 'post-Christian' and 'messianic' groups. They were thought to accommodate the pre-Christian past and to be linked with traditional divination, ancestor rituals and the like. However, these and many other indigenous churches have made an important contribution to the localization of Pentecostal theology.

The Background of American Pentecostalism

Although many reports of the appearance of ecstatic spiritual gifts have been documented throughout church history, Pentecostalism's immediate background was the North American Holiness movement based on the teaching of John Wesley. The Moravian movement, which had sprung from German Pietism, had a profound effect upon Wesley and the Methodist revival (R. M. Anderson, 1979: 28). Wesley's contact with Moravians in Georgia and in England led him to his Aldersgate conversion experience. Pietism gave emphasis to the importance of feeling in Christian experience and encouraged a personal relationship with God. In some early Methodist revivals, there were unusual manifestations of the Spirit. Wesley said that charismatic gifts were withdrawn when dry, formal, orthodox men began to ridicule them, and that these gifts had returned to some of his fellow Methodists (Dayton, 1987: 44–5). Wesley's doctrine of a second blessing, a crisis experience subsequent to conversion (which he called 'sanctification' or 'perfect love'), was a central emphasis of early Methodism and had a great influence on Pentecostalism. Eventually there was a polarization within Methodism between those who believed Wesley's 'second blessing' teaching (who subsequently formed the 'Holiness Movement') and those who did not. There was, in fact, some ambiguity as to what Wesley meant by his 'perfect love' doctrine and this caused some confusion. It was apparently Wesley's theologian John Fletcher who first spoke of the experience of sanctification as the 'baptism of the Holy Spirit', the key Pentecostal concept.

The understanding of Wesley's teaching in the Holiness Movement was shaped by the emphasis on experience of the Reformed revivalism of Jonathan Edwards and the 'Oberlin Perfectionism' of revivalists Charles Finney and Asa Mahan. Another Holiness leader, Phoebe Palmer, stressed 'perfection' (sanctification) as an instantaneous experience. There was a gradual separation between the Reformed and Wesleyan forms of the Holiness Movement (Faupel, 1996: 59, 64, 66, 68–9). American revivalism stressed the role of the emotions in changing lives. Charles Finney's dependence on the presence of the Holy Spirit gave his message a profound emotional impact, and his revivalist theology was another great influence on American Pentecostalism. A revival in 1858 in the Northeast USA created a new expectancy throughout the Holiness movement linking the 'second blessing' experience of sanctification with a worldwide revival, the 'latter rain' that would precede the return of Christ (Faupel, 1996: 73–5). The early Pentecostals continued this eschatological emphasis.

The Holiness movement was a reaction to liberalism in established churches and stood for biblical literalism, the need for a personal and individual experience of conversion, and moral perfection – or holiness. None of the major Protestant churches emphasized these principles any longer, so gradually 'Holiness Churches' separated, characterized by revivalism and accompanied by ecstatic phenomena and 'camp meetings' which swept across the country. Between 1895 and 1905 over 20 separate Holiness denominations were set up, including the Church of God (1886), the Christian and Missionary Alliance (1887), the Church of the Nazarene (1895), the Pilgrim Holiness Church and the Wesleyan Methodist Church – thus creating a precedent for the further fragmentation that was to occur in Pentecostalism. Many of the early Pentecostals came from these churches.

The Keswick Convention, which began annual gatherings in England in 1875, recognized two distinct experiences of the 'new birth' and the 'fullness of the Spirit'. Increasingly in the Holiness movement the phrase 'baptism with the Spirit' was used to indicate the 'second blessing'. Towards the end of the nineteenth century, Spirit baptism was no longer understood in terms of holiness, but as an empowering for service (Faupel, 1996: 85). In particular, evangelist R. A. Torrey taught this change in emphasis, saying that the form of the power received varied according to different gifts of the Spirit. Some Holiness teachers began to say that spiritual gifts were connected to the power of the Spirit and should still be in operation, and some spoke of Spirit baptism as a 'third blessing' to be sought. The end of the nineteenth century also saw the rise of the healing movement in North America and Europe. The foundation had been laid for the birth of Pentecostalism.

With few exceptions, most Holiness people and subsequently most early Pentecostals accepted the premillennial 'secret rapture' dispensational eschatology of John Nelson Darby from the Plymouth Brethren. The reasons for this are complicated, and included an increasingly pessimistic reaction to theological liberalism and the 'social gospel'. But more significantly, this eschatology was based on the same assumptions as those of the emerging liberalism that evangelicals were trying to counteract. Because the Keswick movement was at first an expression of Reformed evangelicalism, it accepted premillennialism early. As other Holiness groups gradually accepted the pneumatological centre of the Keswick position, they also accepted its eschatology with its stress on the coming of a new Pentecost to usher in the return of Christ (Faupel, 1996: 104–5, 110–12). The Pentecostals declared that this eschatological Pentecost had arrived.

The Azusa Street Revival

A number of interrelated events occurring during the first two decades of the twentieth century marked the birth of the Pentecostal movement. Most American accounts trace the beginning to events in Topeka, Kansas, where a former Methodist minister, Charles Parham, instructed his Bethel Bible College students to look for 'some certain common evidence' of the baptism in the Spirit. They reached the conclusion that the biblical evidence of Spirit baptism (based largely on the book of Acts) was speaking in tongues, which discovery they told Parham on his return. Throughout the next two days they prayed and waited until finally, at 11 p.m. on 1 January 1901, Agnes Ozman asked Parham to lay hands on her to receive the gift of the Spirit. She was the first to speak in tongues, followed by others in the next three days, including Parham. In 1903 Parham preached at Holiness missions in Kansas and Missouri, where there were many experiences of tongues and healings. By 1905 there were said to be about a thousand people who had received Spirit baptism, and the movement was known as the 'Apostolic Faith' (Faupel, 1996: 158–80). Parham's doctrine of 'evidential tongues' became the hallmark of American classical Pentecostalism but unlike the latter, Parham's rather eccentric theology included a belief that tongues were authentic languages given for the proclamation of the gospel in the end times. These tongues were the second Pentecost that would usher in the end, achieve world evangelization within a short period, and seal the Bride of Christ. Unlike his Pentecostal successors, however, Parham did not engage in world evangelization and did not provide the 'spark' that transformed Pentecostalism into an international movement (Faupel, 1996: 185).

William Joseph Seymour, an African American preacher, did that. When the ultra-conservative Parham began a Bible school in Houston, Texas, in 1905, Seymour, the son of freed slaves, was only allowed to listen to Parham's lectures through a half-opened door, but he was convinced of these views. Seymour was then invited to be pastor of a Holiness Church in Los Angeles in 1906, but his sermon on tongues caused the church building to be locked against him. Members of this church continued meeting with Seymour in prayer in a house, soon joined by others. After a few days Seymour's Baptist host asked the preacher to lay hands on him, fell to the floor as if unconscious and began speaking in tongues. Seven others, including Seymour, were 'struck from their chairs' the same day, receiving the same experience. For three days and nights the house was filled with people praying and rejoicing continuously and loudly, until a few whites joined in and the house became too small. They moved into an old storage shed in Azusa Street where the Apostolic Faith Mission was born (Faupel, 1996: 200–2). With a sawdust-sprinkled floor and planks as benches, daily meetings commenced at about 10 in the morning and usually lasted well into the night. They were completely spontaneous, without planned programs or speakers. The racial integration in these meetings was unique at that time and people from ethnic minorities discovered a sense of dignity and community that was denied them in the larger urban culture (R. M. Anderson, 1979: 69).

For the next three years the revival in Azusa Street was the centre of Pentecostalism. People went there from all over the continent to see what was happening and to be baptized in the Spirit. The adverse press reports helped to publicize the revival. Parham came to 'control' it, was disgusted (particularly by the interracial fellowship), was rejected as leader, never reconciled with Seymour and went into obscurity and eventual disgrace (Faupel, 1996: 182–6, 202–5, 208–9; Robeck, 1993: 174–5). The leadership of the new movement passed to Seymour and took on international dimensions. Seymour later repudiated Parham's 'initial evidence' doctrine and was later rejected as leader by white Pentecostals; but 26 different American Pentecostal denominations trace their origins to Azusa Street, including the largest, the Assemblies of God. From the beginning, the movement placed an emphasis on evangelism and missions. People came from Europe and went back with the 'baptism', and Pentecostal missionaries were sent out all over the world, reaching over 25 nations in two years (Faupel, 1996: 212–16; Robeck, 1993: 176–8). But within 10 years the movement in the USA had split into numerous organizations and three major streams that remain to this day: the original Holiness Pentecostals, the Baptistic or 'Finished Work' Pentecostals (since 1911), and the 'Oneness' or Unitarian Pentecostals (since 1916).

Azusa Street was certainly significant in reminding American Pentecostals of their non-racial, ecumenical origins and ethos. A choice between Parham and Seymour as founder of American Pentecostalism is an important ideological decision to make in defining the essence of Pentecostalism. The Azusa Street revival has given inspiration to many, including black South African Pentecostals, for many decades denied basic human dignities by their white counterparts, often in the same Pentecostal denomination. Emissaries from Azusa Street founded the first Pentecostal churches in South Africa in 1908 (Anderson, 2000b: 57–60). Missionaries from Azusa Street went as far afield as Liberia, China and India.

The Beginnings of Global Charismatic Christianity

For the overwhelming majority of Pentecostals in the world, the question of the significance of Azusa Street is largely an academic Western debate. There were several places in the world where Pentecostal revival broke out quite independently of the Azusa Street revival and in some cases even predated it. The 'Korean Pentecost' began in 1903 and greatly influenced the present dominance of the charismatic movement in the Presbyterian and Methodist churches there, many of whose characteristic practices have been absorbed by 'classical' Pentecostal churches like Yonggi Cho's famous Yoido Full Gospel Church (the largest Christian congregation in the world) that came much later. Korean Pentecostals with American origins acknowledge the contribution of the earlier revival to their own movement. Furthermore, in spite of North American missionary participation in this revival, early Korean revival leaders in the Presbyterian and Methodist churches were much more 'Pentecostal' than the missionaries would have wanted them to be (Lee Jae Bum, 1986; Lee Young Hoon, 1996). In India, the 1905–7 revival at Pandita Ramabai's Mukti Mission in Poona, in which young women baptized by the Spirit had seen visions, fallen into trances and spoken in tongues, was understood by Ramabai herself to be the means by which the Holy Spirit was creating an indigenous form of Indian Christianity (Adhav, 1979: 216; Ramabai, 1905: 9). Pentecostal missionaries worked with the Mukti Mission for many years and Ramabai received support from the fledgling Pentecostal movement in Britain (Boddy, 1908: 10). However, the original Pentecostal revival in India took place much earlier than Mukti, in Tamil Nadu in 1860 under the Tamil evangelist Aroolappen (Satyavrata, 1999: 205).

The Mukti revival had far-reaching consequences penetrating parts of the world untouched by Azusa Street. Methodist missionary Minnie Abrams received Spirit baptism at Mukti and communicated the news to her Methodist missionary friends the Hoovers in Chile, where the first Pentecostal revival in South America began in 1909. The Chilean movement was unconnected with American Pentecostalism and Willis Hoover became founder of an autonomous and indigenous Chilean church (Sepúlveda, 1999: 205). The Assembléias de Deus (Assemblies of God) was formed by Swedish missionaries from Chicago in Brazil in 1911 as the Apostolic Faith Mission, three years before the denomination was constituted in the USA. There are far more Assemblies of God members in Brazil than in the USA today, and more than in any other country.

There were revivals all over the world unconnected with North American Pentecostalism. In the Côte d'Ivoire and the Gold Coast (Ghana), Liberian prophet William Wade Harris spearheaded a revival in 1914 with many Pentecostal phenomena including healing and speaking in tongues, the largest ingathering of Africans to Christianity the continent had ever seen. Chinese evangelists criss-crossed that vast nation with a Pentecostal message similar to but distinct from its Western counterpart. In fact, untold thousands of Pentecostal preachers in Latin America, Africa and Asia were responsible for the spread of the Pentecostal message into the furthest corners of the globe. One of the greatest disservices done to the worldwide Pentecostal movement is to assume that this is a 'made in the USA' product. Los Angeles becomes the 'Jerusalem' from which the 'full gospel' reaches out to the nations of earth (McClung, 1999: 49, n.11), but there were in fact many 'Jerusalems': Pyongyang in Korea, Beijing in China, Poona in India, Lagos in Nigeria, Wakkerstroom in South Africa, Valparaiso in Chile, Belem in Brazil, Oslo in Norway, and Sunderland in England – among others. Pentecostalism has had many beginnings, and there are many 'Pentecostalisms' (Wilson, 1999: 107). An obscure history of Pentecostalism has been taken for granted for so long that the multitudes of nameless ones responsible for the grassroots expansion of the movement have passed into history unremembered, and their memory is now difficult to retrieve (Wilson, 1999: 103–4, 106, 109; Anderson, forthcoming).

Walter Hollenweger believes that Pentecostalism's essential nature lies in its character as an expression of oral and narrative spirituality, and not because of its adherence to any particular doctrine (like that of 'initial evidence'). This is why the 'African' or 'Black' roots of Pentecostalism are so important for him (Hollenweger, 1999). Harvey Cox expresses this as the resurgence of 'primal spirituality', the fulfillment of the human longing for a direct experience of God, and not 'abstract religious ideas' (Cox, 1996: 5). For this reason, Cox maintains that Pentecostals are quite unlike, and should not be equated with, Christian fundamentalists, who are 'text-oriented believers', whereas he says that Pentecostals are more akin to mystics. But American Pentecostalism has undergone some fundamental changes. Cox contrasts the 'other-worldliness' of early Pentecostals with the 'this-worldliness' of some American Pentecostals, particularly manifested in the 'prosperity gospel'. A rebellion against creeds has given way to dogmatism and the 'techniques of raptures' have become a preoccupation instead of the original message of 'signs and wonders' as a portent of the coming kingdom of God. He charts the changes from the early Pentecostal pacifists who were imprisoned as conscientious objectors during the First World War to the 'super-patriots' of today, and the change from a race and gender-inclusive fellowship to white male-dominated denominationalism (Cox, 1996: 15–17).

The Charismatic Movement in the West

Although there are many examples of Pentecostal phenomena in older churches in the 1950s, the attention of the Western world was focused on events relating to the resignation of Dennis Bennett as rector of St Mark's Episcopal Church, Van Nuys, California in April 1960, regarded as the commencement of the charismatic movement in the Western world. In a Sunday sermon, Bennett testified to his baptism in the Spirit with speaking in tongues. He was asked to resign, which he did in a pastoral letter explaining the compatibility of his experience with Episcopalian teaching. His story was reported in *Time* and *Newsweek*, other 'charismatics' were encouraged to come out of hiding and the 'charismatic movement' or 'neo-Pentecostalism' was out of the closet. Bennett was appointed rector of St Luke's in Seattle, Washington, and was able to communicate his experience to his congregation. The church grew rapidly and was soon the largest Episcopal church in the diocese. Bennett became a national figure and through him other ministers became involved in the charismatic movement, including Episcopalians, Methodists, Reformed, Baptists, Lutherans and Presbyterians.

The charismatic movement spread during the 1960s throughout North America. Early leaders received Spirit baptism through attending Pentecostal meetings. Reformed minister Harold Bredesen brought the charismatic experience to students from several denominations at Yale University in October 1962, and Lutheran pastor Larry Christenson visited Europe in 1963 and discovered Lutherans there who had spoken in tongues for 60 years. Charismatics were not universally welcomed in their churches, however, and opposition often caused them to leave, resulting in divided churches. In the 1970s, Pentecostal experiences in older churches were encouraged by news reports of charismatic happenings and by hundreds of popular publications – particularly John Sherrill's *They Speak with Other Tongues* (1964) and David Wilkerson's *The Cross and the Switchblade* (1963). Wilkerson, a rural Assemblies of God pastor, started Teen Challenge in Brooklyn, New York in 1959, a remarkably successful rehabilitation center for drug addicts that established other such centers throughout the world.

The charismatic movement was further publicized by television broadcasts – particularly those of Oral Roberts and Pat Robertson (Southern Baptist contender for the 1988 Republican presidential nomination) and the 'Jesus People' movement that commenced in California among former hippies in the late 1960s. Television evangelists in the USA were many, and among the most notorious were Jimmy Swaggart and Jim Bakker, whose sensational falls in the late 1980s were a source of embarrassment for Pentecostals. But Robertson's Christian Broadcasting Network and Paul Crouch's Trinity Broadcasting Network continue from strength to strength. Oral Roberts left the Pentecostal Holiness Church to join the United Methodist Church in 1968 to more firmly anchor himself within the older churches. Many well-known personalities, by being part of the charismatic movement, made it more socially acceptable – singers Pat Boone and Johnny Cash, and General Ralph Haines, Jr were examples. David du Plessis (1905–80), nicknamed 'Mr. Pentecost', had since 1951 travelled around the world as a spokesperson for Pentecostalism in ecumenical circles. He was warmly received by the World Council of Churches and in congregations and seminaries of all denominations. His work opened many within older churches to the Pentecostal experience, but the result of his ecumenical contacts was that he was 'disfellowshipped' from the Assemblies of God in 1962, which was caught up in the evangelical–ecumenical divide of the time (Hollenweger,

1972: 7). In 1953 the Full Gospel Businessmen's Fellowship International (FGBFI) was organized and grew quickly, emphasizing bringing the Pentecostal experience to laypersons. Soon it attracted people from older churches as well as Pentecostals, encouraging its members to be active in and loyal to their own churches. This was an instrument to bring Pentecostal experience to older churches, and it introduced Pentecostal healing evangelists to them, especially Oral Roberts. It also helped finance the ultramodern Oral Roberts University in Tulsa, Oklahoma.

As the charismatic movement expanded in North America, so it spread in Western Europe. In Germany, Lutheran pastor Arnold Bittlinger became a leader in the movement. In Britain, the first home for the movement was the Anglican church of All Souls in London, where the well-known evangelical John Stott was rector – although he himself was clearly not a charismatic. Early British charismatic leaders were Anglicans David Watson, Stott's curate Michael Harper (who received Spirit baptism in 1962), and Baptist pastor David Pawson. Harper was director of the Fountain Trust from 1964 to 1975, the leading organization in Britain promoting the charismatic renewal, which closed in 1980 (McBain, 1997: 31–6, 72–4).

In 1967 the charismatic movement made a spectacular new entrance into the Catholic Church. Beginning with four people at Duquesne University in Pittsburgh, it spread steadily to include 300,000 people by 1976. From 1971 Cardinal Leo Suenens, primate of Belgium and one of the moderators of the Second Vatican Council was acknowledged leader of Catholic charismatics with papal approval (McBain, 1997: 63). In 1975 Pope Paul VI addressed a Congress of 10,000 Catholic charismatics in Rome. This was the climax for a movement whose doors had been opened 10 years earlier by Pope John XXIII and the Second Vatican Council, which had called for spiritual renewal. By 1992 there were an estimated 72 million Catholic charismatics in the world (Synan, 1992: 11).

As the charismatic movement in the older churches began to decline in the late 1970s, a 'non-denominational' neo-Pentecostal movement with much weaker links with older churches began, emphasizing house groups and radical discipleship. Networks of rapidly growing independent churches emerged in the 1980s all over North America and Britain. By 1982 there were an estimated 100,000 house groups in Britain, attended by one million people (McBain, 1997: 89). In a quite different camp, and in more continuity with the Pentecostal healing evangelists, were the 'prosperity' preachers of the US Bible Belt. The father of this movement was Kenneth Hagin (b. 1917), who founded the Rhema Bible Training Center in Tulsa in 1974 where he taught his 'faith gospel of health, wealth and success' and sold more than 33 million copies of his booklets. Even more successful than Hagin is his more radical disciple Kenneth Copeland of Fort Worth, Texas, who has taken this 'faith message' all around the world. Many Pentecostals and charismatics rejected this movement and distanced themselves from it (Gifford, 1993: 147–8). In 1990 there were an estimated 33 million 'Pentecostals/charismatics' in the USA, 13 per cent of the total population.

In the 1980s the 'Third Wave' in evangelicalism emerged. This was a term coined in Los Angeles by Fuller Theological Seminary's Peter Wagner, following the two 'waves' of the Classical Pentecostal movement and the charismatic movement. Wagner identified the 'Third Wave' with John Wimber (1934–97), who taught a 'Signs and Wonders' course at Fuller and whose Vineyard Christian Fellowship spearheaded a new emphasis on renewal in the established churches throughout the English-speaking world, especially in Britain. The Third Wave moved away from the idea of a 'second blessing' experience of the Spirit to an emphasis on the gifts of the Spirit in evangelism and as part of Christian life. Wimber's first visit to Britain and his laid-back ministry there in 1982 resulted in widespread acceptance of his message of 'power evangelism' among older churches, especially in evangelical Anglicanism. In 1994 a new phenomenon emerged in the Toronto Airport Vineyard Church in Canada pastored by John Arnott, to become known as the 'Toronto Blessing'. This 'revival' was characterized by unusual manifestations, especially 'holy laughter'. Holy Trinity, Brompton in London became the leading center of this phenomenon in Britain, and of the rapidly expanding interdenominational Alpha evangelism program. In December 1995 Wimber dissociated himself and his movement from Toronto (McBain, 1997: 159), the church in Toronto had to withdraw from the Vineyard Association, and is now known as the Toronto Airport Christian Fellowship. In 1996 a revival in an Assemblies of God church in Brownsville, Pensacola, Florida attracted international interest, in which the emphasis seems to be upon 'old-fashioned' repentance. Both Toronto and Pensacola have become places of pilgrimage for the new revival movements.

The Globalization of Pentecostalism

Pentecostalism has become a form of Christianity found in almost every country on earth. If 'globalization' refers to geographical extent, then Pentecostalism is certainly 'globalized'. But if we are talking about some 'supra-cultural' quality of Pentecostalism that is its dominant feature, then 'globalization' may not be taken for granted. Pentecostalism has at least as many different expressions as has the rest of Protestantism, and probably far more divisions. Sociologist David Martin (1994: 747) says that while there are many connections between Latin American Pentecostals and North America, the most important feature of Latin American Pentecostalism is its 'indigenous character'. Pentecostalism's strengths lie especially in its ability to adjust itself and 'incarnate' in any culture, and so the particular local expressions are more important than any 'global' or 'supra-cultural' quality. Its emphasis on the 'freedom of the Spirit' militates against any homogenizing or dispassionate standardizing tendencies.

Nevertheless, there is a sense in which access to modern electronic media, communications and rapid travel, and the consequential interdependence of Pentecostals and charismatics the world over, have resulted in certain commonalities within the movements themselves that have affected any local character. This is particularly true of the emphasis on the power and gifts of the Spirit and the sense and experience of the immediacy of God that pervades Pentecostalism throughout the globe, but is also found in such characteristics as an emphasis on prayer, a high view of the Bible, participation of all believers in Christian service and witness, the use of an indigenous leadership, and a conservative Christian morality. These continually expanding movements have established themselves to be among the most significant expressions of Christianity in the twenty-first century.

References

Adhav, Shamsundar M. (1979). *Pandita Ramabai*. Madras: Christian Literature Society.

Anderson, Allan (2000a). Pentecostalism in East Asia: Indigenous Oriental Christianity? *Pneuma: The Journal for the Society for Pentecostal Studies* 22, 1: 115–32.

Anderson, Allan (2000b). *Zion and Pentecost: The Spirituality and Experience of Pentecostal and Zionist/Apostolic Churches in South Africa*. Pretoria: University of South Africa Press.

Anderson, Allan (forthcoming). Revising Pentecostal History in Global Perspective. In Allan Anderson and Edmond Tang (eds.), *Asian and Pentecostal: The Charismatic Face of Asian Christianity*. Kualar Lumpur and Oxford: Regnum.

Anderson, Robert Mapes (1979). *Vision of the Disinherited: The Making of American Pentecostalism*. Peabody, MA: Hendrickson.

Barrett, David B., and Johnson, Todd M. (2002). Annual Statistical Table on Global Mission: 2002. *International Bulletin of Missionary Research* 26, 1: 23–5.

Boddy, Alexander A. (1908). Editorial. *Confidence: A Pentecostal Paper for Great Britain*, 1: 6. Sunderland, UK, September: 10.

Cox, Harvey (1996). *Fire from Heaven: The Rise of Pentecostal Spirituality and the Reshaping of Religion in the Twenty-First Century*. London: Cassell.

Dayton, Donald W. (1987). *Theological Roots of Pentecostalism*. Metuchen, NJ: Scarecrow Press.

Deng, Zhaoming (forthcoming). Indigenous Chinese Pentecostal Denominations. In Allan Anderson and Edmond Tang (eds.), *Asian and Pentecostal: The Charismatic Face of Asian Christianity*. Kualar Lumpur and Oxford: Regnum.

Faupel, D. William (1996). *The Everlasting Gospel: The Significance of Eschatology in the Development of Pentecostal Thought*. Sheffield, UK: Sheffield Academic Press.

Gifford, Paul (1993). *Christianity and Politics in Doe's Liberia*. Cambridge, UK: Cambridge University Press.

Gifford, Paul (1998). *African Christianity: Its Public Role*. London: Hurst.

Hollenweger, Walter J. (1972). *The Pentecostals*. London: SCM Press.

Hollenweger, Walter J. (1999). The Black Roots of Pentecostalism. In Allan Anderson and W. J. Hollenweger (eds.), *Pentecostals After a Century: Global Perspectives on a Movement in Transition*. Sheffield, UK: Sheffield Academic Press, pp. 33–4.

Lee Jae Bum (1986). Pentecostal Type Distinctives and Korean Protestant Church Growth. PhD thesis, Fuller Theological Seminary, Los Angeles.

Lee Young Hoon (1996). The Holy Spirit Movement in Korea: Its Historical and Doctrinal Development. PhD thesis, Temple University, Philadelphia.

McBain, Douglas (1997). *Fire over the Waters: Renewal among Baptists and Others from the 1960s to the 1990s*. London: Darton, Longman and Todd.

McClung, L. Grant (1999). 'Try to Get People Saved': Revisiting the Paradigm of an Urgent Pentecostal Missiology. In M. W. Dempster, B. D. Klaus, and D. Petersen (eds.), *The Globalization of Pentecostalism: A Religion Made to Travel*. Oxford: Regnum, pp. 30–51.

McGee, Gary B. (1994). Pentecostal Missiology: Moving Beyond Triumphalism to Face the Issues. *Pneuma* 16, 2: 257–81.

Martin, David (1994). Evangelical and Charismatic Christianity in Latin America. In Karla Poewe (ed.), *Charismatic Christianity as a Global Culture*. Columbia: University of South Carolina Press, pp. 73–86.

Maxwell, David (1995). Witches, Prophets and Avenging Spirits: The Second Christian Movement in North-East Zimbabwe. *Journal of Religion in Africa* 25, 3: 309–39.

Oblau, Gotthard (forthcoming). Pentecostals by Default? Contemporary Christianity in China. In Allan Anderson and Edmond Tang (eds.), *Asian and Pentecostal: The Charismatic Face of Asian Christianity*. Kualar Lumpur and Oxford: Regnum.

Ramabai, Pandita (1905). Stray Thoughts on the Revival. *The Bombay Guardian and Banner of Asia* 7 November 1905: 9–10.

Robeck, Cecil M. (1993). Pentecostal Origins in Global Perspective. In Harold D. Hunter and Peter D. Hocken (eds.), *All Together in One Place: Theological Papers from the Brighton Conference on World Evangelization*. Sheffield, UK: Sheffield Academic Press, pp. 166–80.

Satyavrata, Ivan M. (1999). Contextual Perspectives on Pentecostalism as a Global Culture: A South Asian View. In M. W. Dempster, B. D. Klaus, and D. Petersen (eds.), *The Globalization of Pentecostalism: A Religion Made to Travel*. Oxford: Regnum, pp. 203–21.

Sepúlveda, Juan (1999). Indigenous Pentecostalism and the Chilean Experience. In Allan Anderson and W. J. Hollenweger (eds.), *Pentecostals After a Century: Global Perspectives on a Movement in Transition*. Sheffield, UK: Sheffield Academic Press, pp. 111–34.

Sherrill, John (1964). *They Speak with Other Tongues*. Grand Rapids, MI: Fleming H. Revell.

Synan, Vinson (1992). *The Spirit said 'Grow': The Astounding Worldwide Expansion of Pentecostal and Charismatic Churches*. Monrovia, CA: MARC.

Tang, Edmund (forthcoming). 'Yellers' and Healers: Pentecostalism and the Study of Grassroots Christianity in China. In Allan Anderson and Edmond Tang (eds.), *Asian and Pentecostal: The Charismatic Face of Asian Christianity*. Kualar Lumpur and Oxford: Regnum.

Wilkerson, David R. (1963). *The Cross and the Switchblade*. New York: B. Geis.

Wilson, Everett A. (1999). They Crossed the Red Sea, Didn't They? Critical History and Pentecostal Beginnings. In M. W. Dempster, B. D. Klaus, and D. Petersen (eds.), *The Globalization of Pentecostalism: A Religion made to Travel*. Oxford: Regnum.

Further Reading

Anderson, Allan, and Hollenweger, W. J. (eds.) (1999). *Pentecostals After a Century: Global Perspectives on a Movement in Transition*. Sheffield, UK: Sheffield Academic Press.

Dempster, Murray W., Klaus B. D., and Petersen, D. (eds.) (1999). *The Globalization of Pentecostalism: A Religion Made to Travel*. Oxford: Regnum.

Hollenweger, Walter J. (1997). *Pentecostalism: Origins and Developments Worldwide*. Peabody, MA: Hendrickson.

Land, Steven J. (1993). *Pentecostal Spirituality: A Passion for the Kingdom*. Sheffield, UK: Sheffield Academic Press.

Lederle, Henry I. (1988). *Treasures Old and New: Interpretations of 'Spirit-baptism' in the Charismatic Renewal Movement*. Peabody, MA: Hendrickson.

Martin, David (1990). *Tongues of Fire: The Explosion of Protestantism in Latin America*. Oxford: Blackwell.

Martin, David (2002). *Pentecostalism: The World Their Parish*. Oxford: Blackwell.

Poewe, Karla (ed.) (1994). *Charismatic Christianity as a Global Culture*. Columbia: University of South Carolina Press.

Shaull, Richard, and Cesar, W (2000). *Pentecostalism and the Future of the Christian Churches: Promises, Limitations, Challenges*. Grand Rapids, MI: Eerdmans.

Synan, Vinson (1997). *The Holiness-Pentecostal Tradition: Charismatic Movements in the Twentieth Century*. Grand Rapids, MI: Eerdmans.

CHAPTER 40

The Future of Protestantism: Postmodernity

Graham Ward

I am going to begin with a provocative statement and proceed to argue for why I believe this statement is an accurate description of where Protestantism (and Christianity more generally) is in the West. I deliberately construct this analysis and examination as a polemic, recognizing that there are and will be other views from elsewhere – views supporting, modifying and countering my arguments. The justification for the polemical nature of this chapter then is the desire to orchestrate a debate. The statement is this: postmodernity tolls the bell for the cultural demise of Protestantism. Let me now demonstrate why I hold this view.

Argument One: Postmodernity is Antithetical to Protestantism

In brief: Protestantism is one of the key developments in modernity and, to the extent that postmodernity offers itself as a critique of modernity, then the ethos it fosters is antithetical to Protestantism.

More analytically: the cultural agendas and values of modernity – the autonomy of the reasoning subject, free from the fetters of tradition, and the cultivation of a private sensibility not only able to question and debate all forms of external authority, but confident that this is one of the rights of 'man' – was shaped fundamentally by both the theology and the politics of early Protestantism. Of course, the invention of printing that made books more available and fostered the interiorities of reading is not insignificant. Neither are the struggles of the various princes against the imperial ambitions of the papacy to be forgotten – struggles that gave rise to the nation-state and redefined the secular unit to which people should give their allegiance. But in the cultural ethos – or what could be called a social imaginary saturated and governed by Christian construals of salvation and the kingdom of God – all the cultural factors contributing to the development of modernity are filtered through hopes and fears fashioned by the language, dreams, myths and stories of Christianity.

A major shift, then, in the understanding of what it is to be human and of the human condition itself – a shift driven, in part, by the new economics of global trading and geographical expansion, and the rise and confidence of a merchant-bourgeois mentality – finds a cultural catalyst in dramas such as Luther's stand upon his personal integrity at the Diet of Worms or the assassination by a Jesuit of the Protestant King of France, Henry IV.[1] These phenomena suddenly crystallize, and then come to symbolize, a change in sensibility. They become not occurrences but events – that is, occurrences which, because of the weight of significance given to them, are viewed as (or come to be viewed as) historical turning points. As such they are not simply historical happenings but cultural events. Something new is brought about by such 'events' because of what they come to symbolize. In their wake, Luther's declaration and the violent stabbing in 1610 on the rue de la Ferronnerie were recognized as triggering responses that shook the pillars and foundations of an aging Christendom. The point to be made here is that in the sixteenth and seventeenth centuries, Protestantism constituted a speculum through which a new cultural consciousness could be understood and legitimated by the very highest authority: God.

Although Weber's thesis on the correlation of capitalism and Protestantism has been critiqued for its lack of hard and cumulative evidence, its sweeping understanding of Calvinism and its thin treatment of Catholicism, nevertheless what Weber pointed to was the way in which Protestantism, and the Christian sectarianism that it fostered, announced a new social order (Weber, 1992). It is an order in which individuals in their fallen condition are viewed as radical promoters of their own self-worth, at the expense of everyone else's. Human beings are defined both by their insecurity and their acquisitiveness. As Hobbes expressed it: each threatens and is threatened in a struggle to maintain oneself. This new social atomism mapped onto a Protestant conviction in each having to work out their salvation. A sacred cosmology in which the social emphasis was upon corporatism, through an ontological correspondence between various bodies (the body of Christ, the body of the king, the body of the church, the body of the Commonwealth) – became no longer credible. A new fragmentation, which gave birth to the autonomy and rights of the subject, fostered imaginary communities: societies whose members may never meet each other, but nevertheless who believe their existence is founded upon social consensus, covenant, contract (see Anderson, 1983). Christendom gradually became Christian denominationalism as Protestant collectivities fought back the inner principle of their original sin of acquisitiveness in a striving to create new regimes, new social disciplines, new technologies for the shaping and policing of autocratic selves. Sin turned social atomism into Milton's *Pandemonium*; faith turned social atomism into covenanted societies – societies where each was bound to the other by a recognized and regulated agreement.

The newly emerging social order at the end of the seventeenth century was both aggressively entrepreneurial and, following Locke, Toland, Addison and Steele, buoyed up by a developing sense of civility. This new sensibility towards the social as a public realm of human interchange free from religious control and guaranteed by the newly emerging secular state encouraged its own self-analysis (sociology). And as Pierre Manent has recently reminded us: 'sociology presupposes the humanity of man without further inquiry into what constitutes his humanity' (Manent, 1998: 64). At one time, inquiries into the humanity of 'man' were inseparable from theological teachings on Christ, the incarnation and being made in the image of God. Now modernity's dream was for the city of 'man', for a nonhierarchical social order in which the responsibilities of each (and the fulfilment of those responsibilities) were transparent to each. Modernity as a self-regulating panopticon is impossible to conceive outside of the new understanding of the human and the social fostered by 'the great disembedding' (Taylor, forthcoming) that Protestantism both exemplified and generated.

By 'disembedding' Charles Taylor refers to the way Protestantism fostered a new cosmology, a secular reality divorced from sacral significance. The spiritual became unhooked from the social and political. For example, the overthrowing of the images of saints, the abrogation of several saint days in the liturgical calendar and the demand that at certain times in the year (particularly harvesttime) the worker's responsibility was towards providing food for the nation (not the worship of God in religious holidays), effected the nature of time and space. Each, in turn, was desacralized. The sovereignty of the newly attained autonomous self could rethink time (as France did after the Revolution), and the idea that certain locations were sacred (pilgrimage sites, the altar in the parish church) was viewed as irrational, superstitious, even (under certain rulers) seditious. A new public space of opinion was created, the entry into which demanded the privatization of religious beliefs and the outward toleration of differences. It took some time to effect and expand such toleration. In England,[2] the Act of Toleration was passed in 1689, the year in which Locke published his *Letter Concerning Toleration*, but while the latter sought to allow the different beliefs of Christian, Jews and Muslims, the former merely allowed Protestant Dissenters the right to worship alongside members of the Church of England. Catholics remained excluded from such an advocacy of tolerance, and so the new public space for opinion was one structured according to a Protestant ethos. This space, in which consensus on truth was sought, announced a new form of secularity. The older form recognized the secular as a realm instituted and maintained by the sacral order. Its autonomy rested upon the graciousness of God in giving human beings the freedom to seek God and understand divine operations in the world. Here was an autonomous space, safeguarded by the state (through parliamentary law); a pragmatic realm in which the acquisitive and self-serving nature of being human could be given both scope and defined parameters.

In the creation of this social space lay the origin of liberal humanism (with its concern to define and implement notions of individual liberty, rights and justice), and its Christian counterpart – liberal theology. If God is not yet dead, God is certainly well hidden – a *deus absconditus*, a divine architect, a divine mechanic, a divine mathematician and a divine bookkeeper. Divine presence was now difficult to discern in the world; providence was increasingly understood as 'an invisible hand' (Adam Smith). The 'disembedding' brought about what Weber described as a 'disenchantment', a demystification, a demythologizing that continued well into the twentieth century. If the modern can be defined as the pursuit of the new and the rejection of the past as authoritatively shaping the possibilities of the present, Protestantism can be viewed as another aspect of the cultural change that ushered in such a pursuit. In its own way it demanded that each person should begin again, and discover the truth for themselves by paying only sceptical heed to what tradition had deemed necessary. It demanded new accounts of time and materiality and it gave a new valorization to the human will. At the height of Renaissance humanism, before Protestantism, Pico della Mirandola could already announce that human beings (in imitation of God) can 'become what we will' (Mirandola, 1948). But it was Protestantism that lent to this announcement theological and existential necessity. The development of the secular social space in which 'man's' Promethean will might engineer new prosperities, and new secular forms of salvation from the world-besetting ills (accident, disease, the arbitrary whims of nature), lay in Protestantism's demythologizing the Christian faith. And while Catholicism, as we will see, was not always a counterforce to this process, Francis Fukuyama (in his account of the rise of global democracy and the marketplace) states a case that several social scientists, cultural historians and even theologians have already made: 'Christianity in a certain sense had to abolish itself through a secularisation of its goals before liberalism could emerge. The generally accepted agent for this secularisation in the West was Protestantism' (Fukuyama, 1992: 216; see also Cox, 1964).

As I will demonstrate later, postmodernity announces the implosion of secularism, or rather the implosion of an autonomous realm of human affairs – transparent; regulated; governed by liberty, fraternity and equality; and philosophically underpinned by an empirical method of inductive reasoning. Postmodernity radically questions the politics and possibilities of the panopticon state, devalorizes subjective agency, mimics the literacy and elitism of liberal humanism, is sceptical of panaceas for social amelioration, and refuses the ideology of a neutral space and the unmediated arrival of social consensus. Liberalism itself is understood as an ideology, not the triumph over and liberation from ideology. As the political scientist, John Gray, has described it in his account of today's postliberalism:

> humanism is merely an atavistic anomaly, a curious relic of theism . . . It is not the individual that is the bottom line in the theory of rights. For the well-being of the individual is owed to his participation in a form of life [and] . . . we at the same time find ourselves in the interstices of many such forms. . . . No determinate set of principles about liberty, rights or justice has been stated which is not disabled by deep indeterminacies. (Gray, 1993: 307–13)

The social is now saturated with conflicting politics so that pragmatic strategy rather than management is the order of the day, and there is no essence of being human and no essential identity to each self. For what defines a subject is the consumer choices he or she makes. The social scientist Alain Touraine (who advocates, like Habermas, the need to return to some critical form of liberal humanism) writes: 'Politics no longer claims to be able to "change life" and parliaments no longer represent social demands. They are no more than sites for the ever more pragmatic definition of a power base for managerial and, above all, financial executive. Actors have ceased to be social actors' (Touraine, 1995: 188). The social order that Protestantism fostered and fought to define is coming to end, the substantial content of that form of the Christian faith having been secularized, criticized and made one of multiple forms of religious belief. We can take this further.

Argument Two: Advancing Nominalism and the Liquidation of the Protestant Faith

In brief: Protestantism's alliance with the cultural trajectories of modernity accommodated themselves to its secular and theologically demythologized aspiration – liberal humanism. Postmodernity expresses the *apotheosis* of such theological liberalism, which announces the triumph of nominalism and the liquidation of the Protestant faith.

More analytically: from the late mediaeval period we find the emergence and development of two forms of thought. The first is nominalism and the second is the univocity of being. According to Michel de Certeau, the nominalism of Ockhamist linguistics produced a certain 'opacification'.[3] For signs were no longer recognized as participating in the unfolding of an understanding about the world; they became names (instituted by repeated and conventional use) labelling the world, but whether the world in any sense corresponded to these names could never be proven. In accounts of creation, less attention was given to the sustaining of nature's being by the grace of the threefold God, and more attention was given to the omnipotence of the divine which rendered anything possible. So that, on the one hand, there developed a set of ideas concerning the separation of minds from what was 'out there' or from matter: as Descartes surmises in his *Meditations*, God may be a deceiving demon. On the other, a new voluntarism (forerunner of Mirandola's belief that we can make of ourselves what we will, itself a forerunner of Nietzsche's will-to-power) submitted the old sacramental view of nature to an absolute and arbitrary power. Deity proceeds towards domination.[4] This opacification led to a new understanding of nature itself – an understanding that finds parallels with the autonomy of the social, that is, secular, realm. Grace and nature were unlinked from each other, soon to be divorced. Confidence in reading nature as God's second book became increasingly unsustainable as signs no longer held a correspondence with the cosmos (for the cosmos could no longer be recognized as a semiotic system). This led to an epistemological crisis – what is known and how is it known – that set the philosophical (and scientific) agendas of modernity. Michel Foucault defined the '*episteme*' of modernity in terms of the gaze (Foucault, 1976, 1974). The gaze gives rise to the positivisms and empiricisms that foster scientific rationality from the eighteenth century onwards. But the gaze is only possible when what is seen is an end in itself, and can be treated as such – as an object of the gaze. The gaze is a product of nominalism and it eventually offered the way out of the epistemological crisis.

Prior to the development of scientific rationalism, Protestantism proffered new certitudes in the loss of confidence, even melancholy, that beset Western culture in the sixteenth century by appeal to self-validating revelation.[5] The personal conviction based upon having been spoken to by God, the experiential basis for *sola fidei*, was one way of handling this crisis of knowing and knowledge. In the older Catholic tradition, revelation was always mediated by the church, but now there was both a democratizing of 'being called' (the priesthood of all believers) and a new immediacy of God's voice – as the journals of George Fox and the autobiography of John Bunyan testify. Nominalism had placed an emphasis upon the omnipotence of God's will and the vast difference between Creator and created. From the human perspective it developed an account of cognition as an event (Cunningham, 2002: 44–58). These elements fostered a new religious epistemology in which the arbitrary and punctiliar nature of God's will with respect to the world was answered by an imitative (and also arbitrary) act on the part of the human subject. This manner of responding to the crisis of knowledge can also be found in Catholic circles, with appeals to mystical experience (the mystical as an altogether distinctive kind of experience) evident from the seventeenth century onwards. The cry of divine rapture saw its demonic counterpart in the glossolalia of the possessed.[6] But, as the likes of Saint Teresa discovered, the Catholic Church remained committed to the mediation of revelation governed by a centralized authority. Protestantism, on the other hand, splintered under the new social atomism grounded in the integrity of each to discover their divine calling.

The splintering, and the warring factions it gave rise to, generated the search for the essence of religion. Protestantism was at the forefront of developing the category of 'religion' as distinct from the pious practices of a particular faith; religion as a universal condition of being human. An impressive line of Protestant thinkers from Grotius to Schleiermacher and Hegel, from William James to Paul Tillich, sought in 'religion' a principle of ultimate reality. It is out of this search that theological liberalism emerged as a spiritual counterpart to the social and political liberalism of the nation-state. With theological liberalism the liquidation of Protestantism became inevitable (the liquidation also of the Protestant-established category of 'religion' itself) (Ward, 2002a). Once more, it is nominalism that provides the philosophical basis for this liberalism. It provided the metaphysical warrant for the dualism of the ultimate reality that can never be defined or grasped as such (God, the noumenal) and its various symbolic codings (the different religions, the different cultures, religion as the cultural). In the wake of this liberalism the doctrines of the Protestant faith – incarnation, resurrection, virgin birth, the trinity, Christ, salvation and the eschaton – became so many metaphors and myths that must be demythologized or at least seen for what they are – religious rhetoric. The secular theologies and atheologies of the self-appointed postmodern theologians – Robert Scharlemann, John D. Caputo, Charles Winquist, Don Cupitt, Mark C. Taylor and so on – simply announce the apotheosis of this Protestant liberalism. They offer an account of the theological sublime as negation *en abyme*; the collapse of identity that enters the endless *kenosis* these thinkers enjoin means that Protestantism too is emptied of all its meaning and content. We have now moved beyond the absence of God to the death of God – a notion, again, with a Protestant pedigree in Hegel, Nietzsche and Heidegger. Caputo recognizes the philosophical roots of this belief in the absence of belief or religion without religion:[7] 'a kind of felicitous nominalism, a happy, anti-essentialist open-endedness' (Caputo, 2000: 16).

The liquidation of religion that began with the existential turn towards subjective experience parallels the expansion of the secular. As Charles Taylor has recently observed, 'the drive to personal religion has been part of the impetus toward different facets of secularization' (Taylor, 2002: 13–14). But if nominalism was one of the philosophical roots of secularism, another root lay in the univocity of being. The univocity of being established the secular as an independent and self-regulating domain. As I suggested earlier, this begins to emerge in the late Middles Ages and is frequently associated with Duns Scotus. For the purposes of this chapter we need not enter into the thickets of the debates on this point. Suffice it to say, the new distance of creator from creation, and the lack of emphasis upon the participation of the created orders within the divine operations and effects, gave rise to a world that was not only opaque (as I have said) but one distinct ontological nature. The being of the world became increasingly separated from the being of God, and as the absence of God developed into the death of God, so the independence of the being of the world was increasingly established. The world has to explain itself – this is axiomatic for the emergence of scientific rationalism and procedure. No appeal can be made to any transcendent principle of origin, maintenance or order. Metaphysics gives way to natural philosophy. The profound role Protestantism played in the rise of instrumental reasoning, I leave to others better qualified than I to describe; likewise the resistance in Catholicism to what Weber defined as the 'dis-enchanted' world.[8] Beyond nominalism and on the far side of subjective, self-validating experience, on the basis of the univocity of being, science established the fable of an objective world that framed the liberalism of *laissez-faire*. Both were the cultural products of a Protestant dispensation, and both are called radically into question by postmodernity. John Gray makes plain that 'none of the four constitutive elements of doctrinal liberalism – universalism, individualism, egalitarianism and meliorism – survives the ordeal of value-pluralism, and that liberalism . . . is therefore dead' (Gray, 1993: 284). Thomas Kuhn, Bruno Latour and Donna Haraway are among several philosophers of science to emphasize the social production of scientific truth (see, e.g., Latour & Woolgar, 1979). The point is simply that the ethos of modernity, philosophically founded upon nominalism and the univocity of being, was defined in and through Protestantism; so the end of modernity announces the end of Protestantism.

Argument Three: Postmodernity's 'Re-enchantment' is Antithetical to Protestantism

In brief: the cultural agendas and values of postmodernity re-enchant and remythologize the world. New age spirituality brings with it a new sacramentalism, and therefore a new cosmology, but these new cultural orders of the sacred are antithetical to Protestantism.

More analytically: postmodernity must be viewed as both a development in the cultural logic of modernity and a resistance to its ideologies.[9] With respect to modernity's own projects, postmodernity remains concerned with critique and the freedoms of consciousness and *praxis* that might follow from such critique. One could say that postmodernity indeed accelerates critique. Its commitment to irony, double-coding and open-ended reflexivity fashions a constant critique of critique. Thus the grand explanatory narratives developed through modernity's critiques (belief in historical progress, scientific realism, evolution etc.), summed up in the different projects of Hegel, Marx, Darwin, Freud, and others, in postmodernity become themselves subject to critique. More than one cultural critic of postmodernity has viewed its sensibility as fundamentally 'treason of the clerks' – a new form of intellectual and academic productivity.[10] As such postmodernity is not contesting modernity but developing it. Furthermore, the current postliberalism, with its differential calculus, its recognition of irreducible plurality and the right of the other to remain other, is not opposed to liberalism but its *apotheosis*. As Owen Chadwick noted at the beginning of his book, *The Secularization of the European Mind in the Nineteenth Century*: 'From the moment that European opinion decided for toleration, it decided for an eventual free market in opinion' (Chadwick, 1975: 21).

Nevertheless, the structures of Western feeling since the 1970s have changed (see Harvey, 1989; Jameson, 1998). If modernity thought in regular shapes from the Georgian square and the hermeneutical circle, to the pyramids of institutional hierarchies and linear teleologies of progress, then postmodernity thinks in irregular hybrid figures – like the rhizome (Deleuze and Guattari, 1986: 21), the heteroclite (Foucault, 1974: xviii) and the *khora*. For example, the *khora* (taken from Plato's *Timeaus* in which it appears as the womb from which all things proceed) is a mytheme that appears in the work of Julia Kristeva, Luce Irigaray and Jacques Derrida. Derrida asks: 'Not having any essence, how could the *khora* be beyond its name? The *khora* is anachronistic; it "is" the anachrony within being, or better: the anachrony of being. It anachronizes being. . . . Rich, numerous, inexhaustible, the interpretations come, in short to give form to the meaning of *khora*' (see Derrida, 1993: 94). We will return to this passage below, but for the moment let us continue with marking the differences between modernity and postmodernity. For if the dominant modes of representation in modernity aspired to the realism of photography, then the dominant modes of representation in postmodernity aspire to the pastiche of the drag queen. Culturally, modernity's concern with the sublime has inverted to become postmodernity's concern with the kitsch.[11] The deep and profound is now viewed as the depthless reflective surface. This cultural turn resists, deconstructs and renders relative (now no grand narratives, but only little stories) the concerns of modernity, and it is the effect of this work that terminally challenges the cultural ethos fostered by Protestantism. It overthrows the dualisms that modernity spawned – public/private, immanent/transcendent, sacred/secular, subject/object, faith/reason – and it raises the question of whether we have ever been modern at all (Latour, 1993). It challenges the strong identities modernity forged, showing how they are internally unstable, externally policed and constituted in and through the myriad processes of a cultural politics. In doing this, postmodernity has 're-enchanted' the world such that postmodernity is also postsecular.

The quotation from Derrida above points, in part, to what I would argue is taking place in contemporary Western culture. There is an appeal to a new ontology; a broken or, to use Derrida's phrase, an 'anachronized' ontology. Derrida will speak of 'quasi-transcendence' (Derrida, 1982: 1–28). Irigaray will speak of a 'sensible transcendent' (Irigaray, 1993: 57–72) and critics comment upon the 'Catholic imaginary' that subtends the work of Julia Kristeva, Michel de Certeau, Michel Foucault, Jacques Lacan (see Oliver, 1993: 128). The postmodern concerns for the wholly other, the unpresentable, for the aporetic, has made metaphysics respectable again. It has reopened questions on negative theology, disciplines of desire and economies of love. In the rejection of Weber's description of the modern as a 'disenchanted' worldview, Zygmunt Bauman (1992: vii–xxviii) will speak of the new 're-enchantment'. Religious imagery and myth are back on the cultural agenda. The gothic imagination haunts once more, with a panoply of angels and demons. Life after death, spirituality, the soul's relation to the body, the nature of evil have all been the subject of recent box-office films and internationally acclaimed novels. Cyberspace thunders with the battles between mythic forces of good and evil. There are defences of the Christian legacy by cultural critics (Slavoj Zizek, Alain Badiou), rejections of the secular thesis by social and political scientists (William Connelly, Charles Taylor), the revival of paganisms, the spawning of new age cults and the naming of shops after biblical events.[12] The sacred is being reinvented; a new sacramentalism is emerging.

The nature of this sacramentalism can be appreciated by returning to that figure of the *khora* which articulates not so much a doctrine of the real presence as an account of an ontology that forever escapes and alludes becoming present as such. It is a sacramentalism that arrives with an opening onto endless aporia, the infinitely unpresentable, an indeterminate flow of time, space and materiality. Michel Serres (Serres, 1995: 79) and Emmanuel Levinas (Levinas, 1987: 46) have both likened this amorphousness from which events are torn to the background 'noise' or 'interference' for radio communication. A more current figure would be cyberspace.[13] I suggest this is not a sacramentalism conducive to the Protestant ethos for the following reasons:

1   While paying attention to the excess of meaning, this sacramentalism cannot take its own experience of the "sacralization of a presence–absence" (Derrida, 1998: 64) too seriously. It is always aware of the mediating and ineradicable rhetoric. It does not need to be named religiously for it can be named in so many other ways. There is no immediate or authentic experience of it, for the experience is always and only a mediatized experience. Thus this sacramentalism remains locked into the logics of both nominalism and the univocity of being – as my citation from Caputo demonstrates – but its ironization means we are far from the religious experience detailed by William James in his Protestant classic *The Varieties of Religious Experience*.

2   It is anti-individual. In fact, several critics (of Foucault, for example, but also Lacan and Derrida) have drawn attention to the erasure of agency in a fixation upon the anonymous economies of power or *différance* or desire. The postmodern 're-enchantment' bears a closer resemblance to both gnosticism and paganism than Protestantism. The assertion of will is always an arbitrary act, an adventure into the undecideable. The absence of a teleology for this sacramentalism renders liberal notions of 'education' as a civilizing progress, and consciousness raising as a stage towards a true freedom and integrity of the self, fundamentally flawed.

3   It is anti-institutional because it is a born from a critique of all structures, frames, taxonomies and boundaries. It trades in transgression and so floats free of the authorized practices of piety (church-going, catechism, Bible-reading, sermon-hearing, public prayers etc.) that once disciplined and socialized the faithful. Spirituality (even Christian spirituality) has moved beyond denominationalism.

4   It is fundamentally syncretistic. The move beyond denominationalism is a further dissemination of Christian discourse. The Catholic/Protestant divide and Established/Nonconformist divide are no longer tenable as axes along which the Christian tradition can be mapped today. Postmodern sacramentalism, then, is not one which conforms to either Catholic or Protestant Eucharistic teaching. It is fused with other, not necessarily Christian, elements: ecological concerns, self-enlightenment and development techniques, various Western takes on eastern mysticism, and appreciations of native traditions (the Celtic, for example, or the religions of the American Indian). The sacramentalism is hybrid, eclectic and glocal.[14] It borders sometimes on sport because of its concern with the body, fitness and health. It has been linked to virtual reality (Heim, 1991). It is rooted in an erotic drive deeper than sexuality, but which draws it close to certain traditional Catholic

teachings on human desire and divine *eros*. It will have nothing whatsoever to do with the more Protestant dualism of *eros* and *agape*.

5   Rooted in an erotic drive, this sacramental emphasizes the power of the image, the logo or the icon. The sign is not a *sign of* something; the sign presents itself, it performs upon its readers or observers. The sign is part of a persuasive force, a pragmatic (rather than teleological) creativity issuing from the anachronized or disruptive ontology (some might say nihilistic drift) that postmodernity espouses. The point here is that Protestantism has always been iconoclastic, whereas postmodernity is a culture in which there is a new and pervasive iconolatry; an iconolatry in which the distinction between idol and icon depends not upon the visual or auditory content of the image but its power. The icon is a persuasive force; it participates, its produces. The idol is an inert sign – the failed logo, the brand name or image that does not 'pull', does not persuade the consumer of its value.

Of course Catholicism and Orthodoxy will also both be affected by the postmodern cultural turn, but I suggest less so because of their own resistances to liberalism, their continuing emphasis upon the iconic and a mediated revelation, and their attention not to individualism but corporatism. The waning of Protestantism, I suggest, might be somewhat akin to the waning of Catholic Christendom. For it too spawned a culture, an *ethos*, out of its religion and had to undergo a radical transformation with the creation of new structures of feeling and value. What has already gone is the way both Protestantism and Catholicism defined their position with respect to countering the position of the other – and this has already had implications for ecumenical dialogues, like those sponsored by the Anglican–Roman Catholic International Commission (ARCIC) and the World Council of Churches. Such dialogues will increasingly lack conviction and enthusiasm. And if Protestantism can no longer define itself with respect to Catholicism (one recalls it has always been a reactive stance and the 'protest' still remains at the heart of its self-image), it will become a term of the past, a cultural anachronism. Though we might see fundamentalism as its own reactive successor.

Epilogue: Fundamentalism and Neo-orthodoxy

I am being brief and provocative here. Furthermore I am aware I am not defining what I include and exclude under the labels 'fundamentalism' and 'neo-orthodoxy'. Nevertheless, I would contend that Christian fundamentalism (whose history really only goes back to the beginning of the twentieth century) and neo-orthodoxy (for Protestants, the Barth-inspired neo-orthodoxy[15]) are anti-cultural moves, dictated by a fortress mentality. They are defensive forms of Christian living in a complex world; attempts to remain free of or withdraw from the various cultural pressures that are thought to compromise their biblical-based accounts of Christian *praxis*. Manuel Castells calls them 'resistance communities' (Castells, 1997: 5–67). In their desire to extract themselves as separate domains from the larger cultural and secular sphere, they are fundamentally antimodern – and for that reason I distinguish them from Protestantism and the cultural ethos it fostered. This obviously needs another essay to develop. Here I only offer the observations as a coda. But the main point Castells makes with respect to 'resistance communities' is significant: they do not stem the rising tides of postmodernity's rampant, celebratory pluralism – they accelerate them. They establish certain cultural incommensurables and increase the fragmentation in their formation of interest groups or neo-tribal units. Sociologists like Zygmunt Bauman (1992: xxiii, 136, 148, 204) and Michel Maffesoli (1988, 1991) views such neo-tribalism as characteristic of postmodernity.

Notes

1 For an account of the way in which the assassination of Henry IV of Francis provoked a religious and cultural crisis see Toulmin (1990: 45–56).
2 Jürgen Habermas points out that the development of a public sphere took place first in England in the late seventeenth and early eighteenth centuries. See Habermas (1989: 14–26, 57–66).
3 See Certeau (1992: 79–112). Certeau's thesis on Ockham echoes here the thought of his teacher, Henri de Lubac. Several of the *nouvelle théologie* group spoke of a cultural turn in late mediaeval scholasticism that encouraged the divorce between nature and grace. The same thesis can be found in Yves Congar's work as in Hans Urs von Balthasar It is a line of thought continued today in the work of John Milbank, Catherine Pickstock and Conor Cunningham. Each of these thinkers also traces the relationship between nominalism and the univocity of being (often attributed to Duns Scotus).
4 See Nicholls (1989) for an account of the development of political construal of autarky and absolutism sanctioned in the name of God.
5 For an account of this melancholy see Cunningham and Grell (2000) and Balthasar (1991: 9–140).
6 See Michel de Certeau for accounts of both these phenomena as they emerged in the sixteenth and seventeenth centuries in his *The Mystic Fable* (1992) and *The Possession of Loudon* (2000).
7 This is a formulation of Derrida's that Caputo cites and supports.
8 Two classics in this field are Webster (1976) and Shapin and Schaffer (1985).
9 We have to recognize that to some extent these ideologies of modernity – sovereignty of the subject, the panoptical gaze, the production of universal laws and so on – are constructs after the event, in the same way as, following the cultural shifts in the 1970s, early thinkers of postmodernity (e.g., Lyotard, 1984) constructed maps of modernity, reducing its complexity and heterogeneity.
10 See Eagleton (1996) and Boyle (1998). Boyle writes sharply: 'Post-Modernism is the pessimism of an obsolete class – the salaried official intelligensia – whose fate is closely bound up with the declining nation-state' (p. 318).

11   For an account of the relation between the sublime and the kitsch, see Ward (2002b).
12   There is a chain of sandwich shops called 'Feed the Five Thousand' and a hairdressing/tattooing service in Manchester calls itself 'The Parting of the Waves'. For other such examples of the contemporary faces of public religion see Ward (2002a).
13   Derrida draws upon metaphors related to cyberspace in his essay 'Faith and Knowledge' (1998). For an account of postmodern notions of presence see Ward (2000), *Cities of God* (London: Routledge) pp. 152–88.
14   'Glocal' is a term used in discourses about globalism. It describes situations where a local, indigenous culture is already affected by global consumer motifs.
15   I reserve the right to distinguish between Barth's own theology and that liberal evangelical Christian theology that is said to be an interpretation of his work.

References

Anderson, Benedict (1983). *Imaginary Communities*. London: Verso.

Balthasar, Hans Urs von (1991). *The Realm of Metaphysics in the Modern Age*, vol. 5 of *The Glory of the Lord*, trans. Oliver Davies et al. Edinburgh: T & T Clark.

Bauman, Zygmunt (1992). *Intimations of Postmodernity*. Oxford: Blackwell.

Boyle, Nicholas (1998). *Who Are We Now? Christian Humanism and the Global Market from Hegel to Heaney*. Edinburgh: T & T Clark.

Caputo, John D. (2000). *More Radical Hermeneutics: On Not Knowing Who We Are*. Bloomington: Indiana University Press.

Castells, Manuel (1997). *The Power of Identity*, vol. 2 of *The Information Age*. Oxford: Blackwell.

Certeau, Michel de (1992). *The Mystic Fable: The Sixteenth and Seventeenth Centuries*, trans. M. B. Smith. Chicago: University of Chicago Press.

Certeau, Michel de (2000). *The Possession of Loudon*, trans. M. B. Smith. Chicago: University of Chicago Press.

Chadwick, Owen (1975). *The Secularization of the European Mind in the Nineteenth Century*. Cambridge, UK: Cambridge University Press.

Cox, Harvey (1964). *The Secular City*. London: SCM.

Cunningham, Andrew and Grell, Ole Peter (2000). *The Four Horsemen of the Apocalypse*. Cambridge, UK: Cambridge University Press.

Cunningham, Conor (2002). *Genealogy of Nihilism*. London: Routledge.

Deleuze, Giles and Guattari, Felix (1986). *A Thousand Plateaux: Capitalism and Schizophrenia*. London: Althone.

Derrida, Jacques (1982). *Margins of Philosophy*, trans. Alan Bass. Brighton: Harvester Press.

Derrida, Jacques (1993). *On the Name*, trans. D. Wood et al. Stanford, CA: Stanford University Press.

Derrida, Jacques (1998). Faith and Knowledge: The Two Sources of 'Religion' at the Limits of Reason Alone, trans. Samuel Weber. In Jacques Derrida and Gianni Vattimo (eds.), *Religion*. Cambridge, UK: Polity Press, pp. 1–78.

Eagleton, Terry (1996). *The Illusions of Postmodernity*. Oxford: Blackwell.

Foucault, Michel (1974). *The Order of Things: An Archaeology of the Human Sciences*. London: Tavistock.

Foucault, Michel (1976). *Birth of the Clinic: An Archaeology of Medical Perception*, trans. A. Sheridan. London: Tavistock.

Fukuyama, Francis (1992). *The End of History and the Last of Man*. Harmondsworth, UK: Penguin.

Gray, John (1993). *Post-Liberalism: Studies in Political Thought*. London: Routledge.

Habermas, Jürgen (1989). *The Structural Transformation of the Public Sphere*, trans. T. Burger. Cambridge, UK: Polity Press.

Harvey, David (1989). *The Condition of Postmodernity*. Oxford: Blackwell.

Heim, Michael (1991). The Erotic Ontology of Cyberspace. In M. Benedikt (ed.), *Cyberspace: First Steps*. Cambridge, MA: MIT Press, pp. 63–87.

Irigaray, Luce (1993). *Sexes and Genealogies*, trans. Gillian C. Gill. New York: Columbia University Press.

Jameson, Fredric (1998). *The Cultural Turn: Selected Writings on the Postmodern, 1983–1998*. London: Verso.

Latour, Bruno (1993). *We Have Never Been Modern*, trans. C. Porter. Hemel Hempstead, UK: Harvester Wheatsheaf.

Latour, Bruno and Woolgar, Steve (1979). *Laboratory Life: The Constitution of Scientific Facts*. Princeton, NJ: Princeton University Press.

Levinas, Emmanuel (1987). *Time and the Other*, trans. R. Cohen. Pittsburgh: Duquesne University Press.

Lyotard, Jean-François (1984). *The Postmodern Condition*, trans G. Bennington and B. Masumi. Manchester, UK: Manchester University Press.

Maffesoli, Michel (1988). Jeux de masques: postmoderne tribalism. *Design Issues* 4: 1–22.

Maffesoli, Michel (1991). The Ethic of Aesthetics. *Theory Culture and Society* 8, 7–20.

Manent, Pierre (1998). *The City of Man*, trans. Marc A LePain. Princeton, NJ: Princeton University Press.

Mirandola, Pico della (1948). *Oration of the Dignity of Man*, trans. Elizabeth Livermore Forbes. In Ernest Cassirer, Paul Oskar Kristaller and John Herman Randall (eds.), *The Renaissance Philosophy of Man*. Chicago: University of Chicago Press.

Nicholls, David (1989). *Diety and Domination: Images of God and State in the Nineteenth and Twentieth* Centuries. London: Routledge.

Oliver, Kelly (1993). *Reading Kristeva: Unraveling the Double-bind*. Bloomington: Indiana University Press.

Serres, Michel (1995). *Angels: A Modern Myth*, trans. Francis Cowper. Paris: Flammarion.

Shapin, Steven and Schaffer, Simon (1985). *Leviathan and the Air-Pump: Hobbes, Boyle and the Experimental Life*. Princeton, NJ: Princeton University Press.

Taylor, Charles (2002), *Varieties of Religion Today: William James Revisited*. Cambridge, MA: Harvard University Press.

Taylor, Charles (forthcoming). *Modern Social Imaginaries* (book-length study of article in *Public Culture* 14, 1, Winter 2002).

Toulmin, Stephen (1990). *Cosmopolis: The Hidden Agenda of Modernity*. Chicago: University of Chicago Press.

Touraine, Alain (1995). *Critique of Modernity*, trans. D. Macey. Oxford: Blackwell.

Ward, Graham (2000). *Cities of God*. London: Routledge.

Ward, Graham (2002a). *True Religion*. Oxford: Blackwell.

Ward, Graham (2002b). Language and Silence. In Denys Turner and Oliver Davies (eds.), *Silence and the Word: Negative Theology and Incarnation*. Cambridge, UK: Cambridge University Press, pp. 159–84.

Weber, Max (1992). *The Protestant Ethic and the Spirit of Capitalism*, trans. T. Parsons. London: Routledge.

Webster, Charles (1976). *The Great Instauration: Science, Medicine, and Reform, 1626–60*. New York: Holes and Meier.

CHAPTER 41

The Future of Protestantism: The Non-Western Protestant World

Allan Anderson

The Shifting Centre of Gravity

In this chapter, the term 'Protestantism' is used broadly, to include Pentecostal, Independent and Anglican denominations together with the historic Protestant denominations like Lutherans, Baptists, Methodists, and Reformed. The traditional categories of Christianity used in the West like 'Protestant', 'evangelical', 'ecumenical' and so on, are becoming increasingly meaningless in Africa, Asia and Latin America. Protestant Christianity has grown to such an extent during the twentieth century in these three continents that the vast majority of Protestants in the world today live there. What has been called 'the seismic shift in Christian identity' (Robert, 2000: 50) and 'the southward swing of the Christian center of gravity' (Walls, 2000: 1) has made Christianity more African and Asian than Western. What in the past were regarded as the continents of the so-called 'pagan religions' are now where most of the Christians are (Bediako, 2000: 6). The two largest Presbyterian denominations in the world are in Korea, and the largest Pentecostal one is in Brazil. More Anglicans attend church in Nigeria today than in England, and Africa is the continent with the most Anglicans (Robert, 2000: 53). That only a small proportion of a large book like this one is given to Protestantism outside the Western world may indicate first that the information resources are scarcer than they are for Protestantism in Europe and North America, and secondly that there is still a disproportionate emphasis on Western forms of Protestantism in our Western universities and seminaries. Protestantism is still regarded by many as the religion of northern Europe and North America, but nothing could be further from the truth.

It is also important to refrain from popular generalizations like speaking of 'non-Western' as if it were a homogeneous whole. Not only does this term suggest a presumption of a Western centre, but it leads to mistaken impressions of the rest of the world as being of the same composition. Christianity generally, and Protestantism in particular outside the West, is extremely diversified and consists of a complex variety. As this chapter attempts to show, the future of Protestantism lies increasingly outside the Western world, and we cannot understand Protestantism today without giving due attention to the contribution of African, Asian and Latin American forms of it. These are much more diverse than Western Protestantism is, and would in many cases appear 'strange' to Western Protestants. Dana Robert points out that Christianity was losing its Western character as 'ordinary people were receiving the gospel message and retranslating it into cultural modes that fitted their worldviews and met their needs' (Robert, 2000: 53).

To start with some basic facts: Christianity began in Asia, it was present in Africa before it reached Europe, and Latin America is proportionately today the most Christian continent in the world. At the beginning of the twentieth century, there were an estimated 90 million Christians in Asia, Africa and Latin America, 16 per cent of the world's Christian population, compared to 428 million or 77 per cent in Europe (including Russia) and North America. A century later, according to Barrett and Johnson's statistics, there were 1,118 million Christians in Asia, Africa and Latin America, 59 per cent of the world's Christians, while those of the two northern continents only constituted 39 per cent (Barrett and Johnson, 2002: 23). Barrett and Johnson's statistics give dramatic evidence of how rapidly the 'Western' share of world Christianity decreased in the twentieth century. The demographic balance of Christianity has been shifting steadily southwards. They estimate that if present trends continue, 68 per cent of the world's Christians will live in the South by 2025, with only 31 per cent in the North (Barrett and Johnson, 2002: 25). But it is not just in terms of numbers that there have been fundamental changes.

These statistics also indicate that Christianity is growing most often in Pentecostal and charismatic forms, and that many of these are independent of Western 'mainline' Protestant denominations. The 'southward swing' is possibly more evident in Pentecostalism than in other forms of Protestantism. Most of the dramatic church growth in the twentieth century in Asia, Africa and Latin America has taken place in Pentecostal and indigenous and independent Pentecostal-like churches, and probably at least three-quarters of Pentecostalism today is found in the Third World (EATWOT, 1998: 36). Classical Pentecostal churches with roots in North America, like the Assemblies of God, have probably only some 8 per cent of their world associate membership in North America, with at least 80 per cent in the Third World. One estimate puts the total number of adherents of the World Assemblies of God Fellowship in 1997 at some 30 million, of which only about 2.5 million are in North America (Wilson, 1997: 3, 107, 183). In the subtitle of his intriguing book *Fire from Heaven*, Harvey Cox (1996) suggests that throughout the world 'the rise of Pentecostal spirituality' has contributed to the 'reshaping of religion in the twenty-first century'. Although he does not only refer to Pentecostal forms of Christianity in this assessment, he may indeed be correct. Furthermore, his concept of 'Pentecostal spirituality' is widely inclusive and must be clarified for his conclusions to be understood. Pentecostalism has certainly contributed towards the global reshaping of Protestantism, but in any discussion of the 'globalization' of Protestantism, due recognition must also be given to the 'localization' of indigenous and independent forms that is probably its greatest strength.

Half the world's Christians today live in developing, presently poor countries. The historic forms of Protestantism have been profoundly affected by several factors in these countries, including the desire to have a more contextual and culturally relevant form of Christianity, the rise of nationalism, a reaction to what were perceived as 'colonial' forms of Christianity, and the burgeoning Pentecostal and Charismatic renewal. In addition to this is a further complication to understanding the term 'Protestant'. Barrett and Johnson have drawn attention to what they call the 'latest in a long line of major historical realignments within global Christianity', the emergence of the Independents, alternatively termed 'postdenominationalists' and 'neo-apostolics'. They state that this 'megabloc' consists of over 20,000 movements with 394 million members scattered across the world. According to these estimates, there are more Independents (African and Chinese Independents being the largest groups) than there are historic Protestants today (Barrett and Johnson, 2001: 24–5). These Independents have emerged, in a large part, from Protestant and Pentecostal churches.

One of the principal factors in the emergence of an autonomous, self-assertive Protestantism in the South has been the fall of colonialism, and the nationalism and increasing anti-Western feeling that followed the independence of former colonies after the Second World War. The independence of India in 1949 began a domino-like fall of colonies culminating with South Africa in 1994. The end of colonialism gave rise to a new and strident nationalism, and more recently there has emerged a new continentalism that emphasizes human dignity. South African President Thabo Mbeki gave an example of this in his inaugural speech in 1999, when he spoke of an 'African renaissance'. The emergence of ' African theology' and 'Asian theology' are but two examples of the changing scenario in Protestantism. The decline of Western power was accompanied by a loss of prestige for 'colonial' religions like Protestantism. Protestant missionaries had been given privileges like land grants not afforded the local people. Churches in Asia and Africa had to adjust to this change in status, not only by rapidly changing their leadership from expatriate to national, but also in loosening their ties with the West and expressing the character of the churches in African and Asian ways. In Latin America, as well as in the Philippines and African nations that were formerly 'Catholic' colonies, the situation was rather different, as in these areas Catholicism was perceived as the religion of the oppressor. In those countries occupied by Japan, Protestantism was seen as the champion of nationalism. In Korea during the Japanese occupation in 1935, a disproportionate number of Protestants led the resistance to the imposition of Shinto worship. In these and other cases, Protestantism was regarded as the bearer of liberation, but in all instances it had to reckon with the rising tide of nationalism. In several

countries in Africa, Protestantism was involved in the foundation of nationalism, as many African nationalists came from the ranks of its mission education.
Korean nationalists were trained in Protestant schools during Japanese occupation (Robert, 2000: 51). In South Africa and Rhodesia (now Zimbabwe), the historic Protestant churches joined the Catholics in their vocal opposition to white
settler rule and the injustices of apartheid.

Protestantism today, therefore, is very different and much more fragmented
in Africa, Asia and Latin America than its European and North American missionary originators intended it to be. Although there is some doubt as to whether
the proportion of Christians in the world's population is declining or increasing,
it is definitely increasing in Asia and Africa, and the overall constitution of Christianity dramatically changed in the twentieth century. Whereas Protestants in
Europe and even in North America are experiencing ever-decreasing church
attendance and membership, those in Asia, Africa and Latin America have
grown exponentially, especially since the 1970s. In the West, not only are immigrant communities from these continents setting up their own Christian communities, but secularized, post-Christian Europe in particular is seen as a needy
mission field for evangelization by missionaries from such places as Nigeria,
Brazil and Korea. Larry Pate estimated that by 1998 the majority of Protestant
missionaries would come from the non-Western world. The leading missionary
sending nations would no longer be the United States, Britain, or Germany, but
India, South Korea, Brazil and Nigeria (Pate, 1991: 35).

Protestantism in Asia

Although Christianity has been in Asia for two millennia, and Protestantism
there since the Dutch conquest of Indonesia from the Portuguese in 1605, the
earliest Protestant missionaries from Europe, Bartholomäus Ziegenbalg and
Heinrich Plütschau, went to South India with the Danish-Halle Mission in 1706.
Thousands of missionaries from the West have followed them ever since. But
despite the activities of these many tireless and often sacrificial workers, it was
the Asian evangelists and 'native' workers, and indigenous revival movements
that were mainly responsible for the rapid growth of Protestantism there. The
same is true in Latin America and Africa. Since the Second World War, Protestantism has grown so significantly in Asia that by the end of the twentieth
century its rate of growth was higher than that of any other continent (Brierley, 1998: 38). The fastest growing form of Christianity is a Pentecostal type,
and here 'charismatic' Christianity dominates the older Protestant churches.
One can now speak of the 'Pentecostalization' of Asian Christianity, particularly
among Chinese, Korean, Filipino and Indian churches.

It was estimated that Christians formed about 8 per cent of the population of
Asia in 2000, some 316 million people. Of this number, there were at least 87
million Pentecostals and charismatic Protestants, more than a quarter of the

Christian population (Johnstone and Mandryk, 2001: 41). The greatest increase in Christian adherence took place during the 1980s, when the number of evangelicals doubled; and there may be as many Asian evangelicals today as there are in the entire Western world. However, most of the growth has taken place in three countries: China, South Korea and Indonesia, and that mainly among Pentecostals (Johnstone, 1993: 42–3). Cox speaks of 'the rapid spread of the Spirit-oriented forms of Christianity in Asia' (Cox, 1996: 214).

South Korea is a pluralistic society that has been 'exposed to religious and cultural radiation from the USA' (Martin, 1990: 135). Despite this influence, Protestantism has taken on a distinctive form in Korea that is quite different from that found in the West. Observers who have tried to emphasize the 'American' nature of Pentecostalism throughout the world or the 'Americanization' of Christianity in Africa, Korea and elsewhere often miss this important fact. Creative innovations and the selective transformation of 'foreign' symbols are constantly occurring, and naturally, a synthesizing process takes place as new religious forms interact with older ones (Anderson, 2000a: 115). Since the arrival of Presbyterian and Methodist missionaries in Korea in 1884, the Protestant population has grown from zero to 12 million, a quarter of the population. There are now more Protestants in South Korea than Buddhists, and this is the foremost Protestant country in Asia. All but one of the 11 largest Christian (Protestant) congregations in the world are in Seoul. The majority of Korean Protestantism is Presbyterian, but it is dominated by a charismatic and conservative evangelical character that has its roots in a series of revivals that began with the 1903 and 1907 revivals in Wonsan and Pyongyang. Reinforced by the remarkable growth of Pentecostalism from the 1960s onwards (especially in the world's largest congregation, the Yoido Full Gospel Church led by Yonggi Cho), Korean Protestantism today represents one of the most vigorous forms of Protestantism in the world today. Some 11 thousand Korean Protestant missionaries (only exceeded by the USA) serve in 156 countries of the world, the greatest concentration being in Japan, the Philippines, and Russia (Johnstone and Mandryk, 2001: 387). Thousands of South Koreans are poised for the re-evangelization of North Korea after the expected reunification takes place. On the downside, Korean Protestantism is plagued by schism, with over 200 separate denominations, almost a hundred being Presbyterian ones.

In China, the most populous nation on earth, there has been a remarkable growth of independent Protestant house churches since 1949, when the Western missionaries left. These churches bear little resemblance whatever to Protestant (or Pentecostal) churches in the West, but are characterized by conservative evangelical piety, an emphasis on prayer, healing, exorcism and other spiritual gifts, and leadership often by women. These independent, non-registered churches are often in opposition to the political order, but reflect popular Chinese spirituality. Understandably, statistics of people in Chinese house churches are hard to come by, but one estimate put the number at 45 million in 2000 (Johnstone and Mandryk, 2001: 161), and many of these are rapidly growing Pentecostal-like groups. Some current estimates are much higher than this figure, but an accurate estimate is impossible. It may be that

China has the largest numbers of Pentecostals of any country in the world. The differences between these indigenous and independent churches, and forms of Protestantism found in the West are considerable and may be likened to distinctively African forms of Christianity which have consciously rejected Western forms. Chinese independent churches have developed in isolation from the rest of Christianity for at least 50 years, and grew rapidly at a time when they were faced with severe opposition from the 'Anti-Christian Movement'. Three of the largest of these churches, the True Jesus Church, the Jesus Family, and the Little Flock/ Local Church/ Christian Assembly churches are referred to in China as 'Old Three-Self' churches. They have been in conflict with the government-recognized union of Protestant churches, the Three-Self Patriotic Movement (referring to the three principles of being self-supporting, self-governing and self-propagating) which resulted in their banning during the 1950s as promoters of 'American imperialism, feudalism and capitalism', the 'unlawful activities' of faith healing and exorcism, and the 'immoralities' of 'spiritual dance' (Anderson, 2000a: 116). But these house churches have emerged at the beginning of the twenty-first century as the most resilient form of Chinese Christianity and probably the most widespread.

In South East Asia independent Protestant churches have also grown significantly. In the Philippines they have emerged on the backs of a dominant Catholicism and a Protestantism imported with the American colonialism that replaced that of the Spanish in 1898. Indonesia experienced a 'revival' after the overthrow of the Sukarno regime in 1965, and there are an estimated 18 million Protestants, Pentecostals and Independents there today, most of whom have become Christian since 1965. Some of the largest Protestant denominations in Asia are in Indonesia. Perhaps as much as three-quarters of South-East and East Asian Protestantism is charismatic or Pentecostal.

India has the first successful united Protestant church in the world, the Church of South India, formed in 1947 when Congregationalists, Presbyterians, Anglicans and Methodists came together. The impact of this event on Protestant ecumenism throughout the world was enormous, although Indian Christians have pointed out that the divisions were not of their making in the first place. Revival movements have also been characteristic of Indian Christianity, and Pentecostal phenomena were recorded as early as 1860–1 in the revival associated with Tamil Anglican evangelist John Christian Aroolappen in Tamil Nadu, followed by another in Travancore (Kerala) in 1874–5 (Satyavrata, 1999: 205). In the 1905–7 revival that occurred at Pandita Ramabai's Mukti Mission at Pune, Ramabai (1858–1922) understood this to be the means by which the Holy Spirit was creating an indigenous form of Indian Christianity (Adhav, 1979: 216). All this occurred before Pentecostalism came to Asia from the West. In the north-east Indian states of Nagaland and Mizoram, revival movements that began there in the 1950s have resulted in over 85 per cent of the population becoming Protestant, mainly Baptist and Presbyterian (Johnstone and Mandryk, 2001: 330–1). But Christianity in Asia still represents a minority of less than 10 per cent, and it faces difficult challenges in its encounter with the ancient religions that dominate most Asian countries.

Protestantism in Africa

Protestantism came to Africa with the seventeenth-century Dutch settlers, but was first introduced to African people by Georg Schmidt, a Moravian missionary to Khoisan people in the Cape of Good Hope in 1738. After a rather slow beginning, the growth of African Christianity in the twentieth century has been one of the most amazing stories in the history of the church. Although Western missionaries introduced Protestantism to Africa, its rapid growth is not primarily attributable to their efforts as much as to the innovative dynamics of African preachers that outlasted the colonialism with which the introduction of Protestantism was intimately associated. By the end of the twentieth century, African Christianity had grown to over 300 million, almost half the population of Africa and more than 60 per cent of the sub-Sahara. This is a vibrant, active Christianity, as church buildings, cathedrals and auditoriums are filled every Sunday and often during the week. Since the independence of African nations from European colonizing powers, beginning with Ghana in 1957, Africans have replaced expatriates as church leaders.

Protestantism is probably more difficult to define in Africa than anywhere else, because there are several thousand independent churches, some of which have existed since the end of the nineteenth century. Some were protest movements against European ecclesiastical domination and control, but the great majority are churches of a Pentecostal nature: the older African Initiated Churches (AICs),[1] and the new charismatic churches that have arisen since the 1970s. In these churches the emphasis is on the power and gifts of the Spirit, particularly healing, exorcism and prophecy, which have been interpreted within an African context dealing with daily witchcraft and rampant disease. The older AICs arose as a movement of religious resistance to colonialism in the late nineteenth and early twentieth centuries, and have become a major part of Christianity in Africa, particularly in southern Africa, Kenya, the West African coast and the Congo. In South Africa and Nigeria, AICs constitute almost half of the Christian population.

The influence of the AICs is enormous, amounting to a fundamental reformation of Protestant Christianity in Africa. Most African churches have now followed the example of the AICs and have incorporated into their worship more of the popular oral culture with its rich symbolism and rituals, expressing their Christianity with the rhythms of African song, dance and charismatic public oratory. In some countries, particularly Anglophone ones like Nigeria, Ghana, and Zimbabwe, the new charismatic churches have become the dominant form of Christianity there, influenced much more by a globalized Pentecostalism of the mass media and (in some cases) by the 'health and wealth' gospel from the USA. In south-western Nigeria, Pentecostal forms of Christianity now overwhelmingly dominate the religious scene. The size of the new Christian congregations in southern Nigeria is breathtaking, and some of the largest church buildings and Christian gatherings in the world are found there. In Ghana, the largest Protestant church is the Church of Pentecost and in Zimbabwe, the Zimbabwe Assemblies of God Africa (Johnstone and Mandryk, 2001: 274, 689). Each of these churches claims over a million affiliates. Most of these new African churches, while sometimes having links with the West, are independent of Western control and represent a form of African Christianity that is particularly successful in the cities (Anderson, 2001a).

The important role of this rapidly growing new form of African Christianity has now been recognized (Maxwell, 1995: 313; Gifford, 1998: 31; Anderson, 2000b: 237–55). Ogbu Kalu calls this the 'third response' to white cultural domination and power in the church, the former two responses being Ethiopianism and the Aladura/ Zionist churches (Kalu, 1998: 2–3). 'Ethiopianism' refers to those AICs that separated from European Protestant churches as 'Ethiopian' or 'African' churches at the turn of the twentieth century. The first AICs were secessions from Protestant churches that were identified with European colonial power. The 'Aladura/Zionist' churches are the much larger group of churches that seceded as 'Spirit' or 'prophet-healing' churches some 20 years later, and are now found all over Africa. These churches were more innovative and accommodating to African religious and cultural values, and their influence on the nature and future direction of African Christianity was immense (Anderson, 2001a: 15–18). The new Pentecostal movement is not *fundamentally* different from the Spirit movements that preceded it in the AICs, but is a continuation of them in a different context. The older AICs, the 'classical' Pentecostal churches brought to Africa by Western missionaries, and the newer independent Pentecostal and charismatic churches have all responded in differing yet similar ways to the existential needs of the African worldview. They have all offered a personal encounter with God through the power of the Spirit, healing from sickness and deliverance from evil in all its manifestations, spiritual, social and structural. This is not to say that there are no tensions or differences between the new and the old churches, which are sometimes painful. There is a paradox in most historic forms of Protestantism in Africa: although there is a desire to make the churches more 'African' in character, there is also a reluctance to change Western traditions like vestments, liturgies, music and church architecture for more authentically African expressions.

Many new Protestant movements in Africa have begun as movements of youth and women, giving opportunities not afforded them by patriarchal and gerontocratic religions that have lost their charismatic power (Maxwell, 1995: 316–17). The entrance and pervading influence of many new and different kinds of African churches now makes it even more difficult, if not impossible, to put African Protestantism into types and categories. Some of the 'classical' Pentecostal churches have become vibrant and rapidly expanding African churches, in particular the Assemblies of God, which operates in most countries of the sub-Sahara. But throughout the history of AICs there has been a predominance of Pentecostal features and phenomena. Harvey Cox (1996: 246) refers to the Apostolic/Zionist, Lumpa and Kimbanguist churches as 'the African expression of the worldwide Pentecostal movement', and although these churches do not usually define themselves in this way, not enough attention has been given to this resonance. Gifford, however, is right to question whether the older AICs can be regarded as *paradigmatic* of the Pentecostal movement in Africa (Gifford, 1998: 33).

Protestantism in Latin America

Protestant settlers in South America in the sixteenth century kept their faith largely to themselves, and it was not until the nineteenth century that Protestant missionaries arrived, mainly from Britain and the USA. At the beginning of the twentieth century, Latin America was still almost entirely Catholic. It was recognized, however, that this was a 'folk Catholicism', a synthesis of traditional Catholicism with pre-Christian and spiritistic beliefs. This, coupled with a reaction against Catholicism (often perceived as a colonizing religion), made the situation favorable to the growth of Protestantism (especially Pentecostalism) in the twentieth century. Latin America is also the birthplace of Liberation Theology, a theology that seeks to apply Christian faith to the economical and political oppression that many Latinos have faced. Although the first proponents of Liberation Theology were Catholics, it has also been embraced by Protestant theologians, among whom are the Argentinian Methodist José Míguez Bonino, the Brazilian Rubem Alves, and the Uruguayan Methodist leader, Emilio Castro, who worked for many years for the World Council of Churches in Geneva.

Most Latin Americans today are either Catholic or Pentecostal. In some countries like Brazil, Chile, El Salvador, Puerto Rico and Guatemala, Pentecostals number over a fifth of the total population. The growth of Pentecostalism in Latin America has been most extensively studied, particularly by sociologists, and an estimated 10 per cent of the continent's population are now Pentecostal. Most of this growth has occurred in the second half of the twentieth century. In Guatemala the figure might be as high as 30 per cent, and in Chile and Brazil some 20 per cent (Martin, 1994: 74–5). According to present growth rates, several Latin American countries could have a majority of Protestants (mostly Pentecostals) by 2010 (Cox, 1996: 168). Pope John Paul II warned against the 'invasion of the sects' and the 'ravenous wolves' that were threatening the traditional Catholic hold on Latin America (Cleary and Stewart-Gambino, 1997: 228).

And yet, Protestantism in Latin America is fundamentally an indigenous phenomenon. Recent studies show that Catholicism has proportionately far more foreign priests in Latin America than Pentecostal churches have foreign missionaries, an astonishing 94 per cent in Venezuela (Cleary and Stewart-Gambino, 1997: 231). Many Pentecostal denominations were founded in Latin America before the major ones in the USA from which they are sometimes erroneously presumed to have emerged. David Martin explains that Pentecostalism expanded in Brazil during a time of rapid population growth and urbanization.

Because it was 'fully indigenous' it was 'able to provide an all-encompassing world-view for marginalized people'. It offered 'the fruits of honesty and thrift and a surrogate family, as well as the chance of participation, and a sense of worth, meaning and empowerment' (Martin, 1994: 65).

Míguez Bonino writes of three 'faces' of Latin American Protestantism. First, the 'liberal face' is found in the older Protestant denominations and the ecumenical movements, including the efforts to reflect on the liberation theology of the time (Bonino, 1997: 20–1). Second is the 'evangelical face', which Bonino sees as the result of the evangelical missionary and holiness movements of the late nineteenth century, with a strong pietistic and other-worldly spirituality, premillennialism and fundamentalism. He says that these features still affect Latin American Protestantism today (Bonino, 1997: 31–7). Third is the 'Pentecostal face', clearly the dominant feature of Latin American Protestantism today and for years to come (Bonino, 1997: 54–5). The growth of Pentecostalism in Latin America has been so dramatic that scholars are asking whether the continent is 'turning Protestant' (Stoll, 1990). In Latin America, however, the terms 'evangelical', 'Protestant' and 'Pentecostal' are interchangeable. Bonino questions whether the term 'Protestant' is appropriate for Latin American *evangélicos* (evangelicals), the term by which they are known there. He points out that 'the heritage has been reshaped in other lands and with other molds, and ignorance of these mediation processes has been a grave obstacle for us to understand ourselves as Protestants' (Bonino, 1997: ix).

Protestants in Latin America tend to be politically and theologically conservative. The open support of many Chilean Pentecostal leaders for the dictator Augusto Pinochet is a case in point. Although there are exceptions, the great majority of Protestant churches in Latin America are not affiliated to the World Council of Churches or to national ecumenical organizations. An important development pioneered by Latin American Protestants has been the emergence and development of Theological Education by Extension (TEE), by which ministers are trained in their local contexts without isolating them in theological seminaries and universities, and the need for trained lay leaders is also met. The TEE system has been very effective in providing trained leaders for a rapidly expanding church, and it has spread widely.

Challenges for the Future

The changing nature of Protestantism brings with it many challenges for the church. First, there is need to acknowledge that although Protestantism began in Europe, its strength today lies in its diversity and spirituality in other continents. The founders, evangelists and leaders of the 'younger' churches in the South must be given due recognition. Globalization has brought about a world in which more interaction between South and North is inevitable. No longer can dependent relationships between 'mission partners' from the North and 'younger churches' in the South be sustained.

Second, there is the challenge of adapting to a Protestantism that is more flexible, charismatic and spiritual, more easily able to utilize elements of the prevailing culture to become more relevant to a new generation. Although globalization is an increasing factor, the need for a contextualized Christian witness in each local situation is a pressing need. Asian Protestants are mostly evangelical in theological orientation, and they are engaged in efforts to evangelize their fellow Asians. The Church in India has reportedly sent out over 14,000 cross-cultural missionaries in recent years (mostly within India), South Korea over 5,800, Brazil 2,200, and Nigeria over 1,200 (Moreau, 2000: 144, 480, 546, 692). These missionaries, although sometimes repeating the mistakes of their Western counterparts, are also going to places inaccessible to Western missionaries, and are breaking the stereotypes that often hinder their work.

Third, there is the challenge of theological education, of finding creative ways to overcome the shortage of trained leaders for the burgeoning churches in these continents. This includes the need to train lay leaders. At the same time, there is need for a theological education that does not blindly copy Western models but seeks to be creatively relevant to local contexts (Anderson, 2001b). The drastic transformation in Christian demographics has made little impact on Western, rationalistic, theological education, which continues to be the leading model in seminaries across the globe. Africans, Latinos and Asians do not become Pentecostals or Presbyterians for precisely the same reasons that North Americans do. They have an increasing sense of self-identity. Academic appointments in 'Third World Theology' in Western institutions often serve as smokescreens to camouflage the reality or to further marginalize the 'voices from the margin' (Sugirtharajah, 1995), whereas actually little has changed in the way most educators think of and teach theology. Although Western theology has adjusted of late to the particular challenges of post-modernism, feminism and religious pluralism, the presuppositions remain. The rise of post-modernism has profoundly challenged the autonomous rationalism and empirical scepticism of Western theology, but has not yet shaken the foundations of the theology taught in most Protestant seminaries. The fundamental flaws in these structures exist particularly because they are Western models foisted onto the rest of the world, part of the legacy of the colonial past with its cultural imperialism and ethnocentrism. Hwa Yung points out that the many theological institutions that have sprung up all over Asia have been 'conditioned by the methodologies, agenda, and content of Western theology'. He says, 'This approach must be changed if the Asian church is to come to terms more adequately with its own identity, context, and mission' (Hwa Yung, 1995: 1).

Fourth is the challenge of the proliferation of Protestant denominations. Despite the efforts of the pan-continental ecumenical organizations like the All African Council of Churches, independent churches continue to multiply, especially in Africa. It does not seem that this is likely to diminish in the near future. New forms of independent Pentecostal and charismatic churches emerge in their thousands, spurred on by a non-institutional ecclesiology and individual charismatic leadership. Protestantism is much more fragmented than it has ever been. The challenge of these divisions for the ecumenical vision of a united church is obvious.

In conclusion, the globalization of Protestantism brings a host of criticisms by those who tend to see conspiracy or a 'deprivation theory' behind every religious movement. This is particularly the case with those who consider 'globalization' and 'Americanization' as essentially the same thing. It is expounded in *Exporting the American Gospel*, where Brouwer, Gifford and Rose say that US Americans have a belief in 'America's special place among nations' and 'a conviction that other peoples ought to be guided and ruled by American principles, both civil and religious' (Brouwer, Gifford, and Rose, 1996: 14). The result is, they maintain, that regions like sub-Saharan Africa with 'phenomenal economic and social collapse' have 'a rapidly growing sector of Christianity that is closely related to and heavily dependent on the United States' (Brouwer et al., 1996: 151, 154). Although at least once these authors deny a 'conspiracy theory' (p. 250), their study abounds with suggestions that globalization has resulted in the 'Americanization' of Christianity in struggling nation states all over the world.

With reference to Africa, Paul Gifford has become a leading and voluminous exponent of this theory. He suggests that the biggest single factor in the emergence of the new churches is the collapse of African economies by the 1980s and the subsequent increasing dependence on the USA. He proposes that it is 'Americanization' rather than any 'African quality' that is responsible for the growth of these churches. He sees this new phenomenon as a type of neo-colonialism propagated by American 'prosperity preachers'– in effect, a type of conspiracy theory (Gifford, 1993: 196–9, 294, 314–15). Gifford suggests that all types of African Christianity have Western links and are part of a globalized religious network, and that Christianity is 'one of Africa's best remaining ways of opting *into* the global order' (Gifford, 1998: 321). But this rather exaggerated and one-sided view, which has been somewhat modified more recently (Gifford, 1998: 236–44), has been accepted in many church and academic circles in the West, although Gifford has not been short of critics from within Africa itself.

This 'Americanization' theory seems to ignore fundamental features of Protestantism in Africa, where experience and practice are more important than formal ideology or even theology. As Ogbu Kalu points out, the relationship between the African pastor and his or her 'Western patron' is entirely eclectic. The 'dependency' has actually been mutual, as the Western supporters often need the African pastor to bolster their own international image and financial resources. Kalu observes that in the 1990s, since the public disgracing of American 'televangelists', the mood in Africa has changed, and churches are now 'characterised by independence and an emphasis on the Africanist roots of the ministries' (Kalu, 1998: 8). Daneel points out that in Africa, 'wealth and success are naturally signs of the blessing of God', so it is no wonder that such a message should be uncritically accepted there (Daneel, 1987: 46; Gifford, 1993: 188).

There *are* connections between some of the new churches and the American 'health and wealth' movement, and it is also true that some of these churches reproduce and promote 'health and wealth' teaching and literature. But identifying them with the American 'prosperity gospel' is a generalization that particularly fails to appreciate the reconstructions and innovations made by these new African movements in adapting to a radically different context, just as the older AICs did years before.

David Martin, discussing Latin American Protestantism, also takes issue with the presuppositions of those who identify 'globalization' with 'Americanization'. He says that while there are many connections between Latin American Pentecostalism and North America, the most important feature of the former is its 'indigenous character': 'The main thrust is local, powered by commitment, and thoroughly Latin American, down to the elements of authoritarianism and patronage. If pastors brook no internal dissidence and act as brokers in the web of patronage, that indicates an affinity to and an assimilation of local culture' (Martin, 1994: 75).

Not enough attention has been given to how the so-called 'global culture' is itself changed and formed by its encounter with a local context. 'Globalization' must not be construed to mean an overarching hegemony of an 'international culture' that neatly separates the 'global' from the 'local' and, in the African context, is often seen as the 'Americanization' of African Christianity. In fact, 'globalization' is both defined and limited by the local context. As Dana Robert observes, 'What at first glance appears to be the largest world religion is in fact the ultimate local religion'. She says that the strength of world Christianity lies in its ability to interweave 'the warp of a world religion with the woof of its local contexts' (Robert, 2000: 56). All the common features of Protestantism like those mentioned above are reinterpreted and conditioned by the social and religio-cultural contexts in which they appear. The new Protestantism challenges older Christian churches throughout the world. They are demonstrations of a form of Christianity that appeals to a new generation, and from which older churches can learn. The future of world Protestantism is now in the hands of the younger churches in the three continents of the 'South'.

Note

1   The terms 'African Independent Church' and 'African Indigenous Church' have been substituted more recently with 'African Initiated Church' 'African Instituted Church' or 'African Initiatives in Christianity', all using the now familiar acronym 'AIC'.

References

Adhav, Shamsundar M. (1979). *Pandita Ramabai*. Madras: Christian Literature Society.
Anderson, Allan (2000a). Pentecostalism in East Asia: Indigenous Oriental Christianity? *Pneuma: The Journal for the Society for Pentecostal Studies* 22, 1: 115–32.

Anderson, Allan (2000b). *Zion and Pentecost: The Spirituality and Experience of Pentecostal and Zionist/Apostolic Churches in South Africa*. Pretoria: University of South Africa Press.

Anderson, Allan (2001a). *African Reformation: African Initiated Christianity in the 20th Century*. Trenton, NJ: Africa World Press.

Anderson, Allan (2001b). The 'Fury and Wonder'? Pentecostal-Charismatic Spirituality in Theological Education. *Pneuma: The Journal of the Society for Pentecostal Studies* 23, 2: 287–302.

Barrett, David B. and Johnson, Todd M. (2001). Annual Statistical Table on Global Mission: 2001. *International Bulletin of Missionary Research* 25, 1: 24–5.

Barrett, David B. and Johnson, Todd M. (2002). Annual Statistical Table on Global Mission: 2002. *International Bulletin of Missionary Research* 26, 1: 23–5.

Bediako, Kwame (2000). A Half Century of African Christian Thought: Pointers to Theology and Theological Education in the Next Half Century. *Journal of African Christian Thought* 3, 1: 5–11.

Bonino, José Míguez (1997). *Faces of Latin American Protestantism*. Grand Rapids, MI: Eerdmans.

Brierley, Peter (1998). *Future Church: A Global Analysis of the Christian Community to the Year 2010*. London: Monarch Books & Christian Research.

Brouwer, Steve, Gifford, Paul, and Rose, Susan (1996). *Exporting the American Gospel: Global Christian Fundamentalism*. New York and London: Routledge.

Cleary, Edward L. and Stewart-Gambino, Hannah W. (eds.) (1997). *Power, Politics and Pentecostals in Latin America*. Boulder, CO: Westview Press.

Cox, Harvey (1996). *Fire from Heaven: The Rise of Pentecostal Spirituality and the Reshaping of Religion in the Twenty-First Century*. London: Cassell.

Daneel, Inus (1987). *Quest for Belonging*. Gweru, Zimbabwe: Mambo Press.

EATWOT (1998). Fourth General Assembly Final Statement, Search for a New Just World Order: Challenges to Theology. *Ministerial Formation* 81 (April): 27–36.

Gifford, Paul (1993). *Christianity and Politics in Doe's Liberia*. Cambridge, UK: Cambridge University Press.

Gifford, Paul (1998). *African Christianity: Its Public Role*. London: Hurst.

Hwa Yung (1995). Critical Issues Facing Theological Education in Asia. *Transformation* October–December: 1–6.

Johnstone, Patrick (1993). *Operation World*. Carlisle, UK: OM Publishing.

Johnstone, Patrick and Mandryk, Jason (2001). *Operation World: 21st Century Edition*. Carlisle, UK: Paternoster.

Kalu, Ogbu U. (1998). The Third Response: Pentecostalism and the Reconstruction of Christian Experience in Africa, 1970–1995. *Journal of African Christian Thought* 1, 2: 3–16.

Martin, David (1990). *Tongues of Fire: The Explosion of Protestantism in Latin America*. Oxford: Blackwell.

Martin, David (1994). Evangelical and Charismatic Christianity in Latin America. In Karla Poewe (ed.), *Charismatic Christianity as a Global Culture*. Columbia: University of South Carolina Press, pp. 73–86.

Maxwell, David (1995). Witches, Prophets and Avenging Spirits: The Second Christian Movement in North-East Zimbabwe. *Journal of Religion in Africa* 25, 3: 309–39.

Moreau, A. Scott (ed.) (2000). *Evangelical Dictionary of World Missions*. Grand Rapids, MI: Baker Books and Carlisle, UK: Paternoster Press.

Pate, Larry D. (1991). The Dramatic Growth of Two-Thirds World Missions. In William D. Taylor (ed.), *Internationalising Missionary Training*. Exeter: The Paternoster Press, pp. 27–40.

Robert, Dana (2000). Shifting Southward: Global Christianity since 1945. *International Bulletin of Missionary Research* 24, 2: 50–8.

Satyavrata, Ivan M. (1999). Contextual Perspectives on Pentecostalism as a Global Culture: A South Asian View. In M. W. Dempster, B. D. Klaus, and D. Petersen (eds.), *The Globalization of Pentecostalism: A Religion Made to Travel*. Oxford: Regnum, pp. 203–21.

Stoll, David (1990). *Is Latin America Turning Protestant? The Politics of Evangelical Growth*. Berkeley: University of California Press.

Sugirtharajah, R. S. (ed.) (1995). *Voices from the Margin: Interpreting the Bible in the Third World*. Maryknoll, NY: Orbis and London: SPCK.

Walls, Andrew F. (2000). Of Ivory Towers and Ashrams: Some Reflections on Theological Scholarship in Africa. *Journal of African Christian Thought* 3, 1: 1–4.

Wilson, Everett A. (1997). *Strategy of the Spirit: J Philip Hogan and the Growth of the Assemblies of God Worldwide 1960–1990*. Carlisle, UK: Regnum.

Index

Note: Page references in **bold** type indicate main references to major topics.

Aagaard, Johannes 142
Aberhart, Bill 351, 354 n.15
abortion 105–6, 290, 294, 304, 352
Abrams, Minnie 445
Act of Union (1707) 112
Act of Union (1800) 126
affaire des placards 54
Africa **239–47**, 474–6
   and Americanization 478–80
   balkanization 242
   denominationalism 240–1
   and evangelicalism 432–3, 435
   messianic movements 245–6
   and missions 240–3, 246–7
   and Pentecostalism 246, 440, 445–6,
      474–6
   post-Independence 243
   prophetic movements 245
   religious pluralism 239–40
   spirituality 389
   theologies 244–5
African Americans 170–1, 178, 293,
     304, 388
   and evangelicalism 430
   and Pentecostalism 176
   see also race and racism
African Initiated Churches (AIC) 245–7,
     423, 440–1, 470, 474–6, 480
African Methodist Episcopal Church
   (AME) 170

African Methodist Episcopal Zion Church
   (AMEZ) 170–1
Agassiz, Jean-Louis Rodolphe 363
Agricola, Mikael 132
Ainslie, Peter 407
Aladura churches 245, 423, 440, 475
Albrecht, Archbishop of Mainz 43
Alexander, Archibald 262
All Africa Conference of Churches 246,
     478
All-Union Council of Evangelical
     Christian-Baptists 159
Allen, Horace 216
Allen, Richard 170–1
Allen, Young J. 229
Alline, Henry 193
Alves, Rubem 476
American Baptist Convention 176, 367
American Board of Commissioners for
     Foreign Missions 202, 210, 225,
     417, 430
Amish 167, 290
Anabaptists 147–8, 155, 431
   and Calvin 13, 54
   and the Eucharist 12
   and separatism 3, 300, 385
   and spirituality 385
ancestor worship 228, 441
Andraea, James, and *Book of Concord* 15
Andrews, C. F. 204

Andrewes, Lancelot 385
Anglicanism
  in Africa 240, 242, 245, 468
  in Australia and New Zealand 232–4,
    235–6
  in Canada 189–93, 195, 196
  in China 224, 225
  as classical Protestant denomination 4
  and ecumenism 144, 146, 407, 411,
    413
  High Church 427
  in India 204
  in Korea 216
  and mission see Church Missionary
    Society
  in South-East Asia 207
  in United States 167, 169
  in Wales 120–2
  see also Church of England
Anglo-Catholicism 105, 194, 233, 386
Angus, Samuel 236
Anselm of Canterbury 26, 37, 80
anthropology
  in Barth 92
  in liberal Protestantism 9, 86, 88, 317
  Reformation 301, 332–3, 396
antisemitism see Judaism
apartheid 64, 246, 287, 293, 389, 471
Appasamy, A. J. 204
Aquinas, St Thomas 42, 59
  and images 271
  and Schleiermacher 80–1
Aristotle 25, 44, 60, 81, 309, 311
Arminianism 102, 125
Arminius, Jacob 102, 149
Arndt, Johann 133
Arnold, Thomas 327
Arnott, John 449
Aroolappen, John Christian 445, 473
arts 268–83
  and aesthetic gaze 282–3
  in late medieval thought 270–3
  and literature 279
  post-Reformation 278–81
  and Reformation iconoclasm 268,
    273–8, 281
  see also music
Asbury, Francis 170, 430
Asia 471–3
  evangelicalism 432–3, 478

Pentecostalism 439–40, 445–6,
    471–2
  spirituality 389–90
  see also South-East Asia
Assemblies of God 4, 469
  in Africa 475
  in Brazil 445
  and ecumenism 447
  in Korea 218
  and mission 176
  origins 176, 444
  and televangelism 178
Associated Churches in Japan
    (Nihon Kumiai Kyokai) 210
assurance 140, 257, 386, 428
astronomy 62, 307–8, 309
atonement
  disputes over 235
  subjective/objective 136, 140
  substitutionary 211, 422
Auburn Declaration (1924) 175
Augsburg Confession (1530) 6, 14–16,
    46, 258
  and historical particularity 16
  as normative 15–16
  as witness 15–16
  and Zwingli 28
Augsburg, Diet of (1530) 46
Augustine of Hippo, St
  and grace 253
  and Luther 8, 42, 44, 50
  and philosophy 80
  and predestination 8, 360
Australia and New Zealand 232–8
  conservatism 234, 236
  denominational diversity 232–3,
    238
  evangelicalism 232, 233, 235–6, 432,
    434
  indigenous peoples 235
  liberalism 234–5, 236
  social change 236–7
authority of the Bible 122, 131, 234,
    309
  in evangelicalism 422, 429
  in fundamentalism 317, 345
  and liberal theology 262
  in Luther and Lutheranism 5, 17, 48,
    51, 254–5
  in Reformed thought 6

Authorized Version of the Bible *see* King James (Authorized) Bible
Ayandele, E. A. 242–3
Azariah, V. S. 204, 407, 422
Azusa Street Revival 175, 388, 423, 443–4, 445

Bach, J. S. 280
Badiou, Alain 461
Baeta, Christian G. 244
Bakker, Jim and Tammy 178, 447
Ballagh, James H. 210
Ballou, Adin 288
Balthasar, Hans Urs von 464 n.3
Banerjea, Krishna Mohan 202
baptism
    in Holy Spirit 175–6, 388, 423, 442, 443–4, 445, 446–7
    of infants 2, 26, 101, 102, 149, 385
    Luther 44, 384
    Zwingli 26
Baptist Bible Union 347–8, 349
Baptist Missionary Society (BMS) 201–2, 240, 396, 430
Baptists
    in Australia and New Zealand 233
    Calvinist v. Arminian 102
    in Canada 189–90, 191
    in China 225
    and church government 57, 115
    in Eastern Europe 155, 157, 158–9
    in England 101, 102
    and Haldane movement 115–16
    in India 202, 204, 430, 473
    in Ireland 124
    in Italy 163
    in Korea 216
    in Nordic countries 142, 146
    in Scotland 115–16
    in United States 3, 4, 169, 302–3, 347–8, 424
    in Wales 120, 121
    see also American Baptist Convention; Northern Baptist Convention; Southern Baptist Convention
Barbour, Ian G. 319
Barmen Declaration (1934) 86
Barrett, David 432–3, 439, 440, 469–70

Barth, Karl **83–94**
    and the Bible 85, 87–8, 91, 264
    and Calvin 64, 89
    Christian Dogmatics 86
    and Christology 9, 92
    and the church 89, 94
    Church Dogmatics 83, 84, 86–7, 89, 90–3
    and "Dialectical Theology" 84, 85, 87, 141
    earlier work 84, 87–90
    The Epistle to the Romans 85, 87–8
    and ethics 86, 89, 92
    Ethics 89
    and faith and reason 37
    The Göttingen Dogmatics 85
    influence 122, 142, 212, 213
    life 84–7
    and political theology 86
    Protestant Theology in the Nineteenth Century 78, 88
    on Schleiermacher 67, 78–80, 85, 88
    and science and religion 316, 320
    The Theology of Schleiermacher 88
    and Word of God 79, 89, 90–1, 264
    see also liberalism
Basel Mission 140, 202, 227, 241, 242
Bashkin, Matthew 156
Bauman, Zygmunt 461, 464
Baxter, Richard 64
Bea, Augustin 411
beauty of God, in Jonathan Edwards 183–4, 387
Bebbington, David 422
Beecher, Henry Ward 172
Beecher, Lyman 169–70
Belgic Confession (1561) 27, 62
Bennett, Dennis 446–7
Berger, Carl 198 n.5
Bergreav, Bishop 142
Berlin, Isaiah 394–5
Bernard of Clairvaux 41, 42
Beyerhaus, Peter 418
Bèze (Beza), Théodore de 55, 62, 394
Bible **251–66**
    canon 68–9
    and the church 23
    and commentaries 57
    content and purpose 252–4
    and feminism 335, 337

Bible (*cont.*)
  inerrancy: and American
    evangelicalism 303; and
    fundamentalism 175, 195, 317,
    345–6, 350, 352, 422–3; and
    historical criticism 262, 264; and
    Protestant scholasticism 57, 264,
    309; in Scotland 117
  as inspired 117, 150, 195, 257, 261,
    309, 429
  and reason 30
  and spirituality 382, 390
  and tradition 23–8, 31, 138–9
  as Word of God 253–4, 257, 261–2,
    264
  see also authority of the Bible; Barth,
    Karl; Calvin, John; criticism;
    hermeneutics; literalism, biblical;
    Luther, Martin; *sola scriptura*
    principle
Bible translations 279, 334–5, 382,
    393, 398
  Chinese 222
  English 58, 96–7, 98, 100, 101, 106
  in India 201–2
  and Luther 46, 50, 97, 167
  in Nordic countries 131–2, 134, 143,
    145
  in South-East Asia 207
  Welsh 120
Biel, Gabriel 40, 42, 43
Billing, Einar 144
Biró, Matthias Dévai 156
Bittlinger, Arnold 448
Bjørnson, Bjørnstjerne 139
Blaisdell, Charmarie Jenkins 334
Bliss, Kathleen 409
Blix, Elias 139, 143
Blumhardt, Christoph Friedrich 292
Boesak, Allan 244
Bogue, David 116
Bohemia 157
Bolsec, Jerome, and predestination 27,
    62
Bonaventura, St 271–2, 275, 276
Bonhoeffer, Dietrich 387
Bonino, José Míguez 476–7
Book of Common Prayer 98, 99, 100,
    120, 385

Book of Concord (1580) 15, 16
Book of Confessions 339
Bovell, James 195
Bowie, Andrew 75
Boyle, Nicholas 464 n.10
Boyle, Robert 311
Brazil
  and evangelicalism 433
  and Pentecostalism 439, 445,
    476
Bredesen, Harold 447
Brent, Charles 407
Bridgman, Elijah C. 224
British and Foreign Bible Society 104,
    157
Brochmand, Jesper 133
Brooke, John Hedley 306
Brooks, Phillips 172
Brorson, Hans Adof 135
Brouwer, Steve 479
Brovallius, Johan 137
Brown, William Adams 328
Brunner, Emil, and "Dialectical Theology"
    85
Brunvoll, Arve 143
Bryan, William Jennings 175, 303, 317,
    347, 348
Bucer, Martin 10, 46, 54, 98
Buchman, Frank 177
Budé, Guillaume 53
Bugenhagen, Johannes 14, 131
Bullinger, Johann Heinrich 27, 373
Bultmann, Rudolph 36–7, 316
  and Barth 85, 86
Bunyan, John 269–70, 385, 396, 426,
    458
Buren, Paul M. van 379
Burton, John 190
Bushnell, Horace 172, 328
Businessman's Revival 171–2, 176
Buthelezi, Manas 244

Cajetan, Thomas de Vio 43, 47
Calvin, John **53–64**, 161
  and Anabaptists 13, 54
  and Barth 64, 89
  and the Bible 57–8, 253, 256, 264,
    309, 334–5
  and biblical theology 58

and the church 12–14, 56–7, 60
and church and state 2, 13, 161
Commentary on Genesis 308
and confessions of faith 54, 62
Ecclesiastical Ordinances 57
and Eucharist 9, 10, 12, 27, 28, 54
and the Holy Spirit 27
and humanism 45, 53, 279
and images and art 276–8
influence 55–64, 161
Institutes of the Christian Religion 2, 5,
    28, 54, 58–61, 62–4, 276, 334–5
and law and gospel 9–10
Little Treatise of the Lord's Supper 54
and Luther 53
and natural theology 61–2
and preaching 58
priesthood of all believers 13–14
and science 62, 64, 308, 313
and spirituality 384–5
and women 333
see also Calvinism; Christology;
    Judaism; justification by faith;
    predestination
Calvinism
and political thought 289
spread 55, 56–7
see also Reformed thought
Cambridge Platform (1649) 166
Cameron, Peter 236
Cameroon 241
Camille, Michael 272
camp meetings 169, 442
Campbell, Alexander 169
Campus Crusade for Christ 425
Canada **189–97**
conformity v. nonconformity 191–3
as cultural mosaic 189–91, 196–7
evangelicalism 192–3, 194–6, 429,
    432–3, 434
fundamentalism 195–6, 344, 348,
    349, 351–2, 353 n.3
indigenous peoples 196, 198 n.7
mission 194
modernity 194–6, 432
Candidius, George 395
Cannon, Katie Geneva 244–5, 338
capitalism 2, 64, 234, 287, 290–2, 454
Caputo, John D. 459, 462

Carey, William 201–2, 396, 430
Carnegie, Andrew 172
Carpenter, Joel 345
Carroll, Charles 364
Castells, Manuel 464
Castro, Emilio 476
Catherine of Aragon 97, 98
Cauvin, Gérard 53
Certeau, Michel de 457, 461
Chadwick, Owen 460
Chakkarai, V. 204
Chang Ding 227
Channing, William Ellery 171
charismatic movement: in Africa 246,
    474
in Asia 471–2
in Australia and New Zealand 236
growth 1, 105, 388, 469
in Korea 217, 218, 445, 472
and mainline denominations 4,
    107–8, 122, 423, 447–9, 469
in the West 163, 445–6, 448
Charles I of Britain and Ireland 101–2,
    111
Charles II of Britain and Ireland 103,
    111, 125
Charles V, Emperor
and Dutch Revolt 147
and Henry VIII 97
and Luther 14, 43, 48
Chauncy, Charles 168–9
Chemnitz, Martin, and *Book of Concord*
    15
Chen Dao Ren 224
Chen Mengnan 224
Chenchiah, P. 204
Cheng Jianye 225
Childs, Brevard 265
Chillingworth, William 57
China **222–30**, 424
future propects 228–30
indigenous Christianity 222–8, 230,
    440–1
origins of Protestantism 222–6, 399
Pentecostalism 440, 445, 472–3
social reform 228–9
spirituality 389
China Inland Mission 229
Cho Yong–gi 218, 445, 472

Christenson, Larry 447
Christian III of Denmark 131
Christian Brethren, in Scotland 116–17
Christian Church (Disciples of Christ)
    169, 176, 204, 294
Christian Coalition (US) 177, 178, 290,
    304, 351
Christian and Missionary Alliance (US)
    431, 442
Christian Socialism 105, 292
Christo Samaj 204
Christology
    in Barth 9, 92
    in Calvin 2, 6–7, 8–9, 10, 49, 278,
        334
    and Eucharist 8, 11–12
    exegetical 6–7
    in Luther 2, 6–7, 8, 9–12, 48–50, 372
    in Schleiermacher 78–9, 88
Chung Hyun Kyung 338
church
    in Barth 89, 94
    as continually reforming 17, 51, 333
    as visible and invisible 12–13, 96
    as witness 12–13, 299, 414–15, 416
    see also Calvin, John; church and
        society; church and state; Luther,
        Martin
Church of England
    and Anglo-Catholicism 105
    and Broad Church 326–7
    and Civil War 101–2
    contemporary 107
    and Elizabethan Settlement 99–100
    and evangelicals 103, 104–5, 106,
        386, 431
    and Henry VIII 97–8
    and liberalism 326
    and mission 396
    and Puritans 100–1, 385, 425
    restoration 103
    revival 104–5
    and spirituality 385, 386
    see also Anglicanism; Book of Common
        Prayer; Thirty-Nine Articles
Church of God (US) 176, 442
Church of God in Christ (US) 176
church government 299, 408
    and Baptists 57, 115
    and Calvin 57

congregational 218
episcopacy 111, 124, 132, 142, 144
    in Nordic countries 132, 141–2,
        144
    and Presbyterianism 57, 102, 111,
        112
    and Puritanism 166
church history, in Schleiermacher 69
Church of Ireland 123–5, 126, 127–8
Church of Jesus Christ of Latter Day
    Saints (Mormons) 171
Church of the Lord (Aladura) 245, 423,
    440, 475
Church Missionary Society (CMS) 202,
    211, 232, 240–2, 396, 417, 430
Church of the Nazarene (US) 156, 431,
    442
Church of North India (CNI) 204,
    412–13
Church of Scotland 111–12
    divisions 112–14, 117, 125, 412
    and Irish Catholics 118
    and revival 114
church and society 287–95, 301
Church of South India (CSI) 204,
    412–13, 473
church and state
    in Africa 243
    in Australia and New Zealand 232–3
    in Canada 191–3, 194
    in Eastern Europe 159, 160
    in England 96–104, 105, 426
    in Germany 324–5
    in Ireland 123–6, 127
    in Japan 212–13
    and magisterial Reformation 13, 17,
        289, 299–300
    in Netherlands 148–9, 150–2
    in Nordic countries 130–2, 133, 135,
        138–40, 142, 144–5
    and Radical Reformation 2–3
    and Schleiermacher 67, 324
    in Scotland 111, 117, 406, 426
    in United States 166, 169, 328
    in Wales 121
    see also Calvin, John; Luther, Martin
Church in Wales 121
churches, independent 448–9, 470
Churches of Christ, in Australia and New
    Zealand 233, 235

civil rights movement (US) 178, 293, 304, 351, 359, 366–7
Civil War, English 101–3
clergy
  celibacy 98
  education 98, 100, 109, 132, 251–2
  marriage 44, 98
  and politics 50
Coleridge, Samuel Taylor 326–7, 328
Colet, John 96
colonialism 3, 470
  and missions 201–2, 241–3, 392, 395, 396, 398, 399, 474
commentaries, biblical 57
Commission on World Mission and Evangelism 417
communicatio idiomatum 11
compatibilism, in Jonathan Edwards 184
Confessing Church (Germany) 86
Confucianism, and Christianity 223, 227–8
Congar, Yves 409, 411, 464 n.3
Congregationalism
  in Australia and New Zealand 233, 235
  in Canada 189–90, 191–2
  in China 225
  in Eastern Europe 156
  in England 102–3
  in India 204
  in United States 169
Connelly, William 461
conscience see freedom of religion
consciousness
  in Kant 72, 314
  in Schleiermacher 33, 73–4, 78–9, 81, 85, 315
conservatism, religious see fundamentalism; traditionalism
conservatism, social 105, 423
Constance, Council of (1415) 43
consubstantiation, in Luther 11
contract theory 289, 301, 454
conversion
  in Jonathan Edwards 168, 186–7
  and evangelicalism 126, 303, 422, 426, 429
  and fundamentalism 345
  and Holiness Movement 442
  and Pietism 158

and Puritanism 165, 186
and revivalism 168, 169, 171
Cooper, Samuel 169
Cop, Nicholas 54
Copeland, Kenneth 448–9
Copernicus, Nicholas 307–8, 309, 311
Corrymeela Community 128
Cotton, John 166
Counter-Reformation 156–7, 308
Couturier, Paul 411
covenant
  and baptism 26
  in Barth 37, 89, 92
  in Calvin 7–8, 10, 373–4
  in Luther 40
  in Puritanism 165, 166, 360–1
  and social contract 289, 301, 454
Covenanters, Scottish 111–12
Cox, Harvey 446, 469–70, 472, 475
Cranach, Lucas "the Elder" 280, 281
Cranmer, Thomas, Archbishop of Canterbury 97, 98–9, 299, 385
Cranston, Maurice 322
creation
  in Barth 92
  in Calvin 61–2
  as contingent 306, 312
  continuous 318
  in Jonathan Edwards 183
  and Puritanism 360
creationism 175, 317, 352, 431
criticism, historical 195, 251–2, 253, 327
  and Barth 87, 264
  and biblical literalism 256, 259
  conservative approaches 261–2
  and Enlightenment 24, 259, 265–6, 323
  and fundamentalism 175, 345, 347
  and history of religions school 260–1, 263
  origins 258–9
  and Presbyterianism 117
  and reason 24, 34
  and Schleiermacher 68–9, 77–8
  and search for the historical Jesus 260
  source criticism 259–60, 265
  and Spinoza 259
Croatia 157
Cromwell, Oliver 102–3, 124, 395

Cromwell, Thomas 97, 98, 110
cross 422
  in Luther 41, 43, 47, 51, 384
Crouch, Paul 447
Crowther, Samuel Ajayi 242, 421
culture, and Protestantism xiv, 2–3,
  107–8, 424
Cunningham, Conor 464 n.3
Cupitt, Don 459

Daly, Mary 338
Daneel, Inus 479
Daniel, J. E. 122
Darby, J. N. 258, 346, 443
Darwin, Charles, *Origin of Species* 105,
  194–5, 316–17, 348
Dass, Peter 133
Datta, S. K. 204
Davies, Richard, Bishop of St David's 120
Davies, Samuel 429, 430
Day, Lal Behari 202
Dayton, Donald 354 n.13
Deane-Drummond, Celia 319
"death of God" theology 459
Defenders of the Christian Faith (US)
  177
Defoe, Daniel 396–7
deism 310, 326
democracy 2, 211, 289–90, 295, 301–2
Denmark
  Church Ordinance 131, 132
  Conventicle Act 135, 136, 138, 139,
    140
  and ecumenism 142
  and liberalism 141
  Lutheranism 130, 131, 132–3, 135,
    138, 386
  pietism and Enlightenment 135,
    137–8
denominations
  African-American 170–1, 176
  charismatic and Pentecostal 4–5
  classical *see* Anglicanism; Lutheranism;
    Reformed thought
  evangelical 4
  growth in number 1, 399, 423–4,
    458, 472, 478–9
  and Radical Reformation *see* Baptists;
    Mennonites

Western decline 1, 107, 471
  see also ecumenism
Dentière, Marie 335
dependence, in Schleiermacher 33,
  73–4, 375
Derrida, Jacques 460–1, 462, 464 n.7,
  465 n.13
Descartes, René 30, 134
Devanandan, P. D. 204
dialectic, in Schleiermacher 76
Dickson, Kwesi A. 244
Dike, K. N. 242
Dillenberger, John 312, 315
Dippel, Joseph Konrad 136–7, 140
direction, spiritual 383, 388
Disciples of Christ 169, 176, 204,
  294
dispensationalism 345–6, 347, 350,
  352, 430, 443
dissent
  in England 102–3, 104, 455
  in Ireland 124–5, 126
  in North America 192
diversity 1–2, 3–5, 294–5, 390, 458,
  477–8
  and Schleiermacher 68
Dixon, A. C. 346
doctrine
  in Barth 83, 88–9, 90–3
  and Bible as authoritative 5, 6, 17, 48,
    131, 234, 254–5
  and individual conscience 14
  in Schleiermacher 69–70, 74
Dodd, C. H. 409
Dohi Akio 214
Donne, John 385
Dort (Dordrecht), Synod of (1619) 149,
  281
Douglass, Frederic 170
Douglass, Jane Dempsey 335
Du Plessis, David 447
dualism 16, 325
Duff, Alexander 202
Dukhobors 158
Dulles, John Foster 177
Dunkers 167
Duns Scotus, Johannes 42, 459
Durandus, William 271
Dürer, Albrecht 281

Dutch Reformed Church (South Africa)
240, 389
Dwight, Timothy 169

Eastern Europe **155–60**
Protestantism and Catholicism 155–6
Protestantism and Orthodoxy 157–9
Ebina Danjo 211, 212
Eck, Johann 43, 47, 373
ecology, and spirituality 388
economics **290–3**, 295, 329, *see also*
capitalism
ecumenism **405–19**
in Africa 245, 246
in Australia and New Zealand 235–6
and Barth 86
in Canada 194
and church unions 196, 204, 225,
412–13, 419, 473
and councils of churches 416
and dialogue 410–12, 413–14, 418,
419, 463
in England 107
and interfaith dialogue 142, 143, 417
in Ireland 128, 129
methodology 408–10
and mission 225, 246, 399, 405–7,
412, 416–17
in Nordic countries 134, 141, 142,
144, 145–6
and Protestant identity 418–19, 429,
477, 478–9
and sociopolitical activity 414–15
in United States 177
see also Faith and Order movement; Life
and Work Movement; World Council
of Churches
education 234
and liberalism 326–7
and mission 207, 229, 396–7, 398
and state 150–1, 152, 300
education, theological 478
and Calvin 56
by extension (TEE) 477
and Schleiermacher 67–71, 81
Edward VI of England 98
Edwards, D. Miall 122
Edwards, Jonathan 168, **181–8**
Dissertation Concerning the End 183

The Distinguishing Marks 168, 186
Freedom of the Will 168, 182, 184,
187
life 182
The Narrative of Surprising Conversions
186
Original Sin 168, 182, 184
and revivalism 114
significance 64, 181–2, 187–8,
427–8, 442
Some Thoughts Concerning the Revival
186
theology 182–7, 368
Treatise on Religious Affections 168,
185, 186–7, 387
True Virtue 182
Edwards, Lewis 121
Egede, Hans 136
Ekman, Ulf 144
election *see* predestination
Elias, John 121
Eliot, John 395
Elizabeth I of England 55, 99–101, 120
Ellingsen, Svein 143
Ellus, Jacques 162
Emerson, Ralph Waldo 172
Engelbrektsdatter, Dorothe 133
Engelbrektsson, Olav 131
England **96–108**
and the Bible 101
and Civil War 101–3
contemporary 106–8
divisions 102–3
and Elizabethan Settlement 99–101
and English Reformation 98–9, 106
and evangelicalism 103–4, 202, 384,
427–9, 431–2
and influence of Calvinism 55, 98
and liberalism 326–8
origins of Protestantism 96–8
and pluralism and secularization
104–6
and social reforms 104, 105
Enlightenment
and historical criticism 24, 259,
265–6
and liberalism 7, 122, 139, 323–4,
326
and mission 396–8

Enlightenment (*cont.*)
  in Nordic countries 135–7, 139
  in North America 168, 185, 187–8,
    192, 195
  and skepticism 103
  and sociopolitical thought 104, 287,
    289
  and spirituality 385, 386
episcopacy
  in England *see* Church of England
  in Ireland 123–4, 126
  in Nordic countries 132
  in Scotland 111–12
Episcopal Church of the USA 169, 171,
    176, 179, 211, 294, 367, 446–7
epistemology, and modernity 458
Erasmus, Desiderius
  and the arts 268
  A Discourse Concerning Free Choice 45
  and humanism 96, 253
  Institutio principis Christiani 59
  and predestination 8
Erastianism 111, 148
Erfurt, as humanist center 40
Erskine, Ebenezer 112–13
eschatology
  and Pentecostalism 442, 443
  and two-kingdom theology 16
  see also Kingdom of God
ethics
  in Barth 86, 89–90, 92
  and free will 184–5
  in Schleiermacher 69, 70–1
Ethiopianism 242–3, 475
Eucharist
  in both kinds 44
  and Christology 8, 11–12
  and confessions of faith 28
  and consubstantiation 11
  and memorialism 10, 12
  see also Calvin, John; Luther, Martin;
    Melanchthon, Philip; Real Presence;
    transubstantiation; Zwingli, Uldrich
Evangelical Alliance 364, 406, 429
Evangelical Fellowship of Canada 432
Evangelical Lutheran Church in America
    176, 179, 373, 421
Evangelical Union (Scotland) 114–15
evangelicalism **421–35**
  and the Bible 4, 17, 422–3, 429

  definition 421–6
  and denominations 4
  and ecumenism 417–18, 429, 447
  and evolution and creationism 177,
    317
  future prospects 433–5
  history 426–33
  and law 302–3
  and mission 425, 429, 434
  and origins of Protestantism 2, 53–4
  and scholarship 105, 236, 431–2
  and science and theology 320
  and voluntary organizations 170,
    193, 303, 427, 434, 435
  see also Australia and New Zealand;
    Canada; charismatic movement;
    England; fundamentalism; Ireland;
    Korea; Netherlands; Pentecostalism;
    Pietism; revivalism; Scotland;
    United States; Wales
Evangeliska Fosterlandstiftelsen 140
Evans, Christmas 121
evolution 64, 105, 175, 316–17, 347,
    348–9, 352
  and evangelicalism 177, 317
  and racism 364
experience 126, 263, 397, 441
  and justification 137
  and reason 314
  in Schleiermacher 33, 73

faith
  in Bultmann 36–7
  and emotion 186
  and justification 5, 6–8, 36, 41, 166
  and Pietism 29–30
  practical 32
  and reason 29, 30–6, 37, 314–15
  in Ritschl 35
  in Schleiermacher 73
  and verification 31–2
Faith and Order movement 407–10,
    412, 413, 415, 419
Falwell, Jerry 178, 290, 351
Farel, Guillaume 54
feeling, in Schleiermacher 24, 32, 33–5,
    72–4, 76, 88, 375, 386
feminism 196, 236, 244–5, **332–40**
  contemporary 338–9
  future prospects 339–40

Latina 338
and racism 359
and Reformation 332–5
and suffrage movement 336–7
Fenn, Eric 409
Feuerbach, Ludwig 34, 35, 37, 282
Fichte, Johan Gottlieb 67, 73, 254
Finland
and church architecture 145
and ecumenism 145–6
and Lutheran orthodoxy 134
and pietism and Enlightenment 137, 140
Reformation 132
and revivalism 137, 140–1, 145
Finn, Daniel 296 n.5
Finney, Charles Grandison 170, 421, 442
Fjellstedt, Peter 140
Fletcher, John 442
forgiveness, and Eucharist 11–12
Formula of Agreement (US) (1997–8) 413
Formula of Concord (1578) 4, 6, 10, 15, 28, 134
Forsyth, P. T. 212, 273, 284 n.16
Foucault, Michel 458, 461, 462
Foursquare Gospel Church (US) 176
Fox, George 385, 458
France 161–2
and Calvinism 55, 56–7, 161
and Lutheranism 53–4, 161
Francke, August H. 29, 30, 427
Frank, Manfred 75
Frankenhausen, battle of (1525) 45
Franklin, Benjamin 168
Fredrik IV of Denmark 135, 201
Free Church of Scotland 117–18
Free Presbyterian Church (Ireland) 128
Free Presbyterian Church (Scotland) 117
free will
in Jonathan Edwards 184–5
in Erasmus 45
in Luther 45, 322
in Melanchthon 25
in Spinoza 72
freedom of God
in Barth 37, 89, 92
in Calvin 63
and justification 7, 9
in Zwingli 46

freedom of religion 14, 17, 300
in Australia and New Zealand 234
in Nordic countries 135, 137, 138, 139, 145
in North America 166, 169, 191–2, 302–3, 304
in South-East Asia 208
Frei, Hans 264–5
Frelinghuysen, Theodore 168
French Confession (1559) 27
Fukuyama, Francis 456
Full Gospel Businessmen's Fellowship International 448
Fuller, Charles 349
fundamentalism 295, **344–53**, 431
in Africa 240
in Canada 195–6, 344, 348, 349, 351–2, 353 n.3
definition 344–6, 422–3
denominations 349
division 350
and evolution and creationism 105, 175, 177, 317, 347, 348–9, 352, 431
in Ireland 126, 127–8, 129
in Latin America 477
and liberalism 346–7, 422
and missions 228, 344, 350, 352
politicized 290, 350–3
and postmodernity 463–4
The Fundamentals 10, 175, 346–7
Furuya Yasuo 213

Gadamer, Hans-Georg 75
Galileo Galilei 309–10, 311
Garborg, Arne 139
Garrison, William Lloyd 170
Geering, Lloyd 236
Gejer, E. G. 139
Geneva
and Calvin 53–5, 57–8, 161, 385
and iconoclasm 276–7
and influence on Reformation 5, 55, 56, 100, 110, 149
St Peter's Cathedral 58
Geneva Bible 58, 100
Geneva Confession (1536) 6
George, David 190, 392, 430
George, Duke of Saxony 50
Gerhard, Paul 133

German Christians 378
German Protestantism **23–37**
  and Bible and tradition 23–8
  Church Crisis of 1930s 16, 86
  and critique of confessional orthodoxy
    24, 29–31
  and development of confessional
    orthodoxy 24, 27–8
  and liberalism 324–6
  in modern world 36–7
  and reason and revelation 31–6
  see also Barth, Karl; Calvin, John;
    Luther, Martin; Schleiermacher,
    F. D. E.
Gezelius the Younger 137
Ghana 240–2, 243, 246, 445, 474–5
Gibson, James Campbell 224
Giertz, Bo 144
Gifford, Paul 476, 479
gifts of the Spirit 106, 175–6, 423,
  440–1, 442, 443, 449–50
Gilkey, Langdon 316
Gladden, Washington 173, 328
Glencree Reconciliation Centre 128
globalization, and Americanization of
    Christianity 478–80
glory of God, in Jonathan Edwards
    183–4, 387
glossolalia 175, 423, 441, 443–4,
  446–7, 458
Gomarus, Franciscus 149
Goodall, Norman 414
Goodman, Ellen 358
Gordon, Dorcas 199 n.15
Goreh, Nehemiah 202–3
Gorringe, Tim 281
gospel, and law *see* law and gospel
grace
  in Barth 89
  in Calvin 7–8, 27, 62, 89
  "cheap" 43, 387
  in Luther 7, 36, 40–2, 43, 45, 50
  and nature 457–8, 464 n.3
  and sacraments 26, 27
  and salvation 7, 8, 36, 41, 253,
    295
  in Zwingli 26
Graf, Karl Heinrich 260, 265
Graham, Billy 388, 422

and evangelical ecumenism 236, 418,
  425, 435
and fundamentalism 175, 349–50
and revivalism 177–8
Grane, Leif 142
Grant, George P. 197
Gray, John 456, 459
Great Awakening
  First 168, 169, 182, 185–6, 302, 390
  Second 169–70, 302
Greaves, Richard L. 335–6, 340 n.7
Green, T. H. 327
Gregg, John, Archbishop of Armagh
    127
Gregory of Rimini, and predestination 63
Grimke, Sarah and Angelina 170, 336–7
Gruchy, John de 244, 270, 274, 278
Grumbach, Argula von 335
Grundtvig, N. F. S. 138–9, 140, 141
Gunnerus, Johan Ernst 136
Gustav I Vasa of Sweden 131, 132
Gutzlaff, Charles 224

Habermas, Jurgen 457, 464 n.1
Hagin, Kenneth 448
Haldane, James and Robert 115
Hall, Douglas John 197
Hallesby, Ole 142
Hamilton, Patrick 110
Haraway, Donna 459
Hare, Julius 327
Harnack, Adolf von 84–5, 144, 325,
    375–7
Harper, Michael 448
Harris, Harriet 350
Harris, Howell 121, 427
Harris, William Wade 445
Hart, Joseph 428–9
Harvard College 56
Haselden, Kyle 369
Hauge, Hans Nielsen 139, 140
healing *see* gifts of the Spirit
Hedberg, F. G. 141
Hedenius, Ingemar 144
Hefner, Philip 319
Hegel, G. W. F. 67, 254, 386, 399, 458
  and consciousness 73
  and knowledge of God 32–3, 37,
    73–4, 282

and speculative reason 31, 32–3, 34,
    35
Hegelianism, in Denmark 138
Heidegger, Martin 37, 254
Heidelberg Catechism 28, 148
Heidelberg Disputation (1518) 47
Heidelberg University 28, 56, 149
Helgason, Jon 143
Henry IV of France 454
Henry VIII of England 97–8, 120, 123
Henry, Carl F. H. 425
Herbert, George 385
hermeneutics
    in Barth 87–8, 264
    and Bible as own interpreter 256
    in Calvin 6–7, 308
    canonical 265
    conservative 261–2, 431
    and ecumenism 409
    and feminism 335
    liberal 262–4
    in Luther 6–7, 48, 307–8
    narrative 264–5
    postcritical 264–5
    and *Quadriga* 255
    in Schleiermacher 69, 75–8, 80,
        263
Herrmann, Wilhelm 36, 37, 85, 325
Herrnhuter movement 155, 158, 240
Hiraethog, Gwilym 121
history
    and divine intervention 3
    and Lessing 31
    and liberalism 327, 328
Ho Tsun Sheen 223
Hobbes, Thomas 289, 454
Hobhouse, L. T. 327
Hobson, J. A. 327
Hodge, A. A. 345
Hodge, Charles 175, 262, 345
Hoffman, Melchior 147
Holbein, Hans "the Younger" 268, 281
Holberg, Ludvig 135
Holiness movement 176, 388, 421, 431,
    441–4
Hollenweger, Walter 446
Holy Spirit
    in Barth 79, 91, 94
    in Calvin 27

in evangelicalism 429
in Schleiermacher 74, 79
in Zwingli 25–6
see also Pentecostalism
homosexuality 16, 106, 107, 179, 263,
    290, 294, 339
Hong Kong 223
Hong Xiuquan 223
Hooker, Richard 385
Hoover, Willis 445
Hopkins, Samuel 430
house churches 122, 448
    in China 226, 424, 441, 472–3
Hovden, Anders 143
Hubmaier, Balthasar, and Zwingli 26
Hughes, Stephen 120
Hugolino of Orvieto, and predestination
    63
Huguenots 148, 161, 302, 410–11
human rights 64, 289, 295, 301–2,
    325, 328
humanism
    and Calvin 45, 53, 279
    Chinese 227
    influence on Reformation 3, 45, 96,
        130–1, 274
    liberal 455–7
    and Luther 40, 43, 253
Hume, David 314
Hungary, and Lutheranism 156, 157
Hus, Jan 43, 96
Hussite Church 155, 157
Hutchinson, Abigail 428–9
Hutchinson, Anne 166, 336
Hutterites, in United States 167, 290
Hwa Yung 478
hymns 279, 383
    in evangelicalism 104, 428–9, 435
    in Nordic countries 132, 133, 134,
        135, 139, 143

Iceland
    and liberalism 143
    and Lutheranism 133, 138
    and Reformation 131
iconoclasm 44, 268, 273–7, 281,
    463
icons 271
Idowu, Bolaji 244

images
    in late medieval thought 271–3
    opposition to 26, 269, 270–1, 273–8,
        281
    and painting 280–1
Imbart de la Tour, Pierre 58
immanentism 85, 87, 88, 282
incarnation
    and the arts 270–1, 278, 281, 282
    and creation 339
    in Luther 11–12, 46, 49
Independent churches 448–9, 470, 474,
    478–9
Independents
    English 102–3
    Irish 124
    Welsh 120, 121
India **201–5**
    and church union 204, 412–13, 473
    and conversion of Dalits 203
    and evangelicalism 433
    indigenous Christianity 202–3, 204,
        445, 475
    and missions 201–3, 204, 205, 430,
        478
    and national identity 204, 205
    and Pentecostalism 440, 445, 473
    spirituality 389, 424
indigenization 398, 417, 470, 478
    in Africa 242–3, 423–4, 440–1,
        474–6
    in Australia and New Zealand 237
    and the Bible 266
    in China 222–8, 230, 440–1, 472–3
    and evangelicalism 423–4
    in India 202–3, 204, 445, 475
    in Japan 213, 214
    in Latin America 476–7, 480
individualism 191, 237, 244, 454
    and Kierkegaard 138
    and liberalism 325, 326–7, 328
    and nationalism 150
    and Protestant problematic 14
Indonesia 206–7, 440, 472, 473
indulgences, and Luther 40, 43, 49
Inglis, Charles, Bishop of Nova Scotia
    191–2
International Missionary Council 417
InterVarsity Christian Fellowship 425

intuition
    in Schleiermacher 72–4, 76
    in Unitarianism 172
Ireland **123–9**
    early Protestantism 123–4
    and evangelicalism 126, 129, 431
    fragmentation of Protestantism 124–5
    and political divide 127–8
    revivalism 126–7, 428
Irigaray, Luce 460, 461
Irish School of Ecumenics 128
Isasi-Díaz, Ada Maria 338
Islam, in Africa 240, 435
Italy **163**

Jackson, John 190
James VI of Scotland and I of England
    101, 111, 123
James VII of Scotland and II of England
    103, 111, 125
James, William 458, 462
Janes, Leroy L. 210
Japan **210–14**
    future tasks 214
    origins of Protestantism 210–11
    postwar theology 213
    spirituality 389
    theological and social issues 211–12
    and United Church of Christ 212–13
Japan Holy Catholic Church (*Nihon Seo Ko
    Kai*) 211
Japan Methodist Church (*Nihon
    Mesojisuto Kyokai*) 211
Jefferson, Thomas 169
Jeremias, Joachim 377
Jesus Christ
    as divine 11, 34, 49, 79, 93
    as exemplar 172
    as human 11–12, 28, 49, 93
    and Judaism 35, 376–7
    in Kierkegaard 35–6
    as sinless archetype 33–4, 35
"Jesus People" 447
Jews *see* Judaism
John XXIII, Pope 411, 448
John of Damascus 271
John Paul II, Pope 476
Johnson, Todd M. 439, 440, 469–70
Jon Arason 131

Jonas, Justus 14
Jones, Griffith 120
Jones, John Morgan 122
Jones, William 273
Jordan, Winthrop D. 362
Joseph II of Austro-Hungary 157
Jospin, Lionel 162
Jowett, Benjamin 327
Judaism and Jews 258, **372–9**
  and Calvin 373–4
  and Harnack 375–7
  and Jewish–Christian relations 378–9
  and Kittel 378
  and Luther 13, 372–3
  and Schleiermacher 374–5
  in United States 174, 177
Jüngel, Eberhard 51
justification
  and experience 137
  by works 24, 41, 42, 166, 253, 374
justification by faith 121, 122, 234, 382,
    429
  and Barth 89
  and Calvin 6–8, 42, 299
  and Cranmer 98, 299
  and definition of Protestantism 17
  and Luther 5, 6–7, 10, 15, 36, 41, 47,
    51, 253, 299, 383
  and Melanchthon 5, 7, 42

Kagawa Toyohiko 212
Kalu, Ogbu 475, 479
Kalweit, Martin 159
Kant, Immanuel
  and beauty 27
  Critique of Pure Reason 71, 314
  and knowledge of God 32, 72, 85, 314
  and liberalism 323, 326
  and morality 31, 34–5, 72, 314–15
  and practical reason 31–2
  Religion Within the Limits of Reason
    Alone 71
  and the transcendent 76
Kanyoro, Musimbi R. A. 244
Kargel, Ivan 159
Karlstadt, Andreas Bodenstein von
  and Eucharist 46
  and images 25, 26, 274, 276
  and Luther's reforms 25, 44–5

Keble, John 386
Kelsey, Morton 388
Kennedy, David 413
kenosis theology 11
Kenya 240–1, 245, 474
Kepler, Johannes 309–10
Keswick Convention 442–3
Kierkegaard, Søren 35–6, 37, 138, 141,
    386
Kilham, Hannah 398
King James (Authorized) Bible 58, 101,
    106, 167
King, Martin Luther Jr. 178, 293,
    359–60, 366
Kingdom of God
  in Ritschl 35
  and Social Gospel 173, 328–9
  in Weiss 35
Kingo, Thomas 133, 134
Kirisuto Kokai 210
Kirschbaum, Charlotte von 87
Kitamori Kazo 51, 213
Kittel, Gerhard 378
Knopken, Andreas 156
knowledge of God
  in Barth 37, 91
  in Calvin 61–2
  in Hegel 32–3, 37, 73–4, 282
  in Kant 32, 72, 85, 314
  in Schleiermacher 73–4, 78–80
  and science 310–11
  in Spinoza 71–2, 73–4
Knox, John 110, 114
Knudson, Albert C. 293
Koch, Hal 141
Korea **216–20**, 389, 468
  from democratic transition to present
    219–20
  and evangelicalism 217–18, 219,
    424, 433
  future prospects 220
  from liberation to democratic transition
    217–19, 470–1
  and missionary Protestantism
    216–17, 395, 471–2, 478
  and Pentecostalism 440, 445, 471–2
Kraemer, Henrik 417
Kristeva, Julia 460, 461
Ku Klux Klan 174, 177

Kuhn, Thomas 459
Kuyper, Abraham 151–2, 153, 282, 283

Lacan, Jacques 461, 462
Landstad, Magnus Brostrup 139, 143
language, religious
  in Feuerbach 34
  inclusive 264, 294
  in Ritschl 35
  in Schleiermacher 75–8
Lasius, Balthasar (printer) 59
Lästadius, Lars Levi 140
Latimer, Hugh 99
Latin America 470, 476–7
  evangelicalism 432–3, 435
  Pentecostalism 390, 439, 445–6, 449,
    468, 476–7, 480
  spirituality 390, 424, 477
  see also liberation theology
Latour, Bruno 459
Latourette, Kenneth Scott 406
Latvia, and Reformation 156
Laud, William, Archbishop of Canterbury
  101–2, 124
Lausanne Articles (1536) 6
Lausanne Covenant 417–18
Lausanne Faith and Order Conference
  (1927) 408
law 298–304
  and evangelicalism 302–3
  modern views 303–4
  natural 30, 32, 300, 314
  and Reformation 97, 298–300
law and gospel
  in Barth 86
  in Calvin 9–10
  in Luther 9–10, 24–5, 281
Law, William 193
Lawrence, William 172, 292
Laws, Curtis Lee 175, 345
lectio continua 58
Lee Ang Fu 227
Legge, James 223, 227
Legge, Marilyn 199 n.15
Legion of Silver Shirts (US) 177
Leimena, Johannes 207
Leslie, Charles 313
Lessing, Gotthold 31
Levinas, Emmanuel 462
Lewis, C. S. 387

Liang Ah Fa 223
liberalism 322–9
  anthropological 9, 86, 88, 139
  in Australia and New Zealand 234–5,
    236
  and Barth 84–8, 89, 264, 325
  and the Bible 254, 262–4
  in Canada 192, 196, 197
  in England 105, 326–8
  in Germany 324–6
  in Japan 211
  and Judaism 375–7
  and modernity 455–6, 458–60
  negative 322–3, 325, 326, 328, 329
  in Netherlands 151–2
  in Nordic countries 139, 141
  positive 324–5, 327–9
  and racism 359, 366–9
  and science and religion 315, 316,
    317, 327
  and secularization 105
  and spirituality 386, 387
  and traditionalism 4, 107, 121–2
  in United States 172, 174–5, 178–9,
    197, 328–9
  see also Enlightenment
liberation theology 218–19, 244, 292,
  390, 418, 476–7
Life and Work Movement 144, 414–15
Lima Report 410, 413
Linné, Carl von 136, 139
literalism, biblical 240, 442
  and fundamentalism 344, 345–6
  and historical criticism 256, 259
  and levels of meaning 255–6
  and Luther 307, 372
  and racism 360
  and Schleiermacher 75–6
Lithuania 157
liturgy
  and music 279–80, 383
  vernacular 51, 97–8, 120, 132
Liu Tingfeng 225
Livingstone, David 397
Lloyd-Jones, Martin 122, 431
Locke, John 181, 187, 289, 315, 323,
  455
  and miracles 30, 313
  and preaching of Paul 30, 36
Løgstrup, K. E. 142, 144

Lollards 96, 110
London Missionary Society (LMS) 202,
    207, 225, 241, 398, 430
Louis XIV of France 161
love of God 92, 295
Lowell, James Russell 295
Lund Principle 409
Luther, Martin **40–51**, 454
    and *Augsburg Confession* 14–15
    "autobiographical fragment" 41
    and the Bible 45, 47–8, 49, 51, 253,
        255, 264, 307, 309, 334
    and Calvin 53
    and the church 12–14, 23, 43, 51,
        56
    and church and state 2, 13, 43–4, 45,
        131–2
    Confessio Augustana 131
    de Servo Arbitrio 8
    and divisions 44–6
    and the Eucharist 10–12, 26–7, 44,
        46, 49–50, 54
    excommunication 43
    The Freedom of a Christian 322, 384
    and Henry VIII 98
    and images 275–6
    influence 40, 48, 51
    Large Catechism 5, 28, 384
    and law and gospel 9–10, 24–5
    Lectures on Romans 36
    and medieval theology 40–3, 44, 51
    and mission 393–4
    and music 279
    "Ninety-Five Theses" 41, 43, 299,
        333–4
    On Secular Authority 50
    and political theology 50–1
    and predestination 8–9
    priesthood of all believers 13–14,
        43–4, 383
    and Radical Reformation 2
    and reason and faith 24, 30, 47
    and "Reformation breakthrough"
        42–3
    reforming programme 43–4
    and revelation 47, 48
    and Roman captivity of the church
        24–5
    and sacraments 42, 43, 44, 46, 255
    and science 307–8, 313

Small (Lesser) Catechism 5, 15, 28, 59,
    131, 132
    and spirituality 383–4
    Sunday Postilla 131
    and the vernacular 47, 50, 51, 97,
        167
    and women 333
    and Word of God 24–5, 31, 41–2, 44,
        48
    and Wycliffe 96–7
    and Zwingli 5, 26–7, 28, 46, 48, 54
    see also Christology; cross; Judaism;
        justification by faith
Lutheran World Federation, and
    ecumenism 411–12
Lutheranism 4
    in Australia and New Zealand 233,
        235, 236
    in Canada 190
    in China 225
    and confessional orthodoxy 27–8
    and confessions of faith 6, 14–16, 28
    and ecumenism 411–12, 413
    in India 201–2, 421
    in Nordic countries 130, 131, 132–4,
        135, 136, 138, 140, 386
    and Reformed theology 27–8
    in Scotland 110
    spread 56
    and two-kingdom theology 16
    in United States 167–8, 176, 294,
        303, 421
    see also Denmark; England;
        Melanchthon, Philip; Pietism;
        Sweden
Lutherska evangeliförsamlingen 141

McFague, Sallie 338–9
McGiffert, A. C. 328
McGrath, Alister E. 319
Machen, J. Gresham 347
MacInnis, Donald E. 230
McIntire, Carl 350
Mackie, Robert 409
McLaurin, John 427
McMullin, Ernan 318
McPherson, Aimee Semple 176
Maffesoli, Michel 464
magistracy *see* church and state
Mahan, Asa 442

Malaysia 208
Manent, Pierre 454
Mannermaa, Prof. 145–6
Marburg Colloquy (1529) 14, 46
Marcion, and Jewish Scriptures 375–6
Marees, Pieter de 241
Marian Exiles, and Calvinism 55, 99,
    100
Marprelate tracts 100–1
marriage
    and law 300
    as vocation 334, 339, 383
Marsden, George 344, 346, 353 n.4,
    354 n.13
Marsden, Samuel 232
Martensen, Hans 138
Martin, David 218, 449, 472, 476–7,
    480
Martin, W. A. P. 227, 228, 229
Marx, Karl 34
Mary II *see* William III and Mary II
Mary, Queen of Scots 110
Mary Tudor 55, 98–9, 100, 110
Mason, Charles H. 176
Mastricht, Peter van 183
Mather, Cotton 361–2
Mathews, Shailer 328
Matthiae, Johannes 134
Maurice, F. D. 292, 327
Mayhew, Jonathan 168–9
Mbeki, Thabo 470
Mbiti, John 244
meaning, in Schleiermacher 76–7
Melanchthon, Philip
    and *Augsburg Confession* 14–15
    and Calvin 10, 27–8
    and the Eucharist 10, 15
    and humanism 45
    influence 132, 133
    and justification by faith 5, 7, 42
    Loci Communes 5, 14, 25, 28, 60–1,
        131
    and Luther 10, 373
    and Marburg Colloquy 46
    and predestination 27
    Saxon Visitations 131
    and science 308
    and the Trinity 25
    and university-based theology 25

Melanesia 235–6
memorialism, Eucharistic 10, 12
Men and Religion Forward Movement
    173
Meng Juezi 227
Mennander, Carl Fredrik 137
Mennonites
    and Baptists 101
    in Eastern Europe 155, 159
    in Netherlands 148
    in North America 3, 4, 167, 168,
        190, 431
    and pacifism 148, 288, 431
metaphysics
    and Kant 85
    and Schleiermacher 71, 72, 74
    and Spinoza 71
Methodism
    in Australia and New Zealand 233,
        234, 235
    in Canada 190–1, 192–3, 195, 196
    in Eastern Europe 156
    in England 104, 291, 386
    in India 204
    in Ireland 125, 128
    in Italy 163
    and mission 397
    in Nordic countries 143
    in South-East Asia 207, 211, 216,
        218, 225–6, 445, 472
    in United States 169, 171, 293, 294,
        302–3, 424
    in Wales 121
    see also Wesley, John
Methodist Episcopal Church, South 171
Meyer, Harding 419
Meyer, Louis 346
middle classes, and Reformation 3
Milbank, John 464 n.3
Mill, John Stuart 322
millenarianism 106, 258, 345–6, 350,
    352
Milman, H. H. 327
Milne, William 207, 222–3, 227
Milton, John 385, 454
ministry, in Calvin 57
minjung theology 218–19
miracles 30, 311, 313–14
Mirandolo, Pico della 456, 457

missions **392–400**
  in Africa 240–3, 246–7, 392, 471,
    474
  in Australia and New Zealand 232,
    235
  in China 222–5, 227, 399
  and colonialism 201–2, 241–3, 392,
    395, 396, 398, 399, 470, 474
  current trends 399–400
  and dialogue 417
  and ecumenism 225, 246, 399,
    405–7, 412, 416–17
  in England 104, 106, 392
  and evangelicalism 425, 429, 434
  history 392–5
  in India 201–3, 204, 205, 430,
    478
  in Ireland 126–7
  in Japan 210
  in Korea 216–17, 219, 395, 471–2,
    478
  in Nordic countries 135–6, 139, 140,
    143, 144–5, 445
  and Pentecostalism 444, 445
  and spirituality 386–7
  in United States 176
Miyahira Nozomo 213
Miyata Mitsuo 214
modernity
  and Barth 94, 325
  and crisis of epistemology 458
  and Jonathan Edwards 187–8
  and fundamentalism 195, 344–5,
    347–9, 353
  and liberalism 325–6, 455–60
  Protestantism as xiv, 7, 217, 453–60
Moffat, Robert 241
Molokany 158, 159
Moltmann, Jürgen 16, 51
Moody, Dwight L. 173, 422
Moral Majority 178, 290, 304, 351
Moral Re-armament movement 177
morality
  in Kant 31, 34–5, 72, 314–15
  religion as 72, 74, 135, 150
Moravia 157
Moravianism
  in Africa 240, 474
  influence 384, 386, 427, 441

in Nordic countries 135, 136, 137,
    139, 393
  in North America 167, 190, 393
Morgan, William 120
Morison, James 114–15
Mormons *see* Church of Jesus Christ of
    Latter Day Saints
Morrison, John Robert 224
Morrison, Robert 222–3, 224, 399
Mott, John 235, 406
Movinckel, Sigmund 143
Muhlenberg, Henry 167–8
Muirhead, William 229
Mukyokai (Non-Church Movement)
    211
Munck, Kaj 141
Müntzer, Thomas 45, 254
Muromaa, Urko 145
Murphy, Nancey 319
music 278, 279–80, 423
Myanmar (Burma) 207, 389
Mynster, Jakob Peter 138
mysticism 133

Nakajima Shigeru 212
Nantes, Edict (1598) 56, 161, 411
National Council of Churches (US) 173,
    304, 366, 416
nationalism 287
  and colonialism 204, 217, 470–1
  and liberalism 325–7
Native Americans 388, 395, 430
nature
  and grace 457–8, 464 n.3
  and science 62, 310–11
Naude, Beyers 389
Nee, Watchman 225–6
Neo-Calvinism 151, 153, 283
neo-orthodoxy, and postmodernity
    463–4
"Neology" 323
Netherlands **147–53**
  and the arts 280
  as confessional state 148–9
  and Dutch Revolt 147–8, 302
  and evangelicalism 153
  and Lutheranism 147, 148, 153
  and mass politics 151
  as Protestant nation 150, 151–2

Netherlands (*cont.*)
  and renewal 152–3
  and secessionist movement 150–1
Netherlands Missionary Society 207
New Age Movement 388, 460, 461
New England
  and Puritan settlements 64, 101,
    165–6, 182
  revivalism 114
  and women 336
New Light Movement (US and Canada)
  193, 302
New Light Presbyterians (Ireland) 125,
  126
New Zealand *see* Australia and New
  Zealand
Newbigin, Lesslie 409, 413, 417, 419
Newman, John Henry 327, 386
Newton, John 429, 435
Newton, Sir Isaac 181, 188, 311–13
Niebuhr, H. Richard 2, 287–8, 304,
  329, 368
Niebuhr, Reinhold 290, 296 n.6, 304,
  316, 329, 368
Nielsson, Haraldur 143
Nietzsche, Friedrich 2, 457
Nigeria 240–2, 245, 433, 468, 471,
  474, 478
Niijima Jo 210
Niinivaara, Erki 145
Nishida Kitaro 213
Nketia, J. H. 242
Nkrumah, Kwame 241, 243
nominalism, in postmodernity 457–60,
  462
Nordic countries **130–46**
  and confessionalism and liberation
    137–41, 146
  and Lutheran orthodoxy 132–4, 135,
    136, 140
  and pietism and Enlightenment 134–7
  and Reformation 130–2
  and vernacular Bible 131–2, 134, 143
Norris, J. Frank 348, 349
Northern Baptist Convention (US) 175,
  345, 347–8
Norway
  Church Ordinance 131
  liberalism 142

Lutheran orthodoxy 133, 138
national liberation 138–9
pietism and Enlightenment 135–6,
  139
revivalism 139
secularization 143
Noyes, John Humphrey 171
Nygren, Anders 144

Oceania 232, 235–8
Ockenga, Harold J. 350
Ödmann, S. 139
Oduyoye, Mercy Amba 244, 338
Oecolampadius, John 46
Old Testament
  and Harnack 375–6
  and Judaism 375–6
  in magisterial Reformation 255–6
  and Schleiermacher 78, 375
Oldham, Joseph 406
Olivétan, Robert 53
Oncken, Johann Gerhard 159
Oneida Community 171
ontology
  "anachronized" 460–2
  Trinitarian 9, 78–9
  and univocity of being 457, 459–60,
    462
Orange Order 127, 233
ordination of women 16, 332
  in Australia and New Zealand 236
  in England 106
  in Nordic countries 141, 142, 143,
    144, 145
  in United States 174, 179, 294, 337,
    339
Orthodox Churches, and ecumenism
    407, 414–15, 416, 417
orthodoxy
  Lutheran 27–8, 132–4, 136–7, 138
  in Schleiermacher 69
Osiander, Andreas 46, 308
Oxford Movement 105, 125, 386

pacifism 148, 287, 288–90, 385, 431
Packer, J. I. 425, 435
Paisley, Ian 128
Paley, William 195
Palmer, Phoebe 421, 442

Pannenberg, Wolfhart 320
papacy
   and Jonathan Edwards 184
   and English Reformation 99, 100
   and Luther 43, 44, 48, 51
Parham, C. F. 175, 443–4
Paris University 53–4, 161
Parker, Peter 224
Pashkovism 158–9
Pate, Larry 471
patriarchy
   and feminism 335, 337
   and fundamentalism 344
patronage, in Scotland 112
Paul VI, Pope 448
Paul
   in Barth 85, 87–8
   in Calvin 360
   in Kierkegaard 36
   in Locke 30
   in Luther 24, 29
Paul, K. T. 204
Pavlov, Vassili 159
Pawson, David 448
Peacocke, Arthur R. 318, 319
Peasants' Revolt 45
Pelagianism, and Luther 8, 43, 51
Pelikan, Jaroslav 373
Pentecostalism **439–50**
   in Africa 246, 440, 445–6, 474–6
   in Asia 208, 439–40, 445–6, 471–2
   in Australia and New Zealand 236
   in Eastern Europe 155, 159
   and evangelicalism 423, 439
   and fragmentation 442, 444, 449–50
   globalization 439, 449–50, 474
   growth 1, 4, 121, 423, 435, 445–6,
      469
   in Latin America 390, 439, 445–6,
      468, 476–7, 490
   and mission 444, 445
   in Nordic countries 143, 144–5, 146
   in North America 175–6, 179, 196,
      388, 443–4, 446–9
   origins 175–6, 441–3
   "third wave" 449
   in the West 153, 163, 446–9
   see also Azusa Street Revival; gifts of
      the Spirit; glossolalia

perfections of God, in Barth 93
Peter Lombard, Sentences 44, 60
Pethrus, Lewi 144
Petri, Olaus 131
Petursson, Hallgrimur 133
Pfleiderer, Otto 325
Philip II of Spain 99
Philip of Hesse 46
Philippines 207–8, 389, 424, 440, 473
Pickstock, John 464 n.3
pietism 262, 263, 426–7, 430, 441
   in Canada 192–3
   in Eastern Europe 158, 159
   and Francke 29, 30, 427
   Nordic 133, 134–7, 138–9, 140
   radical 136–7, 302
   and Spener 29, 137, 257–8, 384, 427
   in United States 197
   and Zinzendorf 29–30, 136, 427
Pilgrim Holiness Church 442
pisteology 7
Plato 25, 366
Platter, Thomas (printer) 59
pluralism 287, 324–5, 399
   in Africa 239–40
   in England 104–6, 326, 327
   in Japan 213
   in Nordic countries 134, 141–6
   and postmodernity 464
   in United States 167–8
Plütschau, Henry 201, 471
Plymouth Brethren 115–16, 207, 346,
      443
Pobee, John xiv
Poland, and Calvinism 156, 157
politics 2, **288–90**, 295, 303–4
   and evangelicalism 423, 434–5
   and fundamentalism 178, 290, 304,
      351
   and liberalism 325, 328
   and minjung theology 219
   and pietism 192–3
   and radicalism 121
   see also democracy; law
Polkinghorne, John 319
Polynesia 232, 236
Pontoppidan, Eric 135, 136, 139
Porvoo Common Statement 146, 413
postliberalism 460

postmillennialism 346
postmodernity 187–8, 237, **453–64**
  and advancing nominalism 457–60
  as antithetical to Protestantism xiv,
    453–7
  and Barth 94
  "re-enchantment" 460–3
  and secularism 456
  and theology 81, 458, 478
power *see* politics
preaching
  in Barth 89, 91
  and creation of faith 29
  expository 58, 111
  in Luther 42
  and rhetoric 56
  as role of the church 12–13
predestination
  and Arminianism 102, 125, 149
  in Barth 92
  in Calvin 8–9, 27, 62–4, 149, 360, 384
  double 8, 63, 89, 124, 149, 184–5,
    384
  in Jonathan Edwards 183–5
  in Luther 8–9
  and providence 64
  in Wesley 104
premillennialism 176, 177, 345–6, 347,
    350, 352, 443, 477
Prenter, Regin 142
Presbyterian Church in the US 171, 176,
    339, 347–8, 374
Presbyterianism
  in Africa 242
  in Australia and New Zealand 233,
    234, 235–6
  in Canada 189–91, 192, 196
  in China 225–6
  and church government 57, 102, 111,
    112
  and confession of faith 102
  and divisions 112–14, 117, 125, 126
  in England 103
  in India 202, 204, 473
  in Ireland 124–5, 126, 128, 415
  in Japan 210
  in Korea 216, 218, 395, 445, 468,
    472
  and monarchy 102, 103

  in Scotland 111–12, 302, 431
  and Unitarianism 103
  in United States 182, 262: divisions in
    294, 303; and fundamentalism
    175, 347–8, 350; and ordination of
    women 179; and revivalism 168,
    169
Preston, Richard 190
Prierias, Sylvester 43, 47
priesthood of all believers 254, 458
  in Calvin 13–14
  and feminism 333–4, 339
  in Luther 13–14, 43–4, 383
  in Spener 29
Prokhanov, Ivan 159
prophecy *see* gifts of the Spirit
prosperity, gospel of 446, 448–9, 474,
    479–80
"Protestant problematic" 14
Protestantism
  classical denominations *see*
    Anglicanism; Lutheranism;
    Reformed thought
  classical theology 5–14
  and evangelicalism 4
  and the future 469, 477–80
  as heterogeneous 1–2, 3–5
  and modernity xiv, 7, 217, 453–60
  non-Western **468–80**
  origins 2, 3
  of Radical Reformation *see* Baptists;
    Mennonites
  self-definition 1–17
providence
  in Barth 92
  in Calvin 64
  in Jonathan Edwards 184
Puritans
  in England 100–3, 302, 385, 426
  in North America 64, 101, 165–6,
    183–4, 186, 189, 302, 387
  and racism 358–9, 360–4
  in Wales 120
Pusey, Edward 386

Quakers (Religious Society of Friends)
  in Canada 189–90
  in Eastern Europe 158
  in England 102

in Ireland 124
in New England 166, 167, 168
and pacifism 288, 385
and spirituality 385
Quenstedt, Johannes 57

race and racism 287, 293–4, **357–69**, 378, 388, 430
and gender 338
and liberal Protestantism 178, 359, 366–9
and Puritanism 358–9, 360–4
in Reformed thought 360–4
in Scotland 118
see also slavery
Rade, Martin 325
Radical Reformation 2–3, 4, 100, 254, 258, 263, *see also* Anabaptists; Baptists; Mennonites
Rahner, Karl, and Protestant problematic 14
Ramabai, Pandita 445, 473
Ramos, Fidel 208
Ramsey, Michael 409
Ratana Church (New Zealand) 235
rationalism
and missions 244
in Nordic countries 135, 136, 138
in North America 191
scientific 458, 459
and spirituality 385
Rauschenbusch, Walter 36
and racism 364–6
and Social Gospel 173, 292, 303, 328–9, 365
Rawls, John 322
Real Presence
in Luther 46, 49–50
in Wycliffe 96
realism 290, 318
reason
and faith 29, 30–6, 37, 195–6, 314–15, 328, 458
instrumental 459
in Kant 31–2, 72, 314–15
in Luther 24, 30, 47
practical 24, 31, 32
speculative 24, 31, 32–3
reconciliation, in Barth 92–3

Reconstructionism (US) 290
Reed, Ralph 290, 351
Rees, David 121
Rees, Thomas 121–2
Reformation
centers *see* Geneva; Wittenberg; Zurich
divisions 44–6
in England 98–9
and iconoclasm 268, 273–8
magisterial 2–3, 13, 156
Scottish 109, 114
see also Radical Reformation
Reformed Church in America 176, 210
Reformed theology 2, 4, 55–64
in Africa 241
and confessional orthodoxy 27–8
and confessions of faith 6, 15, 16, 27–8, 62
and ecumenism 413
and fourfold ministry 57
and law 301–2
and Lutheranism 27–8, 63
in Netherlands 148–9, 153, 374
and predestination 63–4
and racism 360–4
and spirituality 384–5
in United States 56, 167, 182–7
see also Barth, Karl; Calvin, John; Calvinism; Scotland; Zwingli, Uldrich
Reichelt, Karl Ludvig 143
Reimarus, Hermann Samuel 30–1, 32, 35, 36, 260
Relief Church (Scotland) 113
religion
"essence" 458
and experience 73
as morality 72, 74, 150
Religionsgeschichtliche Schule 260–1, 263
Religious Society of Friends *see* Quakers
Rembrandt van Rijn 281
reprobation, in Calvin 27
retreats 383, 388
Reuterdahl, Henrik 140
revelation
in Barth 88, 89, 90–1, 320
in Luther 47, 49
and reason 30–6, 37, 195–6, 458
in Schleiermacher 68, 79–80
and the Trinity 89, 90–1

revivalism 427–9
  Canada 190, 193, 195
  China 225–6
  and ecumenism 406
  England 103–4, 202, 427–8
  Ireland 126–7, 428
  New England 114
  Nordic countries 137, 139–40,
    145
  Scotland 113, 116, 427–8
  United States 168–70, 171–3, 177,
    182, 427, 442, *see also* Edwards,
    Jonathan
  Wales 121, 122, 427–8
Rhenius, C. T. E. 202
Richard, Timothy 229
Ridley, Nicholas 99
righteousness of God, in Luther 24, 41,
  42, 49
Riley, William Bell 347–8
Ringeltaube, W. T. 202
Ritschl, Albrecht 34–5, 144, 315, 325
Robert, Dana 468, 469, 480
Roberts, Evan 121
Roberts, Oral 447, 448
Robertson, Marion Gordon "Pat" 178,
  290, 351, 447
Roman Catholic Church
  in Africa 240
  and the arts 269
  in Australia and New Zealand 233,
    236–7
  and Barth 93–4
  in Canada 190–3, 194
  and canon law 97, 131, 298–300
  and charismatic movement 448
  in Eastern Europe 155–7
  and ecumenism 407, 409–10,
    411–12, 416, 417, 418
  in England 98–100, 103, 104, 107
  in France 162
  in Ireland 124, 125, 126–8, 129
  in Italy 163
  and Jews 378–9
  in Korea 216
  in Latin America 476
  and Luther 23, 24–5
  in Netherlands 148, 149, 151–2
  in Nordic countries 131, 134
  and science 308–9

in Scotland 109–10, 111, 119
in South-East Asia 206–7, 208
and spirituality 383, 388, 390
in United States 165, 174, 176, 177
in Wales 120, 122
Romanticism, German 67, 72, 74, 78,
  80–1, 282, 386
Rose, Susan 479
Rosenius, Karl Olof 140, 141
Rosenkrantz, Holger 133
Rothe, Richard 324
Rothovius, Isak 134
Rousseau, Jean-Jacques 289
Rowland, Daniel 121
Roxborogh, J. 432
Rudra, S. K. 204
Ruether, Rosemary Radford 334, 338–9,
  379
Ruotsalainen, Paavo 140
Rushdoony, Rousas 290
Russell, Letty 338
Russell, Robert John 319
Russia, and Reformation 156, 158
Russian Bible Society 158
Russian Orthodox Church, in Eastern
  Europe 155, 156, 158–9
Ryerson, Egerton 192

Sabbath observance 234, 303
sacramentalism, "new" 461–3
sacraments
  in Calvin 27
  in Luther 42, 43, 44, 46, 255
  number 111, 255
  in Zwingli 26
  see also baptism; Eucharist
Saffin, John 361–2, 365
Sahlin, Margit 144
St Bartholomew's Day Massacre 161
Saiving, Valerie 337–8
Salesbury, William 120
Salonga, Jovito 208
salvation
  and the church 13
  and the cross 47
  by grace 7, 8, 36, 41–2, 43, 45, 360
  see also predestination
Salvation Army 233, 234, 431
Samartha, S. J. 204
Samuel, V. K. 204

sanctification 17, 303, 382
  in Barth 89
  in Calvin 7–8, 385
  in Wesley 386, 388, 441–2
Sanders, E. P. 377
Saravia, Adrianus 394
Sawyerr, Harry 244
Schaff, Philip 405–6
Schama, Simon 280, 281
Scharlemann, Robert 459
Schartau, Henrik 139
Schelderup, Bishop 142
Schelling, F. W. J. von 67, 74, 282
Schlegel, Friedrich 67
Schleiermacher, F. D. E. **66–81**, 315
  and *Augsburg Confession* 15
  and Barth 67, 78–80, 85, 88
  *Brief Outline of Theology as a Field of
    Study* 67–71
  and Bultmann 36, 37
  *The Christian Faith (Der Christliche
    Glaube)* 66, 71–4, 77, 78–9
  Dialectics 75
  and experience 31–2, 73
  and feeling, consciousness, and religion
    32, 33–5, 71–4, 76, 85, 88, 375,
    386, 458
  and hermeneutics and language 75–8,
    80, 263
  influence 66–7
  and Judaism 374–5
  and liberalism 324, 328
  On Religion 71–3, 78
Schmidt, Georg 474
Schmidt, Leigh Eric 433
Schmucker, Samuel 405–6
scholasticism
  medieval 40–3, 44, 51, 63, 306, 457,
    459, 464 n.3
  Protestant 9, 86, 254, 257, 262, 264,
    309, 434
Schroeder, H. P. S. 139
Schüssler Fiorenza, Elizabeth 338
Schwabach Articles (1529) 14
Schwartz, C. F. 201
Schweitzer, Albert 260
Schwenkfelders, in United States
    167
science and religion 36, 195–6, 236,
    306–20, 327
  in Calvin 62, 64, 308
  and Copernican revolution 306,
    307–11
  and hypothetical consonance
    318–20
  in Kant 314–15
  and liberalism 174, 459–60
  and Linné 136
  and Newtonian physics 311–13
  and two-language view 315–16, 317,
    318
  see also evolution; miracle
Scofield, C. I. 258, 346
Scopes, John 175, 317, 348
Scotland **109–18**, 406, 424
  and Baptists 115–16
  and Christian Brethren 116–17
  early Protestants 109–11
  and evangelicalism 114, 115, 116,
    424, 431–2
  and National Covenant 111–12
  Relief Church 113
  revivalism 113, 116, 427–8
  Scottish Reformation 109, 114
  Secession Church 112–13, 114, 125
  twentieth-century 117–18
Secession Church (Scotland) 112–13,
    114, 125
Second Helvetic Confession (1566) 6, 28
Second Vatican Council 304, 378–9,
    411, 448
sectarianism 102, 118, 126–8, 295,
    434, *see also* separatism
secularization
  in Canada 194, 195, 432
  in Eastern Europe 160
  in England 105–6
  in France 162
  and fundamentalism 351
  and modernity 455–7, 459
  in Nordic countries 130, 141–6
  in Wales 121–2
Seippel, Alexander 143
Semler, Johann Salomo 323
sense of the heart, in Jonathan Edwards
    186–7
separatism 13, 288, 302
  and Anabaptists 3, 300, 385
  and fundamentalism 349–50, 352,
    422, 431

separatism (*cont.*)
  and pietists 137
  and Puritans 101
sermon *see* preaching
Serres, Michel 462
Servetus, Michael 13, 25, 255
Seventh Day Adventism, in Eastern
    Europe 155, 157
Seymour, William Joseph 443–4
Shakers 171
Shen, Philip 230
Sherrill, John 447
Shields, Thomas T. 199 n.16, 348, 349
Sibbes, Richard 242
Sierra Leone 241, 392, 430
Simeon, Charles 116, 421
Simons, Menno 148, 299
sin
  and baptism 26
  in Calvin 360
  in Chinese Protestantism 228
  in Jonathan Edwards 184
  in feminist theology 337–8
  in Kant 32
  and law 10, 301–2
  in Luther 41
  and politics 289, 301–2
  and works 24
Singapore 207, 208
Singh, Sadhu Sundar 204
Skydsgaard, Kristen 142
slavery
  abolition 104, 170, 171, 295, 303,
    359, 430
  and racism 293, 357–8, 361–3, 406
Slovenia 157
Smith, Adam 456
Smith, Joseph 171
Smith, Wilfred C. 196
Sobrino, Jon 390
Social Gospel 173, 194, 212, 229, 292,
    303, 328–9, 365
socialism 287, 292, 327
society **287–95**, 301, 454–5
Society for the Propagation of Christian
    Knowledge (SPCK) 120, 201
Society for the Propagation of the Gospel
    (SPG) 190, 201, 211, 240–2, 396
sociology **293–4**, 328–9, 455

sociopolitical thought *see* economics;
    politics; sociology; wealth
Söderblom, Nathan 144, 414
Søe, Niels Hansen 142
sola fide principle 5, 6–7, 253, 458
sola scriptura principle 101, 309–10, 393
  and feminism 334–5
  implications 254–5, 309
  and magisterial Reformation 2, 5, 6,
    47, 251
soli Christo principle 7, 47, 253
Song, C. S. 230
Soskice, Janet Martin 284 n.18
Soulen, R. Kendall 375, 379
South Africa 240, 242, 246, 389, 471,
    474
  and evangelicalism 432, 433
  and Pentecostalism 444
South-East Asia **206–8**
  and indigenous churches 207–8, 473
  and missions 206–7
  and spirituality 217, 389–90
Southern Baptist Convention (US) 171,
    176, 179, 294, 341 n.12, 348, 352
speaking in tongues *see* glossolalia
Spener, Philipp Jakob 29, 137, 257–8,
    384, 427
Speyer, Diet of (1529) 2
Spinoza, Baruch
  and historical criticism 259
  and knowledge 71, 72, 73–4
spiritism 143
spirituality **382–90**, 462
  African 389
  Asian 389–90
  common themes and practices 382–3
  European 383–7
  Latin American 390
  North American 387–8
  Pentecostal 218, 446, 469–70
Spittler, L. T. 323
Spurgeon, Charles Haddon 421
Stackhouse, John 354 n.15
Stanley, A. P. 327
Stanton, Elizabeth Cady 174, 336, 337
stewardship 172, 197, 291, 339
Stone, Barton W. 169
Stott, John 418, 422, 425, 435, 448
Strachan, John, Bishop of Toronto 192

Strasbourg, and Calvin 54–5, 59
Strauss, David Friedrich 33–4, 35
Strong, Charles 235
Strong, Josiah 174, 364
Student Christian Movement 144, 235,
    406, 409, 413
Stundist movement 158, 159
subjectivity
    and Fichte 73
    and modernity 7, 397, 455–7, 459
    and Schleiermacher 81, 315
Sudan 240, 246
Suenens, Card. Leo 448
Sunday, Billy 173, 174
Sundkler, Bengt 245
Sung, John 226
Svedberg, Jesper 134, 136
Swaggart, Jimmy 178, 447
Sweden
    and Eastern Europe 155
    and ecumenism 144
    and Lutheran orthodoxy 133–4,
        136–7, 140
    and Lutheranism 130, 132
    pietism and Enlightenment 136–7,
        139
    and Reformation 131–2
    and religious freedom 139, 140
    and revivalism 139–40
Swedenborg, Emanuel 137
Switzerland, and humanism 45
syncretism 222, 245–7, 400, 441,
    462–3

Takakura Tokutaro 212
Takenaka Masao 213
Takizawa Katsumi 213
Tamez, Elsa 338
Tanner, Mary 413
Tanzania 240, 242
Tappa, Louise 333
Tausen, Hans 131
Taylor, Charles 455, 459, 461
Taylor, Edward 426
Taylor, Jeremy 385
Taylor, Mark C. 459
Tear Fund 107, 425
Teinonen, Seppo 145
televangelism (US) 178, 447, 479

Temple, Frederick 327
Temple, William 328, 405, 412, 414
Ten Theses of Berne (1528) 6
Tennent, Gilbert 168, 427
Terserus, Prof. 134
Tetrapolitan Confession (1530) 6
Tetzel, Johann 43
theology
    African 244–5, 470
    as anthropology 9, 86, 88
    Asian 470
    biblical 58
    and the church 89
    classical Protestant 5–14
    contextual 219, 236
    "dialectical" 84, 85, 87, 141, 244,
        329
    dogmatic 69–71, 73, 79–80, 85–6
    exegetical 48, 68–9
    historical 68–70, 85
    moral 89
    narrative 244
    natural 47, 61–2, 311
    as object of study 66, 67–71, 81, 107,
        133
    philosophical 67–8, 80–1
    political 50–1, 86, 104, 219–20
    postmodern 81, 459
    practical 70
    womanist 244–5, 338
    see also Christology; feminism;
        liberation theology
Thielicke, Helmut 16
Thirty Years' War 134, 324
Thirty-nine Articles 4, 99, 100, 120, 124
Thomas, M. M. 204
Thomas, R. S. 268, 283
Thommison, Hans 131
Thompson, Thomas 241
Thrasher, John B. 242, 363
Three Self Patriotic Movement 226, 230,
    473
Tiililä, Osmo 145
Tilak, N. V. 204
Tillich, Paul 278, 280, 316, 368–9, 458
tolerance
    and Enlightenment 137, 157
    in Netherlands 149
    in Schleiermacher 68

Toleration Acts (England) 103, 125, 455
Tolstoy, Leo 288
Tomkins, Oliver 408–9
"Toronto Blessing" 106, 449
Torrance, Thomas Forsyth 320
Torrey, Reuben A. 317, 346, 442
Touraine, Alain 457
Tractarianism 105, 121, 194.
tradition
  and authority 23–4
  critique 37
  in Schleiermacher 69
  and Scripture 23–8, 31, 138–9
traditionalism
  and evangelicalism 106, 424–5
  and interpretation 260–1
  and liberalism 4, 107, 121–2, 218,
    219–20, 234–5
  and science 174–5, 315, 316
Traherne, Thomas 385
Tranquebar (Trankebar) Mission 135,
  201, 240, 394, 395
transcendence
  in Barth 84, 85, 89, 93, 213
  in Calvin 276
  in Japanese theology 213
  in Kant 76
  in Schleiermacher 76
  and science 318
transubstantiation 11, 12, 46, 98, 273
Trible, Phyllis 338
Trinity
  in Barth 89–91, 94
  in Calvin 9
  in evangelicalism 429, 435
  in Hegel 32–3, 34, 74
  in Japanese theology 213
  in Melanchthon 25
  and revelation 90–1
  in Schleiermacher 74, 78–80
Troeltsch, Ernst 85, 261, 263, 288,
  325–6
truth
  in Hegel 32, 34
  in Kant 32
  in Schleiermacher 33, 76
Truth, Sojourner 336
Turretin, François 182
Tutu, Desmond 244, 389

two-kingdom theology 16, 50–1, 58,
  131–2
Tyndale, William 96–7

Uchimura Kanzo 211
Uemura Masahisa 211
Uganda 240–1
Ukraine 158–9
Ulster Protestantism 127–8, 129
unio mystica
  in Calvin 384–5
  in Luther 10, 11, 12
Union Church of Christ in Japan (Nihon
    Kirisuto Icchi Kyokai) 210
Union of Evangelical Christians (Russia)
  159
Unitarianism
  in Eastern Europe 156
  in England 103
  in United States 172, 176, 179
United Church of Canada 196, 412
United Church of Christ in Japan (Nihon
    Kirisuto Kyodan) 212–13
United Church of Christ (US) 176, 294,
  367
United Free Church (Scotland) 118
United Methodist Church (US) 176, 179,
  367, 447
United Presbyterian Church (Scotland)
  113, 117
United Presbyterian Church (US) 176,
  367, 374
United Reformed Church (England) 107
United States 165–79
  Calvinism 56
  and challenges of modernity 173–7,
    178
  conservatism 177–8, 290
  and election 64
  evangelicalism 176, 177–9, 290,
    302–3, 424, 429–33, 434
  liberalism 172, 174–5, 178–9, 197,
    328–9
  pluralism 167–8
  Puritan settlements 64, 101, 165–6,
    183–4, 186
  revivalism and reform 114, 168–70,
    171–3, 177, 182, 185–6, 303,
    427

utopian and communal movements 171

Virginia settlement 167, 169

see also African Americans; charismatic movement; fundamentalism; Native Americans; Pentecostalism; race and racism; slavery

Uniting Church (Australia) 235, 236

univocity of being 457, 459–60, 462

Urquhart, David 224

Ussher, James, Archbishop of Armagh 124

Valentine, Lewis 122

Varick, James 171

Venn, Henry 242

via moderna, and Luther 40, 43

Vineyard Christian Fellowship 449

Viret, Pierre 54

Visser't Hooft, W. A. 398, 409

vocation 64, 291, 301, 313, 334

voluntarism 193, 195, 300, 457

Wagner, Peter 449

Waldenses 163

Waldenström, P. P. 140

Wales 120–2, 424

and evangelicalism 122, 424

and revivalism 121, 122, 427–8

Walls, Andrew F. 468

Wang Mingdao 226, 229

Wang Zhai 226

Warfield, Benjamin B. 64, 175, 345

Warneck, Gustav 392–5

Wars of Religion 55, 161

Watson, David 448

Watts, Isaac 279

wealth 291–2, 424

gospel of 172, 292, 446, 448–9, 474, 479–80

Weber, Max 2, 64, 290–1, 454, 456, 459, 461

Week of Prayer for Christian Unity 411

Weiss, Johannes 35, 36

Weld, Theodore 170

Wellhausen, Julius 260, 265

Welsh Calvinistic Methodist Connexion 121

Welz, Justinian von 394

Wesley, Charles 279, 386, 428, 435

Wesley, John 258, 279, 386, 388

and economics 291

and Holiness movement 441–2

and revivalism 104, 125, 427–9

and science 313

Wesley, Samuel and Susannah 427

Wesleyans see Methodism

Westen, Thomas von 135

Westminster Confession of Faith (1647) 4, 6, 102, 112, 117, 125

Wette, W. M. L. de 324

Whitefield, George 114, 168, 182, 185, 427, 430, 435

Wilberforce, Samuel, Bishop of Oxford 317

Wilberforce, William 435

Wilkerson, David 447

will of God 458

in Barth 93

in Calvin 8–9, 10, 63

in Luther 8, 10

William III and Mary II 103, 111

William of Ockham 40, 457

William of Orange, in Ireland 125, 127, see also William III and Mary II

Williams, Delores 338

Williams, Peter 171

Williams, Roger 166, 302

Williams, William 121, 428

Williamson, Alexander 229

Wilson, Bryan 412

Wilson, Marvin 379

Wimber, John 449

Wingren, Gustav 144, 145

Winquist, Charles 459

Winthrop, John 360, 362

Wise, S. F. 198 n.5

witch-hunts 132, 166–7

Wittenberg

and Copernicanism 308

and Luther 40–1, 46

and Reformation 5, 14, 28, 130–2, 394

and Wycliffe 97

Wolff, Christian 135, 136

Wolmar, Melchior 53

Wolsey, Card. Thomas 97

women
  and Calvin 333
  liberation 333, 397
  and Luther 333
  New England 336
  see also feminism; ordination of women
Wood, Forest G. 357, 369 n.3
Woods, Edward 409
Word of God 253–4, 257
  in Barth 79, 89, 90–1, 264
  in Luther 24–5, 31, 41–2, 44, 48
  in Spener 29
  in Zwingli 25–6
work ethic 64, 291
works, and justification 24, 41, 42, 166, 253, 374
  see also Karlstadt, Andreas Bodenstein von; Luther, Martin; Melanchthon, Philip
World Council of Churches 236, 304, 350, 408, 411, 415, 419
  and evangelicalism 143, 417–18
  and fundamentalism 350
  and Jews 379
  and Pentecostalism 447, 477
  Programme to Combat Racism 415, 418
  and the responsible society 289
World Methodist Council 411
World Missionary Conference (Edinburgh) 225, 246, 399, 406–7, 412, 414
World Student Christian Federation 406
World Vision 425
Worms, Diet of (1521) 2, 43, 48, 274, 454
Worms, Edict of (1521) 46
worship *see* liturgy
Wren, Brian 296 n.7
Wright, J. Elwin 350

Wu Leiquan 229
Wu Yaozong 226, 229
Wycliffe, John 96

Yagi Seiichi 213
Yanaihara Tadao 212
Yoder, John Howard 288, 290
Yoido Full Gospel Church 218, 445, 472
Yoshino Sakuzo 211
Young Men's Christian Association (YMCA) 143, 173, 406
Young Women's Christian Association (YWCA) 143, 406
Youth for Christ 349
Youth with a Mission 425
Yuan Ang Bong 227

Zaire 246
Zhao Zichen 225, 228, 229
Ziegenbalg, Bartholomäus 201, 395, 471
Zimbabwe 242, 471, 474–5
Zinzendorf, Nicholas Ludwig, Count von 29–30, 136, 427
Zizek, Slavoj 461
Zurich, and Reformation 5, 26–8, 149, 274
Zurich Consensus (1551) 27, 28
Zwingli, Uldrich
  and baptism 26
  and Calvin 61, 384
  and Christology 49
  and the church 2, 5
  and the Eucharist 10, 11, 12, 26–7, 46, 48, 49, 54
  and Holy Spirit 25–6
  and humanism 45, 274
  and images 26, 274–5, 276
  and Luther 5, 26–7, 46, 48, 54
  and Marburg Colloquy 46
  and Word of God 25–6

DATE DUE